Lecture Notes in Computer Science 16443

The series Lecture Notes in Computer Science (LNCS), including its subseries Lecture Notes in Artificial Intelligence (LNAI) and Lecture Notes in Bioinformatics (LNBI), has established itself as a medium for the publication of new developments in computer science and information technology research, teaching, and education.

LNCS enjoys close cooperation with the computer science R & D community, the series counts many renowned academics among its volume editors and paper authors, and collaborates with prestigious societies. Its mission is to serve this international community by providing an invaluable service, mainly focused on the publication of conference and workshop proceedings and postproceedings. LNCS commenced publication in 1973.

Paolo D'Arco · Alin Zamfiroiu
Editors

Innovative Security Solutions for Information Technology and Communications

18th International Conference, SecITC 2025
Bucharest, Romania, November 20–21, 2025
Revised Selected Papers

Editors
Paolo D'Arco
University of Salerno
Fisciano, Salerno, Italy

Alin Zamfiroiu
Bucharest University of Economic Studies
Bucharest, Romania

ISSN 0302-9743 ISSN 1611-3349 (electronic)
Lecture Notes in Computer Science
ISBN 978-3-032-17442-0 ISBN 978-3-032-17443-7 (eBook)
https://doi.org/10.1007/978-3-032-17443-7

This Springer imprint is published by the registered company Springer Nature Switzerland AG
The registered company address is: Gewerbestrasse 11, 6330 Cham, Switzerland

Preface

The International Conference on Security for Information Technology and Communications (SecITC) is an annual international event held in Romania. It brings together computer security researchers, cryptographers, industry representatives, and graduate students interested in all aspects of information security and privacy.

Its primary goal is to connect people from different communities by providing a forum for informal exchanges and fostering the emergence of new scientific and industrial collaborations. Since 2015, the post-proceedings of the conference have been published in the Springer LNCS series.

The 18th edition of the conference, SecITC 2025, took place both in person and online from 20 to 21 November 2025, in Bucharest. It was jointly organized by the Bucharest University of Economic Studies, the Advanced Technologies Institute, and the Military Technical Academy "Ferdinand I". The on-site event was hosted in the magnificent Aula Magna of the Bucharest University of Economic Studies and in the Robert Schumann Room.

The submission and reviewing process was managed through the EasyChair platform. SecITC 2025 received 44 submissions. Each Program Committee (PC) member was assigned an average of three papers to review, and every submission received at least three reviews. The PC was further supported by reports and opinions from 8 external reviewers. As in previous years, the reviewing process followed a double-blind model. Reviewers and authors were required to declare conflicts of interest, and EasyChair was configured to automatically detect potential conflicts. The system ensured that PC members, including the PC chairs, could not access reviewer assignments or reviews for papers in conflict. Based on the reviews and an in-depth discussion phase, a total of 20 submissions were selected for presentation at the conference. The full papers published in these proceedings cover a wide spectrum of topics across all areas of information security and privacy.

The SecITC 2025 program featured two keynote speeches by Maria Isabel González Vasco from Universidad Carlos III de Madrid (Spain) and Peter Scholl from Aarhus University (Denmark). We are grateful to both keynote speakers for their outstanding contributions and for the interest they generated, especially among young students and early-career researchers.

SecITC 2025 was co-chaired by Paolo D'Arco (University of Salerno, Italy) and Alin Zamfiroiu (Bucharest University of Economic Studies, Romania), who coordinated the PC members and guided the selection of the papers included in this volume. The PC consisted of 56 members from 20 countries: 14 from Europe and 6 from Asia, North America, and Africa.

We would like to thank everyone who contributed to the success of SecITC 2025. We are especially grateful to all PC members and external reviewers for their commitment, time, and efforts, which ensured a careful and fair reviewing process for all submissions.

We also thank the members of the organizing committee for their professional support, with special thanks to our colleague Cristian Toma for his invaluable contribution to the on-site organization of the conference.

Last but not least, we extend our sincere gratitude to all authors who submitted their work to SecITC 2025 and to all participants for making the conference a fruitful, pleasant, and enjoyable experience.

November 2025

Paolo D'Arco
Alin Zamfiroiu

Organization

Program Committee Chairs

Paolo D'Arco	University of Salerno, Italy
Alin Zamfiroiu	Bucharest University of Economic Studies, Romania

Steering Committee

Ion Bica	Military Technical Academy "Ferdinand I", Romania"
Andrei-George Oprina	Advanced Technologies Institute, Romania
Cristian Toma	Bucharest University of Economic Studies, Romania

Program Committee

Iulian Aciobanitei	Military Technical Academy,Romania
Raja Naeem Akram	University of Aberdeen, UK
Claudio Ardagana	Università degli Studi di Milano,Italy
Lasse Berntzen	University of South-Eastern Norway, Norway
Ion Bica	Military Technical Academy, Romania
Catalin Boja	Bucharest University of Economic Studies, Romania
Guillaume Bouffard	French National Cybersecurity Agency (ANSSI), France
Francesco Buccafurri	Università di Reggio Calabria,Italy
Luca Campa	University of Innsbruck, Austria
Xavier Carpent	University of Nottingham, UK
Mihai Chiroiu	Bucharest Politehnica University, Romania
Michele Ciampi	University of Edimburgh, UK
Vanesa Daza	Pompeu Fabra University, Spain
Roberto De Prisco	Università degli Studi di Salerno, Italy
Eric Diehl	Sony Pictures, USA
Mihai Doinea	Bucharest University of Economic Studies, Romania

Vlad Drăgoi	Aurel Vlaicu University of Arad, Romania
Petr Dzurenda	Brno University of Technology, Czech Republic
Navid Nasr Esfahani	Toronto Metropolitan University, Canada
Anna Lisa Ferrara	Università del Molise, Italy
Joe Francom	Utah Tech University, USA
Eric Freyssinet	Loria Laboratory, France
Dieter Gollmann	University of Hamburg, Germany
Johann Großschädl	University of Luxembourg, Luxemburg
Shoichi Hirose	University of Fukui, Japan
Paul Irofti	University of Bucharest, Romania
Mehmet Sabir Kiraz	De Montfort University, UK
Diana Maimut	Advanced Technologies Institute, Romania
Stig Mjolsnes	Norwegian University of Science and Technology, Norway
Luciana Morogan	Military Technical Academy, Romania
David Naccache	École Normale Supérieure - PSL, France
Anderson Nascimento	Washington University,USA
Svetla Nikova	KU Leuven, Belgium
Ruxandra Olimid	Bucharest University, Romania
Andrei-George Oprina	Advanced Technologies Institute, Romania
Carles Padro	Universitat Politècnica de Catalunya, Spain
Elena Pagnin	Chalmers University of Technology, Sweden
Angel Perez del Pozo	Universidad Rey Juan Carlos, Spain
Marius Popa	Bucharest University of Economic Studies, Romania
Silvio Ranise	FBK and Università di Trento, Italy
Sara Ricci	Brno University of Technology, Czech Republic
Peter Rønne	University of Luxembourg, Luxemburg
Palash Sarkar	Indian Statistical Institute, Kolkata, India
Emil Simion	Politehnica University of Bucharest, Romania
Luisa Siniscalchi	Technical University of Denmark, Denmark
El Mamoun Soudi	University Mohammed V in Rabat, Morocco
Pantelimon Stanica	Naval Postgraduate School, USA
Rainer Steinwandt	University of Alabama in Huntsville, USA
George Teseleanu	Advanced Technologies Institute, Romania
Ferucio Laurențiu Țiplea	Alexandru Ioan Cuza University of Iași, Romania
Mihai Togan	Military Technical Academy, Romania
Cristian Toma	Bucharest University of Economic Studies, Romania
Denis Trcek	University of Ljubljana, Slovenia
Ivan Visconti	Sapienza University of Rome, Italy

Sule Yildirim-Yayilgan	Norwegian University of Science and Technology, Norway
Lei Zhang	East China Normal University, China

Additional Reviewers

Syed Ali
Stefano Berlato
Filip Ceara
Ramona Corbeanu
Ruslan Kasheparov
Marius Lombard-Platet
Riccardo Longo
Luca Piras

Keynotes Talks

The Best of Both Worlds: Bridging Classical and Quantum Technologies for Secure Communication

Maria Isabel González Vasco

Universidad Carlos III de Madrid

Abstract: The advent of large-scale quantum computers poses a structural threat to currently deployed public-key cryptography, motivating the transition towards quantum-safe communication infrastructures. Two main approaches have emerged: quantum key distribution (QKD), which leverages quantum physics to provide information-theoretic security, and post-quantum cryptography (PQC), which relies on classical primitives designed to withstand quantum adversaries. In practice, neither paradigm alone is sufficient: QKD deployments are expensive, heterogeneous and often lack a clean theoretical security model, while PQC is typically analysed in classical models that only partially capture quantum capabilities. Hybrid designs that combine keys from multiple sources are therefore increasingly recommended in standardisation and policy documents. However, existing work largely focuses on two-party settings and does not directly address scalable, authenticated group key establishment in heterogeneous networks where classical and quantum users coexist.

In this talk we present a framework for analysing and constructing hybrid group key establishment protocols spanning both QKD- and PQC-capable nodes (joint work with R. Steinwandt). We first adapt a modern key-exchange model from to the setting of parties equipped with both classical and quantum channels, explicitly tracking partner identities, session identifiers and long-term security, and enforcing an integrity notion that binds keys to their intended communication context. Within this model we introduce a generic compiler that, given secure building blocks (QKD-based or PQ KEM-based two-party and group authenticated key establishment with integrity, plus suitable commitment and MAC primitives), yields a provably secure hybrid group protocol in the quantum random oracle model. This work has been published in and has been carried over in the NATO SPS project G5985 *Secure Communication via Classical and Quantum Technologies.*

References

Michele, M., Stebila, D., Ustaolu, B.: "Quantum Key Distribution in the Classical Authenticated Key Exchange Framework", pp.136–154. In: Post-Quantum Cryptography. Ed. by Philippe Gaborit. Berlin, Heidelberg: Springer Berlin Heidelberg, (2013)

Maria, V., González, I., Steinwandt.: "Scalable Authenticated Group Key Establishment in Quantum and Post-Quantum Networks", pp. 315–335. In: Informatica 36.2 (2025)

Zero-Knowledge Proofs and Post-Quantum Signatures from VOLE-in-the-Head

Peter Scholl

Aarhus University, Aarhus, Denmark

Abtsract: Zero-knowledge proofs are a powerful cryptographic primitive with numerous applications, including secure authentication, anonymous credentials and proving properties of blockchain transactions. Many state-of-the-art zero-knowledge proof systems achieve very compact proof sizes and fast verification times, but often at the cost of high proving times, which makes it challenging to scale to large statements or resource-constrained environments. Furthermore, many of these proof systems rely on cryptographic assumptions that may be vulnerable to attacks by quantum computers.

In this talk, I begin with an overview of the different tools available for building post-quantum cryptography, and discuss the ongoing NIST standardization process. Then, I introduce a recent paradigm for building zero-knowledge proofs based on vector oblivious linear evaluation (VOLE). VOLE is a tool from secure two-party computation, which underpins a number of recent advances in protocols for oblivious transfer, private set intersection, and more. In the setting of zero-knowledge, VOLE offers a conceptually simple approach to building general-purpose proofs without any heavy machinery. At the same time, VOLE-based proofs are powerful, enabling efficient proofs of complex statements with linear proof size but very fast proving times [1]. In recent work, we introduced the VOLE-in-the-head paradigm [2], which allows upgrading VOLE-based schemes to support public verifiabity. This is particularly important for digital signatures, and has led to the use of VOLE-in-the-head in a number of recent post-quantum signature algorithms, such as FAEST, which has at its heart a proof of knowledge of an AES secret key. This gives practical, post-quantum security under very conservative security guarantees, while offering competitive performance compared with the state-of-the-art.

References

1. Yang, K., Sarkar, P., Weng, C., Wang X.,. QuickSilver: Efficient and affordable zero-knowledge proofs for circuits and polynomials over any field. In: Giovanni Vigna and Elaine Shi, editors, ACM CCS 2021, pp. 2986–3001. ACM Press, Nov (2021)

2. Baum, C., et al.: Publicly verifiable zeroknowledge and post-quantum signatures from VOLE-in-the-head. In: Helena Handschuh and Anna Lysyanskaya, editors, CRYPTO 2023, Part V, volume 14085 of LNCS, pp. 581–615. Springer, Cham, Aug (2023)

Contents

Artificial Intelligence Techniques for Security

Application, System and Network Security

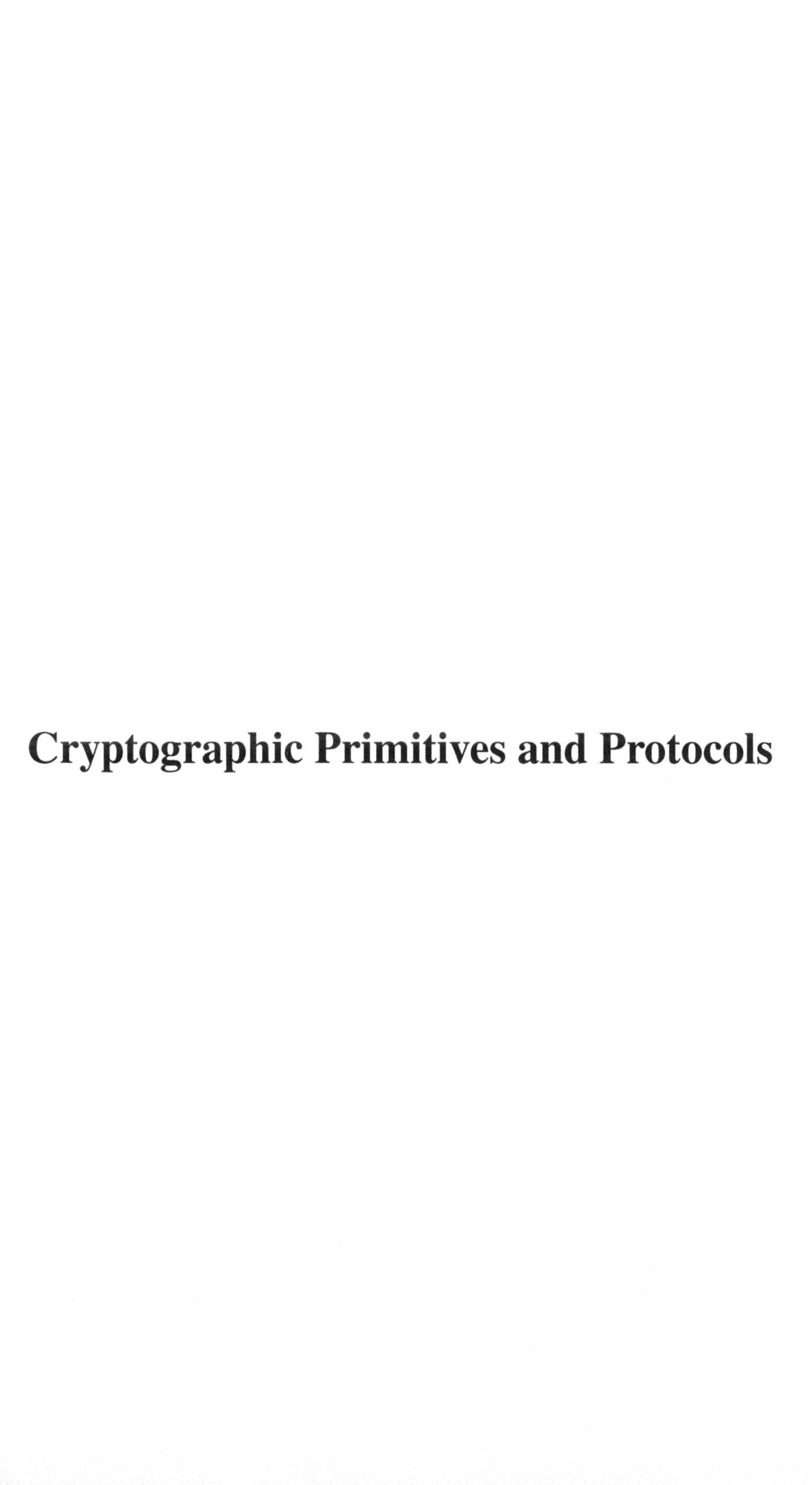

Cryptographic Primitives and Protocols

Adding Two Easy Functions Is Always Hard to Invert

Hayato Gibo[1(✉)], Yohei Watanabe[1,2], and Mitsugu Iwamoto[1]

[1] The University of Electro-Communications, Tokyo, Japan
{h.gibo,watanabe,mitsugu}@uec.ac.jp
[2] National Institute of Advanced Industrial Science and Technology, Tokyo, Japan

Abstract. One-way functions play a fundamental role in the theory of cryptography; however, proving their existence remains a long-standing open problem. Ghosal and Sahai proposed a novel information-theoretic framework for constructing a one-way function by combining two easy functions, each modeled as a random oracle paired with its inverse oracle, both of which are accessible to the distinguisher. They demonstrated that the resulting function f is hard to invert in the sense of indifferentiability, assuming that the gap between output and input lengths satisfies $m-n = \Omega(\log^{1+\varepsilon} n)$ for all $\varepsilon > 0$. However, this condition is somewhat artificial, and their claim that combining easy functions yields hardness holds only under this restricted – prompting the natural question of whether such a constraint can be eliminated. In this work, we answer this question affirmatively: the condition is not necessary. We prove that adding two easy functions always results in a one-way function, regardless of the gap between m and n. Our proof relies on a careful simulation of the inverse oracle using a polynomial-time sampling algorithm in n that generates outputs ϵ-close to the binomial distribution.

Keywords: One-way Function · Random function · Indifferentiability

1 Introduction

1.1 Background

One-way functions play a fundamental role in the theory of cryptography and form a cornerstone of theoretical computer science [6]. A function $f : \{0,1\}^n \rightarrow \{0,1\}^m$ is said to be *one-way* if it satisfies the following two properties: (1) For any input x, the value $f(x)$ can be computed efficiently; (2) Given $f(x)$ for a uniformly random x from the domain, it is computationally hard to find any x' such that $f(x') = f(x)$. Despite their foundational importance, the existence of one-way functions remains one of the most significant open problems in theoretical computer science. Traditionally, a (strong) one-way function is defined via the negligible success probability of any computationally efficient adversary in inverting it [6].

An alternative and arguably more natural characterization of one-wayness is to show that a function is essentially as hard to invert as a truly random function

P. D'Arco and A. Zamfiroiu (Eds.): SecITC 2025, LNCS 16443, pp. 3–22, 2026.
https://doi.org/10.1007/978-3-032-17443-7_1

R. Following this perspective, Ghosal and Sahai [4] introduced an information-theoretic framework for constructing one-way functions via the existence of so-called *easy* functions. Loosely speaking, an easy function g is one that is efficiently computable in both directions, given access to oracles for g and its inverse g^{-1}. Namely, such a function g is represented by a pair of oracles: a random oracle O and its inverse oracle O^{-1}, corresponding to g and g^{-1}, respectively.

This approach is analyzed within the framework of *indifferentiability* [9], in which one shows that any computationally unbounded distinguisher D, given *polynomial-time* oracle access to both O and O^{-1}, cannot distinguish the composed function f from a truly random function R. One may find this framework somewhat puzzling, yet it has been used to construct a pseudorandom function by adding two pseudorandom permutations [7], which serves as the ideal model of AES. Constructing a pseudo-random function from AES plays a central role in symmetric-key cryptography.

In this framework, Ghosal and Sahai proposed two approaches for constructing one-way functions: the first involves adding two easy functions, while the second introduces linear noise into an easy function. This paper focuses on the former, that is, we consider the case where the sum of two easy functions yields a one-way function. Given a domain size n and a codomain size m, the results for this setting are further divided into two cases depending on the class of easy functions: one where the easy functions are drawn from all functions mapping $\{0,1\}^n$ to $\{0,1\}^m$ [3–5], and another where they are drawn from all bijective functions mapping $\{0,1\}^n$ to $\{0,1\}^n$ (i.e., when $n = m$) [5].

1.2 Motivation and Technical Challenges

It is important to note that the results in prior works [3–5] hold only under certain restrictions on m and n. In [4,5], the claims apply when m is sufficiently larger than n, specifically when $m - n = \Omega(\log^{1+\varepsilon} n)$ for all $\varepsilon > 0$. In contrast, [3] studies the case $m = n$, but assumes a slightly modified oracle behavior compared to that in [4,5], which makes the problem easier. Our motivation and research question is whether these restrictions on m and n can be removed. We answer this question in the affirmative, showing that the addition of two easy functions can yield a one-way function without any restriction on m and n.

The necessity of such restrictions on m and n arises from the techniques used to construct simulators for proving one-wayness via indifferentiability. In the indifferentiability framework, a simulator $\mathsf{Sim}^{\mathsf{R}}$ interacting with a truly random function R must be designed to emulate the random oracles $\mathsf{O}_1, \mathsf{O}_2$ and their inverse oracles $\mathsf{O}_1^{-1}, \mathsf{O}_2^{-1}$. Our goal is to show that any computationally unbounded distinguisher D cannot distinguish $(f, (\mathsf{O}_1, \mathsf{O}_2, \mathsf{O}_1^{-1}, \mathsf{O}_2^{-1}))$ from $(\mathsf{R}, \mathsf{Sim}^{\mathsf{R}})$, thereby establishing the one-wayness of f. Consequently, the core of the proof lies in the simulation of the oracles, particularly the *inverse oracles*, which, in the results of [1,4,5], require certain restrictions on n and m to establish one-wayness. The details are as follows:

In simulating the inverse oracle, for a fixed element in the codomain, we must simulate its preimage and then randomly select an element from it. A straightforward approach is to first determine the size of the preimage according to the binomial distribution, and then sample a random subset of the domain of that size to serve as the preimage.

Keeping this approach in mind, Ghosal and Sahai [4,5] simulated the inverse oracle in a particularly simple setting. Specifically, they considered the case where $m - n = \Omega(\log^{1+\varepsilon} n)$ for all $\varepsilon > 0$. In this regime, since the output length is sufficiently larger than the input length, the preimage set is empty with overwhelming probability, and its size is zero in most cases. Consequently, simulating the inverse oracle becomes straightforward; that is, it simply outputs an empty set, i.e., no element is returned from the preimage.

In the case of Eisenberg et al. [3], they assumed $n = m$. Under this assumption, combinatorial arguments show that the probability of a preimage having size greater than n is negligible. Consequently, their simulation of the inverse oracle proceeds by sampling a preimage size $s \leq n$ according to a binomial distribution and assigning s input-output correspondences. As a result, [3] allows the inverse oracle to output all elements of the preimage. Specifically, they assumed $\mathsf{O}^{-1} : \{0,1\}^m \to \mathcal{P}(\{0,1\}^n)$, where $\mathcal{P}(\{0,1\}^n)$ means the power set of $\{0,1\}^n$, whereas the original setting in [4,5] assumes $\mathsf{O}^{-1} : \{0,1\}^m \to \{0,1\}^n \cup \{\perp\}$. However, this assumption in [3] regarding the inverse oracle is *not valid* for general values of m and n, as the preimage size can become exponential in n when $n \gg m$. In contrast, when the preimage size is at most n, as in the setting of [3], it becomes feasible to efficiently select a random element from the preimage returned by the inverse oracle.

In summary, in all of [3–5], the restrictions on m and n play a critical role in enabling the simulation of inverse oracles. Lifting these restrictions appears to be highly nontrivial and would likely require fundamentally new techniques or insights.

1.3 Our Ideas Behind the Proposed Simulators

As explained in the previous section, our main concern is the construction of inverse oracles for proving one-wayness within the indifferentiability framework. Specifically, our goal is to develop a new simulation method for inverse oracles that does not impose any restrictions on m and n, which distinguishes our result from previous works such as [3–5].

The key challenge in simulating the inverse oracle is to randomly sample the size of the preimage in *polynomial time*. A naive approach is to sample the preimage size according to the binomial distribution $\mathsf{Bin}(N, p)$, where $N := 2^n$ and $p = 2^{-m}$. However, this is infeasible in practice, as it requires time polynomial in N, which is exponential in n. To overcome this problem, we employ the sampling algorithm $\mathsf{DiscBB}(N, p)$ proposed by Kawachi et al. [8]. This algorithm efficiently generates samples that are ϵ-close to the binomial distribution. By selecting appropriate parameters, we can ensure that the output distribution is sufficiently accurate while preserving polynomial-time efficiency.

However, even if we can sample the preimage sizes efficiently, it is not always feasible to store all elements in the preimage, as their number can be exponential in n. To address this issue, we introduce a *virtual allocation strategy*, which forms the other core component of our inverse oracle simulation. Instead of explicitly storing all preimage elements, the simulator records only the preimage size and incrementally assigns actual input-output correspondences by manipulating the probability of selecting an element from the preimage in response to the distinguisher's queries. This approach is sound because the inverse oracle reveals at most as many correspondences as the number of queries made by the distinguisher. As a result, the distinguisher cannot distinguish between the real inverse oracle and our simulator, which assigns at most one new correspondence per inverse query, even though the simulator does not store the entire preimage.

By combining these new technical ideas, we succeed in constructing a simulator that emulates both the random oracle and the inverse oracle in polynomial time for all values of n and m. In particular, we can conclude that the sum of two easy functions is always one-way and hard to invert, thereby overcoming the restrictions on m and n imposed in previous works such as [3–5].

1.4 Organization

The rest of this paper is organized as follows. Section 2 introduces our notation and defines the notion of an *easy function*, characterized by the availability of oracles that compute the function and its inverse. We also summarize the previous result of [4], which shows that the sum of two easy functions becomes hard to invert under a certain condition. Section 3 is devoted to removing this condition, and we prove that the sum of any two easy functions is always hard to invert. In the Appendices, we present the lengthy proof of (6) and provide the pseudocodes used in the proof of the main theorem (Theorem 2).

2 Preliminaries

2.1 Notation

For a binary string x, let $\|x\|$ be the bit length of x. For integers $n, m \in \mathbb{N}$ with $n \leq m$, define $[n] := \{1, 2, \ldots, n\}$ and $[n : m] := \{n, \ldots, m\}$. For a finite set $\mathcal{S}$, $\#\mathcal{S}$ stands for the size of $\mathcal{S}$. The notation $s \xleftarrow{\$} \mathcal{S}$ means that an element $s \in \mathcal{S}$ is chosen uniformly at random from $\mathcal{S}$. For two random variables X and Y over a finite set $\mathcal{S}$, the corresponding probability distributions are denoted by P_X and P_Y, respectively. The statistical distance of P_X and P_Y is defined to be $\Delta(P_X, P_Y) := (1/2)\sum_{w \in \mathcal{S}} |P_X(w) - P_Y(w)|$. We say that P_X is ϵ-close to P_Y if $\Delta(P_X, P_Y) \leq \epsilon$ holds. Let $\mathsf{Bin}(N, p)$ be the binomial distribution with $N \in \mathbb{N}$ and $p \in [0, 1]$, i.e., $\mathsf{Bin}(N, p)$ outputs $n \in [0 : N]$ with probability $\binom{N}{n} p^n (1-p)^{N-n}$.

2.2 Easy Functions, One-Way Functions via Indifferentiability

We first introduce an *easy* function[1] as a component for building a one-way function. An easy function is characterized by the existence of a pair of oracles

[1] In [4,5], there is another example of an easy function based on a model of adding random noise.

that simulate the function and its inverse. If we can access both oracles, we say that the function is easy (to invert).

Definition 1 (Easy Functions [4,5]). *For a random function $g : \{0,1\}^n \to \{0,1\}^m$, g is said to be an easy function if there exists a pair of oracles $(\mathsf{O}_g, \mathsf{O}_g^{-1})$ that satisfies the following:*

- *An oracle O_g satisfies $\mathsf{O}_g = g$ over $\{0,1\}^n$, and;*
- *An inverse oracle O_g^{-1} simulates the inverse map of g. Concretely, for every $b \in \{0,1\}^m$, $\mathsf{O}_g^{-1}(b)$ outputs an element from $g^{-1}(\{b\})$ uniformly at random.*

We abuse the notation of an easy function by using O without g. One of the main contributions of [4,5] is to show that adding easy functions *can be* hard to invert, namely, one-way. The one-wayness of adding two easy functions is formalized by the framework of indifferentiability [2,9], since we prove indistinguishability of the addition of easy functions from the random function via polynomial-time oracle accesses. For this purpose, we introduce the notion of indifferentiability.

Definition 2 (Polynomial-Query-Bounded Oracle Turing Machine [4]). *We say that an oracle Turing machine $\mathsf{T}^{(\cdot)}$ is polynomial-query-bounded if there exits a polynomial $p(\cdot) : \mathbb{N} \to \mathbb{N}$ such that for any input $x \in \{0,1\}^*$ and for any oracle O, the execution of $\mathsf{T}^{\mathsf{O}}(x)$ makes at most $p(\|x\|)$ many queries to O.*

Definition 3 (Indifferentiability [2,9]). *Let $\mathsf{C} : \{0,1\}^n \to \{0,1\}^{m(n)}$ be an algorithm that has oracle access to functions denoted by F mapping from $\{0,1\}^{p(n)}$ to $\{0,1\}^{q(n)}$ and implements a functionality based on F, where $p(n)$, $q(n)$, $m(n) = \mathsf{poly}(n)$. We say that C is indifferentiable from a random function $\mathsf{R} : \{0,1\}^n \to \{0,1\}^m$, if there exists a polynomial time simulator Sim with oracle access to R such that for all polynomial-query-bounded distinguishers D, $|\Pr[\mathsf{D}^{\mathsf{C}^{\mathsf{F}},\mathsf{F}}(1^n) = 1] - \Pr[\mathsf{D}^{\mathsf{R},\mathsf{Sim}^{\mathsf{R}}}(1^n) = 1]|$ is negligible in n.*

2.3 Previous Results on Adding Easy Functions

Under the indifferentiability framework, Ghosal–Sahai claimed that adding two easy functions $g_1, g_2 : \{0,1\}^n \to \{0,1\}^m$ yields a one-way function, which is one of the main contributions of [4,5]. Let $\mathsf{O}_1 : \{0,1\}^n \to \{0,1\}^m$ and $\mathsf{O}_2 : \{0,1\}^n \to \{0,1\}^m$ be two random oracles corresponding to g_1 and g_2, respectively. We claim that the function $((\mathsf{O}_1 + \mathsf{O}_2) \mod 2^m)$, that is, $x \mapsto (\mathsf{O}_1(x) + \mathsf{O}_2(x)) \mod 2^m$ is *indifferentiable* from a random function upon giving oracle access to $(\mathsf{O}_1, \mathsf{O}_2, \mathsf{O}_1^{-1}, \mathsf{O}_2^{-1})$ where O_1^{-1} and O_2^{-1} denote the corresponding inverse oracles. Formally, the inverse oracles are defined as $\mathsf{O}_1^{-1} : \{0,1\}^m \to \{0,1\}^n \cup \{\perp\}$ and $\mathsf{O}_2^{-1} : \{0,1\}^m \to \{0,1\}^n \cup \{\perp\}$, where $\perp$ means that no symbol is output from O_i^{-1} since the inverse map g^{-1} is the empty set. We note again that O_i^{-1} takes an element $b \in \{0,1\}^m$ as input and output an element of $\{0,1\}^n$ which is randomly selected from $g^{-1}(\{b\}) \subseteq \{0,1\}^n$.

Roughly speaking, the following theorem states that adding two easy functions is hard to invert, but such a claim does *not always* hold because the theorem holds under a restricted condition on the input and output lengths. This motivated our work, which will be described in the next section.

Theorem 1 (Ghosal–Sahai [4]). *Let* $\mathsf{O}_1, \mathsf{O}_2$ *be random oracles and* R *be a random function from* $\{0,1\}^n$ *to* $\{0,1\}^m$, $m, n \in \mathbb{N}$ *and* $m = \mathsf{poly}(n)$. *For all polynomial-query-bounded distinguishers* D *making at most* $q = \mathsf{poly}(n)$ *queries to each oracle, there exists a polynomial time oracle simulator* $\mathsf{Sim}^{(\cdot)}$ *and a constant* $c > 0$ *such that*

$$\left| \Pr\left[\mathsf{D}^{(\mathsf{O}_1+\mathsf{O}_2),(\mathsf{O}_1,\mathsf{O}_2,\mathsf{O}_1^{-1},\mathsf{O}_2^{-1})}(1^n) = 1\right] - \Pr\left[\mathsf{D}^{\mathsf{R},\mathsf{Sim}^{\mathsf{R}}}(1^n) = 1\right] \right| \leq \frac{cq}{2^{m-n}} + \frac{q^2}{2^m},$$

which is negligible when $m - n = \Omega(\log^{1+\varepsilon} n)$, $\varepsilon > 0$.

A similar result was shown in [3] for the case where $m = n$, as briefly mentioned in Sect. 1.2. We omit the details here.

3 Adding Two Easy Functions Always One-Way

3.1 Motivation and Main Result

Although Theorem 1 states that the addition of two easy functions is hard to invert, this claim holds only under the restriction that $m-n = \Omega(\log^{1+\varepsilon} n)$. This leaves open the possibility that adding two easy functions is *not always* hard to invert. As seen in the proof of [4,5], this restriction simplified the analysis, but the condition itself is rather artificial. The same applies to [3], where the case $m = n$ is assumed. It is clearly preferable to remove such restrictions, as this would allow us to conclude that adding two easy functions is *always* hard to invert for arbitrary values of n and m.

Therefore, our main concern in this paper is to clarify whether adding two easy functions is hard or not when $m - n \neq \Omega(\log^{1+\varepsilon} n)$. Based on such motivation, we prove the following theorem.

Theorem 2. *Let* $\mathsf{O}_1, \mathsf{O}_2$ *be random oracles and* R *be a random function from* $\{0,1\}^n$ *to* $\{0,1\}^m$, $m, n \in \mathbb{N}$ *and* $m = \mathsf{poly}(n)$. *For all polynomial-query-bounded distinguishers* D *making at most* $q = \mathsf{poly}(n)$ *queries to each oracle, there exists a polynomial time oracle simulator* $\mathsf{Sim}^{(\cdot)}$ *such that*

$$\left| \Pr\left[\mathsf{D}^{(\mathsf{O}_1+\mathsf{O}_2),(\mathsf{O}_1,\mathsf{O}_2,\mathsf{O}_1^{-1},\mathsf{O}_2^{-1})}(1^n) = 1\right] - \Pr\left[\mathsf{D}^{\mathsf{R},\mathsf{Sim}^{\mathsf{R}}}(1^n) = 1\right] \right|$$
$$\leq \frac{q}{2^n} + \frac{q(q+1)(3q^2+11q+22)}{12(2^n+1)}.$$

Theorem 2 claims that D's advantage is negligible in n since q is polynomial in n, which asserts the one-wayness of $\mathsf{O}_1 + \mathsf{O}_2$ for *arbitrary* $m = \mathsf{poly}(n)$. Comparing with Theorem 1, it turns out that Theorem 2 succeeded in removing the condition $m - n = \Omega(\log^{1+\varepsilon} n)$ from Theorem 1 to prove that adding two easy functions is hard to invert.

3.2 Proof Idea via Sampling Binomial Distributions

Before proving Theorem 2, we give several ideas for the proof. Let $g_i : \{0,1\}^n \to \{0,1\}^m$, $i = 1, 2$ be easy functions with oracles denoted by $(\mathsf{O}_i, \mathsf{O}_i^{-1})$. In order to prove that $g_1 + g_2$ is as hard to invert as a random function R in the framework of indifferentiability, we construct a polynomial time simulator $\mathsf{Sim}^{\mathsf{R}}$ that simulates O_1, O_2, O_1^{-1}, O_2^{-1}. The basic strategy of our simulator $\mathsf{Sim}^{\mathsf{R}}$ on simulating random oracles O_i is the same as [4,5], whereas a more intricate treatment is necessary in our simulator for the inverse oracles O_i^{-1}.

To see this, we first explain the construction of the inverse oracle according to [4,5], and the reason why Theorem 1 requires the artificial condition $m - n = \Omega(\log^{1+\varepsilon} n)$. In simulating O_i^{-1}, we have to estimate the preimage size of g_i, which follows the binomial distribution. However, [4,5] only treated the case where *the preimage is the empty set* with high probability, because it is sufficient for the inverse oracle O_i^{-1} to always output $\perp$ (meaning that the preimage is empty) for successful simulation in such a case.

Therefore, to remove the restriction from Theorem 1, we have to consider the case where $\mathsf{O}_i^{-1}(b)$ outputs other than $\perp$. Concretely, in our proof of Theorem 2, we carefully estimate the preimage size using a binomial distribution, which succeeds in eliminating the extra condition on m and n. Considering such issues in mind, we will sketch how the inverse function O_i^{-1} behaves in our proof. Here, recall that O_i^{-1} takes an element $b \in \{0,1\}^m$ as input, and outputs an element of $\{0,1\}^n$ which is randomly chosen from $g_i^{-1}(\{b\}) \subseteq \{0,1\}^n$. To simulate this in a naïve manner, we first sample the size of $g_i^{-1}(\{b\})$, and we choose $\#g_i^{-1}(\{b\})$ elements from $\{0,1\}^n$ randomly. Then, it outputs an element randomly selected from $g_i^{-1}(\{b\})$. However, there are two obstacles in this simulation.

The first obstacle is the sampling algorithm for the preimage size. For $g_i : \{0,1\}^n \to \{0,1\}^n$, $\#g_i^{-1}(\{b\})$ follows the distribution $\mathsf{Bin}(2^n, 2^{-m})$. Since the simulator deals with values represented by bits within polynomial time, we construct sampling algorithms by combining random bits while maintaining their efficiency. However, the computational complexity of sampling $\mathsf{Bin}(N, p)$ based on random bits is in $N = 2^n$ [8], which is exponential in our case.

This obstacle is resolved by the algorithm called $\mathsf{DiscBB}(N, p)$, which was introduced by Kawachi et al. [8], whose output distribution is ϵ-close to the binomial distribution with parameters N and p. Note that the running time of $\mathsf{DiscBB}(N, p)$ is in the polynomial time of $\log N$, $\log p$, and $-\log \epsilon$. A more formal statement is the following lemma.

Lemma 1 (Kawachi et al. [8]). *There is a sampling algorithm* $\mathsf{DiscBB}(N, p)$ *such that for any positive integer* N*, any rational number* $p \in [0,1]$ *represented by* l *bits, and any positive real number* ϵ*, the following properties are satisfied:*

- *the distribution of the output of the algorithm is* ϵ*-close to the binomial distribution* $\mathsf{Bin}(N, p)$ *and*
- *the running time of the algorithm is a polynomial in* $\log N$, l, *and* $-\log \epsilon$.

In our simulator, we leverage $\mathsf{DiscBB}(N, p)$ with parameters $N = 2^n$, $p = 2^{-m}$, $l = m$ and $\epsilon = 2^{-n}$. Since m is polynomial in n, the running time is polynomial in n.

The second obstacle is that even if we can sample the preimage sizes, it is not always possible to store all elements in the preimage of $\{b\}$ because it can be exponential in n. To resolve this issue, we virtually allocate elements of the preimage using a list that registers tuples of b and its preimage size, which is sampled from $\mathsf{DiscBB}(N, p)$.

3.3 Behavior of Simulatior

The proof of Theorem 2 will consist of a sequence of hybrids described by pseudocode. In this section, we explain the pseudocode in hybrid H^1 that describes the real world. In the pseudocodes, $i, i' \in \{1, 2\}$ are used to represent that O_i is either one of O_1 or O_2, and $\mathsf{O}_{i'}$ is the other. For $a \in \{0,1\}^n$ and $b \in \{0,1\}^m$, the notations "query $\mathsf{O}_i(a)$" and "query $\mathsf{O}_i^{-1}(b)$" denote forward and inverse queries to O_i and O_i^{-1}, respectively. For $i \in \{1, 2\}$, the series of hybrids use five lists Reg_i, $\mathsf{InvIm}_{i,b}$, $\mathsf{InvSize}_i$, $\mathsf{FullList}_i$, Inpt_i, and a counter c_i, which are dynamically updated based on accesses to D by the simulator.

Simulation of Oracles: Note that a random oracle returns a uniformly random output for any input that has not been queried before. If the same input is queried again, the oracle returns the same output as previously generated. The list $\mathsf{Reg}_i \subseteq \{0,1\}^n \times \{0,1\}^m$ is used to register input-output correspondences for $\mathsf{O}_i : \{0,1\}^n \to \{0,1\}^m$.

Concretely, for a query $\mathsf{O}_i(a)$, the behavior of our simulator is as follows: If there exists b such that $(a, b) \in \mathsf{Reg}_i$, the simulator outputs b. If a is not registered in Reg_i, the simulator outputs b_i randomly chosen from $\{0,1\}^m$, and register (a, b_i) to Reg_i. Then, the simulator registers the pair $(a, \mathsf{R}(a) - b_i)$ to the list $\mathsf{Reg}_{i'}$ because it holds that $\mathsf{O}_i(a) + \mathsf{O}_{i'}(a) = b_i + (\mathsf{R}(a) - b_i) = \mathsf{R}(a)$, where $\mathsf{R}(a)$ is the output of the random function.

More precisely, the simulator has to choose an output b from $\{0,1\}^m$, excluding those m-bit strings for which all preimage elements have already been registered in Reg_i. We denote this set as $\mathsf{FullList}_i$.

Simulation of Inverse Oracles: Then, we describe how our simulator operates to emulate inverse oracles. The core idea behind simulating inverse oracles is to estimate the sizes of preimages and to virtually allocate inputs accordingly. To formalize this, we introduce a list $\mathsf{InvSize}_i \subseteq \{0,1\}^m \times [0 : 2^n]$ to store pairs (b, s), where b represents an output and s denotes the estimated size of its preimage.

Note that an inverse oracle outputs $\perp$ for a query $\mathsf{O}_i^{-1}(b)$ if the size of its preimage is zero. Accordingly, for a query $\mathsf{O}_i^{-1}(b)$, the simulator's behavior is divided into the following three cases: (i) b is not registered in $\mathsf{InvSize}_i$; (ii) b is registered in $\mathsf{InvSize}_i$ with a preimage size of 0; (iii) b is registered in $\mathsf{InvSize}_i$ with a positive preimage size.

(i) The simulator determines the preimage size of b. Since some values are already paired with b in Reg_i, the simulator samples an integer t from $\mathsf{DiscBB}(N, p)$ to estimate how many additional values are paired with b in Reg_i. We use a list $\mathsf{InvIm}_{i,b}$ to register values paired with b in Reg_i. Then, it registers the tuple $(b, t + \#\mathsf{InvIm}_{i,b})$ to $\mathsf{InvSize}_i$. The behavior after determining the preimage size is the same as in cases (ii) or (iii). The details of parameters N and p in $\mathsf{DiscBB}(N, p)$ are provided later.

(ii) Since the preimage size is zero, the simulator outputs $\perp$.

(iii) In this case, let b be paired with a positive integer s in $\mathsf{InvSize}_i$ The simulator generates a response for query $\mathsf{O}_i^{-1}(b)$ by probabilistically executing one of the following two algorithms: (1) with probability $(\#\mathsf{InvIm}_{i,b})/s$, it outputs $a \xleftarrow{\$} \mathsf{InvIm}_{i,b}$, or (2) with probability $1 - (\#\mathsf{InvIm}_{i,b})/s$, it outputs $a \xleftarrow{\$} \{0,1\}^n \setminus \mathsf{Inpt}_i$, where Inpt_i is the set of n-bit strings registered in Reg_i. Then it adds (a, b) to Reg_i.

The Parameters of the Sampling Algorithm. Before we determine the parameters N and p used in the algorithm $\mathsf{DiscBB}(N, p)$, we first explain the distribution that the preimage sizes of a random oracle follow. For $\mathsf{O}_i : \{0,1\}^n \to \{0,1\}^m$ and a value $b \in \{0,1\}^m$, the preimage size of b is $s \in [0 : 2^n]$ with probability $\binom{2^n}{s}(2^{-m})^s(1-2^{-m})^{2^n - s}$. Although it may seem natural to set $N = 2^n$ and $p = 2^{-m}$, our simulator instead determines input–output correspondences, and thus the parameters N and p, dynamically in response to the queries.

For instance, after outputting an element b_1 for the first query $\mathsf{O}_i(a_1)$, the preimage size of $b_2 (\neq b_1)$ follows $\mathsf{Bin}(2^n - 1, 2^{-m})$. This is because, under this condition, the random oracle O_i is equivalent to a random function mapping from $\{0,1\}^n \setminus \{a\}$ to $\{0,1\}^m$. And then, after outputting a_2 for the subsequent query $\mathsf{O}_i^{-1}(b_2)$, the random oracle O_i becomes identical to a random function mapping from $\{0,1\}^n \setminus (g_i^{-1}(\{b_2\}) \cup \{a_1\})$ to $\{0,1\}^m \setminus \{b_2\}$.

Therefore, $N = 2^n - c_i$, where c_i counts the n-bit strings registered in Reg_i or virtually allocated via $\mathsf{InvSize}_i$, and $p = (2^m - \#\mathsf{InvSize}_i)^{-1}$. Initially, before the distinguisher issues its first query, the lists Reg_i, $\mathsf{InvSize}_i$, and $\mathsf{FullList}_i$ are all empty, and the counter c_i is set to 0.

3.4 Proof of Theorem 2

We prove Theorem 2 using a sequence of intermediate indifferentiable hybrids from H^1 to H^8, where H^1 is the ideal world and H^8 is the real world. Therefore, due to the triangular inequality, we have

$$\left| \Pr\left[\mathsf{D}^{\mathsf{H}^8} = 1\right] - \Pr\left[\mathsf{D}^{\mathsf{H}^1} = 1\right] \right| \leq \sum_{j=1}^{7} \left| \Pr\left[\mathsf{D}^{\mathsf{H}^{j+1}} = 1\right] - \Pr\left[\mathsf{D}^{\mathsf{H}^j} = 1\right] \right|. \quad (1)$$

For notational simplicity, we use $(\mathsf{LOra}_j, \mathsf{ROra}_j)$ to denote the two oracles accessed by D in Hybrid j. In the hybrid H^1 (real world), LOra_1 and ROra_1 correspond to R and $\mathsf{Sim}^{\mathsf{R}}$, respectively, and are modified in the hybrids H^2–H^8.

Hybrid H^1: This represents the case where D interacts with oracles $(\mathsf{R}, \mathsf{Sim}^{\mathsf{R}})$.

- LOra_1 is the random function R.
- ROra_1 is the simulator $\mathsf{Sim}^{\mathsf{R}}$ and is defined as follows.
  - a) On the queries of the form $\mathsf{O}_i(a)$,
    - i) if $\nexists b \in \{0,1\}^m$ s.t. $(a, b) \in \mathsf{Reg}_i$,
      1. $b \overset{\$}{\leftarrow} \{0,1\}^m \setminus \mathsf{FullList}_i$.
      2. set v as $\mathsf{R}(a)$.
      3. set b' as $v - b$.
      4. add (a, b) to Reg_i.
      5. add (a, b') to $\mathsf{Reg}_{i'}$.
      6. if $\nexists s \in [2^n]$ s.t. $(b, s) \in \mathsf{InvSize}_i$, then $c_i = c_i + 1$.
      7. if $\nexists s \in [2^n]$ s.t. $(b', s) \in \mathsf{InvSize}_{i'}$, then $c_{i'} = c_{i'} + 1$.
      8. add a to Inpt_i, $\mathsf{InvIm}_{i,b}$.
      9. add a to $\mathsf{Inpt}_{i'}$, $\mathsf{InvIm}_{i',b'}$.
      10. if $(\exists s \in [2^n]$ s.t. $(b, s) \in \mathsf{InvSize}_i)$ and $(\#\mathsf{InvIm}_{i,b} = s)$, then add b to $\mathsf{FullList}_i$.
      11. if $(\exists s \in [2^n]$ s.t. $(b, s) \in \mathsf{InvSize}_{i'})$ and $(\#\mathsf{InvIm}_{i',b'} = s')$, then add b' to $\mathsf{FullList}_{i'}$.
    - ii) return $\mathsf{Reg}_i(a)$.
  - b) On the queries of the form $\mathsf{O}_i^{-1}(b)$,
    - i) if $\nexists s \subset [0 : 2^n]$ s.t. $(b, s) \in \mathsf{InvSize}_i$,
      1. $t \leftarrow \mathsf{DiscBB}(2^n - c_i, (2^m - \#\mathsf{InvSize}_i)^{-1})$, and $c_i = c_i + t$.
      2. add $(b, t + \#\mathsf{InvIm}_{i,b})$ to $\mathsf{InvSize}_i$.
    - ii) set s as the value paired with b on $\mathsf{InvSize}_i$.
    - iii) if $s = 0$, return $\perp$.
    - iv) $u \overset{\$}{\leftarrow} [s]$.
    - v) if $u \leq \#\mathsf{InvIm}_{i,b}$, then $a \overset{\$}{\leftarrow} \mathsf{InvIm}_{i,b}$.
    - vi) else,
      1. set v as $\mathsf{R}(a)$.
      2. set b' as $b - v$.
      3. $a \overset{\$}{\leftarrow} \{0,1\}^n \setminus \mathsf{Inpt}_i$.
      4. add (a, b) to Reg_i.
      5. add (a, b') to $\mathsf{Reg}_{i'}$.
      6. if $\nexists s \in [2^n]$ s.t. $(b, s) \in \mathsf{InvSize}_i$, then $c_i = c_i + 1$.
      7. if $\nexists s' \in [2^n]$ s.t. $(b', s') \in \mathsf{InvSize}_{i'}$, then $c_{i'} = c_{i'} + 1$.
      8. add a to Inpt_i, $\mathsf{InvIm}_{i,b}$.
      9. add a to $\mathsf{Inpt}_{i'}$, $\mathsf{InvIm}_{i',b'}$.
      10. if $\#\mathsf{InvIm}_{i,b} = s$, then add b to $\mathsf{FullList}_i$.
      11. if $(\exists s' \in [2^n]$ s.t. $(b', s') \in \mathsf{InvSize}_{i'})$ and $(\#\mathsf{InvIm}_{i',b'} = s')$, then add b' to $\mathsf{FullList}_{i'}$.
    - vii) return a.

By definition, we have

$$\Pr\left[\mathsf{D}^{\mathsf{R},\mathsf{Sim}^{\mathsf{R}}} = 1\right] = \Pr\left[\mathsf{D}^{\mathsf{H}^1} = 1\right]. \tag{2}$$

Hybrid H^2: In this hybrid, we replace the sampling algorithm DiscBB in the previous hybrid with the binomial distribution Bin. Formally, we replace step 1) in b-i) in H^1 with the following step.

- $s \leftarrow \mathsf{Bin}(2^n - c_i, (2^m - \#\mathsf{InvSize}_i)^{-1})$

The only difference between H^1 and H^2 lies solely in how preimage sizes are sampled. To analyze this difference, we decompose $\mathsf{Sim}^{\mathsf{R}}$ into the sampling algorithm DiscBB and the remaining components of the algorithm. In H^1, the remaining components interact with DiscBB, whereas in H^2 they interact with Bin. This clarifies that D has indirect access to the sampling algorithms via the same remaining components. As a result, distinguishing H^1 from H^2 is no easier than distinguishing DiscBB from Bin.

From this observation, we calculate the success probability of distinguishing H^1 from H^2 by using a sequence of intermediate indifferentiable hybrids from B^1 to B^{q+1}, where B^1 is H^1 and B^{q+1} is H^2. These hybrids progressively replace the sample algorithm DiscBB with Bin. In the hybrid B^j, D has access to Bin up to the $(j-1)$-th query and to the sampling algorithm DiscBB starting from the j-th query. Hence, B^j differs from B^{j+1} only in the sampling algorithm that D accesses at the j-th query.

For notational simplicity, we use the following notation to denote sampling algorithms that D accesses in B^j : $[(1)\mathsf{DiscBB}, \ldots, (j-1)\mathsf{DiscBB}, (j)\mathsf{Bin}, \ldots, (q)\mathsf{Bin}]$. The sequence of intermediate indifferentiable hybrids from B^1 to B^{q+1} is described as B^1 : $[(1)\mathsf{DiscBB}, \ldots, (q-1)\mathsf{DiscBB}, (q)\mathsf{DiscBB}]$, B^2 : $[(1)\mathsf{DiscBB}, \ldots, (q-1)\mathsf{DiscBB}, (q)\mathsf{Bin}]$, $\cdots$, B^{q+1} : $[(1)\mathsf{Bin}, \ldots, (q-1)\mathsf{Bin}, (q)\mathsf{Bin}]$.

For any D and any ϵ, the probability that D distinguishes B^j and B^{j+1} is at most ϵ as DiscBB is ϵ-close to Bin. Hence, we substitute 2^{-n} for ϵ and we have

$$\left|\Pr\left[\mathsf{D}^{\mathsf{H}^1} = 1\right] - \Pr\left[\mathsf{D}^{\mathsf{H}^2} = 1\right]\right| \leq \frac{q}{2^n}. \tag{3}$$

Hybrid H^3:

- ROra_3 remains identical as ROra_2.
- On an input $a \in \{0,1\}^n$, LOra_3 outputs $b_1 + b_2$, where b_1, b_2 are the responses of ROra_3 when a is queried for both O_1 and O_2 to ROra_3.

Since we register $b_{i'}$ to $\mathsf{Reg}_{i'}$ as $\mathsf{R}(a) - b_i$, the output of LOra_3 $b_1 + b_2$ remains $\mathsf{R}(a)$, which is the output of ROra_2 Hence, we have

$$\Pr\left[\mathsf{D}^{\mathsf{H}^2} = 1\right] = \Pr\left[\mathsf{D}^{\mathsf{H}^3} = 1\right]. \tag{4}$$

Hybrid H^4: We replace the random function R with random values and no longer use R in H^4. To be specific, we construct H^4 by replacing step 2) in a-i) and step 1) in b-vi) in H^3 with the step such that $v \xleftarrow{\$} \{0,1\}^m$.

Since the distribution of outputs in ROra_3 and ROra_4 remains identical,

$$\Pr\left[\mathsf{D}^{\mathsf{H}^3} = 1\right] = \Pr\left[\mathsf{D}^{\mathsf{H}^4} = 1\right]. \tag{5}$$

Hybrid H^5: We set H^5 is constructed by adding the following step between steps 5) and 6) in both a-i) and b-vi) in H^4.

- if $b' \in \mathsf{FullList}_{i'}$, then abort.

H^4 and H^5 are identical given the aborts do not occur. Therefore, we have $|\Pr[\mathsf{D}^{\mathsf{H}^4} = 1] - \Pr[\mathsf{D}^{\mathsf{H}^5} = 1]| = \Pr[\mathsf{Abort}] = \Pr[\bigvee_{j=1}^{q}(\mathsf{Abort}^{(j)})] \leq \sum_{j=1}^{q} \Pr[\mathsf{Abort}^{(j)}]$, where Abort denotes the event that the abort statement occurs in H^5 and $\mathsf{Abort}^{(j)}$ denotes the event that the abort statement occurs on the jth access of D to oracles in H^5. $\Pr[\mathsf{Abort}^{(j)}]$ is bounded as

$$\Pr\left[\mathsf{Abort}^{(j)}\right] \leq \frac{j(j+1)(j+2)}{2(2^n+1)}. \tag{6}$$

The proof of (6) is provided in the Appendix, as it is somewhat lengthy. Hence, we have

$$\begin{aligned} &\left|\Pr[\mathsf{D}^{\mathsf{H}^4} = 1] - \Pr[\mathsf{D}^{\mathsf{H}^5} = 1]\right| \\ &\leq \sum_{j=1}^{q} \frac{j(j+1)(j+2)}{2(2^n+1)} = \frac{q(q+1)(3q^2+11q+22)}{24(2^n+1)}. \end{aligned} \tag{7}$$

Hybrid H^6: In the previous hybrid, LOra_5 uses a random value v to register the pair $(a, v - b_i)$ in $\mathsf{Reg}_{i'}$ whenever it registers the pair (a, b_i) in Reg_i, so that $\mathsf{O}_i(a) + \mathsf{O}_{i'}(a)$ is uniformly distributed. In this hybrid, however, we no longer make such a technical adjustment for consistency, i.e., no longer treat b'. Concretely, we eliminate steps 5, 6, 8, 10, and 12 in a-i) and b-v) in H^5.

Since both b_i and $b_{i'}$ are chosen uniformly at random, their sum $b_i + b_{i'}$ is also uniformly distributed. Hence, selecting $b_{i'}$ uniformly at random is equivalent to setting $b_{i'} = R(a) - b$, which ensures that ROra_5 is identical to ROra_6 when the abort statement does not occur. As a result, we have

$$\left|\Pr\left[\mathsf{D}^{\mathsf{H}^5} = 1\right] - \Pr\left[\mathsf{D}^{\mathsf{H}^6} = 1\right]\right| \leq \frac{q(q+1)(3q^2+11q+22)}{24(2^n+1)}. \tag{8}$$

Hybrid H^7:

- LOra_7 remains identical as LOra_6.

– Before the distinguisher forwards their first query, ROra_7 executes the setup algorithm once, which determines all input-output correspondences.

Setup-i) for a in $\{0,1\}^n$
1. $b \xleftarrow{\$} \{0,1\}^m$ and $b' \xleftarrow{\$} \{0,1\}^m$.
2. add (a,b) to Reg_1 and (a,b') to Reg_2.
3. add a to $\mathsf{InvIm}_{1,b}$ and $\mathsf{InvIm}_{2,b'}$.

Setup-ii) for (b,i) in $\{0,1\}^m \times \{1,2\}$, if $\#\mathsf{InvIm}_{i,b} = 0$, add $\perp$ to $\mathsf{InvIm}_{i,b}$.
a) On the queries of the form $\mathsf{O}_i(a)$, output b s.t. $(a,b) \in \mathsf{Reg}_i$.
b) On the queries of the form $\mathsf{O}_i^{-1}(b)$, output $a \xleftarrow{\$} \mathsf{InvIm}_{i,b}$.

In this hybrid, the input–output correspondences are determined all at once based on the input, whereas in the previous hybrid, they are determined progressively, sometimes based on the output. However, the two algorithms produce the same output distribution because the correspondences are determined according to the binomial distribution in the output-based case. Hence, we have

$$\Pr\left[\mathsf{D}^{\mathsf{H}^6} = 1\right] = \Pr\left[\mathsf{D}^{\mathsf{H}^7} = 1\right]. \tag{9}$$

Hybrid H^8:

– LOra_8 remains identical as LOra_7.
– In ROra_8, we replace all simulators and oracles with $(\mathsf{O}_1, \mathsf{O}_2, \mathsf{O}_1^{-1}, \mathsf{O}_2^{-1})$.

Constructing a function by assigning all input–output correspondences uniformly at random is equivalent to selecting a function uniformly at random from the set of all functions. Hence,

$$\Pr\left[\mathsf{D}^{\mathsf{H}^7} = 1\right] = \Pr\left[\mathsf{D}^{\mathsf{H}^8} = 1\right] \tag{10}$$

Substituting (2)–(5) and (7)–(10) into (1) completes the proof.

Acknowledgments. The authors are grateful to Keita Xagawa for introducing them to the result in [8]. They also thank Takashi Yamakawa for his comments and for drawing their attention to [1]. This work was partially supported by JSPS KAKENHI Grant Numbers JP23H00468, JP23H00479, JP23K17455, JP23K21644, JP23K24846, and JST K Program Grant Number JPMJKP24U2, Japan.

A The Proof of (6)

In this appendix, we provide the proof of (6). $\mathsf{Abort}^{(j)}$ happens when the programmed value b on the jth access belongs to $\mathsf{FullList}_i$, which registers values satisfying the following two conditions: the values are defined in $\mathsf{InvSize}_i$ and paired with s such that $s \leq j$. Due to the independence of these two events, we evaluate the probability that the programmed value b on the jth access belongs to $\mathsf{FullList}_i$ as follows.

$$\begin{aligned}
&\Pr[\mathsf{Abort}^{(j)}] \\
&\quad \leq \Pr[(\mathsf{InvSize}_i(b) \text{ is defined}) \wedge (\mathsf{InvSize}_i(b) \leq j)] \\
&\quad = \Pr[\mathsf{InvSize}_i(b) \text{ is defined}] \Pr[\mathsf{InvSize}_i(b) \leq j \mid \mathsf{InvSize}_i(b) \text{ is defined}] \\
&\quad = \Pr[\mathsf{InvSize}_i(b) \text{ is defined}] \Pr\left[\bigvee_{k=0}^{j} (\mathsf{InvSize}_i(b) = k) \mid \mathsf{InvSize}_i(b) \text{ is defined}\right] \\
&\quad = \Pr[\mathsf{InvSize}_i(b) \text{ is defined}] \sum_{k=0}^{j} \Pr\left[\mathsf{InvSize}_i(b) = k \mid \mathsf{InvSize}_i(b) \text{ is defined}\right].
\end{aligned}$$

The probability that $\mathsf{InvSize}_i(b)$ is defined is at most $\frac{j}{2^m}$ because the size of $\mathsf{InvSize}_i$ is at most j on the jth access of D to oracles and because b is chosen randomly from $\{0,1\}^m$. The conditional probability of $\#\mathsf{InvSize}_i(b) = k$ given the event that $\mathsf{InvSize}_i(b)$ is defined is evaluated by the following inequality due to $\binom{2^n+1}{k+1} = \frac{k+1}{2^n+1}\binom{2^n}{k}$ and the binomial theorem.

$$\begin{aligned}
&\Pr[\mathsf{InvSize}_i(b) = k \mid \mathsf{InvSize}_i(b) \text{ is defined}] \\
&\quad = \binom{2^n}{k}\left(\frac{1}{2^m}\right)^j \left(1 - \frac{1}{2^m}\right)^{2^n - k} \\
&\quad = \frac{(k+1)2^m}{2^n+1}\binom{2^n+1}{k+1}\left(\frac{1}{2^m}\right)^{k+1}\left(1 - \frac{1}{2^m}\right)^{2^n - k} \\
&\quad \leq \frac{(k+1)2^m}{2^n+1}.
\end{aligned}$$

Hence, abort statements on the jth access of D to oracles can be triggered with the probability at most

$$\frac{j}{2^m}\left(\sum_{k=0}^{j}\frac{(k+1)2^m}{2^n+1}\right) = \frac{j(j+1)(j+2)}{2(2^n+1)}.$$

B Pseudocodes of the Simulator in Eash Hybrid

We describe pseudocodes of hybrids in Sect. 3.4. For ease of comparison, we highlight codes of hybrid Hs that differ from previous pseudocodes in red.

B.1 Hybrid H^2:

We define H^2 by the following steps.

– LOra_2 remains identical as LOra_1.

- ROra_2 use the binomial distribution Bin instead of DiscBB to sample the size of preimages.
  a) On the queries of the form $\mathsf{O}_i(a)$,
    i) if $\nexists b \in \{0,1\}^m$ s.t. $(a,b) \in \mathsf{Reg}_i$,
      1. $b \xleftarrow{\$} \{0,1\}^m \setminus \mathsf{FullList}_i$.
      2. set v as $\mathsf{R}(a)$.
      3. set b' as $v - b$.
      4. add (a,b) to Reg_i.
      5. add (a,b') to $\mathsf{Reg}_{i'}$.
      6. if $\nexists s \in [2^n]$ s.t. $(b,s) \in \mathsf{InvSize}_i$, then $c_i = c_i + 1$.
      7. if $\nexists s \in [2^n]$ s.t. $(b',s) \in \mathsf{InvSize}_{i'}$, then $c_{i'} = c_{i'} + 1$.
      8. add a to Inpt_i, $\mathsf{InvIm}_{i,b}$.
      9. add a to $\mathsf{Inpt}_{i'}$, $\mathsf{InvIm}_{i',b}$.
      10. if ($\exists s \in [2^n]$ s.t. $(b,s) \in \mathsf{InvSize}_i$) and ($\#\mathsf{InvIm}_{i,b} = s$), then add b to $\mathsf{FullList}_i$
      11. if ($\exists s' \in [2^n]$ s.t. $(b',s') \in \mathsf{InvSize}_{i'}$) and ($\#\mathsf{InvIm}_{i',b'} = s'$), then add b' to $\mathsf{FullList}_{i'}$
    ii) return $\mathsf{Reg}_i(a)$
  b) On the queries of the form $\mathsf{O}_i^{-1}(b)$,
    i) if $\nexists s \in [2^n]$ s.t. $(b,s) \in \mathsf{InvSize}_i$,
      1. $s \leftarrow \mathsf{Bin}(2^n - c_i, (2^m - \#\mathsf{FullList}_i)^{-1})$,
      2. add $(b, s + \#\mathsf{InvIm}_{i,b})$ to $\mathsf{InvSize}_i$.
      3. $c_i = c_i + s$.
    ii) set s as the value paired with b on $\mathsf{InvSize}_i$,
    iii) $u \xleftarrow{\$} [s]$.
    iv) if $u \leq \#\mathsf{InvIm}_{i,b}$, then $a \xleftarrow{\$} \mathsf{InvIm}_{i,b}$.
    v) else,
      1. set v as $\mathsf{R}(a)$
      2. set b' as $\mathsf{R}(a) - b$
      3. $a \xleftarrow{\$} \{0,1\}^n \setminus \mathsf{Inpt}_i$
      4. add (a,b) to Reg_i.
      5. add (a,b') to $\mathsf{Reg}_{i'}$.
      6. if $\nexists s \in [2^n]$ s.t. $(b,s) \in \mathsf{InvSize}_i$, then $c_i = c_i + 1$.
      7. if $\nexists s' \in [2^n]$ s.t. $(b',s') \in \mathsf{InvSize}_{i'}$, then $c_{i'} = c_{i'} + 1$.
      8. add a to Inpt_i, $\mathsf{InvIm}_{i,b}$.
      9. add a to $\mathsf{Inpt}_{i'}$, $\mathsf{InvIm}_{i',b}$.
      10. if $\#\mathsf{InvIm}_{i,b} = s$, then add b to $\mathsf{FullList}_i$.
      11. if ($\exists s' \in [2^n]$ s.t. $(b',s') \in \mathsf{InvSize}_{i'}$) and ($\#\mathsf{InvIm}_{i',b'} = s'$), then add b' to $\mathsf{FullList}_{i'}$.
    vi) return a.

B.2 Hybrid H^4:

H^4 is defined by the following steps.

- LOra_4 remains identical as LOra_3.
- ROra_4 use random values instead of R.
  a) On the queries of the form $\mathsf{O}_i(a)$,
    i) if $\nexists b \in \{0,1\}^m$ s.t. $(a,b) \in \mathsf{Reg}_i$,
      1. $b \xleftarrow{\$} \{0,1\}^m \setminus \mathsf{FullList}_i$.
      2. $v \xleftarrow{\$} \{0,1\}^m$
      3. set b' as $v - b$
      4. add (a,b) to Reg_i.
      5. add (a,b') to $\mathsf{Reg}_{i'}$.
      6. if $\nexists s \in [2^n]$ s.t. $(b,s) \in \mathsf{InvSize}_i$, then $c_i = c_i + 1$.
      7. if $\nexists s' \in [2^n]$ s.t. $(b',s') \in \mathsf{InvSize}_{i'}$, then $c_{i'} = c_{i'} + 1$.
      8. add a to Inpt_i, $\mathsf{InvIm}_{i,b}$.
      9. add a to $\mathsf{Inpt}_{i'}$, $\mathsf{InvIm}_{i',b}$.
      10. if $(\exists s \in [2^n]$ s.t. $(b,s) \in \mathsf{InvSize}_i)$ and $(\#\mathsf{InvIm}_{i,b} = s)$, then add b to $\mathsf{FullList}_i$
      11. if $(\exists s' \in [2^n]$ s.t. $(b',s') \in \mathsf{InvSize}_{i'})$ and $(\#\mathsf{InvIm}_{i',b'} = s')$, then add b' to $\mathsf{FullList}_{i'}$
    ii) return $\mathsf{Reg}_i(a)$
  b) On the queries of the form $\mathsf{O}_i^{-1}(b)$,
    i) if $\nexists s \in [2^n]$ s.t. $(b,s) \in \mathsf{InvSize}_i$,
      1. $s \leftarrow \mathsf{Bin}(2^m - c_i, (2^n - \#\mathsf{FullList}_i)^{-1})$,
      2. add $(b, s + \#\mathsf{InvIm}_{i,b})$ to $\mathsf{InvSize}_i$.
      3. $c_i = c_i + s$.
    ii) set s as the value paired with b on $\mathsf{InvSize}_i$,
    iii) $u \xleftarrow{\$} [s]$.
    iv) if $u \leq \#\mathsf{InvIm}_{i,b}$, then $a \xleftarrow{\$} \mathsf{InvIm}_{i,b}$.
    v) else,
      1. $v \xleftarrow{\$} \{0,1\}^m$
      2. set b' as $v - b$
      3. $a \xleftarrow{\$} \{0,1\}^n \setminus \mathsf{Inpt}_i$
      4. add (a,b) to Reg_i.
      5. add (a,b') to $\mathsf{Reg}_{i'}$.
      6. if $\nexists s \in [2^n]$ s.t. $(b,s) \in \mathsf{InvSize}_i$, then $c_i = c_i + 1$.
      7. if $\nexists s' \in [2^n]$ s.t. $(b',s') \in \mathsf{InvSize}_{i'}$, then $c_{i'} = c_{i'} + 1$.
      8. add a to Inpt_i, $\mathsf{InvIm}_{i,b}$.
      9. add a to $\mathsf{Inpt}_{i'}$, $\mathsf{InvIm}_{i',b}$.
      10. if $\#\mathsf{InvIm}_{i,b} = s$, then add b to $\mathsf{FullList}_i$.
      11. if $(\exists s' \in [2^n]$ s.t. $(b',s') \in \mathsf{InvSize}_{i'})$ and $(\#\mathsf{InvIm}_{i',b'} = s')$, then add b' to $\mathsf{FullList}_{i'}$.
    vi) return a.

B.3 Hybrid H^5:

H^5 becomes the following:

- LOra_5 remains identical as LOra_4.
- ROra_5 is identical to ROra_4 except that we abort if a value programmed in $\mathsf{Reg}_{i'}(a)$ during an invocation of a O_i already belongs to $\mathsf{FullList}_{i'}$. Formally, on queries of the form $\mathsf{O}_i(a)$, ROra_5 works as above except if $\mathsf{Reg}_{i'}(a) \in \mathsf{FullList}_{i'}$, then abort.
  a) On the queries of the form $\mathsf{O}_i(a)$,
     i) if $\nexists b \in \{0,1\}^m$ s.t. $(a, b) \in \mathsf{Reg}_i$,
        1. $b \xleftarrow{\$} \{0,1\}^m \setminus \mathsf{FullList}_i$.
        2. $v \xleftarrow{\$} \{0,1\}^m$
        3. set b' as $v - b$
        4. add (a, b) to Reg_i.
        5. add (a, b') to $\mathsf{Reg}_{i'}$.
        6. if $b' \in \mathsf{FullList}_{i'}$, then abort.
        7. if $\nexists s \in [2^n]$ s.t. $(b, s) \in \mathsf{InvSize}_i$, then $c_i = c_i + 1$.
        8. if $\nexists s' \in [2^n]$ s.t. $(b', s') \in \mathsf{InvSize}_{i'}$, then $c_{i'} = c_{i'} + 1$.
        9. add a to Inpt_i, $\mathsf{InvIm}_{i,b}$.
        10. add a to $\mathsf{Inpt}_{i'}$, $\mathsf{InvIm}_{i',b}$.
        11. if $(\exists s \in [2^n]$ s.t. $(b, s) \in \mathsf{InvSize}_i)$ and $(\#\mathsf{InvIm}_{i,b} = s)$, then add b to $\mathsf{FullList}_i$
        12. if $(\exists s' \in [2^n]$ s.t. $(b', s') \in \mathsf{InvSize}_{i'})$ and $(\#\mathsf{InvIm}_{i',b'} = s')$, then add b' to $\mathsf{FullList}_{i'}$
     ii) return $\mathsf{Reg}_i(a)$
  b) On the queries of the form $\mathsf{O}_i^{-1}(b)$,
     i) if $\nexists s \in [2^n]$ s.t. $(b, s) \in \mathsf{InvSize}_i$,
        1. $s \leftarrow \mathsf{Bin}(2^m - c_i, (2^n - \#\mathsf{FullList}_i)^{-1})$,
        2. add $(b, s + \#\mathsf{InvIm}_{i,b})$ to $\mathsf{InvSize}_i$.
        3. $c_i = c_i + s$.
     ii) set s as the value paired with b on $\mathsf{InvSize}_i$,
     iii) $u \xleftarrow{\$} [s]$.
     iv) if $u \leq \#\mathsf{InvIm}_{i,b}$, then $a \xleftarrow{\$} \mathsf{InvIm}_{i,b}$.
     v) else,
        1. $v \xleftarrow{\$} \{0,1\}^m$
        2. set b' as $v - b$
        3. $a \xleftarrow{\$} \{0,1\}^n \setminus \mathsf{Inpt}_i$
        4. add (a, b) to Reg_i.
        5. add (a, b') to $\mathsf{Reg}_{i'}$.
        6. if $b' \in \mathsf{FullList}_{i'}$, then abort.
        7. if $\nexists s \in [2^n]$ s.t. $(b, s) \in \mathsf{InvSize}_i$, then $c_i = c_i + 1$.
        8. if $\nexists s' \in [2^n]$ s.t. $(b', s') \in \mathsf{InvSize}_{i'}$, then $c_{i'} = c_{i'} + 1$.
        9. add a to Inpt_i, $\mathsf{InvIm}_{i,b}$.
        10. add a to $\mathsf{Inpt}_{i'}$, $\mathsf{InvIm}_{i',b}$.
        11. if $\#\mathsf{InvIm}_{i,b} = s$, then add b to $\mathsf{FullList}_i$.
        12. if $(\exists s' \in [2^n]$ s.t. $(b', s') \in \mathsf{InvSize}_{i'})$ and $(\#\mathsf{InvIm}_{i',b'} = s')$, then add b' to $\mathsf{FullList}_{i'}$.

vi) return a.

B.4 Hybrid H^6:

We eliminate several steps in H^5. We use strikethroughs to eliminate steps. H^6 becomes the following:

- LOra_6 remains identical as LOra_5.
- ROra_6 is identical to ROra_5 except that we abort if a value programmed in $\mathsf{Reg}_{i'}(a)$ during an invocation of a O_i already belongs to $\mathsf{FullList}_{i'}$. Formally, on queries of the form $\mathsf{O}_i(a)$, ROra_5 works as above except if $\mathsf{Reg}_{i'}(a) \in \mathsf{FullList}_{i'}$, then abort.
  a) On the queries of the form $\mathsf{O}_i(a)$,
    i) if $\nexists b \in \{0,1\}^m$ s.t. $(a, b) \in \mathsf{Reg}_i$,
      1. $b \xleftarrow{\$} \{0,1\}^m \setminus \mathsf{FullList}_i$.
      2. $v \xleftarrow{\$} \{0,1\}^m$
      3. set b' as $v - b$
      4. add (a, b) to Reg_i.
      5. ~~add (a, b') to $\mathsf{Reg}_{i'}$.~~
      6. ~~if $b' \in \mathsf{FullList}_{i'}$, then abort.~~
      7. if $\nexists s \in [2^n]$ s.t. $(b, s) \in \mathsf{InvSize}_i$, then $c_i = c_i + 1$.
      8. ~~if $\nexists s' \in [2^n]$ s.t. $(b', s') \in \mathsf{InvSize}_{i'}$, then $c_{i'} = c_{i'} + 1$.~~
      9. add a to Inpt_i, $\mathsf{InvIm}_{i,b}$.
      10. ~~add a to $\mathsf{Inpt}_{i'}$, $\mathsf{InvIm}_{i',b'}$.~~
      11. if $(\exists s \in [2^n]$ s.t. $(b, s) \in \mathsf{InvSize}_i)$ and $(\#\mathsf{InvIm}_{i,b} = s)$, then add b to $\mathsf{FullList}_i$
      12. ~~if $(\exists s' \in [2^n]$ s.t. $(b', s') \in \mathsf{InvSize}_{i'})$ and $(\#\mathsf{InvIm}_{i',b'} = s')$, then add b' to $\mathsf{FullList}_{i'}$.~~
    ii) return $\mathsf{Reg}_i(a)$
  b) On the queries of the form $\mathsf{O}_i^{-1}(b)$,
    i) if $\nexists s \in [2^n]$ s.t. $(b, s) \in \mathsf{InvSize}_i$,
      1. $s \leftarrow \mathsf{Bin}(2^m - c_i, (2^n - \#\mathsf{FullList}_i)^{-1})$,
      2. add $(b, s + \#\mathsf{InvIm}_{i,b})$ to $\mathsf{InvSize}_i$.
      3. $c_i = c_i + s$.
    ii) set s as the value paired with b on $\mathsf{InvSize}_i$,
    iii) $u \xleftarrow{\$} [s]$.
    iv) if $u \leq \#\mathsf{InvIm}_{i,b}$, then $a \xleftarrow{\$} \mathsf{InvIm}_{i,b}$.
    v) else,
      1. $v \xleftarrow{\$} \{0,1\}^m$
      2. set b' as $v - b$
      3. $a \xleftarrow{\$} \{0,1\}^n \setminus \mathsf{Inpt}_i$
      4. add (a, b) to Reg_i.
      5. ~~add (a, b') to $\mathsf{Reg}_{i'}$.~~

6. ~~if $b' \in \mathsf{FullList}_{i'}$, then abort.~~
7. if $\nexists s \in [2^n]$ s.t. $(b, s) \in \mathsf{InvSize}_i$, then $c_i = c_i + 1$.
8. ~~if $\nexists s' \in [2^n]$ s.t. $(b', s') \in \mathsf{InvSize}_{i'}$, then $c_{i'} = c_{i'} + 1$.~~
9. add a to Inpt_i, $\mathsf{InvIm}_{i,b}$.
10. ~~add a to $\mathsf{Inpt}_{i'}$, $\mathsf{InvIm}_{i',b}$.~~
11. if $\#\mathsf{InvIm}_{i,b} = s$, then add b to $\mathsf{FullList}_i$.
12. ~~if $(\exists s' \in [2^n]$ s.t. $(b', s') \in \mathsf{InvSize}_{i'})$ and $(\#\mathsf{InvIm}_{i',b'} = s')$, then add b' to $\mathsf{FullList}_{i'}$.~~

vi) return a.

B.5 Hybrid B^j

We introduce a counter co that counts how many times the distinguisher forwards inverse queries. Hence, we initiarize co as 0 and define $\mathsf{B}^j, (j = 1, 2, \ldots, q + 1)$ by the following steps.

a) On the queries of the form $\mathsf{O}_i(a)$,
  i) if $\nexists b \in \{0, 1\}^m$ s.t. $(a, b) \in \mathsf{Reg}_i$,
    1. $b \xleftarrow{\$} \{0, 1\}^m \setminus \mathsf{FullList}_i$.
    2. set v as $\mathsf{R}(a)$.
    3. set b' as $v - b$.
    4. add (a, b) to Reg_i.
    5. add (a, b') to $\mathsf{Reg}_{i'}$.
    6. if $\nexists s \in [2^n]$ s.t. $(b, s) \in \mathsf{InvSize}_i$, then $c_i = c_i + 1$.
    7. if $\nexists s \in [2^n]$ s.t. $(b', s) \in \mathsf{InvSize}_{i'}$, then $c_{i'} = c_{i'} + 1$.
    8. add a to Inpt_i, $\mathsf{InvIm}_{i,b}$.
    9. add a to $\mathsf{Inpt}_{i'}$, $\mathsf{InvIm}_{i',b}$.
    10. if $(\exists s \in [2^n]$ s.t. $(b, s) \in \mathsf{InvSize}_i)$ and $(\#\mathsf{InvIm}_{i,b} = s)$, then add b to $\mathsf{FullList}_i$
    11. if $(\exists s' \in [2^n]$ s.t. $(b', s') \in \mathsf{InvSize}_{i'})$ and $(\#\mathsf{InvIm}_{i',b'} = s')$, then add b' to $\mathsf{FullList}_{i'}$
  ii) return $\mathsf{Reg}_i(a)$
b) On the queries of the form $\mathsf{O}_i^{-1}(b)$,
  i) if $\nexists s \in [2^n]$ s.t. $(b, s) \in \mathsf{InvSize}_i$,
    1. $co = co + 1$.
    2. if $co \leq q - j + 1$, $s \leftarrow \mathsf{DiscBB}((,2)^n - c_i, (2^m - \#\mathsf{FullList}_i)^{-1})$,
    3. else, $s \leftarrow \mathsf{Bin}(2^n - c_i, (2^m - \#\mathsf{FullList}_i)^{-1})$,
    4. add $(b, s + \#\mathsf{InvIm}_{i,b})$ to $\mathsf{InvSize}_i$.
    5. $c_i = c_i + s$.
  ii) set s as the value paired with b on $\mathsf{InvSize}_i$,
  iii) $u \xleftarrow{\$} [s]$.
  iv) if $u \leq \#\mathsf{InvIm}_{i,b}$, then $a \xleftarrow{\$} \mathsf{InvIm}_{i,b}$.
  v) else,
    1. set v as $\mathsf{R}(a)$

2. set b' as $\mathsf{R}(a) - b$
3. $a \xleftarrow{\$} \{0,1\}^n \setminus \mathsf{Inpt}_i$
4. add (a, b) to Reg_i.
5. add (a, b') to $\mathsf{Reg}_{i'}$.
6. if $\nexists s \in [2^n]$ s.t. $(b, s) \in \mathsf{InvSize}_i$, then $c_i = c_i + 1$.
7. if $\nexists s' \in [2^n]$ s.t. $(b', s') \in \mathsf{InvSize}_{i'}$, then $c_{i'} = c_{i'} + 1$.
8. add a to Inpt_i, $\mathsf{InvIm}_{i,b}$.
9. add a to $\mathsf{Inpt}_{i'}$, $\mathsf{InvIm}_{i',b}$.
10. if $\#\mathsf{InvIm}_{i,b} = s$, then add b to $\mathsf{FullList}_i$.
11. if $(\exists s' \in [2^n]$ s.t. $(b', s') \in \mathsf{InvSize}_{i'})$ and $(\#\mathsf{InvIm}_{i',b'} = s')$, then add b' to $\mathsf{FullList}_{i'}$.

vi) return a.

References

1. Coron, J.S., Holenstein, T., Künzler, R., Patarin, J., Seurin, Y., Tessaro, S.: How to build an ideal cipher: the indifferentiability of the feistel construction. J. Cryptol. **29**, 61–114 (2014)
2. Dachman-Soled, D., Katz, J., Thiruvengadam, A.: 10-round feistel is indifferentiable from an ideal cipher. In: Fischlin, M., Coron, J.-S. (eds.) EUROCRYPT 2016. LNCS, vol. 9666, pp. 649–678. Springer, Heidelberg (2016). https://doi.org/10.1007/978-3-662-49896-5_23
3. Eisenberg, Y., Havens, C., Korb, A., Sahai, A.: Building hard problems by combining easy ones: Revisited. Cryptology ePrint Archive, Paper 2025/223 (2025). https://eprint.iacr.org/2025/223
4. Ghosal, R., Sahai, A.: Building hard problems by combining easy ones. In: IEEE ISIT 2023, pp. 1770–1775 (2023)
5. Ghosal, R., Sahai, A.: Building hard problems by combining easy ones. Cryptology ePrint Archive, Paper 2023/1088 (2023). https://eprint.iacr.org/2023/1088
6. Goldreich, O.: The Foundations of Cryptography - Volume 1: Basic Techniques. Cambridge University Press (2001)
7. Gunsing, A., Bhaumik, R., Jha, A., Mennink, B., Shen, Y.: Revisiting the indifferentiability of the sum of permutations. In: Handschuh, H., Lysyanskaya, A. (eds.) Advances in Cryptology - CRYPTO 2023, pp. 628–660. Springer Nature Switzerland, Cham (2023)
8. Kawachi, A., Numayama, A., Tanaka, K., Xagawa, K.: Security of encryption schemes in weakened random oracle models. In: Nguyen, P.Q., Pointcheval, D. (eds.) Public Key Cryptography - PKC 2010, pp. 403–419. Springer, Berlin Heidelberg, Berlin, Heidelberg (2010)
9. Maurer, U., Renner, R., Holenstein, C.: Indifferentiability, impossibility results on reductions, and applications to the random oracle methodology. In: Theory of Cryptography, pp. 21–39 (2004)

Adaptively Secure Matchmaking Encryption from Witness Encryption

Taisei Matsushita[1(✉)], Sohto Chiku[1,2,3], Keisuke Hara[2,3], and Junji Shikata[2,4]

[1] Graduate School of Environment and Information Sciences, Yokohama National University, Yokohama, Japan
{matsuhsita-taisei-bk,chiku-sohto-tw}@ynu.jp
[2] Institute of Advanced Science, Yokohama National University, Yokohama, Japan
[3] National Institute of Advanced Industrial Science and Technology (AIST), Tokyo, Japan
hara-keisuke@aist.go.jp
[4] Faculty of Environment and Information Sciences, Yokohama National University, Yokohama, Japan
shikata-junji-rb@ynu.ac.jp

Abstract. Matchmaking encryption (ME) is a generalization of attribute-based encryption in which both the sender and the receiver (each with their own attributes) can specify access policies for the other party. While prior work has clarified privacy and authenticity for ME, achieving adaptive privacy has typically required non-standard assumptions such as indistinguishability obfuscation (iO) or intricate selective-to-adaptive upgrades under strong assumptions, leading to impractical parameters. Moreover, the match condition is known to imply iO. In this work, we focus on the "mismatch" condition and give a simple construction of adaptively secure ME from witness encryption (WE), a weaker assumption than iO. The resulting scheme reduces reliance on strong assumptions while preserving the core functionality of ME, advancing the feasibility of practical ME under weaker assumptions than previously known schemes.

1 Introduction

Backgrounds. Matchmaking encryption (ME) is an advanced encryption scheme in a multi-user setting proposed by Ateniese et al. [1], in which both a sender and a receiver can specify their policies so that the underlying message is decrypted if both policies are satisfied. Specifically, in ME, the sender specifies an attribute for a legitimate sender; and the receiver also specifies an attribute for a legitimate sender; and the receiver can decrypt the ciphertext if and only if both policies match. Formally, let σ and $\mathbb{R}$ be an attribute and a policy specified by the sender, respectively, and let ρ and $\mathbb{S}$ be an attribute and a policy specified by the receiver respectively; and the receiver successfully decrypts the ciphertext if and only if $\mathbb{R}(\rho) = 1 \wedge \mathbb{S}(\sigma) = 1$. The security requirements for ME consist of two notions: privacy and authenticity. Privacy ensures that no

P. D'Arco and A. Zamfiroiu (Eds.): SecITC 2025, LNCS 16443, pp. 23–42, 2026.
https://doi.org/10.1007/978-3-032-17443-7_2

information about the message is leaked from the ciphertext, while authenticity guarantees that a ciphertext is not forged. In particular, with respect to privacy, there are two variants depending on the types of keys available to an adversary, the mismatch and match conditions. Ateniese et al. [1] first introduced the concept of ME, defined its security, and presented constructions based on either functional encryption for randomized functions or two-input functional encryption. For a practical ME, an identity-based construction of ME under the bilinear Diffie-Hellman assumption was proposed in [2]. Subsequently, Francati et al. [5] showed how to construct ME from two-key predicate encryption (PE). In their construction, it is shown that the CPA-1-sided security of PE is enough to satisfy the mismatch condition of ME, and the CPA-2-sided security of PE is enough to meet the match condition of ME. It should be noted that Bitansky and Vaikuntanathan [3] showed that even for "plain" predicate encryption (without the two-key setting), achieving CPA-2-sided security implies the existence of iO. Their result strongly indicates that the match condition is unlikely to be realizable from a standard assumption in constructions of ME. Furthermore, even if the mismatch condition is restricted, achieving adaptive privacy of ME seems to require a rather strong assumption. In fact, all known constructions of ME either rely on iO, or use a complicated way to upgrade selective to adaptive security by assuming another strong assumption, such as sub-exponential hardness, leading to yet losing realistic parameters. Therefore, the purpose of this paper is to construct an ME scheme satisfying the mismatch condition under a weaker assumption in a simple way.

Our Contribution. In this paper, we construct an adaptively secure ME scheme under an assumption weaker than iO, namely witness encryption (WE)[1], in a simple way. Specifically, we construct ME from WE [7], a commitment, non-interactive zero-knowledge (NIZK) proof system, functional tag system [11], and lockable obfuscation (LO) [8,12] in a simple and generic way. Technically, the main idea of our construction is inspired by the idea of Waters and Wichs [11], which enables us to construct adaptively secure attribute-based encryption from WE. In this paper, we extend it in the context of constructing ME, and in particular, we prove adaptive privacy in the mismatch condition in our construction of ME.

2 Preliminaries

Here, we introduce the notation and cryptographic primitives used throughout this paper.

Notation. For any string $x \in \{0,1\}^*$, let $|x|$ denote its length. Let $[a,b]$ be a set that holds $[a,b] = \{k \in \mathbb{N} | a \leq k \leq b\}$, and $[n]$ denotes $[1,n]$. Let $\mathcal{X}$ be a set. We write $x \leftarrow_{\$} \mathcal{X}$ to denote that x is chosen uniformly at random from $\mathcal{X}$. We write $y \leftarrow \mathsf{A}(x)$ to denote that algorithm A is executed on input x and outputs

[1] Regarding the relationship between WE and iO, WE is known to be implied by iO [6], whereas no method is currently known for constructing iO from WE.

y. If A is a randomized algorithm, then y is a random variable, and we write $\mathsf{A}(x; r)$ to denote the execution of A on input x with randomness r. Moreover, if A is randomized and for all inputs x, $r \in \{0,1\}^*$ the computation of $\mathsf{A}(x; r)$ terminates in a number of steps polynomial in the input size, then we say that A is a probabilistic polynomial-time (PPT) algorithm. Throughout this paper, we denote the security parameter by $\lambda \in \mathbb{N}$ and assume that all algorithms take λ as an implicit input. A function $v : \mathbb{N} \to [0,1]$ is said to be negligible in the security parameter λ if $v(\lambda)$ decreases faster than the inverse of any polynomial in λ; that is, for every positive polynomial $p(\lambda)$, it holds that $v(\lambda) \in O(\frac{1}{p(\lambda)})$. We denote by $\mathsf{negl}(\cdot)$ a negligible function in the security parameter when the specific function is left unspecified.

2.1 Matchmaking Encryption

In this section, we introduce matchmaking encryption (ME) [1,2]. Since this paper does not consider authentication, we omit the sender's attribute key generation algorithm SKGen introduced in [1]. Nevertheless, authenticity can easily be achieved by employing NIZK proofs.

Definition 1 (Matchmaking Encryption). *A matchmaking encryption scheme consists of the following* PPT *algorithms* $\mathsf{ME} = (\mathsf{Setup}, \mathsf{RKGen}, \mathsf{PolGen}, \mathsf{Enc}, \mathsf{Dec})$.

- $\mathsf{Setup}(1^\lambda) \to (\mathsf{mpk}, \mathsf{msk})$: *The setup algorithm takes as input a security parameter* 1^λ, *and outputs a master public key and master secret key* $(\mathsf{mpk}, \mathsf{msk})$.
- $\mathsf{RKGen}(\mathsf{msk}, \rho) \to \mathsf{dk}_\rho$: *The receiver key generation algorithm takes as input the master secret key* msk *and an attribute* ρ, *and outputs a decryption key* dk_ρ *corresponding to* ρ.
- $\mathsf{PolGen}(\mathsf{msk}, \mathbb{S}) \to \mathsf{dk}_\mathbb{S}$: *The policy key generation algorithm takes as input the master secret key* msk *and a policy* $\mathbb{S}$, *and outputs a decryption key* $\mathsf{dk}_\mathbb{S}$ *corresponding to* $\mathbb{S}$.
- $\mathsf{Enc}(\mathsf{mpk}, \sigma, \mathbb{R}, \mathsf{m}) \to \mathsf{ct}$: *The encryption algorithm takes as input the master public key* mpk, *an attribute* σ, *a policy* $\mathbb{R}$, *and a message* m, *and outputs a ciphertext* ct.
- $\mathsf{Dec}(\mathsf{mpk}, \mathsf{dk}_\rho, \mathsf{dk}_\mathbb{S}, \mathsf{ct}) \to \mathsf{m}/\perp$: *The decryption algorithm takes as input the master public key* mpk, *a decryption key* dk_ρ *for attribute* ρ, *a decryption key* $\mathsf{dk}_\mathbb{S}$ *for policy* $\mathbb{S}$, *and a ciphertext* ct, *and outputs either the message* m *or the failure symbol* $\perp$.

We define correctness and security requirements for matchmaking encryption.

<u>**Correctness:**</u> *A matchmaking encryption scheme* ME *is said to satisfy correctness if, for any* $\lambda \in \mathbb{N}$, *for any* $\mathbb{R}$, ρ *such that* $\mathbb{R}(\rho) = 1$, *for any* $\mathbb{S}$, σ *such that* $\mathbb{S}(\sigma) = 1$, *and for any message* m, *it holds that* $\Pr[\mathsf{Dec}(\mathsf{mpk}, \mathsf{dk}_\rho, \mathsf{dk}_\mathbb{S}, \mathsf{ct}) = \mathsf{m}] = 1$, *where* $(\mathsf{mpk}, \mathsf{msk}) \leftarrow \mathsf{Setup}(1^\lambda)$, $\mathsf{dk}_\rho \leftarrow \mathsf{RKGen}(\mathsf{msk}, \rho)$, $\mathsf{dk}_\mathbb{S} \leftarrow \mathsf{PolGen}(\mathsf{msk}, \mathbb{S})$, $\mathsf{ct} \leftarrow \mathsf{Enc}(\mathsf{mpk}, \sigma, \mathbb{R}, \mathsf{m})$.

<u>**Privacy:**</u> *For matchmaking encryption, we define the following security game between an adversary* $\mathcal{A}$ *and a challenger, denoted by* $\mathsf{Expt}^{\mathsf{privacy}}_{\mathcal{A},\mathsf{ME}}(\lambda)$:

Setup Phase: *The challenger chooses a challenge bit* $b \leftarrow_\$ \{0,1\}$, *runs* $(\mathsf{mpk}, \mathsf{msk}) \leftarrow \mathsf{Setup}(1^\lambda)$, *and gives* mpk *to the adversary* $\mathcal{A}$.

Query Phase: *When* $\mathcal{A}$ *issues oracle queries, the challenger responds as follows:*

- **Decryption-Key Generation Oracle:** $\mathcal{A}$ *makes polynomially many decryption key generation queries. For each query,* $\mathcal{A}$ *chooses* ρ. *The challenger runs* $\mathsf{dk}_\rho \leftarrow \mathsf{RKGen}(\mathsf{msk}, \rho)$ *and returns* dk_ρ *to* $\mathcal{A}$.
- **Policy Generation Oracle:** $\mathcal{A}$ *makes polynomially many generation queries. For each query,* $\mathcal{A}$ *chooses* $\mathbb{S}$. *The challenger runs* $\mathsf{dk}_\mathbb{S} \leftarrow \mathsf{PolGen}(\mathsf{msk}, \mathbb{S})$ *and returns* $\mathsf{dk}_\mathbb{S}$ *to* $\mathcal{A}$.
- **Challenge Ciphertext:** $\mathcal{A}$ *issues exactly one challenge ciphertext query.* $\mathcal{A}$ *chooses* $(\sigma_0, \sigma_1, \mathbb{R}_0, \mathbb{R}_1, \mathsf{m}_0, \mathsf{m}_1)$. *The challenger runs* $\mathsf{ct} \leftarrow \mathsf{Enc}(\mathsf{mpk}, \sigma_b, \mathbb{R}_b, \mathsf{m}_b)$ *and returns* ct *to* $\mathcal{A}$.

Guess Phase: *Finally,* $\mathcal{A}$ *outputs a guess* $b' \in \{0,1\}$. *If* $b = b'$, *the challenger outputs 1; otherwise, it outputs 0.*

We say that an adversary $\mathcal{A}$ *is valid if, for all queries made with* $\rho, \mathbb{S}$ *the following conditions hold:*

1. *Mismatch Condition: Either*

$$(\mathbb{R}_0(\rho) = \mathbb{R}_1(\rho) = 0) \vee (\mathbb{S}(\sigma_0) = \mathbb{S}(\sigma_1) = 0) \vee \\ (\mathbb{R}_0(\rho) = \mathbb{S}(\sigma_1) = 0) \vee (\mathbb{S}(\sigma_0) = \mathbb{R}_1(\rho) = 0)$$

2. *Match Condition: Or*

$$(\mathsf{m}_0 = \mathsf{m}_1) \wedge (\mathbb{R}_0(\rho) = \mathbb{R}_1(\rho)) \wedge (\mathbb{S}(\sigma_0) = \mathbb{S}(\sigma_1))$$

The advantage of the adversary is defined as $\mathsf{Adv}^{\mathsf{privacy}}_{\mathcal{A},\mathsf{ME}}(\lambda) := \left| \Pr\left[\mathsf{Expt}^{\mathsf{privacy}}_{\mathcal{A},\mathsf{ME}}(\lambda) \Rightarrow 1\right] - \frac{1}{2} \right|$. *A matchmaking encryption scheme* ME *satisfies privacy if for any valid PPT adversary* $\mathcal{A}$, *there exists a negligible function* $\mathsf{negl}(\cdot)$ *s.t.* $\mathsf{Adv}^{\mathsf{privacy}}_{\mathcal{A},\mathsf{ME}}(\lambda) = \mathsf{negl}(\lambda)$.

2.2 Commitment

In this section, we define statistically binding commitments in the common reference string (CRS) model [10].

Definition 2 (Commitment). *A commitment scheme consists of the following* PPT *algorithms* $\mathsf{COM} = (\mathsf{Setup}, \mathsf{Commit})$*:*

- $\mathsf{Setup}(1^\lambda) \rightarrow \mathsf{crs}$*: The setup algorithm takes as input a security parameter* 1^λ, *and outputs a common reference string* crs.
- $\mathsf{Commit}_{\mathsf{crs}}(x; r) \rightarrow \mathsf{com}$*: The commit algorithm takes as input the common reference string* crs, *a string* x *and a randomness* r, *and outputs a commitment* com.

A commitment scheme must satisfy the following two properties:

Hiding: *For* $\mathsf{crs} \leftarrow \mathsf{Setup}(1^\lambda), \mathsf{com}_b \leftarrow \mathsf{Commit}_{\mathsf{crs}}(b)$, *it holds that* $(\mathsf{crs}, \mathsf{com}_0) \overset{c}{\approx} (\mathsf{crs}, \mathsf{com}_1)$.

Statistical Binding: *A commitment scheme is said to be binding if there do not exist randomness* r_0, r_1 *such that* $\mathsf{Commit}_{\mathsf{crs}}(x_0; r_0) = \mathsf{Commit}_{\mathsf{crs}}(x_1; r_1)$, *where* $\mathsf{crs} \leftarrow \mathsf{Setup}(1^\lambda)$.

Assuming the existence of one-way functions, statistically binding commitments exist [10].

2.3 Non-interactive Zero-Knowledge Proofs

In this section, we define statistically sound non-interactive zero-knowledge (NIZK) proof system in the CRS model with witness indistinguishability [4,9].

Definition 1 (NIZK). *For an NP language* $L_\lambda = \{x : \exists w \ \ (x, w) \in R_\lambda\}$ *with an NP relation* $R_\lambda \subseteq \{0,1\}^{n(\lambda)} \times \{0,1\}^{m(\lambda)}$, *a NIZK proof system consists of the following* PPT *algorithms* $\mathsf{NIZK} = (\mathsf{Setup}, \mathsf{Prove}, \mathsf{Verify})$:

- $\mathsf{Setup}(1^\lambda) \to \mathsf{crs}$: *The setup algorithm takes as input a security parameter* 1^λ, *and outputs a common reference string* crs.
- $\mathsf{Prove}_{\mathsf{crs}}(x, w) \to \pi$: *The proof generation algorithm takes as input the common reference string* crs, *an intance* x *and a witness* w, *and outputs a proof* π.
- $\mathsf{Verify}_{\mathsf{crs}}(x, \pi) \to 1/0$: *The verification algroithm takes as input the common reference string* crs, *an instance* x *and the proof* π, *and outputs a bit* $b \in \{0,1\}$, *where* $b = 1$ *indicates acceptance and* $b = 0$ *indicates rejection.*

A NIZK proof system must satisfy the following three properties:

Completeness: *For all* $\lambda \in \mathbb{N}$, $(x, w) \in R_\lambda$, *there exists a negligible function* $\mathsf{negl}(\cdot)$ *such that*

$$\Pr\left[\mathsf{Verify}_{\mathsf{crs}}(x, w) = 1 : \ \mathsf{crs} \leftarrow \mathsf{Setup}(1^\lambda), \ \pi \leftarrow \mathsf{Prove}_{\mathsf{crs}}(x, w)\right] \geq 1 - \mathsf{negl}(\lambda).$$

Statistical Soundness: *For all* $x \notin L_\lambda$ *and for all* π, *if* $\mathsf{Verify}_{\mathsf{crs}}(x, \pi) = 0$, *then* crs *is said to be sound, and it hold that*

$$\Pr\left[\mathsf{crs} \text{ is sound} : \ \mathsf{crs} \leftarrow \mathsf{Setup}(1^\lambda)\right] = 1 - \mathsf{negl}(\lambda).$$

Witness Indistinguishability: *We say* NIZK *satisfies witness indistinguishability if for any* $b \in \{0,1\}$ *and for any* x, w_0, w_1 *such that* $(x, w_0) \in R_\lambda \wedge (x, w_1) \in R_\lambda$, *it holds that*

$$\left| \Pr\left[b = b' \ \middle| \ \begin{array}{l} \mathsf{crs} \leftarrow \mathsf{Setup}(1^\lambda) \\ b \leftarrow_\$ \{0,1\} \\ \pi \leftarrow \mathsf{Prove}_{\mathsf{crs}}(x, w_b) \\ b' \leftarrow \mathcal{A}(\mathsf{crs}, \pi) \end{array} \right] - \frac{1}{2} \right| = \mathsf{negl}(\lambda).$$

2.4 Functional Tag System

In this section, we introduce the functional tag system [11].

Definition 3 (Functional Tag System). *A functional tag system consists of the following* PPT *algorithms:*

- $\mathsf{DInputTag}(x) \to \mathsf{tag}_x$*: The dummy input-tag generation algorithm takes as input* x *and outputs a tag* tag_x *corresponding to* x*.*
- $\mathsf{DFunctionTag}(f) \to \mathsf{tag}_f$*: The dummy function-tag generation algorithm takes a function* f *as input and outputs a tag* tag_f *corresponding to* f*.*
- $\mathsf{KGen}(1^\lambda) \to \mathsf{tsk}$*: The key generation algorithm takes the security parameter* 1^λ *as input and outputs a tag-generation key* tsk*.*
- $\mathsf{SInputTag}(\mathsf{tsk}, x) \to \mathsf{tag}_x$*: The smart input-tag generation algorithm takes a tag-generation key* tsk *and an input* x*, and outputs a tag* tag_x *corresponding to* x*.*
- $\mathsf{SFunctionTag}(\mathsf{tsk}, f) \to \mathsf{tag}_f$*: The smart function-tag generation algorithm takes a tag-generation key* tsk *and a function* f*, and outputs a tag* tag_f *corresponding to* f*.*
- $\mathsf{Trigger}(\mathsf{tag}_x, \mathsf{tag}_f) \to 1/0$*: The trigger algorithm takes as input a tag* tag_x *corresponding to an input* x *and a tag* tag_f *corresponding to a function* f*, and outputs either 1 or 0.*

We define correctness and security requirements for a functional tag system.

Dummy Correctness: *A functional tag system* FTS *satisfies dummy correctness if, for any* $\lambda \in \mathbb{N}$*,* f*, and* x*, there exists a negligible function* $\mathsf{negl}(\cdot)$ *such that*

$$\Pr[\mathsf{Trigger}(\mathsf{DInputTag}(x), \mathsf{DFunctionTag}(f)) = 1] = \mathsf{negl}(\lambda)$$

Smart Correctness: *A functional tag system* FTS *satisfies smart correctness if, for any* $\lambda \in \mathbb{N}$*, any* f*,* x *such that* $f(x) = 1$*, and any* $\mathsf{tsk} \leftarrow \mathsf{KGen}(1^\lambda)$*, it holds that*

$$\Pr[\mathsf{Trigger}(\mathsf{SInputTag}(\mathsf{tsk}, x), \mathsf{SFunctionTag}(\mathsf{tsk}, f)) = 1] = 1.$$

Security: *For a functional tag system, consider the following security game* $\mathsf{Expt}^{\mathsf{IND}}_{\mathcal{A},\mathsf{FTS}}(\lambda)$ *between an adversary* $\mathcal{A}$ *and a challenger:*

Setup Phase: *The challenger samples a challenge bit* $b \leftarrow_\$ \{0, 1\}$ *uniformly at random and runs* $\mathsf{tsk} \leftarrow \mathsf{KGen}(1^\lambda)$*.*

Query Phase: *For each oracle query made by* $\mathcal{A}$*, the challenger responds as follows:*

- *Function-tag generation oracle:* $\mathcal{A}$ *may make polynomially many queries by selecting a function* f*. Depending on* b*, the challenger returns*

$$\begin{cases} \mathsf{tag}_f \leftarrow \mathsf{DFunctionTag}(f) & \textbf{if } b = 0 \\ \mathsf{tag}_f \leftarrow \mathsf{SFunctionTag}(\mathsf{tsk}, f) & \textbf{if } b = 1 \end{cases}$$

- *Input-tag generation oracle: $\mathcal{A}$ may make exactly one query by selecting an input x. Depending on b, the challenger returns*

$$\begin{cases} \mathsf{tag}_x \leftarrow \mathsf{DInputTag}(x) & \textbf{if } b = 0 \\ \mathsf{tag}_x \leftarrow \mathsf{SInputTag}(\mathsf{tsk}, x) & \textbf{if } b = 1 \end{cases}$$

Guess Phase: *Finally, $\mathcal{A}$ outputs a guess $b' \in \{0,1\}$. If $b = b'$, the challenger outputs 1; otherwise, it outputs 0.*

An adversary $\mathcal{A}$ is said to be valid if, for all queried functions f, it holds that $f(x) = 0$. The advantage of adversary $\mathcal{A}$ is defined as

$$\mathsf{Adv}^{\mathsf{IND}}_{\mathcal{A},\mathsf{FTS}}(\lambda) := \left| \Pr\left[\mathsf{Expt}^{\mathsf{IND}}_{\mathcal{A},\mathsf{FTS}}(\lambda) \Rightarrow 1 \,\middle|\, b = 0\right] - \Pr\left[\mathsf{Expt}^{\mathsf{IND}}_{\mathcal{A},\mathsf{FTS}}(\lambda) \Rightarrow 1 \,\middle|\, b = 1\right] \right|$$

A functional tag system is secure if, for every valid PPT *adversary $\mathcal{A}$ there exists a negligible function* $\mathsf{negl}(\cdot)$ *such that* $\mathsf{Adv}^{\mathsf{IND}}_{\mathcal{A},\mathsf{FTS}}(\lambda) = \mathsf{negl}(\lambda)$.

2.5 Witness Encryption

In this section, we define Witness Encryption [7].

Definition 4 (Witness Encryption. *Witness Encryption for an NP language L with the corresponding witness relation R consists of the following pair of* PPT *algorithms:*

- $\mathsf{Enc}(1^\lambda, x, \mu) \to \mathsf{ct}$*: The encryption algorithm takes as input the security parameter 1^λ, an instance x, and a plaintext μ, and outputs a ciphertext* ct.
- $\mathsf{Dec}(w, \mathsf{ct}) \to \mu$*: The decryption algorithm takes as input a witness w and a ciphertext* ct*, and outputs the plaintext μ.*

We define the correctness and security requirements for Witness Encryption.

<u>**Correctness:**</u> *A Witness Encryption scheme* WE *satisfies correctness if, for any $\lambda \in \mathbb{N}$, any x, w such that $R(x, w) = 1$, and any $\mu \in \{0,1\}$, the following holds:*

$$\Pr\left[\mathsf{Dec}(w, \mathsf{Enc}(1^\lambda, x, \mu)) = \mu\right] = 1.$$

<u>**Security:**</u> *For a witness encryption scheme* WE*, let us define security game* <u>WEGame</u> *as follows:*

Setup Phase: *The challenger samples a challenge bit $b \leftarrow\!\$\, \{0,1\}$ uniformly at random.*

Query Phase: *$\mathcal{A}$ makes exactly one query by selecting (x, μ_0, μ_1). Depending on b, the challenger returns $\mathsf{ct}_b \leftarrow \mathsf{Enc}(1^\lambda, x, \mu_b)$.*

Guess Phase: *Finally, $\mathcal{A}$ outputs a guess $b' \in \{0,1\}$. If $b = b'$, the challenger outputs* 1*; otherwise, it outputs* 0.

The advantage of the adversary $\mathcal{A}$ is defined as

$$\mathsf{Adv}^{\mathsf{IND}}_{\mathcal{A},\mathsf{WE}}(\lambda) := \left| \Pr\left[\mathsf{WEGame}^{\mathcal{A}}_{\mathsf{WE}}(\lambda) \Rightarrow 1 \,\middle|\, b = 0\right] - \Pr\left[\mathsf{WEGame}^{\mathcal{A}}_{\mathsf{WE}}(\lambda) \Rightarrow 1 \,\middle|\, b = 1\right] \right|.$$

A WE is said to be secure if for any PPT *adversary $\mathcal{A}$, there exists a negligible function* $\mathsf{negl}(\lambda)$ *such that* $\mathsf{Adv}^{\mathsf{IND}}_{\mathcal{A},\mathsf{WE}}(\lambda) = \mathsf{negl}(\lambda)$.

2.6 Lockable Obfuscation

In this section, we define Lockable Obfuscation (LO) [8].

Definition 5 (Lockable Obfuscation). *For a class of circuits $\mathcal{C}_{n,m,d}$ with depth $d(\lambda)$, input length $n(\lambda)$ bits, and output length $m(\lambda)$ bits, and for a message space $\mathcal{M}$, a Lockable Obfuscation consists of the following* PPT *algorithms:*

- $\mathsf{Obf}(1^\lambda, P, \mathrm{msg}, \alpha) \rightarrow \tilde{P}$: *The obfuscation algorithm takes as input the security parameter λ, a program $P \in \mathcal{C}_{n,m,d}$, a message $\mathrm{msg} \in \mathcal{M}$, and a lock string $\alpha \in \{0,1\}^{m(\lambda)}$, and outputs an obfuscated program $\tilde{P}$.*
- $\mathsf{Eval}(\tilde{P}, x) \rightarrow y \in \mathcal{M} \cup \{\perp\}$: *The evaluation algorithm takes as input an obfuscated program $\tilde{P}$ and a string $x \in \{0,1\}^{n(\lambda)}$, and outputs $y \in \mathcal{M} \cup \{\perp\}$.*

We now define the correctness and security requirements for LO.

Correctness: *An LO scheme satisfies correctness if, for any $\lambda \in \mathbb{N}$, input $x \in \{0,1\}^{n(\lambda)}$, program $P \in \mathcal{C}_{n,m,d}$, message $\mathrm{msg} \in \mathcal{M}$, the following holds:*

- *If $P(x) = \alpha$:* $\Pr\left[\mathsf{Eval}(\mathsf{Obf}(1^\lambda, P, \mathrm{msg}, \alpha), x) = \mathrm{msg}\right] = 1$,
- *If $P(x) \neq \alpha$:* $\Pr\left[\mathsf{Eval}(\mathsf{Obf}(1^\lambda, P, \mathrm{msg}, \alpha), x) = \mathrm{msg}\right] \leq \mathrm{negl}(\lambda)$.

Security: *For a lockable obfuscation scheme* LO, *let us define security game* LOGame *as follows:*

Setup Phase: *The challenger samples a challenge bit $b \leftarrow\$ \{0,1\}$ uniformly at random.*

Query Phase: *$\mathcal{A}$ makes exactly one query by selecting $(P, \mathrm{msg}, \mathrm{st})$. Depending on b, the challenger returns*

$$\begin{cases} \tilde{P}_0 \leftarrow \mathsf{Obf}(1^\lambda, P, \mathrm{msg}, \alpha) & b = 0 \\ \tilde{P}_1 \leftarrow \mathsf{Sim}(1^\lambda, 1^{|P|}, 1^{|\mathrm{msg}|}) & b = 1. \end{cases}$$

Guess Phase: *Finally, $\mathcal{A}$ outputs a guess $b' \in \{0,1\}$. If $b = b'$, the challenger outputs 1; otherwise, it outputs 0.*

The advantage of the adversary $\mathcal{A}$ is defined as

$$\mathsf{Adv}^{\mathsf{SIM}}_{\mathcal{A},\mathsf{LO}}(\lambda) := \left|\Pr\left[\mathsf{LOGame}^{\mathcal{A}}_{\mathsf{LO}}(\lambda) \Rightarrow 1 \,\middle|\, b = 0\right] - \Pr\left[\mathsf{LOGame}^{\mathcal{A}}_{\mathsf{LO}}(\lambda) \Rightarrow 1 \,\middle|\, b = 1\right]\right|.$$

A lockable obfuscation is said to be secure if for any PPT *adversary $\mathcal{A}$, there exists a negligible function $\mathsf{negl}(\lambda)$ such that $\mathsf{Adv}^{\mathsf{SIM}}_{\mathcal{A},\mathsf{LO}}(\lambda) = \mathsf{negl}(\lambda)$.*

3 Our Construction

In this section, we present a generic construction of adaptively secure ME based on Witness Encryption (WE), together with its security proof. The main idea is based on the technique of constructing adaptively secure Attribute-Based Encryption (ABE) from functional tag systems, as proposed by Waters and

Wichs [11]. Furthermore, we incorporate LO, as introduced by Goyal et al. [8], into our construction to hide the sender's attribute and the receiver's policy from the ciphertexts.

Ingredients. Our construction of ME employs the following building blocks:

- A Witness Encryption scheme $\mathsf{WE} = (\mathsf{WE.Enc}, \mathsf{WE.Dec})$ that satisfies soundness.
- A statistically binding commitment scheme $\mathsf{COM} = (\mathsf{Setup}, \mathsf{Commit})$.
- A statistically sound NIZK proof system $\mathsf{NIZK} = (\mathsf{Setup}, \mathsf{Prove}, \mathsf{Verify})$.
- A functional tag system $\mathsf{FTS} = (\mathsf{DInputTag}, \mathsf{DFunctionTag}, \mathsf{SGen}, \mathsf{SInputTag}, \mathsf{SFunctionTag}, \mathsf{Trigger})$
- A Lockable Obfuscation scheme $\mathsf{LO} = (\mathsf{Obf}, \mathsf{Eval})$.

Construction. Let the function class $\mathcal{F}_\lambda$ be a subset of Boolean functions $\mathcal{F}_\lambda \subseteq \{f : \{0,1\}^{n(\lambda)} \to \{0,1\}\}$. Our ME scheme ME is described as follows[2]:

- $\mathsf{Setup}(1^\lambda)$: It runs $\mathsf{NIZK.crs}_0 \leftarrow \mathsf{NIZK.Setup}(1^\lambda)$, $\mathsf{NIZK.crs}_1 \leftarrow \mathsf{NIZK.Setup}(1^\lambda)$, and $\mathsf{Com.crs} \leftarrow \mathsf{Com.Setup}(1^\lambda)$. Next, it chooses $r_{\mathsf{rcv},0}, r_{\mathsf{snd},0}, r_{\mathsf{rcv},1}, r_{\mathsf{snd},1} \leftarrow_\$ \{0,1\}^{4\lambda}$. Then, it computes $\mathsf{com}_{\mathsf{rcv},0} \leftarrow \mathsf{Commit}_{\mathsf{Com.crs}}(0; r_{\mathsf{rcv},0})$, $\mathsf{com}_{\mathsf{rcv},1} \leftarrow \mathsf{Commit}_{\mathsf{Com.crs}}(0^{\ell(\lambda)}; r_{\mathsf{rcv},1})$, $\mathsf{com}_{\mathsf{snd},0} \leftarrow \mathsf{Commit}_{\mathsf{Com.crs}}(0; r_{\mathsf{snd},0})$, and $\mathsf{com}_{\mathsf{snd},1} \leftarrow \mathsf{Commit}_{\mathsf{Com.crs}}(0^{\ell(\lambda)}; r_{\mathsf{snd},1})$. Finally, it outputs $\mathsf{mpk} := (\mathsf{Com.crs}, \mathsf{NIZK.crs}_0, \mathsf{NIZK.crs}_1, \mathsf{com}_{\mathsf{rcv},0}, \mathsf{com}_{\mathsf{rcv},1}, \mathsf{com}_{\mathsf{snd},0}, \mathsf{com}_{\mathsf{snd},1})$ and $\mathsf{msk} := (r_{\mathsf{rcv},0}, r_{\mathsf{snd},0})$.
- $\mathsf{RKGen}(\mathsf{msk}, \rho)$: It defines $f_\rho : \mathcal{F}_\lambda \to \{0,1\}$ that takes a policy $\mathbb{R} \in \mathcal{F}_\lambda$ as input and outputs $\mathbb{R}(\rho) \in \{0,1\}$, and runs $\mathsf{tag}_{f_\rho} \leftarrow \mathsf{DFunctionTag}(1^\lambda, f_\rho)$. Now, consider the following NP relation NIZK.R^0:

$$\text{NIZK}.R^0 = \left\{ (x_0, w_0) : \begin{array}{c} x_0 = (\mathsf{Com.crs}, \mathsf{com}_{\mathsf{rcv},0}, \mathsf{com}_{\mathsf{rcv},1}, \rho, \mathsf{tag}_{f_\rho}) \\ \text{either } w_0 = r_{\mathsf{rcv},0} \\ : \mathsf{com}_{\mathsf{rcv},0} = \mathsf{Commit}_{\mathsf{Com.crs}}(0; r_{\mathsf{rcv},0}) \\ \text{or } w_0 = (\mathsf{tsk}_{\mathsf{rcv}}, r_{\mathsf{rcv},1}, r_{\mathsf{rcv},2}) \\ : \mathsf{com}_{\mathsf{rcv},1} = \mathsf{Commit}_{\mathsf{Com.crs}}(\mathsf{tsk}_{\mathsf{rcv}}; r_{\mathsf{rcv},1}) \\ \wedge \mathsf{tag}_{f_\rho} = \mathsf{SFunctionTag}(\mathsf{tsk}_{\mathsf{rcv}}, f_\rho; r_{\mathsf{rcv},2}) \end{array} \right\}.$$

Then, it sets $x_0 := (\mathsf{Com.crs}, \mathsf{com}_{\mathsf{rcv},0}, \mathsf{com}_{\mathsf{rcv},1}, \rho, \mathsf{tag}_{f_\rho})$, $w_0 := r_{\mathsf{rcv},0}$, and computes $\pi_0 \leftarrow \mathsf{Prove}_{\mathsf{NIZK.crs}_0}(x_0, w_0)$ with respect to the relation NIZK.R^0. Finally, it outputs $\mathsf{dk}_\rho := \left(\rho, \mathsf{tag}_{f_\rho}, \pi_0\right)$.

[2] As mentioned above, although the security of ME should in principle also consider Authenticity, we omit its proof here since it can be straightforwardly established by combining NIZKs and digital signatures using the method of [1].

- $\mathsf{PolGen}(\mathsf{msk}, \mathbb{S})$: It runs $\mathsf{tag}_{\mathbb{S}} \leftarrow \mathsf{DFunctionTag}(1^\lambda, \mathbb{S})$. Now, consider the following NP relation NIZK.R^1:

$$\text{NIZK}.R^1 = \left\{ (x_1, w_1) : \begin{array}{c} x_1 = (\mathsf{Com.crs}, \mathsf{com}_{\mathsf{snd},0}, \mathsf{com}_{\mathsf{snd},1}, \mathbb{S}, \mathsf{tag}_{\mathbb{S}}) \\ \text{either } w_1 = r_{\mathsf{snd},0} \\ : \mathsf{com}_{\mathsf{snd},0} = \mathsf{Commit}_{\mathsf{Com.crs}}(0; r_{\mathsf{snd},0}) \\ \text{or } w_1 = (\mathsf{tsk}_{\mathsf{snd}}, r_{\mathsf{snd},1}, r_{\mathsf{snd},2}) \\ : \mathsf{com}_{\mathsf{snd},1} = \mathsf{Commit}_{\mathsf{Com.crs}}(\mathsf{tsk}_{\mathsf{snd}}; r_{\mathsf{snd},1}) \\ \wedge\, \mathsf{tag}_{\mathbb{S}} = \mathsf{SFunctionTag}(\mathsf{tsk}_{\mathsf{snd}}, \mathbb{S}; r_{\mathsf{snd},2}) \end{array} \right\}.$$

  Then, it sets $x_1 := (\mathsf{Com.crs}, \mathsf{com}_{\mathsf{snd},0}, \mathsf{com}_{\mathsf{snd},1}, \mathbb{S}, \mathsf{tag}_{\mathbb{S}}), w_1 := r_{\mathsf{snd},0}$ and compute $\pi_1 \leftarrow \mathsf{Prove}_{\mathsf{NIZK.crs}_1}(x_1, w_1)$ with respect to the relation NIZK.R^1. Finally, it outputs $\mathsf{dk}_{\mathbb{S}} := (\mathbb{S}, \mathsf{tag}_{\mathbb{S}}, \pi_1)$.
- $\mathsf{Enc}(\mathsf{mpk}, \sigma, \mathbb{R}, \mathsf{m})$: It computes $\mathsf{tag}_\sigma \leftarrow \mathsf{DInputTag}(1^\lambda, \sigma)$ and $\mathsf{tag}_{\mathbb{R}} \leftarrow \mathsf{DInputTag}(1^\lambda, \mathbb{R})$. Now, consider the following NP relation WE.R:

$$\text{WE}.R = \left\{ (x_{WE}, w_{WE}) : \begin{array}{l} x_{WE} = (\mathsf{Com.crs}, \mathsf{NIZK.crs}_0, \mathsf{NIZK.crs}_1, \mathsf{com}_{\mathsf{rcv},0}, \\ \qquad \mathsf{com}_{\mathsf{rcv},1}, \mathsf{com}_{\mathsf{snd},0}, \mathsf{com}_{\mathsf{snd},1}, \sigma, \mathsf{tag}_\sigma, \mathbb{R}, \mathsf{tag}_{\mathbb{R}}) \\ w_{WE} = (\rho, \mathsf{tag}_{f_\rho}, \mathbb{S}, \mathsf{tag}_{\mathbb{S}}, \pi_0, \pi_1) : \\ \mathbb{R}(\rho) = 1 \wedge \mathsf{Verify}_{\mathsf{NIZK.crs}_0}(x_0, \pi_0) = 1 \\ \wedge \mathbb{S}(\sigma) = 1 \wedge \mathsf{Verify}_{\mathsf{NIZK.crs}_1}(x_1, \pi_1) = 1 \\ \wedge \mathsf{Trigger}(\mathsf{tag}_{\mathbb{S}}, \mathsf{tag}_\sigma) = 0 \wedge \mathsf{Trigger}(\mathsf{tag}_{\mathbb{R}}, \mathsf{tag}_{f_\rho}) = 0 \end{array} \right\}.$$

  Next, it samples a lock string $\alpha \leftarrow\!\$\, \{0,1\}^{d(\lambda)}$ for LO. Then, it sets $x_{WE} := (\mathsf{Com.crs}, \mathsf{NIZK.crs}_0, \mathsf{NIZK.crs}_1, \mathsf{com}_{\mathsf{rcv},0}, \mathsf{com}_{\mathsf{rcv},1}, \mathsf{com}_{\mathsf{snd},0}, \mathsf{com}_{\mathsf{snd},1}, \sigma, \mathsf{tag}_\sigma, \mathbb{R}, \mathsf{tag}_{\mathbb{R}})$ and $w_{WE} := (\rho, \mathsf{tag}_{f_\rho}, \mathbb{S}, \mathsf{tag}_{\mathbb{S}}, \pi_0, \pi_1)$, and runs $\mathsf{WE.ct}_\alpha \leftarrow \mathsf{WE.Enc}(1^\lambda, x_{WE}, \alpha)$ and $\tilde{P} \leftarrow \mathsf{Obf}(1^\lambda, \mathsf{WE.Dec}(\cdot, \mathsf{WE.ct}_\alpha), \mathsf{m}, \alpha)$. Finally, it outputs $\mathsf{ct} := \tilde{P}$.
- $\mathsf{Dec}(\mathsf{dk}_\rho, \mathsf{dk}_{\mathbb{S}}, \mathsf{ct})$: It computes $\mathsf{m} \leftarrow \mathsf{Eval}(\tilde{P}, (\mathsf{dk}_\rho, \mathsf{dk}_{\mathbb{S}}))$, and outputs m.

4 Security Proof

In this section, we prove the correctness and the adaptive privacy under the mismatch condition of our proposed scheme ME.

Theorem 1. *Assume the existence of a WE scheme for NP relations that is sound, a statistically sound NIZK proof system for NP relations, a statistically binding commitment scheme, and a functional tag system for circuits. Then there exists an ME scheme for circuits achieving adaptive privacy under the mismatch condition.*

Proof. First, we prove the correctness. For all security parameters $\lambda \in \mathbb{N}$, attributes σ, ρ, policies $\mathbb{S}, \mathbb{R}$ such that $\mathbb{S}(\sigma) = 1 \wedge \mathbb{R}(\rho) = 1$, first compute correctly $(\mathsf{mpk}, \mathsf{msk}) \leftarrow \mathsf{Setup}(1^\lambda)$, $\mathsf{sk}_\rho \leftarrow \mathsf{RKGen}(\mathsf{msk}, \rho)$, $\mathsf{dk}_{\mathbb{S}} \leftarrow \mathsf{PolGen}(\mathsf{msk}, \mathbb{S})$, and $\mathsf{ct} \leftarrow \mathsf{Enc}(\sigma, \mathbb{R}, \mathsf{m})$. In this case, since the NIZK proofs and the functional tag system contained in the generated decryption key and policy key satisfy

$\mathsf{Verify}_{\mathsf{NIZK.crs}_0}(x_0, \pi_0) = 1 \wedge \mathsf{Verify}_{\mathsf{NIZK.crs}_1}(x_1, \pi_1) = 1 \wedge \mathsf{Trigger}(\mathsf{tag}_{\mathbb{S}}, \mathsf{tag}_\sigma) = 0 \wedge \mathsf{Trigger}(\mathsf{tag}_{\mathbb{R}}, \mathsf{tag}_{f_\rho}) = 0$ it follows that $\mathsf{WE}.R(x_{WE}, w_{WE}) = 1$. Therefore, by the correctness of WE, $\mathsf{WE.Dec}((\mathsf{dk}_\rho, \mathsf{dk}_{\mathbb{S}}), \mathsf{WE.ct}_\alpha) = \alpha$. Hence, for $\mathsf{Dec}(\mathsf{dk}_\rho, \mathsf{dk}_{\mathbb{S}}, \mathsf{ct})$, by the correctness of LO, it holds that

$$\mathsf{Eval}(\tilde{P}, (\mathsf{dk}_\rho, \mathsf{dk}_{\mathbb{S}})) = \mathsf{Eval}(\mathsf{Obf}(1^\lambda, \mathsf{WE.Dec}(\cdot, \mathsf{WE.ct}_\alpha), \mathsf{m}, \alpha), (\mathsf{dk}_\rho, \mathsf{dk}_{\mathbb{S}})) = \mathsf{m}.$$

Next, we prove the adaptive privacy under the mismatch condition. Let $\mathcal{A}$ be an adversary attempting to break the adaptive Privacy of ME under the mismatch condition. From the definition of privacy under the mismatch condition the queries allowed to the adversary fall into the following four cases:

$$① \ \mathbb{R}_0(\rho) = \mathbb{R}_1(\rho) = 0 \ \vee \ ② \ \mathbb{S}(\sigma_0) = \mathbb{S}(\sigma_1) = 0 \ \vee$$
$$③ \ \mathbb{R}_0(\rho) = \mathbb{S}(\sigma_1) = 0 \ \vee \ ④ \ \mathbb{S}(\sigma_0) = \mathbb{R}_1(\rho) = 0$$

In the following, we use $\epsilon_i := \Pr\left[\mathrm{PMEGame}_i^b(\lambda) \Rightarrow 1\right]$ for the probability that $\mathcal{A}$ submits correct guess in $\mathrm{PMEGame}_i^b(\lambda)$.

Now, we consider the case ① $\mathbb{R}_0(\rho) = \mathbb{R}_1(\rho) = 0$. To prove the security, we consider the following sequence of hybrids:

- $\mathrm{PMEGame}_0^b(\lambda)$: This is the original security game $\mathsf{Expt}^{\mathsf{privacy}}_{\mathcal{A},\mathsf{ME}}(\lambda)$.
- $\mathrm{PMEGame}_1^b(\lambda)$: In this game, we modify how tags for the receiver's attributes and policy are generated. At the beginning of the game, the challenger samples a "smart tag key" $\mathsf{tsk}_{\mathsf{rcv}} \leftarrow \mathsf{KGen}(1^\lambda)$. For decryption-key generation queries, instead of producing dummy tags, the challenger computes $\mathsf{tag}_{f_\rho} \leftarrow \mathsf{SFunctionTag}(\mathsf{tsk}_{\mathsf{rcv}}, f_\rho)$ and uses it in the response. For encryption queries, instead of using dummy tags, the challenger computes $\mathsf{tag}_{\mathbb{R}_b} \leftarrow \mathsf{SInputTag}(\mathsf{tsk}_{\mathsf{rcv}}, \mathbb{R}_b)$ and incorporates it into the challenge ciphertext.
- $\mathrm{PMEGame}_2^b(\lambda)$: In this game, we modify the generation of the master public key. When choosing $\mathsf{com}_{\mathsf{rcv},1}$, the challenger sets $\mathsf{com}_{\mathsf{rcv},1} := \mathsf{Commit}_{\mathsf{Com.crs}}(\mathsf{tsk}_{\mathsf{rcv}}; r_{\mathsf{rcv},1})$ instead of committing to $0^{\ell(\lambda)}$.
- $\mathrm{PMEGame}_3^b(\lambda)$: In this game, we modify how the proof π_0 is generated for decryption key queries. When answering such a query, the challenger uses the witness $w_0 = (\mathsf{tsk}_{\mathsf{rcv}}, r_{\mathsf{rcv},1}, r_{\mathsf{rcv},2})$ instead of $w_0 = r_{\mathsf{rcv},0}$. That is, $\pi_0 \leftarrow \mathsf{Prove}_{\mathsf{NIZK.crs}_0}\Big(x_0 = (\mathsf{Com.crs}, \mathsf{com}_{\mathsf{rcv},0}, \mathsf{com}_{\mathsf{rcv},1}, \rho, \mathsf{tag}_{f_\rho}), w_0 = (\mathsf{tsk}_{\mathsf{rcv}}; r_{\mathsf{rcv},1}, r_{\mathsf{rcv},2})\Big)$, where $r_{\mathsf{rcv},2}$ denotes the randomness used in generating $\mathsf{tag}_{f_\rho} \leftarrow \mathsf{SFunctionTag}(\mathsf{tsk}_{\mathsf{rcv}}, f_\rho; r_{\mathsf{rcv},2})$.
- $\mathrm{PMEGame}_4^b(\lambda)$: In this game, we modify the generation of the master public key. When choosing $\mathsf{com}_{\mathsf{rcv},0}$, the challenger sets $\mathsf{com}_{\mathsf{rcv},0} := \mathsf{Commit}_{\mathsf{Com.crs}}(1; r_{\mathsf{rcv},0})$ instead of committing to 0.
- $\mathrm{PMEGame}_5^b(\lambda)$: In this game, we modify how the ciphertext generated in the encryption algorithm. Specifically, when answering encryption queries, the challenger computes $\mathsf{WE.ct}$ using the fixed value $\alpha = 0^{d(\lambda)}$. As a result, the challenge ciphertext no longer depends on α.

- $\mathrm{PMEGame}_6^b(\lambda)$: In this game, we modify how the challenge ciphertext is generated. Instead of computing $\mathsf{ct} := \tilde{P} \leftarrow \mathsf{Obf}(1^\lambda, \mathsf{ME.Dec}(\cdot, \mathsf{WE.ct}_\alpha, \mathsf{m}_b, \alpha))$, the challenger $\mathcal{C}$ uses the simulator Sim and sets $\mathsf{ct} := \tilde{P} \leftarrow \mathsf{Sim}(1^\lambda, 1^{|\mathsf{ME.Dec}(\cdot,\cdot)|}, 1^{|\mathsf{m}_b|})$.

By definition, since $\mathrm{PMEGame}_0^b(\lambda)$ is exactly same as $\mathsf{Expt}_{\mathcal{A},\mathsf{ME}}^{\mathsf{privacy}}(\lambda)$, we have $\epsilon_0 = \Pr\left[\mathsf{Expt}_{\mathcal{A},\mathsf{ME}}^{\mathsf{privacy}}(\lambda) \Rightarrow 1\right]$. Therefore, it suffices to show that

$$\{|\epsilon_i - \epsilon_{i+1}| \leq \mathsf{negl}(\lambda)\}_{i\in[0,5]}, \text{ and } \left|\epsilon_6 - \frac{1}{2}\right| \leq \mathsf{negl}(\lambda).$$

Lemma 1. *Assuming the security of* FTS, *we have* $|\epsilon_0 - \epsilon_1| \leq \mathsf{negl}(\lambda)$.

Proof. To show the difference between $\mathrm{PMEGame}_0^b(\lambda)$ and $\mathrm{PMEGame}_1^b(\lambda)$ is negligible, we construct $\mathcal{B}$ that breaks the security of the functional tag system by using $\mathcal{A}$.

1. At the beginning of the game, $\mathcal{B}$ runs $\mathsf{NIZK.crs}_0 \leftarrow \mathsf{NIZK.Setup}(1^\lambda)$, $\mathsf{NIZK.crs}_1 \leftarrow \mathsf{NIZK.Setup}(1^\lambda)$, and $\mathsf{Com.crs} \leftarrow \mathsf{Com.Setup}(1^\lambda)$. Next, $\mathcal{B}$ chooses $r_{\mathsf{rcv},0}, r_{\mathsf{snd},0}, r_{\mathsf{rcv},1}, r_{\mathsf{snd},1} \leftarrow\$ \{0,1\}^{4\lambda}$. Then, $\mathcal{B}$ computes $\mathsf{com}_{\mathsf{rcv},0} \leftarrow \leftarrow\$ \mathsf{Commit}_{\mathsf{Com.crs}}(0; r_{\mathsf{rcv},0})$, $\mathsf{com}_{\mathsf{rcv},1} \leftarrow \mathsf{Commit}_{\mathsf{Com.crs}}(0^{\ell(\lambda)}; r_{\mathsf{rcv},1})$, $\mathsf{com}_{\mathsf{snd},0}$ $\mathsf{Commit}_{\mathsf{Com.crs}}(0; r_{\mathsf{snd},0})$, and $\mathsf{com}_{\mathsf{snd},1} \leftarrow \mathsf{Commit}_{\mathsf{Com.crs}}(0^{\ell(\lambda)}; r_{\mathsf{snd},1})$. Finally, $\mathcal{B}$ executes $\mathcal{A}$ on input $\mathsf{mpk} := (\mathsf{Com.crs}, \mathsf{NIZK.crs}_0, \mathsf{NIZK.crs}_1, \mathsf{com}_{\mathsf{rcv},0}, \mathsf{com}_{\mathsf{rcv},1}, \mathsf{com}_{\mathsf{snd},0}, \mathsf{com}_{\mathsf{snd},1})$. Additionally, $\mathcal{B}$ samples $\hat{b} \leftarrow\$ \{0,1\}$.
2. When $\mathcal{A}$ issues some oracle queries $\mathcal{B}$ responses as follows:
   - **Decryption key generation:** When $\mathcal{A}$ makes a decryption key generation query on input ρ, $\mathcal{B}$ makes function tag query on input ρ and receives tag_{f_ρ}. Next, $\mathcal{B}$ runs $\pi_0 \leftarrow \mathsf{Prove}_{\mathsf{NIZK.crs}_0}((\mathsf{Com.crs}, \mathsf{com}_{\mathsf{rcv},0}, \mathsf{com}_{\mathsf{rcv},1}, \rho, \mathsf{tag}_{f_\rho}), r_{\mathsf{rcv},0})$, and returns $\mathsf{dk}_\rho := (\rho, \mathsf{tag}_{f_\rho}, \pi_0)$ to $\mathcal{A}$.
   - **Policy generation:** When $\mathcal{A}$ makes a policy generation query on input $\mathbb{S}$, $\mathcal{B}$ makes function tag query on input $\mathbb{S}$ and receives $\mathsf{tag}_{\mathbb{S}}$. Next, $\mathcal{B}$ runs $\pi_1 \leftarrow \mathsf{Prove}_{\mathsf{NIZK.crs}_0}((\mathsf{Com.crs}, \mathsf{com}_{\mathsf{snd},0}, \mathsf{com}_{\mathsf{snd},1}, \mathbb{S}, \mathsf{tag}_{\mathbb{S}}), r_{\mathsf{snd},0})$ and returns $\mathsf{dk}_{\mathbb{S}} := (\mathbb{S}, \mathsf{tag}_{\mathbb{S}}, \pi_1)$ to $\mathcal{A}$.
   - **Challenge ciphertext:** When $\mathcal{A}$ makes a challenge ciphertext query on input $(\sigma_0, \sigma_1, \mathbb{R}_0, \mathbb{R}_1, \mathsf{m}_0, \mathsf{m}_1)$, $\mathcal{B}$ makes input tag queries on $\sigma_{\hat{b}}$ and $\mathbb{R}_{\hat{b}}$, and receives $\mathsf{tag}_{\sigma_{\hat{b}}}$ and $\mathsf{tag}_{\mathbb{R}_{\hat{b}}}$. Next, It runs $\mathsf{WE.ct}_\alpha \leftarrow \mathsf{WE.Enc}(1^\lambda, (\mathsf{Com.crs}, \mathsf{NIZK.crs}_0, \mathsf{NIZK.crs}_1, \mathsf{com}_{\mathsf{rcv},0}, \mathsf{com}_{\mathsf{rcv},1}, \mathsf{com}_{\mathsf{snd},0}, \mathsf{com}_{\mathsf{snd},1}, \sigma_{\hat{b}}, \mathsf{tag}_{\sigma_{\hat{b}}}, \mathbb{R}_{\hat{b}}, \mathsf{tag}_{\mathbb{R}_{\hat{b}}}), \alpha)$. Then, $\mathcal{B}$ samples a lock string $\alpha \leftarrow\$ \{0,1\}^{d(\lambda)}$, runs $\tilde{P} \leftarrow \mathsf{Obf}(1^\lambda, \mathsf{WE.Dec}(\cdot, \mathsf{WE.ct}_\alpha), \mathsf{m}_{\hat{b}}, \alpha)$, and returns $\mathsf{ct} := \tilde{P}$ to $\mathcal{A}$.
3. Finally, $\mathcal{A}$ submits a guess coin $\hat{b}' \in \{0,1\}$, $\mathcal{B}$ outputs $b' := \hat{b} \oplus \hat{b}'$.

In the decryption key generation oracle and challenge ciphertext oracle described above, if $b = 0$, the tag_{f_ρ} and $\mathsf{tag}_{\mathbb{R}_{\hat{b}}}$ queried by $\mathcal{B}$ are generated by $\mathsf{tag}_{f_\rho} \leftarrow \mathsf{DFunctionTag}(1^\lambda, f_\rho)$ and $\mathsf{tag}_{\mathbb{R}_{\hat{b}}} \leftarrow \mathsf{DInputTag}(1^\lambda, \mathbb{R}_{\hat{b}})$. Also, if $b = 1$, they are generated by $\mathsf{tag}_{f_\rho} \leftarrow \mathsf{SFunctionTag}(\mathsf{tsk}_{\mathsf{rcv}}, f_\rho)$ and $\mathsf{tag}_{\mathbb{R}_{\hat{b}}} \leftarrow$

$\mathsf{SInputTag}(\mathsf{tsk}_{\mathsf{rcv}}, \mathbb{R}_{\hat{b}})$ such that $\mathsf{tsk}_{\mathsf{rcv}} \leftarrow \mathsf{KGen}(1^\lambda)$. If $b = 0$, $\mathcal{B}$ perfectly simulates $\text{PMEGame}_0^{\hat{b}}(\lambda)$ to $\mathcal{A}$. On the otherhand, if $b = 1$, $\mathcal{B}$ perfectly simulates $\text{PMEGame}_1^{\hat{b}}(\lambda)$ to $\mathcal{A}$. Also, if $\mathcal{A}$ is admissible adversary in case ①, the attributes and policies queried by $\mathcal{A}$ all satisfy $\mathbb{R}_0(\rho) = \mathbb{R}_1(\rho) = 0$, and the queries of $\mathcal{B}$ correspond to this restriction, hence $\mathcal{B}$ is admissible. Thus, we have $\epsilon_0 = \Pr\left[\hat{b} = \hat{b}' \,\middle|\, b = 0\right]$ and $\epsilon_1 = \Pr\left[\hat{b} = \hat{b}' \,\middle|\, b = 1\right]$. Due to the construction of $\mathcal{B}$, $\hat{b} = \hat{b}'$ implies $b' = 0$. Therefore, we have $|\epsilon_0 - \epsilon_1| = \left|\Pr\left[\mathsf{Expt}^{\mathsf{IND}}_{\mathcal{A},\mathsf{FTS}}(\lambda) \Rightarrow 1 \,\middle|\, b = 0\right] - \Pr\left[\mathsf{Expt}^{\mathsf{IND}}_{\mathcal{A},\mathsf{FTS}}(\lambda) \Rightarrow 1 \,\middle|\, b = 1\right]\right| = \mathsf{Adv}^{\mathsf{IND}}_{\mathcal{A},\mathsf{FTS}}(\lambda) = \mathsf{negl}(\lambda)$. □

Lemma 2. *Assuming the hiding property of* COM, *we have* $|\epsilon_1 - \epsilon_2| = \mathsf{negl}(\lambda)$ *and* $|\epsilon_3 - \epsilon_4| = \mathsf{negl}(\lambda)$.

Proof. The only difference between $\text{PMEGame}_1^b(\lambda)$ and $\text{PMEGame}_2^b(\lambda)$ is the way of computing $\mathsf{com}_{\mathsf{rcv},1}$. Also, assuming the hiding property of COM, $\mathcal{A}$ cannot distinguish $\mathsf{com}_{\mathsf{rcv},1} = \mathsf{Commit}_{\mathsf{Com.crs}}(0^{\ell(\lambda)}; r_{\mathsf{rcv},1})$ and $\mathsf{com}_{\mathsf{rcv},1} = \mathsf{Commit}_{\mathsf{Com.crs}}(\mathsf{tsk}_{\mathsf{rcv}}; r_{\mathsf{rcv},1})$. Thus $|\epsilon_1 - \epsilon_2| = \mathsf{negl}(\lambda)$ holds. Also, we have $|\epsilon_3 - \epsilon_4| = \mathsf{negl}(\lambda)$ by the same way. □

Lemma 3. *Assuming witness indistinguishability of* NIZK, *we have* $|\epsilon_2 - \epsilon_3| = \mathsf{negl}(\lambda)$.

Proof. The only difference between $\text{PMEGame}_2^b(\lambda)$ and $\text{PMEGame}_3^b(\lambda)$ is the value of witness w_0. Also, assuming the witness indistinguishability of NIZK, $\mathcal{A}$ cannot distinguish $\pi_0 \leftarrow \mathsf{Prove}_{\mathsf{NIZK.crs}_0}(x_0, r_{\mathsf{rcv},0})$ and $\pi_0 \leftarrow \mathsf{Prove}_{\mathsf{NIZK.crs}_0}(x_0, (\mathsf{tsk}_{\mathsf{rcv}}, r_{\mathsf{rcv},1}, r_{\mathsf{rcv},2}))$. Thus $|\epsilon_2 - \epsilon_3| = \mathsf{negl}(\lambda)$ holds. □

Lemma 4. *Assuming soundness of WE, we have* $|\epsilon_4 - \epsilon_5| \leq \mathsf{negl}(\lambda)$.

Proof. First, since Com.crs is statistically binding and $\mathsf{NIZK.crs}_0$ is statistically sound, the NP statement x_{WE} must be false. Suppose for contradiction that there exists $w_{WE} = (\rho, \mathsf{tag}_{f_\rho}, \mathbb{S}, \mathsf{tag}_{\mathbb{S}}, \pi_0, \pi_1)$ such that $(x_{WE}, w_{WE}) \in \mathsf{WE}.R$. Then, with $x_0 = (\mathsf{Com.crs}, \mathsf{com}_{\mathsf{rcv},0}, \mathsf{com}_{\mathsf{rcv},1}, \rho, \mathsf{tag}_{f_\rho})$, $x_1 = (\mathsf{Com.crs}, \mathsf{com}_{\mathsf{snd},0}, \mathsf{com}_{\mathsf{snd},1}, \mathbb{S}, \mathsf{tag}_{\mathbb{S}})$, the conditions $\mathsf{Verify}_{\mathsf{NIZK.crs}_0}(x_0, \pi_0) = 1 \wedge \mathsf{Verify}_{\mathsf{NIZK.crs}_1}(x_1, \pi_1) = 1 \wedge \mathbb{S}(\sigma) = 1 \wedge \mathbb{R}(\rho) = 1 \wedge \mathsf{Trigger}(\mathsf{tag}_{\mathbb{S}}, \mathsf{tag}_\sigma) = 0 \wedge \mathsf{Trigger}(\mathsf{tag}_{f_\rho}, \mathsf{tag}_{\mathbb{R}}) = 0$ must hold simultaneously. However, with $\mathsf{com}_{\mathsf{rcv},0} = \mathsf{Commit}_{\mathsf{Com.crs}}(1; r_{\mathsf{rcv},0})$, $\mathsf{com}_{\mathsf{rcv},1} = \mathsf{Commit}_{\mathsf{Com.crs}}(\mathsf{tsk}_{\mathsf{rcv}}; r_{\mathsf{rcv},1})$, $\mathsf{com}_{\mathsf{snd},0} = \mathsf{Commit}_{\mathsf{Com.crs}}(0; r_{\mathsf{snd},0})$, $\mathsf{com}_{\mathsf{snd},1} = \mathsf{Commit}_{\mathsf{Com.crs}}(0^{\ell(\lambda)}; r_{\mathsf{snd},1})$, and with $\mathsf{tag}_{f_\rho} = \mathsf{SFunctionTag}(\mathsf{tsk}_{\mathsf{rcv}}, f_\rho; r_{\mathsf{rcv},2})$, $\mathsf{tag}_{\mathbb{S}} = \mathsf{DFunctionTag}(1^\lambda, \mathbb{S})$, $\mathsf{tag}_{\mathbb{R}} = \mathsf{SInputTag}(\mathsf{tsk}_{\mathsf{rcv}}, \mathbb{R})$, $\mathsf{tag}_\sigma = \mathsf{DInputTag}(1^\lambda, \sigma)$, the smart correctness of the functional tag system implies that $\mathsf{Trigger}(\mathsf{tag}_{\mathbb{S}}, \mathsf{tag}_\sigma) = 1 \wedge \mathsf{Trigger}(\mathsf{tag}_{f_\rho}, \mathsf{tag}_{\mathbb{R}}) = 1$, contradicting the above. Thus, the NP statement x_{WE} is false. Therefore, if adversary $\mathcal{A}$ could distinguish $\mathsf{WE.Enc}(1^\lambda, x_{WE}, \alpha)$ from $\mathsf{WE.Enc}(1^\lambda, x_{WE}, 0^{d(\lambda)})$ with non-negligible probability. To show the difference between $\text{PMEGame}_4^b(\lambda)$ and $\text{PMEGame}_5^b(\lambda)$ is negligible, we construct $\mathcal{B}$ that breaks the security of WE by using $\mathcal{A}$.

1. At the beginning of the game, $\mathcal{B}$ runs $\mathsf{NIZK.crs}_0 \leftarrow \mathsf{NIZK.Setup}(1^\lambda)$, $\mathsf{NIZK.crs}_1 \leftarrow \mathsf{NIZK.Setup}(1^\lambda)$, and $\mathsf{Com.crs} \leftarrow \mathsf{Com.Setup}(1^\lambda)$. Next, $\mathcal{B}$ chooses $r_{\mathsf{rcv},0}, r_{\mathsf{snd},0}, r_{\mathsf{rcv},1}, r_{\mathsf{snd},1} \leftarrow\!\$ \{0,1\}^{4\lambda}$. Then, $\mathcal{B}$ computes $\mathsf{com}_{\mathsf{rcv},0} \leftarrow \mathsf{Commit}_{\mathsf{Com.crs}}(0; r_{\mathsf{rcv},0})$, $\mathsf{com}_{\mathsf{rcv},1} \leftarrow \mathsf{Commit}_{\mathsf{Com.crs}}(0^{\ell(\lambda)}; r_{\mathsf{rcv},1})$, $\mathsf{com}_{\mathsf{snd},0} \leftarrow \mathsf{Commit}_{\mathsf{Com.crs}}(0; r_{\mathsf{snd},0})$, and $\mathsf{com}_{\mathsf{snd},1} \leftarrow \mathsf{Commit}_{\mathsf{Com.crs}}(0^{\ell(\lambda)}; r_{\mathsf{snd},1})$. Finally, $\mathcal{B}$ executes $\mathcal{A}$ on input $\mathsf{mpk} := (\mathsf{Com.crs}, \mathsf{NIZK.crs}_0, \mathsf{NIZK.crs}_1, \mathsf{com}_{\mathsf{rcv},0}, \mathsf{com}_{\mathsf{rcv},1}, \mathsf{com}_{\mathsf{snd},0}, \mathsf{com}_{\mathsf{snd},1})$. Additionally, $\mathcal{B}$ samples $\hat{b} \leftarrow\!\$ \{0,1\}$.
2. When $\mathcal{A}$ issues some oracle queries $\mathcal{B}$ responses as follows:
   - **Decryption key generation:** When $\mathcal{A}$ makes a decryption key generation query on input ρ, $\mathcal{B}$ runs $\mathsf{tag}_{f_\rho} \leftarrow \mathsf{SFunctionTag}(\mathsf{tsk}_{\mathsf{rcv}}, f_\rho)$, $\pi_0 \leftarrow \mathsf{Prove}_{\mathsf{NIZK.crs}_0}((\mathsf{Com.crs}, \mathsf{com}_{\mathsf{rcv},0}, \mathsf{com}_{\mathsf{rcv},1}, \rho, \mathsf{tag}_{f_\rho}), r_{\mathsf{rcv},0})$. Then, $\mathcal{B}$ returns $\mathsf{dk}_\rho := (\rho, \mathsf{tag}_{f_\rho}, \pi_0)$ to $\mathcal{A}$.
   - **Policy generation:** When $\mathcal{A}$ makes a policy generation query on input $\mathbb{S}$, $\mathcal{B}$ makes function tag query on input $\mathbb{S}$ and receives $\mathsf{tag}_{\mathbb{S}}$. Next, $\mathcal{B}$ runs $\pi_1 \leftarrow \mathsf{Prove}_{\mathsf{NIZK.crs}_0}((\mathsf{Com.crs}, \mathsf{com}_{\mathsf{snd},0}, \mathsf{com}_{\mathsf{snd},1}, \mathbb{S}, \mathsf{tag}_{\mathbb{S}}), r_{\mathsf{snd},0})$ and returns $\mathsf{dk}_{\mathbb{S}} := (\mathbb{S}, \mathsf{tag}_{\mathbb{S}}, \pi_1)$ to $\mathcal{A}$.
   - **Challenge ciphertext:** When $\mathcal{A}$ makes a challenge ciphertext query on input $(\sigma_0, \sigma_1, \mathbb{R}_0, \mathbb{R}_1, \mathsf{m}_0, \mathsf{m}_1)$, $\mathcal{B}$ makes input tag queries on $\sigma_{\hat{b}}$ and receives $\mathsf{tag}_{\sigma_{\hat{b}}}$. Next, $\mathcal{B}$ runs $\mathsf{tag}_{\mathbb{R}_{\hat{b}}} \leftarrow \mathsf{SInputTag}(\mathsf{tsk}_{\mathsf{rcv}}, \mathbb{R}_{\hat{b}})$, and sends $(x_{WE} = (\mathsf{Com.crs}, \mathsf{NIZK.crs}_0, \mathsf{NIZK.crs}_1, \mathsf{com}_{\mathsf{rcv},0}, \mathsf{com}_{\mathsf{rcv},1}, \mathsf{com}_{\mathsf{snd},0}, \mathsf{com}_{\mathsf{snd},1}, \sigma_{\hat{b}}, \mathsf{tag}_{\sigma_{\hat{b}}}, \mathbb{R}_{\hat{b}}, \mathsf{tag}_{\mathbb{R}_{\hat{b}}}), \mathsf{m}_0, \mathsf{m}_1)$ to its challenger, and receives $\mathsf{WE.ct}_\alpha$. Also, $\mathcal{B}$ sends $\mathsf{WE.ct}_\alpha$ its challenger, and receives $\tilde{P}$, and returns $\mathsf{ct} := \tilde{P}$ to $\mathcal{A}$.
3. Finally, $\mathcal{A}$ submits a guess coin $\hat{b}' \in \{0,1\}$, $\mathcal{B}$ outputs $b' := \hat{b} \oplus \hat{b}'$.

In the challenge ciphertext oracle described above, the $\mathsf{WE.ct}_\alpha$ queried by $\mathcal{B}$ are generated by $\mathsf{WE.ct}_\alpha \leftarrow \mathsf{WE.Enc}(1^\lambda, (\mathsf{Com.crs}, \mathsf{NIZK.crs}_0, \mathsf{NIZK.crs}_1, \mathsf{com}_{\mathsf{rcv},0}, \mathsf{com}_{\mathsf{rcv},1}, \mathsf{com}_{\mathsf{snd},0}, \mathsf{com}_{\mathsf{snd},1}, \sigma_{\hat{b}}, \mathsf{tag}_{\sigma_{\hat{b}}}, \mathbb{R}_{\hat{b}}, \mathsf{tag}_{\mathbb{R}_{\hat{b}}}), \alpha)$ such that $\alpha \leftarrow\!\$ \{0,1\}^{d(\lambda)}$ if $b = 0$, $\alpha = 0^{d(\lambda)}$ if $b = 1$. If $b = 0$, $\mathcal{B}$ perfectly simulates $\mathrm{PMEGame}_4^{\hat{b}}(\lambda)$ to $\mathcal{A}$. On the otherhand, if $b = 1$, $\mathcal{B}$ perfectly simulates $\mathrm{PMEGame}_5^{\hat{b}}(\lambda)$ to $\mathcal{A}$. Also, if $\mathcal{A}$ is admissible adversary in case ①, the attributes and policies queried by $\mathcal{A}$ all satisfy $\mathbb{R}_0(\rho) = \mathbb{R}_1(\rho) = 0$, and the queries of $\mathcal{B}$ correspond to this restriction, hence $\mathcal{B}$ is admissible. Thus, we have $\epsilon_4 = \Pr\left[\hat{b} = \hat{b}' \;\middle|\; b = 0\right]$ and $\epsilon_5 = \Pr\left[\hat{b} = \hat{b}' \;\middle|\; b = 1\right]$. Due to the construction of $\mathcal{B}$, $\hat{b} = \hat{b}'$ implies $b' = 0$. Therefore, we have

$$\begin{aligned}|\epsilon_4 - \epsilon_5| &= \left|\Pr\left[\mathsf{WEGame}_{\mathsf{WE}}^{\mathcal{A}}(\lambda) \Rightarrow 1 \;\middle|\; b = 0\right] - \Pr\left[\mathsf{WEGame}_{\mathsf{WE}}^{\mathcal{A}}(\lambda) \Rightarrow 1 \;\middle|\; b = 1\right]\right| \\ &= \mathsf{Adv}_{\mathcal{A},\mathsf{WE}}^{\mathsf{IND}}(\lambda) = \mathsf{negl}(\lambda).\end{aligned}$$

□

Lemma 5. *If lockable obfuscation satisfies security, it holds that* $|\epsilon_5 - \epsilon_6| \leq \mathsf{negl}(\lambda)$.

Proof. To show the difference between $\text{PMEGame}_5^b(\lambda)$ and $\text{PMEGame}_6^b(\lambda)$ is negligible, we construct $\mathcal{B}$ that breaks the security of LO by using $\mathcal{A}$.

1. At the beginning of the game, $\mathcal{B}$ runs $\mathsf{NIZK.crs}_0 \leftarrow \mathsf{NIZK.Setup}(1^\lambda)$, $\mathsf{NIZK.crs}_1 \leftarrow \mathsf{NIZK.Setup}(1^\lambda)$, and $\mathsf{Com.crs} \leftarrow \mathsf{Com.Setup}(1^\lambda)$. Next, $\mathcal{B}$ chooses $r_{\mathsf{rcv},0}, r_{\mathsf{snd},0}, r_{\mathsf{rcv},1}, r_{\mathsf{snd},1} \leftarrow\$ \{0,1\}^{4\lambda}$. Then, $\mathcal{B}$ computes $\mathsf{com}_{\mathsf{rcv},0} \leftarrow \mathsf{Commit}_{\mathsf{Com.crs}}(0; r_{\mathsf{rcv},0})$, $\mathsf{com}_{\mathsf{rcv},1} \leftarrow \mathsf{Commit}_{\mathsf{Com.crs}}(0^{\ell(\lambda)}; r_{\mathsf{rcv},1})$, $\mathsf{com}_{\mathsf{snd},0} \leftarrow \mathsf{Commit}_{\mathsf{Com.crs}}(0; r_{\mathsf{snd},0})$, and $\mathsf{com}_{\mathsf{snd},1} \leftarrow \mathsf{Commit}_{\mathsf{Com.crs}}(0^{\ell(\lambda)}; r_{\mathsf{snd},1})$. Finally, $\mathcal{B}$ executes $\mathcal{A}$ on input $\mathsf{mpk} := (\mathsf{Com.crs}, \mathsf{NIZK.crs}_0, \mathsf{NIZK.crs}_1, \mathsf{com}_{\mathsf{rcv},0}, \mathsf{com}_{\mathsf{rcv},1}, \mathsf{com}_{\mathsf{snd},0}, \mathsf{com}_{\mathsf{snd},1})$. Additionally, $\mathcal{B}$ samples $\hat{b} \leftarrow\$ \{0,1\}$.
2. When $\mathcal{A}$ issues some oracle queries $\mathcal{B}$ responses as follows:
   - **Decryption key generation:** When $\mathcal{A}$ makes a decryption key generation query on input ρ, $\mathcal{B}$ runs $\mathsf{tag}_{f_\rho} \leftarrow \mathsf{SFunctionTag}(\mathsf{tsk}_{\mathsf{rcv}}, f_\rho)$, $\pi_0 \leftarrow \mathsf{Prove}_{\mathsf{NIZK.crs}_0}((\mathsf{Com.crs}, \mathsf{com}_{\mathsf{rcv},0}, \mathsf{com}_{\mathsf{rcv},1}, \rho, \mathsf{tag}_{f_\rho}), r_{\mathsf{rcv},0})$. Then, $\mathcal{B}$ returns $\mathsf{dk}_\rho := (\rho, \mathsf{tag}_{f_\rho}, \pi_0)$ to $\mathcal{A}$.
   - **Policy generation:** When $\mathcal{A}$ makes a policy generation query on input $\mathbb{S}$, $\mathcal{B}$ makes function tag query on input $\mathbb{S}$ and receives $\mathsf{tag}_\mathbb{S}$. Next, $\mathcal{B}$ runs $\pi_1 \leftarrow \mathsf{Prove}_{\mathsf{NIZK.crs}_0}((\mathsf{Com.crs}, \mathsf{com}_{\mathsf{snd},0}, \mathsf{com}_{\mathsf{snd},1}, \mathbb{S}, \mathsf{tag}_\mathbb{S}), r_{\mathsf{snd},0})$ and returns $\mathsf{dk}_\mathbb{S} := (\mathbb{S}, \mathsf{tag}_\mathbb{S}, \pi_1)$ to $\mathcal{A}$.
   - **Challenge ciphertext:** When $\mathcal{A}$ makes a challenge ciphertext query on input $(\sigma_0, \sigma_1, \mathbb{R}_0, \mathbb{R}_1, \mathsf{m}_0, \mathsf{m}_1)$, $\mathcal{B}$ makes input tag queries on $\sigma_{\hat{b}}$ and receives $\mathsf{tag}_{\sigma_{\hat{b}}}$. Next, $\mathcal{B}$ runs $\mathsf{tag}_{\mathbb{R}_{\hat{b}}} \leftarrow \mathsf{SInputTag}(\mathsf{tsk}_{\mathsf{rcv}}, \mathbb{R}_{\hat{b}})$, $\mathsf{WE.ct}_\alpha \leftarrow \mathsf{WE.Enc}(1^\lambda, (\mathsf{Com.crs}, \mathsf{NIZK.crs}_0, \mathsf{NIZK.crs}_1, \mathsf{com}_{\mathsf{rcv},0}, \mathsf{com}_{\mathsf{rcv},1}, \mathsf{com}_{\mathsf{snd},0}, \mathsf{com}_{\mathsf{snd},1}, \sigma_{\hat{b}}, \mathsf{tag}_{\sigma_{\hat{b}}}, \mathbb{R}_{\hat{b}}, \mathsf{tag}_{\mathbb{R}_{\hat{b}}}), \alpha = 0^{d(\lambda)})$. Also, $\mathcal{B}$ sends $(\mathsf{ME.Dec}(\cdot, \mathsf{WE.ct}_\alpha), \mathsf{m}_0, \mathsf{m}_1)$ to its challenger, and receives $\tilde{P}$. Finally, $\mathcal{B}$ returns $\mathsf{ct} := \tilde{P}$ to $\mathcal{A}$.
3. Finally, $\mathcal{A}$ submits a guess coin $\hat{b}' \in \{0,1\}$, $\mathcal{B}$ outputs $b' := \hat{b} \oplus \hat{b}'$.

In the challenge ciphertext oracle described above, the $\tilde{P}$ queried by $\mathcal{B}$ are generated by $\tilde{P} \leftarrow \mathsf{Obf}(1^\lambda, \mathsf{ME.Dec}(\cdot, \mathsf{WE.ct}_\alpha, \mathsf{m}_{\hat{b}}, 0^{d(\lambda)}))$ if $b = 0$, and $\tilde{P} \leftarrow \mathsf{Sim}(1^\lambda, 1^{|\mathsf{ME.Dec}(\cdot,\cdot)|}, 1^{|\mathsf{m}_{\hat{b}}|})$ if $b = 1$. If $b = 0$, $\mathcal{B}$ perfectly simulates $\text{PMEGame}_5^{\hat{b}}(\lambda)$ to $\mathcal{A}$. On the otherhand, if $b = 1$, $\mathcal{B}$ perfectly simulates $\text{PMEGame}_6^{\hat{b}}(\lambda)$ to $\mathcal{A}$. Also, if $\mathcal{A}$ is admissible adversary in case ①, the attributes and policies queried by $\mathcal{A}$ all satisfy $\mathbb{R}_0(\rho) = \mathbb{R}_1(\rho) = 0$, and the queries of $\mathcal{B}$ correspond to this restriction, hence $\mathcal{B}$ is admissible. Thus, we have $\epsilon_5 = \Pr\left[\hat{b} = \hat{b}' \,\middle|\, b = 0\right]$ and $\epsilon_6 = \Pr\left[\hat{b} = \hat{b}' \,\middle|\, b = 1\right]$. Due to the construction of $\mathcal{B}$, $\hat{b} = \hat{b}'$ implies $b' = 0$. Therefore, we have

$$\begin{aligned}|\epsilon_5 - \epsilon_6| &= \left|\Pr\left[\mathsf{LOGame}_{\mathsf{LO}}^{\mathcal{A}}(\lambda) \Rightarrow 1 \,\middle|\, b = 0\right] - \Pr\left[\mathsf{LOGame}_{\mathsf{LO}}^{\mathcal{A}}(\lambda) \Rightarrow 1 \,\middle|\, b = 1\right]\right| \\ &= \mathsf{Adv}_{\mathcal{A},\mathsf{LO}}^{\mathsf{SIM}}(\lambda) = \mathsf{negl}(\lambda).\end{aligned}$$

□

Here,

$\left|\epsilon_6 - \frac{1}{2}\right|$ can be rewritten as $\left|\epsilon_6 - \frac{1}{2}\right| = \left|\Pr\left[\text{PMEGame}_6^b(1^\lambda) = 1\right] - \frac{1}{2}\right| =$

$\frac{1}{2}\left|\Pr\left[\text{PMEGame}_6^0(1^\lambda)=1\right]-\Pr\left[\text{PMEGame}_6^1(1^\lambda)=1\right]\right|$. Since $\text{PMEGame}_6^b(1^\lambda)$ is independent of the bit b, we have $\Pr\left[\text{PMEGame}_6^0(1^\lambda)=1\right]=\Pr\left[\text{PMEGame}_6^1(1^\lambda)=1\right]$, and therefore we have

$$\left|\epsilon_6-\frac{1}{2}\right|=\frac{1}{2}\left|\Pr\left[\text{PMEGame}_6^0(1^\lambda)=1\right]-\Pr\left[\text{PMEGame}_6^1(1^\lambda)=1\right]\right|=0.$$

Thus, since $|\epsilon_i-\epsilon_{i+1}|\ (for\ i=0,\cdots,5)\le \mathsf{negl}(\lambda)$, $\left|\epsilon_6-\frac{1}{2}\right|\le \mathsf{negl}(\lambda)$, Privacy under the Mismatch Condition in Pattern ① is proven.

Next, we consider ② $\mathbb{S}(\sigma_0)=\mathbb{S}(\sigma)=0$. To prove the security, we consider the following sequence of hybrids:

- $\text{PMEGame}_0^b(\lambda)$: This is the original security game $\mathsf{Expt}_{\mathcal{A},\mathsf{ME}}^{\mathsf{privacy}}(\lambda)$.
- $\text{PMEGame}_1^b(\lambda)$: In this game, we modify how tags for the sender's attributes and policy are generated. For decryption-key generation queries, instead of producing dummy tags, the challenger computes $\mathsf{tag}_{\mathbb{S}} \leftarrow \mathsf{SFunctionTag}(\mathsf{tsk}_{\mathsf{snd}},\mathbb{S})$ and uses it in the response. For encryption queries, instead of using dummy tags, the challenger computes $\mathsf{tag}_{\sigma_b} \leftarrow \mathsf{SInputTag}(\mathsf{tsk}_{\mathsf{snd}},\sigma_b)$ and incorporates it into the challenge ciphertext.
- $\text{PMEGame}_2^b(\lambda)$: In this game, we modify the generation of the master public key. When choosing $\mathsf{com}_{\mathsf{snd},1}$, the challenger sets $\mathsf{com}_{\mathsf{snd},1} := \mathsf{Commit}_{\mathsf{Com.crs}}(\mathsf{tsk}_{\mathsf{snd}};r_{\mathsf{snd},1})$ instead of committing to $0^{\ell(\lambda)}$.
- $\text{PMEGame}_3^b(\lambda)$: In this game, we modify how the proof π_1 is generated for policy generation queries. When answering such a query, the challenger uses the witness $w_1=(\mathsf{tsk}_{\mathsf{snd}},r_{\mathsf{snd},1},r_{\mathsf{snd},2})$ instead of $w_1=r_{\mathsf{snd},0}$. That is, $\pi_1 \leftarrow \mathsf{Prove}_{\mathsf{NIZK.crs}_1}(x_1=(\mathsf{Com.crs},\mathsf{com}_{\mathsf{snd},0},\mathsf{com}_{\mathsf{snd},1},\mathbb{S},\mathsf{tag}_{\mathbb{S}}),w_1=(\mathsf{tsk}_{\mathsf{snd}};r_{\mathsf{snd},1},r_{\mathsf{snd},2}))$, where $r_{\mathsf{snd},2}$ denotes the randomness used in generating $\mathsf{tag}_{\mathbb{S}} \leftarrow \mathsf{SFunctionTag}(\mathsf{tsk}_{\mathsf{snd}},\mathbb{S};r_{\mathsf{snd},2})$.
- $\text{PMEGame}_4^b(\lambda)$: In this game, we modify the generation of the master public key. When choosing $\mathsf{mpk}=(\mathsf{Com.crs},\mathsf{NIZK.crs}_0,\mathsf{NIZK.crs}_1,\mathsf{com}_{\mathsf{snd},0},\mathsf{com}_{\mathsf{snd},1})$, the challenger sets $\mathsf{com}_{\mathsf{snd},0} := \mathsf{Commit}_{\mathsf{Com.crs}}(1;r_{\mathsf{snd},0})$ instead of committing to 0.
- $\text{PMEGame}_5^b(\lambda)$: In this game, we modify how the ciphertext generated in the encryption algorithm. Specifically, when answering encryption queries, the challenger computes $\mathsf{WE.ct}$ using the fixed value $\alpha=0^{d(\lambda)}$. As a result, the challenge ciphertext no longer depends on α.
- $\text{PMEGame}_6^b(\lambda)$: In this game, we modify how the challenge ciphertext is generated. Instead of computing $\mathsf{ct} \leftarrow \mathsf{Obf}(1^\lambda,\mathsf{ME.Dec}(\cdot,\mathsf{WE.ct}_\alpha,\mathsf{m}_b,\alpha))$, the challenger $\mathcal{C}$ uses the simulator Sim and sets $\mathsf{ct} := \widetilde{P} \leftarrow \mathsf{Sim}(1^\lambda,1^{|\mathsf{ME.Dec}(\cdot,\cdot)|},1^{|\mathsf{m}_b|})$.

By definition, since $\text{PMEGame}_0^b(\lambda)$ is exactly same as $\mathsf{Expt}_{\mathcal{A},\mathsf{ME}}^{\mathsf{privacy}}(\lambda)$, we have $\epsilon_0=\Pr\left[\mathsf{Expt}_{\mathcal{A},\mathsf{ME}}^{\mathsf{privacy}}(\lambda)\Rightarrow 1\right]$. Therefore, it suffices to show that

$$\{|\epsilon_i-\epsilon_{i+1}|\le \mathsf{negl}(\lambda)\}_{i\in[0,5]},\ \text{and}\ \left|\epsilon_6-\frac{1}{2}\right|\le \mathsf{negl}(\lambda).$$

Lemma 6. *Assuming the security of* FTS, *we have* $|\epsilon_0 - \epsilon_1| \leq \mathsf{negl}(\lambda)$.

Proof. To show the difference between $\mathrm{PMEGame}_0^b(\lambda)$ and $\mathrm{PMEGame}_1^b(\lambda)$ is negligible, we construct $\mathcal{B}$ that breaks the security of the functional tag system by using $\mathcal{A}$.

1. At the beginning of the game, $\mathcal{B}$ runs $\mathsf{NIZK.crs}_0 \leftarrow \mathsf{NIZK.Setup}(1^\lambda)$, $\mathsf{NIZK.crs}_1 \leftarrow \mathsf{NIZK.Setup}(1^\lambda)$, and $\mathsf{Com.crs} \leftarrow \mathsf{Com.Setup}(1^\lambda)$. Next, $\mathcal{B}$ chooses $r_{\mathsf{rcv},0}, r_{\mathsf{snd},0}, r_{\mathsf{rcv},1}, r_{\mathsf{snd},1} \leftarrow\!\$ \{0,1\}^{4\lambda}$. Then, $\mathcal{B}$ computes $\mathsf{com}_{\mathsf{rcv},0} \leftarrow \mathsf{Commit}_{\mathsf{Com.crs}}(0; r_{\mathsf{rcv},0})$, $\mathsf{com}_{\mathsf{rcv},1} \leftarrow \mathsf{Commit}_{\mathsf{Com.crs}}(0^{\ell(\lambda)}; r_{\mathsf{rcv},1})$, $\mathsf{com}_{\mathsf{snd},0} \leftarrow \mathsf{Commit}_{\mathsf{Com.crs}}(0; r_{\mathsf{snd},0})$, and $\mathsf{com}_{\mathsf{snd},1} \leftarrow \mathsf{Commit}_{\mathsf{Com.crs}}(0^{\ell(\lambda)}; r_{\mathsf{snd},1})$. Finally, $\mathcal{B}$ executes $\mathcal{A}$ on input $\mathsf{mpk} := (\mathsf{Com.crs}, \mathsf{NIZK.crs}_0, \mathsf{NIZK.crs}_1, \mathsf{com}_{\mathsf{rcv},0}, \mathsf{com}_{\mathsf{rcv},1}, \mathsf{com}_{\mathsf{snd},0}, \mathsf{com}_{\mathsf{snd},1})$. Additionally, $\mathcal{B}$ samples $\hat{b} \leftarrow\!\$ \{0,1\}$.
2. When $\mathcal{A}$ issues some oracle queries $\mathcal{B}$ responses as follows:
   - **Decryption key generation:** When $\mathcal{A}$ makes a decryption key generation query on input ρ, $\mathcal{B}$ makes function tag query on input ρ and receives tag_{f_ρ}. Next, $\mathcal{B}$ runs $\pi_0 \leftarrow \mathsf{Prove}_{\mathsf{NIZK.crs}_0}((\mathsf{Com.crs}, \mathsf{com}_{\mathsf{rcv},0}, \mathsf{com}_{\mathsf{rcv},1}, \rho, \mathsf{tag}_{f_\rho}), r_{\mathsf{rcv},0})$, and returns $\mathsf{dk}_\rho := (\rho, \mathsf{tag}_{f_\rho}, \pi_0)$ to $\mathcal{A}$.
   - **Policy generation:** When $\mathcal{A}$ makes a policy generation query on input $\mathbb{S}$, $\mathcal{B}$ makes function tag query on input $\mathbb{S}$ and receives $\mathsf{tag}_{\mathbb{S}}$. Next, $\mathcal{B}$ runs $\pi_1 \leftarrow \mathsf{Prove}_{\mathsf{NIZK.crs}_0}((\mathsf{Com.crs}, \mathsf{com}_{\mathsf{snd},0}, \mathsf{com}_{\mathsf{snd},1}, \mathbb{S}, \mathsf{tag}_{\mathbb{S}}), r_{\mathsf{snd},0})$ and returns $\mathsf{dk}_{\mathbb{S}} := (\mathbb{S}, \mathsf{tag}_{\mathbb{S}}, \pi_1)$ to $\mathcal{A}$.
   - **Challenge ciphertext:** When $\mathcal{A}$ makes a challenge ciphertext query on input $(\sigma_0, \sigma_1, \mathbb{R}_0, \mathbb{R}_1, \mathsf{m}_0, \mathsf{m}_1)$, $\mathcal{B}$ makes input tag queries on $\sigma_{\hat{b}}$ and $\mathbb{R}_{\hat{b}}$, and receives $\mathsf{tag}_{\sigma_{\hat{b}}}$ and $\mathsf{tag}_{\mathbb{R}_{\hat{b}}}$. Next, It runs $\mathsf{WE.ct}_\alpha \leftarrow \mathsf{WE.Enc}(1^\lambda, (\mathsf{Com.crs}, \mathsf{NIZK.crs}_0, \mathsf{NIZK.crs}_1, \mathsf{com}_{\mathsf{rcv},0}, \mathsf{com}_{\mathsf{rcv},1}, \mathsf{com}_{\mathsf{snd},0}, \mathsf{com}_{\mathsf{snd},1}, \sigma_{\hat{b}}, \mathsf{tag}_{\sigma_{\hat{b}}}, \mathbb{R}_{\hat{b}}, \mathsf{tag}_{\mathbb{R}_{\hat{b}}}), \alpha)$. Then, $\mathcal{B}$ samples a lock string $\alpha \leftarrow\!\$ \{0,1\}^{d(\lambda)}$, runs $\tilde{P} \leftarrow \mathsf{Obf}(1^\lambda, \mathsf{WE.Dec}(\cdot, \mathsf{WE.ct}_\alpha), \mathsf{m}_{\hat{b}}, \alpha)$, and returns $\mathsf{ct} := \tilde{P}$ to $\mathcal{A}$.
3. Finally, $\mathcal{A}$ submits a guess coin $\hat{b}' \in \{0,1\}$, $\mathcal{B}$ outputs $b' := \hat{b} \oplus \hat{b}'$.

In the Policy generation oracle and challenge ciphertext oracle described above, if $b = 0$, the $\mathsf{tag}_{\mathbb{S}}$ and $\mathsf{tag}_{\sigma_{\hat{b}}}$ queried by $\mathcal{B}$ are generated by $\mathsf{tag}_{\mathbb{S}} \leftarrow \mathsf{DFunctionTag}(1^\lambda, \mathbb{S})$ and $\mathsf{tag}_{\sigma_{\hat{b}}} \leftarrow \mathsf{DInputTag}(1^\lambda, \sigma_{\hat{b}})$. If $b = 1$, they are generated by $\mathsf{tag}_{\mathbb{S}} \leftarrow \mathsf{SFunctionTag}(\mathsf{tsk}_{\mathsf{snd}}, \mathbb{S})$ and $\mathsf{tag}_{\sigma_{\hat{b}}} \leftarrow \mathsf{SInputTag}(\mathsf{tsk}_{\mathsf{snd}}, \sigma_{\hat{b}})$ such that $\mathsf{tsk}_{\mathsf{snd}} \leftarrow \mathsf{KGen}(1^\lambda)$. Also, if $b = 0$, $\mathcal{B}$ perfectly simulates $\mathrm{PMEGame}_0^{\hat{b}}(\lambda)$ to $\mathcal{A}$. On the otherhand, if $b = 1$, $\mathcal{B}$ perfectly simulates $\mathrm{PMEGame}_1^{\hat{b}}(\lambda)$ to $\mathcal{A}$. Also, if $\mathcal{A}$ is admissible adversary in case ②, the attributes and policies queried by $\mathcal{A}$ all satisfy $\mathbb{S}(\sigma_0) = \mathbb{S}(\sigma) = 0$, and the queries of $\mathcal{B}$ correspond to this restriction, hence $\mathcal{B}$ is admissible. Thus, we have $\epsilon_0 = \Pr\left[\hat{b} = \hat{b}' \,\middle|\, b = 0\right]$ and $\epsilon_1 = \Pr\left[\hat{b} = \hat{b}' \,\middle|\, b = 1\right]$. Due to the description of $\mathcal{B}$, $\hat{b} = \hat{b}'$ implies $b' = 0$. Thus, we have $|\epsilon_0 - \epsilon_1| = \left|\Pr\left[\mathsf{Expt}_{\mathcal{A},\mathsf{FTS}}^{\mathsf{IND}}(\lambda) \Rightarrow 1 \,\middle|\, b = 0\right] - \Pr\left[\mathsf{Expt}_{\mathcal{A},\mathsf{FTS}}^{\mathsf{IND}}(\lambda) \Rightarrow 1 \,\middle|\, b = 1\right]\right| = \mathsf{Adv}_{\mathcal{A},\mathsf{FTS}}^{\mathsf{IND}}(\lambda) = \mathsf{negl}(\lambda)$. □

It should be noted that $\{|\epsilon_i - \epsilon_{i+1}| \leq \mathsf{negl}(\lambda)\}_{i\in[1,5]}$, and $\left|\epsilon_6 - \frac{1}{2}\right| \leq \mathsf{negl}(\lambda)$ can be proved using the same technique as in Pattern ①. Thus, Privacy under the Mismatch Condition in Pattern ② is proven.

Next, we consider ③ $\mathbb{R}_0(\rho) = \mathbb{S}(\sigma_1) = 0$. To prove the security, we consider the following sequence of hybrids:

- PMEGame$^b_0(\lambda)$: This is the original security game $\mathsf{Expt}^{\mathsf{privacy}}_{\mathcal{A},\mathsf{ME}}(\lambda)$ in case $b = 0$.
- PMEGame$^b_1(\lambda)$: In this game, we modify how tags for the receiver's attributes and policy are generated. For decryption-key generation queries, instead of producing dummy tags, the challenger computes $\mathsf{tag}_{f_\rho} \leftarrow \mathsf{SFunctionTag}(\mathsf{tsk}_{\mathsf{rcv}}, f_\rho)$ and uses it in the response. For encryption queries, instead of using dummy tags, the challenger computes $\mathsf{tag}_{\mathbb{R}_0} \leftarrow \mathsf{SInputTag}(\mathsf{tsk}_{\mathsf{rcv}}, \mathbb{R}_0)$ and incorporates it into the challenge ciphertext.
- PMEGame$^b_2(\lambda)$: In this game, we modify the generation of the master public key. When choosing $\mathsf{com}_{\mathsf{rcv},1}$, the challenger sets $\mathsf{com}_{\mathsf{rcv},1} := \mathsf{Commit}_{\mathsf{Com.crs}}(\mathsf{tsk}_{\mathsf{rcv}}; r_{\mathsf{rcv},1})$ instead of committing to $0^{\ell(\lambda)}$.
- PMEGame$^b_3(\lambda)$: In this game, we modify how the proof π_0 is generated for decryption key queries. When answering such a query, the challenger uses the witness $w_0 = (\mathsf{tsk}, r_{\mathsf{rcv},1}, r_{\mathsf{rcv},2})$ instead of $w_0 = r_{\mathsf{rcv},0}$. That is, $\pi_0 \leftarrow \mathsf{Prove}_{\mathsf{NIZK.crs}_0}\big(x_0 = (\mathsf{Com.crs}, \mathsf{com}_{\mathsf{rcv},0}, \mathsf{com}_{\mathsf{rcv},1}, \rho, \mathsf{tag}_{f_\rho}), w_0 = (\mathsf{tsk}_{\mathsf{rcv}}, r_{\mathsf{rcv},1}, r_{\mathsf{rcv},2})\big)$, where $r_{\mathsf{rcv},2}$ denotes the randomness used in generating $\mathsf{tag}_{f_\rho} \leftarrow \mathsf{SFunctionTag}(\mathsf{tsk}_{\mathsf{rcv}}, f_\rho; r_{\mathsf{rcv},2})$.
- PMEGame$^b_4(\lambda)$: In this game, we modify the generation of the master public key. When choosing $\mathsf{com}_{\mathsf{rcv},0}$, the challenger sets $\mathsf{com}_{\mathsf{rcv},0} := \mathsf{Commit}_{\mathsf{Com.crs}}(1; r_{\mathsf{rcv},0})$ instead of committing to 0.
- PMEGame$^b_5(\lambda)$: In this game, we modify how the ciphertext generated in the encryption algorithm. Specifically, when answering encryption queries, the challenger computes $\mathsf{WE.ct}$ using the fixed value $\alpha = 0^{d(\lambda)}$.
- PMEGame$^b_6(\lambda)$: In this game, we modify the generation of the master public key. When choosing $\mathsf{com}_{\mathsf{rcv},0}$, the challenger commit 0 instead of computing $\mathsf{com}_{\mathsf{rcv},0} := \mathsf{Commit}_{\mathsf{Com.crs}}(1; r_{\mathsf{rcv},0})$.
- PMEGame$^b_7(\lambda)$: In this game, we modify how the proof π_0 is generated for decryption key queries. When answering such a query, the challenger uses the witness $w_0 = r_{\mathsf{rcv},0}$ instead of $w_0 = (\mathsf{tsk}_{\mathsf{rcv}}, r_{\mathsf{rcv},1}, r_{\mathsf{rcv},2})$. That is, $\pi_0 \leftarrow \mathsf{Prove}_{\mathsf{NIZK.crs}_0}\big(x_0 = (\mathsf{Com.crs}, \mathsf{com}_{\mathsf{rcv},0}, \mathsf{com}_{\mathsf{rcv},1}, \rho, \mathsf{tag}_{f_\rho}), w_0 = (r_{\mathsf{rcv},0})\big)$, where $r_{\mathsf{rcv},2}$ denotes the randomness used in generating $\mathsf{tag}_{f_\rho} \leftarrow \mathsf{SFunctionTag}(\mathsf{tsk}_{\mathsf{rcv}}, f_\rho; r_{\mathsf{rcv},2})$.
- PMEGame$^b_8(\lambda)$: In this game, we modify the generation of the master public key. When choosing $\mathsf{com}_{\mathsf{rcv},1}$, the challenger commits $0^{\ell(\lambda)}$ instead computing $\mathsf{com}_{\mathsf{rcv},1} := \mathsf{Commit}_{\mathsf{Com.crs}}(\mathsf{tsk}_{\mathsf{rcv}}; r_{\mathsf{rcv},1})$.
- PMEGame$^b_9(\lambda)$: In this game, we modify how tags for the receiver's attributes and policy are generated. For decryption-key generation queries, instead of producing dummy tags, the challenger computes $\mathsf{tag}_{f_\rho} \leftarrow \mathsf{DFunctionTag}(1^\lambda, f_\rho)$ and uses it in the response. For encryption queries,

instead of using dummy tags, the challenger computes $\mathsf{tag}_{\mathbb{R}_0} \leftarrow \mathsf{DInputTag}(1^\lambda, \mathbb{R}_0)$ and incorporates it into the challenge ciphertext.

- $\text{PMEGame}^b_{10}(\lambda)$: In this game, we modify how the challenge ciphertext is generated. Instead of computing $\mathsf{ct} \leftarrow \mathsf{Obf}(1^\lambda, \mathsf{ME.Dec}(\cdot, \mathsf{WE.ct}_\alpha, \mathsf{m}_b, \alpha))$, the challenger $\mathcal{C}$ uses the simulator Sim and sets $\mathsf{ct} := \tilde{P} \leftarrow \mathsf{Sim}(1^\lambda, 1^{|\mathsf{ME.Dec}(\cdot,\cdot)|}, 1^{|\mathsf{m}|})$.
- $\text{PMEGame}^b_{11}(\lambda)$: In this game, we modify how tags for the sender's attributes and policy are generated. At the beginning of the game, the challenger samples a "smart tag key" $\mathsf{tsk}_{\mathsf{snd}} \leftarrow \mathsf{KGen}(1^\lambda)$. For policy-generation queries, instead of returning a dummy tag, the challenger computes $\mathsf{tag}_{\mathbb{S}} \leftarrow \mathsf{SFunctionTag}(\mathsf{tsk}_{\mathsf{snd}}, \mathbb{S})$ and uses it in the response. For encryption queries, the challenger likewise replaces dummy tags by computing $\mathsf{tag}_{\sigma_1} \leftarrow \mathsf{SInputTag}(\mathsf{tsk}_{\mathsf{snd}}, \sigma_1)$ and incorporates it into the challenge ciphertext.
- $\text{PMEGame}^b_{12}(\lambda)$: In this game, we modify the generation of the master public key. When choosing $\mathsf{com}_{\mathsf{snd},1}$, the challenger sets $\mathsf{com}_{\mathsf{snd},1} := \mathsf{Commit}_{\mathsf{Com.crs}}(\mathsf{tsk}_{\mathsf{snd}}; r_{\mathsf{snd},1})$ instead of committing to $0^{\ell(\lambda)}$.
- $\text{PMEGame}^b_{13}(\lambda)$: In this game, we modify how the proof π_1 is generated for policy generation queries. When answering such a query, the challenger $\mathcal{C}$ uses the witness $w_1 = (\mathsf{tsk}_{\mathsf{snd}}, r_{\mathsf{snd},1}, r_{\mathsf{snd},2})$ instead of $w_1 = r_{\mathsf{snd},0}$. That is, $\pi_1 \leftarrow \mathsf{Prove}_{\mathsf{NIZK.crs}_1}(x_1 = (\mathsf{Com.crs}, \mathsf{com}_{\mathsf{snd},0}, \mathsf{com}_{\mathsf{snd},1}, \mathbb{S}, \mathsf{tag}_{\mathbb{S}}), w_1 = (\mathsf{tsk}_{\mathsf{snd}}; r_{\mathsf{snd},1}, r_{\mathsf{snd},2}))$, where $r_{\mathsf{snd},2}$ denotes the randomness used in generating $\mathsf{tag}_{\mathbb{S}} \leftarrow \mathsf{SFunctionTag}(\mathsf{tsk}_{\mathsf{snd}}, \mathbb{S}; r_{\mathsf{snd},2})$.
- $\text{PMEGame}^b_{14}(\lambda)$: In this game, we modify the generation of the master public key. When choosing $\mathsf{com}_{\mathsf{snd},0}$, the challenger sets $\mathsf{com}_{\mathsf{snd},0} := \mathsf{Commit}_{\mathsf{Com.crs}}(1; r_{\mathsf{snd},0})$ instead of committing to 0.
- $\text{PMEGame}^b_{15}(\lambda)$: In this game, we modify how the ciphertext generated in the encryption algorithm. Specifically, when answering encryption queries, the challenger computes $\mathsf{WE.ct}$ using the fixed value m_1.
- $\text{PMEGame}^b_{16}(\lambda)$: In this game, we modify the generation of the master public key. When choosing $\mathsf{com}_{\mathsf{snd},0}$, the challenger commits 0 instead computing $\mathsf{com}_{\mathsf{snd},0} := \mathsf{Commit}_{\mathsf{Com.crs}}(1; r_{\mathsf{snd},0})$.
- $\text{PMEGame}^b_{17}(\lambda)$: In this game, we modify how the proof π_1 is generated for policy generation queries. When answering such a query, the challenger $\mathcal{C}$ uses the witness $w_1 = r_{\mathsf{snd},0}$ instead of $w_1 = (\mathsf{tsk}_{\mathsf{snd}}, r_{\mathsf{snd},1}, r_{\mathsf{snd},2})$. That is, $\pi_1 \leftarrow \mathsf{Prove}_{\mathsf{NIZK.crs}_1}(x_1 = (\mathsf{Com.crs}, \mathsf{com}_{\mathsf{snd},0}, \mathsf{com}_{\mathsf{snd},1}, \mathbb{S}, \mathsf{tag}_{\mathbb{S}}), w_1 = (r_{\mathsf{snd},0}))$.
- $\text{PMEGame}^b_{18}(\lambda)$: In this game, we modify how tags for the sender's attributes and policy are generated. For policy-generation queries, instead of returning a dummy tag, the challenger computes $\mathsf{tag}_{\mathbb{S}} \leftarrow \mathsf{DFunctionTag}(1^\lambda, \mathbb{S})$ and uses it in the response. For encryption queries, the challenger likewise replaces dummy tags by computing $\mathsf{tag}_{\sigma_1} \leftarrow \mathsf{DInputTag}(1^\lambda, \sigma_1)$ and incorporates it into the challenge ciphertext.

We note that the indistinguishability among the above games can be proven by lemmas analogous to Pattern ① and ②. Thus, ③ is omitted. Finally, ④ $\mathbb{S}(\sigma_0) = \mathbb{R}_1(\rho) = 1$ falls into an alternative case of ③, and is therefore omitted.

□

5 Conclusion

In this work, we proposed a new construction of ME from WE, commitments, NIZKs, functional tag systems, and LO. We also proved the adaptive privacy of the proposed ME scheme under the mismatch condition. In particular, our construction does not rely on any strong assumptions other than WE. Therefore, our ME can be viewed as a simpler and more assumption-light realization compared to existing constructions.

Acknowledgments. This work was in part supported by JST K Program Grant Number JPMJKP24U2, Japan. This work was in part supported by JSPS KAKENHI Grant Number JP23K24846, JP25KJ1319.

References

1. Ateniese, G., Francati, D., Nuñez, D., Venturi, D.: Match me if you can: matchmaking encryption and its applications. In: Boldyreva, A., Micciancio, D. (eds.) CRYPTO 2019. LNCS, vol. 11693, pp. 701–731. Springer, Cham (2019). https://doi.org/10.1007/978-3-030-26951-7_24
2. Ateniese, G., Francati, D., Nuñez, D., Venturi, D.: Match me if you can: matchmaking encryption and its applications. J. Cryptol. **34**(3), 16
3. Bitansky, N., Vaikuntanathan, V:. Indistinguishability obfuscation from functional encryption. In: 56th Annual Symposium on Foundations of Computer Science, pp. 171–190, Berkeley, CA, USA (2015)
4. Feige, U., Lapidot, D., Shamir, A.: Multiple non-interactive zero knowledge proofs based on a single random string (extended abstract). In: 31st Annual Symposium on Foundations of Computer Science, pp. 308–317, St. Louis, MO, USA (1990)
5. Francati, D., Friolo, D., Malavolta, G., Venturi, D.: Multi-key and multi-input predicate encryption (for conjunctions) from learning with errors
6. Garg, S., Gentry, C., Halevi, S., Raykova, M., Sahai, A., Waters, B.: Candidate indistinguishability obfuscation and functional encryption for all circuits. SIAM J. Comput. **45**(3), 882–929
7. Garg, S., Gentry, C., Sahai, A., Waters, B.: Witness encryption and its applications. In: 45th Annual ACM Symposium on Theory of Computing, pp. 467–476, Palo Alto, CA, USA (2013)
8. Goyal, R., Koppula, V., Waters, B.: Lockable obfuscation. In: 58th Annual Symposium on Foundations of Computer Science, pp. 612–621, Berkeley, CA, USA (2017)
9. Groth, J., Ostrovsky, R., Sahai, A.: Perfect non-interactive zero knowledge for NP. In: Vaudenay, S. (ed.) EUROCRYPT 2006. LNCS, vol. 4004, pp. 339–358. Springer, Heidelberg (2006). https://doi.org/10.1007/11761679_21
10. Naor, M.: Bit commitment using pseudorandomness. J. Cryptol. **4**
11. Waters, B., Wichs, D.: Adaptively secure attribute-based encryption from witness encryption. In: Theory of Cryptography, pp. 65–90, Cham, (2025)
12. Wichs, D., Zirdelis, G.: Obfuscating compute-and-compare programs under LWE. In: 58th Annual Symposium on Foundations of Computer Science, pp. 600–611, Berkeley, CA, USA (2017)

Deniable Asymmetric One-Round Group Key Agreement

Kashi Neupane(✉)

Department of Mathematics, University of North Georgia, Oakwood, GA, USA
kashi.neupane@ung.edu

Abstract. We propose a secure deniable asymmetric one-round group key agreement protocol based on decisional Bilinear Diffie-Hellman Exponent (BDHE) assumption. This protocol enables a set of users to negotiate shared encryption and decryption keys, rather than establishing a common secret. Each participant can join a protocol session, authenticate messages for other group members, but receivers cannot prove to a third party that such group involvement occurred. For authentication, we employ a ring signature scheme and message authentication code.

Keywords: group key agreement · deniability · ring signature

1 Introduction

Group key agreement is an essential cryptographic mechanism used to establish a common secret among multiple participants. This shared secret facilitates secure exchange of substantial data within the group. Key agreement is universally acknowledged as indispensable yet complex within security frameworks.

Wu et al. [WMS+09] introduced the notion of asymmetric group key agreement, which negotiates a set of shared encryption and decryption keys instead of a common secret key as in traditional group key agreement. Along with the notion of asymmetric group key agreement, they proposed an asymmetric GKA protocol secure under the Decisional Bilinear Diffie-Hellman Exponent (BDHE) assumption, without relying on random oracles. Efficiency in communication is a significant objective in establishing secure keys. The concept of asymmetric group key agreement represents a crucial advancement towards minimizing the number of protocol rounds necessary. Following Wu's proposal of asymmetric group key agreement there have been efforts to incorporate additional features into asymmetric group key agreement protocols. Zhang et al. [ZWQD11] expanded on this concept by introducing a security model for Identity-Based Authenticated Asymmetric Group Key Agreement (IB-AAGKA) protocols and proposed a protocol proven secure under the BDHE assumption. Additionally, Zhang et al. [ZZCC23] introduced a one-round dynamic authenticated asymmetric group key agreement with sender non-repudiation and privacy. Similarly, Braeken [Bra22] proposed a one-round lightweight elliptic curve based alternative adding self-certification to the members of the group. Recent advancements in

P. D'Arco and A. Zamfiroiu (Eds.): SecITC 2025, LNCS 16443, pp. 43–58, 2026.
https://doi.org/10.1007/978-3-032-17443-7_3

this field include [TM19] Teng and Ma's adaptation of Wu's asymmetric key agreement protocol to include traitor traceability, Chen et al. [CWH+21]an identity-based cross-domain authenticated asymmetric group key agreement, and [Neu22] Neupane's extension of asymmetric key agreement to achieve long-term security. In our study, we enhance Wu's protocol [WMS+09] by introducing the feature of deniability.

In a deniable group key agreement protocol, the transcript of the protocol cannot be used to demonstrate that the participant was involved in the session. Essentially, this means that a participant can take part in the protocol session but later deny their involvement altogether. Deniability is important in certain situations where a participant may wish to join a protocol session without leaving any trace or evidence of their participation. In 2002, Mao and Paterson introduced definitions of deniability across various levels and proposed key establishment protocols achieving deniability through identity-based techniques. Building upon a model by Bresson et al. [BCPQ01], Bohli and Steinwandt [BVS07] formalized deniability and presented a group key agreement protocol with provable security. They also proposed a four-round deniable group key agreement protocol with security analysis in the random oracle model, leveraging the Computational Diffie-Hellman assumption and Schnorr's Signature.

Building on Bohli and Steinwandt's research [BVS07], Zhang et al. [ZWL10] expanded the concept of deniable group key establishment and devised a protocol utilizing a variation of Schnorr's zero-knowledge identification scheme along with Burmester's group key establishment protocol in the standard model. Neupane et al. [NSC12] introduced a compiler designed to maintain the round complexity of key agreement protocols while integrating authentication and deniability. They demonstrated the feasibility of implementing a three-round group key agreement protocol using their methodology. The notion of deniability has been widely explored in the context of authenticated key exchange [UG15,UG18,BFG+22], where deniability extends beyond key establishment to the ability to repudiate entire communications conducted under the shared key. Gajland et al. [GJK24] present an extensive study of the use of ring signatures in achieving deniability.

In our research, we introduce a one-round asymmetric deniable group key agreement protocol. We utilize Wu et al.'s asymmetric group key agreement protocol [WMS+09] as the foundation for establishing key agreement. Additional technical components include ring signatures, multiparty key encapsulation, and message authentication codes. Specifically, we extend the existing one-round unauthenticated asymmetric group key agreement protocol proposed by [WMS+09] to an authenticated deniable protocol without introducing any additional rounds

2 Preliminaries

In this section, we briefly review mathematical and cryptographic tools we will use in the protocol. We begin with Bilinear Diffie-Hellman Exponentiation (BDHE) assumption as formalized by Wu et al. [WMS+09] and Zhang et al. [ZWL10]. Then, we discuss the standard definitions of multi key encapsulation mechanism, signature scheme, and symmetric encryption. Finally, we review the main idea of real-or-random indistinguishability as discussed by Bellare et al. [BDJR00].

2.1 Bilinear Maps and the Bilinear Diffie Hellman Assumption

Let G_1, and G_2 be two multiplicative groups of prime order q, where $q > 2^k$ with k being the security parameter. We denote by $\hat{e} : G_1 \times G_1 \longrightarrow G_2$ as an *admissible bilinear map*, i. e. meaning $\hat{e}$ possesses all of the following properties:

Bilinear: For all $a, b \in \mathbb{Z}$ and a generator g of G_1, we have $\hat{e}(g^a, g^b) = \hat{e}(g, g)^{ab}$.
Non-degenerate: There exist $g, h \in G_1$ such that $\hat{e}(g, h) \neq 1$.
Efficiently computable: There exists a polynomial-time algorithm which computes $\hat{e}(g, h)$ for all $g, h \in G_1$.

The Weil and Tate pairings are the most widely used in cryptography. To improve computational efficiency, researchers have developed several alternative pairings, such as the Ate, Eta, reduced Tate, twisted Ate, and R-Ate pairings, among others [DRR+15]. We define the Bilinear Diffie-Hellman Exponentiation (BDHE) problem using a probabilistic polynomial time (ppt) algorithm $\mathcal{G}$. This *BDHE parameter generator* $\mathcal{G}$ takes the security parameter as input, and outputs q and a description of G_1, G_2, and $\hat{e}$. This is denoted by $\langle q, G_1, G_2, \hat{e} \rangle \leftarrow \mathcal{G}(1^k)$.

Definition 1 (n-BDHE Problem). *Given g, h, and $y_i = g^{\alpha^i}$ in G_1 for $i = 1, 2 \cdots n, n+2, \cdots 2n$ as input, compute $\hat{e}(g, h)^{\alpha^{n+1}}$.*

Now consider the following experiment for a ppt algorithm $\mathcal{A}$ that outputs 0 or 1: The challenger chooses α^i for $i = 1, 2 \cdots n, n+1, n+2, \cdots 2n$ and an element $Z \in G_2$ independently and uniformly at random. Additionally, the challenger flips a random coin $\delta \in \{0, 1\}$ uniformly at random.

If $\delta = 0$, the tuple $(g, h, y_1, \cdots y_n, y_{n+2}, \cdots y_{2n}, Z)$ is given to $\mathcal{A}$, whereas for $\delta = 1$ the tuple $(g, h, y_1, \cdots y_n, y_{n+2}, \cdots y_{2n}, \hat{e}(g, h)^{\alpha^{n+1}})$ is given to $\mathcal{A}$. $\mathcal{A}$ wins the game whenever its guessed δ' matches δ. the advantage of $\mathcal{A}$ is denoted by

$$\mathrm{Adv}_{\mathcal{A}}^{\mathsf{n-BDHE}} := \left| \Pr[\delta = \delta'] - \frac{1}{2} \right|.$$

Definition 2 (decisional n-BDHE assumption). *The decisional n-BDHE assumption for $(G_1, G_2, \hat{e})$ holds, if the advantage $\mathrm{Adv}_{\mathcal{A}}^{\mathsf{n-BDHE}}$ in the above experiment is negligible for all ppt algorithms $\mathcal{A}$.*

2.2 Multi Key Encapsulation Mechanism

Cramer and Shoup [CS03] formalized the notion of *key encapsulation mechanism (KEM)* which allows sender and receiver to agree on a shared random session key. In [Sma05], Smart extended this formalization of key encapsulation to accomodate multiple recipients, introducing the concept of *multi key encapsulation mechanism (mKEM)*. Some of the protocols utilizing this primitives include those developed by Gorantla et al. [GBNM10,NSC12]. Here, we briefly revisit the concept this notion as outlined by the above two protocols.

Definition 3 (multi key encapsulation mechanism). *A multi key encapsulation mechanism (mKEM) consists of three polynomial time algorithms:* ($\mathtt{mKeyGen}, \mathtt{mEncaps}, \mathtt{mDecaps}$) *defined as follows:*

- $\mathtt{mKeyGen(D)}$: *A probabilistic key generation algorithm that takes the parameters $\mathbb{D}$ as input and generates a pair of public and secret keys (pk, dk).*
- $\mathtt{mEncaps}(\{\mathtt{pk}_1, \ldots, \mathtt{pk}_n\})$: *A probabilistic key encapsulation algorithm that takes a (polynomial size) set $\{pk_1, \ldots, pk_n\}$ of public keys, and generates a pair (K, C) where $K \in \{0, 1\}^k$ is a session key and C is an encapsulation of this session key under the public keys $\{pk_1, \ldots, pk_n\}$.*
- $\mathtt{mDecaps(dk, C)}$: *A deterministic key decapsulation algorithm that takes a secret key dk and an encapsulation C, and returns the session key K or a special error symbol $\perp$.*

For every key pairs (pk_i, dk_i) generated by $\mathtt{mKeyGen}$, *it holds that* $(K, C) = \mathtt{mEncaps}(\{pk_1, \ldots, pk_n\}) \Longrightarrow \mathtt{mDecaps}_{dk_i}(C) = K$ *for* $i = 1, \ldots, n$.

To characterize security of an mKEM, we adopt a similar approach as in the case of a single recipient.

Definition 4 (IND-CCA security). *An mKEM scheme is* IND-CCA secure *if* $\mathrm{Adv}_{\mathcal{A}}^{IND\text{-}CCA}(k) = |2 \cdot \Pr[b = b'] - 1|$ *is negligible. Here* $\mathrm{Adv}_{\mathcal{A}}$ *is the advantage of any probabilistic polynomial-time adversary $\mathcal{A}$ in a game as described in Fig. 1*

- **Setup:** The challenger $\mathcal{C}$ runs the key generation $\mathtt{mKeyGen}$ to produce n key pairs $(pk_1, dk_1), \ldots, (pk_n, dk_n)$ and hands the public keys $pk_1, \ldots, pk_n$ to adversary $\mathcal{A}$.
- **Phase 1:** The $\mathcal{A}$ is allowed to submit queries to a decapsulation oracle with subsets $\mathcal{P}' \subseteq \{pk_1, \ldots, pk_n\}$ and encapsulations C: given a query $\mathsf{mDecaps}(\mathcal{P}', C)$, $\mathcal{C}$ computes $\mathtt{mDecaps}_{dk_i}(C)$ for each $pk_i \in \mathcal{P}'$. For every $pk_i \in \mathcal{P}'$, if the same output K is produced then K is returned to $\mathcal{A}$. Otherwise, $\perp$ is returned.
- **Challenge:** $\mathcal{A}$ chooses a set $\mathcal{P}^* \subseteq \{pk_1, \ldots, pk_n\}$ and hands it to $\mathcal{C}$. Then $\mathcal{C}$ selects a bit $b \in \{0, 1\}$ uniformly at random and computes $(K_b, C^*) \leftarrow \mathtt{mEncaps}(\mathcal{P}^*)$. Finally, $\mathcal{C}$ selects a key K_{1-b} uniformly at random from the session key space and gives $(\{K_0, K_1\}, C^*)$ to $\mathcal{A}$.
- **Phase 2:** $\mathcal{A}$ can submit decapsulation queries as in Phase 1, subject to the condition that no $\mathsf{mDecaps}$-query is made that returns K_b.
- **Guess:** $\mathcal{A}$ outputs $b' \in \{0, 1\}$ and wins if and only $b = b'$.

Fig. 1. IND-CCA security of a multi key encapsulation mechanism

2.3 Message Authentication Codes and Ring Signatures

We employ a message authentication code along with an appropriate ring signature to address the challenge of authentication while preserving deniability.

Definition 5 (message authentication code).
A message authentication code (MAC) *consists of a tuple* (`MKeyGen`, `Tag`, `Verify`) *comprising polynomial time algorithms:*

- `MKeyGen(D)` : *A probabilistic key generation algorithm that takes the domain parameters* $\mathbb{D}$ *as input and generates secret key* K.
- `Tag(m, K)` : *A probabilistic tag generation algorithm that takes a message* $m \in \{0,1\}^*$ *and a secret key* K *as input, producing a message tag* $\theta := \mathtt{Tag}_K(m) \in \{0,1\}^*$ *on* m.
- `Verify(m, K,` θ`)`: *A deterministic verification algorithm that takes a message* m, *a secret key* K *and a candidate tag* θ *as input. It returns* 1 *if* θ *is a valid tag for the message* m, *and* 0 *otherwise.*

We assume that the message authentication which we use in the protocol is strongly unforgeable under adaptive chosen message attacks. Figure 2 outlines the experiment which explains security notion of a message authentication code. For more detail on this security definition, we refer Bellare and Namprempre [BN00].

Definition 6 (SUF-CMA security).
A message authentication code (`MKeyGen`, `Tag`, `Verify`) *is* strongly unforgeable under adaptive chosen message attacks/secure in the sense of SUF-CMA *if for all probabilistic polynomial time adversaries* $\mathcal{A}$ *the advantage* $\mathrm{Adv}_{\mathcal{A}}^{suf\text{-}cma} = \mathrm{Adv}_{\mathcal{A}}^{suf\text{-}cma}(k) := \Pr[\mathsf{Succ}_{\mathcal{A}}^{suf\text{-}cma}]$ *is negligible. Here* $\mathsf{Succ}_{\mathcal{A}}^{\mathrm{suf-cma}}$ *denotes the event that* $\mathcal{A}$ *wins the experiment in Fig. 2.*

- **Setup:** A secret key $K \leftarrow \mathtt{MKeyGen}(\mathbb{D})$ is created
- **Challenge:** The adversary $\mathcal{A}$ has unrestricted access to the tagging oracle $\mathcal{T}_K(\cdot)$ and the verification oracle $\mathcal{V}_K(\cdot)$.
- **Guess:** $\mathcal{A}$ outputs a (message, tag)-pair (m, θ) and wins if and only if $\mathtt{MVer}_K(m, \theta) = 1$ and either m has never ben queried to $\mathcal{T}_K(\cdot)$ or no query of the form $\mathcal{T}_K(m)$ returned the tag θ. en queried to $\mathcal{T}_K(\cdot)$ or no query of the form $\mathcal{T}_K(m)$ returned the tag θ.

Fig. 2. SUF-CMA security of a message authentication code

The final cryptographic primitive we use for our protocol is a ring signature, allowing a signer to generate signatures that can be verified successfully under several verification keys.

Definition 7 (ring signature scheme). *A* ring signature scheme *is a tuple of polynomial time algorithms* (`RKeyGen`, `RSign`, `RVerify`) *defined as follows:*

- $\texttt{RKeyGen(k)}$: *A probabilistic key generation algorithm that takes the security parameter k as input and outputs a pair of keys (vk, sk), where vk is a public verification key and sk is its corresponding secret signing key.*
- $\texttt{RSign}(\texttt{m}, \texttt{R}, \texttt{sk}_\texttt{s})$: *A probabilistic ring signature algorithm that takes a message m, a polynomial size set (a* ring*) of public verification keys $\mathcal{R} = \{vk_1, \ldots, vk_n\}$ and a secret key sk_s such that $vk_s \in \mathcal{R}$, and produces a signature σ.*
- $\texttt{RVerify}(\texttt{m}, \sigma, \texttt{R})$: *A deterministic ring signature verification algorithm that takes a message m, a signature σ and a ring of public keys $\mathcal{R}$, and returns* 1 *if σ is a valid signature for the message m with respect to the ring $\mathcal{R}$, and* 0 *otherwise.*

We require that for any ring $\mathcal{R}$ comprised of public verification keys produced by RKeyGen *and for any message m, with the secret key sk and verification key $vk \in \mathcal{R}$ the following relation holds:*
$\texttt{RVerify}(m, \texttt{RSign}_{sk}(m, \mathcal{R}), \mathcal{R}) = 1.$

For a ring signature, it is usually expected that the adversary cannot determine which of the group members produced the signature. Figure 3 outlines the experiment which explains security notion of a ring signature. A strong form of this design goal is known as *anonymity against full key exposure* [BKM06]:

- **Setup:** The challenger $\mathcal{C}$ runs the key generation **RKeyGen** n times to produce key pairs $(vk_1, sk_1), \ldots, (vk_n, sk_n)$ and gives the public keys $vk_1, \ldots, vk_n$ to $\mathcal{A}$.
- **Find:** The adversary $\mathcal{A}$ can (adaptively) query for signatures on a message m under a ring $\mathcal{R}$ from users with a public key $vk_s \in \mathcal{R} \cap \{vk_1, \ldots, vk_n\}$.[a] The challenger responds with $\texttt{RSign}_{sk_s}(m, \mathcal{R})$. At the end of this phase, $\mathcal{A}$ hands a message m^*, a ring $\mathcal{R}^*$ and two indices i_0, i_1 to $\mathcal{C}$, such that $vk_{i_0}, vk_{i_1} \in \mathcal{R}^* \cap \{vk_1, \ldots, vk_n\}$.
- **Challenge:** The challenger $\mathcal{C}$ chooses a bit $b \in \{0, 1\}$ uniformly at random, computes a signature $\texttt{RSign}_{sk_{i_b}}(m^*, \mathcal{R}^*)$, and hands this signature to $\mathcal{A}$ along with the random coins used to generate the key pairs $(vk_1, sk_1), \ldots, (vk_n, sk_n)$.[b]
- **Guess:** The adversary outputs a guess b' for b and wins if and only if $b = b'$.

[a] Note that only vk_s must be chosen from $vk_1, \ldots, vk_n$.
[b] In particular, $\mathcal{A}$ can recover the secret keys $sk_1, \ldots, sk_n$.

Fig. 3. RSIG-ANO: anonymity against full key exposure

Definition 8 (anonymity). *A ring signature scheme is* anonymous against full key exposure *if the advantage of any probabilistic polynomial time adversary $\mathcal{A}$ in the game described in Fig. 3 is negligible. Here the* advantage *of an adversary $\mathcal{A}$ is defined as* $\mathrm{Adv}_{\mathcal{A}}^{\mathrm{rsig-ano}}(k) = \left|\Pr[b = b'] - \frac{1}{2}\right|$.

Of course, as for other kinds of digital signatures, for a ring signature scheme we also expect an appropriate form of existential unforgeability. More specifically, we impose the following.

Definition 9 (RSIG-UF security). *A ring signature scheme is called* unforgeable with respect to insider corruption *if for any probabilistic polynomial time adversary $\mathcal{A}$ the advantage* $\mathrm{Adv}_{\mathcal{A}}^{rsig\text{-}uf}(k) := \Pr[\mathsf{Succ}_{\mathcal{A}}^{rsig\text{-}uf}]$ *in the game described in Fig. 4 is negligible. Here* $\mathsf{Succ}_{\mathcal{A}}^{rsig\text{-}uf}$ *denotes the event that $\mathcal{A}$ wins the experiment in Fig. 4.*

- **Setup:** The challenger $\mathcal{C}$ runs the algorithm **KeyGen** n times to obtain key pairs $(vk_1, sk_1), \ldots, (vk_n, sk_n)$ and hands the public keys $vk_1, \ldots, vk_n$ to $\mathcal{A}$.
- **Challenge:** The adversary is allowed to ask (adaptively) queries for:
  - private keys for a public key vk_i ($i \in \{1, \ldots, n\}$). The challenger returns sk_i.
  - signatures for a message m and a ring $\mathcal{R}$ under a secret key sk_s such that $vk_s \in \mathcal{R} \cap \{vk_1, \ldots, vk_n\}$. The challenger responds with $\mathbf{RSign}_{sk_s}(m, \mathcal{R})$.[a]
- **Guess:** The adversary outputs a tuple $(\mathcal{R}^*, m^*, \sigma^*)$ and wins if and only if all of the following hold:
  - $\mathtt{RVerify}(m^*, \sigma^*, \mathcal{R}^*) = 1$;
  - in the challenge phase, no secret key sk_i for a $vk_i \in \mathcal{R}^*$ has been queried;
  - in the challenge phase, the pair $(m^*, \mathcal{R}^*)$ was not part of a signature query.

[a] Note that only vk_s must be chosen from $vk_1, \ldots, vk_n$.

Fig. 4. RSIG-UF security of a ring signature

2.4 Real-or-Random Indistinguishability

We base our treatment of real-or-random indistinguishability on the framework established by Bellare et al. in [BDJR00]. For a comprehensive discussion, we direct readers to their work. Prior to presenting the definition of real-or-random indistinguishability, we revisit the definition of a symmetric encryption scheme.

Definition 10 (Symmetric Key Encryption Scheme).
A symmetric key encryption scheme $\mathcal{SE} = (\mathsf{Gen}, \mathsf{Enc}, \mathsf{Dec})$ *consists of three polynomial-time algorithms:*

- Gen *is a randomized key generation algorithm that takes the security parameter* 1^k*, and outputs a secret key* $K \in \{0,1\}^*$*;*
- Enc *is a randomized encryption algorithm that takes a secret key K and a message* $M \in \{0,1\}^*$ *as its input, and produces a ciphertext* $C \in \{0,1\}^*$*;*
- Dec *is a deterministic decryption algorithm that takes the key K and a ciphertext C as its inputs, and returns either a message M or an error symbol* $\perp$.

To ensure *correct decryption*, the scheme guarantees that for any secret key K and any message M such that ciphertext $C \leftarrow \mathsf{Enc}_K(M)$, it holds that $\mathsf{Dec}_K(C) = M$.

To formalize the security notion needed later, we utilize a *real-or-random oracle* $\mathcal{E}_K(\mathcal{RR}(\cdot, b))$ with the following specifications:

When given $b \in \{0,1\}$ and a plaintext $M \in \{0,1\}^*$,

- if $b = 1$, the oracle returns the encryption C obtained from $\mathsf{Enc}_K(M)$.
- if $b = 0$, the oracles returns returns an encryption C generated from $\mathsf{Enc}_K(r)$, where r is a randomly chosen bitstring of length $|M|$ from $\{0,1\}$.

For a ppt algorithm $\mathcal{A}$ now consider the following experiment where $b \in \{0,1\}$ is fixed and unknown to $\mathcal{A}$: a secret key $K \leftarrow \mathsf{Gen}(1^k)$ is created, and $\mathcal{A}$ has unrestricted access to $\mathcal{E}_K(\mathcal{RR}(\cdot, b))$. Further, $\mathcal{A}$ has access to a decryption oracle $\mathcal{D}_K(\cdot)$ which executes $\mathsf{Dec}_K(\cdot)$, subject to the restriction that no messages must be queried to $\mathcal{D}_K(\cdot)$ that have been output by the real-or-random oracle. We measure $\mathcal{A}$'s advantage as the difference $\mathrm{Adv}_{\mathcal{A}}^{\mathsf{ror-cca}} =$

$$\begin{aligned}\mathrm{Adv}_{\mathcal{A}}^{\mathsf{ror-cca}}(k) := \Pr\left[1 \leftarrow \mathcal{A}^{\mathcal{E}_K(\mathcal{RR}(\cdot,1)),\mathcal{D}_K(\cdot)}(1^k) \,\middle|\, K \leftarrow \mathsf{Gen}(1^k)\right] - \\ \Pr\left[1 \leftarrow \mathcal{A}^{\mathcal{E}_K(\mathcal{RR}(\cdot,0)),\mathcal{D}_K(\cdot)}(1^k) \,\middle|\, K \leftarrow \mathsf{Gen}(1^k)\right]\end{aligned}$$

Definition 11 (Real-or-Random Indistinguishability). *A symmetric encryption scheme* $\mathcal{SE}$ *is* secure in the sense of real-or-random indistinguishability (ROR-CCA), *if for all ppt algorithms* $\mathcal{A}$*, the advantage* $\mathrm{Adv}_{\mathcal{A}}^{\mathsf{ror-cca}}$ *is negligible (in* k*).*

3 Security Model

The security model adopted for analyzing our protocol builds upon the framework introduced by Bohli et al. [BVS07] and Neupane et al. [NSC12], which extends the model originally proposed by Bresson et al. [BCPQ01]. In this section we quickly revisit the relevant terminology and definitions from the literature.

Protocol Participants. The set of participants in the protocol, denoted as $\mathcal{U} = \{U_0, \ldots.., U_n\}$, consists of individuals capable of concurrently executing a polynomial number of protocol instances Π_U^s (where $s \in \mathbb{N}$). Each participant $U \in \mathcal{U}$ is identified by a bitstring of identical length k. For simplicity in notation, we treat the bitstring identifying a participant U itself as interchangeable. Each protocol instance Π_U^s is associated with the following seven variables:

sk_U^s: This variable stores the set of encryption and decryption keys of each user participating in a session.

acc_U^s: This variable indicates whether the session keys stored in sk_U^s have been accepted.

pid_U^s: This variable stores the identities of users in $\mathcal{U}$ with whom a key agreement is intended, including U itself.

sid_U^s: This variable stores a non-secret session identifier that serves as public reference to the session keys stored in sk_U^s.

state_U^s: This variable stores state information related to the protocol instance.

used_U^s: This variable indicates whether this instance is used, i. e., actively involved in a protocol run.

Initialization. Prior to commencing actual protocol executions, a trusted initialization phase is conducted to prevent adversarial interference. During this phase:

- Each user U_i generates a (public key, secret key)-pair (pk_i, dk_i) for multi key encapsulation scheme. The public keys pk_i are made available to all users, including the adversary.
- Each user U_i also generates a set of (verification key, signing key)-pair (vk_i, sk_i) for ring signature scheme. The signing keys sk_i are distributed to the users, while verification keys vk_i are made available to all the users, including the adversary.

Adversarial Capabilities and Communication Network. We assume that the network allows arbitrary point-to-point connections among users, is non-private, and operates fully asynchronously. The adversary $\mathcal{A}$ is modeled as ppt algorithm with full control over the communication network. More specifically, the following *oracles* are employed to capture the capabilities of the adversary $\mathcal{A}$:

$\mathsf{Send}(U, s, M)$: sends the message M to instance Π_U^s of user U and returns the protocol message output by that instance after receiving M. The Send oracle also enables $\mathcal{A}$ to initialize a protocol execution by sending a special message $M = \{U_{i_1}, \ldots, U_{i_r}\}$ to an unused instance $\prod_U^s$. After such a query, $\prod_U^s$ sets $\mathsf{pid}_U^s := \{U_{i_1}, \ldots, U_{i_r}\}$, $\mathsf{used}_U^s :=$ TRUE, and processes the first step of the protocol.

$\mathsf{Reveal}(U, s)$: returns the set of encryption and decryption keys in sk_U^s if $\mathsf{acc}_U^s =$ TRUE and a NULL value otherwise.

$\mathsf{Corrupt}(U)$: for a user $U \in \mathcal{U}$ this query returns U's long term signing key sk_U^{sig}.

In addition to the mentioned oracles, $\mathcal{A}$ has access to a Test oracle, which can be queried only once: the query $\mathsf{Test}(U, s)$ can be made with an instance Π_U^s that has accepted the set of session keys. Upon the query, a bit $b \leftarrow \{0, 1\}$ is chosen uniformly at random; for $b = 0$, the set of session keys stored in sk_U^s is returned, and for $b = 1$ a uniformly at random chosen elements from the space of session keys is returned. In order to exclude useless protocols we consider only *correct* group key establishments, and our correctness definition follows Katz and Yung [KY03].

Definition 12 (Correctness). *A group key establishment is* correct *if for all instances $\Pi_i^{s_i}$, $\Pi_j^{s_j}$ that have accepted with $\mathsf{sid}_i^{s_i} = \mathsf{sid}_j^{s_j}$ and $\mathsf{pid}_i^{s_i} = \mathsf{pid}_j^{s_j}$, the encryption and decryption keys stored in $\mathsf{sk}_i^{s_i}$ and $\mathsf{sk}_j^{s_j}$ are meaningful keys.*

To ensure non-triviality, we require that key establishment protocols be correct: they must establish a valid set of session keys in the absence of active adversaries, with consistent session identifiers and matching partner identifiers. Subsequently, we adopt the concept of partnered instances based on the following principle. It should be noted that each session is inherently partnered with itself

Definition 13 (Partnering). *Two instances* $\prod_{U_i}^{s_i}$ *and* $\prod_{U_j}^{s_j}$ *are* partnered *if* $\mathsf{sid}_{U_i}^{s_i} = \mathsf{sid}_{U_j}^{s_j}$, $\mathsf{pid}_{U_i}^{s_i} = \mathsf{pid}_{U_j}^{s_j}$ *and* $\mathsf{acc}_{U_i}^{s_i} = \mathsf{acc}_{U_j}^{s_j} = \text{TRUE}$.

We define an instance as fresh if the adversary lacks knowledge of its session keys. Building upon this concept of pattern, we formally define freshness as follows

Definition 14 (Freshness). *An instance* $\prod_{U_i}^{s_i}$ *is considered* fresh *if, before any query of the form* $\mathsf{Send}(U_k, s_k, *)$ *with* $U_k \in \mathsf{pid}_{U_i}^{s_i}$*, the adversary has not queried* $\mathsf{Corrupt}(U_j)$ *for some* $U_j \in \mathsf{pid}_{U_i}^{s_i}$ *nor* $\mathsf{Reveal}(U_j, s_j)$ *for an instance* $\prod_{U_j}^{s_j}$ *partnered with* $\prod_{U_i}^{s_i}$.

We denote by $\mathsf{Succ}_{\mathcal{A}}$ the event where $\mathcal{A}$ queries a fresh instance and guesses correctly the bit output by the Test oracle. The *advantage* of $\mathcal{A}$ is defined as

$$\mathrm{Adv}_{\mathcal{A}}^{\mathsf{ke}} = \mathrm{Adv}_{\mathcal{A}}^{\mathsf{ke}}(k) := \left| \Pr[\mathsf{Succ}_{\mathcal{A}}] - \frac{1}{2} \right|.$$

Definition 15 (Semantic security). *A key establishment protocol is said to be* (semantically) secure, *if* $\mathrm{Adv}_{\mathcal{A}}^{\mathsf{ke}} = \mathrm{Adv}_{\mathcal{A}}^{\mathsf{ke}}(k)$ *is negligible for all ppt algorithms* $\mathcal{A}$.

In addition to semantic security, another important security goal is *strong entity authentication*:

Definition 16 (Strong entity authentication). strong entity authentication *for an instance* $\Pi_{U_i}^{s_i}$ *is provided if* $\mathsf{acc}_{U_i}^{s_i} = \text{TRUE}$ *implies that for all uncorrupted* $U_j \in \mathsf{pid}_{U_i}^{s_i}$*, there exists with overwhelming probability an instance* $\Pi_{U_j}^{s_j}$ *with* $\mathsf{sid}_{U_j}^{s_j} = \mathsf{sid}_{U_i}^{s_i}$ *and* $U_i \in \mathsf{pid}_{U_j}^{s_j}$.

3.1 A Privacy Goal: Deniability

In addition to semantic security and authentication, the protocol also achieves deniability. In this section, we explore a privacy objective of the protocol, focusing on the concept of deniability as defined by Neupane et al. [NSC12] and grounded in the research of Bohli and Steinwandt [BS06]. Now we revisit this notion briefly as discussed in [NSC12,BS06].

Let $\mathcal{A}_d$ denote a probabilistic polynomial time algorithm that takes security parameter 1^k and public information pk from the initialization phase as inputs. In a first phase $\mathcal{A}_d$ has access only to the $\mathsf{Corrupt}$-oracle, enabling it to (adaptively) corrupt an arbitrary subset of the users, including the scenarios where no user or all users being corrupted. Subsequently, in a second phase, $\mathcal{A}_d$ interacts with the protocol participants via the Reveal- and Send-oracle without querying Corrupt nor Test during this phase. $\mathcal{A}_d$ outputs a bitstring $T_{\mathcal{A}_d} = T_{\mathcal{A}_d}(k, pk)$ to indicate the involvement of a specific user in the establishment of encryption and encryption keys. Let $T_{\mathcal{A}_d} = T_{\mathcal{A}_d}(k)$ denote the random variable describing $T_{\mathcal{A}_d}(k, pk)$ with randomness chosen uniformly at random for $\mathcal{A}_d$, for all protocol instances, and during the initialization phase.

The probabilistic polynomial time simulator $\mathcal{S}_d$ receives the same input as $\mathcal{A}_d$, but is restricted to accessing only the Corrupt oracle—without access to Reveal, Send, or Test. $\mathcal{S}_d$ outputs a bitstring $T_{\mathcal{S}_d}(k, pk)$, and similarly to $\mathcal{A}_d$, we define a random variable $T_{\mathcal{S}_d}(k)$ based on uniformly chosen randomness. Consider the following experiment involving a probabilistic polynomial time distinguisher $\mathcal{X}$ which outputs 0 or 1: the challenger flips a random coin $b \in \{0, 1\}$ uniformly at random. If $b = 1$, the transcript $T_{\mathcal{A}_d}(k)$ is provided to $\mathcal{X}$: if $b = 0$ the transcript $T_{\mathcal{S}_d}(k)$ is provided to $\mathcal{X}$. The distinguisher $\mathcal{X}$ wins if its guessed b' matches b; the advantage of $\mathcal{X}$ is denoted by $\mathrm{Adv}_{\mathcal{X}}^{\mathsf{den}} := \left|\Pr[b = b'] - \frac{1}{2}\right|$.

Definition 17 (deniability). *A group key establishment protocol is* deniable *if for every polynomial time adversary $\mathcal{A}_d$ as specified above there exists a probabilistic polynomial time simulator $\mathcal{S}_d$ such that the following holds:*

- *With overwhelming probability, the number of* Corrupt*-queries made by $\mathcal{S}_d$ is less than or equal to the number made by $\mathcal{A}_d$.*
- *For each probabilistic polynomial time distinguisher $\mathcal{X}$, the advantage* $\mathrm{Adv}_{\mathcal{X}}^{\mathsf{den}}$ *in the experiment described above is negligible.*

4 The Proposed Group Key Establishment Protocol

4.1 Description of the Protocol

In this protocol, we adopt the notation from Sect. 2.1. Here g serves as a generator of the group G_1 with prime order q, as defined in the n-BDHE assumption. The terms Enc and Dec represent the encryption and decryption algorithms of a symmetric encryption scheme that ensures security under ROR-CCA notion. The symbol σ denotes an existentially unforgeable ring signature scheme. The protocol involves participants denoted as $U_0, \ldots, U_n$ who aim to negotiate encryption and decryption keys. Initially, the initiator has to broadcast a message. subsequently, open receiving the message this message, all the other participants broadcast a single message each. Following successful verification of signatures and Message Authentications Code (MAC) tag, all the participants can compute encryption and decryption keys.

4.2 Security Analysis

The protocol described in Sect. 4.1 achieves semantic security under the condition that the underlying ring signature scheme is existentially unforgeable and the symmetric encryption scheme used satisfies the security requirements of ROR-CCA. To elaborate further:

Setup. Takes a security parameter $k \in Z^+$ and outputs BDHE parameters $(q, G_1, G_2, \hat{e})$. An element $h_i \in G_1$ is randomly chosen for each user U_i.

Computation. First of all, the initiator U_0 creates a key $K_0 \leftarrow \texttt{MKeyGen}(\mathbb{D})$ for a message authentication code, produces a ring signature $\sigma := \texttt{RSig}_{sk_0}(K_0, \mathsf{pid}_0)$, and computes $(K, C) \leftarrow \texttt{mEncaps}(\mathsf{pid}_0)$. Then the initiator produces a ciphertext $E := \texttt{Enc}_K(K_0||\mathsf{pid}_0||\sigma)$ and computes a tag $\mathsf{tag}_0 = \mathsf{Tag}_{K_0}(C, E)$. The initiator publishes $(C, E)||\mathsf{tag}_0$. First, each user except the initiator, recovers $K := \texttt{mDecaps}_{dk_i}(C)$ and decrypts the ciphertext E. Then each U_i randomly chooses $X_i \in G_1$, $r_i \in \mathbb{Z}_q^*$ and computes $\gamma_{i,j} = X_i h_j^{r_i}$, $R_i = g^{-r_i}$, $A_i = \hat{e}(X_i, g)$. Furthermore, each U_i computes a tag t_i on $\{\gamma_{i,j}, R_i, A_i\}_{i \neq j}$ and signs the message $\{t_i, \gamma_{i,j}, R_i, A_i\}_{i \neq j}$ to produce a ring signature σ_i.

Broadcast. Each U_i broadcasts $(pid, \{t_i, \gamma_{i,j}, R_i, A_i\}_{i \neq j}, \sigma_i)$.

Group encryption key derivation. Upon receipt of broadcast messages from each party, U_j accepts the messages from U_i if:
- the signature σ_i is successfully verified
- t_i is a valid tag on the message.

If all the verifications are successful, then each party U_i computes the group encryption key (R, A):
$R = \prod_{j=1}^{n} R_j = g^{-\sum_{j=1}^{n} r_j}$, $A = \prod_{j=1}^{n} A_j = \hat{e}(\prod_{j=1}^{n} X_j, g)$.

Decryption key derivation. Using the private input (X_i, r_i) during the protocol execution phase, player U_i can calculate its secret decryption key from the public communication:
$\gamma_i = X_i h_i^{r_i} \prod_{j=1}^{n, j \neq i} \gamma_{j,i} = \prod_{j=1}^{n} X_j h_i^{r_j} = (\prod_{j=1}^{n} X_j) h_i^{\sum_{j=1}^{n} r_j}$

Encryption. For a plaintext $m \in G_2$, any user who has the group encryption key can compute the ciphertext $c = (c_1, c_2, c_3)$, where $t \leftarrow \mathbb{Z}_p$, $c_1 = g^t$, $c_2 = R^t$, $c_3 = mA^t$.

Decryption. Since each player U_i has the symmetric encryption key $\hat{e}(\gamma_i, g)\hat{e}(h_i, R) = A$, U_i can recover the plaintext m:
$m = \frac{c_3}{\hat{e}(\gamma_i, c_1)\hat{e}(h_i, c_2)}$.

Fig. 5. Deniable asymmetric group key agreement

Proposition 1. *If the signature scheme employed in the protocol depicted in Fig. 5 is secure under the UF-CMA notion, and the symmetric encryption scheme adheres to ROR-CCA security, then the protocol in Fig. 5 achieves semantic security and provides entity authentication for all participating entities. These assurances hold under the condition that the n-BDHE assumption for the underlying BDHE instance generator remains valid.*

We establish the security of the protocol through a series of "game hopping" steps, where the adversary $\mathcal{A}$ interacts with a simulator $\mathcal{S}$. The adversary's success and advantage in Game Game i are denoted as $\mathsf{Succ}_{\mathcal{A}}^{\text{Game } i}$ and $\text{Adv}_{\mathcal{A}}^{\text{Game}}$ i, respectively. This approach involves proving the protocol's security by transitioning through a concise sequence of these games.

Game 0: This game is identical to the original attack game for the adversary, with all oracles being simulated faithfully. In particular,

$$\text{Adv}_{\mathcal{A}} = \text{Adv}_{\mathcal{A}}^{\text{Game } 0}.$$

Game 1: Let $\mathsf{ForgeRS}$ be the event that, for the Test-instance, $\mathcal{A}$ succeeds in forging a new ring signature for the initiator U_0 when the session is initiated or for any users when they broadcast the message before querying $\mathsf{Corrupt}(U_i)$ for some $U_i \in \mathsf{pid}_0$. Whenever the event $\mathsf{ForgeRS}$ occurs, we abort the simulation and consider $\mathcal{A}$ as successful. Otherwise, Game 1 is identical to Game 0. Consequently $|\mathrm{Adv}_{\mathcal{A}}^{\text{Game 1}} - \mathrm{Adv}_{\mathcal{A}}^{\text{Game 0}}| \leq \mathrm{Adv}_{\mathcal{A}_{\text{rsig}}}^{\text{rsig-uf}}$.

Game 2: In this game everything remains the same as Game 1 except the simulator $\mathcal{S}$ generates the ciphertext E using an encryption of a freshly generated key $K' \leftarrow \mathtt{KeyGen}(1^k)$ instead of using the real key K. Whenever the adversary notices the difference, we abort the protocol and consider $\mathcal{A}$ as successful. Otherwise, Game 2 is identical to Game 1. Consequently $|\mathrm{Adv}_{\mathcal{A}}^{\text{Game 2}} - \mathrm{Adv}_{\mathcal{A}}^{\text{Game 1}}| \leq \mathrm{Adv}_{\mathcal{A}_{\text{mkem}}}^{\text{IND-CCA}}$

Game 3: Now, in the protocol the simulator replaces the ciphertext E with an encryption of a uniformly chosen random bitstring of the appropriate length. To bound $|\mathrm{Adv}_{\mathcal{A}}^{\text{Game 2}} - \mathrm{Adv}_{\mathcal{A}}^{\text{Game 1}}|$ we can derive a challenger $\mathcal{C}$ to attack the $\mathsf{ROR\text{-}CCA}$ security of the underlying symmetric encryption scheme: whenever the protocol requires to encrypt or decrypt a message using the symmetric key K, $\mathcal{C}$ queries its encryption or decryption oracle, respectively, simulating $\mathsf{Corrupt}$, Reveal, Send and Test in the obvious way. Consequently, we obtain

$$|\mathrm{Adv}_{\mathcal{A}}^{\text{Game 3}} - \mathrm{Adv}_{\mathcal{A}}^{\text{Game 2}}| \leq \mathrm{Adv}_{\mathcal{C}}^{\mathsf{ror-cca}}$$

Game 4: In this game, simulator's behavior deviates from that in Game 3 when computing the decryption key for user U_i, rather than using X_i, as specified in the protocol, the simulator computes γ_i with a uniformly at random chosen element $Y_i \in G_1$.
We have $|\mathrm{Adv}_{\mathcal{A}}^{\text{Game 4}} - \mathrm{Adv}_{\mathcal{A}}^{\text{Game 3}}| \leq |\Pr(\mathsf{Succ}_{\mathcal{A}}^{\text{Game 4}}) - \Pr(\mathsf{Succ}_{\mathcal{A}}^{\text{Game 3}})|$, and the latter is negligible since we can derive an algorithm $\mathcal{B}$ to solve the n-BDHE problem, i.e.,

$$\left|\Pr[\mathsf{Succ}_{\mathcal{A}}^{\text{Game 4}}] - \Pr[\mathsf{Succ}_{\mathcal{A}}^{\text{Game 3}}]\right| \leq \mathrm{Adv}_{\mathcal{B}}^{\mathsf{n-BDHE}}$$

Game 5: Let $\mathsf{ForgeMAC}$ denote the event that $\mathcal{A}$ succeeds in forging a new valid (message, tag)-pair for a user U_i before queing $\mathsf{Corrupt}(U_j)$ for user some $U_j \in \mathsf{pid}_j$. This game is identical to Game 4 with the only exception that we abort the simulation and consider $\mathcal{A}$ as successful whenever the event $\mathsf{ForgeMAC}$ occurs. The occurrence of this event immediately yields an adversary $\mathcal{A}_{\text{mac}}$ against the message authentication code. Therefore, $|\mathrm{Adv}_{\mathcal{A}}^{\text{Game 5}} - \mathrm{Adv}_{\mathcal{A}}^{\text{Game 4}}| \leq \mathrm{Adv}_{\mathcal{A}_{\text{mac}}}^{\text{suf-cma}}$.

By construction $\mathrm{Adv}_{\mathcal{A}}^{\text{Game 5}} = 0$, and we recognize the protocol in Fig. 5 as secure.

Proposition 2. *The protocol Fig. 5 is deniable in the sense of Definition 17.*

Proof. We establish the deniability of the protocol using the 'game hopping' technique. We allow the probabilistic polynomial time adversary $\mathcal{A}_d$ of the protocol and the simulator $\mathcal{S}_d$ interact with the challenger $\mathcal{C}$. We denote the advantage of the distinguisher $\mathcal{X}$ in Game i by $\mathrm{Adv}_{\mathcal{X}}^{\text{Game}}i$.

Game 0: This game is identical to the original deniability game, where all oracles of the adversary and simulator are faithfully simulated by $\mathcal{C}$. Consequently, $\mathrm{Adv}_{\mathcal{X}}^{\mathrm{den}} = \mathrm{Adv}_{\mathcal{X}}^{\mathrm{Game\ 0}}$.

Game 1: This game is identical to Game 0, except that if no participant $U_i \in \mathsf{pid}_0$ has been corrupted, the challenger $\mathcal{C}$ produces the ciphertext E in simulation for U_0 by encrypting a random bitstring of the appropriate length. It can be argued that the advantage of the distinguisher $\mathcal{X}$ in Game 0 and Game 1 differs only negligibly by considering adversary $\mathcal{D}$ against the real-or-random indistinguishability of the symmetric encryption scheme and derive
$\left|\mathrm{Adv}_{\mathcal{X}}^{\mathrm{Game\ 1}} - \mathrm{Adv}_{\mathcal{X}}^{\mathrm{Game\ 0}}\right| \leq |\mathrm{Adv}^{\mathrm{ror-cca}}(k)|$, which is negligible.

Game 2: This game is identical to Game 1 except that $\mathcal{C}$ changes the simulation of the Send-oracle for Round 0 messages for the initiator U_0 if some participant $U_j \in \mathsf{pid}_0$ has been corrupted. In such cases, the adversary possesses a secret key pair (sk_j, dk_j); if multiple key pairs exists, one is randomly selected. The challenger faithfully simulates all computations of U_0 using sk_j to compute the required ring signature. If the distinguisher $\mathcal{X}$ detects the discrepancies between the simulation and that in Game 2, it could be used as a black-box to attack the anonymity of the ring signature, yielding
$\left|\mathrm{Adv}_{\mathcal{X}}^{\mathrm{Game\ 2}} - \mathrm{Adv}_{\mathcal{X}}^{\mathrm{Game\ 1}}\right| \leq 2 \cdot \mathrm{Adv}_{\mathcal{F}}^{\mathrm{rsig-ano}}(k)$, which is negligible.
Note that the simulation provided now to $\mathcal{A}_d$ by the challenger $\mathcal{C}$ matches what $\mathcal{S}_d$ would provide, thus the distinguisher's advantage in this scenario is 0.
Combining all advantages, we get: $\mathrm{Adv}_{\mathcal{X}}^{\mathrm{den}} \leq |\mathrm{Adv}_{\mathcal{D}}^{\text{ror-cca}}(k)| + 2 \cdot \mathrm{Adv}_{\mathcal{F}}^{\text{rsig-ano}}(k)$, which is negligible.

Therefore, we affirm that the protocol in Fig. 5 is deniable.

Entity Authentication. Successful verification of the signatures and message authentication codes on the messages ensures the existence of a used instance for each intended communication partner and that the respective (R, A)-values are computed as expected. Consequently, it implies the equality of both the pid_i- and the sid_i-values. □

5 Conclusion

The one-round deniable asymmetric group key agreement protocol we introduced extends an existing asymmetric group key agreement by incorporating deniability. This protocol utilizes both a ring signature scheme and a multi key encapsulation scheme. It becomes particularly advantageous in scenarios where communication costs are high, participants can only broadcast a single message, and deniability is a necessary feature. Furthermore, the security guarantees offered by the protocol are robust and substantial.

References

[BCPQ01] Bresson, E., Chevassut, O., Pointcheval, D., Quisquater, J.-J.: Provably Authenticated group Diffie-Hellman key exchange. In: Proceedings of the 8th ACM Conference on Computer and Communications Security CCS'01, pp. 255–264. ACM (2001)

[BDJR00] Bellare, M., Desai, A., Jokipii, E., Rogaway. P.: A Concrete Security Treatment of Symmetric Encryption. Available at http://cseweb.ucsd.edu/mihir/papers/sym-enc.html (Sept 2000)

[BFG+22] Brendel, J., Fiedler, R., Günther, F., Janson, C., Stebila, D.: Post-quantum asynchronous deniable key exchange and the signal handshake. In: Hanaoka, G., Shikata, J., Watanabe, Y., editors, Public-Key Cryptography - PKC 2022 - 25th IACR International Conference on Practice and Theory of Public-Key Cryptography, Virtual Event, March 8-11, 2022, Proceedings, Part II, volume 13178 of Lecture Notes in Computer Science, pages 3–34. Springer (2022)

[BKM06] Bender, A., Katz, J., Morselli, R.: Ring signatures: stronger definitions, and constructions without random oracles. In: Halevi, S., Rabin, T. (eds.) TCC 2006. LNCS, vol. 3876, pp. 60–79. Springer, Heidelberg (2006). https://doi.org/10.1007/11681878_4

[BN00] Bellare, M., Namprempre, C.: Authenticated encryption: relations among notions and analysis of the generic composition paradigm. In: Okamoto, T. (ed.) ASIACRYPT 2000. LNCS, vol. 1976, pp. 531–545. Springer, Heidelberg (2000). https://doi.org/10.1007/3-540-44448-3_41

[Bra22] Braeken, A.: Pairing free asymmetric group key agreement protocol. Comput. Commun. **181**, 267–273 (2022)

[BS06] Bohli, J.-M., Steinwandt, R.: Deniable group key agreement. In: Nguyen, P.Q. (ed.) VIETCRYPT 2006. LNCS, vol. 4341, pp. 298–311. Springer, Heidelberg (2006). https://doi.org/10.1007/11958239_20

[BVS07] Bohli, J.-M., González Vasco, M. I., Steinwandt, R.: Secure group key establishment revisited. Int. J. Inform. Secur. **6**(4), 243–254 (2007)

[CS03] Cramer, R., Shoup, V.: Design and analysis of practical public-key encryption schemes secure against adaptive chosen ciphertext attack. SIAM J. Comput. **33**(1), 167–226 (2003)

[CWH+21] Chen, Q., Wu, T., Hu, C., Chen, A., Zheng, Q.: An identity-based cross-domain authenticated asymmetric group key agreement. Information **12**(3) (2021)

[DRR+15] Moody, D., Peralta, R., Perlner, R., Regenscheid, A., Roginsky, A., Chen, L.: Report on pairing-based cryptography. J. Res. National Inst. Stand. Technol. **2015**(120-11), November 2015

[GBNM10] Choudary Gorantla, M., Boyd, C., González Nieto, J.M., Manulis, M.: Generic one round group key exchange in the standard model. In D. Lee and S. Hong, editors, Information Security and Cryptology – ICISC 2009, volume 5984 of LNCS, pp. 1–15. Springer (2010)

[GJK24] Phillip Gajland, Jonas Janneck, and Eike Kiltz. Ring signatures for deniable AKEM: gandalf's fellowship. In Leonid Reyzin and Douglas Stebila, editors, *Advances in Cryptology - CRYPTO 2024 - 44th Annual International Cryptology Conference, Santa Barbara, CA, USA, August 18-22, 2024, Proceedings, Part I*, volume 14920 of *Lecture Notes in Computer Science*, pages 305–338. Springer, 2024

[KY03] Katz, J., Yung, M.: Scalable protocols for authenticated group key exchange. In: Boneh, D. (ed.) CRYPTO 2003. LNCS, vol. 2729, pp. 110–125. Springer, Heidelberg (2003). https://doi.org/10.1007/978-3-540-45146-4_7

[Neu22] Neupane, K.: Long-term secure asymmetric group key agreement. In: Ryan, P.Y.A., Toma, C., eds, Innovative Security Solutions for Information Technology and Communications, pp. 296–307. Springer International Publishing (2022)

[NSC12] K. Neupane, R. Steinwandt, and A. Suárez Corona. Scalable deniable group key establishment. In Joaquín García-Alfaro, Frédéric Cuppens, Nora Cuppens-Boulahia, Ali Miri, and Nadia Tawbi, editors, *Foundations and Practice of Security - FPS 2012*, volume 7743 of *LNCS*, pages 365–373. Springer, 2012

[Sma05] Smart, N.P.: Efficient key encapsulation to multiple parties. In: Blundo, C., Cimato, S., eds, Security in Communication Networks - SCN 2004, vol. 3352 LNCS, pp. 208–219. Springer (2005)

[TM19] Teng, J., Ma, H.: Dynamic asymmetric group key agreement protocol with traitor traceability. IET Inf. Secur. **13**(6), 703–710 (2019)

[UG15] Unger, N., Goldberg, I.: Deniable key exchanges for secure messaging. In: Proceedings of the 22nd ACM SIGSAC Conference on Computer and Communications Security, CCS '15, pp. 1211–1223, New York, NY, USA, 2015. Association for Computing Machinery (2015)

[UG18] Unger, N., Goldberg, I.: Improved strongly deniable authenticated key exchanges for secure messaging. Proc. Priv. Enhancing Technol. **2018**(1), 21–66 (2018)

[WMS+09] Wu, Q., Mu, Y., Susilo, W., Qin, B., Domingo-Ferrer, J.: Asymmetric group key agreement. In: Joux, A. (ed.) EUROCRYPT 2009. LNCS, vol. 5479, pp. 153–170. Springer, Heidelberg (2009). https://doi.org/10.1007/978-3-642-01001-9_9

[ZWL10] Zhang, Y., Wang, K., Li, B.: A deniable group key establishment protocol in the standard model. In: Kwak, J., Deng, R.H., Won, Y., Wang, G. (eds.) ISPEC 2010. LNCS, vol. 6047, pp. 308–323. Springer, Heidelberg (2010). https://doi.org/10.1007/978-3-642-12827-1_23

[ZWQD11] Zhang, L., Qianhong, W., Qin, B., Domingo-Ferrer, J.: Provably secure one-round identity-based authenticated asymmetric group key agreement protocol. Inf. Sci. **181**(19), 4318–4329 (2011)

[ZZCC23] Zhang, R., Zhang, L., Raymond Choo, K.-K., Chen, T.: Dynamic authenticated asymmetric group key agreement with sender non-repudiation and privacy for group-oriented applications . IEEE Trans. Depend. Secure Comput. **20**(01), 492–505 (2023)

Efficiency Improvement of Deniable FHE: Tighter Deniability Analysis and TFHE-Based Construction

Towa Toyooka[1(✉)], Yohei Watanabe[1,2], and Mitsugu Iwamoto[1]

[1] The University of Electro-Communications, Chofu, Japan
{t.toyooka,watanabe,mitsugu}@uec.ac.jp
[2] National Institute of Advanced Industrial Science and Technology, Tokyo, Japan

Abstract. Fully homomorphic encryption (FHE) is a cryptographic scheme that can take ciphertexts as inputs and compute a new ciphertext of a function of the underlying messages without decryption. FHE has been attracting attention along with the growing interest in privacy-preserving technologies. In terms of privacy-preserving technology, deniable encryption is also important. Deniable encryption enables a user, who may be forced to reveal the messages corresponding to the user's public ciphertexts, to lie about which messages the user encrypted. Agrawal et al. (CRYPTO 2021) introduced deniable FHE (DFHE) that combines FHE with deniable encryption, and proposed a transformation from an FHE scheme that satisfies specific special requirements, called special FHE, to a DFHE scheme. They also showed a construction of a special FHE scheme based on the BGV (Brakerski–Gentry–Vaikuntanathan) scheme. However, in the construction by Agrawal et al., one must store all the extensive randomness used for encryption in order to lie, and a bootstrapping operation, which takes a long time to execute, is a bottleneck in execution speed. In this paper, we show that by providing a tighter upper bound on deniability, we can reduce the size of the stored randomness and the required number of bootstrapping in the construction by Agrawal et al. In addition, we show that TFHE (Chillotti et al., J. Cryptol., 2020; Joye, CT-RSA 2024), which is known as a FHE scheme with fast bootstrapping, satisfies the requirements of special FHE, and thus can realize a faster DFHE scheme than the BGV-based construction.

Keywords: Deniable fully homomorphic encryption · Deniability · TFHE

1 Introduction

1.1 Background

In recent years, there has been a growing interest in privacy-preserving data utilization. Consequently, research on techniques for secure cross-organizational data collaboration and analysis of sensitive information has become an active

P. D'Arco and A. Zamfiroiu (Eds.): SecITC 2025, LNCS 16443, pp. 59–78, 2026.
https://doi.org/10.1007/978-3-032-17443-7_4

field. In this context, secure computation, a class of cryptographic techniques that enables computation on private inputs without revealing them, is attracting significant attention. Multi-party computation [17,26] and homomorphic encryption [23] are primary examples of techniques used to realize secure computation.

Homomorphic encryption is a cryptographic scheme that enables computation on messages by performing certain operations on ciphertexts without decryption. In particular, a scheme that can perform both additions and multiplications for an arbitrary number of times is called fully homomorphic encryption (FHE) [15]. Since the first FHE construction was proposed by Gentry [14,15], various FHE schemes have been proposed, such as BGV [6], B/FV [5,13], GSW [16], DM (or FHEW) [12], CGGI (or TFHE) [11], and CKKS [9,10].

In the context of privacy-preserving technologies, one relevant cryptographic primitive is deniable encryption, proposed by Canetti et al. [8]. Deniable encryption is a cryptographic scheme that enables a user, who may be coerced to reveal the messages corresponding to the user's public ciphertexts, to lie about which messages the user encrypted. This property is useful in scenarios such as electronic voting and cloud computing, where computations are performed on encrypted data provided by other parties.

Agrawal et al. [2] proposed deniable FHE (DFHE), a cryptographic scheme that satisfies the properties of both FHE and deniable encryption, and provided its security model and a construction. They proposed a concrete construction of DFHE by first showing a generic method to convert any FHE scheme that satisfies certain properties (which they term a special FHE) into a DFHE scheme. They then demonstrated how to construct such a special FHE based on the BGV scheme [6].

However, the DFHE construction proposed by Agrawal et al. [2] suffers from two drawbacks in terms of efficiency. The first is that in order to lie about a one-bit message, one must store all $\mathcal{O}\left(\lambda \cdot \mathsf{poly}(\lambda)^2 \cdot \delta(\lambda)^2 \cdot (\ell'_c + \ell)\right)$ bits of the randomness used for encryption, where λ is the security parameter, $\mathsf{poly}(\lambda)$ is a positive polynomial, $\delta(\lambda)$ is a parameter for deniability, ℓ'_c is the bit length of elements in ciphertext space, and ℓ is a parameter for encryption. The second is the heavy use of bootstrapping operations, which plays a crucial role in existing FHE constructions but is computationally expensive. Indeed, Agrawal et al.'s construction [2] requires $\mathcal{O}\left(\lambda \cdot \mathsf{poly}(\lambda)^2 \cdot \delta(\lambda)^2\right)$ bootstrapping operations to encrypt a one-bit message, where λ is the security parameter, $\mathsf{poly}(\lambda)$ is a positive polynomial, and $\delta(\lambda)$ is a parameter for deniability. Consequently, the overall performance of the DFHE scheme is significantly impacted by the speed of a single bootstrapping operation.

1.2 Our Contributions

In this paper, we propose methods to mitigate two efficiency drawbacks in Agrawal et al.'s DFHE scheme [2]: the large randomness size and the performance overhead caused by the heavy use of bootstrapping.

First, in Sect. 4, we provide a tighter upper bound on deniability of Agrawal et al.'s DFHE scheme [2]. Since the bit length of the randomness and the number of bootstrapping operations in the encryption algorithm depend on the deniability, these values can be reduced by achieving a tighter upper bound on deniability. By providing the tighter bound, both the bit length of the randomness and the number of bootstrapping operations can be reduced by 84%.

Second, in Sect. 5, we show that TFHE [11,20], which is known as a FHE scheme with fast bootstrapping, satisfies the requirements of special FHE, and thus can realize a faster DFHE scheme than the BGV-based construction.

2 Preliminaries

2.1 Notations

Throughout the paper, we use $\lambda \in \mathbb{N}$ to denote the security parameter. We write $y \leftarrow A(x)$ to denote that the probabilistic polynomial-time (PPT) algorithm A takes x as input and outputs y. To explicitly show that A uses randomness r, we write $y \leftarrow A(x; r)$. For a distribution D, we denote by $d \leftarrow D$ the operation of sampling d according to D. For a finite set S, we denote by $s \xleftarrow{\$} S$ the operation of sampling s uniformly at random from S. For a positive integer $n \in \mathbb{N}$, we denote by $[n]$ the set $\{1, 2, \ldots, n\}$. For a real number $x \in \mathbb{R}$, we denote by $\lfloor x \rceil$ the closest integer to x. For integers $a \in \mathbb{Z}$ and $b \in \mathbb{Z} \setminus \{0\}$, we use $b|a$ to denote that b divides a. $\varphi(\cdot)$ denotes Euler's totient function. We use bold lowercase letters (e.g., $\boldsymbol{v}$) to denote vectors. For two vectors $\boldsymbol{a}$ and $\boldsymbol{b}$ of the same dimension, we denote by $\langle \boldsymbol{a}, \boldsymbol{b} \rangle$ the inner product of $\boldsymbol{a}$ and $\boldsymbol{b}$. For a bit string $\boldsymbol{x} = (x_1, \ldots, x_n) \in \{0,1\}^n$, we define the multiplicity of 1 as $M_1(\boldsymbol{x}) := \#\{i \in [n] \mid x_i = 1\}$. We use $\mathsf{poly}(\lambda)$ and $\mathsf{negl}(\lambda)$ to denote a positive polynomial function of λ and a negligible function of λ, respectively.

2.2 Useful Lemmas

We will use the following lemmas throughout this paper.

Lemma 1. *For all $n \in \mathbb{N}$ and all $k \in [0, n]$, we have*

$$\binom{n+1}{k} = \binom{n}{k-1} + \binom{n}{k} \quad \text{and} \quad \binom{n}{k+1} = \frac{n-k}{k+1}\binom{n}{k}.$$

Lemma 2 ([24])**.** *For all $n \in \mathbb{N}$, we have*

$$\sqrt{2\pi n}\left(\frac{n}{e}\right)^n e^{\frac{1}{12n+1}} < n! < \sqrt{2\pi n}\left(\frac{n}{e}\right)^n e^{\frac{1}{12n}}.$$

Lemma 3 ([4])**.** *For all $n \in \mathbb{N}$, we have*

$$\left(1 + \frac{1}{n}\right)^n < e.$$

2.3 Fully Homomorphic Encryption

We recall the definition of FHE.

Definition 1 (Fully Homomorphic Encryption). *A public-key fully homomorphic encryption scheme* FHE *for a message space* $\mathcal{M}$ *consists of PPT algorithms* $(\mathsf{Gen}, \mathsf{Enc}, \mathsf{Eval}, \mathsf{Dec})$ *with the following syntax:*

- $\mathsf{Gen}(1^\lambda) \to (\mathsf{pk}, \mathsf{sk})$*: On input the unary representation of the security parameter* λ*, the key-generation algorithm* Gen *outputs a public key* pk *and secret key* sk.
- $\mathsf{Enc}(\mathsf{pk}, m) \to \mathsf{ct}$*: On input a public key* pk *and a message* m*, the encryption algorithm* Enc *outputs a ciphertext* ct.
- $\mathsf{Eval}(\mathsf{pk}, C, \mathsf{ct}_1, \ldots, \mathsf{ct}_k) \to \mathsf{ct}$*: On input a public key* pk*, a circuit* $C \colon \mathcal{M}^k \to \mathcal{M}$*, and ciphertexts* $\mathsf{ct}_1, \ldots, \mathsf{ct}_k$*, the evaluation algorithm* Eval *outputs a ciphertext* ct.
- $\mathsf{Dec}(\mathsf{sk}, \mathsf{ct}) \to m$*: On input a secret key* sk *and a ciphertext* ct*, the decryption algorithm* Dec *outputs a message* $m \in \mathcal{M}$.

We omit the definitions of correctness, compactness, and IND-CPA security of FHE scheme here. For the formal definitions of them, see Definitions 6, 7 and 8 in Appendix A.1.

In FHE, performing operations on ciphertexts increases the amount of noise they contain. This noise growth limits the number of homomorphic operations that can be performed on a ciphertext. A technique to reduce this noise without decrypting the ciphertext was introduced by Gentry [14,15] and is known as bootstrapping. All currently known FHE schemes are constructed based on this bootstrapping technique. The definition of bootstrapping is as follows.

Definition 2 (Bootstrapping Procedure). *Let* $\mathsf{FHE} = (\mathsf{Gen}, \mathsf{Enc}, \mathsf{Eval}, \mathsf{Dec})$ *be a public-key FHE scheme for a message space* $\mathcal{M}$ *with a ciphertext space* $\mathcal{R}^{\ell_c}$. *The bootstrapping procedure, denoted by* $\mathsf{boot} \colon \mathcal{R}^{\ell_c} \to \mathcal{R}^{\ell_c}$*, is defined as*

$$\mathsf{boot}(x) = \mathsf{Eval}(\mathsf{pk}, \mathsf{Dec}_x, \mathsf{ct}_{\mathsf{sk}}),$$

where $(\mathsf{pk}, \mathsf{sk}) \leftarrow \mathsf{Gen}(1^\lambda)$, $\mathsf{ct}_{\mathsf{sk}} \leftarrow \mathsf{Enc}(\mathsf{pk}, \mathsf{sk})$, *and* $\mathsf{Dec}_x(\mathsf{sk}) = \mathsf{Dec}(\mathsf{sk}, x)$.

2.4 Deniable Fully Homomorphic Encryption

We recall the definition of DFHE.

Definition 3 (Deniable FHE [2]). *A public-key deniable fully homomorphic encryption scheme* DFHE *for a message space* $\mathcal{M}$ *consists of PPT algorithms* $(\mathsf{Gen}, \mathsf{Enc}, \mathsf{Eval}, \mathsf{Dec}, \mathsf{Fake})$ *with the following syntax:*

- $\mathsf{Gen}(1^\lambda) \to (\mathsf{dpk}, \mathsf{dsk})$*: On input the unary representation of the security parameter* λ*, the key-generation algorithm* Gen *outputs a public key* dpk *and secret key* dsk.

- $\mathsf{Enc}(\mathsf{dpk}, m; r) \rightarrow \mathsf{dct}$: *On input a public key* dpk *and a message* m, *the encryption algorithm* Enc *uses an* ℓ*-bit randomness* r *and outputs a ciphertext* dct.
- $\mathsf{Eval}(\mathsf{dpk}, C, \mathsf{dct}_1, \ldots, \mathsf{dct}_k) \rightarrow \mathsf{dct}$: *On input a public key* dpk, *a circuit* $C: \mathcal{M}^k \rightarrow \mathcal{M}$, *and ciphertexts* $\mathsf{dct}_1, \ldots, \mathsf{dct}_k$, *the evaluation algorithm* Eval *outputs a ciphertext* dct.
- $\mathsf{Dec}(\mathsf{dsk}, \mathsf{dct}) \rightarrow m$: *On input a secret key* dsk *and a ciphertext* dct, *the decryption algorithm* Dec *outputs a message* $m \in \mathcal{M}$.
- $\mathsf{Fake}(\mathsf{dpk}, m, r, m^*) \rightarrow r^*$: *On input a public key* dpk, *an original message* m, *an original* ℓ*-bit randomness* r, *and a fake message* $m^* \in \mathcal{M}$, *the fake algorithm* Fake *outputs a fake* ℓ*-bit randomness* r^*.

We say that a DFHE scheme $\mathsf{DFHE} = (\mathsf{Gen}, \mathsf{Enc}, \mathsf{Eval}, \mathsf{Dec}, \mathsf{Fake})$ is correct, compact, and IND-CPA secure if the scheme $(\mathsf{Gen}, \mathsf{Enc}, \mathsf{Eval}, \mathsf{Dec})$ satisfies correctness, compactness, and IND-CPA security of FHE, as in Definitions 6, 7 and 8, respectively. The notions of deniability and deniability compactness of DFHE were defined by Agrawal et al. [2]. Deniability is defined as follows.

Definition 4 (Deniability [2]). *A DFHE scheme* $\mathsf{DFHE} = (\mathsf{Gen}, \mathsf{Enc}, \mathsf{Eval}, \mathsf{Dec}, \mathsf{Fake})$ *is* $1/\delta(\lambda)$*-deniable if for all PPT adversaries* $\mathcal{A}$, *we have*

$$\left|\Pr\left[\mathsf{DenGame}_{\mathcal{A}}^{0} = 1\right] - \Pr\left[\mathsf{DenGame}_{\mathcal{A}}^{1} = 1\right]\right| \leq \frac{1}{\delta(\lambda)},$$

where $\mathsf{DenGame}_{\mathcal{A}}^{b}$ *is a game between a challenger and a PPT adversary* $\mathcal{A}$ *with a challenge bit* b *defined as follows:*

- *The challenger samples* $(\mathsf{dpk}, \mathsf{dsk}) \leftarrow \mathsf{Gen}(1^\lambda)$, *and sends* dpk *to* $\mathcal{A}$.
- *The adversary* $\mathcal{A}$ *chooses* $m, m^* \in \mathcal{M}$, *and sends* (m, m^*) *to the challenger.*
- *The challenger samples* $r \xleftarrow{\$} \{0,1\}^\ell$ *and computes* $r^* \leftarrow \mathsf{Fake}(\mathsf{dpk}, m, r, m^*)$; *if* $b = 0$ *sends* $(m^*, r, \mathsf{Enc}(\mathsf{dpk}, m^*; r))$ *to* $\mathcal{A}$, *else if* $b = 1$, *sends* $(m^*, r^*, \mathsf{Enc}(\mathsf{dpk}, m; r))$ *to* $\mathcal{A}$.
- *The adversary* $\mathcal{A}$ *outputs a bit* b' *which we define as the output of the game.*

We omit the definition of deniability compactness here. For the formal definition of deniability compactness, see Definition 12 in Appendix A.2.

3 Agrawal et al.'s DFHE Scheme

The DFHE constructions proposed by Agrawal et al. [2] rely on an FHE scheme, called special FHE, that satisfies some special properties. They proposed two variants of special FHE schemes in the full version [1]: a strong version and a weak version. In this paper, we employ the latter, defined as follows.

Definition 5 (Special FHE (Weak Version) [1]). *An FHE scheme* $\mathsf{FHE} = (\mathsf{Gen}, \mathsf{Enc}, \mathsf{Eval}, \mathsf{Dec})$ *for the message space* $\mathcal{M} = \{0,1\}$ *with ciphertext space* $\mathcal{R}^{\ell_c}$ *is a special FHE scheme if* FHE *satisfies the following additional properties:*

1. *The evaluation algorithm* Eval *and the decryption algorithm* Dec *are deterministic.*
2. *The distribution* $\mathsf{Enc}(\mathsf{pk}, m; U^\ell)$ *is computationally indistinguishable from* $\mathcal{R}^{\ell_c}$*, where* U^ℓ *is a uniform distribution over* $\{0,1\}^\ell$*,* $(\mathsf{pk}, \mathsf{sk}) \leftarrow \mathsf{Gen}(1^\lambda)$*, and* $m \in \mathcal{M}$*. Moreover, the distribution* $\mathsf{boot}(\mathcal{R}^{\ell_c})$ *is computationally indistinguishable from* $\mathcal{R}^{\ell_c}$*.*
3. *The decryption algorithm* Dec *always outputs a message from the message space* $\mathcal{M}$*.*
4. *On input a secret key* sk *and random element in the ciphertext space* $\mathcal{R}^{\ell_c}$*, the decryption algorithm* Dec *outputs* 0 *with non-negligible probability.*
5. *The scheme* FHE *is circular secure.*[1]

We recall Agrawal et al.'s DFHE scheme [1, Section 7.1] below.

Construction 1 (DFHE [1]**).** *Let a scheme* $\mathsf{FHE} = (\mathsf{Gen}, \mathsf{Enc}, \mathsf{Eval}, \mathsf{Dec})$ *be a special FHE scheme for the message space* $\mathcal{M} = \{0,1\}$ *with ciphertext space* $\mathcal{R}^{\ell_c}$*. We let* $n = 100\delta(\lambda)^2$ *and* $k' = \lambda(\mathsf{poly}(\lambda))^2$*. Let* $\oplus_2 \colon (\mathcal{R}^{\ell_c})^n \to \mathcal{R}^{\ell_c}$ *be a homomorphic evaluation of addition modulo 2.*[2] *A compact public-key* $1/\delta(\lambda)$*-deniable FHE scheme for the message space* $\mathcal{M} = \{0,1\}$*,* $\mathsf{DFHE} = (\mathsf{Gen}, \mathsf{Enc}, \mathsf{Eval}, \mathsf{Dec}, \mathsf{Fake})$*, is described below.*

- $\mathsf{DFHE.Gen}(1^\lambda) \to (\mathsf{dpk}, \mathsf{dsk})$*: On input the unary representation of the security parameter* λ*, do the following:*
  1. $(\mathsf{pk}, \mathsf{sk}) \leftarrow \mathsf{FHE.Gen}(1^\lambda)$.
  2. $\mathsf{ct}_{\mathsf{sk}} \leftarrow \mathsf{FHE.Enc}(\mathsf{pk}, \mathsf{sk})$.
  3. *Output* $\mathsf{dpk} = (\mathsf{pk}, \mathsf{ct}_{\mathsf{sk}})$ *and* $\mathsf{dsk} = \mathsf{sk}$.
- $\mathsf{DFHE.Enc}(\mathsf{dpk}, m) \to \mathsf{dct}$*: On input a public key* dpk *and a message* m*, do the following:*
  1. *Parse* $\mathsf{dpk} := (\mathsf{pk}, \mathsf{ct}_{\mathsf{sk}})$.
  2. $x_1, \ldots, x_n \xleftarrow{\$} \{0,1\}$ *s.t.* $\sum_{i=1}^n x_i = m \pmod 2$.
  3. *For all* $i \in [n]$*, if* $x_i = 0$*, select* R_i *as follows:*
     (a) *For all* $j \in [k']$*,* $A_{i,j} \xleftarrow{\$} \mathcal{R}^{\ell_c}$ *and set* $T_{i,j} = \mathsf{boot}(A_{i,j})$.
     (b) *Set* $R_i = \mathsf{FHE.Eval}(\mathsf{pk}, \mathsf{AND}, T_{i,1}, \ldots, T_{i,k'})$.
  4. *For all* $i \in [n]$*, if* $x_i = 1$*, select* R_i *as follows:*
     1. *For all* $j \in [k']$*,* $r_{i,j} \xleftarrow{\$} \{0,1\}^\ell$*,* $A_{i,j} \leftarrow \mathsf{FHE.Enc}(\mathsf{pk}, 1; r_{i,j})$*, and set* $T_{i,j} = \mathsf{boot}(A_{i,j})$.
     2. *Set* $R_i = \mathsf{FHE.Eval}(\mathsf{pk}, \mathsf{AND}, T_{i,1}, \ldots, T_{i,k'})$.
  5. *Output* $\mathsf{dct} = \oplus_2(\mathsf{boot}(R_1), \ldots, \mathsf{boot}(R_n))$.
- $\mathsf{DFHE.Eval}(\mathsf{dpk}, C, \mathsf{dct}_1, \ldots, \mathsf{dct}_k) \to \mathsf{dct}$*: On input a public key* dpk*, a circuit* $C \colon \mathcal{M}^k \to \mathcal{M}$*, and ciphertexts* $\mathsf{dct}_1, \ldots, \mathsf{dct}_k$*, do the following:*
  1. *For all* $i \in [k]$*, interpret* dct_i *as a* FHE *ciphertext* ct_i.
  2. *Output* $\mathsf{dct} = \mathsf{FHE.Eval}(\mathsf{pk}, C, \mathsf{ct}_1, \ldots, \mathsf{ct}_k)$.
- $\mathsf{DFHE.Dec}(\mathsf{dsk}, \mathsf{dct}) \to m$*: On input a secret key* dsk *and a ciphertext* dct*, do the following:*

[1] For the formal definition of circular security [7], see Definition 9 in Appendix A.1.
[2] For the formal definition of $\oplus_2$, see Definition 11 in Appendix A.1.

1. *Interpret* dsk *and* dct *as* FHE *secret key* sk *and* FHE *ciphertext* ct.
2. *Output* FHE.Dec(sk, ct).

- DFHE.Fake(dpk, m, rand, m^*) $\rightarrow$ rand*: *On input a public key* dpk, *an original message* m, *an original* ℓ*-bit randomness* rand, *and a fake message* $m^* \in \mathcal{M}$, *do the following:*
  1. *If* $m = m^*$, *output* rand* = rand.
  2. *Parse* dpk := (pk, ct$_{\mathsf{sk}}$) *and* rand $= (x_1, \ldots, x_n, \boldsymbol{r}_1, \ldots, \boldsymbol{r}_n)$, *where* $x_1, \ldots, x_n \in \{0,1\}$, *and for all* $i \in [n]$, *if* $x_i = 1$, *then* $\boldsymbol{r}_i = (r_{i,1}, \ldots, r_{i,k'})$; *else if* $x_i = 0$, *then* $\boldsymbol{r}_i = (A_{i,1}, \ldots, A_{i,k'})$.
  3. $i^* \xleftarrow{\$} [n]$ *s.t.* $x_{i^*} = 1$. *If there is no such* i^*, *output "cheating impossible"; else:*
     (a) *For all* $j \in [k']$, $A_{i^*,j} \leftarrow$ FHE.Enc(pk, 1; $r_{i^*,j}$).
     (b) *Set* $x^*_{i^*} = 0$ *and* $\boldsymbol{r}^*_{i^*} = (A_{i^*,1}, \ldots, A_{i^*,k'})$.
     (c) *For all* $i \in [n] \setminus \{i^*\}$, *set* $x^*_i = x_i$ *and* $\boldsymbol{r}^*_i = \boldsymbol{r}_i$.
  4. *Output* rand$^* = (x^*_1, \ldots, x^*_n, \boldsymbol{r}^*_1, \ldots, \boldsymbol{r}^*_n)$.

Regarding the deniability of the DFHE scheme (Constrction 1), Proposition 1 holds as follows.

Proposition 1 ([1]). *For all PPT adversaries* $\mathcal{A}$, *we have*

$$\begin{aligned} &\left|\Pr\left[\mathsf{DenGame}^0_{\mathcal{A}} = 1\right] - \Pr\left[\mathsf{DenGame}^1_{\mathcal{A}} = 1\right]\right| \\ &\le \frac{1}{2^n}\left\{\sum_{k \ge n/2}\binom{n}{k}\left(1 - \frac{n-k}{k+1}\right) + \sum_{k<n/2}\binom{n}{k}\left(\frac{n-k}{k+1} - 1\right)\right\} \quad (1) \\ &\le \frac{10}{\sqrt{n}}. \quad (2) \end{aligned}$$

If we let $n = 100\delta(\lambda)^2$, DFHE = (Gen, Enc, Eval, Dec, Fake) *is* $1/\delta(\lambda)$*-deniable.*

We here emphasize that the parameter n drastically affects the efficiency of the above DFHE scheme, since the randomness size and the number of bootstrapping operations depend on n. Let us look into it below.

Let $\boldsymbol{x} = (x_1, \ldots, x_n)$. We denote by ℓ'_c the bit length of elements in the ciphertext space $\mathcal{R}^{\ell_c}$ (that is, $\ell'_c = \lceil \ell_c \log_2(|\mathcal{R}|) \rceil$). The bit length of rand is $n + k'\ell'_c(n - M_1(\boldsymbol{x})) + k'\ell M_1(\boldsymbol{x})$. Since we can set $M_1(\boldsymbol{x}) = cn$ for $0 \le c \le 1$, the bit length of rand is as follows:

$$\underbrace{n}_{\boldsymbol{x}} + \underbrace{k'\ell'_c(n - M_1(\boldsymbol{x}))}_{(A_{i,j}) \text{ in Step 3}} + \underbrace{k'\ell M_1(\boldsymbol{x})}_{(r_{i,j}) \text{ in Step 4}} = (1 + (1-c)k'\ell'_c + ck'\ell)n. \quad (3)$$

Since both addition modulo 2 and an AND gate can be evaluated homomorphically with a single bootstrapping operation, the total number of bootstrapping operations in the encryption algorithm is as follows:

$$\underbrace{(k' + (k'-1))(n - M_1(\boldsymbol{x}))}_{\text{Step 3}} + \underbrace{(k' + (k'-1))M_1(\boldsymbol{x})}_{\text{Step 4}} + \underbrace{n + (n-1)}_{\text{Step 5}} = (2k'+1)n - 1. \quad (4)$$

4 Tighter Upper Bound on Deniability

In this section, we show that the bit length of the randomness and the number of bootstrapping operations in the encryption algorithm can be reduced by providing a tighter upper bound on deniability of Sect. 1. In Sect. 4.1, we revisit the analysis of the deniability provided by Agrawal et al. [1]. In Sect. 4.2, we analyze how our tighter deniability bound reduces the bit length of the randomness and the number of bootstrapping operations in encryption algorithm.

4.1 Deniability Analysis

We provide a tighter bound for the upper bound given in Equation (2) of Proposition 1. Specifically, we prove the following Theorem 1.

Theorem 1. *For all PPT adversaries $\mathcal{A}$, we have*

$$\left|\Pr\left[\mathsf{DenGame}^0_{\mathcal{A}} = 1\right] - \Pr\left[\mathsf{DenGame}^1_{\mathcal{A}} = 1\right]\right| \leq \frac{4}{\sqrt{n}}.$$

If we let $n = 16\delta(\lambda)^2$, the DFHE scheme $\mathsf{DFHE} = (\mathsf{Gen}, \mathsf{Enc}, \mathsf{Eval}, \mathsf{Dec}, \mathsf{Fake})$ *is $1/\delta(\lambda)$-deniable.*

Proof (Sketch). We have

$$\sum_{k\geq n/2}\binom{n}{k}\left(1-\frac{n-k}{k+1}\right)\overset{(a)}{=}\sum_{k=\lceil n/2\rceil}^{n}\binom{n}{k}-\sum_{k=\lceil n/2\rceil}^{n}\binom{n}{k+1}\overset{(b)}{=}\binom{n}{\lceil\frac{n}{2}\rceil} \tag{5}$$

and

$$\sum_{k<n/2}\binom{n}{k}\left(\frac{n-k}{k+1}-1\right)\overset{(a)}{=}\sum_{k<n/2}\binom{n}{k+1}-\sum_{k<n/2}\binom{n}{k}. \tag{6}$$

Equation (a) follows from Lemma 1, and Equation (b) follow from $\binom{n}{k} = 0$ when $n < k$.

In addition, when n is an even number, we have

$$\sum_{k<n/2}\binom{n}{k+1}-\sum_{k<n/2}\binom{n}{k}=\sum_{k=0}^{\frac{n}{2}-1}\binom{n}{k+1}-\sum_{k=0}^{\frac{n}{2}-1}\binom{n}{k}=\left(1+\frac{2}{n}\right)\binom{n}{\lceil\frac{n}{2}\rceil-1}-1 \tag{7}$$

and when n is an odd number, we have

$$\sum_{k<n/2}\binom{n}{k+1}-\sum_{k<n/2}\binom{n}{k}=\sum_{k=0}^{\lfloor\frac{n}{2}\rfloor}\binom{n}{k+1}-\sum_{k=0}^{\lfloor\frac{n}{2}\rfloor}\binom{n}{k}=\binom{n}{\lceil\frac{n}{2}\rceil-1}-1. \tag{8}$$

For full proofs of Equations (7) and (8) see Appendix B.1.

Hence, according to Equations (6), (7) and (8) we have

$$\sum_{k<n/2} \binom{n}{k}\left(\frac{n-k}{k+1}-1\right) \leq \left(1+\frac{2}{n}\right)\binom{n}{\lceil \frac{n}{2}\rceil - 1} - 1. \tag{9}$$

Therefore, we have

$$\begin{aligned}
&\left|\Pr\left[\mathsf{DenGame}_{\mathcal{A}}^{0}=1\right]-\Pr\left[\mathsf{DenGame}_{\mathcal{A}}^{1}=1\right]\right| \\
&\overset{(c)}{\leq} \frac{1}{2^n}\left\{\binom{n}{\lceil \frac{n}{2}\rceil}+\left(1+\frac{2}{n}\right)\binom{n}{\lceil \frac{n}{2}\rceil - 1}-1\right\} < \frac{1}{2^n}\left(1+\frac{2}{n}\right)\binom{n+1}{\lceil \frac{n}{2}\rceil}.
\end{aligned} \tag{10}$$

Inequality (c) follows from Equations (1), (5) and (9). For a full proof of Equations (10), see AppendixB.2.

Furthermore, according to Equations (7) and (8), the equality in Equations (9) holds when n is an even number. Hence, according to Equation (10), we have

$$\left|\Pr\left[\mathsf{DenGame}_{\mathcal{A}}^{0}=1\right]-\Pr\left[\mathsf{DenGame}_{\mathcal{A}}^{1}=1\right]\right| < \frac{1}{2^n}\left(1+\frac{2}{n}\right)\binom{n+1}{\frac{n}{2}}. \tag{11}$$

Moreover, we have

$$\begin{aligned}
\binom{n+1}{\frac{n}{2}} &= \frac{(n+1)!}{\frac{n}{2}!\,(n+1-\frac{n}{2})!} = \frac{(n+1)!}{\frac{n}{2}!\,(\frac{n}{2}+1)!} \\
&\overset{(d)}{<} \frac{\sqrt{2\pi(n+1)}\left(\frac{n+1}{e}\right)^{n+1} e^{\frac{1}{12(n+1)}}}{\sqrt{2\pi\frac{n}{2}}\left(\frac{n}{2e}\right)^{\frac{n}{2}} e^{\frac{1}{12\cdot\frac{n}{2}+1}} \cdot \sqrt{2\pi(\frac{n}{2}+1)}\left(\frac{\frac{n}{2}+1}{e}\right)^{\frac{n}{2}+1} e^{\frac{1}{12\left(\frac{n}{2}+1\right)+1}}} \\
&< \frac{2\sqrt{2}\cdot 2^n (n+1)^{n+\frac{3}{2}}}{\sqrt{\pi} n^{\frac{n+1}{2}} (n+2)^{\frac{n+3}{2}}}
\end{aligned} \tag{12}$$

Inequality (d) follows from Lemma 2. For a full proof of Equation (12), see Appendix B.3.

Therefore, according to Equaton (11), we have

$$\begin{aligned}
&\left|\Pr\left[\mathsf{DenGame}_{\mathcal{A}}^{0}=1\right]-\Pr\left[\mathsf{DenGame}_{\mathcal{A}}^{1}=1\right]\right| \\
&< \frac{1}{2^n}\left(1+\frac{2}{n}\right)\binom{n+1}{\frac{n}{2}} \overset{(e)}{<} \frac{1}{2^n}\cdot\frac{n+2}{n}\cdot\frac{2\sqrt{2}\cdot 2^n (n+1)^{n+\frac{3}{2}}}{\sqrt{\pi} n^{\frac{n+1}{2}} (n+2)^{\frac{n+3}{2}}} \\
&< \frac{2\sqrt{2}}{\sqrt{\pi}}\cdot\frac{1}{\sqrt{n}}\left(1+\frac{1}{n}\right)\sqrt{\left(1+\frac{1}{n}\right)^n} \overset{(f)}{<} \frac{2\sqrt{2}}{\sqrt{\pi}}\cdot\frac{1}{\sqrt{n}}\cdot\frac{3}{2}\cdot\sqrt{e} < \frac{4}{\sqrt{n}}.
\end{aligned} \tag{13}$$

Inequality (e) follows from Equation (12), and Inequality (f) follows from $1+1/n \leq 3/2$ when $n \geq 2$ and Lemma 3. For a full proof of Equation (13), see Appendix B.4.

Thus, we have

$$\left|\Pr\left[\mathsf{DenGame}^0_{\mathcal{A}} = 1\right] - \Pr\left[\mathsf{DenGame}^1_{\mathcal{A}} = 1\right]\right| \leq \frac{4}{\sqrt{n}},$$

and if we let $n = 16\delta(\lambda)^2$, the DFHE scheme $\mathsf{DFHE} = (\mathsf{Gen}, \mathsf{Enc}, \mathsf{Eval}, \mathsf{Dec}, \mathsf{Fake})$ is $1/\delta(\lambda)$-deniable. □

4.2 Efficiency Analysis

According to Equations (3) and (4), the bit length of the randomness is $(1+(1-c)k'\ell'_c + ck'\ell)n$ and the number of bootstrapping operations in the encryption algorithm is $(2k'+1)n-1$. Therefore, when n is reduced from $100\delta(\lambda)^2$ to $16\delta(\lambda)^2$, the two values are reduced by 84%.

5 Faster DFHE Using TFHE

In FHE, the execution time of bootstrapping is extremely long. Accelerating bootstrapping is crucial for the practical applications of FHE. The DFHE scheme proposed by Agrawal et al., as described in Construction 1, also employs bootstrapping. Employing an FHE scheme with a faster bootstrapping than the BGV scheme [6] employed by Agrawal et al. can lead to a faster DFHE scheme. Therefore, we employ TFHE [11], known for its fast bootstrapping.

TFHE is a concrete FHE construction proposed by Chillotti et al. [11]. While the original TFHE proposed by Chillotti et al. is a symmetric-key FHE, Agrawal et al.'s DFHE construction requires a public-key FHE. Hence, we employ a public-key variant of TFHE. Several public-key TFHE schemes have been proposed by Joye [19,20]. We employ the scheme proposed in [20, Section 3] due to its smaller public key size and smaller noise variance.

We recall Joye's public-key TFHE scheme [20, Section 3] below. According to the functional completeness of the NAND gate [25], which states that any logic circuit can be constructed solely from NAND gates, we describe $\mathsf{TFHE.Eval}$ below specifically for homomorphic NAND computation.

Construction 2 (TFHE [20]). *Let $\circledast\colon \mathbb{Z}^n \times \mathbb{Z}^n \to \mathbb{Z}^n$ be a reverse negative wrapped convolution.*[3] *A public-key TFHE scheme for the message space $\mathcal{M} = \{0,1\}$, $\mathsf{TFHE} = (\mathsf{Gen}, \mathsf{Enc}, \mathsf{Eval}, \mathsf{Dec})$, is described below.*

- $\mathsf{TFHE.Gen}(1^\lambda) \to (\mathsf{pp}, \mathsf{pk}, \mathsf{sk})$*: On input the unary representation of the security parameter λ, do the following:*
  1. *Set $n = \varphi(M)$ for some $M \in \mathbb{N}$.*
  2. *Select $q \in \mathbb{Z}_{\geq 0}$ with $2|q$ and set $\Delta = q/2$.*
  3. *Set two discretized error distributions χ_1 and χ_2 over $\mathbb{Z}$ with a variance σ.*

[3] For the formal definition of reverse negative wrapped convolution [20], see Definition 13 in Appendix A.3.

4. *Set* $\widetilde{\boldsymbol{b}} = \widetilde{\boldsymbol{a}} \circledast \boldsymbol{s} + \boldsymbol{e}$ *with* $\boldsymbol{s} = (s_1, \ldots, s_n) \xleftarrow{\$} \{0,1\}^n, \widetilde{\boldsymbol{a}} = (\widetilde{a}_1, \ldots, \widetilde{a}_n) \xleftarrow{\$} (\mathbb{Z}/q\mathbb{Z})^n$, *and* $\boldsymbol{e} \leftarrow \chi_1^n$.
5. *Output* $\mathsf{pp} = (n, \sigma, 2, q, \Delta)$, $\mathsf{pk} = (\widetilde{\boldsymbol{a}}, \widetilde{\boldsymbol{b}})$, *and* $\mathsf{sk} = \boldsymbol{s}$.

- $\mathsf{TFHE.Enc}(\mathsf{pk}, m) \to \mathsf{ct}$: *On input a public key* pk *and a message* m, *do the following:*
  1. *Set* $\boldsymbol{a} = \widetilde{\boldsymbol{a}} \circledast \boldsymbol{r} + e_1$ *and* $b = \langle \widetilde{\boldsymbol{b}}, \boldsymbol{r} \rangle + \Delta m + e_2$ *with* $\boldsymbol{r} \xleftarrow{\$} \{0,1\}^n$, $e_1 \leftarrow \widehat{\chi}_1^n$, *and* $e_2 \leftarrow \widehat{\chi}_2$.
  2. *Output* $\mathsf{ct} = (\boldsymbol{a}, b)$.
- $\mathsf{TFHE.Eval}((\mathsf{BRK}, \mathsf{KSK}), \mathsf{NAND}, \mathsf{ct}_1, \mathsf{ct}_2) \to \mathsf{ct}$: *On input a blind rotation key* BRK, *a key switching key* KSK, *a circuit for NAND computation, and two ciphertexts* ct_1 *and* ct_2, *do the following:*[4]
  1. *Output* $\mathsf{ct} = \mathsf{boot}((\mathsf{BRK}, \mathsf{KSK}), (\mathbf{0}, 5q/8) - \mathsf{ct}_1 - \mathsf{ct}_2)$.
- $\mathsf{TFHE.Dec}(\mathsf{sk}, \mathsf{ct}) \to m$: *On input a secret key* sk *and a ciphertext* ct, *do the following:*
  1. *Output* $\lfloor ((b - \langle \boldsymbol{a}, \boldsymbol{s} \rangle) \bmod q)/\Delta \rceil \bmod 2$.

To show that the TFHE scheme (Construction 2) can be transformed into a DFHE scheme using Agrawal et al.'s construction (Construction 1), we prove the following Theorem 2.

Theorem 2. *The public-key TFHE scheme* $\mathsf{TFHE} = (\mathsf{Gen}, \mathsf{Enc}, \mathsf{Eval}, \mathsf{Dec})$ *described in Construction 2 is a weak version of special FHE scheme.*

Proof (Sketch). We prove that the FHE scheme $\mathsf{TFHE} = (\mathsf{Gen}, \mathsf{Enc}, \mathsf{Eval}, \mathsf{Dec})$ satisfies the five properties of special FHE (Definition 5).

1. The $\mathsf{TFHE.Eval}$ is deterministic because its underlying boot is deterministic when the keys BRK and KSK are fixed (see [11,18] for details on bootstrapping). The $\mathsf{TFHE.Dec}$ is also deterministic. Hence, the scheme TFHE satisfies property 1 of special FHE.
2. The scheme TFHE satisfies property 2 of special FHE, assuming the hardness of the learning with errors (LWE) problem [22].
3. For all $\mathsf{ct} = (\boldsymbol{a}, b) \in (\mathbb{Z}/q\mathbb{Z})^{n+1}$ and all $(\mathsf{pk}, \mathsf{sk}) \leftarrow \mathsf{TFHE.Gen}(1^\lambda)$, we have

$$\mathsf{TFHE.Dec}(\mathsf{sk}, \mathsf{ct}) = \left\lfloor \frac{(b - \langle \boldsymbol{a}, \boldsymbol{s} \rangle) \bmod q}{\Delta} \right\rceil \bmod 2 \in \{0,1\} = \mathcal{M}.$$

   Hence, the scheme TFHE satisfies property 3 of special FHE.
4. We have

$$\begin{aligned} &\Pr\left[\mathsf{TFHE.Dec}(\mathsf{sk}, \mathsf{ct}) = 0\right] \\ &= \Pr\left[\left\lfloor \frac{(b - \langle \boldsymbol{a}, \boldsymbol{s} \rangle) \bmod q}{\Delta} \right\rceil \bmod 2 = 0\right] \end{aligned}$$

[4] Although we omitted them from this paper for simplicity, the blind rotation key BRK and the key switching key KSK are the bootstrapping keys generated by the $\mathsf{TFHE.Gen}$ algorithm. These keys are made public as part of the public key.

$$= \Pr\left[0 \leq (b - \langle \boldsymbol{a}, \boldsymbol{s} \rangle) \bmod q \leq \frac{1}{4}q\right] + \Pr\left[\frac{3}{4}q < (b - \langle \boldsymbol{a}, \boldsymbol{s} \rangle) \bmod q \leq q - 1\right], \tag{14}$$

where $\mathsf{ct} = (\boldsymbol{a}, b) \xleftarrow{\$} (\mathbb{Z}/q\mathbb{Z})^{n+1}$ and $(\mathsf{pk}, \mathsf{sk}) \leftarrow \mathsf{TFHE.Gen}(1^\lambda)$. For a full proof of Equation (14), see Appendix B.5.
Furthermore, for all $k \in \{0, 1, \ldots, q-1\}$, we have

$$\Pr\left[(b - \langle \boldsymbol{a}, \boldsymbol{s} \rangle) \bmod q = k\right] = \frac{1}{q}, \tag{15}$$

where $\mathsf{ct} = (\boldsymbol{a}, b) \xleftarrow{\$} (\mathbb{Z}/q\mathbb{Z})^{n+1}$ and $(\mathsf{pk}, \mathsf{sk}) \leftarrow \mathsf{TFHE.Gen}(1^\lambda)$. For a full proof of Equation (15), see Appendix B.6.
Hence, we have

$$\begin{aligned}
&\Pr\left[\mathsf{TFHE.Dec}(\mathsf{sk}, \mathsf{ct}) = 0\right] \\
&\stackrel{(a)}{=} \sum_{k=0}^{\lfloor \frac{1}{4}q \rfloor} \Pr\left[(b - \langle \boldsymbol{a}, \boldsymbol{s} \rangle) \bmod q = k\right] + \sum_{k=\lceil \frac{3}{4}q \rceil}^{q-1} \Pr\left[(b - \langle \boldsymbol{a}, \boldsymbol{s} \rangle) \bmod q = k\right] \\
&\stackrel{(b)}{=} \left\{\frac{1}{q}\left(\left\lfloor \frac{1}{4}q \right\rfloor - 0 + 1\right) + \left(q - 1 - \left\lfloor \frac{3}{4}q \right\rfloor + 1\right)\right\} \\
&\stackrel{(c)}{>} \frac{1}{q}\left\{\frac{1}{4}q - 1 + 1 + q - \left(\frac{3}{4}q + 1\right)\right\} = \frac{1}{2} - \frac{1}{q},
\end{aligned}$$

where $\mathsf{ct} = (\boldsymbol{a}, b) \xleftarrow{\$} (\mathbb{Z}/q\mathbb{Z})^{n+1}$ and $(\mathsf{pk}, \mathsf{sk}) \leftarrow \mathsf{TFHE.Gen}(1^\lambda)$. Equation (a) follows from Equation (14). Equation (b) follows from Equation (15). Inequality (c) follows from $x - 1 < \lfloor x \rfloor, \lceil x \rceil < x + 1$ for all $x \in \mathbb{R}$.
Thus, the scheme TFHE satisfies property 4 of special FHE.

5. TFHE assumes circular security [11,21]. Hence, the scheme TFHE satisfies property 5 of special FHE.

Thus, the scheme $\mathsf{TFHE} = (\mathsf{Gen}, \mathsf{Enc}, \mathsf{Eval}, \mathsf{Dec})$ is a weak version of special FHE scheme. □

A single bootstrapping operation in the BGV scheme has a latency of 15 s, whereas in TFHE it is merely 0.0295 s [3]. In the DFHE construction by Agrawal et al., which relies on frequent sequential bootstrapping operations, using TFHE instead of BGV results in a significant speedup, even accounting for BGV's single instruction multiple data (SIMD) bootstrapping operations.

6 Conclusion

In this work, we improved the efficiency of the DFHE scheme by Agrawal et al. using two techniques. First, we reduced the bit length of the randomness and the number of bootstrapping operations in the encryption algorithm by deriving a tighter upper bound on the scheme's deniability. Second, we constructed a faster DFHE scheme by showing that TFHE, which is known for its fast bootstrapping, is a special FHE.

Future work includes investigating constructions of DFHE based on other FHE schemes and further improving the algorithm's efficiency. Our research did not achieve an asymptotic (i.e., order-level) improvement in performance. For real-world applications, achieving such an order-level efficiency improvement is a crucial next step.

Acknowledgments. This work was supported by JSPS KAKENHI Grant Numbers JP23H00468, JP23H00479, JP23K17455, JP23K21644, JP23K24846, and JST K Program Grant Number JPMJKP24U2, Japan.

A Additional Preliminaries

A.1 Omitted Definitions for FHE

Definition 6 (Correctness). *An FHE scheme* $\mathsf{FHE} = (\mathsf{Gen}, \mathsf{Enc}, \mathsf{Eval}, \mathsf{Dec})$ *is correct if for all security parameters* λ*, all polynomial-time circuits* $C\colon \mathcal{M}^k \to \mathcal{M}$*, and all messages* $m_i \in \mathcal{M}$ *for* $i \in [k]$*, we have*

$$\Pr\left[\begin{array}{c}\mathsf{Dec}(\mathsf{sk}, \mathsf{Eval}(\mathsf{pk}, C, \mathsf{ct}_1, \ldots, \mathsf{ct}_k)) \\ = C(m_1, \ldots, m_k)\end{array} : \begin{array}{c}(\mathsf{pk}, \mathsf{sk}) \leftarrow \mathsf{Gen}(1^\lambda) \\ \forall i \in [k], \mathsf{ct}_i \leftarrow \mathsf{Enc}(\mathsf{pk}, m_i)\end{array}\right] \geq 1 - \mathsf{negl}(\lambda).$$

Definition 7 (Compactness). *An FHE scheme* $\mathsf{FHE} = (\mathsf{Gen}, \mathsf{Enc}, \mathsf{Eval}, \mathsf{Dec})$ *is compact if there exists a polynomial* $\mathsf{poly}(\cdot)$ *such that for all security parameters* λ*, all polynomial-time circuits* $C\colon \mathcal{M}^k \to \mathcal{M}$*, and all messages* $m_i \in \mathcal{M}$ *for* $i \in [k]$*, we have*

$$\Pr\left[|\mathsf{Eval}(\mathsf{pk}, C, \mathsf{ct}_1, \ldots, \mathsf{ct}_k)| \leq \mathsf{poly}(\lambda) : \begin{array}{c}(\mathsf{pk}, \mathsf{sk}) \leftarrow \mathsf{Gen}(1^\lambda) \\ \forall i \in [k], \mathsf{ct}_i \leftarrow \mathsf{Enc}(\mathsf{pk}, m_i)\end{array}\right] = 1.$$

Definition 8 (IND-CPA Security). *An FHE scheme* $\mathsf{FHE} = (\mathsf{Gen}, \mathsf{Enc}, \mathsf{Eval}, \mathsf{Dec})$ *is IND-CPA secure if for all PPT adversaries* $\mathcal{A}$*, we have*

$$\left|\Pr\left[\mathsf{CPAGame}_{\mathcal{A}}^0(\lambda) = 1\right] - \Pr\left[\mathsf{CPAGame}_{\mathcal{A}}^1(\lambda) = 1\right]\right| \leq \mathsf{negl}(\lambda),$$

where $\mathsf{CPAGame}_{\mathcal{A}}^b(\lambda)$ *is a game between a challenger and a PPT adversary* $\mathcal{A}$ *with a challenge bit* b *defined as follows:*

- *The challenger samples* $(\mathsf{pk}, \mathsf{sk}) \leftarrow \mathsf{Gen}(1^\lambda)$*, and sends* pk *to* $\mathcal{A}$*.*
- *The adversary* $\mathcal{A}$ *chooses* $m_0, m_1 \in \mathcal{M}$*, and sends* (m_0, m_1) *to the challenger.*
- *The challenger computes* $\mathsf{ct} \leftarrow \mathsf{Enc}(\mathsf{pk}, m_b)$*, and sends* ct *to* $\mathcal{A}$*.*
- *The adversary* $\mathcal{A}$ *outputs a bit* b' *which we define as the output of the game.*

Definition 9 (Circular Security). *A public-key encryption scheme with key generation algorithm* Gen *and encryption algorithm* Enc *is circular secure if for all PPT adversaries* $\mathcal{A}$, *we have*

$$\left|\Pr\left[\mathsf{CircGame}^0_{\mathcal{A}}(\lambda)=1\right]-\Pr\left[\mathsf{CircGame}^1_{\mathcal{A}}(\lambda)=1\right]\right|\le\mathsf{negl}(\lambda),$$

where $\mathsf{CircGame}^b_{\mathcal{A}}(\lambda)$ *is a game between a challenger and a PPT adversary* $\mathcal{A}$ *with a challenge bit* b *defined as follows:*

- *The challenger samples* $(\mathsf{pk},\mathsf{sk})\leftarrow\mathsf{Gen}(1^\lambda)$, *computes* $\mathsf{ct}_{\mathsf{sk}}\leftarrow\mathsf{Enc}(\mathsf{pk},\mathsf{sk})$, *and sends* $(\mathsf{pk},\mathsf{ct}_{\mathsf{sk}})$ *to* $\mathcal{A}$.
- *The adversary* $\mathcal{A}$ *chooses* $m_0,m_1\in\mathcal{M}$, *and sends* (m_0,m_1) *to the challenger.*
- *The challenger computes* $\mathsf{ct}\leftarrow\mathsf{Enc}(\mathsf{pk},m_b)$, *and sends* ct *to* $\mathcal{A}$.
- *The adversary* $\mathcal{A}$ *outputs a bit* b' *which we define as the output of the game.*

Definition 10 (Valid Ciphertext). *A ciphertext* ct *of an FHE scheme* $\mathsf{FHE}=(\mathsf{Gen},\mathsf{Enc},\mathsf{Eval},\mathsf{Dec})$ *is a valid ciphertext of* m *if either*

$$\mathsf{ct}\leftarrow\mathsf{Enc}(\mathsf{pk},m),$$

or for all polynomial-sized circuits $C\colon\mathcal{M}\to\mathcal{M}$, *we have*

$$\Pr\left[\mathsf{Dec}(\mathsf{sk},\mathsf{Eval}(\mathsf{pk},C,\mathsf{ct}))=C(m):(\mathsf{pk},\mathsf{sk})\leftarrow\mathsf{Gen}(1^\lambda)\right]\ge1-\mathsf{negl}(\lambda).$$

Definition 11 (Addition Modulo 2). *The homomorphic evaluation of addition modulo 2 circuit, denoted by* $\oplus_2\colon(\mathcal{R}^{\ell_c})^k\to\mathcal{R}^{\ell_c}$, *is defined as*

$$\oplus_2\left(\mathsf{ct}_1,\ldots,\mathsf{ct}_k\right)=\mathsf{ct},$$

where $x_i\in\{0,1\}$ *for* $i\in[k]$, ct_i *is a valid ciphertext of* x_i *for* $i\in[k]$, *and* ct *is a valid ciphertext of* $\sum_{i=1}^k x_i \pmod 2$.

A.2 Omitted Definition for DFHE

Definition 12 (Deniability Compactness [2]). *A* $1/\delta(\lambda)$*-deniable scheme* DFHE *is deniability compact if there exists a polynomial* $\mathsf{poly}(\cdot)$ *such that for all security parameters* λ *and all messages* $m\in\mathcal{M}$, *we have*

$$\Pr\left[\left|\mathsf{Enc}(\mathsf{dpk},m)\right|\le\mathsf{poly}(\lambda)\right]=1,$$

regardless of the encryption running time.

A.3 Omitted Definition for TFHE

Definition 13 (Reverse Negative Wrapped Convolution [20]). *For* $n\in\mathbb{N}$ *and* $i\in[n]$, *the reverse negative wrapped convolution of two vectors* $\boldsymbol{u}=(u_1,\ldots,u_n),\boldsymbol{v}=(v_1,\ldots,v_n)\in\mathbb{Z}^n$ *is the vector* $\boldsymbol{w}=\boldsymbol{u}\circledast\boldsymbol{v}=(\boldsymbol{u}\circledast_1\boldsymbol{v},\ldots,\boldsymbol{u}\circledast_n\boldsymbol{v})\in\mathbb{Z}^n$ *defined by*

$$\boldsymbol{u}\circledast_i\boldsymbol{v}:=\sum_{j=1}^{i}u_jv_{n+j-i}-\sum_{j=i+1}^{n}u_jv_{j-i}.$$

B Omitted Proofs

B.1 Proof of Equation (7) and (8)

Proof. When n is an even number, we have

$$\begin{aligned}
\sum_{k<n/2}\binom{n}{k+1}-\sum_{k<n/2}\binom{n}{k} &= \sum_{k=0}^{\frac{n}{2}-1}\binom{n}{k+1}-\sum_{k=0}^{\frac{n}{2}-1}\binom{n}{k}\\
&= \binom{n}{\frac{n}{2}}-\binom{n}{0}\\
&= \binom{n}{\lceil\frac{n}{2}\rceil}-1\\
&\overset{(a)}{=} \frac{n-\lceil\frac{n}{2}\rceil+1}{\lceil\frac{n}{2}\rceil}\binom{n}{\lceil\frac{n}{2}\rceil-1}-1\\
&= \left(1+\frac{2}{n}\right)\binom{n}{\lceil\frac{n}{2}\rceil-1}-1
\end{aligned}$$

and when n is an odd number, we have

$$\begin{aligned}
\sum_{k<n/2}\binom{n}{k+1}-\sum_{k<n/2}\binom{n}{k} &= \sum_{k=0}^{\lfloor\frac{n}{2}\rfloor}\binom{n}{k+1}-\sum_{k=0}^{\lfloor\frac{n}{2}\rfloor}\binom{n}{k}\\
&= \binom{n}{\lfloor\frac{n}{2}\rfloor+1}-1\\
&= \binom{n}{n-(\lfloor\frac{n}{2}\rfloor+1)}-1\\
&\overset{(b)}{=} \binom{n}{\lceil\frac{n}{2}\rceil-1}-1.
\end{aligned}$$

Equation (a) follows from Lemma 1 and Equation (b) follows from $\lfloor\frac{n}{2}\rfloor+\lceil\frac{n}{2}\rceil=n$ for all $n\in\mathbb{Z}$. □

B.2 Proof of Equation (10)

Proof. According to Equation (1) in Proposition 1, we have

$$\begin{aligned}
&\left|\Pr\left[\mathsf{DenGame}_{\mathcal{A}}^{0}=1\right]-\Pr\left[\mathsf{DenGame}_{\mathcal{A}}^{1}=1\right]\right|\\
&\le \frac{1}{2^n}\left\{\sum_{k\ge n/2}\binom{n}{k}\left(1-\frac{n-k}{k+1}\right)+\sum_{k<n/2}\binom{n}{k}\left(\frac{n-k}{k+1}-1\right)\right\}\\
&\overset{(a)}{\le} \frac{1}{2^n}\left\{\binom{n}{\lceil\frac{n}{2}\rceil}+\left(1+\frac{2}{n}\right)\binom{n}{\lceil\frac{n}{2}\rceil-1}-1\right\}
\end{aligned}$$

$$
\begin{aligned}
&= \frac{1}{2^n}\left\{\binom{n}{\lceil\frac{n}{2}\rceil} + \binom{n}{\lceil\frac{n}{2}\rceil - 1} + \frac{2}{n}\binom{n}{\lceil\frac{n}{2}\rceil - 1} - 1\right\} \\
&\overset{\text{(b)}}{=} \frac{1}{2^n}\binom{n+1}{\lceil\frac{n}{2}\rceil} + \frac{2}{n2^n}\binom{n}{\lceil\frac{n}{2}\rceil - 1} - \frac{1}{2^n} \\
&< \frac{1}{2^n}\binom{n+1}{\lceil\frac{n}{2}\rceil} + \frac{2}{n2^n}\binom{n}{\lceil\frac{n}{2}\rceil - 1} \\
&= \frac{1}{2^n}\binom{n+1}{\lceil\frac{n}{2}\rceil} + \frac{2}{n2^n}\left\{\binom{n}{\lceil\frac{n}{2}\rceil - 1} + \binom{n}{\lceil\frac{n}{2}\rceil} - \binom{n}{\lceil\frac{n}{2}\rceil}\right\} \\
&\overset{\text{(b)}}{=} \frac{1}{2^n}\binom{n+1}{\lceil\frac{n}{2}\rceil} + \frac{2}{n2^n}\binom{n+1}{\lceil\frac{n}{2}\rceil} - \frac{2}{n2^n}\binom{n}{\lceil\frac{n}{2}\rceil} \\
&< \frac{1}{2^n}\left(1 + \frac{2}{n}\right)\binom{n+1}{\lceil\frac{n}{2}\rceil}
\end{aligned}
$$

Inequality (a) follows from Equations (5) and (9), and Equation (b) follows from Lemma 1. □

B.3 Proof of Equation (12)

Proof. We have

$$
\begin{aligned}
\binom{n+1}{\frac{n}{2}} &= \frac{(n+1)!}{\frac{n}{2}!\,\left(n+1-\frac{n}{2}\right)!} = \frac{(n+1)!}{\frac{n}{2}!\,\left(\frac{n}{2}+1\right)!} \\
&\overset{\text{(a)}}{<} \frac{\sqrt{2\pi(n+1)}\left(\frac{n+1}{e}\right)^{n+1} e^{\frac{1}{12(n+1)}}}{\sqrt{2\pi\frac{n}{2}}\left(\frac{n}{2e}\right)^{\frac{n}{2}} e^{\frac{1}{12\cdot\frac{n}{2}+1}} \cdot \sqrt{2\pi\left(\frac{n}{2}+1\right)}\left(\frac{\frac{n}{2}+1}{e}\right)^{\frac{n}{2}+1} e^{\frac{1}{12\left(\frac{n}{2}+1\right)+1}}} \\
&= \sqrt{\frac{n+1}{n\pi\left(\frac{n}{2}+1\right)}}\,\frac{(n+1)^{n+1}}{\left(\frac{n}{2}\right)^{\frac{n}{2}}\left(\frac{n}{2}+1\right)^{\frac{n}{2}+1}} \cdot e^{-\frac{108n^2+228n+155}{12(n+1)(6n+1)(6n+13)}} \\
&\overset{\text{(b)}}{<} \sqrt{\frac{n+1}{n\pi\left(\frac{n}{2}+1\right)}}\,\frac{(n+1)^{n+1}e^{0}}{\left(\frac{n}{2}\right)^{\frac{n}{2}}\left(\frac{n}{2}+1\right)^{\frac{n}{2}+1}} \\
&= \frac{2\sqrt{2}\cdot 2^n (n+1)^{n+\frac{3}{2}}}{\sqrt{\pi}n^{\frac{n+1}{2}}(n+2)^{\frac{n+3}{2}}}
\end{aligned}
$$

Inequality (a) follows from Lemma 2, and Inequality (b) follows from $f(n) < 0$ for all $n \in \mathbb{N}$ if we let $f(n) := -\frac{108n^2+228n+155}{12(n+1)(6n+1)(6n+13)}$. □

B.4 Proof of Equation (13)

According to Equation (11), we have

$$
\left|\Pr\left[\mathsf{DenGame}_{\mathcal{A}}^{0} = 1\right] - \Pr\left[\mathsf{DenGame}_{\mathcal{A}}^{1} = 1\right]\right|
$$

$$
\begin{aligned}
&< \frac{1}{2^n}\left(1+\frac{2}{n}\right)\binom{n+1}{\frac{n}{2}} \\
&\overset{\text{(a)}}{<} \frac{1}{2^n}\cdot\frac{n+2}{n}\cdot\frac{2\sqrt{2}\cdot 2^n(n+1)^{n+\frac{3}{2}}}{\sqrt{\pi}n^{\frac{n+1}{2}}(n+2)^{\frac{n+3}{2}}} = \frac{2\sqrt{2}}{\sqrt{\pi}}\cdot\frac{(n+1)^{n+\frac{3}{2}}}{n^{\frac{n+3}{2}}(n+2)^{\frac{n+1}{2}}} \\
&< \frac{2\sqrt{2}}{\sqrt{\pi}}\cdot\frac{(n+1)^{n+\frac{3}{2}}}{n^{\frac{n+3}{2}}(n+1)^{\frac{n+1}{2}}} = \frac{2\sqrt{2}}{\sqrt{\pi}}\cdot\frac{1}{\sqrt{n}}\left(1+\frac{1}{n}\right)\sqrt{\left(1+\frac{1}{n}\right)^n} \\
&\overset{\text{(b)}}{<} \frac{2\sqrt{2}}{\sqrt{\pi}}\cdot\frac{1}{\sqrt{n}}\cdot\frac{3}{2}\cdot\sqrt{e} = \sqrt{\frac{18e}{\pi}}\frac{1}{\sqrt{n}} = \frac{3.946\cdots}{\sqrt{n}} \\
&< \frac{4}{\sqrt{n}}.
\end{aligned}
$$

Inequality (a) follows from Equation (12), and Inequality (b) follows from $1 + 1/n \leq 3/2$ when $n \geq 2$ and Lemma 3.

B.5 Proof of Equation (14)

Proof. We have

$$
\begin{aligned}
&\Pr\left[\mathsf{TFHE.Dec}(\mathsf{sk},\mathsf{ct}) = 0\right] \\
&= \Pr\left[\left\lfloor\frac{(b-\langle \boldsymbol{a},\boldsymbol{s}\rangle) \bmod q}{\Delta}\right\rceil \bmod 2 = 0\right] \\
&\overset{\text{(a)}}{=} \sum_{i=-\infty}^{\infty} \Pr\left[\left\lceil\frac{4\{(b-\langle \boldsymbol{a},\boldsymbol{s}\rangle) \bmod q\} - q}{2q}\right\rceil = 2i\right] \\
&\overset{\text{(b)}}{=} \sum_{i=-\infty}^{\infty} \Pr\left[2i-1 < \frac{4\{(b-\langle \boldsymbol{a},\boldsymbol{s}\rangle) \bmod q\} - q}{2q} \leq 2i\right] \\
&= \sum_{i=-\infty}^{\infty} \Pr\left[\frac{4i-1}{4}q < (b-\langle \boldsymbol{a},\boldsymbol{s}\rangle) \bmod q \leq \frac{4i+1}{4}q\right] \\
&\overset{\text{(c)}}{=} \Pr\left[0 \leq (b-\langle \boldsymbol{a},\boldsymbol{s}\rangle) \bmod q \leq \frac{1}{4}q\right] + \Pr\left[\frac{3}{4}q < (b-\langle \boldsymbol{a},\boldsymbol{s}\rangle) \bmod q \leq q-1\right],
\end{aligned}
$$

where $\mathsf{ct} = (\boldsymbol{a}, b) \xleftarrow{\$} (\mathbb{Z}/q\mathbb{Z})^{n+1}$ and $(\mathsf{pk},\mathsf{sk}) \leftarrow \mathsf{TFHE.Gen}(1^\lambda)$. Equation (a) follows from $\Delta = q/2$, $\lfloor x \rceil = \lceil x - 1/2 \rceil$ for all $x \in \mathbb{R}$, and a property of the modulo-2 operation. Equation (b) follows from the definition of the ceiling function. Equation (c) follows from $\Pr\left[\frac{4i-1}{4}q < (b-\langle \boldsymbol{a},\boldsymbol{s}\rangle) \bmod q \leq \frac{4i+1}{4}q\right] = 0$ for all $i \in \mathbb{Z} \setminus \{0, 1\}$ and a property of the modulo-q operation. $\square$

B.6 Proof of Equation (15)

Proof. Since $(\boldsymbol{a}, b) \xleftarrow{\$} (\mathbb{Z}/q\mathbb{Z})^{n+1}$, we have

$$\Pr[b = 0] = \cdots = \Pr[b = q - 1] = \frac{1}{q}. \tag{16}$$

In addition, for all $j \in \{0, 1, \ldots, q - 1\}$, let $p(j) := \Pr[\langle \boldsymbol{a}, \boldsymbol{s} \rangle \bmod q = j]$. Then, we have

$$\sum_{j=0}^{q-1} p(k) = 1. \tag{17}$$

Hence, for all $k \in \{0, 1, \ldots, q - 1\}$, we have

$$\begin{aligned}
&\Pr[(b - \langle \boldsymbol{a}, \boldsymbol{s} \rangle) \bmod q = k] \\
&= \Pr[b = q - 1]\, p(q - 1 - k) + \cdots + \Pr[b = k]\, p(0) \\
&\quad + \Pr[b = k - 1]\, p(q - 1) + \cdots + \Pr[b = 0]\, p(q - k) \\
&\overset{(a)}{=} \frac{1}{q}(p(q - 1 - k) + \cdots + p(0) + p(q - 1) + \cdots + p(q - k)) \\
&\overset{(b)}{=} \frac{1}{q},
\end{aligned}$$

where $\mathsf{ct} = (\boldsymbol{a}, b) \xleftarrow{\$} (\mathbb{Z}/q\mathbb{Z})^{n+1}$ and $(\mathsf{pk}, \mathsf{sk}) \leftarrow \mathsf{TFHE.Gen}(1^\lambda)$. Equation (a) follows from Equation (16). Equation (b) follows from Equation (17). □

References

1. Agrawal, S., Goldwasser, S., Mossel, S.: Deniable fully homomorphic encryption from LWE. Cryptology ePrint Archive, Report 2020/1588 (2020). https://eprint.iacr.org/2020/1588
2. Agrawal, S., Goldwasser, S., Mossel, S.: Deniable fully homomorphic encryption from learning with errors. In: Malkin, T., Peikert, C. (eds.) Advances in Cryptology – CRYPTO 2021, Part II. Lecture Notes in Computer Science, vol. 12826, pp. 641–670. Springer, Cham (2021). https://doi.org/10.1007/978-3-030-84245-1_22
3. Al Badawi, A., Polyakov, Y.: Demystifying bootstrapping in fully homomorphic encryption. Cryptology ePrint Archive, Report 2023/149 (2023). https://eprint.iacr.org/2023/149
4. Barnes, C.W.: Euler's constant and e. Am. Math. Mon. **91**(7), 428–430 (1984). https://doi.org/10.2307/2322999
5. Brakerski, Z.: Fully homomorphic encryption without modulus switching from classical GapSVP. In: Safavi-Naini, R., Canetti, R. (eds.) Advances in Cryptology – CRYPTO 2012. Lecture Notes in Computer Science, vol. 7417, pp. 868–886. Springer, Berlin, Heidelberg (2012). https://doi.org/10.1007/978-3-642-32009-5_50
6. Brakerski, Z., Gentry, C., Vaikuntanathan, V.: (leveled) fully homomorphic encryption without bootstrapping. ACM Trans. Comput. Theor. (TOCT) **6**(3), 1–36 (2014). https://doi.org/10.1145/2633600

7. Camenisch, J., Lysyanskaya, A.: An efficient system for non-transferable anonymous credentials with optional anonymity revocation. In: Pfitzmann, B. (ed.) Advances in Cryptology – EUROCRYPT 2001. Lecture Notes in Computer Science, vol. 2045, pp. 93–118. Springer, Berlin, Heidelberg (2001). https://doi.org/10.1007/3-540-44987-6_7
8. Canetti, R., Dwork, C., Naor, M., Ostrovsky, R.: Deniable encryption. In: Kaliski, B.S. (ed.) CRYPTO 1997. LNCS, vol. 1294, pp. 90–104. Springer, Heidelberg (1997). https://doi.org/10.1007/BFb0052229
9. Cheon, J.H., Han, K., Kim, A., Kim, M., Song, Y.: Bootstrapping for approximate homomorphic encryption. In: Nielsen, J.B., Rijmen, V. (eds.) Advances in Cryptology – EUROCRYPT 2018, Part I. Lecture Notes in Computer Science, vol. 10820, pp. 360–384. Springer, Cham (2018). https://doi.org/10.1007/978-3-319-78381-9_14
10. Cheon, J.H., Kim, A., Kim, M., Song, Y.S.: Homomorphic encryption for arithmetic of approximate numbers. In: Takagi, T., Peyrin, T. (eds.) Advances in Cryptology – ASIACRYPT 2017, Part I. Lecture Notes in Computer Science, vol. 10624, pp. 409–437. Springer, Cham (2017). https://doi.org/10.1007/978-3-319-70694-8_15
11. Chillotti, I., Gama, N., Georgieva, M., Izabachène, M.: TFHE: fast fully homomorphic encryption over the torus. J. Cryptol. **33**(1), 34–91 (2019). https://doi.org/10.1007/s00145-019-09319-x
12. Ducas, L., Micciancio, D.: FHEW: Bootstrapping homomorphic encryption in less than a second. In: Oswald, E., Fischlin, M. (eds.) Advances in Cryptology – EUROCRYPT 2015, Part I. Lecture Notes in Computer Science, vol. 9056, pp. 617–640. Springer, Berlin, Heidelberg (2015). https://doi.org/10.1007/978-3-662-46800-5_24
13. Fan, J., Vercauteren, F.: Somewhat practical fully homomorphic encryption. Cryptology ePrint Archive, Report 2012/144 (2012). https://eprint.iacr.org/2012/144
14. Gentry, C.: A Fully Homomorphic Encryption Scheme. Phd thesis, Stanford University (2009). https://crypto.stanford.edu/craig/
15. Gentry, C.: Fully homomorphic encryption using ideal lattices. In: Mitzenmacher, M. (ed.) 41st Annual ACM Symposium on Theory of Computing, pp. 169–178. ACM Press (2009). https://doi.org/10.1145/1536414.1536440
16. Gentry, C., Sahai, A., Waters, B.: Homomorphic encryption from learning with errors: Conceptually-simpler, asymptotically-faster, attribute-based. In: Canetti, R., Garay, J.A. (eds.) Advances in Cryptology – CRYPTO 2013, Part I. Lecture Notes in Computer Science, vol. 8042, pp. 75–92. Springer, Berlin, Heidelberg (2013). https://doi.org/10.1007/978-3-642-40041-4_5
17. Goldreich, O., Micali, S., Wigderson, A.: How to play any mental game or a completeness theorem for protocols with honest majority. In: Aho, A. (ed.) 19th Annual ACM Symposium on Theory of Computing, pp. 218–229. ACM Press (1987). https://doi.org/10.1145/28395.28420
18. Hwang, I., Min, S., Song, Y.: Practical circuit privacy/sanitization for TFHE. Cryptology ePrint Archive, Report 2025/216 (2025). https://eprint.iacr.org/2025/216
19. Joye, M.: SoK: Fully homomorphic encryption over the [discretized] torus. IACR Trans. Cryptograph. Hardw. Embed. Syst. **2022**(4), 661–692 (2022). https://doi.org/10.46586/tches.v2022.i4.661-692
20. Joye, M.: TFHE public-key encryption revisited. In: Oswald, E. (ed.) Topics in Cryptology – CT-RSA 2024. Lecture Notes in Computer Science, vol. 14643, pp. 277–291. Springer, Cham (2024). https://doi.org/10.1007/978-3-031-58868-6_11

21. Micciancio, D., Vaikuntanathan, V.: SoK: Learning with errors, circular security, and fully homomorphic encryption. In: Tang, Q., Teague, V. (eds.) PKC 2024: 27th International Conference on Theory and Practice of Public Key Cryptography, Part IV. Lecture Notes in Computer Science, vol. 14604, pp. 291–321. Springer, Cham (2024). https://doi.org/10.1007/978-3-031-57728-4_10
22. Regev, O.: On lattices, learning with errors, random linear codes, and cryptography. J. ACM (JACM) **56**(6), 1–40 (2009). https://doi.org/10.1145/1568318.1568324
23. Rivest, R.L., Adleman, L., Dertouzos, M.L.: On data banks and privacy homomorphisms. Found. Secure Comput. **4**(11), 169–180 (1978)
24. Robbins, H.: A remark on stirling's formula. Am. Math. Mon. **62**(1), 26–29 (1955). https://doi.org/10.2307/2308012
25. Sheffer, H.M.: A set of five independent postulates for Boolean algebras, with application to logical constants. Trans. Am. Math. Soc. **14**(4), 481–488 (1913). https://doi.org/10.2307/1988701
26. Yao, A.C.C.: Protocols for secure computations (extended abstract). In: 23rd Annual Symposium on Foundations of Computer Science, pp. 160–164. IEEE Computer Society Press (1982). https://doi.org/10.1109/SFCS.1982.38

Card-Based Representation of Floating-Point Numbers and Arithmetic Operations

Shun Odaka and Yuichi Komano(✉)

Chiba Institute of Technology, 2–17–1, Tsudanuma, Narashino, Japan
yuichi.komano@chibatech.ac.jp

Abstract. Card-based cryptography uses physical cards to realize cryptographic protocols, such as secure multiparty computation. At the last SecITC, card-based arithmetic operations using integer commitments were proposed with their application to statistical processing. In statistical processing, the statistical value increases as the number of data points increases, so the number of cards required for processing also increases. To address this issue, this paper introduces a new representation of commitments, named floating-point numerical commitments, for floating-point numbers. The floating-point numerical commitments allow us to represent a wide range of numbers, including negative and arbitrary-precision integers. We also propose a protocol that converts a conventional integer commitment to a floating-point numerical commitment and protocols for arithmetic operations using floating-point numerical commitments as inputs. We then discuss that our new representation and operations enhance the application of card-based cryptography to statistical processing.

Keywords: card-based cryptography · integer commitment · floating-point numbers · statistical operations

1 Introduction

Card-based cryptography [1] is a technique that implements cryptographic protocols by encoding information on physical playing cards and rearranging them by hand. For example, it can realize secure computation protocols for computing a product or sum of two secret inputs without revealing the inputs [4]. Card-based cryptography has been applied to education because it helps beginners to understand the principles of cryptographic protocols. Another advantage is that it enables secure protocol execution without a black-box computer.

In the card-based cryptography, there are two conventional ways to represent integers. The first one is *a binary integer commitment*, in which an integer is expressed as a binary integer, and each bit is represented by a pair of ♣ and ♡ cards. Using this representation, we can compute bitwise operations for addition and multiplication in a secure manner, and therefore, arbitrary arithmetic

P. D'Arco and A. Zamfiroiu (Eds.): SecITC 2025, LNCS 16443, pp. 79–95, 2026.
https://doi.org/10.1007/978-3-032-17443-7_5

operations can be realized by combining them. With this approach, the number of cards can be kept logarithmic in the size of the integer, but the computation requires complex combinations of bitwise operations, resulting in a large number of card operations.

The second way is *an integer commitment* [3,11,14], in which an integer is expressed with one ♡ and $k-1$ ♣ cards. In this commitment, the position of ♡ represents the value. Compared to the binary integer commitment, protocols for arithmetic operations using the integer commitment are simple, and we can reduce the number of card operations.

1.1 Related Work

At the last SecITC, card-based protocols, *using integer commitments*, that efficiently execute arithmetic operations such as multiplication, division, and square root were proposed [7] (and in its full paper [8]). They also proposed a protocol to compute a correlation coefficient and introduced an application of card-based cryptography to statistical processing. However, it is a drawback that these protocols with the integer commitment require a large number of cards.

Eriguchi and Shinagawa [2] proposed efficient protocols for arithmetic operations, *using the binary integer commitments*. Their protocols use a constant number of cards with respect to the bit length ℓ of the integers. The numbers of card operations for addition and subtraction are $O(\ell)$, and those for multiplication and division are $O(\ell^2)$.

This paper introduces a new representation of commitments using floating-point numbers with sign, significand, and exponent bits. This representation allows us to approximately express large integers with fewer cards, as well as a uniform handling of negative and/or fractional numbers in the same format.

1.2 Our Contribution

The contributions of this paper are as follows.

- We introduce a new notion of a *floating-point numerical commitment*, consisting of sign, significand, and exponent bits, which is analogous to the conventional floating-point numbers. This representation allows us to uniformly handle not only positive and negative numbers but also large integers and fractional numbers by assigning positive and negative values to the exponent bits, respectively.
- We propose protocols that convert the integer commitments into a multi-digit integer commitments or floating-point numerical commitments. These protocols enable us to transform the conventional integer commitments into the floating-point numerical commitments.
- We also propose protocols for performing arithmetic operations using the floating-point numerical commitments as inputs. Since two floating-point numerical commitments may have different exponent bits, their significand must be aligned before the computation. Therefore, we first propose a protocol

for exponent alignment, and then, propose protocols for addition, subtraction, multiplication, and division. These protocols allow us to compute numbers in arbitrary precision with fewer cards than the conventional protocols with the integer commitments.
- Finally, we discuss applications of floating-point numerical commitments to statistical processing, by demonstrating that they require significantly fewer cards than the protocol with the integer commitment.

The remainder of this paper is organized as follows. Section 2 reviews the background of card-based cryptography and protocols for arithmetic operations proposed in [7,8]. Section 3 introduces a floating-point numerical commitment and gives protocols for converting the integer commitment into the multi-digit integer commitment or the floating-point numerical commitments, as well as protocols for arithmetic operations using the floating-point numerical commitments as inputs. Then, Sect. 5 discusses applications of floating-point numerical commitments to statistical processing. Finally, Sect. 6 concludes this paper.

2 Preliminaries

In this section, we first describe properties of the physical cards and encoding rules of integers with the cards. We then explain the shuffle and arithmetic operations proposed in [7,8].

2.1 Physical Cards

We use a set of physical cards where each card has a ♣ or ♡ symbol on its face, and the back of every card has the same pattern ?. We call these cards black-red cards.

2.2 Commitments

Let us represent an integer $i \in [0, k-1]$ ($[a, b]$ denotes a set of integers from a to b) with one red card and $k-1$ black cards as

$$\overset{0}{\clubsuit}\overset{1}{\clubsuit}\cdots\overset{i-1}{\clubsuit}\overset{i}{\heartsuit}\overset{i+1}{\clubsuit}\cdots\overset{k-1}{\clubsuit}.$$

A card sequence by turning over these k cards is called an *integer commitment with a base* k [3,7,8,11,14] which is denoted by ??···? or ?, and written as $E_k(i)$.

As a variant of the integer commitment, Mizuki et al. [13] introduced a representation of an integer in $[-k+1, k-1]$. In this paper, we call it a *extended integer commitment*. It consists of $2k-2$ black cards and one red card and an integer i is represented with face-down cards of

$$\overset{-k+1}{\clubsuit}\ \overset{-k+2}{\clubsuit}\cdots\overset{i-1}{\clubsuit}\overset{i}{\heartsuit}\overset{i+1}{\clubsuit}\cdots\overset{k-1}{\clubsuit}.$$

Ruangwises [11] proposed a secure addition protocol for the integer commitments. The idea is as follows: place $E_k(j)$ in reversed order below $E_k(i)$, to arrange a $2 \times k$ card matrix. After applying a pile-shifting shuffle (see next subsection), rearrange the second row back to its original order. In this matrix, the first and second rows are $E_k(i + r \bmod k)$ and $E_k(j - r \bmod k)$. We then turn over the cards in the second row and set $\ell = j - r \bmod k$ from the position of ♡ in the sequence. Therefore, we have $E_k(i + j \bmod k)$ by cyclically shifting the card sequence in the first row to the right by ℓ.

Recently, Igari et al. [9,15] proposed a secure addition protocol for a *multi-digit integer commitment*. In the multi-digit integer commitment, an integer i is represented as a multi-digit integer with base k and, for each digit, an integer commitments with base k is arranged. An example of the multi-digit integer commitment is

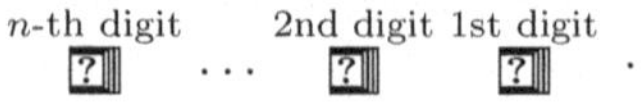

$$\overset{n\text{-th digit}}{\boxed{?}} \cdots \overset{\text{2nd digit}}{\boxed{?}} \; \overset{\text{1st digit}}{\boxed{?}} \; .$$

With the multi-digit integer commitment, we can reduce the number of cards to represent an integer i with black-red cards. For example, if the integer i has three digits in its decimal representation, the multi-digit integer commitment consists of 30 cards (three integer commitments with base $k = 10$), while the conventional integer commitment to i requires at most 1000 cards. We will explain an addition protocol for the multi-digit integer commitment later.

2.3 Pile-Shifting Shuffle

A *pile-shifting shuffle* [6,12] is a shuffling operation in which several piles of cards of the same size are cyclically shifted at random.

A pile-shifting shuffle was applied to k piles, considering two cards in the same column as a single pile. The transition is:

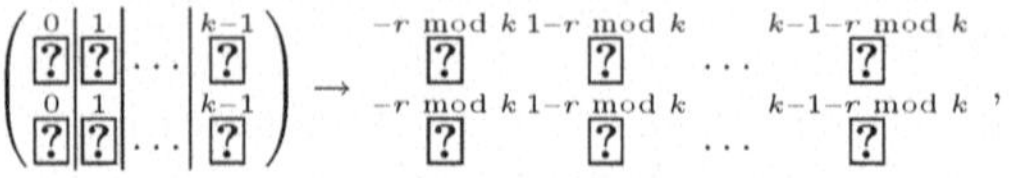

$$\left(\begin{array}{c|c|c|c} \overset{0}{\boxed{?}} & \overset{1}{\boxed{?}} & \cdots & \overset{k-1}{\boxed{?}} \\ \overset{0}{\boxed{?}} & \overset{1}{\boxed{?}} & \cdots & \overset{k-1}{\boxed{?}} \end{array} \right) \rightarrow \begin{array}{cccc} \overset{-r \bmod k}{\boxed{?}} & \overset{1-r \bmod k}{\boxed{?}} & \cdots & \overset{k-1-r \bmod k}{\boxed{?}} \\ \overset{-r \bmod k}{\boxed{?}} & \overset{1-r \bmod k}{\boxed{?}} & \cdots & \overset{k-1-r \bmod k}{\boxed{?}} \end{array},$$

where $r \in [0, k-1]$ is a random number corresponding to the cyclic shift generated by the pile-shifting shuffle.

2.4 Protocols with Integer Commitments

In this subsection, let us briefly review protocols. Due to the page limit, we omit the details of each protocol, and therefore, refer [7,8] for details.

Base Extension: Given an integer commitment $E_k(x)$ to $x \in [0, k-1]$ with base k, appending $(k' - k)$ additional ♣ cards to the right yields an integer commitment $E_{k'}(x)$ with base $k'(> k)$.

The number of additional cards required is $(k' - k)$, and no shuffles are used in this protocol.

Secure Squaring: Given an integer commitment $E_k(i)$ of $i \in [0, k-1]$, the protocol outputs an integer commitment of $i^2 \in [0, (k-1)^2]$ with base $(k-1)^2+1$.

In this protocol, $\clubsuit$ cards are inserted between each card such that the j-th card of $E_k(i)$ is moved to the $\{(j-1)^2+1\}$-th position. Since $E_k(i)$ contains $\heartsuit$ at the $(i+1)$-th position, in the resulting sequence, $\heartsuit$ is moved to the (i^2+1)-th position which is an integer commitment to i^2.

The output consists of $(k-1)^2+1$ blackred cards by using (k^2-3k+2) additional $\clubsuit$ cards. No shuffle operation is required.

Secure Multiplication with Constant: Given an integer commitment $E_k(i)$ to $i \in [0, k-1]$ and a public integer $n \geqslant 1$, this protocol outputs an integer commitment to $ni \in [0, n(k-1)]$ with base $n(k-1)+1$.

In this protocol, $(n-1)$ $\clubsuit$ cards are inserted between each card in $E_k(i)$. The protocol uses $(n-1)(k-1)$ additional cards and requires no shuffle.

Secure Division with Constant: Given an integer commitment $E_k(i)$ to $i \in [0, k-1]$ and a public integer $n \geqslant 1$, where $k = \ell n$ (if necessary, applying the base extension in advance so that $k = \ell n$), this protocol securely outputs integer commitments to the quotient $q(= \lfloor i/n \rfloor)$ with base ℓ and the remainder r with base n.

In this protocol, the card sequence of $E_k(i)$ is rearranged into an $n \times \ell$ card matrix. Then, by applying shuffle operations, we can obtain the commitments to q and r in the row and column, respectively.

The output consists of $\ell+n$ blackred cards and this protocol requires $k+\ell+n$ cards in total and two shuffle operations.

Secure Multiplication: Given two integer commitments $E_k(x)$ and $E_k(y)$ to integers $x, y \in [0, k-1]$, this protocol outputs an integer commitment to the product $xy \in [0, (k-1)^2]$ with base $(k-1)^2+1$. This protocol is based on the following equation:

$$xy = \left\{(x+y)^2 - x^2 - y^2\right\}/2. \tag{1}$$

Moreover, by substituting $x/2$ and $y/2$ into Eq. (1), we have another protocol that requires fewer cards while the number of shuffles increases.

Secure Absolute Value: Given an output of the secure subtraction protocol of [13], this protocol computes the absolute value together with its sign information. It requires $k+2$ additional cards and two shuffle operations.

Addition of Multi-digit Integer Commitments [9]*:* Given two multi-digit integer commitments represented in decimal notation, this protocol outputs a multi-digit integer commitment to their sum. In this paper, we generalize the base of multi-digit integer commitment from ten (decimal) to an arbitrary integer n.

3 Floating-Point Numerical Commitment

In this section, we first introduce a new representation of a commitment in card-based cryptography, named a *floating-point numerical commitment.*

We then present two conversion protocols: from an integer commitment to a multi-digit integer commitment expressed in base n, and from a multi-digit integer commitment to a floating-point numerical commitment. By combining these two protocols, an integer commitment can be converted into a floating-point numerical commitment.

3.1 Floating-Point Numerical Commitment

A floating-point numerical commitment is represented by three sequences of cards corresponding to a sign, a mantissa, and an exponent.

The *sign part* is represented with two cards: ♡♣ denotes a negative number, and ♣♡ denotes a positive number. If subtraction is not applied or numbers should not be negative throughout statistical processing, the sign part can be omitted to reduce the numbers of cards and operations.

The *mantissa part* is a sequence of p multi-digit integer commitments in base n. Each digit is encoded as a multi-digit integer commitment consisting of n cards. Thus, the mantissa requires pn cards in total.

The *exponent part* is expressed as an extended integer commitment to an integer between $-k+1$ and $k-1$ capable of representing negative values, using $2k-1$ cards [13].

3.2 Conversion to Multi-digit Integer Commitment

We propose a protocol that, given an integer commitment $E_k(x)$ as input, outputs a multi-digit integer commitment $E_n(d_j^{(x)})$ in base n, where

$$x = \sum_{j=1}^{\ell} d_j^{(x)} n^{j-1}.$$

The protocol takes k cards as an input and produces $\ell = \lfloor \log_n(k-1) \rfloor + 1$ digits of multi-digit integer commitments with ℓn cards.

Protocol 1 (Conversion to Multi-Digit Integer Commitment)

1. Perform a base extension from $E_k(x)$ to $E_{n^\ell}(x)$ using the method described in Sect. 2.4.
2. For $i = 1, 2, \ldots, \ell-1$, repeat the following steps:
   (a) If $i = 1$, divide $E_{n^\ell}(x)$ by n with the constant division protocol. If $i \geqslant 2$, divide the commitment for the quotient obtained in Step 2(a) of the previous iteration by n.
   (b) Store the commitment for the remainder as $E_n(d_i^{(x)})$.
3. Store the commitment for the quotient obtained in Step 2(a) of the $(\ell-1)$-th iteration as $E_n(d_\ell^{(x)})$.

This protocol requires $n^\ell + n^{\ell-1} + n$ cards and $2(\ell-1)$ shuffles.

3.3 Conversion to Floating-Point Numerical Commitment

Suppose the input is a multi-digit integer commitment of x, consisting of ℓ piles of $E_n(d_j^{(x)})$ for $j = 1, 2, \ldots, \ell$. We propose a protocol that outputs a floating-point numerical commitment corresponding to

$$x = \left(\sum_{j=1}^{p} f_j^{(x)} \times n^{j-p} \right) \times n^{x_{\exp}},$$

where the mantissa consists of p piles $E_n(f_j^{(x)})$ and the exponent is represented by $E_{2\ell-1}(x_{\exp})$.

Protocol 2 (Conversion to Floating-Point Numerical Commitment)

1. Prepare ℓ ♣ cards to store the exponent.
2. Prepare two card sequences, ♡♡ and ♣♣, and flip the left card of each to obtain ?♡ and ?♣.
3. For $i = \ell, \ell - 1, \ldots, 2$, repeat the following:
   (a) Place the leftmost card of $E_n(d_i^{(x)})$ in the first row, and arrange the remaining sequence left-to-right to form the second row in the reverse order. Append $(n-1)$ face-down ♣ cards to the left of the first row, and one face-down ♣ card to the right of the second row.
   (b) Place the card sequence whose rightmost card is ♣ (from Step 2 or the previous iteration of 3(g)) at the right end of the first row. Similarly, place the sequence whose rightmost card is ♡ at the right end of the second row. Then turn over the face-up cards.
   (c) In the third row, place one face-down ♡ and $(n-1)$ face-down ♣.
   (d) Apply a pile-shifting shuffle to the top two rows.
   (e) Apply a pile-shifting shuffle to the leftmost n columns.
   (f) Reveal the leftmost n columns of the top two rows. Rotate cards in the leftmost n columns so that ♡ move to the n-th column, and store the n cards of the third row as $E_n(d_i^{(x)})$.
   (g) Swap the second card from the right of the row containing ♡ (from Step 3(f)) with the i-th card of the exponent sequence prepared in Step 1.
   (h) Apply a pile-shifting shuffle to the rightmost two columns together. Then, turn over the rightmost card of each row.
4. In Step 3(h) of the $(\ell-1)$-th iteration, swap the second card from the right of the row where ♡ appears with the leftmost card of the exponent sequence.
5. Arrange the copies of $E_n(d_i^{(x)})$ obtained in Step 3(f) for $i = \ell, \ell-1, \ldots, 2$, followed by $E_n(d_1^{(x)})$, in the first row. Place the exponent sequence in the reverse order in the second row. In the third row, place $(\ell-1)$ face-down ♣ and one face-down ♡.
6. Apply a pile-shifting shuffle to the columns.
7. Reveal the second row, and cyclically shift the sequence so that ♡ moves to the leftmost column. Output the first p piles from the first row as the mantissa $E_n(f_p^{(x)}), E_n(f_{p-1}^{(x)}), \ldots, E_n(f_1^{(x)})$.

8. Append $(\ell - 1)$ face-down ♣ to the left of the third row, and output it as the exponent part extended to negative values.
9. If an absolute-value protocol was applied during conversion from integer to multi-digit integer commitment, output the corresponding sign information as the sign part. Otherwise, output ♣♡ (denoting positivity) as the default sign.

If subtraction is not required or if it is clear that negative inputs do not appear, the sign part can be omitted. This protocol requires $\ell n + \ell + 2n + 4$ cards and $3\ell - 2$ shuffles.

4 Protocols for Floating-Point Numerical Commitments

In this section, we present protocols for performing arithmetic operations on floating-point numerical commitments.

4.1 Exponent Alignment Protocol

This protocol takes as input two floating-point numerical commitments and aligns their exponents by adjusting the mantissa of the number with the smaller exponent so that the exponent is equal to the larger one. The floating-point numerical commitment with the larger exponent is output as is, representing number x. The other number is adjusted so that its mantissa aligns with the larger exponent, and its sign and mantissa are output as the floating-point numerical commitment of number y.

Protocol 3 (Exponent Alignment Protocol)

1. Using the copy protocol [10], duplicate both $E_{2k-1}(x_{exp})$ and $E_{2k-1}(y_{exp})$.
2. Arrange $E_{2k-1}(x_{exp})$ in the first row and arrange $E_{2k-1}(y_{exp})$ in the reverse order in the second row. Place $(k-1)$ face-down ♣ cards on both sides of each row.
3. Apply a pile-shifting shuffle column-wise and reveal the second row. Apply a cyclic shift so that the ♡ card moves to the $(2k-1)$-th column from the left. Apply a secure absolute value protocol, described in Sect. 2.4, to the first row and obtain both the absolute value and sign information.
4. Place the sign, mantissa, and exponent parts of x in the first row, and those of y in the second row. Then, place the first card of the sign information obtained in Step 3 at the leftmost position of the first row, and the second card at the leftmost position of the second row.
5. Apply a pile-shifting shuffle to the rows and reveal the leftmost cards. Store the cards in the row with ♡ as x (its sign, mantissa, and exponent), and the cards in the row with ♣ as the sign of y.
6. If $p > 2k - 1$, append $(p - (2k - 1))$ face-down ♣ cards to the right of the absolute value obtained in Step 3.

7. Arrange the absolute value obtained in Step 3 or Step 6 in the reverse order in the first row.
8. In the second row, arrange the mantissa of y (from the p-th digit to the first digit) obtained in Step 5, followed by commitments of $E_n(0)$ so that the row has the same number of columns as the first row.
9. Apply a pile-shifting shuffle to the columns and reveal the first row.
10. Apply a cyclic shift so that the ♡ card in the first row moves to the rightmost column. Store the first p piles from the left of the second row as the adjusted mantissa of y.

The above protocol requires $O((p+k)n)$ cards and 7 shuffles.

4.2 Addition and Subtraction of Floating-Point Numerical Commitments

This protocol takes as input two floating-point numerical commitments x, y (sign, mantissa, and exponent) and outputs the floating-point numerical commitment of $x \pm y$. Logical operations within the protocol are defined with ♡♣ $= 0$ and ♣♡ $= 1$. When no subtraction occurs or when it is clear that no negative values appear, the multi-digit integer commitment addition protocol in reference [9] can be used to reduce the number of shuffles.

Protocol 4 (Addition and Subtraction Protocol)

1. If subtraction is required, rearrange the cards of the sign part of y in the reverse order.
2. Apply a exponent alignment protocol of Sect. 4.1 to inputs x and y.
3. Compute the exclusive OR of the sign parts of x and y using the XOR protocol [5], then duplicate the result three times.
4. Duplicate $E_n(f_i^{(y)})(i = 1, 2, \cdots, p)$ twice using the copy protocol [10].
5. Arrange the two copies of $E_n(f_i^{(y)})$ in the first and second rows. Place one face-down ♣ card to the right of each $E_n(f_1^{(y)})$.
6. Rearrange each card pile in the second row in the reverse order.
7. Place the first card of the XOR obtained in Step 3 at the rightmost end of the first row, and the second card at the rightmost end of the second row.
8. Apply a pile-shifting shuffle to the rows and reveal the rightmost cards.
9. Apply a multi-digit integer commitment addition protocol to $E_n(f_i^{(x)})(i = 1, \ldots, p)$ and the row with ♡ revealed in Step 8. When placing $E_n(0)$ in the third row, by placing $E_n(0)$ in the fourth row additionally, obtain two copies of the addition result.
10. Use copy protocol [10] to obtain three copies of $E_n(f_{p+1}^{x+y})$ obtained in Step 9.
11. Place the first card of the XOR obtained in Step 3 at the leftmost of the first row, and the second card at the leftmost of the second row. Place $E_n(f_{p+1}^{x+y})$ in the first row and $E_n(0)$ in the second row. Apply a pile-shifting shuffle to the rows, reveal the leftmost cards, and store the row containing ♡ as $E_n(f_{p+1}^{x+y})$.

12. Rearrange the cards of the row containing ♣ (appeared in Step 11) in the reverse order, and apply a the AND protocol [5] to the rearranged cards and the XOR result of Step 3.
13. Use copy protocol [5] to obtain three copies of the AND result obtained in Step 12.
14. Apply the XOR protocol [5] to the sign part of x and the AND result obtained in Step 13, and store the result as the sign of $x \pm y$.
15. Arrange $E_n(f_i^{x+y})(i = 1, \ldots, p+1)$ in both the first and second rows. Rearrange card sequence in the second row in the reverse order. Place the first card of the AND result (obtained in Step 13) at the leftmost of the first row, and the second card at the leftmost of the second row.
16. Apply a pile-shifting shuffle to the rows and reveal the leftmost cards.
17. Apply a base extension protocol to the AND result (obtained in Step 13) so that the base is extended to n and add it to the row with ♡ (obtained in Step 16).
18. Apply the floating-point conversion protocol to the addition of Step 17. Store the mantissa part as the result. Cyclically shift the exponent left by $(p-1)$.
19. Place the exponent obtained in Step 2 with one face-down ♣ card on each side in the first row. Place the exponent obtained in Step 18 with $(k-p)$ face-down ♣ cards on each side in the second row.
20. Apply a pile-shifting shuffle to the columns and reveal the second row. Apply a cyclically shift so that the ♡ card moves to the $(k+1)$-th columns, then store the first row as the exponent.

The above protocol requires $O((p+k)n)$ cards and $O(p)$ shuffles.

4.3 Multiplication of Floating-Point Numerical Commitments

In this section, we explain idea to construct our multiplication protocol for the floating-point numerical commitments. Due to the page limit, we give the concrete procedure of our protocol in Appendix B.

Our protocol outputs the result by computing the product of the mantissas and the sum of the exponents of two floating-point numerical commitments.

The computation of the mantissa is similar to the procedure of hand-written multiplication. For two mantissas of inputs each consisting of multi-digit integer commitments, each digit of multi-digit integer commitments of the output is derived by multiplying the digits of inputs sequentially.

Let r_ℓ denote the ℓ-th digit of the mantissa of the output, which is initialized to zero. Using the secure multiplication protocol for integer commitments, the product $x_i \times y_j$ is computed for the i-th digit x_i of the first floating-point numerical commitment and the j-th digit y_j of the second. The result is then divided by n to obtain the carry: the quotient is added to r_{i+j} and the remainder to r_{i+j-1}. This process is repeated for all digit pairs of the two floating-point numerical commitments.

For the computation of exponent, note that the exponent is extended so that it can represent negative values. An extended integer commitment to the exponent of the output is computed by the sum of extended integer commitments to the exponents of inputs. In addition, if a carry occurs in the most significant digit during the mantissa multiplication, one is added to the exponent. Since both the mantissa and the exponent are kept confidential while their product and sum are computed, our protocol is designed to add one to the exponent without revealing whether a carry occurred.

Our multiplication protocol for the floating-point numerical commitments requires $O(n^2 + pn)$ cards and $O(p^2)$ shuffles.

4.4 Division of Floating-Point Numerical Commitments

Similar to previous section, we explain idea to construct our division protocol and we give the concrete procedure of our protocol in Appendix C.

Our protocol outputs the result by computing the quotient of the mantissas and the difference of the exponents of two floating-point numerical commitments to x and y. In addition, it outputs a flag indicating whether the divisor y is zero.

The computation of the quotient is based on a repetition of subtractions and comparisons, which is optimized by multiplying the divisor y by powers of two with the secure multiplication with constant. First, each value of $2^i y$ for powers of two less than or equal to n is computed. Then, for each $2^i y$, a comparison is performed between the higher digits of x and those of $2^i y$. If the higher digits of x are larger, $2^i y$ is added to the quotient, which is initially set to zero, and $2^i y$ is subtracted from the higher digits of x. When x is smaller, zero is added and subtracted respectively, so that no information is leaked. By repeating this operation for all digit positions, the quotient can be obtained.

An (extended) integer commitment of the exponent of the output is computed with the difference of the (extended) integer commitments to exponents of inputs. Furthermore, since the mantissa may have leading zeros in its higher digits, the exponent is decreased with our conversion protocol from a multi-digit integer commitment to a floating-point numerical commitment.

Our division protocol for the floating-point numerical commitments requires $O(pn \log n)$ cards and $O(p^2 \log n)$ shuffles.

5 Discussion

In this section, we discuss an application of floating-point numerical commitments with an example of computing the average score of 100 students.

When using the integer commitments, one would first compute the total sum of scores with 2×10^4 cards and then apply the constant division to round up the average score.

Then, let us consider the use of floating-point numerical commitments. In this example, we do not need negative numbers. Thus, the sum of scores can first be computed using decimal multi-digit integer commitment, then converted to the floating-point numerical commitment before performing the division. This enables an efficient computation of the average. Moreover, instead of preparing all 100 scores at once, scores can be added sequentially, reducing the number of required cards to about 1×10^2. After conversion to the floating-point numerical commitment and setting the exponent to -2, the average score including decimal fractions can be obtained.

As shown above, the floating-point numerical commitments reduce the number of required cards compared to the integer commitments, while also enabling representation of fractional values. The advantage becomes even more significant when dealing with larger numbers. Another strength is the unified treatment of negative numbers. In certain cases, the number of shuffles can also be reduced depending on the computation.

6 Conclusion

In this work, we proposed floating-point numerical commitments and protocols for the fundamental arithmetic operations. We demonstrated that floating-point numerical commitments enable arithmetic computations with arbitrary precision while requiring fewer cards than integer commitments. Future work will focus on constructing protocols for additional operations such as square roots, which are important in statistical processing.

Acknowledgements. We thank the anonymous reviewers, whose comments have helped us improve the presentation of the paper. This work was supported by Grant-in-Aid for Scientific Research (JP24K14951).

A Addition of Multi-digit Integer Commitments

Following the reference [9,15], let us review an addition protocol where the base of each commitment for digit is ten.

Protocol 5 (Addition of multi-digit integer commitments)

1. Repeat the following steps for $j = 0, 1, 2, \cdots, s-1$.
   (a) Put ten ♣ cards to the right of each of $(j+1)$-th piles $E_{10}(d_j^{(x)})$ and $E_{10}(d_j^{(y)})$. The resulting piles are $E_{20}(d_j^{(x)})$ and $E_{20}(d_j^{(y)})$. When $j > 0$, put eighteen ♣ cards right to the sequence of cards $E_2(c_{j-1})$, obtained in the $(j-1)$-th iteration as a commitment to a carry $c_{j-1} \in \{0, 1\}$, to generate $E_{20}(c_{j-1})$.
   (b) Compute the sum of commitments[1] $E_{20}(d_j^{(x)}), E_{20}(d_j^{(y)})$, and $E_{20}(c_{j-1})$, obtained in Step 1(a). Then, place the leftmost and rightmost ten cards of the result in the first and second rows, respectively. After that, rearrange cards in each row in the reverse order:

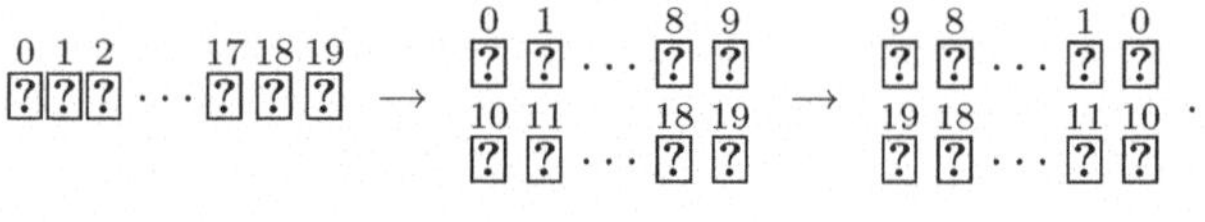

$$\begin{array}{c} 0\ 1\ 2 \quad\quad 17\ 18\ 19 \\ ?\,?\,? \cdots ?\,?\,? \end{array} \rightarrow \begin{array}{c} 0\ \ 1 \quad\quad 8\ \ 9 \\ ?\ ? \cdots ?\ ? \\ 10\ 11 \quad 18\ 19 \\ ?\ ? \cdots ?\ ? \end{array} \rightarrow \begin{array}{c} 9\ \ 8 \quad\quad 1\ \ 0 \\ ?\ ? \cdots ?\ ? \\ 19\ 18 \quad 11\ 10 \\ ?\ ? \cdots ?\ ? \end{array}.$$

[1] For $j = 0$, the addition of $E_{20}(c_{j-1})$ is skipped.

(c) Place ♡ and ♣ to the right of the ten face-down cards in each row. Then, turn over these face-up cards:

```
9 8       1 0              9 8       1 0
? ? ··· ? ? ♡              ? ? ··· ? ? ?
19 18     11 10      →     19 18     11 10      .
? ? ··· ? ? ♣              ? ? ··· ? ? ?
```

(d) Apply a pile-scramble shuffle:

```
[ 9 8       1 0   ]
[ ? ? ··· ? ? ?   ]         ? ? ··· ? ? ?
[ 19 18     11 10 ]    →    ? ? ··· ? ? ?  .
[ ? ? ··· ? ? ?   ]
```

(e) Put $E_{10}(0)$ as the third row and turn it over:

```
? ? ··· ? ? ?         ? ? ··· ? ? ?
? ? ··· ? ? ?    →    ? ? ··· ? ? ?  .
♡ ♣ ··· ♣ ♣           ? ? ··· ? ?
```

(f) Apply a pile-shifting shuffle to the left ten columns:

```
( ?|?|···|?|? )  ?          ? ? ··· ? ? ?
( ?|?|···|?|? )  ?    →     ? ? ··· ? ? ?  .
( ?|?|···|?|? )             ? ? ··· ? ?
```

(g) Turn over the leftmost ten cards in the first and second rows. Note that one of the face-up cards is ♡ and the others are ♣'s. Then, shift the left ten columns cyclically so that ♡ is in the 10-th column. As a result, the face-down cards in the third row become a $(j+1)$-th digit of commitment to $x+y$. Therefore, output the commitment in the third row as $(j+1)$-th pile of a result.
Moreover, among the first and second rows, rearrange the rightmost card of the row including face-up ♡ and the rightmost card of the other row into a two-card sequence from left to right. Then, forward the sequence as a carry, $E_2(c_j)$, to the addition of $(j+1)$-th digit. In the following example, the rightmost card in the second row and the rightmost card in the first row are the first and second cards from the left of $E_2(c_j)$, respectively:

```
♣ ♣ ··· ♣ ♣ ?         ♣ ♣ ··· ♣ ♣ ?
♣ ♣ ··· ♡ ♣ ?    →    ♣ ♣ ··· ♣ ♡ ?    →    ? ? .
? ? ··· ? ?           ? ? ··· ? ?
```

The face-up cards can be reused in the following steps.

2. Put eight ♣'s to the right of $E_2(c_{s-1})$, which is obtained as the $(s-1)$-th carry. Then, output it as the $(s+1)$-th digit of the commitment to $x+y$.

We can compare integers encoded in the multi-digit integer commitment as follows. Assume that we want to determine whether $x \geq y$ for two digit integer commitments to x and y. Each of the commitments consists of s piles of ten colored cards, $E_{10}(d_i)$ where $i \in \{0, 1, \cdots, s-1\}$ and d_i is a digit of x or y. To compare x and y, we first rearrange the order of each $E_{10}(d_i^{(y)})$ in the reverse order. Note that the resulting piles represent a (commitment to) 9's complement of y. Then, we add it to a digit integer commitment to one (with s piles of ten colored cards) to obtain a (commitment to) 10's complement of y. After that, we add it to a digit integer commitment to x and check whether the topmost pile (final carry) is $E_{10}(0)$ or $E_{10}(1)$. If it is $E_{10}(1)$, then $x \geq y$ holds; otherwise, $x < y$ holds.

B Detail of Multiplication of Floating-Point Numerical Commitments

Given floating-point numerical commitments of x and y as input, this protocol outputs the floating-point numerical commitment of their product. By changing the formula applied in the secure multiplication protocol, we can obtain variations of multiplication protocol to prioritize the number of shuffles or the number of cards required.

Protocol 6 (Multiplication of Floating-Point Numerical Commitments)

1. For $i = 1, 2, \cdots, p$, repeat the following steps:
   (a) For $j = 1, 2, \cdots, p$, repeat the following steps:
      i. Compute $E_n(f_i^{(x)}) \times E_n(f_j^{(y)})$ using the secure multiplication protocol in Sect. 2.4.
      ii. Divide the result by n using constant division. Extend the bases of the quotient and remainder to np, and denote the quotient as $E_{np}(d_{i+j}^{(r)})$ and the remainder as $E_{np}(d_{i+j-1}^{(r)})$. If the corresponding variable already has an associated commitment, add the extended quotient or remainder securely to the existing commitment.

2. For $i = 1, 2, \cdots, 2p$, perform the following:
   (a) If $i \geqslant 2$, add $E_{np}(d_i^{(c)})$, which was stored in Step 2(c) of the previous iteration, to $E_{np}(d_i^{(r)})$.
   (b) Divide $E_{np}(d_i^{(r)})$ by n using constant division. Store the remainder as $E_n(d_i^{(xy)})$.
   (c) Extend the base of the quotient obtained in Step 2(b) to np and store it as $E_{np}(d_{i+1}^{(c)})$.
3. Store $E_{np}(d_{2p+1}^{(c)})$ as $E_n(d_{2p+1}^{(xy)})$.
4. Using $E_n(d_i^{(xy)})(i = 1, 2, \cdots, 2p+1)$ as input, apply a conversion protocol to a floating-point numerical commitment in Sect. 3.3.

5. Cyclically shift the exponent part obtained in Step 4 to the left by $(2p-1)$.
6. Arrange $E_{2k-1}(x_{exp})$ in the first row, and arrange $E_{2k-1}(y_{exp})$ in reverse order in the second row. Place $(k-1)$ cards of ♣ on both sides of each row. Apply a pile-shifting shuffle to the columns, and cyclically shift the colmuns so that ♡ moves to the $(2k-1)$-th column.
7. Place one additional face-down ♣ card on both sides of the exponent part obtained in Step 6, and arrange them in the first row. Place $(2k-p-1)$ face-down ♣ cards on both sides of the exponent part obtained in Step 5, rearrange the card sequence in the reverse order, and arrange it in the second row.
8. Apply a pile-shifting shuffle to columns. Reveal the second row, and cyclically shift so that ♡ moves to the $2k$-th column. Store the first row as the exponent part.
9. With regarding ♡♣ $= 1$ and ♣♡ $= 0$, compute the XOR of the sign bits of x and y using the XOR protocol in [5], and store it as the sign bit of the product.

The above protocol requires $O(n^2 + pn)$ cards and $O(p^2)$ shuffles.

C Detail of Division of Floating-Point Numerical Commitments

Given two floating-point numerical commitments x and y as input, the protocol outputs a floating-point numerical commitment of $q = x/y$. In the case where $y = 0$, the protocol instead outputs a two-card commitment.

Protocol 7 (Division of Floating-Point Numerical Commitments)

1. Insert n face-down ♣ cards between the first and second cards of $E_n(d_p^{(y)})$.
2. Apply a constant division by n on the card sequence obtained in Step 1.
3. Output the quotient obtained in Step 2 as a flag that indicates whether $y = 0$. The output is ♡♣ when $y = 0$, and ♣♡ when $y \neq 0$.
4. Regard the remainder obtained in Step 2 again as $E_n(d_p^{(y)})$.
5. Duplicate $E_n(f_i^{(y)})(i = 1, 2, \cdots, p)$ using the copy protocol in [10].
6. For $i = 0, 1, \cdots, \lfloor \log_2 n \rfloor - 1$, repeat the following steps:
   (a) Repeat the following operations for $j = 1, 2, \cdots, p+1$. However, when $i = 0$, skip the step for $j = p+1$.
      i. Multiply $E_n(f_i^{(2^i y)})$ by 2 with a constant multiplication protocol.
      ii. If $j \geqslant 2$, extend the base of $E_n(c_j)$ to $2n-1$ and add it to the card sequence obtained in Step 6(a)(i).
      iii. Divide the card sequence obtained in Step 6(a)(ii) by n with a constant division protocol. Append an additional zero commitment to the 4th row to obtain two remainders. Store the remainder as $E_n(f_i^{(2^{i+1} y)})$ and the quotient as $E_k(c_j)$. When $i = 0$ and $j = p$, store the result also as $E_n(f_{p+1}^{(2y)})$.

7. For $i = p+1, p, \cdots, 1$, repeat the following steps:
   (a) Prepare $E_n(0)$ to store the quotient commitment $E_n(d_i^{(q)})$.
   (b) If $i = p+1$, prepare $E_n(0)$ for storing $E_n(f_{i+1}^{(x)})$; if $i \leqslant p$, prepare $E_n(0)$ for storing $E_n(f_1^{(x)})$.
   (c) For $j = \lfloor \log_2 n \rfloor, \lfloor \log_2 n \rfloor - 1, \cdots, 0$, repeat:
      i. For $m = 1, 2, \cdots, p+1$, repeat the following steps:
         A. Extend the base of $E_n(f_m^{(2^j y)})$ and $E_2(c_{m-1})$ to $n+1$ and apply a secure addition (with $c_0 = 0$ when $m = 1$).
         B. Extend the base of $E_n(f_m^{(x)})$ to $n+1$ and apply a secure subtraction protocol [13] with the card sequence obtained in Step 7(c)(i)(A).
         C. Remove the rightmost card of the sequence and divide by n with a constant division protocol. Rearrange the card sequence of the quotient in the reverse order and store it as $E_2(c_m)$. Also store the remainder as $E_n(r_m)$.
      ii. Place the first card of $E_2(c_{p+1})$ in the first row and the second card in the second row. In the first row, append $E_n(r_i)(i = 1, \cdots, p+1)$ followed by $E_n(2^j)$. In the second row, append $E_n(f_i^{(x)})(i = 1, \cdots, p+1)$ and $E_n(0)$.
      iii. Apply a pile-shifting shuffle to the rows and reveal the leftmost card.
      iv. Add the rightmost card sequence of the row where ♡ appeared in Step 7(c)(iii) to $E_n(d_i^{(q)})$.
      v. Use the card sequence in the middle of the row where ♡ appeared in Step 7(c)(iii) as $E_n(f_i^{(x)})(i = 1, \cdots, p+1)$, which will be used in the next iteration.
   (d) Store $E_n(d_i^{(q)})$ as part of the quotient.
   (e) Update $E_n(f_{i+1}^{(x)}) = E_n(f_i^{(x)})(i = 1, 2, \cdots, p+1)$ from Step 7(c)(v), and remove $E_n(f_{p+2}^{(x)})$.
8. Place $E_{2k-1}(x_{exp})$ in the first row and $E_{2k-1}(y_{exp})$ in the second row, append $(k-1)$ face-down ♣ cards to each side. Apply a pile-shifting shuffle to the columns, then cyclically shift so that ♡ moves to the $(2k-1)$-th column.
9. Apply a conversion protocol to floating-point representation using $E_n(d_i^{(q)})(i = 1, 2, \cdots, p+1)$. The output mantissa $E_n(f_i^{(q)})(i = 1, 2, \cdots, p)$ represents the quotient.
10. Pad the exponent from Step 9 with $(2k - p - 1)$ face-down ♣ cards on both sides, then cyclically shift left by p.
11. Place the exponent from Step 8 with one ♣ on each side in the first row. Place the exponent from Step 10 reversed in the second row. Apply a pile-shifting shuffle to the columns, reveal the second row, and cyclically shift so that ♡ moves to the $2k$-th column. The first row is then output as the exponent.
12. Compute the XOR of the sign parts of x and y using the XOR protocol [5], regarding ♡♣ $= 1$ and ♣♡ $= 0$, and output it as the sign of the quotient.

The above protocol requires $O(pn \log n)$ cards and $O(p^2 \log n)$ shuffles.

References

1. Boer, B.: More efficient match-making and satisfiability *The Five Card Trick*. In: Quisquater, J.-J., Vandewalle, J. (eds.) EUROCRYPT 1989. LNCS, vol. 434, pp. 208–217. Springer, Heidelberg (1990). https://doi.org/10.1007/3-540-46885-4_23
2. Eriguchi, R., Shinagawa, K.: Efficient card-based protocols for basic arithmetic operations. IEICE Trans. Fundam. (2025). https://doi.org/10.1587/transfun.2025CIP0014
3. Miyahara, D., Hayashi, Y.I., Mizuki, T., Sone, H.: Practical card-based implementations of Yao's millionaire protocol. Theor. Comput. Sci. **803**, 207–221 (2020). https://doi.org/10.1016/j.tcs.2019.11.005
4. Mizuki, T., Shizuya, H.: Computational model of card-based cryptographic protocols and its applications. IEICE Trans. Fundam. Electron. Commun. Comput. Sci. **E100.A**(1), 3–11 (2017). https://doi.org/10.1587/transfun.E100.A.3
5. Mizuki, T., Sone, H.: Six-card secure AND and four-card secure XOR. In: Deng, X., Hopcroft, J.E., Xue, J. (eds.) FAW 2009. LNCS, vol. 5598, pp. 358–369. Springer, Heidelberg (2009). https://doi.org/10.1007/978-3-642-02270-8_36
6. Nishimura, A., Hayashi, Y.-I., Mizuki, T., Sone, H.: Pile-shifting scramble for card-based protocols. IEICE Trans. Fundam. Electron. Commun. Comput. Sci. **101**(9), 1494–1502 (2018). https://doi.org/10.1587/transfun.E101.A.1494
7. Odaka, S., Komano, Y.: Card-based arithmetic operations and application to statistical data aggregation. In: SecITC 2024. LNCS, vol. 15595, pp. 118–134. Springer (2025)
8. Odaka, S., Komano, Y.: Card-based arithmetic operations using integer commitments and their application to statistical data aggregation. IEICE Trans. Fundam. (2025). https://doi.org/10.1587/transfun.2025CIP0006
9. Igari, R., Odaka, S., Komano, Y., Mizuki, T.: Digitized integer commitment and addition protocol for card-based cryptography. In: SCIS 2025, 3D2-3 (2025). (in Japanese)
10. Ruangwises, S.: Using five cards to encode each integer in Z/6Z. In: Ryan, P.Y.A., Toma, C. (eds.) SecITC 2021. LNCS, vol. 13195, pp. 165–177. Springer (2021)
11. Ruangwises, S., Itoh, T.: Securely computing the n-variable equality function with $2n$ cards. Theor. Comput. Sci. **887**, 99–110 (2021). https://doi.org/10.1016/j.tcs.2021.07.007
12. Shinagawa, K., et al.: Card-based protocols using regular polygon cards. IEICE Trans. Fundam. Electron. Commun. Comput. Sci. **E100.A**(9), 1900–1909 (2017). https://doi.org/10.1587/transfun.E100.A.1900
13. Mizuki. T., Kuzuma, T., Hirano, T., Oshima, R., Yasuda, M.: Gakmoro: an application of physical secure computation to card game. In: Formenti, E., Manzoni, L. (eds.) Unconventional Computation and Natural Computation. UCNC 2025. LNCS, pp. 344–360. Springer, Cham (2025)
14. Takashima, K., et al.: Card-based protocols for secure ranking computations. Theor. Comput. Sci. **845**, 122–135 (2020). https://doi.org/10.1016/j.tcs.2020.09.008
15. Igari, R., Odaka, S., Komano, Y., Mizuki, T.: Efficient physical ZKP protocols for Hamiltonian cycle problem and traveling salesman problem. IEICE Trans. Fundam. Electron. Commun. Comput. Sci., 2026, to appear

Suken BINGO: An Application of Card-Based Cryptography to Psychological Board Games

Ren Igari[1], Yuichi Komano[1(✉)], and Takaaki Mizuki[2]

[1] Chiba Institute of Technology, 2–17–1 Tsudanuma, Narashino, Japan
yuichi.komano@chibatech.ac.jp

[2] Cyberscience Center, Tohoku University, 6–3 Aramaki-Aza-Aoba, Aoba-ku, Sendai, Japan
mizuki+lncs@tohoku.ac.jp

Abstract. BINGO is a classic game where players compete to complete a line on a 5×5 grid card. Since it typically requires a specialized bingo machine, spontaneous BINGO play is challenging. To overcome this, we introduce Suken BINGO, a new board game that allows players to declare integers verbally, similar to the Japanese hand game Suken, eliminating the need for a bingo machine. Furthermore, we propose Secret Suken BINGO by combining Suken BINGO with card-based cryptography. In this secure variant, players conceal the integers on their BINGO cards throughout the game, which enhances the enjoyment of psychological maneuvering and strategic depth. We then detail the implementation and discuss the security and efficiency of the proposed protocol.

Keywords: BINGO · Suken · card-based cryptography

1 Introduction

BINGO is a classic game played by two or more players using BINGO cards and a dedicated bingo machine. A standard BINGO card features a 5×5 grid, excluding the center square, which is often pre-marked as 'open.' The 24 unique integers written on the card are randomly chosen from the range 1 to 75, typically following the established column rules: $1 \sim 15$ for the leftmost column, $16 \sim 30$ for the second, and so on.

During the game, the bingo machine draws integers from 1 to 75 in a random order. Players mark the drawn numbers on their cards if applicable, and the first player to complete a line (row, column, or diagonal) declares 'BINGO' and wins. However, this traditional game has a significant practical limitation: the mandatory requirement of a specialized bingo machine makes spontaneous or impromptu play difficult.

To find a solution that enables spontaneous play easily, we drew inspiration from *Suken*, a traditional Japanese hand game. In Suken, two players simultaneously extend random numbers of fingers in their right hands and declare an

P. D'Arco and A. Zamfiroiu (Eds.): SecITC 2025, LNCS 16443, pp. 96–115, 2026.
https://doi.org/10.1007/978-3-032-17443-7_6

integer from 0 to 10 verbally. Each player (or a designated judge) then counts the extended fingers of the two players. The player who correctly guesses the sum is the winner. This mechanism demonstrates that a random drawing can be replaced by players' verbal declarations, leading to a game that is highly spontaneous and requires no equipment such as the bingo machine.

This paper introduces two kinds of new psychological games: *Suken BINGO* by combining BINGO with Suken, and *Secret Suken BINGO* by combining Suken BINGO with card-based cryptography.

1.1 Our Contribution

The contributions of this paper are as follows.

- We first propose *Suken BINGO* (Section 3.2), a novel board game designed to address the spontaneity issue of traditional BINGO. By integrating the concept of players' declarations from Suken into BINGO's integer drawing, Suken BINGO eliminates the need for a dedicated bingo machine and can be played anywhere with just BINGO cards.
- Furthermore, we propose *Secret Suken BINGO*, a secure and strategic variant that integrates Suken BINGO with card-based cryptography. In this new variant, the integers on players' BINGO cards are kept secret throughout the game using cryptographic commitments. This concealment transforms the game from a matter of pure luck into a deep strategic challenge, significantly enhancing the enjoyment of psychological maneuvering.
- We also propose another variant of Secret Suken BINGO, *Secret binary Suken BINGO*, to improve the efficiency. We then discuss the security and efficiency of the proposed methods.

The remainder of this paper is organized as follows. Section 1.2 provides an overview of existing research on games applying card-based cryptography. Section 2 introduces the preliminary notations from card-based cryptography required for our proposed games. Section 3 details the rules of Suken BINGO and Secret Suken BINGO. Section 4 then analyzes the security, efficiency, and player experience. Finally, Section 5 concludes this paper.

1.2 Related Works

This section reviews the related works that exemplify the application of card-based cryptography to board games.

Examples in card games include a protocol for creating virtual players in UNO [11], a secret group assignment protocol applicable to Werewolf [1], and a virtual player protocol for the game of Old Maid [13]. In addition, a new game, Gakmoro [7], was created by making use of card-based cryptography.

Furthermore, card-based cryptography has also been applied to games other than card games, such as a protocol that can uniformly and randomly generate problems for the 15-puzzle and Rubik's Cube [12], a protocol that determines the first and second players in shogi or chess based on player preferences [15], a method for enhancing the Hit and Blow game [3], and a method for obtaining new variants of Tagiron [5].

Table 1. Correspondence between Integers and Integer Commitments

integer	integer commitment
0	♡♣♣♣♣♣♣♣♣♣
1	♣♡♣♣♣♣♣♣♣♣
2	♣♣♡♣♣♣♣♣♣♣
3	♣♣♣♡♣♣♣♣♣♣
4	♣♣♣♣♡♣♣♣♣♣
5	♣♣♣♣♣♡♣♣♣♣
6	♣♣♣♣♣♣♡♣♣♣
7	♣♣♣♣♣♣♣♡♣♣
8	♣♣♣♣♣♣♣♣♡♣
9	♣♣♣♣♣♣♣♣♣♡

2 Preliminaries

This section provides preparatory explanations of the cards and card operations utilized in this paper, as well as the concept of Secret Suken BINGO.

2.1 Physical Cards

In this paper, two types of physical cards are used:

Integer Cards: Each card has an integer from 1 to n written on its face, such as [1][2][3] $\cdots$ [n] . The reverse side of every card has the same pattern [?] .

Colored Cards: Each card has a ♣ or ♡ symbol on its face, and the back of every card has the same pattern [?] .

We use the notation

$$\underset{i}{\boxed{?}}$$

to denote a face-down integer card whose face is [i] for an integer i, $1 \leq i \leq n$.

2.2 Commitments

This section describes integer representations using cards: integer commitments, multi-digit integer commitments, and binary integer commitments [6].

Integer Commitment: An integer $i \in \{0, 1, 2, \cdots, k-1\}$ is represented using $k-1$ ♣ cards and one ♡ card. Table 1 summarizes the integer commitments to integers from 0 to 9. The face-down card sequence is called an *integer commitment*. The integer commitment is denoted by ? ? ··· ? or ?‖ , and is written as $E_k(i)$.

Multi-Digit Integer Commitment: A *multi-digit integer commitment* is a representation of an integer k as an n-digit decimal number ($n > \log_{10} k$), where each digit is encoded using an integer commitment above:

n-th digit		2nd digit	1st digit
?‖	···	?‖	?‖ .

By using multi-digit integer commitments, an integer k can be represented using $10n$ cards, resulting in a card complexity of $O(\log_{10} k)$.

In Secret Suken BINGO, bundles of cards (*i.e.*, multi-digit integer commitments) are used to conceal (i) integers from 0 to 74 placed on the BINGO card grid and (ii) the sum of the numbers declared by the players, which is in the range of 0 to 79.

In Secret Suken BINGO, the maximum integer is 79, requiring $n = 2$ decimal digits. Since the integer commitment to the first digit (0 to 7) requires eight cards, a total of 18 cards is sufficient to represent an integer from 0 to 79.

Binary Integer Commitment: We call the encoding scheme that represents bit 0 as a sequence of cards with ♣ ♡ flipped and bit 1 as a sequence with ♡ ♣ flipped *a binary commitment*. Furthermore, we define *a binary integer commitment* as the method that represents an integer k as an n-bit binary number ($n > \log_2 k$) using the binary commitments as

n-th bit		2nd bit	1st bit
? ?	···	? ?	? ? .

Later, we propose a variant of Secret Suken BINGO, named Secret Binary Suken BINGO, that reduces the number of cards by utilizing the binary integer commitments.

2.3 Basic Operations

Next, we explain the card operations which are used in Secret Suken BINGO.

Pile-Scramble Shuffle: A *pile-scramble shuffle* [4] is an operation that shuffles several piles of cards of the same size (e.g., by securing them with rubber bands).

As an example, suppose that we have two lines of n face-down cards as follows:

$$\begin{array}{cccc} 1 & 2 & & n \\ \boxed{?} & \boxed{?} & \cdots & \boxed{?} \\ \boxed{?} & \boxed{?} & \cdots & \boxed{?} \end{array},$$

where the numbers above the cards represent indices for convenience.

Considering each card and its underlying card as a pile, we apply a pile-scramble shuffle to the n piles, then the transition is as follows:

$$\left[\begin{array}{c|c|c|c} \boxed{?} & \boxed{?} & \cdots & \boxed{?} \\ \boxed{?} & \boxed{?} & \cdots & \boxed{?} \end{array}\right] \rightarrow \begin{array}{cccc} r^{-1}(1) & r^{-1}(2) & & r^{-1}(n) \\ \boxed{?} & \boxed{?} & \cdots & \boxed{?} \\ \boxed{?} & \boxed{?} & \cdots & \boxed{?} \end{array},$$

where $r \in S_n$ is a uniformly distributed random permutation generated by the pile-scramble shuffle, and S_n denotes the symmetric group of degree n.

Pile-Shifting Shuffle: A *Pile-shifting shuffle* [9,14] is an operation that cyclically shifts piles of the same size uniformly at random.

As an example, consider two commitments consisting of k cards each, arranged face-down as follows:

$$\begin{array}{cccc} 0 & 1 & & k-1 \\ \boxed{?} & \boxed{?} & \cdots & \boxed{?} \\ 0 & 1 & & k-1 \\ \boxed{?} & \boxed{?} & \cdots & \boxed{?} \end{array},$$

where the numbers on the cards are used as convenient indices indicating their positions.

Considering the top and bottom cards as a single pile and applying a pile-shifting shuffle, then the transition is as follows:

$$\left\langle\begin{array}{c|c|c|c} 0 & 1 & & k-1 \\ \boxed{?} & \boxed{?} & \cdots & \boxed{?} \\ 0 & 1 & & k-1 \\ \boxed{?} & \boxed{?} & \cdots & \boxed{?} \end{array}\right\rangle \rightarrow \begin{array}{cccc} -r \bmod k & 1-r \bmod k & & k-1-r \bmod k \\ \boxed{?} & \boxed{?} & \cdots & \boxed{?} \\ -r \bmod k & 1-r \bmod k & & k-1-r \bmod k \\ \boxed{?} & \boxed{?} & \cdots & \boxed{?} \end{array},$$

where r is a uniformly random integer generated by the pile-shifting shuffle.

Addition of Commitments: Each of Secret Suken BINGO and Secret Binary Suken BINGO requires an addition protocol for multi-digit integer commitments and binary integer commitments, respectively. The idea to construct such addition protocols is similar to an addition of integers: for each digit or bit, we compute a sum of integer commitments or binary commitments with a carry. Due to the space limit, we omit the detail here and give a protocol in Appendices A.1 and A.2.

Equality Check of Commitments: Each of Secret Suken BINGO and Secret Binary Suken BINGO requires an equality check protocol for multi-digit integer commitments and binary integer commitments, respectively. The idea to construct such equality check protocols is similar to an equality check of integer commitments. Due to the space limit, we omit the detail here and give a protocol in Appendix B.

3 Suken BINGO and Variants

In this section, we first explain our idea to construct Suken BINGO and Secret Suken BINGO. Then, we propose Suken BINGO, Secret Suken BINGO, and Secret Binary Suken BINGO.

3.1 Our Idea

Conventional BINGO cards typically feature integers from 1 to 75. In contrast, Suken BINGO and its variants described in this section utilize cards with integers ranging from 0 to 74, excluding one number[1]. In this configuration, the integers on the BINGO cards are constrained to the ranges 0-14, 15-29, 30-44, 45-59, and 60-74 for the leftmost column and subsequent columns, respectively. Furthermore, we define $\mathcal{D}$ as a set of numbers declared by a player (called a saboteur, later); in this paper, we assume that $\mathcal{D} = \{0, 1, 2, 3, 4\}$.

Suken BINGO: Suken BINGO involves two distinct players: a progressor (P_i) and a saboteur (P_j). The progressor is a player who is trying to mark an integer on his own BINGO card by declaring an integer $d_i \in \{0, 1, \cdots, 74\}$. The saboteur is a player who obstructs the progressor from marking an integer on the progressor's BINGO card. For simplicity, this paper assumes only one saboteur, though we can assume two or more saboteurs. The saboteur declares an integer d_j from $\mathcal{D}$.

Subsequently, each player marks the square on their card that contains the sum $d_i + d_j (\text{mod } 75)$. This process is repeated by alternating the roles of the progressor and the saboteur. As in traditional BINGO, players compete to be the first to complete a line (row, column, or diagonal) on their card.

Secret Suken BINGO: Secret Suken BINGO is constructed by placing multi-digit integer commitments corresponding to integers from 0 to 74 in each square of the Suken BINGO card. In this variant, the progressor and the saboteur declare integers by placing the corresponding multi-digit integer commitments on the table. The progressor or saboteur runs an addition protocol to sum up the commitments and, with an equality check protocol, checks whether the sum is equal to each of the commitments placed in their BINGO card.

[1] We can use standard BINGO cards numbered 1 to 75 by defining the value to be marked as the sum of the players' declared integers modulo 75, plus one.

Since the declared integers are concealed throughout the game using these commitments, Secret Suken BINGO significantly enhances the psychological maneuvering compared to Suken BINGO by preventing players from knowing the integers on their opponents' cards.

Secret Binary Suken BINGO: This variant utilizes BINGO cards where each square contains a binary integer commitment. For efficiency, the maximum integer value assigned to a square is set to $2^n - 1$ for some integer n. The candidate maximum values are $15 = 2^4 - 1, 31 = 2^5 - 1$, and $127 = 2^7 - 1$. However, 15 and 31 are considered too small, which could lead to a premature game end and diminish enjoyment. Conversely, a maximum value of 127 is deemed too large, making BINGO difficult to achieve. Therefore, we assume a maximum card value of 63 (*i.e.*, $n = 6$). A key difference is that while conventional BINGO and Secret Suken BINGO utilize a 5×5 grid card, Secret Binary Suken BINGO requires a smaller grid card.

When integers from 0 to 63 are placed on a 5×5 grid card, the probability of a square being marked, assuming random placement and declaration, is $\frac{25}{64}$. This probability is higher than that of conventional BINGO or Secret Suken BINGO ($\approx \frac{1}{3}$), potentially diminishing the player's enjoyment. This is because, in Secret Suken BINGO and Secret Binary Suken BINGO, the progressor declares integers to target holes on their own card, whereas the saboteur declares small integers to prevent this. Consequently, the declarations are not random for the progressor, unlike standard BINGO. Conversely, saboteurs may unintentionally mark squares on their own card. Thus, to maintain players' enjoyments, the size of BINGO card is reduced to a 4×4 grid.

Specifically, Secret Binary Suken BINGO utilizes a 4×4 matrix of binary integer commitments ranging from 0 to 63. Hereinafter, we call this matrix *a* 4×4 *grid card* or *BINGO card* simply. Under the assumption of random placement and declaration, the probability of a hole appearing is $\frac{1}{4}$. Although this probability is lower than that of conventional BINGO or Secret Suken BINGO, it is deemed acceptable as it preserves the satisfaction of marking a square.

In Secret Binary Suken BINGO, the progressor and the saboteur compute the remainder of the sum of their declared integers modulo 64. This remainder is computed efficiently through the bitwise addition of the two binary integer commitments by ignoring the carry to the 7th bit.

3.2 Suken BINGO

This section proposes Suken BINGO. As explained in Section 3.1, players use standard BINGO cards in Suken BINGO. The procedure is as follows.

1. Distribute one 5×5 grid card to each of players P_1 and P_2.
2. Assign initial roles. Assume that the progressor is P_1 and the saboteur is P_2.
3. Repeat the following steps until either player declares 'BINGO'.
   (a) The progressor and saboteur simultaneously declare integers $d_1 \in \{0, 1, \cdots, 74\}$ and $d_2 \in \mathcal{D}$.

(b) Calculate $d = d_1 + d_2 \bmod 75$ and mark a square that match d on their BINGO cards.
(c) If the mark is fourth one in a line (row, column, or diagonal), declare 'Reach.'
(d) Else if the mark is fifth one in a line (row, column, or diagonal), declare 'BINGO'. If only one player declares 'BINGO,' she wins. If both players declare 'BINGO' simultaneously, the game ends in a draw.
(e) Otherwise, switch the roles and go to the next iteration.

3.3 Secret Suken BINGO

Secret Suken BINGO is a variant of Suken BINGO that enhances the enjoyment of psychological maneuvering and strategic depth.

In Secret Suken BINGO, players arrange multi-digit integer commitments from 0 to 74 in each square of the Suken BINGO card. During the game, the progressor and saboteur place multi-digit integer commitments, instead of declaring integers as in Suken BINGO. Then, the progressor and saboteur add them by using the addition protocol and check whether their BINGO cards contain the same commitment as the sum by using the equality check protocol.

Note that, allowing players to freely arrange multi-digit integer commitments on their BINGO cards would degrade the enjoyment of the game. Suppose that a player arranges four multi-digit commitments corresponding to integers 10 through 14 in the first column. If the player (as a progressor) places a commitment corresponding to 10, the progressor can mark a square on own BINGO card, regardless of which commitment to integers 0 through 4 the saboteur places. Therefore, Secret Suken BINGO requires a step to randomly arrange multi-digit integer commitments on BINGO cards.

The procedure of Secret Suken BINGO is as follows.

1. Let players P_1 and P_2 each create their own 5×5 grid cards (BINGO cards) as follows. In this step, each player creates their own BINGO card where integers (represented by multi-digit integer commitments) of squares on the card are known only by the card holder (that is, each player has no information about the integers of squares on the opponent's card).
   (a) Player P_1 arranges seventy-five multi-digit integer commitments corresponding to the integers from 0 to 74 in a single line. Apply a pile-scramble shuffle. Place the leftmost twenty-five multi-digit integer commitments in a 5×5 matrix. At this point, P_1 privately looks at the commitments to check the integers on P_1's BINGO card grid without showing them to P_2. Arrange eighteen times fifty cards of the remaining fifty multi-digit integer commitments in a line. Then, apply a pile-scramble shuffle to the card sequence and turn them over to be face-up. These free cards are used in the next step.
   (b) Player P_2 adds fifty $\boxed{\heartsuit}$ cards and sixteen times twenty-five $\boxed{\clubsuit}$ cards to the free cards obtained in Step 1(a). Then, P_2 prepares P_2's BINGO card in the same manner as Step 1(a).

   (c) Player P_i places a face-up ♣ next to each multi-digit integer commitment arranged on the 5×5 grid card which indicates that the square is not marked.
2. Let P_1 be the progressor and P_2 be the saboteur.
3. Repeat the following steps until either player declares 'BINGO.'
   (a) The progressor and saboteur select an integer d_1 from $0 \sim 74$ and an integer d_2 from $0 \sim 4$, respectively. Place the corresponding multi-digit integer commitments on the table.
   (b) Apply the addition protocol in Appendix A.1 to obtain a multi-digit integer commitment corresponding to $d = d_1 + d_2 \in \{0, 1, 2, \cdots, 79\}$. Then, using the protocol described in Appendix C, compute a multi-digit integer commitment to $d \bmod 75$.
   (c) Each of P_1 and P_2 applies the equality check protocol to check whether a multi-digit integer commitment in a square with an indicator ♣ is equal to the multi-digit integer commitment to $d \bmod 75$ as follows:
      i. P_i $(i = 1, 2)$ checks the equality of the multi-digit integer commitments using the equality check protocol described in Appendix B. Note that, due to the properties of the protocol, the original two multi-digit integer commitments are recovered after the equality check and are used in the subsequent steps.
      ii. If the two multi-digit integer commitments are identical, replace ♣ in that square with ♡ which indicates that the square is marked. Otherwise, place the recovered multi-digit integer commitment back to the square next to the indicator ♣ . Then, return to the previous step and check the equality of a multi-digit integer commitment on the next square with the multi-digit integer commitment to $d \bmod 75$.
   (d) If the equality check in Step 3(c)(i) leads a new line (row, column, or diagonal) where four indicators out of five squares are ♡ , the card holder declares 'Reach.'
   (e) If the equality check in Step 3(c)(i) leads a new line (row, column, or diagonal) where every indicator in the five square is ♡ , the card holder declares 'BINGO.' If only one player declares 'BINGO,' that player wins. If both players declare 'BINGO' simultaneously, end the game in a draw.
   (f) Otherwise, switch the roles and go to the next iteration.

3.4 Secret Binary Suken BINGO

In this section, we propose a variant of Secret Suken BINGO, named a *Secret Binary Suken BINGO*, that reduces the number of colored cards from Secret Suken BINGO. As explained in Section 3.1, this is achieved by arranging binary integer commitments on the players' BINGO cards instead of multi-digit integer commitments.

The procedure of Secret Binary Suken BINGO is as follows.

1. Let players P_1 and P_2 each create their own BINGO cards, so that each player knows the integers corresponding to the squares on own BINGO card and cannot know the integers corresponding to the squares on the opponent's BINGO card, as follows.
   (a) Player P_1 arranges sixty-four binary integer commitments corresponding to the integers from 0 to 63 in a single line. Apply a pile-scramble shuffle. Place the leftmost sixteen binary integer commitments in a 4×4 matrix. At this point, P_1 privately looks at the commitments to check the integers on $P_1's$ BINGO card grid without showing them to P_2. Arrange twelve times forty-eight cards of the remaining forty-eight binary integer commitments in a line. Then, apply a pile-scramble shuffle to the card sequence and turn them over to be face-up. These free cards are used in the next step.
   (b) Player P_2 adds six times sixteen ♣ and six times sixteen ♡ cards to the free cards obtained in Step 1(a). Then, P_2 prepares P_2's BINGO card in the same manner as Step 1(a).
   (c) Player P_i places a face-up ♣ next to each binary integer commitment arranged on the 4×4 grid card which indicates that the square is not marked.
2. Let P_1 be the progressor and P_2 be the saboteur.
3. Repeat the following steps until either player declares 'BINGO.'
   (a) The progressor and saboteur select an integer d_1 from $0 \sim 63$ and an integer d_2 from $0 \sim 4$, respectively. Place the corresponding binary integer commitments on the table.
   (b) Apply the addition protocol in Appendix A.2 with ignoring carry to the 7th bit, which brings a binary integer commitment corresponding to $d = (d_1 + d_2 \bmod 64) \in \{0, 1, 2, \cdots, 63\}$.
   (c) Each of P_1 and P_2 applies the equality check protocol to check whether a binary integer commitment in its own square with an indicator ♣ is equal to the binary integer commitment as follows:
      i. P_i $(i = 1, 2)$ checks the equality of the binary integer commitments using the equality check protocol described in Appendix B. Note that, due to the properties of the protocol, the original two binary integer commitments are recovered after the equality check and are used in the subsequent steps.
      ii. If the two binary integer commitments are identical, replace ♣ in that square with ♡ which indicates that the square is marked. Otherwise, place the recovered binary integer commitment back to the square next to the indicator ♣ . Then, return to the previous step and check the equality of a binary integer commitment on the next square with the binary integer commitment.
   (d) If the equality check in Step 3(c)(i) leads a new line (row, column, or diagonal) where three indicators out of four squares are ♡ , the card holder declares 'Reach.'
   (e) If the equality check in Step 3(c)(i) leads a new line (row, column, or diagonal) where every indicator in the four square is ♡ , the card holder

declares 'BINGO.' If only one player declares 'BINGO,' that player wins. If both players declare 'BINGO' simultaneously, end the game in a draw.

(f) Otherwise, switch the roles and go to the next iteration.

4 Discussion

Let us discuss the security and efficiency of Secret Suken BINGO and Secret Binary Suken BINGO. The discussion on the security and efficiency of Secret Suken BINGO is similar to that on Secret Binary Suken BINGO. Therefore, in this section, we only discuss the security and efficiency of Secret Binary Suken BINGO and compare it with Secret Suken BINGO.

4.1 Security

This section discusses the security of Secret Binary Suken BINGO for integrity and confidentiality. The integrity means that, if players follow the rule of game, the winner of the game is correctly determined. On the other hand, the confidentiality means that information on the squares other than those with holes during game execution[2] does not leak.

Integrity: In Secret Binary Suken BINGO, the card arrangement in Step 1(a) ensures that each square contains a binary integer commitment corresponding to a distinct integer (that is, it is impossible to place identical binary integer commitments in multiple squares). With BINGO cards arranged in this manner, card-based cryptographic protocols, such as addition and equality check protocols, force players to execute the game correctly. Furthermore, by making status of each square visible, the winner of a game can be correctly determined.

Confidentiality: In Secret Binary Suken BINGO, the addition of declared integers and the equality check are executed using card-based cryptographic protocols. The security of these protocols guarantees the confidentiality of the integers for the unmarked squares of the BINGO card.

4.2 Efficiency

We then discuss the efficiency of Secret Binary Suken BINGO.

The number of cards required in Secret Binary Suken BINGO is $12 \times 64 + 12 \times 16$ cards[3] in Step 1. Therefore, when the number of players is two, 960 cards are required.

[2] In Secret Binary Suken BINGO, if a square of a saboteur's BINGO card is marked, the progressor can know that the integer corresponding to that square is close to the integer declared by the progressor (*i.e.*, within the range of the declared number plus 4).

[3] For the equality check of the two binary integer commitments in Step 3, the colored cards discarded in Step 1(a) can be reused instead of number cards.

The number of shuffles required in Secret Binary Suken BINGO is 2× (number of players) in Step 1, 36 in Step 3(b), and 13× (number of squares to check) × (number of players) in Step 3(c)(i). Step 3 is repeated until the game ends, and since the number of squares to check is at most 16, the total number of shuffles is at most $4 + 452\times$ (number of iterations).

4.3 Comparison with Secret Suken BINGO

Table 2 compares Secret Binary Suken BINGO and Secret Suken BINGO.

Table 2. Comparison of Secret Suken BINGO and Secret Binary Suken BINGO

game	grid	integers	commitments	cards	shuffles
Secret Suken BINGO	5×5	0-74	multi-digit integer	1800	$4 + 264\ell$
Secret Binary Suken BINGO	4×4	0-63	binary integer	960	$4 + 452\ell'$

In Table 2, "grid" indicates the size of the BINGO card, "integers" indicates the range of integers placed on the BINGO card, and "commitments" indicates the representation of integers on the BINGO card. In the last two columns, "cards" indicates the number of cards required in each game executed by two players, and "shuffles" indicates the number of shuffles performed during the game. Here, ℓ and ℓ' represent the number of iterations in the integer declaration in Secret Suken BINGO and Secret Binary Suken BINGO, respectively.

Although comparison is difficult due to the differences in BINGO card size and integer ranges, Secret Binary Suken BINGO can reduce both the number of cards and shuffles compared to Secret Suken BINGO.

5 Conclusion

In this paper, we proposed Suken BINGO and its variants, Secret Suken BINGO and Secret Binary Suken BINGO. Among them, Secret Suken BINGO and Secret Binary Suken BINGO are based on card-based cryptography which enhance the enjoyment of psychological maneuvering and strategic depth. We presented the procedures of these games and discussed their security and efficiency. Constructing efficient protocols such as equality check in batch is one of our future works.

Acknowledgements. We thank the anonymous reviewers, whose comments have helped us improve the presentation of the paper. We also thank Yuji Suga for his fruitful comments on an earlier version of our paper. This work was supported by Grant-in-Aid for Scientific Research (JP23H00479, JP24K14951, and JP24K02938).

A Details of Addition Protocols

In this section, let us give details of addition protocols for multi-digit integer commitments and binary integer commitments.

A.1 Addition Protocol for Multi-Digit Integer Commitments

Recently, Igari et al. [2,16] proposed an addition protocol for multi-digit integer commitments. From two multi-digit integer commitments $\{E_{10}(d_j^{(x)})\}$ and $\{E_{10}(d_j^{(y)})\}$, their protocol computes a multi-digit integer commitment to the sum, $\{E_{10}(d_j^{(x+y)})\}$, as follows.

1. Repeat the following steps for $j = 0, 1, 2, \cdots, s-1$, where we assume s-digit integer commitments as input.
   (a) Put ten $\boxed{\clubsuit}$ cards to the right of each of $(j+1)$-th piles $E_{10}(d_j^{(x)})$ and $E_{10}(d_j^{(y)})$. The resulting piles are $E_{20}(d_j^{(x)})$ and $E_{20}(d_j^{(y)})$. When $j > 0$, put eighteen $\boxed{\clubsuit}$ cards right to the sequence of cards $E_2(c_{j-1})$, obtained in the $(j-1)$-th iteration as a commitment to a carry $c_{j-1} \in \{0, 1\}$, to generate $E_{20}(c_{j-1})$.
   (b) Compute the sum of commitments[4] $E_{20}(d_j^{(x)})$, $E_{20}(d_j^{(y)})$, and $E_{20}(c_{j-1})$, obtained in Step 1(a). Then, place the leftmost and rightmost ten cards of the result in the first and second rows, respectively. After that, rearrange cards in each row in the reverse order:

$$\overset{0}{\boxed{?}}\overset{1}{\boxed{?}}\overset{2}{\boxed{?}}\cdots\overset{17}{\boxed{?}}\overset{18}{\boxed{?}}\overset{19}{\boxed{?}} \rightarrow \begin{array}{c}\overset{0}{\boxed{?}}\overset{1}{\boxed{?}}\cdots\overset{8}{\boxed{?}}\overset{9}{\boxed{?}}\\ \overset{10}{\boxed{?}}\overset{11}{\boxed{?}}\cdots\overset{18}{\boxed{?}}\overset{19}{\boxed{?}}\end{array} \rightarrow \begin{array}{c}\overset{9}{\boxed{?}}\overset{8}{\boxed{?}}\cdots\overset{1}{\boxed{?}}\overset{0}{\boxed{?}}\\ \overset{19}{\boxed{?}}\overset{18}{\boxed{?}}\cdots\overset{11}{\boxed{?}}\overset{10}{\boxed{?}}\end{array}.$$

   (c) Place $\boxed{\heartsuit}$ and $\boxed{\clubsuit}$ to the right of the two rows as a new column. Then, turn over these face-up cards:

$$\begin{array}{c}\overset{9}{\boxed{?}}\overset{8}{\boxed{?}}\cdots\overset{1}{\boxed{?}}\overset{0}{\boxed{?}}\boxed{\heartsuit}\\ \overset{19}{\boxed{?}}\overset{18}{\boxed{?}}\cdots\overset{11}{\boxed{?}}\overset{10}{\boxed{?}}\boxed{\clubsuit}\end{array} \rightarrow \begin{array}{c}\overset{9}{\boxed{?}}\overset{8}{\boxed{?}}\cdots\overset{1}{\boxed{?}}\overset{0}{\boxed{?}}\boxed{?}\\ \overset{19}{\boxed{?}}\overset{18}{\boxed{?}}\cdots\overset{11}{\boxed{?}}\overset{10}{\boxed{?}}\boxed{?}\end{array}.$$

   (d) Apply a pile-scramble shuffle:

$$\left[\begin{array}{c}\overset{9}{\boxed{?}}\overset{8}{\boxed{?}}\cdots\overset{1}{\boxed{?}}\overset{0}{\boxed{?}}\boxed{?}\\ \hline \overset{19}{\boxed{?}}\overset{18}{\boxed{?}}\cdots\overset{11}{\boxed{?}}\overset{10}{\boxed{?}}\boxed{?}\end{array}\right] \rightarrow \begin{array}{c}\boxed{?}\boxed{?}\cdots\boxed{?}\boxed{?}\boxed{?}\\ \boxed{?}\boxed{?}\cdots\boxed{?}\boxed{?}\boxed{?}\end{array}.$$

   (e) Put $E_{10}(0)$ as the third row and turn it over:

$$\begin{array}{l}\boxed{?}\boxed{?}\cdots\boxed{?}\boxed{?}\boxed{?}\\ \boxed{?}\boxed{?}\cdots\boxed{?}\boxed{?}\boxed{?}\\ \boxed{\heartsuit}\boxed{\clubsuit}\cdots\boxed{\clubsuit}\boxed{\clubsuit}\end{array} \rightarrow \begin{array}{l}\boxed{?}\boxed{?}\cdots\boxed{?}\boxed{?}\boxed{?}\\ \boxed{?}\boxed{?}\cdots\boxed{?}\boxed{?}\boxed{?}\\ \boxed{?}\boxed{?}\cdots\boxed{?}\boxed{?}\end{array}.$$

[4] For $j = 0$, the addition of $E_{20}(c_{j-1})$ is skipped.

(f) Apply a pile-shifting shuffle to the left ten columns:

$$\left\langle\!\left\langle \begin{array}{cccccc} ? & ? & \cdots & ? & ? \\ ? & ? & \cdots & ? & ? \\ ? & ? & \cdots & ? & ? \end{array} \right\rangle\!\right\rangle \begin{array}{c} ? \\ ? \\ \end{array} \rightarrow \begin{array}{cccccc} ? & ? & \cdots & ? & ? & ? \\ ? & ? & \cdots & ? & ? & ? \\ ? & ? & \cdots & ? & ? & \end{array}.$$

(g) Turn over the leftmost ten cards in the first and second rows. Note that one of the face-up cards is $\heartsuit$ and the others are $\clubsuit$'s. Then, shift the left ten columns cyclically so that $\heartsuit$ is in the 10-th column. As a result, the face-down cards in the third row become a $(j+1)$-th digit of commitment to $x+y$. Therefore, output the commitment in the third row as the $(j+1)$-th pile of the result.
Moreover, among the first and second rows, rearrange the rightmost card of the row including face-up $\heartsuit$ and the rightmost card of the other row into a two-card sequence from left to right. Then, forward the sequence as a carry, $E_2(c_j)$, to the addition of $(j+1)$-th digit. In the following example, the rightmost card in the second row and the rightmost card in the first row are the first and second cards from the left of $E_2(c_j)$, respectively:

$$\begin{array}{cccccc} \clubsuit & \clubsuit & \cdots & \clubsuit & \clubsuit & ? \\ \clubsuit & \clubsuit & \cdots & \heartsuit & \clubsuit & ? \\ ? & ? & \cdots & ? & ? & \end{array} \rightarrow \begin{array}{cccccc} \clubsuit & \clubsuit & \cdots & \clubsuit & \clubsuit & ? \\ \clubsuit & \clubsuit & \cdots & \clubsuit & \heartsuit & ? \\ ? & ? & \cdots & ? & ? & \end{array} \rightarrow \begin{array}{cc} ? & ? \end{array}.$$

The face-up cards can be reused in the following steps.

2. Put eight $\clubsuit$'s to the right of $E_2(c_{s-1})$, which is obtained as the $(s-1)$-th carry. Then, output it as the $(s+1)$-th digit of the commitment to $x+y$.

We can compare integers encoded in the multi-digit integer commitment as follows. Assume that we want to determine whether $x \geq y$ for two multi-digit integer commitments to x and y. Each of commitments consists of s piles of ten colored cards, $E_{10}(d_i)$ where $i \in \{0, 1, \cdots, s-1\}$ and d_i is a digit of x or y. To compare x and y, we first rearrange the order of each $E_{10}(d_i^{(y)})$ in the reverse order. Note that the resulting piles represent a (commitment to) 9's complement of y. Then, we add it to a multi-digit integer commitment to one (with s piles of ten colored cards) to obtain a (commitment to) 10's complement of y. After that, we add it to a multi-digit integer commitment to x and check whether the topmost pile (final carry) is $E_{10}(0)$ or $E_{10}(1)$. If it is $E_{10}(1)$, then $x \geq y$ holds; otherwise, $x < y$ holds.

A.2 Addition Protocol for Binary Integer Commitments

Mizuki et al. [6] proposed a half-adder to efficiently compute the sum of two binary commitments and a full adder using this half-adder to compute the sum of two binary integer commitments with a carry.

Remember that $\clubsuit\heartsuit$ and $\heartsuit\clubsuit$ represent 0 and 1, respectively. The half-adder which takes bit commitments of two bits a, b as input is constructed as follows.

1. Copy the bit commitment of b using the copy protocol [8]. This requires two each of ♣ and ♡ cards and one shuffle.
2. Arrange the four bit commitments corresponding to a, b, b, and 0 sequentially in a single row.
3. Rearrange the cards so that the second card moves to the fifth position, the third to the second, the fourth to the sixth, the fifth to the third, and the sixth to the fourth.
4. Divide the eight cards into two groups of left and right four cards and apply a pile-shifting shuffle by regarding each of the left and right four cards as a pile.
5. Rearrange the cards so that the second card moves to the third position, the third to the fifth, the fourth to the sixth, the fifth to the second, and the sixth to the fourth.
6. Turn over the two leftmost cards.
7. If the face-up cards are ♣♡ , return the third and fourth cards as $a \oplus b$ (sum), and the seventh and eighth cards as $a \wedge b$ (carry). If the face-up cards are ♡♣ , swap the order of the third and fourth cards and return $a \oplus b$ (sum), and the fifth and sixth cards as $a \wedge b$ (carry).

The above half-adder requires four additional cards and two shuffle operations.

A full adder that takes a bit commitment of a carry c from lower bits and bit commitments to two bits a, b as inputs is constructed as follows. Here, $s' = (a \oplus b) \oplus c$ is the sum of its bits including the carry c from the lower bits, and $c' = (a \wedge b) \vee ((a \oplus b) \wedge c)$ represents a carry to the upper bits.

1. Using the aforementioned half-adder, compute the bit commitments to $a \wedge b$ and $a \oplus b$. Apply a shuffle to the remaining two face-down cards and turn them over. These cards are used as free cards later.
2. Input the bit commitments to $a \oplus b$ and c into the aforementioned half-adder, and obtain the bit commitments of $(a \oplus b) \wedge c$ and $s' = (a \oplus b) \oplus c$.
3. Using the OR protocol [8] (which is obtained by inverting the inputs and outputs of the AND protocol), compute the bitwise OR of the bit commitments to $a \wedge b$ and $(a \oplus b) \wedge c$, which is the bit commitment to c'.

The above full adder requires four additional cards and six shuffling operations.

B Detail of Equality Check Protocol

This section describes details of the equality check protocols for two sets of multi-digit integer commitments or binary integer commitments[5].

In Secret Suken BINGO or Secret Binary Suken BINGO, for each square in the grid card, we determine whether a multi-digit integer commitment or a

[5] While Ruangwises et al.'s overwriting protocol [10] can achieve this, we present a more direct and simple protocol here.

binary integer commitment to an integer on the square matches a multi-digit integer commitment or a binary integer commitment to the sum d, respectively.

If they do not match, we then check the equality between a multi-digit integer commitment or a binary integer commitment in the next square and a multi-digit integer commitment or a binary integer commitment to the sum d, respectively. That is, we require an equality check protocol which restores its input.

Let us first give an equality check protocol for two multi-digit integer commitments.

1. Arrange eighteen integer cards [1], [2], [3], ... from left to right and turn them over.
2. Arrange two sets of eighteen cards for two multi-digit integer commitments in two rows (rows 2 and 3) below the face-down integer cards.
3. Apply a pile-scramble shuffle to the cards in these three rows, by regarding each column of three cards as a pile.
4. Turn over the cards in the third row.
5. Place eighteen cards of the same color as the third row in the fourth row.
6. Place eighteen cards of a different color from the fourth row in the fifth row.
7. Turn over cards in rows 3 to 5.
8. Apply a pile-scramble shuffle to the cards in the five rows, by regarding each column of five cards as a pile.
9. Turn over the cards in the second row and specify two columns where [♡] appears in the second row.
10. Create two bit commitments by arranging two cards in the fourth and fifth rows from left to right in the specified columns. One of the commitments is [♡][♣] or [♣][♡] if tens digits are identical or not, and the other is [♡][♣] or [♣][♡] if ones digits are identical or not.
11. Apply a bitwise AND protocol [8] to the two bit commitments and turn them over. If two multi-digit integer commitments to be compared are identical, they are [♡][♣] ; otherwise, they are [♣][♡] .
12. Apply a pile-scramble shuffle to the cards in the upper three rows.
13. Turn over the cards in the first row.
14. Rearrange the piles of the cards, by regarding three cards in each column of upper three rows as a pile, so that the integer cards in the first row are in ascending order. Then, two multi-digit integer commitments are restored in the second and third rows.
15. Rearrange the cards of the fourth and fifth rows in a line and apply a pile-scramble shuffle. Then, turn them over, which become free cards.

Let us then give an equality check protocol for two binary integer commitments to integers x and y.

1. Arrange twenty-four integer cards [1], [2], [3], ... from left to right and turn them over.

2. Arrange two sets of twelve cards for two binary integer commitments to integers from 0 to 63 into a line in the second row below the face-down integer cards.
3. Apply a pile-scramble shuffle to the cards in these two rows, by regarding each column of two cards as a pile.
4. Turn over the cards in the second row.
5. Place twenty-four cards of the same color as the second row in the third row.
6. Apply a pile-scramble shuffle to the cards in the three rows, by regarding each column of three cards as a pile.
7. Turn over the cards in the first row.
8. Rearrange the piles of the cards, by regarding three cards in each column as a pile, so that the integer cards in the first row are in ascending order. Then, two binary integer commitments are restored in the second row.
9. By using the four-card XOR protocol [8], compute six bit commitments to XOR values of the first two cards (a bit commitment for the first bit of x) and the thirteen to fourteen cards (a bit commitment for the first bit of y), the third to forth cards (a bit commitment for the second bit of x) and the fifteen to sixteen cards (a bit commitment for the second bit of y), and so on.
10. Rearrange two cards of each of six commitments to XOR values in the reverse order.
11. By using the AND protocol [8] five times, compute the AND of the above six rearranged commitments. If two binary integer commitments to be compared are identical, they are ♡♣ ; otherwise, they are ♣♡ .

Instead of the integer cards in the above protocols, we can use a sequence of colored cards corresponding to integers, such as integer commitments, multi-digit integer commitments, or binary integer commitments.

C Secure Reduction Protocol with Modulo 75

In Secret Suken BINGO proposed in Section 3.3, we need to compute a multi-digit integer commitment to $d \bmod 75$ where d is in $\{0, 1, 2, \cdots, 79\}$. Note that the multi-digit integer commitment consists of the tens digit integer $d_1 \in \{0, 1, 2, \cdots, 7\}$ which is represented by $E_8(d_1)$ using eight colored cards, and the ones digit integer $d_0 \in \{0, 1, 2, \cdots, 9\}$ which is represented by $E_{10}(d_0)$ using ten colored cards. Our reduction protocol with modulo 75 is performed as follows:

1. Arrange integer cards from 1 to 14 in order from left to right.
2. Add six ♣ cards to the right of the integer commitment $E_8(d_1)$ to form $E_{14}(d_1)$, then place it below the integer cards arranged in Step 1 from left to right.

3. Divide the integer commitment $E_{10}(d_0)$ into two halves of five cards each (upper and lower). Add two [♣] cards to the right of each half. Then, place the lower five cards (with two [♣] cards added to their right) as the third row of cards, each below the integer cards 1 through 7. Similarly, place the upper five cards (with two [♣] cards added to their right) as the third row cards under the integer cards 8 through 14.
4. As the fourth row cards, place [♣] under the integer card 1 and [♡] under the integer card 8. These cards will later indicate whether the tens digit is seven or not.
5. As the fifth row of cards, place [♣] under the integer card 1 and [♡] under the integer card 8. These cards will later indicate whether the ones digit is more than four or not. At this point, the cards are arranged as shown below. Then, turn over all cards to be face-down.

   [1][2] ⋯ [7][8][9] ⋯ [14] : Integer cards
   [?][?] ⋯ [?][?][?] ⋯ [?] : The tens digit and dummy cards
   [?][?] ⋯ [?][?][?] ⋯ [?] : The ones digit and dummy cards
   [♣] [♡] : Colored cards
   [♣] [♡] : Colored cards

   Note that, when d is 75 or greater (*i.e.*, when the right half of each card sequence in second and third rows contains [♡]), d mod 75 is obtained by swapping the positions of the left and right seven cards in the second and third rows.
6. For rows 1 through 3, apply a pile-scramble shuffle to each of the left seven cards and the right seven cards.
7. For rows 1 through 5, by regarding each of the left twenty-three cards (left seven cards in the upper three rows and two cards in the forth and fifth rows) and right twenty-three cards as piles, apply a pile-scramble shuffle.
8. Turn over the cards in the third row to be face-up. Rearrange the left and right piles so that a pile containing [♡] in the third row moves to the right.
9. Keep the two cards in the fifth row. They are [♣][♡] if the ones digit is five or greater, and [♡][♣] if it is less than five.
10. Turn over the cards in the third row to be face-down. Apply a pile-scramble shuffle to the columns in the rows through 1 to 4 as in Step 7.
11. Turn over the cards in the second row to be face-up. Rearrange the left and right piles so that a pile containing [♡] in the second row moves to the right.
12. Keep the two cards in the fourth row. They are [♣][♡] if the tens digit is seven, and [♡][♣] if it is less than seven.
13. Turn over the cards in the second row to be face-down. Apply a pile-scramble shuffle to the whole fourteen columns in the rows through 1 to 3.
14. Turn over the cards in the first row to be face-up. Rearrange the columns so the integer cards in the first row are in ascending order from left to right. Then, remove the integer cards from the first row.
15. Divide each of the remaining two rows into two halves of seven cards each.

16. Apply the AND protocol [8] to the two sets of two cards kept in Steps 9 and 12 to obtain ? ? . Note that here, 0 is encoded as ♡ ♣ and 1 as ♣ ♡ . The resulting cards are ♣ ♡ if the tens digit is seven and the ones digit is five or greater (that is, $d \geq 75$), and ♡ ♣ otherwise.
17. Place each of the two cards obtained in Step 16 onto the left and right halves of seven cards obtained in Step 15.
18. Divide the three rows of card sequences obtained in Step 17 (the first row contains the two cards from the AND operation, the second row contains a sequence of fourteen cards including the card corresponding to the tens place, and the third row contains a sequence of fourteen cards including the card corresponding to the ones place) into halves. Apply the pile-scramble shuffle to each half as a pile.
19. Turn over the cards in the first row to be face-up. Then, rearrange the cards from the first to the third row so that ♡ among the two cards in the first row moves to the left. Remove the two colored cards from the first row.
20. From the remaining two rows, remove the dummy cards placed in Steps 2 and 3. Consequently, output two sequences of cards in the first and second rows as an integer commitment for the tens place and an integer commitment for the ones place of d mod 75), respectively.

References

1. Hashimoto, Y., Shinagawa, K., Nuida, K., Inamura, M., Hanaoka, G.: Secure grouping protocol using a deck of cards. Trans. Fundam. **E101.A**(9), 1512–1524 (2018). https://doi.org/10.1587/transfun.E101.A.1512
2. Igari, R., Odaka, S., Komano, Y., Mizuki, T.: Digitized integer commitment and addition protocol for card-based cryptography. In: Symposium on Cryptography and Information Security (SCIS) 2025, 3D2-3, 2025. (in Japanese)
3. Ikeda, S., Shinagawa, K.: How to play Mastermind without game master. In: Li, M., Xia, M., Zhang, P.(eds.) Theory and Applications of Models of Computation, TAMC 2025. LNCS, pp. 109–120. Springer, Cham (2025)
4. Ishikawa, R., Chida, E., Mizuki, T.: Efficient card-based protocols for generating a hidden random permutation without fixed points. In: Calude, C.S., Dinneen, M.J. (eds.) UCNC 2015. LNCS, vol. 9252, pp. 215–226. Springer, Cham (2015). https://doi.org/10.1007/978-3-319-21819-9_16
5. Koizumi, K., Mizuki, T.: An application of secure computation to tagiron. In: Advances in Computer Games, LNCS, Cham, to appear. Springer
6. Mizuki, T., Asiedu, I.K., Sone, H.: Voting with a logarithmic number of cards. In: Mauri, G., Dennunzio, A., Manzoni, L., Porreca, A.E. (eds.) UCNC 2013. LNCS, vol. 7956, pp. 162–173. Springer, Heidelberg (2013). https://doi.org/10.1007/978-3-642-39074-6_16
7. Mizuki, T., Kuzuma, T., Hirano, T., Oshima, R., Yasuda, M.: Gakmoro: an application of physical secure computation to card game. In: Formenti, E., Manzoni, L. (eds.) Unconventional Computation and Natural Computation. UCNC 2025. LNCS, pp. 344–360. Springer, Cham (2025)

8. Mizuki, T., Sone, H.: Six-card secure and and four-card secure XOR. In: Deng, X., Hopcroft, J.E., Xue, J. (eds.) FAW 2009. LNCS, vol. 5598, pp. 358–369. Springer, Heidelberg (2009). https://doi.org/10.1007/978-3-642-02270-8_36
9. Nishimura, A., Hayashi, Y., Mizuki, T., Sone, H.: Pile-shifting scramble for card-based protocols. IEICE Trans. Fundam. **101**(9), 1494–1502 (2018). https://doi.org/10.1587/transfun.E101.A.1494
10. Ruangwises, S., Ono, T., Abe, Y., Hatsugai, K., Iwamoto, M.: Card-based overwriting protocol for equality function and applications. In: Cho, D.-J., Kim, J., editors, Unconventional Computation and Natural Computation, volume 14776 of LNCS, pages 18–27, Cham, 2024. Springer. https://doi.org/10.1007/978-3-031-63742-1_2D
11. Ruangwises, S., Shinagawa, K.: Simulating virtual players for UNO without computers. In: Formenti, E., Manzoni, L. (eds.) Unconventional Computation and Natural Computation. UCNC 2025. LNCS, pp. 33–46. Springer, Cham (2025)
12. Shinagawa,K., Kanai, K., Miyamoto, K., Nuida, K.: How to covertly and uniformly scramble the 15 puzzle and rubik's cube. In: Broder, A.Z., Tamir, T., editors, Fun with Algorithms volume 291 of LIPIcs, pp. 30:1–30:15, Dagstuhl, Germany, 2024. Schloss Dagstuhl. https://doi.org/10.4230/LIPIcs.FUN.2024.30
13. Shinagawa, K., Miyahara, D., Mizuki. T.: How to play old maid with virtual players. In: Li, B., Li, M., Sun, X., editors, Frontiers of Algorithmics, volume 14752 of LNCS, pp. 53–65, Singapore (2025). Springer. https://doi.org/10.1007/978-981-97-7752-5_4
14. Shinagawa, K., et al.: Card-based protocols using regular polygon cards. IEICE Trans. Fundam., **E100.A**(9):1900–1909, (2017). https://doi.org/10.1587/transfun.E100.A.1900
15. Shinoda, Y., Miyahara, D., Shinagawa, K., Mizuki, T., Sone, H.: Card-based covert lottery. In: Maimut, D., Oprina, A.-G., Sauveron, D. (eds.) SecITC 2020. LNCS, vol. 12596, pp. 257–270. Springer, Cham (2021). https://doi.org/10.1007/978-3-030-69255-1_17
16. Igari, R., Odaka, S., Komano, Y., Mizuki, T.: Efficient physical ZKP protocols for Hamiltonian cycle problem and traveling salesman problem. IEICE Trans. Fundam. Electron. Commun. Comput. Sci., 2026, to appear

Post-quantum Cryptography

Towards Quantum-Safe Cryptography in 5G Networks

Lucía Muñoz-Solanas(✉) and José Álvaro Fernández-Carrasco

Vicomtech Foundation, Basque Research and Technology Alliance (BRTA), 20009 Donostia/San Sebastián, Spain
{lmunoz,jafernandez}@vicomtech.org

Abstract. The advent of 5G networks raises urgent security concerns as quantum computing threatens to break the classical cryptography protecting their control plane. To address this, this project integrates quantum-resistant mechanisms into a virtualized 5G environment. The project secures traffic using TLS tunnels with NIST-standardized CRYSTALS-Kyber for key exchange and CRYSTALS-Dilithium for authentication in a crypto-agile Public Key Infrastructure; Quantum Key Distribution was also explored. Comparative evaluations demonstrate that Post-Quantum Cryptography solutions are feasible and can deliver unexpected efficiency gains, including reduced authentication latency and improved memory usage. The study also highlights operational challenges like certificate management and resilience under attacks. Overall, the results indicate that PQC algorithms are mature enough for real-world deployment in 5G networks. A successful transition will depend on cryptographic agility, while Quantum Key Distribution offers a valuable complementary layer of security for critical links.

Keywords: Post-Quantum Cryptography · 5G Security · Crypto-Agility · TLS · PKI · QKD

1 Introduction

1.1 The Evolving Threat Landscape: Quantum Computing and 5G Security

The rapid evolution of 5G networks–offering ultra-reliable low-latency communications (URLLC), massive machine-type communications (mMTC), and enhanced mobile broadband (eMBB) [8]–introduces heightened security challenges. Traditional public key cryptography, such as RSA (Rivest · Shamir · Adleman) and Elliptic Curve Cryptography (ECC) [15], is the cornerstone of 5G security, essential for critical functions including Authentication and Key Agreement (AKA), Transport Layer Security (TLS), and the Public Key Infrastructure (PKI). However, the prospective emergence of fault-tolerant quantum computers capable of executing Shor's algorithm [16] threatens to break these systems. This vulnerability is immediate due to the "harvest now, decrypt later"

P. D'Arco and A. Zamfiroiu (Eds.): SecITC 2025, LNCS 16443, pp. 119–131, 2026.
https://doi.org/10.1007/978-3-032-17443-7_7

attack paradigm, where data encrypted today can be stored for decryption once cryptographically relevant quantum computers (CRQCs) become available. Consequently, any long-lifecycle data transmitted over 5G is already at risk.

1.2 Quantum-Resistant Security Approaches: PQC and QKD

To counter the quantum threat, two main defense strategies have emerged: Post-Quantum Cryptography (PQC) and Quantum Key Distribution (QKD). PQC refers to a new generation of cryptographic algorithms designed to be secure against attacks from both classical and quantum computers. The U.S. National Institute of Standards and Technology (NIST) has led a global standardization process to identify and validate robust PQC algorithms. This has resulted in standards that are central to the project, such as CRYSTALS-Kyber (formalized as ML-KEM, Module Lattice Key Encapsulation Mechanism, in FIPS 203) for key establishment and CRYSTALS-Dilithium (formalized as ML-DSA (Module Lattice Digital Signature Algorithm) in FIPS 204) for digital signatures. While these are becoming the de facto industry defaults, PQC adoption presents challenges like potential performance overhead from larger key sizes, greater computational demand, and integration complexities. This proposal provides crucial empirical data to validate these standards in 5G environments.

Alongside software-based solutions, QKD offers an alternative, physical-layer mechanism. Unlike PQC, which relies on computational difficulty, QKD's security is based on the fundamental principles of quantum mechanics, providing information-theoretic security. Despite ongoing standardization efforts by bodies like the European Telecommunications Standards Institute (ETSI), QKD has significant practical limitations, including distance restrictions, high deployment costs, the need for dedicated optical fiber, and a dependency on authenticated classical channels. Due to these constraints, its use cases in 5G are specialized, such as securing critical backhaul links. Therefore, QKD is positioned as a high-assurance complement for critical links rather than a scalable substitute for PQC in general communications.

1.3 Objectives and Contributions

This project is a hands-on research initiative designed to accelerate the adoption of quantum-resistant security within 5G network environments. The central objectives of the project are:

1. **Integration of PQC and QKD:** Develop and implement PQC and QKD solutions within a 5G network, evaluating their impacts on resource consumption (CPU, memory), network delay, and overhead compared to classical approaches to define best practices.
2. **Hybridization Techniques:** Create and measure novel hybrid protocols combining QKD, PQC, and classical methods to secure 5G data and control plane operations.

3. **Quantum-Secure PKI:** Assess and deploy quantum-secure PKI solutions based on crypto-agility policies within our 5G lab to support secure identification and authentication.
4. **Performance Evaluation:** Analyze the impact of integrating PQC and QKD on network performance to define best practices and guidelines for their adoption in 5G and beyond.

1.4 Structure of the Article

Section 2 reviews related work. Section 3 details the implemented architecture (5G lab, PQC/TLS, PKI, QKD). Section 4 explains the experimental design, scenarios, and metrics. Section 5 presents and analyzes the empirical results. Section 6 discusses the findings and their implications, comparing them with the state of the art. Section 7 concludes the paper, summarizing contributions, limitations, and future research.

2 Related Work

With the rise of quantum threats, integrating PQC into 5G networks is a priority. Recent studies have explored its implementation across the 5G architecture, from authentication to the core network and IoT environments. A key focus has been hardening the 5G Authentication and Key Agreement (5G-AKA) [2] protocol, whose reliance on classical cryptography makes it vulnerable.

To mitigate these risks, Ko et al. introduced 5G-AKA-HPQC, a hybrid authentication protocol that combines classical Elliptic Curve Integrated Encryption Scheme (ECIES) with PQC Key Encapsulation Mechanisms (KEM). This approach ensures forward secrecy and quantum resistance while preserving interoperability, though performance evaluations showed a trade-off between security and efficiency [10]. Another proposal, KyberPQ-AKA, uses the lightweight cipher ASCON [3] and Kyber for key exchange [1], demonstrating reduced connection and computation costs compared to standard 5G-AKA while improving security and user privacy [9].

Beyond authentication, research has focused on securing the 5G core network. One study implemented ML-KEM from the Open Quantum Safe (OQS) project [17] the TLS v1.3 for communications between Virtualized Network Functions (VNFs) in free5GC [4]. The findings showed that integration is feasible with minimal overhead and significantly improves protection against "Store Now, Decrypt Later" (SNDL) attacks [14]. Similarly, another study secured UE-to-UE communication by integrating ML-KEM into the TLS handshake within a 5G testbed using Open5GS [12] and UERANSIM [6], paving the way for quantum-resilient mobile devices [7].

PQC has also been evaluated in resource-constrained contexts. In a 5G Narrowband IoT (NB-IoT) study, implementing ML-KEM for key exchange introduced minimal overhead, but post-quantum signature schemes were found to increase latency and reduce throughput, highlighting a need for optimization in IoT environments [13]. For zero-trust environments, Gharib and Afghah proposed the SCC5G architecture, with hardware roots of trust (Physically Unclonable Functions) to achieve tamper-resistant authentication. Simulations demonstrated its high scalability, minimal traffic overhead, and acceptable latency [5].

3 Architecture

The architecture of the project is an experimental framework to evaluate the integration of quantum-resistant technologies into a virtualized 5G core extended with PQC and QKD capabilities.

3.1 Virtualized 5G Laboratory Environment

This project is developed in an advanced 5G laboratory that combines physical and virtualized infrastructures, with Open5GS used to deploy a complete 5G core, including key Network Functions (NFs) such as the Network Repository Function (NRF), Access and Mobility Management Function (AMF), etc. –and UERANSIM for the emulation of the Radio Access Network (RAN). This configuration provides a realistic and controlled platform for testing, traffic generation, network resource management, identity management, and security attack simulation.

3.2 PQC-Enabled TLS Tunnels for 5G NFs

A core component of the project architecture is the integration of PQC directly into the TLS v1.3 handshakes that secure communications between 5G control plane functions. The implementation uses the native support for NIST-approved algorithms OpenSSL 3.5.0 for stability and to streamline deployment. The strategy addresses both authentication and key exchange:

- **Authentication with PQC Certificates:** To secure the identity of NFs, classical certificates based on RSA/ECC are replaced by X.509 certificates signed with the ML-DSA65 algorithm. These certificates are used for the mutual authentication (mTLS) of 5G NFs (e.g., AMF, NRF) during the TLS channel setup, as illustrated in Fig. 1. By using ML-DSA, the project mitigates the risk of quantum adversaries forging digital signatures, a critical step to prevent identity impersonation and maintain trust within the 5G core.
- **Secure Key Exchange with PQC KEM:** For the confidential exchange of session keys, ML-KEM768 is implemented. This quantum-resistant KEM is used during the TLS handshake to establish a symmetric key that encrypts all subsequent communication between the NFs. The architecture also supports hybrid modes (e.g., combining classical ECDH with ML-KEM), which provides both classical and quantum resistance during a transitional period. This approach acts as a "safety net": if one algorithm is eventually broken, the other still ensures the security of the key exchange.

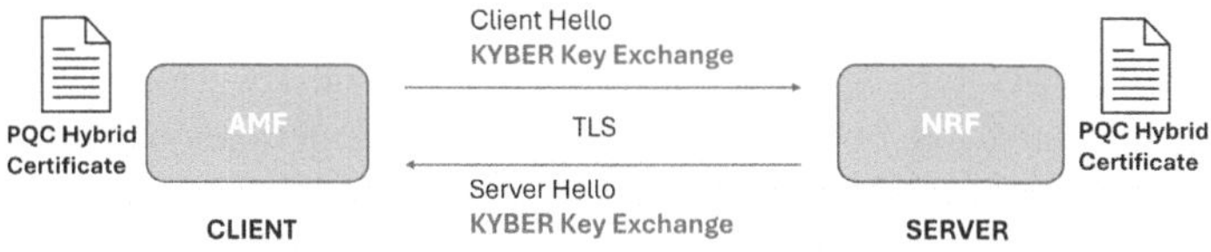

Fig. 1. PQC TLS Exchange Between Client and Server.

3.3 Post-quantum PKI for Enhanced Cryptographic Agility

The project relies on a post-quantum PKI built around a Certificate Authority (CA) that manages ML-DSA-based certificates, as illustrated in Fig. 2. The PKI was implemented using the open-source platform *EJBCA*, which was extended to support post-quantum algorithms and certificate profiles compliant with ML-DSA. This choice ensures compatibility with widely adopted PKI standards while allowing flexibility for experimentation with hybrid and quantum-safe certificate hierarchies.

A fundamental objective is to promote cryptographic agility–the ability to smoothly migrate to new cryptographic standards as threats evolve. This informs how future PKIs can be designed to adapt to any cryptographic transition, addressing the historical weakness of systems rigidly tied to specific algorithms.

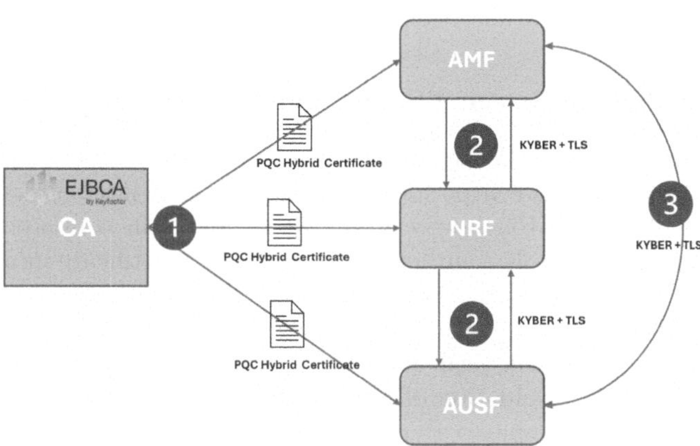

Fig. 2. PQC-enabled architecture, showing the PKI issuing certificates (1) and subsequent secure communications between NFs (2,3)

3.4 Integration of the Open-Source QKD System Quditto

This project integrates Quditto, an open-source QKD orchestrator, to evaluate an additional quantum-resilient layer for key exchange. Quditto [11] emulates

QKD nodes and is compliant with the ETSI QKD 014 API, facilitating interoperability. In the 5G lab, Quditto provides symmetric keys for specific communication links, such as between distributed core functions or MEC nodes. The use of an ETSI-compliant, open-source orchestrator like Quditto signifies a move towards more standardized and accessible QKD experimentation, which can accelerate research by lowering entry barriers and fostering a common framework for testing.

4 Experimental Design and Scenarios

To evaluate the proposed architecture, three quantum-resistant scenarios were deployed. The experiments were conducted in a virtualized 5G lab on OpenStack (KVM). The 5G core was distributed across two nodes (8 vCPUs, 16 GB RAM, Ubuntu 22.04 LTS each) to simulate separated network domains, (hosting NFs like AMF/SMF and NRF/UDM) and test cross-domain security with (PQC/QKD). NFs were deployed as system services managed via `systemctl` and resource usage was measured using `htop` and `pidstat`.

4.1 Baseline Scenario: Classical Cryptography (TLS Based on RSA)

This scenario serves as the baseline, representing the current state where TLS communications are secured using traditional X.509 RSA2048 certificates for authentication and classical algorithms like RSA2048 or ECDH for key exchange.

4.2 Hybrid PQC Scenario: TLS Secured with PQC

All TLS tunnels use ML-KEM768 for quantum-resistant confidentiality, selected as a balanced option between performance and NIST security. Other variants (ML-KEM512, ML-KEM1024) were excluded to maintain consistent security parameters during testing. For authentication, a hybrid certificate infrastructure is deployed: a classical RSA root CA issues two intermediate CAs (one classical RSA2048, one post-quantum ML-DSA65), as shown in Fig. 3, creating a mixed trust architecture where classical and PQC certificates coexist. This setup is designed for a realistic evaluation of crypto-agile infrastructures and the operational implications of a phased PQC migration while maintaining end-to-end quantum-resistant encryption. The focus of this scenario is on the performance of a crypto-agile PKI managing distinct classical and PQC certificates, rather than on the analysis of composite hybrid certificates.

4.3 QKD-Augmented Scenario: Integration of Quditto for Key Exchange

This scenario explores a defense-in-depth strategy by integrating the Quditto QKD system to supply symmetric keys for critical communication channels. The rationale is to provide an additional security layer based on different physical

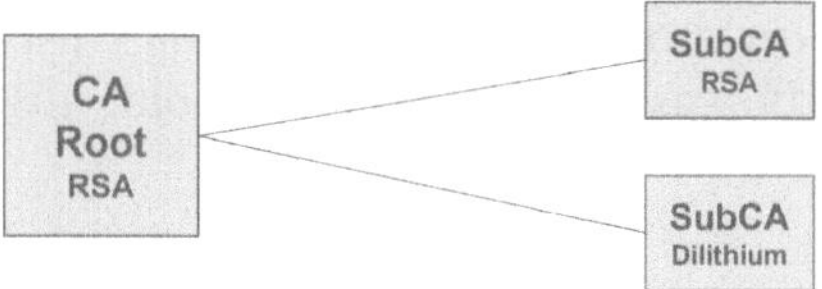

Fig. 3. CA Hierarchy

principles; since QKD's security is based on physics and PQC's on computational hardness, they are not susceptible to the same attacks. QKD thus acts as a valuable fallback in case unforeseen weaknesses are discovered in PQC algorithms.

4.4 Performance and Security Evaluation Metrics

An exhaustive set of Key Performance Indicators (KPIs) and metrics was defined for a rigorous comparison between the scenarios.

Performance-related metrics focused on latency and resource consumption. Latency metrics included: mTLS authentication performance, Certificate Operations (average and standard deviation for issuing/verifying RSA2048 and ML-DSA65 certificates), end-to-end UE Authentication Time (from attach to registration), and QKD key distribution latency. Resource metrics included: Cryptographic Resource Usage (CPU/memory during UE registration and mTLS), Memory footprint per NF registration (measured at the NRF), TLS Cipher Overhead (handshake payload size comparison), and the QKD key generation rate.

Security-related metrics evaluated system robustness, measuring the **Attack detection rate**, the **Impact of attacks** on system resources (CPU, memory) and service availability (downtime), and **Resilience** against specific simulated attacks (e.g., session hijacking, Man-in-the-Middle, and simulation of KEM rupture). The methodology for simulating attacks and generating traffic was designed to emulate realistic network conditions and threat vectors relevant to 5G environments.

The security evaluation was guided by the principle of focusing on realistic and implementation-relevant threats. Certain attack vectors were excluded by design. Brute-force attacks were deemed out of scope, as algorithms like RSA, ML-KEM, and ML-DSA are computationally infeasible to break with current classical hardware. Similarly, theoretical cryptanalysis were not pursued, as the study assumes the security guarantees of the standarized algorithms. Instead, the evaluation focused on practical threats affecting real-world deployments, specifically:

- **Denial-of-Service Against the CA**: An automated attack was launched to degrade the CA by issuing thousands of certificate requests in parallel.
- **Resource Exhaustion of the NRF**: Another test involved flooding the NRF with fake NF registrations signed with different types of certificates.

- **Time Manipulation Attack**: To test temporal trust assumptions, the system time of the AMF was manipulated to a point after the certificate expiration

5 Results and Comparative Analysis

This section is based on the experimental data obtained from the project and presents a comparative evaluation of the three defined scenarios.

5.1 Performance Impact Evaluation

This section evaluates the performance implications of integrating PQC and QKD into 5G control plane communications. Their impact on mutual authentication, certificate operations, and key distribution is analyzed and compared to classical cryptography.

5.1.1 TLS and Mutual Authentication Performance

Table 1 presents a comparison of resource consumption during two key mutual authentication processes in the 5G control plane: the registration of NFs via mutual TLS (AMF to NRF), and the authentication of User Equipment (UE) (AMF to AUSF). Although PQC was expected to impose a higher computational burden, experiments showed that PQC-based authentication achieved better memory efficiency and substantially reduced CPU usage. The end-to-end authentication time was also substantially reduced in the PQC scenario. In the NF registration use case, PQC proved more memory-efficient per operation but showed higher CPU peaks during the TLS handshake.

Table 1. Resource Usage in Mutual Authentication Procedures (NF Registration and UE Authentication).

Procedure	Metric	RSA	PQC	Observations
NF Registration (AMF → NRF)	Memory per Register (MB)	0.30	0.23	PQC 23% more efficient
	Max CPU Usage (%)	5.0	10.0	PQC incurs higher CPU peaks
UE Authentication (AMF → AUSF)	Total Auth Time (ms)	965	519	PQC 46% faster overall
	Max CPU Usage (AMF)	29.9	5.0	PQC significantly lighter
	Memory Increase (MB)	17.5	4.49	PQC 74% more efficient

5.1.2 PQC Certificate Operations and Cryptographic Overhead

Table 2 summarizes the performance of key certificate operations–issuance and validation–for RSA2048 and PQC ML-DSA65 certificates. Surprisingly, certificate issuance was faster on average for PQC, completing approximately 22.5% quicker than RSA, though with slightly greater variance. In contrast, RSA remained marginally faster and more stable during certificate validation.

Table 2. Performance Metrics for Certificate Operations and Authentication.

Operation	RSA2048	ML-DSA65	PQC vs RSA
Certificate Issuance (avg)	6.52 s	5.06 s	PQC 22.5% faster
Standard Deviation	0.085 s	0.124 s	PQC more variable
Certificate Validation (avg)	34.4 ms	37.0 ms	RSA slightly faster
Validation Std. Deviation	4.4 ms	6.6 ms	RSA more stable

5.1.3 Performance of the QKD Quditto System

The Quditto system, being an emulation, provided a Symmetric Key Rate (SKR) and a key distribution latency that are dependent on the emulation's configuration and the assigned resources. For a real application, these values would be dictated by the physical QKD hardware. The emulated Quantum Bit Error Rate (QBER) directly influences the net SKR. The overhead associated with the management and utilization of QKD-derived keys (e.g., integration with the TLS-PSK protocol) was measurable, mainly in terms of initial configuration and key synchronization.

5.2 Security Posture Evaluation

The following results were obtained from the practical attack scenarios defined in Sect. 4.4:

5.2.1 Denial-of-Service Against the CA

Although the CA successfully issued certificates under load, its internal database became saturated, ultimately preventing administrative operations such as certificate lookup and management. The experiment revealed that PQC certificates cause more pressure on the database due to their larger size, meaning a DoS state could be achieved faster using PQC than RSA.

5.2.2 Resource Exhaustion of the NRF

The results of the NRF flooding test showed that with **PQC certificates**, the NRF consistently crashed after 56 entries. The failure was due to exhaustion of the internal client_pool structure, despite low CPU usage (1%). With **RSA certificates**, the NRF endured up to 64 entries, but with higher CPU load (up to 10.8%), failing due to insufficient buffer space.

5.2.3 Time Manipulation Attack ("Time Machine")

As expected, mutual TLS sessions between AMF and other NFs failed due to expired certificates. Additionally, the AMF deregistered connected UEs. The lack of an automated certificate renewal mechanism left the system in an unusable state until a new certificate was manually issued. This highlights a key operational vulnerability unrelated to algorithm type–the absence of crypto-agile automation.

6 Discussion

6.1 Interpretation of the Findings in the Context of 5G Evolution

The empirical results challenge the belief that PQC adoption incurs a significant performance penalty. Instead, the findings show PQC is a viable 5G security upgrade, sometimes offering efficiency improvements. In UE authentication, PQC showed lower end-to-end latency and memory usage than RSA. The observed performance advantage of PQC algorithms may be attributed to the optimized implementation of PQC algorithms in OpenSSL 3.5.0, as well as reduced overhead in asymmetric key scheduling compared to RSA2048 within the same environment. Although simulated attacks primarily stress network components, the results reveal indirect effects of cryptographic overheads on resource saturation and resilience. While a moderate peak CPU rise was seen during NF registration TLS handshakes, the overall effect was manageable. These results suggest PQC algorithms are mature enough for performance-critical 5G.

Beyond performance, the hybrid PKI implementation highlights the importance of cryptographic agility. This model, allowing classical and PQC certificates to coexist under one trust anchor, offers a practical migration path, avoiding disruptive overhauls. This framework addresses the quantum threat and provides a plan for future cryptographic transitions. Adopting an agile PKI is strategic, facilitating the PQC move and simplifying future security updates via a standards-based foundation.

Furthermore, integrating the Quditto system demonstrates QKD as a powerful, complementary security layer. While PQC's security is computational, QKD's is physics-based. In a defense-in-depth approach, QKD can protect critical links (like between separated core networks), providing a valuable fallback should PQC vulnerabilities be found. The evidence supports a strategic move toward hybrid PQC/QKD approaches for a resilient, future-proof security framework for 5G and beyond.

6.2 Comparison with the State of the Art

This research corroborates and expands existing work on PQC in 5G, providing a more holistic and, in key areas, a more optimistic performance analysis.

A key comparison point is the performance of PQC KEMs in the 5G core. The results of the project demonstrates that ML-KEM can be integrated into TLS tunnels with manageable overhead, agree with the findings of Scalise et al. [14]. Their work, which also involved integrating ML-KEM into a 5G core, reported a "negligible increase in connection duration" and found that the integration was feasible with "minimal overhead." This overall viability is further supported by studies on PQC-enhanced authentication, such as KyberPQ-AKA [9], which showed that using ML-KEM could even reduce computation costs compared to the standard 5G-AKA.

However, the main contribution is shifting the discussion beyond "minimal overhead" to reveal real performance benefits. While earlier hybrid proposals mentioned a "trade-off between security and efficiency", this work provides empirical evidence that PQC can outperform classical cryptography in essential procedures. Moreover, the study offers valuable insights into the practicality of PQC digital signatures, an area where other research has raised concerns. For instance, studies on PQC in constrained NB-IoT environments reported that post-quantum signature schemes may cause increased latency and reduced throughput. In contrast, the evaluation of ML-DSA within the 5G core showed that certificate operations were highly practical, with issuance times approximately 22.5% faster than RSA. These results emphasize that performance impacts are context-dependent and that PQC signatures are viable in core network functions.

Finally, the architectural scope and security evaluation methodology of the project are key differentiators. Many studies focus on securing a specific protocol, like 5G-AKA or a single communication path. This project, however, addresses the security of the entire service-based control plane infrastructure. Its practical security tests, which involved launching resource exhaustion and DoS attacks, uncovered implementation-specific vulnerabilities and different stress vectors between PQC (memory-intensive) and RSA (CPU-intensive). This approach offers practical insights for network operators that complement the formal verification methods used in other research.

6.3 Implications for Real-World Deployment and Cryptographic Agility

The practical challenge of migrating 5G networks to a quantum-safe posture is not uniform; instead, it exists on a spectrum defined mainly by an organization's existing cryptographic maturity. The transition can be relatively straightforward for systems built on modern, standardized cryptographic libraries, but presents a monumental task for those reliant on legacy or custom implementations.

The project exemplifies a more streamlined migration path. The implementation was initially developed using the OQS provider for OpenSSL, but was later migrated to the native PQC support introduced in OpenSSL 3.5.0 to simplify deployment and improve stability. This experience demonstrates that the PQC transition becomes a manageable process of software updates, configuration changes, and testing for organizations whose systems already leverage up-to-date, standardized libraries. As standards like ML-KEM and ML-DSA become natively supported in mainstream libraries, the technical barrier for these "cryptographically mature" organizations is significantly lowered.

Conversely, the migration is far more complex for systems that utilize outdated libraries, proprietary cryptographic protocols, or algorithms hardcoded into the application logic. The task transcends a simple library update and becomes a foundational re-engineering effort. It requires an exhaustive discovery phase to identify all instances of non-standard cryptography, followed by a significant redesign of the security architecture before the new PQC standards can even be implemented. This scenario represents the highest risk, cost, and complexity level for operators.

7 Conclusion and Future Work

The project successfully demonstrates the viability of integrating quantum-resistant security strategies within a virtual 5G environment. While a measurable overhead was observed in certain operations, the results revealed unexpected performance gains, such as a substantial reduction in UE authentication latency and more efficient memory usage compared to classical algorithms. These findings suggest PQC technologies are reaching a maturity level viable for deployment. QKD, while more limited, holds promise as a complementary solution for critical links. Continued research and testing in realistic environments are crucial to protect next-generation communications infrastructures.

This study has certain limitations. The tests were performed in a virtualized laboratory; physical 5G hardware and larger-scale evaluations could reveal additional challenges. Furthermore, the research focused exclusively on securing Service-Based Interface (SBI) communications within the control plane using only ML-DSA and ML-KEM. The performance impact of hybrid mechanisms, such as combined classical and PQC KEMs or composite certificates, was not evaluated and remains an area for future investigation. Finally, the attack scenarios, while representative, were not exhaustive and did not cover all possible threats, such as time synchronization attacks.

Future research will focus on addressing these limitations, including performance and security testing in a physical 5G laboratory, larger-scale scalability evaluations, and investigation of other PQC algorithms. The scope will also be expanded to secure user plane communications and critical procedures such as roaming and handovers. Further avenues include developing more sophisticated hybrid PQC-QKD schemes (e.g., using QKD to distribute master keys), exploring AI-based security orchestration, and enhancing PKI crypto-agility with automated certificate management protocols like Automated Certificate Management Environment (ACME).

Acknowledgments. This work was supported by the PQ-REACT project through its Open Call#1. The PQ-REACT project has received funding from the EU Horizon Europe Framework Program under Grant Agreement no 101119547.

References

1. Avanzi, R., et al.: Crystals-kyber algorithm specifications and supporting documentation. NIST PQC Round **2**(4), 1–43 (2019)
2. Basin, D., Dreier, J., Hirschi, L., Radomirovic, S., Sasse, R., Stettler, V.: A formal analysis of 5g authentication. In: Proceedings of the 2018 ACM SIGSAC Conference on Computer and Communications Security, pp. 1383–1396 (2018)
3. Dobraunig, C., Eichlseder, M., Mendel, F., Schläffer, M.: Ascon v1. 2: Lightweight authenticated encryption and hashing. J. Cryptol. **34**, 1–42 (2021)
4. Free5GC: Free5gc: An open-source 5g core network (2025). https://free5gc.org/. Accedido: 2025-03-06
5. Gharib, M., Afghah, F.: Scc5g: a PQC-based architecture for highly secure critical communication over cellular network in zero-trust environment. In: 2023 57th Asilomar Conference on Signals, Systems, and Computers, pp. 11–18. IEEE (2023)
6. Güngör, A.: Ueransim: A 5g ueransim simulator. https://github.com/aligungr/UERANSIM?tab=readme-ov-file (2025). Accedido: 2025-03-06
7. Hoque, S., Aydeger, A., Zeydan, E.: Post-quantum secure ue-to-ue communications. In: 2024 15th International Conference on Network of the Future (NoF), pp. 28–30. IEEE (2024)
8. (ITU), I.T.U.: IMT-2020 standards for 5g networks (2024). https://www.itu.int/en/ITU-R/study-groups/rsg5/imt-2020/
9. Joudah, R.H., Manaa, M.E.: A new approach to improving the security of the 5g-aka using crystals-kyber post-quantum technologies and ascon algorithm. Int. J. Safety Secur. Eng. **14**(6) (2024)
10. Ko, Y., Pawana, I., You, I.: 5g-aka-hpqc: Hybrid post-quantum cryptography protocol for quantum-resilient 5g primary authentication with forward secrecy. arXiv preprint arXiv:2502.02851 (2025)
11. Networks-it-uc3m: Quditto. https://github.com/Networks-it-uc3m/Quditto. access: September 2025
12. Open5GS Project: Open5GS: Open Source 5G Core Project (2025). https://open5gs.org/. Accessed 04 Mar 2025
13. Sabanci, K.: Exploring Post-Quantum Cryptographic Schemes for TLS in 5G Nb-IoT: Feasibility and Recommendations. Master's thesis, Marquette University (2023)
14. Scalise, P., Garcia, R., Boeding, M., Hempel, M., Sharif, H.: An applied analysis of securing 5g/6g core networks with post-quantum key encapsulation methods. Electronics **13**(21), 4258 (2024)
15. Shor, P.W.: Polynomial-time algorithms for prime factorization and discrete logarithms on a quantum computer. SIAM Rev. **41**(2), 303–332 (1999)
16. Shor, P.: Algorithms for quantum computation: discrete logarithms and factoring. In: Proceedings 35th Annual Symposium on Foundations of Computer Science, pp. 124–134 (1994). https://doi.org/10.1109/SFCS.1994.365700
17. Stebila, D., Mosca, M.: Post-quantum key exchange for the internet and the open quantum safe project. In: Avanzi, R., Heys, H. (eds.) Selected Areas in Cryptography (SAC) 2016. Lecture Notes in Computer Science, vol. 10532, pp. 1–24. Springer (2017), https://openquantumsafe.org

DILISAES: An Experimental Lattice-Based Post-quantum Signcryption Scheme

Rownak Borhan(✉), Yuzo Taenaka, and Youki Kadobayashi

Nara Institute of Science and Technology, Ikoma, Japan
rownak.borhan.qx4@naist.ac.jp

Abstract. Signcryption integrates a digital signature with public-key encryption to provide confidentiality and authenticity simultaneously, which is crucial in many applications. Nowadays, most existing signcryption schemes are classical and thus vulnerable to Shor's algorithm on future advanced quantum computers, so quantum-resistant signcryption is an important research direction. Although several post-quantum signcryption designs have been proposed, some exhibit security shortcomings or lack practical instantiations and empirical evaluation. To address this gap, this study proposes DILISAES, a lattice-based experimental signcryption scheme with security proofs achieving IND-iCCA confidentiality and SUF-iCMA unforgeability. Among insider-secure lattice signcryption schemes, DILISAES attains smaller public keys, secret keys, and ciphertexts. In performance, DILISAES delivers lower end-to-end latency than most baselines that apply post-quantum encryption and signatures separately at matched security levels. These results indicate that DILISAES offers a practical path toward efficient, quantum-resistant signcryption.

Keywords: DILISAES · Signcryption · Post-Quantum Cryptography

1 Introduction

Public-key encryption (PKE) and digital signatures are two of the most widely deployed cryptographic primitives. While PKE primarily ensures confidentiality, digital signatures guarantee authentication, integrity, and non-repudiation. In scenarios with a passive adversary who merely eavesdrops, encryption alone can suffice; conversely, if message secrecy is irrelevant, signing alone is often adequate. However, in the presence of an active adversary, a secure communication channel must simultaneously provide privacy, authenticity, and data integrity. Real-world applications such as secure email, as well as Internet of Things (IoT) systems operating in cloud-based infrastructures–including healthcare, smart agriculture, and unmanned aerial systems–demand these properties in unison. A traditional method to achieve such guarantees is the sign-then-encrypt paradigm: the sender first signs a message and then encrypts it. While conceptually straightforward, this composition suffers from drawbacks: increased computational cost due to

P. D'Arco and A. Zamfiroiu (Eds.): SecITC 2025, LNCS 16443, pp. 132–145, 2026.
https://doi.org/10.1007/978-3-032-17443-7_8

performing both signing and encryption, communication overhead from message expansion, and subtle security pitfalls since naïvely concatenating cryptographic primitives can lead to exploitable vulnerabilities [7]. These limitations motivated the introduction of signcryption, which integrates signature and encryption in a single, efficient primitive.

The notion of signcryption was pioneered by Zheng in 1997 [18], who proposed an elegant construction combining ElGamal encryption with signatures. This work sparked a substantial line of research focused on formalizing, analyzing, and improving signcryption schemes. Yet, the majority of classical signcryption protocols are built upon hardness assumptions such as the discrete logarithm problem or integer factorization problem. Both are severely threatened by advances in quantum computing, as algorithms like Shor's can solve them in polynomial time, undermining their long-term security. With progress in quantum technologies worldwide–for example, Google's Willow quantum processor [12] and Microsoft's topological qubits–cryptographers face mounting urgency [13].

The NIST PQC standardization process has evaluated several families of quantum-resistant primitives, including lattice-based, multivariate, isogeny-based, and hash-based cryptography. Lattice-based designs, in particular, have emerged as the leading candidates, with CRYSTALS-Dilithium and Falcon standardized as digital signature schemes, and CRYSTALS-Kyber as a key-encapsulation mechanism [14]. Despite these advances, no lattice-based signcryption scheme has yet been standardized. Although a number of PQC signcryption proposals exist in the literature, most rely on trapdoor constructions, lack of practical instantiations [7] and security [8], and often diverge from NIST-standardized primitives, leaving a significant research gap.

1.1 Contribution

While hybrid signcryption (KEM+DEM+Sig) is known classically (e.g., Chiba et al. [3]), to our knowledge DILISAES is the first post-quantum lattice-based hybrid signcryption that composes a KEM, an AEAD (instantiating the Data Encapsulation Mechanism (DEM)), and a signature, enforcing verify-before-decrypt via a canonical, injective transcript to prevent cross-instance misuse. We prove IND-iCCA confidentiality and SUF-iCMA unforgeability in the random-oracle model. The scheme instantiates NIST-track primitives–CRYSTALS-Dilithium for authenticity, AES-GCM for data encryption, and Saber for key encapsulation–without modifying the underlying algorithms. To the best of our knowledge, among insider-secure lattice signcryption schemes, DILISAES attains smaller public keys, secret keys, and ciphertexts and delivers lower end-to-end latency than most baselines that apply post-quantum encryption and signatures separately at matched security levels. Collectively, these results suggest that signcryption built from NIST-track primitives is both theoretically sound and efficient for IoT, cloud, and secure communications.

2 Related Works

PQC encompasses several approaches, including isogeny-based, multivariate, hash-based, and lattice-based cryptography. Among these, lattice-based cryptography has gained strong support from the research community as the most practical and reliable foundation for post-quantum security, a view reinforced by its central role in the NIST PQC standardization process. For this reason, prior efforts in signcryption have increasingly turned to lattice-based designs. Several schemes have been proposed in this direction. Fagen Li et al. [9] introduced a lattice-based signcryption scheme achieving indistinguishability against adaptive chosen-ciphertext attacks (IND-CCA2) under the Learning With Errors (LWE) assumption, and strong unforgeability against adaptive chosen-message attacks (SUF-CMA) under the inhomogeneous Small Integer Solution (ISIS) assumption in the random oracle model. Xiuhua Lu et al. [11] proposed a scheme that avoids reliance on random oracles, proving IND-CCA2 security under the LWE assumption and existential unforgeability (EUF-CMA) under the SIS assumption in the standard model. Similarly, Sato et al. [16] designed an efficient scheme without random oracles, but Le et al. [8] later pointed out correctness flaws in this construction. Gérard et al. [7] advanced the field with the SETLA scheme, inspired by Malone-Lee's framework, which integrates the NewHope key exchange protocol. However, the encryption component of SETLA was incompletely specified and Le et al. [8] demonstrated that SETLA fails to provide insider security. To address this, Le et al. later introduced a scheme secure against insider attacks under the LWE and SIS assumptions, but their work remained purely theoretical without practical implementation or performance validation.

Taken together, these studies reveal that lattice-based signcryption remains underdeveloped in several aspects. The best of our knowledge, no signcryption scheme has yet been standardized by NIST, and hardly any constructions instantiate with NIST-track primitives such as Kyber or Dilithium. While not strictly necessary, grounding signcryption in such well-studied building blocks is appealing from a deployment perspective, since these components are already undergoing extensive cryptanalysis and standardization. Moreover, many existing proposals rely on bespoke trapdoor public-key encryptions; by contrast, KEM/DEM compositions have emerged as the de facto design paradigm in post-quantum public-key encryption, valued for their modularity and the relative simplicity of their security analysis. Furthermore, most prior studies lack performance evaluations, leaving open questions regarding performance and feasibility in real-world settings. Motivated by these gaps, we propose DILISAES, an insider-secure lattice-based signcryption scheme with concrete performance evaluation.

3 Preliminaries

3.1 Notation

Let $\mathbb{Z}_q \stackrel{\text{def}}{=} \mathbb{Z}/q\mathbb{Z}$, $\mathcal{R} \stackrel{\text{def}}{=} \mathbb{Z}[x]/(x^n+1)$, and $\mathcal{R}_q \stackrel{\text{def}}{=} \mathbb{Z}_q[x]/(x^n+1)$. We denote polynomials by lowercase letters (e.g., a), with $a(x) = \sum_{i=0}^{n-1} a_i x^i$ and coefficients $a_i \in \mathbb{Z}_q$; vectors of polynomials by bold lowercase (e.g., $\mathbf{t}$); and matrices of polynomials by bold uppercase (e.g., $\mathbf{A}$). Polynomial multiplication in $\mathcal{R}_q$ (mod x^n+1) is $a \cdot b$; ssA and ssB the sender's and receiver's shared secrets, respectively; role serves as the domain-separation tag.

3.2 CRYSTALS-Dilithium

CRYSTALS-Dilithium is a lattice-based cryptographic scheme using the hardness of the SelfTargetMSIS problem, Module Short Integer Solution (MSIS) and Module Learning with Errors (MLWE). CRYSTALS-Dilithium consists of three algorithms such as key generation, signing and verification. Among its operations, polynomial multiplication and hashing are the two most computationally intensive operations. For the details about other function such as seed expansion functions ExpandA, Expand and ExpandMask, the reader can refer to the Dilithium official draft [4].

3.3 Saber

Saber is a lattice-based key encapsulation mechanism (KEM) built on the hardness of the Module Learning With Rounding (M-LWR) problem. Its design prioritizes simplicity, efficiency, and flexibility, achieved through several deliberate choices: (1) restricting integer moduli to powers of two, thereby avoiding modular reduction and rejection sampling, (2) adopting LWR in place of LWE, which reduces bandwidth requirements and halves the need for randomness, and (3) employing a modular structure that allows a single core component to support multiple security levels. Comprehensive details are provided in the official submission [15].

3.4 Security Game for Signcryption Scheme

Security for signcryption is analyzed under two complementary adversarial models: (1) the outsider model, where the adversary only has access to public parameters and public keys and (2) the more stringent insider model, where the adversary may also compromise certain private keys. The insider model is considered stronger, as it subsumes the outsider case and captures all essential security attributes. Libert and Quisquater [10] provided a comprehensive formalization of insider security, defining two fundamental requirements: (i) indistinguishability under chosen-ciphertext attack (IND-CCA) for confidentiality, and (ii) existential unforgeability under chosen-message attack (EUF-CMA) for authenticity.

In conventional cryptography, encryption schemes aim to guarantee confidentiality by achieving notions such as IND-CPA or IND-CCA, while digital signature schemes ensure authenticity by satisfying EUF-CMA security. Since signcryption unifies both primitives into a single operation, a secure construction must simultaneously achieve these guarantees: strong confidentiality against ciphertext attacks and robust unforgeability against message forgeries.

Confidentiality (IND-iCCA): Let $\mathcal{C}$ be the challenger and $\mathcal{A}$ the adversary. Here subscript r indicates receiver and subscript s indicates sender. The game proceeds as follows:

- **Initialization.** The challenger $\mathcal{C}$ executes $(\mathsf{PK}_s^\star, \mathsf{SK}_s^\star) \leftarrow \mathsf{KeyGen}_s$ and $(\mathsf{PK}_r^\star, \mathsf{SK}_r^\star) \leftarrow \mathsf{KeyGen}_r$ and gives $(\mathsf{PK}_r^*, \mathsf{PK}_s^*, \mathsf{SK}_s^*)$ to $\mathcal{A}$,while keeping SK_r^* secret.
- **Phase 1.** $\mathcal{A}$ may adaptively issue a polynomial number of unsigncryption queries of the form (C', PK_s). The oracle verifies before decrypting and obtains the corresponding plaintext m from $\mathcal{C}$.
- **Challenge.** $\mathcal{A}$ sends two equal-length plaintext messages (m_0, m_1). The challenger $\mathcal{C}$ chooses a uniformly random $b \in \{0,1\}$, computes $C_b \leftarrow \mathsf{Signcrypt}(m_b, \mathsf{SK}_s^*, \mathsf{PK}_r^*)$, and returns C_b to $\mathcal{A}$. After receiving C_b, A may continue to query C', except any ciphertext whose KEM component equals that of C_b.
- **Guess.** $\mathcal{A}$ returns a bit b'. The adversary wins if $b' = b$.

Unforgeability (EUF-iCMA): This game is defined between a challenger $\mathcal{C}$ and an adversary $\mathcal{A}$.

- **Initialization.** The challenger $\mathcal{C}$ executes $(\mathsf{PK}_s^\star, \mathsf{SK}_s^\star) \leftarrow \mathsf{KeyGen}_s$ and $(\mathsf{PK}_r^\star, \mathsf{SK}_r^\star) \leftarrow \mathsf{KeyGen}_r$ and gives $(\mathsf{PK}_s^\star, \mathsf{PK}_r^\star, \mathsf{SK}_r^\star)$ to $\mathcal{A}$.
- **Signcryption queries.** The adversary $\mathcal{A}$ may adaptively request polynomially many signcryptions. For each query the challenger computes $C \leftarrow \mathsf{Signcrypt}(m, \mathsf{PK}_r^\star, \mathsf{PK}_s^\star, \mathsf{SK}_s^\star)$, and returns C to $\mathcal{A}$.
- **Forgery.** Eventually, $\mathcal{A}$ outputs a tuple $(m^\star, C^\star)$ where $m^\star$ is fresh (not previously used in signcryption queries) and $C^\star$ was not obtained from the signcryption oracle. If $\mathsf{Unsigncrypt}(C^\star, \mathsf{SK}_r^\star, \mathsf{PK}_s^\star) = m^\star$, then $\mathcal{A}$ wins the game; otherwise, it loses.

4 Proposed Signcryption Scheme

The proposed signcryption scheme, DILISAES, illustrated in Fig. 1, is constructed from lattice-based cryptography and consists of three core algorithms: Key Generation, Signcryption, and Unsigncryption. For concreteness, let Alice denote the sender and Bob the receiver. During the setup phase, both parties generate their respective public-private key pairs $(\mathsf{PK}_s, \mathsf{SK}_s)$ and $(\mathsf{PK}_r, \mathsf{SK}_r)$. To transmit a message M, Alice runs the Signcryption algorithm using $(\mathsf{SK}_s, \mathsf{PK}_r)$ to produce a ciphertext C. Bob then applies the Unsigncryption algorithm with $(\mathsf{SK}_r, \mathsf{PK}_s)$ to recover and verify M, ensuring both confidentiality and authenticity. A detailed description of each algorithm follows.

Key Generation

For Alice, the key generation algorithm produces a verification key PK_s and a signing key SK_s. Following the Dilithium design, the public matrix $A \in R_q^{k\times l}$ is expanded from a seed $\zeta \leftarrow \{0,1\}^{256}$ using SHAKE. The corresponding secret vectors s_1, s_2 are sampled and expanded via SHAKE. The complete procedure mirrors the official Dilithium specification [4].

For Bob, the key generation algorithm outputs an encapsulation key PK_r and a decapsulation key SK_r. In line with Saber's KEM construction, a public seed

$seed_A$ is sampled to expand the SABER matrix, while short secret vectors are drawn from Saber's noise distribution. The public component b is then computed through a matrix–vector multiplication followed by rounding, as prescribed by the Module-LWR framework. This yields $(\mathsf{PK}_r, \mathsf{SK}_r)$. The complete method is adapted directly from the Saber specification [15].

Signcryption

To signcrypt a message M, Alice first performs Saber encapsulation using PK_r, obtaining a ciphertext–session key pair (ct, ss). The session key is processed via a key derivation function, $K = \mathsf{KDF}(ssA)$, instantiated with SHAKE-256. With this symmetric key, Alice encrypts the message using AES-256-GCM under a unique nonce IV, binding the KEM layer by setting the AEAD associated data to ct. This yields $C \,\|\, T \;\leftarrow\; \mathsf{AES\text{-}256\text{-}GCM.Encrypt}(K, IV, M;\ \mathrm{AAD} = ct)$.

Next, Alice computes a transcript hash $\mu := H(\mathsf{tr} \,\|\, enc(role, Pk_s, Pk_r, ct, IV, C \,\|\, T))$, and generates a Dilithium signature $\sigma = (\hat{c}, z, h)$ on μ. The signature algorithm employs matrix expansion, NTT-based polynomial multiplication, SHAKE-based hashing, rejection sampling, and other operations specified in the Dilithium official draft. Finally, the DILISAES signcryption outputs the tuple $(ct, IV, C \,\|\, T, \sigma)$.

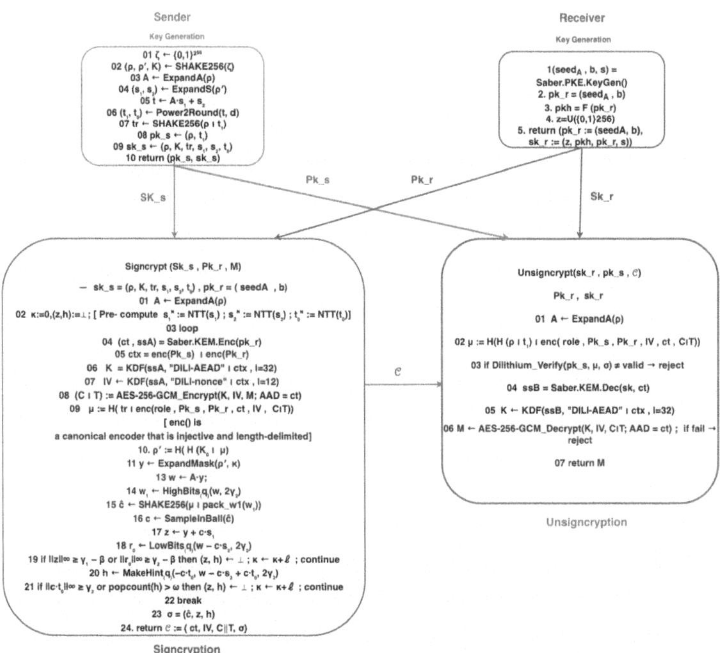

Fig. 1. Proposed Signcryption Scheme DILISAES

Unsigncryption

Upon receiving the ciphertext, Bob parses $(ct, IV, C \parallel T, \sigma)$, recomputes the transcript hash μ, and first verifies the signature via $\mathsf{Dilithium.Verify}(\mathsf{PK}_s, \mu, \sigma)$. If verification fails, the ciphertext is immediately rejected. Otherwise, Bob decapsulates ct using $\mathsf{Saber.Decaps}$ with SK_r to recover the shared secret ssB, derives $K = \mathsf{KDF}(ssB)$, and finally applies AES-256-GCM decryption with associated data ct. If the authentication tag verifies correctly, the plaintext M is output; otherwise, the ciphertext is rejected.

The DILISAES construction signs all components influencing decryption (identities, nonce, ciphertext, and AEAD output), while binding layers through the AEAD associated data. The "verify-before-decrypt" paradigm ensures ciphertexts are only decrypted if a valid signature is present, mitigating oracle misuse. We use an encrypt-then-sign (EtS)âĂŞstyle order of checks within signcryption, thereby enabling verify-before-decrypt; in contrast, sign-then-encrypt (StE) hides the signature and requires decryption before authentication.

5 Security

In this section we show that the DILISAES scheme achieves both IND-iCCA and SUF-iCMA security. Security property underlying encryption and signature scheme are given in following theorems:

Proposition 1. *The concrete security of Dilithium has been analyzed in [4], modeling H as a quantum random oracle. For any PPT adversary $\mathcal{A}$, the strong unforgeability advantage is bounded by*

$$\mathsf{Adv}^{\mathrm{SUF\text{-}CMA}}_{\mathrm{Dilithium}}(\mathcal{A}) \leq \mathsf{Adv}^{\mathrm{MLWE}}_{k,\ell,D}(\mathcal{B}) + \mathsf{Adv}^{\mathrm{SelfTargetMSIS}}_{H,k,\ell+1,\zeta}(\mathcal{C}) + \mathsf{Adv}^{\mathrm{MSIS}}_{k,\ell,\zeta'}(\mathcal{D}) + 2^{-254}.$$

Here, the MLWE assumption protects against key-recovery attacks; the SelfTargetMSIS assumption underlies resistance to "new message" forgeries; and the MSIS assumption is required to obtain strong unforgeability. Thus, assuming MLWE, SelfTargetMSIS, and MSIS hold, Dilithium achieves SUF–CMA security.

Proposition 2. *In the ideal-permutation model, SHAKE-256 [6] is indifferentiable from a random oracle up to negligible advantage [2].*

Proposition 3. *SABER is built on a Module-LWR public-key encryption scheme that is inherently IND-CPA secure. It applies the post-quantum Fujisaki-Okamoto (FO) transform, which re-encapsulates the random seed, hashes the ciphertext together with the public key, and re-derives the session key. This transformation upgrades the underlying IND-CPA security to full IND-CCA security without altering the scheme's parameters [15].*

Proposition 4. *AES-GCM is standardized in NIST SP 800-38D as an authenticated encryption with associated data (AEAD) scheme. When used with unique nonces and properly generated keys, it guarantees both confidentiality and integrity of the protected message [5].*

Theorem 1. *Taking into account the IND-CCA security of Saber, the proposed signcryption scheme DILISAES achieves IND-iCCA security.*

Proof. We argue by contradiction. In the insider model the adversary knows SK_s and can forge signatures. Since the insider knows SK_s, signature validity does not restrict its queries; confidentiality does not rely on the signature–verification merely gates decryption. All decryption queries first compute a canonical, injective transcript $\mathsf{trans} = enc(role, Pk_s, Pk_r, ct, IV, C \| T))$ set $\mu = H(tr \| \mathsf{trans})$, and run $\mathsf{Dilithium.Verify}(\mathsf{pk}_s, \mu, \sigma)$; failure aborts (*verify-before-decrypt*).

The AEAD uses $\mathsf{AAD} = ct$, and the session key is $K = \mathrm{KDF}(ssA)$ derived solely from the Saber shared secret obtained by decapsulating ct with SK_r. Thus any change to identities, IV, ct, C or T that is not signed is rejected *before* decryption, and any validly signed change still requires breaking Saber (to get ssA) or the AEAD to learn the message. However, AES-GCM is used with a fresh, unique IV per key.

Suppose there exists a PPT adversary $\mathcal{A}$ that wins the IND–iCCA game of our signcryption with non-negligible advantage ε. We show how to use $\mathcal{A}$ to construct PPT adversaries $B_{\mathsf{RO}}, B_{\mathsf{AEAD}}, B_{\mathsf{KEM}}$ that respectively distinguish our domain-separated SHAKE-256 from a random oracle, break AES-GCM's AEAD security, or Saber's IND-CCA security.

We proceed via a sequence of games G_0, G_1, G_2, G_3, each step reducing the advantage of $\mathcal{A}$ to one of the underlying components.

Game G_0 (real). This is the real IND-CCA signcryption experiment. By assumption, $\Pr[G_0 : \mathcal{A} \text{ wins}] = \frac{1}{2} + \varepsilon$.

Game G_1. By sponge indifferentiability, replacing the derived key $K = \mathsf{KDF}(ssA)$ used in the challenge by a uniformly random $K \leftarrow \{0,1\}^{256}$ is indistinguishable in the RO model. (Here KDF is instantiated as SHAKE256(ssA, `"DILI- AEAD"` $\| ctx, l = 32$). If $\mathcal{A}$ notices, we obtain a random-oracle distinguisher for SHAKE-256; hence,

$$\left|\Pr[G_1] - \Pr[G_0]\right| \leq \mathrm{Adv}^{\mathrm{RO}}_{\mathrm{SHAKE256}}.$$

Game G_2. Under the random key K of G_1, replace the encryption $\mathsf{AES\text{-}256\text{-}GCM.Enc}(K, IV, m_b;\ \mathsf{AAD} = ct^\star)$ in the challenge with the response of the AEAD challenger oracle. Equivalently, we embed the signcryption challenge into an AEAD indistinguishability experiment. Therefore, any adversary distinguishing G_2 from G_1 yields an AEAD adversary B_{AEAD}. Thus,

$$\left|\Pr[G_2] - \Pr[G_1]\right| \leq \mathsf{Adv}^{\mathsf{AEAD}}_{\mathsf{AES\text{-}GCM}}.$$

Note that $\mathsf{AAD} = ct^\star$ and $\mu = \mu := H(\mathsf{tr} \| enc(role, Pk_s, Pk_r, ct^\star, IV, C \| T))$, so any deviating decryption query is rejected before decryption.

Game G_3. Replace the Saber challenge ciphertext $ct^\star$ (and its associated session key for the KDF) with a uniformly random bit string, and answer all decapsulation queries using the KEM decapsulation oracle. If $\mathcal{A}$ distinguishes G_3 from G_2, we obtain a Saber IND–CCA adversary B_{KEM}. Hence,

$$\Big|\Pr[G_3] - \Pr[G_2]\Big| \leq \mathsf{Adv}^{\mathsf{IND\text{-}CCA}}_{\mathsf{Saber}}.$$

In G_3, the challenge tuple $(ct^\star, K, IV, (C\|T)^\star)$ is independent of b: $ct^\star$ is random, K is random, and the AEAD challenge is random-looking under a random key with fixed associated data. Hence, $\Pr[G_3 : \mathcal{A} \text{ wins}] = \frac{1}{2}$.

By a telescoping sum, we obtain

$$\varepsilon = \left|\Pr[G_0] - \tfrac{1}{2}\right| \leq \mathsf{Adv}^{\mathsf{RO}}_{\mathsf{SHAKE256}} + \mathsf{Adv}^{\mathsf{AEAD}}_{\mathsf{AES\text{-}GCM}} + \mathsf{Adv}^{\mathsf{IND\text{-}CCA}}_{\mathsf{Saber}}.$$

By Proposition 2–4 respectively: (i) SHAKE-256 is modeled as a random oracle / indifferentiable sponge used for the KDF; (ii) AES-256-GCM is an AEAD scheme that provides both confidentiality and integrity under the unique-nonce assumption; (iii) SABER is IND-CCA secure as a KEM, each term is negligible. Hence ε is negligible, contradicting the assumption that $\mathcal{A}$ wins with non-negligible advantage. Therefore, the proposed signcryption scheme is IND-iCCA secure.

Theorem 2. *Taking into account the SUF-CMA security of Dilithium, our proposed signcryption scheme is SUF-iCMA secure. Consequently, since SUF-iCMA implies EUF-iCMA, the scheme is also EUF-iCMA secure.*

Proof. Suppose there exists a PPT adversary $\mathcal{A}$ that wins the SUF–iCMA game of our signcryption with non-negligible probability ε. We construct a PPT forger $\mathcal{F}$ that breaks the SUF–CMA security of the underlying signature scheme Sig with essentially the same advantage.

Setup. $\mathcal{F}$ receives a verification key $\mathsf{PK}_s^\star$ and access to a signing oracle $\mathcal{O}_{\mathsf{Sign}}(\cdot)$ from its Sig challenger. It does not know $\mathsf{SK}_s^\star$. $\mathcal{F}$ generates the receiver's KEM key pair $(\mathsf{PK}_r^\star, \mathsf{SK}_r^\star)$ locally (insider setting already gives $\mathsf{SK}_r^\star$ to the adversary). It then runs $\mathcal{A}$ on input $(\mathsf{PK}_s^\star, \mathsf{PK}_r^\star, \mathsf{SK}_r^\star)$. We call $(C^\star, \sigma^\star)$ *fresh* if either (i) the signed message $\mu^\star$ was never queried to the signing oracle $\mathcal{O}_{\mathsf{Sign}}$, or (ii) $\mu^\star$ was queried before but $\sigma^\star$ differs from the oracle's response on $\mu^\star$ (i.e., a new signature on a previously signed message). Replaying an old (C, σ) pair is not a win.

Signcrypt-Oracle Simulation. Whenever $\mathcal{A}$ queries a message m, the simulator $\mathcal{F}$ computes all non-signature components of the signcryption honestly:

1. $(ct, ssA) \leftarrow \mathsf{Encaps}(\mathsf{PK}_r^\star)$, $ctx = enc(\mathsf{PK}_s^\star) \,\|\, enc(\mathsf{PK}_r^\star)$.
2. $K \leftarrow \mathsf{KDF}(ssA, \texttt{"DILI-AEAD"} \,\|\, ctx, l = 32)$; $IV \leftarrow \mathsf{KDF}(ssA, \texttt{"DILI-nonce"} \,\|\, ctx, l = 12)$.
3. $C \,\|\, T \leftarrow \mathsf{AEAD.Enc}(K, IV, m;\ \mathsf{AAD} = ct)$.
4. $\mu \leftarrow H(tr \,\|\, enc(role, Pk_s^\star, Pk_r^\star, ct, IV, C \,\|\, T))$ (using the injective encoder).
5. $\sigma \leftarrow \mathcal{O}_{\mathsf{Sign}}(\mu)$.

It then returns $C = (ct, IV, C \,\|\, T, \sigma)$ to $\mathcal{A}$ and records the pair (C, μ).

Table 1. Comparison between existing lattice-based signcryption vs DILISAES.

Works	Assumption	Security level	Security model	Insider attack secure
Li [9]	LWE &SIS	IND-CCA2, SUF-CMA	ROM	×
Lu [11]	—	Not secure even with IND-CPA	—	×
Sato [16]	—	Does not work correctly	—	×
Gérard [7]	RLWE &SIS	IND-CPA, EUF-CMA	ROM	×
Yang [17]	RLWE & ideal-SIS	IND-CCA2, EUF-aCMA	SDM	×
le [8]	LWE &SIS	IND-iCCA1, OW-iCCA1, SUF-iCMA	SDM	✓
This work	MLWE & MSIS & M-LWR	IND-iCCA, SUF-iCMA	ROM	✓

Forgery Handling. Eventually, $\mathcal{A}$ outputs a *fresh* accepting pair $(C^\star, m^\star)$ with $C^\star = (ct^\star, \mathrm{IV}^\star, C^\star \parallel T^\star, \sigma^\star)$. Let $\mu^\star = H(\mathsf{tr} \parallel enc(role, Pk_s^\star, Pk_r^\star, ct^\star, IV^\star, C^\star \parallel T^\star))$. Since verification happens before any decryption, acceptance implies that $\mathsf{Verify}(\mathsf{PK}_s^\star, \mu^\star, \sigma^\star) = 1$. Two cases arise:

- **Case 1 (new message).** If $\mu^\star \notin \{\mu_i\}$, then $(\mu^\star, \sigma^\star)$ is a valid signature on a *new message* for Sig. Thus $\mathcal{F}$ outputs this pair and wins.
- **Case 2 (old message, new signature).**If $\mu^\star = \mu_j$ for some recorded μ_j, then by injectivity and collision resistance the covered fields $(\mathrm{IV}, ct, C \parallel T)$ coincide with those of C_j. Freshness gives $\sigma^\star \neq \sigma_j$, so $(\mu_j, \sigma^\star)$ is a new valid signature on a previously signed message, breaking SUF-CMA of Sig. Thus $\mathcal{F}$ outputs $(\mu_j, \sigma^\star)$ and wins.

In either case, $\mathcal{F}$ succeeds whenever $\mathcal{A}$ succeeds, up to negligible probability of a hash collision. Therefore,

$$\mathsf{Adv}_{\mathsf{Sig}}^{\mathsf{SUF\text{-}iCMA}}(\mathcal{F}) \;\geq\; \mathsf{Adv}_{\mathsf{SC}}^{\mathsf{SUF\text{-}CMA}}(\mathcal{A}) - \mathsf{negl}(\lambda).$$

By Proposition 1 Dilithium is SUF-CMA secure so this contradicts the SUF-CMA security of Sig. Hence, our signcryption scheme is SUF-iCMA secure.

6 Performance Analysis

While the concept of signcryption is appealing, its practical relevance arises only when it demonstrably improves upon the straightforward composition of an encryption scheme with a digital signature. For this reason, evaluating the performance of the proposed DILISAES construction is essential.

As summarized in Table 1, most existing lattice-based signcryption proposals are not secure in the insider model [8]. Among them, the scheme of Le et al. is insider-secure, and our proposed DILISAES likewise achieves insider security. In addition, DILISAES is compact: its public key is 2944 B, its secret key is 6336 B, and the per-message ciphertext size is $4409 + |M|$ B.

Le et al. gives the exact counts of items appearing in each object of the scheme: the public key, secret key, and ciphertext contain, respectively, $2mn$ elements of $\mathbb{Z}_q$, $2mnk$ samples from D_{σ_1}, and $3m$ samples from $D_{\alpha q}$ together

Table 2. Baselines (KEM → AEAD → Sig) vs. Proposed Signcryption. Latency [ns].

Algorithm	Key Gen	Signcrypt	Unsigncrypt	Improvement
Saber + Dilithium + AES	125208	318216	124758	3.52% (KeyGen)6.80% (Signcrypt)4.65% (Unsigncrypt)
Kyber +Dilithium + AES	130041	322674	133466	7.11% (KeyGen)8.07% (Signcrypt)10.68% (Unsigncrypt)
NTRU + Dilithium + AES	1312406	327133	147300	90.80% (KeyGen)9.33% (Signcrypt)19.07% (Unsigncrypt)
Saber + Falcon + AES	5009750	343526	87048	97.59% (KeyGen)13.65% (Signcrypt)-36.95% (Unsigncrypt)
Kyber + Falcon + AES	5014583	347984	98756	97.59% (KeyGen)14.76% (Signcrypt)-20.71% (Unsigncrypt)
NTRU + Falcon + AES	6196958	352443	112590	98.05% (KeyGen)15.84% (Signcrypt)-5.88% (Unsigncrypt)
Proposed DILISAES	**120791**	**296625**	**119208**	—

with $(m+nk)$ from D_{σ_2} and $2(m+\ell)$ elements of $\mathbb{Z}_q$ (here $a \cdot S$ means a draws from domain S). Parameters details can be found in official draft [8]. We follow the parameterization used in the construction: $k = \lceil \log_2 q \rceil$ and $m = \bar{m} + nk = O(n \log q)$ with the structural constraint $m \geq nk$ coming from the G-trapdoor setting; the message space is $\mathcal{M} = \{0,1\}^\ell$ (so ℓ is in bits). Turning counts into bits, each $\mathbb{Z}_q$ element incurs k bits while the paper intentionally leaves the *encoding* of discrete-Gaussian samples unspecified. To make the byte totals independent of any truncation policy, we adopt an encoding-agnostic upper bound that assigns k bits to every Gaussian sample; this cannot undercount and can only be improved by any concrete truncation.

Writing $k = \lceil \log_2 q \rceil$ and leaving the Gaussian encodings as $b_\alpha, b_{\sigma_1}, b_{\sigma_2}$ bits per sample, the exact byte sizes are PK $= \left\lceil \frac{2mnk}{8} \right\rceil$, SK $= \left\lceil \frac{2mnk\, b_{\sigma_1}}{8} \right\rceil$, CT $= \left\lceil \frac{(3\,m)b_\alpha + (m+nk)b_{\sigma_2} + 2(m+\ell)k}{8} \right\rceil$. For a Level-3-style instantiation with $n = 256$, $k = \lceil \log_2 2^{23} \rceil = 23$, and the smallest allowed $m = nk = 5888$, we additionally report an *encoding-independent upper bound* by setting $b_\alpha = b_{\sigma_1} = b_{\sigma_2} = k$: PK = 8,667,136 B, SK = 199,344,128 B, CT = 119,968 B.

Any concrete Gaussian truncation yields smaller SK/CT, and our comparative conclusions are unchanged. Even if one assumes maximally aggressive Gaussian truncation, and as long as q satisfies the decisional-LWE hardness requirement stated in [8], Le's ciphertext remains asymptotically and concretely larger than that of DILISAES.

While reviewing existing proposals, only the scheme of Le et al. and the proposed DILISAES construction achieve the desired level of security against insider attacks. On this basis, our contribution is positioned as one of only two lattice-based signcryption schemes with a sound security foundation, and the proposed DILISAES further distinguishes itself by offering smaller public keys, secret keys, and ciphertexts compared to Le's construction.

To be fair, we calculated latency for baselines using NIST-standardized signatures and Round-3 KEM finalists, implemented separately at the same message size, to see how much time each takes. As DILISAES targets NIST security level 3, our baselines use level-3 schemes; for Falcon we report level-5 (Falcon-

1024)[1]. Across all comparisons, AES-256 is adopted as the symmetric encryption layer, chosen for its mature implementations and PQ-robust security with proper key management. For signatures, we restrict attention to Dilithium and Falcon, and deliberately exclude SPHINCS$^+$, since it is hash-based rather than lattice-based and falls outside the scope of this study. For KEMs, only lattice-based third-round finalists are considered, as all remain unbroken and have been carefully vetted by the NIST competition. Table 2 shows that implementing the signature, KEM, and symmetric cipher as separate components is computationally costly, whereas the proposed DILISAES signcryption yields substantial per-operation savings; the sole exception is against Falcon-based baselines, whose fast verification can outpace DILISAES in the unsigncrypt step–a limitation we acknowledge. Although DILISAES uses the same primitives–Dilithium, Saber, and AES–it integrates them via an engineering-oriented hybrid design that reuses common components (e.g., hash/XOF calls) as detailed in the construction, thereby avoiding duplicate work and lowering overall cost. We choose Dilithium as a NIST-selected signature scheme and Saber as a third-round finalist that has been reported relatively faster compared to other finalist scheme, including Kyber [1]. The results in Table 2 were measured macOS 14 on Apple M1 (8 GB), single thread. PQC schemes use reference C implementations; AES-256-GCM uses OpenSSL 3 (ARMv8 crypto). Timings use mach_absolute_time(); we report per-operation medians for a 59 B message; since stages run sequentially, totals equal the sum of the stage medians. We anticipate further speedups from AVX2-optimized polynomial kernels on x86-64—this is the limitation we acknowledge.

7 Conclusion

This study presented DILISAES, an experimental lattice-based signcryption scheme with formal proofs of SUF-iCMA unforgeability and IND-iCCA confidentiality in the insider setting. To the best of our knowledge, among insider-secure lattice signcryption schemes, DILISAES attains smaller public keys, secret keys, and ciphertexts, and outperforms most baselines that apply post-quantum encryption and signatures separately at matched security levels. Our performance evaluation reports per-operation latency ns; a systematic microcontroller study is left to future work to assess efficiency on resource-constrained devices, along with a detailed security analysis of signcryption-specific properties–non-repudiation, public verifiability, and forward secrecy. Finally, our security assessment is theoretical: evaluating robustness against real-world attack scenarios–including side-channel and hardware-based attacks–remains an important direction. Addressing these gaps will help harden DILISAES into a practical, post-quantum signcryption scheme for real-world deployments.

[1] Falcon offers only NIST Levels 1 and 5; therefore Falcon-1024 (L5) is shown for reference.

References

1. Alagic, G., et al.: Status report on the third round of the NIST post-quantum cryptography standardization process (2022)
2. Bertoni, G., Daemen, J., Peeters, M., Van Assche, G.: Keccak sponge function family main document. Submission to NIST (Round 2) **3**(30), 320–337 (2009)
3. Chiba, D., Matsuda, T., Schuldt, J.C.N., Matsuura, K.: Efficient generic constructions of signcryption with insider security in the multi-user setting. In: Lopez, J., Tsudik, G. (eds.) ACNS 2011. LNCS, vol. 6715, pp. 220–237. Springer, Heidelberg (2011). https://doi.org/10.1007/978-3-642-21554-4_13
4. Ducas, L., Lepoint, T., Lyubashevsky, V., Schwabe, P., Seiler, G., Stehlé, D.: Crystals–Dilithium: digital signatures from module lattices (2018)
5. Dworkin, M.J.: SP 800-38d. recommendation for block cipher modes of operation: Galois/counter mode (GCM) and GMAC. National Institute of Standards & Technology (2007)
6. Dworkin, M.J., et al.: SHA-3 standard: permutation-based hash and extendable-output functions (2015)
7. Gérard, F., Merckx, K.: SETLA: signature and encryption from lattices. In: Camenisch, J., Papadimitratos, P. (eds.) CANS 2018. LNCS, vol. 11124, pp. 299–320. Springer, Cham (2018). https://doi.org/10.1007/978-3-030-00434-7_15
8. Le, H.Q., Duong, D.H., Roy, P.S., Susilo, W., Fukushima, K., Kiyomoto, S: Lattice-based signcryption with equality test in standard model. Comput. Standards Interfaces **76**, 103515 (2021)
9. Li, F., Bin Muhaya, F.T., Khan, M.K., Takagi, T.: Lattice-based signcryption. Concurr. Comput. Pract. Exp. **25**(14), 2112–2122 (2013)
10. Libert, B., Quisquater, J.-J.: Efficient signcryption with key privacy from gap Diffie-Hellman groups. In: Bao, F., Deng, R., Zhou, J. (eds.) PKC 2004. LNCS, vol. 2947, pp. 187–200. Springer, Heidelberg (2004). https://doi.org/10.1007/978-3-540-24632-9_14
11. Lu, X., Wen, Q., Jin, Z., Wang, L., Yang, C.: A lattice-based signcryption scheme without random oracles. Front. Comput. Sci. **8**(4), 667–675 (2014)
12. Meet Willow, our state-of-the-art quantum chip – blog.google. https://blog.google/technology/research/google-willow-quantum-chip/. Accessed 22 Sep 2025
13. Microsoft Quantum | Topological qubits – quantum.microsoft.com. https://quantum.microsoft.com/en-us/insights/education/concepts/topological-qubits. Accessed 22 Sep 2025
14. National Institute of Standards and Technology: PQC standardization process: announcing four candidates to be standardized, plus fourth round candidates | NIST (2022). https://www.nist.gov/news-events/news/2022/07/pqc-standardization-process-announcing-four-candidates-be-standardized-plus#standardization. Accessed 08 Oct 2025
15. SABER: Mod-LWR based KEM (round 3 submission). Submission to the NIST's post-quantum cryptography standardization process. https://www.esat.kuleuven.be/cosic/pqcrypto/saber/. Accessed 7 Nov 2025
16. Sato, S., Shikata, J.: Lattice-based signcryption without random oracles. In: Lange, T., Steinwandt, R. (eds.) PQCrypto 2018. LNCS, vol. 10786, pp. 331–351. Springer, Cham (2018). https://doi.org/10.1007/978-3-319-79063-3_16

17. Yan, J., Wang, L., Wang, L., Yang, Y., Yao, W.: Efficient lattice-based signcryption in standard model. Math. Probl. Eng. **2013**(1), 702539 (2013)
18. Zheng, Y.: Digital signcryption or how to achieve cost (signature & encryption)«cost (signature)+ cost (encryption). In: Annual International Cryptology Conference, pp. 165–179. Springer (1997). https://doi.org/10.1007/bfb0052234

Hard-to-Find Bugs in a Post-Quantum Age

Matteo Steinbach(✉), Peter B. Rønne, and Johann Großschädl

DCS and SnT, University of Luxembourg, 6, avenue de la Fonte,
4364 Esch-sur-Alzette, Luxembourg
matteo.steinbach.pro@gmail.com,
{peter.roenne,johann.groszschaedl}@uni.lu

Abstract. The transition of the Internet's public-key infrastructure to Post-Quantum Cryptography (PQC) replaces well-scrutinized schemes with theoretically secure but implementation-wise immature ones based on structured lattices or error-correcting codes. This transition creates a fertile ground for subtle implementation errors, such as Hard-to-Find Bugs (HFBs) in PQC software, that can cause disastrous failures while evading conventional testing procedures. We show that the HFB profile of PQC differs radically from classical cryptography: carry-propagation bugs, common in classical schemes like RSA, ECDH, and ECDSA, are practically absent, while timing side-channels in polynomial arithmetic (e.g., KyberSlash) and precision divergences in floating-point operations in FALCON dominate. To explore this relatively new attack surface, we present a systematic taxonomy of PQC-specific HFBs and introduce an extension of the well-known open-source Wycheproof framework, called `wycheproof-pqc`, that utilizes targeted Known Answer Tests (KATs) to expose elusive bugs. We also provide documentation of 15 weaknesses in common open-source PQC implementations, highlighting the challenges of securing the next generation of public-key cryptosystems.

Keywords: Public Key Cryptography · Hard-to-Find Bugs · Post-Quantum Cryptography · Software Testing · Known Answer Tests

1 Introduction

Cryptographic software is a fundamental pillar of digital security, enabling the confidentiality, authenticity, and integrity of virtually any modern communication infrastructure [5]. However, the real-world security of cryptosystems does not depend only on sound theoretical constructions, but also on the correctness and robustness of their implementations [6,29,31]. Subtle and elusive software defects, commonly denoted as *Hard-to-Find Bugs (HFBs)*, can undermine the security guarantees of cryptosystems by causing rare failures with catastrophic consequences, such as incorrect results that expose confidential data. A typical example is the modular arithmetic bug described in [6], which affected elliptic curve cryptosystems, in particular ECDH, of OpenSSL version 0.9.8g. Due to

P. D'Arco and A. Zamfiroiu (Eds.): SecITC 2025, LNCS 16443, pp. 146–165, 2026.
https://doi.org/10.1007/978-3-032-17443-7_9

a flaw in the modular reduction for the 256-bit NIST prime, the multiplication and squaring modulo this prime produced incorrect results for some rare inputs that occur with a probability of less than $10 \cdot 2^{-29}$. However, by crafting public ECDH keys to deliberately trigger this defect in the modular reduction routine and using TLS handshake success/failure as an oracle, an attacker could obtain a server's entire static ECDH private key with about 633 adaptive queries.

A HFB may manifest not only through incorrect results for certain specific (yet valid) inputs, but also in the form of memory mis-management (e.g., the "Heartbleed" bug of OpenSSL versions from 1.0.1 to 1.0.1f), flawed generation of (pseudo-)random numbers (e.g., the Sony PlayStation3 code-signing failure disclosed in late 2009), or vulnerabilities to timing attacks [29]. Although these classes of defects do not (directly) impact functional correctness, they still pose security risks if, for example, sensitive data, such as a secret key, is not wiped from memory and becomes accessible to an attacker, or if "bad randomness" is used for cryptosystems like ECDSA whose security hinges crucially on random nonces of high quality that are unpredictable and uniformly distributed within a given range. A common property of all HFBs is their ability to remain undetected by conventional software testing (resp., fuzzing), either because they do not produce incorrect outputs at all or incorrect outputs happen only for some extremely rare input combinations. Besides the modular reduction defect from above, the carry-propagation flaw in OpenSSL's long-integer squaring analyzed in [31] is an interesting example of an HFB. This bug is triggered (by random operands) with a probability of 2^{-64} on affected 32-bit processors and 2^{-128} on 64-bit CPUs, respectively. While conventional testing techniques are essential for basic correctness and regression checks, their odds of finding such an elusive bug are practically zero. Thus, it is little surprising that this carry-propagation bug was present in OpenSSL's code-base for almost 10 years.

This paper builds on our earlier work [29], where we provided a formal definition and taxonomy of HFBs in traditional public-key cryptographic software (focusing mainly on RSA and ECC)[1]. In particular, we classified over 50 HFBs and surveyed some approaches for their detection (i.e., testing and fuzzing) and prevention (i.e., tools and techniques for formal verification), respectively. The present paper extends [29] by pivoting to the distinct realities of Post-Quantum Cryptography (PQC). We show that PQC exhibits a markedly different HFB profile; most notably, the carry-propagation defects that repeatedly surfaced in long-integer arithmetic for RSA, ECDH, and ECDSA are largely absent, while subtle timing side-channels, encoding/parsing errors, and precision divergences in floating-point operations now dominate. Equipped with this observation, we develop the first PQC-centric taxonomy of HFBs grounded in the mathematics and implementation properties of standardized (and pre-standardized) schemes across the three main PQC families we study: lattice-based Key-Encapsulation Mechanisms (KEMs) and signature systems (ML-KEM [22], ML-DSA [21], and FN-DSA/Falcon [10]), a hash-based signature algorithm (SLH-DSA [23]), and

[1] An extended version of our previous paper on HFBs in pre-quantum cryptographic software is available at https://github.com/mattc-try/wycheproof-c/.

a representative code-based KEM (HQC [1], which is scheduled to become an official NIST standard in the first half of 2027).

Contributions. We provide a practice-driven foundation for detecting and mitigating HFBs in PQC implementations based on four major contributions. The first is a taxonomy of PQC-specific HFBs: we identify and systematize flaws in PQC software into classes of well-defined HFBs, i.e., classes of rare and elusive bugs that escaped conventional testing/fuzzing efforts. Our second contribution is an analysis of (recurrent) PQC-specific software deficiencies observed in the literature and public code repositories. We document and scrutinize real-world failures, such as non-reproducible FALCON keys and signatures due to floating-point inconsistencies [27] or timing attacks enabled by variable-latency division in coefficient compression [4], and discuss their security implications. Third, we extend the test methodology of Google's project Wycheproof [11] to PQC and generate "adversarial" test vectors for Known Answer Tests (KATs) to expose HFBs. Our test vectors are engineered to trigger precisely those failure states that basic conformance tests and lightweight fuzzers tend to miss: variable-time (especially division-based) coefficient compression, secret-dependent conditional statements in NTT/INTT kernels, non-canonical encodings, and discrepancies in floating-point operations. Using this framework (instrumented with a micro-benchmarking tool for timing measurements), we reproduce 15 concrete HFBs collected from widely-used open-source PQC software. For each identified class of bug, we discuss mitigation strategies and secure-coding practices, and curate code-level guidance for developers to "harden" their implementations, which is our fourth contribution. As complementary material, we release the full source code of `wycheproof-pqc`, an extension of Wycheproof providing PQC-specific KATs: https://github.com/mattc-try/wycheproof-pqc.

Research Questions. This work is guided by three research questions that shape both our analysis of HFBs and the generation of KATs for their detection. The first question is: how do the mathematical and algorithmic properties of PQC schemes (e.g., NTT-based polynomial arithmetic, discrete sampling, and code-decoding loops) give rise to categories of HFBs that are different from those in classical public-key schemes? Second, we ask, which systematic methodology is most effective at detecting, classifying, and reproducing such PQC-specific bugs in software implementations, with a focus on KATs? Third, to what extent can carefully crafted KATs and cross-platform vectors (e.g., division-timing probes and floating-point-drift tests) close the gaps left by standard conformance tests and lightweight fuzzing, thereby improving the robustness of PQC software?

2 Definition and Threat Landscape

In our previous paper [29], we defined a Hard-to-Find Bug (HFB) as "any kind of imperfection of a delivered cryptographic software implementation that can potentially lead to a security vulnerability and remains undetected by state-of-the-art testing techniques." The word *delivered* here implies that only bugs in officially released software (ending up in "production systems") are considered HFBs, i.e., bugs in alpha or beta-level software do not count. However, in this paper, we include bugs discovered in reference and optimized implementations of candidates for the NIST PQC standardization project [2] submitted by the designer teams. As explained in the previous section, an HFB can manifest in different ways, e.g., incorrect results (for very specific and, thus, extremely rare inputs), memory corruption, "bad randomness," and susceptibility to timing-based side-channel attacks. The security implications of such software defects can vary to a large extent and range from complete secret-key compromise to Denial-of-Service (DoS) caused by a crash in a cryptographic library (e.g., due to a buffer overflow). However, as explained in [29], our definition of HFB does not require the existence of an actual exploit; it suffices that the bug has the *potential* to compromise security.

Properties. Most HFBs described in the literature and in bug reports, change logs, mailing lists, and discussion forums of open-source projects share certain properties. In particular, an HFB has a very low probability of occurrence and may manifest only under highly specific and extremely rare conditions, such as unique input combinations, special sequences of inputs or operations (execution orders), compiler settings, micro-architectural features of the target CPU, and other operational contexts. Many HFBs have high complexity and subtlety in common, making them challenging to spot in source-code reviews. An HFB is often a result of complex system interactions, subtle architectural or hardware behavior, or intricate algorithmic details (e.g., an improper handling of "edge cases"). HFBs also share the property of remaining unaffected by conventional measures for software quality assurance, such as simple conformance tests and lightweight fuzzing. As explained in the previous section, HFBs evade software testing regimes because they either do not manifest through incorrect outputs at all, or incorrect outputs happen only with extremely low probability. HFBs are also difficult to reproduce without knowing "the trick."

Hardware/Compiler Problems. Beyond HFBs due to programming errors, PQC software can also face failures that stem from the processor hardware (e.g., the floating-point unit) and/or an optimizing compiler. For example, small changes in the execution order of floating-point operations introduced by vectorization or "fused multiply-add" instructions can alter rounding behaviour and lead to non-reproducible outputs across platforms or build configurations. Embedded devices often lack floating-point hardware, forcing floating-point operations to be emulated in software, either via the compiler's run-time library or a third-party math library. However, the use of emulated floating-point operations can entail some small divergences when the emulation does not exactly match the IEEE-754 semantics. Compilers may also introduce variable-latency operations on integers, e.g., multiplication, division, and modular reduction, or synthesize secret-dependent jumps, which can undermine manually crafted constant-time code. These effects are difficult to detect since they do not necessarily change functional correctness and surface only under specific compiler settings or when executed on CPUs with specific micro-architectures.

Security Risks due to HFBs. The elusive nature of HFBs makes them valuable to adversaries. Exploitation may be possible remotely through carefully crafted inputs (e.g., public keys, ciphertexts, signatures, certificates) or random inputs that trigger rare conditions. Yet, once triggered, an HFB can compromise core security aspects. For example, a rounding divergence in floating-point Gaussian samplers can lead to biased FALCON signatures, while malformed but accepted input encodings may bypass integrity checks. A subtle branch mis-prediction-based timing leak or incomplete parser check, invisible under normal software tests, could remain undetected for years before being exploited.

PQC-Specific Threats. Contrary to classical public-key cryptography, which has benefited from four decades of refinement and accumulated expertise, PQC is comparatively immature. Its algorithms rely on relatively novel mathematical structures (e.g., polynomial rings and matrices, structured lattices, and large linear codes), which differ fundamentally from their classical number-theoretic counterparts. This novelty, combined with a lack of specialized test tools and limited implementation expertise, creates fertile ground for subtle HFBs. These bugs are particularly concerning as they may remain dormant for long periods of time, evading conventional testing/fuzzing, yet still be exploitable.

Deployment Pressure. The risks due to HFBs are amplified by the accelerated deployment roadmaps for PQC, notably those of the NIST [20] and European Commission [7], which target deprecation of classical public-key cryptosystems by 2030. Software engineers, often without deep cryptographic experience, are required to implement and deploy new primitives rapidly across many software and hardware platforms. The very special combination of urgency, novelty, and immaturity increases the probability of HFBs persisting in widely-used crypto libraries. In addition, differing regulatory and certification environments mean that implementations validated in one region will not automatically satisfy the quality assurance requirements in another. This may motivate organizations to maintain independent implementations or evaluation pipelines, which improves local assurance but also entails fragmentation across the PQC ecosystem.

3 Related Work

The landscape of cryptographic implementation testing and vulnerability analysis has evolved significantly, yet substantial gaps remain in addressing PQC unique challenges. This section critically examines existing approaches across three key domains: systematic cryptographic testing frameworks, side-channel detection methodologies, and post-quantum implementation security initiatives.

Systematic Cryptographic Testing Frameworks. Google's Project Wycheproof provides adversarial test vectors for classical algorithms (RSA, ECDSA, ECDH, AEAD, etc.), uncovering 40+ vulnerabilities across libraries [11]. Its scope, however, is limited to classical primitives and attacks (e.g., invalid curves, biased nonces) and does not address PQC-specific issues such as NTT implementations, Gaussian sampling, or non-canonical encodings.

During standardization, NIST offered only basic KATs for functional verification [2], omitting adversarial and misuse testing [14]. As a result, several flawed implementations persisted through multiple evaluation rounds.

Automated Side-Channel Detection. CipherH is the state-of-the-art in automated side-channel detection, combining taint tracking with symbolic execution to identify ciphertext-dependent leaks [9]. Applied to RSA and ECDSA in major libraries, it revealed 236 vulnerabilities within 28 CPU hours, showing better scalability than traditional static analysis.

However, CipherH targets classical cryptographic patterns and does not capture PQC-specific behaviors such as NTT reductions, discrete Gaussian sampling loops, or floating-point rounding effects. Addressing these would require new taint rules and constraint models.

Other tools, such as HACL* and Jasmin, offer formal verification but require full re-implementation in domain-specific languages, limiting their use for existing C/C++ PQC and highly optimized code [5].

Post-quantum Implementation Security Initiatives. The EU's PQCRYPTO project (2015–2018) advanced PQC through over 130 publications, 22 NIST submissions, and reference implementations including the `pqm4` framework [28]. While it noted timing and sampler leakage issues, its implementation security analysis was fragmented and lacked systematic taxonomies for PQC-specific HFBs [28].

The community-driven PQClean project has become the main effort to improve implementation quality [14]. Continuous integration testing across 17 NIST schemes exposed widespread flaws such as memory errors and API violations. However, PQClean mainly addresses general software robustness rather than subtle PQC-specific HFBs like floating-point precision drift, polynomial timing inconsistencies, or sampling deviations.

NIST's PQC evaluation emphasized theoretical cryptanalysis and only documented implementation attacks reactively (e.g., KyberSlash, template, and fault injection) rather than pursuing systematic HFB detection [2].

Critical Gaps and Research Positioning. Mathematical Foundation Analysis: Neither Wycheproof nor CipherH provides systematic analysis of how PQC's underlying mathematical structures (polynomial rings, lattice geometry, discrete distributions) can create implementation vulnerabilities distinct from classical cryptography.

PQC-Specific Vulnerability Taxonomies: While PQClean has improved general software quality, no existing work provides comprehensive taxonomies specifically for PQC HFBs that exploit the mathematics-implementation interface.

Our research directly addresses these limitations by providing the first systematic framework for identifying, classifying, and detecting hard-to-find bugs that arise specifically from the mathematical properties and implementation constraints of PQC systems.

4 Mathematical Foundations and PQC-Specific HFB Manifestations

The transition from classical to PQC represents a fundamental shift in mathematical foundations, with profound implications for implementation security and HFB manifestation patterns. Classical cryptosystems—RSA, ECDSA, and related schemes—rely on number-theoretic problems involving large-integer arithmetic in cyclic groups and finite fields. In contrast, post-quantum cryptosystems derive security from diverse mathematical structures including lattice problems, coding theory, multivariate systems, and isogeny-based constructions.

This mathematical divergence creates distinct HFB profiles. As established in our previous work, HFBs in classical cryptography most frequently involve carry propagation during multi-precision arithmetic operations. However, carry propagation is much less frequent in PQC software, compared to more than 30% in classical systems. This radical reduction stems from fundamental mathematical differences in operand structure and arithmetic domains.

The Absence of Carry Propagation in PQC: Carry propagation bugs arise from the sequential processing of multi-precision integers in classical cryptography. Consider RSA modular exponentiation: computing $c = m^e \mod n$ requires handling integers of size $|n| = 2048$ bits or larger, implemented using multi-limb representations where carries must propagate across limb boundaries:

$$\text{Classical: } \mathbb{Z}_n \text{ with } n \approx 2^{2048} \Rightarrow \text{multi-limb arithmetic} \Rightarrow \text{carry propagation}$$
$$\text{PQC: } R_q = \mathbb{Z}_q[X]/(X^n + 1) \text{ with } q < 2^{16} \Rightarrow \text{single-limb coefficients}$$
$$\Rightarrow \text{no cross-coefficient carries}$$

In lattice-based cryptography, operations occur in polynomial rings $R_q = \mathbb{Z}_q[X]/(X^n + 1)$ where the modulus q is typically small ($q = 3329$ for Kyber, $q = 8380417$ for Dilithium, [21,22]). Coefficients remain bounded within $[0, q-1]$, eliminating the need for carry propagation between polynomial coefficients. Polynomial multiplication in R_q involves coefficient-wise operations modulo q, fundamentally avoiding the multi-precision arithmetic that characterizes classical cryptosystems.

Hash-based schemes such as XMSS and SPHINCS+ [8,23] avoid carry propagation because their security relies on cryptographic hash functions

$$H : \{0,1\}^n \rightarrow \{0,1\}^m$$

implemented as fixed-size Boolean circuits. Operations like XOR, AND, and modular addition over a fixed word size $w \in \{32, 64\}$ are inherently bounded, preventing variable carry chains. Similarly, code-based schemes such as McEliece [16,17] operate over finite fields $\mathbb{F}_q$, where addition and multiplication are algebraic operations (e.g., XOR, AND, or polynomial arithmetic) that are carry-free by construction. In both cases, the arithmetic structure guarantees deterministic, bounded operations without cross-term carry propagation.

4.1 Lattice-Based Cryptography: Where Mathematical Complexity Creates HFBs

Lattice-based schemes, including NIST standards ML-KEM (Kyber), ML-DSA (Dilithium), and FN-DSA (Falcon), form the core of PQC [33]. Their security relies on structured lattices implemented via polynomial arithmetic in quotient rings, creating a distinct attack surface for HFBs, primarily timing side-channels, floating-point inconsistencies, and logical flaws.

4.1.1 Timing Side-Channels in Polynomial Arithmetic Constant-time execution is critical for cryptographic code, yet the complex arithmetic in lattice schemes creates subtle opportunities for timing leaks.

(a) Conditional Reductions in NTT Operations. Lattice-based schemes operate in polynomial rings of the form $R_q = \mathbb{Z}_q[X]/(X^n + 1)$, where polynomial multiplication is accelerated by the Number Theoretic Transform (NTT). The core NTT "butterfly" operation usually contains a conditional modular reduction:

$$(u, v) = (a + \omega b \pmod q, a - \omega b \pmod q).$$

A naive implementation of this reduction introduces a data-dependent branch, creating a vulnerability that leaks information about secret coefficients.

```
1 int32_t t = a + omega * b;
2 if (t >= q) t -= q; // TIMING_GAP: Secret-dependent branch
```

Listing 1.1. Vulnerable conditional reduction in NTT.

The standard mitigation replaces this branch with constant-time arithmetic using bitwise masking.

```
1 // Constant-time modular reduction
2 int32_t t = a + omega * b;
3 t -= q;
4 int32_t mask = t >> 31; // Arithmetic shift: -1 if t < 0, 0
    otherwise
5 t += (q & mask);        // Add q back if original t was < q
```

Listing 1.2. Constant-time modular reduction mitigation.

To verify the mitigation, one can measure the runtime variance of the NTT kernel across a set of crafted inputs. Implementations where timing differs significantly between inputs that trigger the reduction branch and those that do not indicate remaining vulnerabilities.

(b) Variable-Time Division in Coefficient Compression. To reduce the size of public keys and ciphertexts, Kyber compresses polynomial coefficients. This step can inadvertently introduce a timing leak if it compiles to a variable-latency integer division instruction (`idiv` on x86). The KyberSlash [4] attacks demonstrated this vulnerability allows for full private key recovery with only $O(n)$ decapsulation queries.

```
1 // Compiles to a variable-time idiv instruction
2 uint16_t compressed = (coefficient * 16) / KYBER_Q;
```

Listing 1.3. Vulnerable use of integer division for compression.

This is mitigated by replacing division with a constant-time algorithm like Barrett reduction given that it is implemented correctly.

```
1 // Precomputed constant: (1 << 28) / KYBER_Q
2 uint32_t t = (uint32_t)coefficient * BARRETT_MULTIPLIER;
3 uint16_t compressed = t >> 28;
```

Listing 1.4. Constant-time Barrett reduction for compression.

Testing this mitigation can be done using specially crafted ciphertexts to maximize timing variance in the division operation can be detected this way also through KATs. The test fails if timing differences remain after rewriting the code to be division-free.

4.1.2 Precision Divergence in Gaussian Sampling Discrete Gaussian sampling is a fundamental building block of lattice-based signatures. While most NIST lattice standards implement noise generation using integer-only samplers, Falcon is unique in relying on floating-point arithmetic. In Falcon, signatures require sampling from discrete Gaussian distributions over $\mathbb{Z}$, defined as:

$$D_{\mathbb{Z},\sigma}(x) = \frac{\exp(-x^2/2\sigma^2)}{\sum_{y\in\mathbb{Z}} \exp(-y^2/2\sigma^2)}, \quad x \in \mathbb{Z}.$$

To achieve efficient sampling, Falcon employs fast Fourier transforms (FFT) and double-precision floating-point approximations of the exponential function.

Cross-Platform Precision Gaps. Floating-point units (FPUs) are not fully standardized across hardware architectures. For instance, differences between x86 (which supports fused multiply-add, FMA) and ARM architectures can lead to slight variations in floating-point computations. Nguyen et al. (2023) report that up to 7% of exponential evaluations may diverge between platforms [24]. Consequently, identical key-message pairs may yield distinct yet valid Falcon signatures depending on the underlying hardware.

These precision discrepancies can have serious security implications. Potii et al. (2024) demonstrated that collecting approximately 300,000 divergent signatures is sufficient to recover the secret trapdoor with a success rate of 70–76% [26]. Similarly, the PQClean project identified inconsistencies in Falcon implementations on ARM platforms, where mutated signatures were incorrectly accepted, further illustrating the practical impact of these cross-platform precision gaps [27].

Mantissa Leakage. Beyond rounding divergences, Falcon's reliance on FFT-based sampling introduces side-channel risks. Each complex coefficient

$$\widehat{a}_j = u_j + iv_j, \quad u_j, v_j \in \mathbb{R},$$

is stored in IEEE-754 double-precision format with a 52-bit mantissa. On AVX-512 platforms, vectorized loads leak the Hamming weights of mantissas through electromagnetic (EM) emissions:

$$E(t) \propto \sum_j \left[\mathrm{HW}(m_{u,j}) + \mathrm{HW}(m_{v,j}) \right],$$

where $\mathrm{HW}(\cdot)$ denotes the Hamming weight. Correlation Power Analysis (CPA) on such traces enables recovery of FFT coefficients, which after inverse FFT and lattice reduction reveal Falcon's trapdoor polynomials (f, g) [12,15].

4.1.3 Algebraic Correctness and Plaintext-Checking Oracles The algebraic structure of the Ring Learning with Errors (RLWE) problem can be exploited if an implementation's logic reveals information about decryption correctness. During decapsulation, a received ciphertext is used to compute a message, and correctness requires that the coefficients of the resulting error term are small (i.e., $|e_i| < q/2$). A vulnerable implementation might perform an early exit after detecting an invalid coefficient, leaking timing information that an attacker can use as a plaintext-checking oracle.

```
1 int is_valid = 1;
2 for (int i = 0; i < N; ++i) {
3     if (abs(coeffs[i]) > (Q / 2)) {
4         is_valid = 0;
5         break; // TIMING ORACLE: Early exit
6     }
7 }
```

Listing 1.5. Vulnerable early-exit logic in verification.

Such an oracle can be used to recover a Kyber-512 key with just a few thousand queries. The vulnerability is mitigated by ensuring all checks run in constant time, removing any secret-dependent early exits. [4]

```
1 uint16_t mask = 0;
2 for (int i = 0; i < N; ++i) {
3     // Bitwise OR accumulates failure flags without branching
4     mask |= (abs(coeffs[i]) > (Q / 2));
5 }
6 // Final check is based on the accumulated mask
7 int is_valid = (mask == 0);
```

Listing 1.6. Constant-time verification logic.

Testing for this vulnerability can be done by providing pairs of ciphertexts: one valid and one intentionally failing the norm check on the first coefficient. The test fails if the runtime difference exceeds a small, fixed threshold, indicating a potential early-exit vulnerability. [19,32].

4.2 Code-Based Cryptography: Linear Algebraic Core, Concrete HFBs

Code-based cryptography derives its security from the hardness of the syndrome decoding problem for linear codes. Formally, given a parity-check matrix $H \in \mathbb{F}_q^{m\times n}$ and a syndrome $s \in \mathbb{F}_q^m$, the decoding problem asks for an error vector $e \in \mathbb{F}_q^n$ with $\mathrm{wt}(e) \leq t$ such that $He^T = s^T$. This problem is NP-complete [3] in the binary case and naturally extends to higher fields $\mathbb{F}_q$, a foundation that underpins schemes such as Classic McEliece and HQC [25]. The canonical McEliece-style encryption $c = mG + e$ is compact linear algebra over $\mathbb{F}_q$ and, at the algorithmic level, admits implementations without secret-dependent control flow.

However, algebraic simplicity does not guarantee implementation safety: many low-level building blocks (finite-field arithmetic, samplers, decoders, polynomial kernels) are engineering artifacts whose concrete implementations can introduce HFBs. Important implementation hotspots that have produced exploitable leakage include:

- Finite-field and polynomial arithmetic: implementations that rely on table lookups, variable-latency instructions, or non-constant modular reduction can leak through timing or memory-access side channels.
- Constant-weight (weight-t) samplers: naive samplers implemented with variable rejection loops, data-dependent shuffles, or table draws reveal weight patterns unless the sampler is written to enforce fixed iteration counts or is masked.
- Decoder behaviour: iterative decoders (bit-flipping, belief propagation, or hybrid concatenated decoders) whose iteration counts, branch behaviour, or memory accesses depend on secret errors produce reaction channels that an adversary can amplify (chosen-ciphertext strategies) to obtain oracles leaking secret information.
- Structured code surfaces: use of quasi-cyclic or other structured codes reduces key sizes but introduces distinguishers and weak-key regions; these structures broaden the HFB surface by enabling structure-specific attacks and reaction amplification.

HQC provides concrete, instructive examples: timing/division oracles from non-constant modular reductions, chosen-ciphertext amplification to steer decoder failures, pre-reencryption side-channel oracles on the RM/RS path, and single-trace SASCA results against RS syndrome kernels and polynomial multiplies. These attacks demonstrate how finite-field/polynomial kernels and decoders—though algebraically simple—create HFBs unless carefully hardened. [30]

The algebraic simplicity of code-based cryptography makes many building blocks easier to reason about and harden, but does not obviate HFBs. HQC and other real-world studies show that constant-time behaviour, sampler correctness, decoder failure handling, and protection against reaction/fault oracles must be engineered and verified end-to-end. Empirical case studies and KAT-style tests are valuable complements to formal proofs for achieving robust implementations. Both were actively encouraged by the NIST in the course of their post-quantum standardization projects.

4.3 Hash-Based Signatures: Minimal HFB Surface

Hash-based signature schemes (for example, SPHINCS+, XMSS, and LMS) build security solely from standard hash properties (preimage resistance, second-preimage resistance, and—where required—collision resistance), using one-time/one-time-like chains and Merkle trees. This reliance on only hash assumptions yields a minimal algebraic attack surface among the post-quantum families and avoids number-theoretic or lattice assumptions entirely.

Merkle authentication paths are produced by iteratively hashing concatenated sibling nodes up to the root using a cryptographic hash function H; verification recomputes the path and checks equality with the public-key root node. Formally, given leaf L and authentication siblings $S_1, \ldots, S_h$ the root is computed by $R = H\big(\cdots H(H(L\|S_1)\|S_2)\cdots\big)$, and the verifier accepts if the recomputed root equals the public key root.

Winternitz one-time signatures (W-OTS+) are vector-valued chains. Key generation samples l secret seeds $(x_1, \ldots, x_l)$ and computes chain endpoints $\mathsf{pk}_i = F^{w-1}(x_i)$, where F is an iterated hash/compression and w is the Winternitz parameter. The message digest (plus checksum) is encoded in base-w to select which chain positions are revealed; a verifier advances each revealed chain element to its endpoint and authenticates the aggregated endpoints via the Merkle path [13].

SPHINCS+ is a stateless, hypertree-based construction combining many FORS trees, W-OTS+ chains, and layered Merkle trees; it was standardized (as SLH-DSA) by NIST and offers a conservative, stateless alternative to stateful schemes. XMSS and LMS (and their hierarchical variants) are stateful and are profiled in NIST SP 800-208: they require application environments that can enforce strict private-state management such as HSMs or dedicated firmware signing workflows [8,18].

Minimal Attack Surface (and Remaining Pitfalls). Because security reduces to well-studied hash properties, the mathematical attack surface is small compared with algebraic constructions. Nevertheless, implementations must still address practical HFBs and side-channel/fault vectors:

- State management (XMSS/LMS). Stateful schemes are vulnerable to catastrophic key reuse if state updates are lost or mis-synchronized; secure deployment requires atomic state updates and audited backup/restore procedures.

- Side channels and constant-time. SPHINCS+ is stateless but still requires constant-time kernels, robust parsing, and secure randomness/seed handling to avoid timing or microarchitectural leakage.
- Fault injection. Faults that induce inconsistent intermediate W-OTS+ values, Merkle node corruptions, or truncated recomputation can enable forgeries or key recovery; such attacks have been demonstrated against SPHINCS-like designs and adapted to XMSS.

4.4 Comparison Summary Across PQC Families

The manifestations of HFBs differs sharply across PQC families. These differences can be traced directly to the mathematical foundations and implementation requirements of each scheme type. Table 1 provides a structured comparison.

Table 1. Comparison of HFB Characteristics Across PQC Families

Scheme Family	Dominant Mathematics	Primary HFB Types	Underlying Causes/Remarks
Lattice-based (Kyber, Dilithium, Falcon)	Polynomial rings, NTT, discrete Gaussian sampling	Timing side-channels (NTT reductions, coefficient compression); Precision divergences (floating-point sampling, Falcon); Oracle leaks from early-exit logic.	Complex arithmetic with secret-dependent branches; reliance on floating-point units; immaturity of implementations
Code-based (HQC, Classic McEliece)	Linear algebra over finite fields ($\mathbb{F}_q$)	Memory-safety bugs (buffer overflows, API misuse); Rare fault-injection vulnerabilities.	Finite-field operations are inherently constant-time; HFBs mainly stem from conventional programming errors rather than mathematics
Hash-based (SPHINCS+, XMSS, LMS)	Cryptographic hash functions, Merkle trees, hash chains	State-management errors (key reuse in stateful variants); Fault injection in tree structures.	Bit-oriented, deterministic computations with minimal mathematical complexity; HFBs largely software-engineering or physical-attack induced

In summary, lattice-based schemes exhibit the richest and most diverse HFB profiles, with multiple categories of subtle mathematical and platform-dependent vulnerabilities. Code-based schemes show far fewer cryptographic-specific HFBs, with their risks being dominated by classical implementation errors. Hash-based schemes present the smallest mathematical HFB surface, with residual issues restricted to state management and specialized fault attacks.

More information on mitigating these HFBs possibly present in current and future implementations are described in the Appendix A.

5 Implementation Stats and Results

To detect HFBs we provide wycheproof-pqc[2], an extension of the Wycheproof testing framework for PQC. We developed a C-based test harness and a structured methodology for generating KATs, malformed vectors, and adversarial inputs targeting PQC schemes, directly addressing the risks put forward by this paper.

5.1 Research and Vector Generations

The main contribution is the set of vectors targetting ML-KEM, ML-DSA, FN-DSA, SLH-DSA and HQC specifically;

These vectors are targeted at low occurence HFBs and include prior existing HFBs found from open source implementations of PQC.

The researched bugs that were identified around 15 examples are documented methodically and were added to the HFB collection started while working on the first paper. All validated failures were documented with the structured format used throughout the study (Specification, Defect, Impact, Code Snippet) so they can be tracked and reproduced by implementers.

Test generation combined conformance testing with adversarial input crafting:

- Baseline KATs: We integrated official NIST conformance vectors.
- Bug Reproduction: We reproduced known issues from bug research and bugs in open source PQC libraries such as PQClean, LibOQS/liboqs integrations, TLS stacks that include PQC etc.
- Input Mutation: We systematically crafted edge-case vectors by:
  - Bit-flipping signature bytes.
  - Introducing non-canonical encodings and redundant padding.
  - Creating signatures with single-byte offsets.

5.2 Capabilities

Each KAT encodes one of the HFB classes established in Sect. 4. For each vector the tests perform:

1. functional verification (expected true/false);
2. negative/over-acceptance checks (vectors that only a lax parser should accept);
3. timing variability probes (micro-benchmarks around candidate branches compiled with realistic optimization flags);
4. cross-platform comparison (same vector executed on x86/ARM builds to detect precision/FPU differences).

[2] wycheproof-pqc repository, with the technical contribution of the paper is available here: https://github.com/mattc-try/wycheproof-pqc/README.md.

6 Conclusions

The transition to PQC introduces novel and distinct classes of implementation bugs, fundamentally diverging from those of classical schemes, where common carry-propagation bugs are nearly absent. This new HFB profile is dominated by timing side-channels in polynomial arithmetic (e.g., secret-dependent conditional modular reduction in NTT, variable-time division in the compression of coefficients) and very small precision divergences in floating-point Gaussian sampling (required by FALCON), particularly within lattice-based constructions (ML-KEM, ML-DSA, FN-DSA), which exhibit the richest HFB profile.

In order to counter these PQC-specific HFBs, we introduced a systematic taxonomy and released `wycheproof-pqc`, an open-source extension of Google's Wycheproof testing library. This artifact provides tailored test vectors (KATs) that specifically incorporate adversarial vectors, timing variability probes, and cross-platform comparisons to find such defects, leading to the documentation of 15 implementation flaws. These results establish PQC-specific KATs as an effective, yet low-cost, defense mechanism, thereby confirming their importance for securing PQC implementations and deployments.

Limitations. The KAT library and test results come from HFBs reported in the literature and community artifacts (e.g., bug reports on GitHub) so far and are, thus, less complete than our work on classical HFBs [29]. Nonetheless, we hope that this KAT library will help to uncover HFBs that managed to escape standard testing. Some of the discovered issues require a physical side-channel or fault injection to fully validate exploitability; our KATs detect the software precursors but do not substitute for full hardware-level validation. Finally, we emphasize that `wycheproof-pqc` should not be the only effort for testing PQC software; rather, it should be combined with one or more of the other methods for detection and prevention of HFBs discussed in [29], e.g., fuzzing.

A Countermeasures for Hard-to-Find Bugs in PQC

Mitigating HFBs in Post-Quantum Cryptography implementations requires a defense-in-depth strategy that transcends simple conformance testing. The countermeasures detailed in this section address vulnerabilities at the algorithmic, microarchitectural, and compiler levels. These strategies are essential because, as established in this work, the mathematical novelty of PQC schemes introduces HFB profiles distinct from classical cryptography. Effective hardening depends not on the assumed security of the mathematical primitives alone, but on engineering practices that eliminate observable, secret-dependent variations in implementation behavior. This section provides a clear engineering roadmap for achieving robust and secure PQC software.

A.1 Systematic Hardening for Lattice-Based Cryptography

A.1.1 Side-Channel Protection The primary goal of side-channel protection is to eliminate any correlation between secret data and observable non-functional properties of the implementation, such as its execution time, power consumption, or memory access patterns.

A core principle of side-channel hardening is to ensure all arithmetic operations execute in constant time. Secret-dependent branching and variable-latency machine instructions are major sources of timing leakage. For example, integer division instructions like `idiv` on x86 architectures have input-dependent latencies. As demonstrated by the KyberSlash attacks, this specific vulnerability can be exploited to recover the private keys of Kyber. To prevent this, such operations must be replaced with constant-time reduction algorithms, such as Montgomery reduction or a branch-free implementation of Barrett reduction, which use a fixed sequence of multiplications and shifts.

Another critical vulnerability arises from conditional branches within core algorithms. In Number Theoretic Transform (NTT) operations, a naive modular reduction like `if (t >= q) t -= q;` creates a timing vulnerability that leaks information about secret coefficients. This must be replaced with a branch-free equivalent that uses bitwise masking to achieve the same result in a constant number of cycles.

To thwart attacks based on memory access patterns or power analysis, the relationship between secret data and its physical representation must be broken. This can be achieved through blinded memory access techniques. One such technique is arithmetic masking, where polynomial coefficients are combined with fresh random values before processing. The computation is performed on this masked data, and the mask is removed only at the end. Another technique is to randomize the execution order of independent operations, such as the sequence of NTT butterfly calculations, which disrupts an attacker's ability to correlate power traces with specific computations.

Samplers that use rejection loops are another source of leakage, as the number of iterations can depend on secret data. To prevent this, discrete Gaussian samplers should be implemented using constant-time algorithms. Methods based on precomputed Cumulative Distribution Tables (CDT) can be made secure by ensuring they execute with a fixed number of iterations, thereby making their timing independent of the values being sampled.

A.1.2 Oracle Attack Prevention Oracle attacks exploit logical flaws where an implementation's response reveals information about the correctness of an internal computation. This is often achieved by measuring timing variations caused by early-exit logic in verification routines.

To prevent such attacks, all verification steps must execute in constant time. The decapsulation logic, for instance, must not terminate prematurely based on secret-dependent checks. A loop checking the validity of polynomial coefficients must not use a `break` statement upon finding an invalid coefficient, as this creates a clear timing difference. The correct approach is to accumulate failure flags using bitwise operations over the entire set of coefficients and perform a single check only after the loop has completed.

Furthermore, an implementation's observable response must be uniform across all failure conditions. This involves returning a generic error message regardless of the specific internal check that failed. Normalizing the timing of rejection responses, potentially by adding a random delay, also helps prevent an attacker from distinguishing different error pathways and gaining information about the secret data.

A.1.3 Mitigating Floating-Point Vulnerabilities in Falcon A primary issue is precision divergence. Floating-point operations are not fully standardized across different hardware architectures, such as x86 and ARM, which can lead to minute, non-deterministic differences in computation. It has been shown that these divergences can be collected and exploited as an oracle to recover a Falcon secret key. One mitigation is to replace the floating-point logic entirely with deterministic, integer-only sampling methods. A complementary approach is to incorporate rigorous cross-platform validation into testing pipelines, ensuring that signatures generated for identical inputs are bit-for-bit identical across all supported architectures.

Another vulnerability is mantissa leakage. The Hamming weight of the mantissas of floating-point values can be leaked through physical side channels like electromagnetic emissions. This information can be used in attacks to recover the FFT coefficients, which ultimately leads to key recovery. To mitigate this threat, implementers can use fixed-point arithmetic instead of floating-point, or apply masking schemes to the FFT coefficients to decorrelate the mantissa values from the underlying secrets.

A.2 Systematic Hardening for Code-Based Cryptography

A key area of concern is decoder hardening against reaction oracles. Iterative decoders may have iteration counts or memory access patterns that depend on the secret error vector, creating an observable reaction that leaks information. To mitigate this, one must enforce a fixed-time decapsulation wrapper that ensures a constant amount of work is performed, or design decoders with a provably fixed iteration count. The correct implementation of a Fujisaki-Okamoto (FO) style transform can also mask decryption failures, but this is only effective if the re-encryption path is also fully protected from side channels.

Sampler protection is critical. Samplers used for generating constant-weight vectors can leak information through variable-time rejection loops or data-dependent shuffles. Implementations must adopt constant-iteration sampling algorithms or use a fixed-iteration wrapper around rejection-based samplers. Any shuffling operations must be implemented in a data-independent manner.

The finite-field arithmetic in code-based schemes, while simpler than in lattices, can still be a source of leakage. Table-based implementations are particularly vulnerable to cache-timing attacks and should be replaced with bitsliced or purely arithmetic implementations. It is also important to ensure that any polynomial reduction is performed using constant-time algorithms.

Finally, the use of structured codes, such as quasi-cyclic codes, introduces the risk of algebraic weaknesses. While these codes reduce key sizes, they can create vulnerabilities. Implementations should therefore include tests to detect and filter any weak keys and should use conservative parameter choices to limit the effectiveness of structure-specific attacks.

A.3 Compiler-Level and Microarchitectural Protections

Even a securely written implementation can be undermined by compiler optimizations or underlying hardware behaviors.

At the hardware level, microarchitectural hardening is necessary. This includes inserting serialization instructions, such as `lfence` on x86, to prevent out-of-order execution from creating timing leaks. Where feasible, disabling dynamic voltage and frequency scaling (DVFS) during cryptographic operations can ensure a more stable timing baseline, making anomalies easier to detect.

At the build level, developers must enforce strict code generation constraints. This involves using compiler flags that ensure predictable behavior, such as `-fwrapv` for defined integer overflow. For security-critical functions, it may be necessary to use lower optimization levels or specific function attributes to prevent the compiler from making transformations that inadvertently introduce vulnerabilities, such as reintroducing a division instruction where a constant-time reduction was intended.

Lastly, secure memory management is crucial. Sensitive data such as private keys and intermediate states must be securely wiped from memory after use, typically by XORing the data with randomness. Using hardware memory protection features, like guard pages via `mprotect`, can also help prevent accidental reads or writes outside of intended buffers, mitigating a large class of common programming errors.

References

1. Aguilar Melchor, C., Aragon, N., Bettaieb, S., Bidoux, L., Blazy, O., Bos, J., et al.: Hamming Quasi-Cyclic (HQC). Specification (4th round version) (2024). https://pqc-hqc.org/doc/hqc-specification_2024-10-30.pdf
2. Alagic, G., Apon, D., Cooper, D., Dang, Q., Dang, T., Kelsey, J., et al.: Status report on the third round of the NIST post-quantum cryptography standardization process. NIST Interagency/Internal Report 8413, National Institute of Standards and Technology (2022)
3. Berlekamp, E.R., McEliece, R.J., Van Tilborg, H.C.: On the inherent intractability of certain coding problems. IEEE Trans. Inf. Theory **24**(3), 384–386 (1978)
4. Bernstein, D.J., Bhargavan, K., Bhasin, S., Chattopadhyay, A., Chia, T.K., Kannwischer, M.J., et al.: KyberSlash: exploiting secret-dependent division timings in Kyber implementations. IACR Trans. Cryptogr. Hardw. Embed. Syst. **2025**(2), 209–234 (2025)

5. Braga, A., Dahab, R.: A survey on tools and techniques for the programming and verification of secure cryptographic software. In: 15th Brazilian Symposium on Information and Computational Systems Security (SBSeg 2015), pp. 30–43. Brazilian Computing Society (2015)
6. Brumley, B.B., Barbosa, M., Page, D., Vercauteren, F.: Practical realisation and elimination of an ECC-related software bug attack. In: Topics in Cryptology — CT-RSA 2012. Lecture Notes in Computer Science, vol. 7178, pp. 171–186. Springer (2012). https://doi.org/10.1007/978-3-642-27954-6_11
7. Chenu, M., Sportiello, L.: Post-quantum cryptography, the journey so far and the challenges ahead. Tech. Rep. JRC144095, Publications Office of the European Union, Luxembourg (2025)
8. Cooper, D.A., Apon, D.C., Dang, Q.H., Davidson, M.S., Dworkin, M.J., Miller, C.A.: Recommendation for stateful hash-based signature schemes. NIST Special Publication 800-208, National Institute of Standards and Technology (2020)
9. Deng, S., Li, M., Tang, Y., Wang, S., Yan, S., Zhang, Y.: CipherH: automated detection of ciphertext side-channel vulnerabilities in cryptographic software. In: 32nd USENIX Security Symposium (USS 2023), pp. 6843–6860. USENIX (2023)
10. Fouque, P., Hoffstein, J., Kirchner, P., Lyubashevsky, V., Pornin, T., Prest, T., et al.: FALCON: fast-fourier lattice-based compact signatures over NTRU. Specification v1.2 (2020). https://falcon-sign.info/falcon.pdf
11. Google: Project Wycheproof (2020). https://github.com/google/wycheproof
12. Guerreau, M., Martinelli, A., Ricosset, T., Rossi, M.: The hidden parallelepiped is back again: power analysis attacks on Falcon. IACR Trans. Cryptogr. Hardw. Embed. Syst. **2022**(3), 141–164 (2022)
13. Huelsing, A., Butin, D., Gazdag, S.L., Rijneveld, J., Mohaisen, A.: XMSS: eXtended Merkle Signature Scheme. RFC 8391, Internet Engineering Task Force (2018)
14. Kannwischer, M.J., Schwabe, P., Stebila, D., Wiggers, T.: Improving software quality in cryptography standardization projects. In: 6th IEEE European Symposium on Security and Privacy Workshops (EuroS&PW 2022), pp. 19–30. IEEE (2022)
15. Karabulut, E., Aysu, A.: FALCON down: Breaking FALCON post-quantum signature scheme through side-channel attacks. In: 58th ACM/IEEE Design Automation Conference (DAC 2021), pp. 691–696. IEEE (2021)
16. Lidl, R., Niederreiter, H.: Finite Fields, Encyclopedia of Mathematics and its Applications, vol. 20. Cambridge University Press (1997)
17. McEliece, R.J.: A public-key cryptosystem based on algebraic coding theory. In: The Deep Space Network Progress Report 42-44, pp. 114–116. Jet Propulsion Laboratory, California Institute of Technology (1978)
18. McGrew, D.A., Curcio, M.G., Fluhrer, S.: Leighton-Micali hash-based signatures. RFC 8554, Internet Engineering Task Force (2019)
19. Mondal, P., Kundu, S., Bhattacharya, S., Karmakar, A., Verbauwhede, I.: A practical key-recovery attack on LWE-based key-encapsulation mechanism schemes using Rowhammer. In: Applied Cryptography and Network Security — ACNS 2024. LNCS, vol. 14585, pp. 271–300. Springer (2024). https://doi.org/10.1007/978-3-031-54776-8_11
20. Moody, D.: NIST PQC: the road ahead. In: Presentation at the 3rd Annual Workshop on Real World Post-Quantum Cryptography (RWPQC 2025) (2025). https://csrc.nist.gov/presentations/2025/nist-pqc-the-road-ahead
21. National Institute of Standards and Technology (NIST): Module-Lattice-Based Digital Signature Standard. Federal Information Processing Standard (FIPS) 204, U.S. Department of Commerce (2024)

22. National Institute of Standards and Technology (NIST): Module-lattice-based key-encapsulation mechanism standard. Federal Information Processing Standard (FIPS) 203, U.S. Department of Commerce (2024)
23. National Institute of Standards and Technology (NIST): Stateless hash-based digital signature standard. Federal Information Processing Standard (FIPS) 205, U.S. Department of Commerce (2024)
24. Nguyen, D.T., Gaj, K.: Fast Falcon signature generation and verification using ARMv8 NEON instructions. In: Progress in Cryptology — AFRICACRYPT 2023. LNCS, vol. 14064, pp. 417–441. Springer (2023)
25. Overbeck, R., Sendrier, N.: Code-based cryptography. In: Post-Quantum Cryptography, pp. 95–145. Springer (2009). https://doi.org/10.1007/978-3-540-88702-7_4
26. Potii, O., Kachko, O., Kandii, S., Kaptol, Y.: Determining the effect of a floating point on the Falcon digital signature algorithm security. Eastern-Eur. J. Enterprise Technol. **1**(9(127)), 52–59 (2024)
27. PQClean Development Team: PQClean Issue #522: Falcon signature inconsistency across ARM platforms (2023). https://github.com/PQClean/PQClean/issues/522
28. PQCRYPTO Consortium: post-quantum cryptography for long-term security. Deliverables of EU Horizon 2020 Project ICT-645622 (2018). https://pqcrypto.eu.org/deliverables/
29. Steinbach, M., Großschädl, J., Rønne, P.B.: Hard-to-find bugs in public-key cryptographic software: Classification and test methodologies. In: Security, Privacy, and Applied Cryptography Engineering — SPACE 2025. LNCS, vol. 16406, pp. 336–357. Springer (2025). https://doi.org/10.1007/978-3-032-16342-4_19
30. Wafo-Tapa, G., Bettaieb, S., Bidoux, L., Gaborit, P., Marcatel, E.: A practicable timing attack against HQC and its countermeasure. Adv. Math. Commun. **16**(3), 621–642 (2022)
31. Weinmann, R.P.: Assessing and exploiting BigNum vulnerabilities. BlackHat (2015). https://comsecuris.com/slides/slides-bignum-bhus2015.pdf (2015)
32. Xu, Z., Pemberton, O., Sinha Roy, S., Oswald, D., Yao, W., Zheng, Z.: Magnifying side-channel leakage of lattice-based cryptosystems with chosen ciphertexts: the case study of Kyber. IEEE Trans. Comput. **71**(9), 2163–2176 (2021)
33. Zong, C.: The mathematical foundation of post-quantum cryptography. Res. Sci. Partner J. **8**, 0801 (2025)

Combining Digital Signatures and Key Recycling in QKD Authentication: A Performance and Security Analysis

Sara Nikula(✉)

VTT Technical Research Centre of Finland, Kaitoväylä 1, 90590 Oulu, Finland
sara.nikula@vtt.fi

Abstract. Quantum key distribution (QKD) offers a secure mechanism for sharing encryption keys, grounded in the principles of quantum physics, and remains resilient even in the presence of quantum computing capabilities. However, a fundamental challenge in QKD is authentication, which currently depends on classical cryptographic techniques. Post-quantum cryptography (PQC) and public key infrastructure (PKI) are frequently proposed for QKD authentication due to their scalability and efficient node verification, which eliminates the need for pre-shared key pairs across individual links. The practicality of PKI, however, hinges on the current assumption that no known attacks can significantly accelerate the compromise of underlying post-quantum digital signatures, and that public-private key pairs can be refreshed at a manageable rate. This paper investigates a scenario in which post-quantum digital signature algorithms offer only transient security, valid for a limited number of generated signatures. This work analyzes the volume of authentication key renewal data that would need to traverse the network under such conditions to preserve algorithmic security, demonstrating that digital signatures lose their advantage when their usage period is severely constrained. To address this limitation, a novel approach is proposed: integrating PKI with key recycling in QKD reduces the volume of authentication key renewal data required in QKD networks. The security analysis reveals that, given the stringent requirements of post-quantum digital signatures, the overall authentication security is likely to be dominated by the inherent vulnerabilities of QKD sessions, particularly when conventional security parameters on the order of $\sim 10^{-10}$ are employed. These findings provide insights for the future-proof design of QKD networks.

Keywords: Quantum Key Distribution · Authentication · Digital Signatures · Public Key Infrastructure · Key recycling

1 Introduction

In contemporary networks, communication is predominantly encrypted, which helps protect privacy. Encryption requires a shared encryption key at both ends

P. D'Arco and A. Zamfiroiu (Eds.): SecITC 2025, LNCS 16443, pp. 166–179, 2026.
https://doi.org/10.1007/978-3-032-17443-7_10

of the communication channel. Traditionally, key exchange has been accomplished using asymmetric algorithms, such as those based on the factoring of large integers [23]. However, the development of quantum computers and the algorithms they run pose a threat to these traditional key exchange algorithms, necessitating new alternatives. Post-quantum cryptography (PQC) operates on the same principle as classical key exchange algorithms but relies on different mathematical computations that, to the best of current knowledge, cannot be broken by quantum computers. Such new algorithms have been developed and standardized following an initiative by National Institute of Standards and Technology (NIST) in 2016 [15]. The European Commission has established a roadmap for transitioning to post-quantum cryptography [5].

Another method for distributing keys securely is quantum key distribution (QKD), proposed already in 1984 [3]. QKD is based on the no-cloning theorem of quantum physics, which allows a secret key to be shared while ensuring that no eavesdropping has occurred. QKD requires specialized technology and is an evolving field, although some commercial solutions are already available [8,24, 25].

1.1 Authentication Alternatives for QKD

A critical challenge in QKD connections is authentication, which is essential for verifying the identity of the remote party in the link. Authentication relies on classical cryptographic methods, typically implemented through either pre-shared encryption keys or digital signatures. Pre-shared keys allow for authentication by symmetric means, even in an information-theoretically secure manner [28]. Naturally, the challenge is that each link requires its own key pair to be distributed. In a network with N nodes, the total number of key pairs required is $N(N-1)/2$ if each link is to be assigned a key. However, part of the data produced by a QKD session can be saved for the authentication of the next session, thus eliminating the need to distribute a new key for each key exchange session [11], a technique called key recycling.

Authentication of QKD links using quantum-safe digital signatures has been proposed in numerous sources [12,22,27]. At the time of writing, NIST has published standards for two different PQC signatures, one lattice-based (ML-DSA defined in FIPS 204) [17] and one hash-based (SLH-DSA defined in FIPS 205) [19]. Another lattice-based algorithm, FALCON, has also been announced for standardization under the standard FIPS 206, but the standard has not yet been published [6,18]. Since QKD is often considered an alternative to PQC, authenticating with PQC algorithms may seem counterintuitive. However, it is justified by the fact that authentication differs in nature from key exchange: unlike key exchange, authentication cannot be broken retrospectively, so it suffices that the authentication algorithm remains secure for the duration of the authenticated session [14].

To avoid the need to share bilateral authentication key pairs for each link, digital signatures must be integrated into a Public Key Infrastructure (PKI). PKI is a collection of trusted authorities and the certificates they issue. Using these for authentication allows PKI members to verify one another without the need to distribute bilateral encryption keys. An interested reader can find a more thorough explanation of PKI's, even though a somewhat old and thus concentrated on classical asymmetric algorithms, in [4].

PKI's effectiveness relies on computationally secure signature algorithms which allow certificates to be renewed with moderate phase. One of the main use scenarios for QKD technology is a situation where asymmetric key exchange algorithms can no longer be considered secure, that is, their computational breaking has been accelerated by some quantum or classical algorithm. The quantum-safe key exchange algorithms either standardized or included in the NIST competition as of March 2025 are based on lattice problems, isogenies, or codes, while digital signatures are based either on lattice problems or hash functions [21]. Partially, the algorithms used for key exchange and signing are based on the same mathematical problems, making it plausible that the weakening of quantum-safe key exchange algorithms would also lead to the weakening of signature algorithms, or at least some of them.

At the moment, no such attack is known, but if this would happen, one possible attack path could be related to statistical properties resulting from a large number of signatures being created with the same private key. For example, resulting from the fact that two signatures should never be created for the same message, the security of FALCON scales negatively with the number of signatures generated [6]. For SPHINCS+ underlying SLH-DSA, [29] suggests a novel quantum attack, reducing the number of secure signatures that can be produced with the same private key.

1.2 Purpose and Scope of This Paper

This paper examines the authentication of QKD networks starting from the situation to which QKD best responds: that quantum-safe key encapsulation mechanisms have weakened, and the only long-term secure way to share keys is QKD. This work examines how the acceleration of breaking lattice- or hash-based signature algorithms affects the amount of authentication-related data shared in the network and whether PKI can maintain its promise of an efficient authentication method in this scenario, comparing it to the case of pre-shared keys. Furthermore, a new approach combining these two methods is suggested. This approach helps to produce secure keys in QKD networks with only limited number of digital signatures, thus counterfeiting certain attack types that benefit from a large number of signatures. An analysis of the security implications of this method is also provided.

This paper is organized as follows. Sections 2.1 and 2.2 clarify how the need for authentication key renewal data, per authenticated QKD session, has been calculated. In Sect. 3, the results obtained using this method are presented, taking into account the potential weakening of PQC digital signatures. Section 3.2 introduces a new approach, along with a security and performance analysis. Section 4 discusses the benefits and drawbacks of this approach, and Sect. 5 concludes the paper.

2 Methods

In this paper, it is assumed that QKD authentication proceeds as follows: messages in the post-processing protocol do not have individual authentication information, but once the post-processing protocol is completed, both parties authenticate the entire post-processing process by authenticating it once. Thus, each party produces one signature or symmetric authentication tag per key exchange session, resulting in total two signatures or authentication tags per key exchange session. This approach is suggested by e.g. [11]. It was chosen for this work because it minimizes the number of produced signatures or symmetric authentication tags per QKD session, even though also other authentication strategies are possible for QKD.

For modeling the authentication key renewal data related to digital signature algorithms, it is assumed that Certificate Management Protocol [9] (CMP) along with the Lightweight Certificate Management Profile defined in [10] is used for certificate update. For pre-shared keys, it is assumed that the keys are delivered by physical means to the nodes. The calculations are based on an assumption that there exists a maximum number of QKD sessions during which the same signature key or a pre-shared symmetric authentication key pair can be used. Once this limit is reached, it is assumed that the authentication keys are renewed either by obtaining a new certificate (for digital signature protocols) or physically transported (for pre-shared keys). Note that this represents the data needed to refresh the authentication keys in the QKD network, not the data needed to authenticate the QKD sessions.

2.1 Costs of Renewing Authentication Keys for Digital Signatures

In this paper, SLH-DSA and FALCON are used as example digital signature algorithms. This choice was made because SLH-DSA is a standardized hash-based signature algorithm and is based on a mathematical problem different from lattice-based algorithms, so its security may potentially remain intact even if lattice-based algorithms are broken. Among lattice-based algorithms, FALCON was chosen because its signatures and public keys are shorter than those of ML-DSA [6,17], making it a potential choice for PKI use. The algorithms are implementable in several security categories accoring to their computational strength [20]. In both cases, security category 1 was assumed; with FALCON, this meant FALCON512 variant and with SLH-DSA, SLH-DSA-SHA2-128 s/SLH-DSA-SHAKE-128 s variant, which are the variants offering the most compact signature sizes [6,19].

The content of messages related to certificate renewal in PKI varies according to certificate profiles. Lightweight Certificate Management Protocol profile defined by RFC9483 [10] is considered in this work. In this profile, updating a certificate to a new one must be done before the previous certificate expires. The certificate renewal request is made to the certificate authority, and the process involves a total of four messages: Key Update Request, Key Update Response, and two confirmation messages. The Key Update Request includes the unique identifiers of the new and old certificates, the applicant's name, the public key, the signature made with the current public key, and the certificate chain. The Key Update Response includes the unique identifier of the new certificate, the status (indicating whether the request was accepted), the signature, the actual issued certificate (containing at least the certificate serial number, algorithm, issuer, certificate owner, validity period, public key, and the certificate authority's signature), and the associated certificate chain. The confirmation message from the end-user includes the hash function used, the unique identifier of the new certificate, the status, and the signature. The confirmation message from the certificate authority includes an empty field and the signature. Each message also includes a header containing at least the version, sender, receiver, algorithm used, 128-bit event identifier, 128-bit cryptographic nonce, and the certificate profile name.

The certificate profile does not directly define the length of all fields, as some depend on implementation. In this paper, a one-byte load is allocated to fields whose content length is not directly defined. In this way, the amount of other data, excluding signature and public key data, was calculated to be 289 bytes. For FALCON512 at security level 1, the signature length is 666 bytes and the public key length is 897 bytes, so in total renewing the certificate requires $5 \times 666 = 3330$ bytes of signature data and $2 \times 897 = 1794$ bytes of public key data, totaling $289 + 3330 + 1794 = 5413$ bytes. For SLH-DSA at security level 1, the signature length is 7856 bytes and the public key length is 32 bytes, so renewing the certificate requires $5 \times 7856 = 39280$ bytes of signature data and $2 \times 32 = 64$ bytes of public key data, totaling $289 + 39280 + 64 = 39633$ bytes.

This certificate update process must be executed each time the lifespan of a digital signature key pair is reached. Currently, this is primarily determined by the policy of the PKI. In the future, if the compromise of underlying digital signature algorithms is accelerated, more frequent key updates will be required, necessitating the execution of the certificate update process each time.

2.2 Costs of Renewing Authentication Keys for Pre-shared Keys

For pre-shared keys, the use of MAC-type authentication is assumed. A hash of the message is calculated with a 256 bits (32 bytes) long key, as this length can be considered resistant to attacks by quantum computers. Since the same symmetric key must be shared at both ends of the link, renewing such a key pair requires transporting 512 bits (64 bytes) outside the network, for example, via a USB stick.

The frequency of key pair renewal depends on the desired security parameter. The security parameter describes the amount of uncertainty related to the security of the protocol, with a smaller security parameter indicating less uncertainty and thus greater security. More information about the significance of the security parameter can be found in sources such as [26]. In this work, this value is kept constant regardless of the assumed computational capacity of quantum computers. This is because pre-shared keys allow for information-theoretically secure authentication in the so-called Wegman-Carter style [28], which cannot be computationally broken, and thus the development of quantum computers does not affect the need for key renewal. In this work, it is assumed that a portion of the key material from the previous QKD session can be retained for the authentication of the subsequent session. This eliminates the need to distribute an entirely new authentication key for each session. However, this method increases the security parameter, as explained in [2]. After a certain number of rounds, the security parameter becomes a multiple of the original security parameter. For example, if the security parameter for the first session is 10^{-20}, after ten sessions the parameter would be $10 \times 10^{-20} = 10^{-19}$. Thus, the security parameters associated with previous QKD sessions contribute to the overall resulting security parameter. The higher the desired security from the protocol, the more frequently the keys should be renewed. Therefore, the need for pre-shared key material can be described in relation to how much the security parameter can increase from its original value before reaching an unacceptable level. This is illustrated with several scenarios: 1, 100, or 1000 rounds of QKD before renewing the authentication key. The first scenario implies that key material is not reused, but a fresh authentication key is employed for each instance.

3 Results

In its call for quantum-safe signature algorithms, NIST stated that the security assessment must assume an attacker possesses 2^{64} signatures corresponding to a private-public key pair [16]. Under this assumption, SLH-DSA and FALCON are efficient; for a single QKD session, 4.30×10^{-15} bytes (SLH-DSA) or 5.87×10^{-16} bytes (FALCON) of data related to certificate renewal would be required. Thus, at the moment, FALCON appears to be an ideal choice for authenticating QKD when combined with PKI. However, in real-world scenarios, the frequency of public key certificate renewal depends on the policy of the PKI in use and would likely be higher in practice.

3.1 Scenario: Transiently Secure Lattice-Based and Hash-Based Signatures

This subsection concentrates on a scenario in which solving the mathematical problems underlying lattice-based and hash-based algorithms has been somewhat accelerated by a new quantum or classical algorithm, so that only a limited number of signatures can be safely published. Figure 1 illustrates the amount of authentication key renewal data that must be delivered, relative to the acceleration in breaking the signature algorithm. The X-axis shows the number of signatures that could be generated using FALCON or SLH-DSA before the algorithm is compromised, necessitating a key update. The Y-axis represents the amount of authentication data required for certificate renewal, which would be transmitted over the network in this scenario, per one authenticated QKD session. The horizontal lines indicate the amount of pre-shared authentication data per QKD session for different frequencies of authentication key renewal. The left side of Fig. 1, where breaking the algorithm requires 2^{64} signatures, can be considered the current state. Moving to the right, the number of secure signatures decreases.

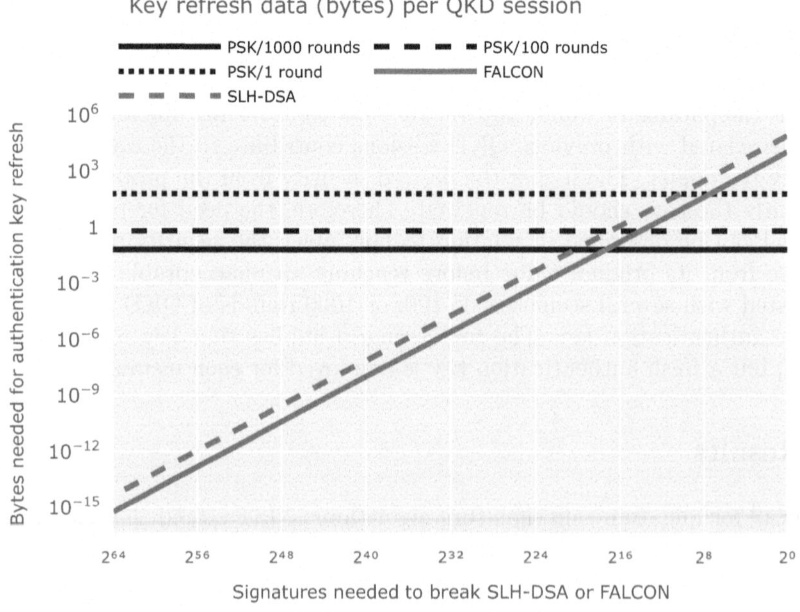

Fig. 1. Key update data required for authentication, when a limited number of FALCON or SLH-DSA signatures can be securely generated by one key pair. Horizontal lines depict amount of key update data needed for pre-shared keys if one key pair is used for 1, 100 or 1000 QKD sessions. Note that both X and Y axes are logarithmic.

As shown in the Figure, FALCON seems like an effective authentication option. It would need to be weakened very much before pre-shared keys become less data consuming: when $2^{17}/2^{14}/2^{7}$ signature pairs are needed to break FALCON, using the same PSK pair for 1000/100/1 QKD rounds becomes less data consuming than updating FALCON keys. Because the SLH-DSA signatures are significantly larger, the amount of data transmitted over the network is approximately ten times greater, reaching impractical levels sooner than its lattice-based counterpart: limitation of $2^{20}/2^{16}/2^{10}$ signature pairs is enough to make using PSK pairs for 1000/100/1 QKD rounds less data consuming than updating SLH-DSA keys.

Genuine impacts would be observed when the number of sessions that can be authenticated becomes so small that it necessitates updating certificates more frequently than PKI's own policy would otherwise require. For instance, if PKI's policy allows a single certificate to be in use for 3 months and one QKD session is authenticated per second, 2^{22} or less secure signatures would be a critical threshold, forcing more frequent certificate renewals than previously. If both lattice-based and hash-based algorithms were to be broken very rapidly, authentication using pre-shared keys could eventually become a more efficient alternative. Depending on how much increase in the security parameter is allowed, the need for authentication data per session is altered: when 256-bit authentication keys are used and one key pair is used 1000/100/1 times, 0.064/0.64/64 bytes of authentication data per QKD session needs to be pre-shared, respectively. In this case, however, authentication keys would need to be distributed separately to each link, which is likely a less practical option for most links than employing PKI.

3.2 Combining PKI and QKD Key Recycling

This subsection introduces a novel approach that combines the advantages of both PKI and QKD key recycling. The protocol proceeds as follows: each node in the QKD network connects to the PKI and obtains a public key along with a corresponding certificate. When two nodes wish to establish a connection within the QKD network, they authenticate the initial session using digital signatures. The subsequent session is authenticated by recycling the data obtained from the previous session. Key recycling can continue until the security parameter reaches an unacceptable level. At this point, the next session is again authenticated with digital signatures, after which the key material obtained in the session can again be recycled for a certain number of rounds, and so on.

This approach best fits the scenario in which only a limited number of secure digital signatures can be generated using a single key pair. It has two advantages: firstly, it allows all node pairs within the PKI to establish connections without pre-shared link-specific keys. Secondly, it permits the use of digital signature algorithms, producing only the minimum number of signatures necessary, effectively preventing those attacks that would be based on statistical analysis on a large number of signatures. Table 1 presents some examples of key renewal data requirements in this case. The required key renewal data can be easily calculated by dividing the digital signature key pair renewal data with the number of QKD rounds during which the key is recycled. As seen in the table, the amount of data needed for refreshing authentication keys depends both on the frequency of refreshing QKD authentication keys and data needed for one certificate update.

Security Analysis of Combining Digital Signatures and Key Recycling. As stated in the previous sections, recycling authentication related data between consecutive QKD sessions increases the overall security parameter of the protocol as the security parameters of all previous sessions accumulate. According to [14], when digital signatures are used to authenticate a QKD session, the security parameter related to authentication can be derived from the strength of the signature scheme.

In this subsection, FALCON is examined as a representative example. The security parameter of FALCON can be assessed using the SUF-CMA (Strong

Table 1. Some examples of key renewal data requirements (bytes per QKD session) in relation to signatures needed to break the algorithm. Notations: PSK/x = Pre-Shared Keys used with key recycling for x rounds; SLH-DSA/100 or FALCON/100 = SLH-DSA or FALCON is used for authenticating the first session and after that, authentication data is recycled for 100 rounds.

Signatures	PSK/100	PSK/1	SLH-DSA	FALCON	SLH-DSA/100	FALCON/100
2^4	0.64	64	4954.13	676.63	49.54	6.76
2^8	0.64	64	309.63	42.29	3.096	0.422
2^{16}	0.64	64	1.21	0.165	0.012	1.65×10^{-3}
2^{24}	0.64	64	4.72×10^{-3}	6.45×10^{-4}	4.72×10^{-5}	6.45×10^{-6}
2^{32}	0.64	64	1.85×10^{-5}	2.52×10^{-6}	1.85×10^{-7}	2.52×10^{-8}
2^{64}	0.64	64	4.30×10^{-15}	5.87×10^{-16}	4.30×10^{-17}	5.87×10^{-18}

Unforgeability under Chosen Message Attack) metric, which has been examined in detail in [7]. SUF-CMA is a probabilistic measure of the algorithm's resistance to forgery, determined by both the hardness of the underlying lattice problem and the number of allowed signature queries. According to [7], with up to 2^{64} signing queries, Falcon's SUF-CMA security is estimated to be at least 89 bits, leading to an authentication related security parameter of 2^{-89}.

In the context of QKD, it is sufficient for the signature algorithm to remain secure for the duration of the key exchange session. This ensures that the resulting key remains secure in the long term, as demonstrated in [14]. On the other hand, when multiple digital signatures are generated using the same key pair, the attacker's effective time window is not limited to the duration of a single QKD session. Instead, the attacker may exploit the entire lifetime of the key pair to perform forgery attempts. Consequently, the SUF-CMA strength should be evaluated based on the maximum number of allowed uses of the key pair, rather than solely on the number of queries feasible within a single QKD session.

Due to the composability theorem [1], the total authentication related security parameter at the last round before refreshing the authentication key can be calculated as a sum over security parameters of all previous QKD sessions and the initial authentication related security parameter, i.e., it is $\epsilon_{auth} + n\epsilon_{QKD}$, where n is the number of rounds before the authentication key is refreshed, ϵ_{auth} is the initial authentication related security parameter and ϵ_{QKD} represents the security parameter associated with the quantum phase of the protocol. In the literature on QKD, robustness and correctness are sometimes included in the total security parameter [13]. However, this work focuses solely on the security component and, therefore, robustness and correctness aspects are omitted.

Figure 2 illustrates how the security parameter is affected when authentication is performed using FALCON512 digital signatures and the same key material is reused for 100 or 1000 rounds. In this case, it is assumed that the overall security parameter for a QKD session is set to 10^{-10}, a commonly adopted value in QKD literature [13,26,30]. In this context, the security parameter of each QKD session depends on three factors: (i) the position of the session within the authentication key recycling cycle, (ii) the security parameter of the authentication scheme, and (iii) the overall QKD session security parameter. As shown in the figure, the authentication-related security parameter during the first session equals that of FALCON512 (2^{-89}), but it increases rapidly in subsequent sessions. This is primarily due to the accumulation of security parameters from previous QKD sessions, where the authentication component becomes non-dominant. Consequently, the convention of targeting a total security parameter of approximately 10^{-10} makes authentication with key recycling significantly less secure than using fresh digital signatures for each session.

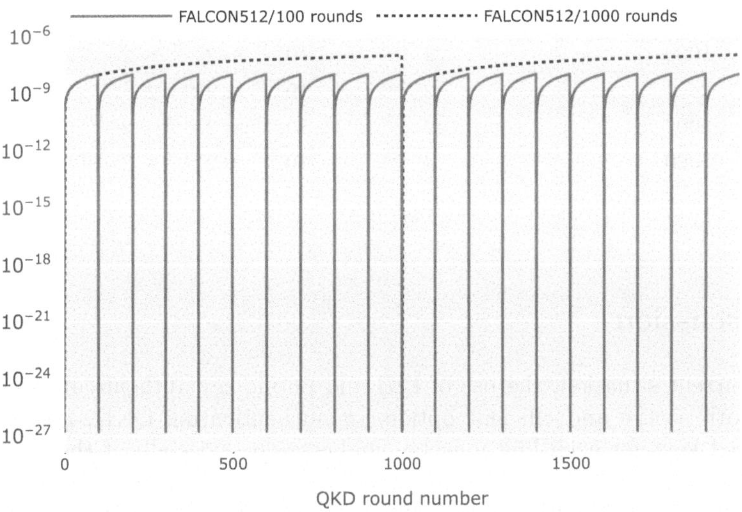

Fig. 2. Security parameter related to authentication, when the first session is authenticated with FALCON512 digital signatures and after that, authentication data is recycled for 100 or 1000 rounds with QKD security parameter $= 10^{-10}$ and authentication parameter for FALCON $= 2^{-89}$ as in [7]. Note that y axis is logarithmic.

As shown in the figure, recycling the key material for 1000 (100) rounds allows the authentication parameter to increase up to $10^{-7} \approx 2^{-23}$ ($10^{-8} \approx 2^{-27}$). Using the data in Table 1 it can be calculated that maintaining authentication-related parameters at or below these levels would require approximately 5.87×10^{-18} (5.87×10^{-19}) bytes of authentication key renewal data.

Compared to the security levels traditionally associated with cryptographic applications, these authentication-related parameters appear relatively high.

This is primarily due to the cumulative effects of QKD-related security parameters. Selecting smaller security parameter values for QKD sessions would reduce these upper bounds. Example configurations are provided in Table 2.

Table 2. Maximum authentication related security parameters (Max. ϵ_{auth}) after a certain number of authentication key recycling rounds with different security parameter choices for authentication (ϵ_{auth}) and QKD session (ϵ_{QKD}). If rounds before key refresh = 1, each session is authenticated with a digital signature.

Rounds before key refresh	Initial ϵ_{auth}	ϵ_{QKD}	Max. ϵ_{auth}
1	2^{-89}	$10^{-10} \approx 2^{-33}$	2^{-89}
100	2^{-89}	$10^{-10} \approx 2^{-33}$	$\sim 2^{-27}$
1000	2^{-89}	$10^{-10} \approx 2^{-33}$	$\sim 2^{-23}$
1	2^{-128}	$10^{-10} \approx 2^{-33}$	2^{-128}
100	2^{-128}	$10^{-10} \approx 2^{-33}$	$\sim 2^{-27}$
1000	2^{-128}	$10^{-10} \approx 2^{-33}$	$\sim 2^{-23}$
1	2^{-128}	$10^{-38} \approx 2^{-128}$	2^{-128}
100	2^{-128}	$10^{-38} \approx 2^{-128}$	$\sim 2^{-119}$
1000	2^{-128}	$10^{-38} \approx 2^{-128}$	$\sim 2^{-116}$

4 Discussion

In the current situation, the use of PKI and public key authentication appears to be both secure and efficient option for authenticating QKD, as delivering pre-shared keys for each link may be cumbersome, especially if the network is large. However, the benefits of using digital signatures start to diminish in case a new mathematical breakthrough is able to weaken their security promises. The method presented in this paper combines digital signatures and key recycling in QKD. In this way, it increases the number of QKD sessions that can be authenticated with one digital signature key pair and decreases the need for authentication related data. This makes digital signatures usable even in the scenario that a very limited number of signatures could be securely generated with them.

The security of the proposed authentication method depends on three things: the security of the used digital signature algorithm, the security parameter for a single QKD session and the maximum number of rounds before authentication key renewal. From key recycling perspective, the security implications of this protocol are the same as with any other type of authentication key recycling in QKD. After the first round, the security of the authentication key material is dependent on the security parameters of the previous QKD sessions, as the authentication data is created in the quantum channel. The authentication related security parameter increases after each round, until the critical limit is reached and a new digital signature is produced. Thus, QKD rounds executed just before a fresh signature is made would have a larger security parameter than the previous ones. Based on the results, it can be seen that the maximum authentication parameter is dominated by the largest value in the chain of QKD sessions; thus, requiring QKD sessions to be run with a security parameter notably smaller than conventionally accepted value of $\approx 10^{-10}$ would greatly decrease the authentication related security parameter and thus enhance security of the protocol. This, however, would come with a cost of decreased key rates, which are at the moment known to be a limiting factor in the current QKD technology, especially with longer links.

The amount of certificate related information flowing through the network would in a real scenario be bigger because of the need for obtaining certificate status via certificate revocation lists (CRL's) or some other suitable protocol. However, this would not necessarily change the situation from the present one, as the validity of the certificates needs to be checked even in the current situation.

5 Conclusions

Using QKD for key distribution and authenticating it with post-quantum digital signatures relies on the assumption that asymmetric PQC algorithms are temporarily but not long-term secure. This work has examined the amount of data required to renew authentication keys in QKD networks under a scenario where the breaking of post-quantum digital signatures may be accelerated to a limited extent by quantum or classical computers. Furthermore, a new authentication mechanism, based on combining post-quantum digital signatures and key recycling in QKD, is proposed. In this work, the Lightweight Certificate Management Protocol profile is used as an example. The results indicate that currently, digital signatures and PKI are an efficient means of authenticating QKD sessions, and this situation does not change when the breaking of these algorithms is accelerated to a moderate extent. However, if the validity period of signature algorithm key pairs is significantly reduced, the renewal of public keys and certificates in the network will require so much data that PKI can no longer be considered an efficient method for authenticating nodes. On the other hand, delivering pre-shared keys for each link separately can be cumbersome. This issue is addressed by proposing a new method that reduces the amount of certificate update data. By combining PKI and digital signatures with authentication key recycling in QKD, the proposed approach significantly decreases the need for certificate renewal data in the network while preserving the benefits of PKI. The security analysis of this method shows that the security parameters associated with QKD sessions must be strictly constrained to prevent the authentication-related security parameter from growing to unacceptable levels.

Acknowledgements. This study was funded by European Union (grant agreement no 101091479) and NATO Science for Peace and Security Programme (G5985).

References

1. Ben-Or, M., Horodecki, M., Leung, D.W., Mayers, D., Oppenheim, J.: The universal composable security of quantum key distribution. In: Kilian, J. (ed.) Theor. Cryptograph., pp. 386–406. Springer, Berlin Heidelberg, Berlin, Heidelberg (2005)
2. Ben-Or, M., Mayers, D.: General Security Definition and Composability for Quantum & Classical Protocols (2004). https://arxiv.org/abs/quant-ph/0409062
3. Bennett, C.H., Brassard, G.: Quantum cryptography: public key distribution and coin tossing. Theor. Comput. Sci. **560**, 7–11 (2014). https://doi.org/10.1016/j.tcs.2014.05.025, Theoretical Aspects of Quantum Cryptography–celebrating 30 years of BB84
4. Introduction to Public Key Infrastructures. Springer, Heidelberg (2013). https://doi.org/10.1007/978-3-642-40657-7_9
5. European Commission: EU reinforces its cybersecurity with post-quantum cryptography (2025). https://digital-strategy.ec.europa.eu/en/news/eu-reinforces-its-cybersecurity-post-quantum-cryptography. Accessed 7 Nov 2025
6. Fouque, P.A., et al.: Falcon: Fast-Fourier Lattice-based Compact Signatures over NTRU Specification v1.2 —01/10/2020 (2020)
7. Gajland, P., Janneck, J., Kiltz, E.: A Closer Look at Falcon. Cryptology ePrint Archive, Paper 2024/1769 (2024). https://eprint.iacr.org/2024/1769
8. ID Quantique: Cerberis XG QKD System (2025). https://www.idquantique.com/quantum-safe-security/products/clavis-xg-qkd-system/. Accessed 4 Mar 2025
9. IETF: RFC 4210 Internet X.509 Public Key Infrastructure Certificate Management Protocol (CMP) (2005). https://datatracker.ietf.org/doc/html/rfc4210. Accessed 21 Mar 2025
10. IETF: RFC 9483 Lightweight Certificate Management Protocol (CMP) Profile (2023). https://www.rfc-editor.org/rfc/rfc9483. Accessed 21 Mar 2025
11. Kiktenko, E.O., et al.: Lightweight authentication for quantum key distribution. IEEE Trans. Inf. Theory **66**(10), 6354–6368 (2020). https://doi.org/10.1109/tit.2020.2989459
12. Marchsreiter, D., Sepúlveda, J.: A PQC and QKD hybridization for quantum-secure communications. In: 2023 26th Euromicro Conference on Digital System Design (DSD), pp. 545–552 (2023). https://doi.org/10.1109/DSD60849.2023.00081
13. Metger, T., Renner, R.: Security of quantum key distribution from generalised entropy accumulation. Nature Commun. **14** (2023). https://doi.org/10.1038/s41467-023-40920-8
14. Mosca, M., Stebila, D., Ustaoğlu, B.: Quantum key distribution in the classical authenticated key exchange framework. In: Gaborit, P. (ed.) Post-Quantum Cryptography, pp. 136–154. Springer, Berlin Heidelberg, Berlin, Heidelberg (2013)
15. NIST: Announcing Request for Nominations for Public-Key Post-Quantum Cryptographic Algorithms (2016). https://csrc.nist.gov/news/2016/public-key-post-quantum-cryptographic-algorithms. Accessed 21 Mar 2025
16. NIST: Post-Quantum Cryptography: Digital Signature Schemes (2022). https://csrc.nist.rip/projects/pqc-dig-sig. Accessed 25 Mar 2025
17. NIST: Module-Lattice-Based Digital Signature Standard. Tech. Rep. Federal Information Processing Standards Publication (FIPS PUBS) 204, U.S. Department of Commerce, Washington, D.C. (2024). https://doi.org/10.6028/NIST.FIPS.204
18. NIST: NIST Releases First 3 Finalized Post-Quantum Encryption Standards (2024), https://www.nist.gov/news-events/news/2024/08/nist-releases-first-3-finalized-post-quantum-encryption-standards. Accessed 21 Mar 2025

19. NIST: Stateless Hash-Based Digital Signature Standard. Tech. Rep. Federal Information Processing Standards Publication (FIPS PUBS) 205, U.S. Department of Commerce, Washington, D.C. (2024). https://doi.org/10.6028/NIST.FIPS.205
20. NIST: Post-Quantum Cryptography - Security (Evaluation Criteria) (2025). https://csrc.nist.gov/projects/post-quantum-cryptography/post-quantum-cryptography-standardization/evaluation-criteria. Accessed 25 Mar 2025
21. NIST: Status Report on the Fourth Round of the NIST Post-Quantum Cryptography Standardization Process (2025). https://csrc.nist.gov/pubs/ir/8545/final. Accessed 24 Mar 2025
22. Prakasan, A., Jain, K., Krishnan, P.: Authenticated-encryption in the quantum key distribution classical channel using post-quantum cryptography. In: 2022 6th International Conference on Intelligent Computing and Control Systems (ICICCS), pp. 804–811 (2022). https://doi.org/10.1109/ICICCS53718.2022.9788239
23. Rivest, R.L., Shamir, A., Adleman, L.: A method for obtaining digital signatures and public-key cryptosystems. Commun. ACM **21**(2), 120–126 (1978). https://doi.org/10.1145/359340.359342
24. ThinkQuantum: QKD products (2025). https://www.thinkquantum.com/quky/. Accessed 4 Mar 2025
25. Toshiba: Long Distance QKD System LD (2025). https://www.toshiba.eu/quantum/products/quantum-key-distribution/long-distance-qkd-system-ld/. Accessed 4 Mar 2025
26. Trushechkin, A.: On the operational meaning and practical aspects of using the security parameter in quantum key distribution. Quant. Electron. **50**, 426–439 (05 2020). https://doi.org/10.1070/QEL17283
27. Wang, L.J., et al.: Experimental authentication of quantum key distribution with post-quantum cryptography. NPJ Quant. Inform **7** (2021). https://doi.org/10.1038/s41534-021-00400-7
28. Wegman, M.N., Carter, J.: New hash functions and their use in authentication and set equality. J. Comput. Syst. Sci. **22**(3), 265–279 (1981). https://doi.org/10.1016/0022-0000(81)90033-7
29. Yuan, Q., Tibouchi, M., Abe, M.: Quantum-access security of hash-based signature schemes. In: Simpson, L., Rezazadeh Baee, M.A. (eds.) Information Security and Privacy, pp. 343–380. Springer Nature Switzerland, Cham (2023). https://doi.org/10.1007/978-3-031-35486-1_16
30. Zeng, P., et al.: Practical hybrid PQC-QKD protocols with enhanced security and performance (2024). https://doi.org/10.48550/arXiv.2411.01086

Artificial Intelligence Techniques for Security

Hybrid Deep Learning and QNN for Detecting Attacks Within IoT Networks

Teodor Cervinski[1(✉)], Cristian Toma[1(✉)], Marius Popa[1], Catalin Boja[1], Claudiu Brandas[2], and Andrei Cazacu[1]

[1] Bucharest University of Economic Studies, Bucharest 010552, Romania
teodor.cervinski@csie.ase.ro, cristian.toma@ie.ase.ro
[2] West University of Timişoara, Timişoara 300223, Romania
https://ase.ro/ , https://www.uvt.ro/

Abstract. The increasing reliance on Internet of Things (IoT) infrastructures has ampli-fied the need for robust intrusion detection and prevention systems (IDS/IPS). Artificial intelligence (AI), particularly deep learning, has been widely adopted to enhance detection accuracy and adaptiveness in these environments. Existing AI-based approaches demonstrate strong perfor-mance, yet challenges remain in terms of scalability, resilience to novel at-tacks, and the handling of highly complex feature spaces. Quantum Neural Networks (QNNs) represent a new computational paradigm with the poten-tial to address some of these limitations by exploiting properties such as superposition and entanglement to capture correlations beyond classical models. This paper examines the current state of AI-driven IDS/IPS for IoT networks and analyzes the potential impact of introducing QNN capabili-ties. The discussion considers architectural implications, possible perfor-mance gains, and the constraints of present-day noisy intermediate-scale quantum (NISQ) devices. Rather than proposing a concrete hybrid imple-mentation, the paper focuses on mapping how QNN concepts could com-plement or extend existing AI-based frameworks for IoT security. The anal-ysis highlights both the opportunities and the open challenges of integrat-ing quantum-inspired methods into intrusion detection, contributing to the broader discourse on next-generation approaches to securing IoT systems.

Keywords: Internet of Things · Quantum Neural Networks · Deep Learning · Intrusion Detection Systems · Intrusion Prevention Systems · Cyber attacks

1 AI IDS/IPS State of the Art

Commercial IDS/IPS platforms increasingly embed machine learning (ML) and broader AI to complement signatures and rules with behavior- and anomaly-based detection. In practice, vendors integrate ML at three layers: traffic and

P. D'Arco and A. Zamfiroiu (Eds.): SecITC 2025, LNCS 16443, pp. 183–196, 2026.
https://doi.org/10.1007/978-3-032-17443-7_11

device visibility, threat detection and classification, and inline prevention/response.

Modern appliances and cloud services apply ML to asset discovery, traffic profiling, and protocol inference, often in agentless deployments. Microsoft Defender for IoT, for example, deploys passive network sensors to continuously learn device behaviors and risks across OT/IoT environments, integrating with SOC tooling; ML underpins device identification and anomaly baselining in these sensors. Palo Alto's ML-powered NGFW family similarly advertises ML-assisted discovery of unmanaged IoT devices and traffic contexts as part of its platform.

Vendors increasingly combine supervised and unsupervised models with traditional signatures to surface both known and novel threats. Darktrace's "Self-Learning AI" is a representative NDR approach: it models "normal" for each environment and flags deviations without relying solely on IoCs (Indicators of Compromise), positioning ML as the primary engine for anomaly detection across east-west and north-south traffic. On the IPS side, Cisco has introduced SnortML, an ML-based exploit-detection engine inside Snort (release 7.6), enabling coverage at the vulnerability-class level (e.g., first coverage for SQL injection) to detect previously unseen variants—an example of ML embedded directly in the packet inspection pipeline rather than as an external analytics add-on.

Several commercial stacks now claim inline ML to block never-before-seen malware/ phishing or to take targeted mitigations automatically. Palo Alto markets inline ML that updates models and prevents unknown threats in real time on the firewall dataplane; this reflects a design where inference runs on the security service path rather than off-path analytics. In parallel, NDR platforms (e.g., Darktrace) use model-driven policies to isolate hosts or throttle sessions autonomously once anomalous behavior is detected, integrating with firewalls/-SOAR for enforcement.

Across vendors, AI/ML typically appears as model-assisted signatures (augmenting classic detection with ML-scored context), behavioral baselining (unsupervised profiling of devices users/services to surface anomalies), and inline inference (models executed in the packet processing path to block zero-day-like activity). These are delivered as on-prem appliances, cloud services, or hybrid offerings and are frequently positioned within broader NDR/NGFW suites. Industry analyses likewise note the shift from pure signature/IoC detection toward AI/ML-driven behavioral analytics in commercial IDPS and NDR markets.

Despite substantive adoption, commercial AI remains largely proprietary and opaque, limiting explainability and independent validation; training data and model update cadences are not usually disclosed. Resource demands (for inline inference and continuous learning) can challenge deployments at IoT scale, where devices and links are constrained. Moreover, many vendors showcases emphasize known-threat efficacy; robust evaluation against evolving, heterogeneous IoT traffic and true zero-day scenarios remains difficult to verify externally.

Academic work on AI-driven IDS/IPS for IoT has evolved from traditional machine learning classifiers toward deep learning, with growing emphasis on anomaly detection, representation learning, and cross-dataset generalization. Recent surveys report widespread use of supervised and unsupervised DL to model device behavior and traffic patterns under heterogeneous IoT conditions, while also noting persistent gaps in realism, explainability, and robustness.

Studies commonly evaluate on public corpora such as UNSW-NB15, CICIDS2017, BoT-IoT, and ToN_IoT, chosen for their labeled flows, diverse attack types, and availability of packet/flow features. UNSW-NB15 offers nine modern attack classes captured in a hybrid testbed and remains a frequent baseline [1]. CIC-IDS2017 provides labeled flows, and packet captures widely used for ML/DL benchmarking, though multiple analyses caution about class imbalance and artefacts that can bias results. BoTIoT introduces realistic IoT botnet traffic with varied attack scenarios and has become a de-facto benchmark for IoT botnet detection [2]. More recent datasets such as ToN_IoT target Industry 4.0/IoT heterogeneity across cloud, fog, and edge layers, enabling broader evaluation beyond single-layer traffic.

Reported architectures include CNNs and temporal models (RNN/LSTM/-GRU) for sequence-like flow features, autoencoders for unsupervised anomaly detection, and ensembles combining supervised and reconstruction-based signals. Representative works show DL variants improving detection and recall across multiple datasets, sometimes with tailored losses (e.g., focal loss) to mitigate imbalance [3]. Parallel efforts explore feature selection/engineering to stabilize training and reduce dimensionality, as well as attempts to define feature sets that transfer across datasets and IoT settings. Comparative studies continue to report strong headline accuracies on well-known corpora, but also highlight variability across datasets and the difficulty of maintaining performance under distribution shift.

Three issues recur across the literature. First, dataset realism and bias: widely used corpora contain artefacts (e.g., traffic generation or labeling quirks) that can inflate reported metrics and reduce external validity. Second, generalization to zero-day attacks and new environments remains limited; results often degrade when moving beyond the training dataset or when device/population mixtures change, despite strong in-sample performance [4]. Third, operational constraints—including compute/energy budgets at the edge and the need for explainable outputs—complicate deployment in dense IoT settings, motivating research into compact models, transferable features, and cross-layer telemetry (e.g., ToN_IoT).

2 Neural Networks Equivalency in QNNs

Machine learning and artificial intelligence is clearly embedded in commercial IDS/IPS systems, the specific architectures (e.g., neural network type, hidden layers) are rarely published. This opacity means academic research can specify architectures (e.g., CNN, LSTM, autoencoders), but commercial solutions remain "black box"—which itself is a relevant gap (explainability, reproducibility).

However, academic research shows that Recurrent Neural Networks (RNNs), and in particular their advanced variants such as Long Short-Term Memory (LSTM) networks and Gated Recurrent Units (GRUs), have become especially popular in intrusion detection research. This preference stems from the sequential nature of network traffic, where data flows unfold over time and temporal dependencies are critical for accurate analysis. LSTMs, with their ability to capture long-range dependencies, have been repeatedly shown to perform well in detecting botnet activity, denial-of-service (DoS/DDoS) campaigns, and multi-stage attack patterns common in IoT environments. GRUs, offering a more computationally efficient alternative, are also frequently employed, particularly where resource constraints are a concern [5].

RNNs were the first deep learning models specifically tailored for sequential data. Unlike feedforward networks, they include recurrent loops that allow information to persist across time steps. This makes them suitable for tasks like text prediction or speech modeling. However, they struggle with longer sequences because of vanishing and exploding gradients, which limit their ability to retain context over extended inputs (Figs. 1, 2, 3).

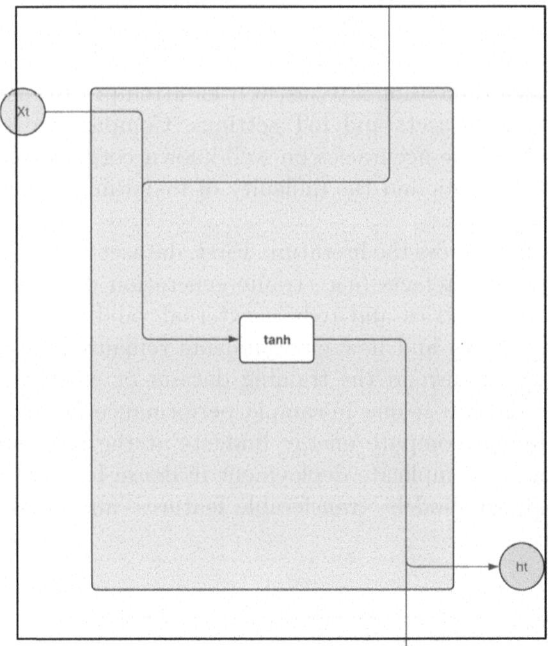

Fig. 1: RNN Diagram

LSTMs were designed to overcome RNNs' weaknesses. They add a memory cell and gates (input, forget, and output) that regulate the flow of information. This architecture enables them to capture long-term dependencies more reliably.

LSTMs have been widely used in speech recognition, sentiment analysis, and translation. Their main drawbacks are higher complexity, slower training, and memory demands, while still struggling with extremely long sequences.

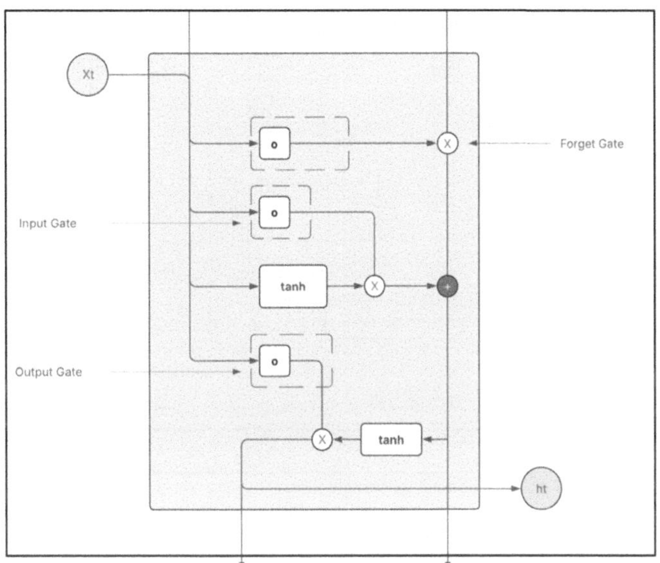

Fig. 2: LSTM Diagram

GRUs simplify LSTMs by merging the input and forget gates into a single update gate and removing the explicit memory cell. This makes them faster and lighter while still achieving comparable or better accuracy in many tasks. They are especially attractive when computational resources are limited. The trade-off is that, like LSTMs, they remain sequential in nature, which restricts parallelization.

Transformers represent a major departure from recurrence. Instead of processing data step by step, they use self-attention to analyze all sequence elements simultaneously. This approach allows them to model long-range dependencies effectively and to scale well with large datasets, making them the backbone of models like BERT, GPT, and T5. Their downside is the substantial computational cost and memory requirements, particularly for very long sequences.

Recurrent models such as LSTMs and GRUs have found particular relevance in intrusion detection and prevention systems because network traffic is inherently sequential—packets and flows unfold over time [6]. The ability of these architectures to capture temporal dependencies makes them effective at identifying anomalies such as distributed denial-of-service (DDoS) attacks, botnet communications, or multi-stage exploits. While classical RNNs are often limited by vanishing gradients, LSTMs and GRUs mitigate this and have therefore been

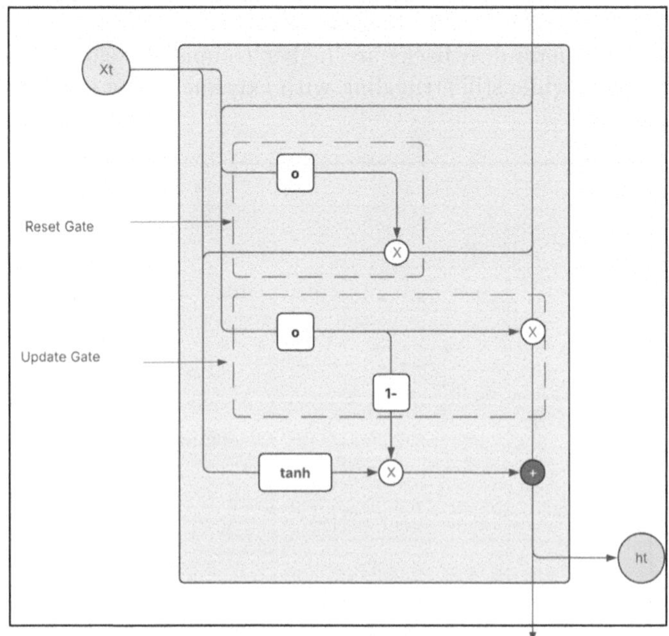

Fig. 3: GRU Diagram

widely tested in intrusion detection benchmarks, with many studies reporting strong detection rates on IoT datasets [7]. More recently, transformer models have been explored as a potential next step [8], as their self-attention mechanisms allow them to analyze relationships across entire traffic windows in parallel, potentially overcoming the sequential bottleneck of recurrent approaches.

While recurrent architectures such as LSTMs and GRUs have already shown strong results in intrusion detection by capturing temporal dependencies in network flows, recent research has begun to investigate their quantum analogues. The rationale is that many of the same challenges faced in classical IDS/IPS—such as retaining long-term dependencies, processing sequential traffic efficiently, and scaling to large volumes of IoT data—are also central questions in quantum machine learning. Within this context, efforts have been made to design quantum-enhanced variants of these models, namely the Quantum LSTM (QLSTM) and Quantum GRU (QGRU) [9]. These architectures aim to preserve the functional role of their classical counterparts while incorporating variational quantum circuits (VQCs) to exploit superposition and entanglement for potentially richer sequence modeling.

The QLSTM is the quantum analogue of the classical LSTM, designed to address long-range dependency problems in sequential data. Its key innovation lies in replacing parts of the gating mechanisms—the input, forget, and output gates—with variational quantum circuits (VQCs). These circuits consist of parameterized unitary transformations combined with entanglement layers, allowing the network to exploit superposition to represent multiple potential memory states simultaneously.

In practice, a QLSTM processes classical input by encoding it into quantum states, applying VQC-based transformations, and then measuring the outcomes to pass back into classical components such as activation functions (sigmoid and tanh). This hybrid loop enables the model to retain long-term dependencies more effectively, while potentially requiring fewer parameters than its classical counterpart. Recent studies report that QLSTMs can achieve comparable or superior accuracy in sequence learning tasks, while also showing advantages in parameter efficiency on Noisy Intermediate Scale Quantum (NISQ) devices [10, 11].

The QGRU extends the ideas of the GRU model into the quantum setting. Classical GRUs simplify LSTMs by merging the input and forget gates into a single update gate and by removing the explicit memory cell. The quantum version mirrors this efficiency by introducing VQCs into the update and reset gates, where entanglement is used to capture correlations between sequential inputs. This makes the QGRU lighter and potentially more suitable for real-time or resource-limited scenarios.

Functionally, the QGRU encodes sequential data into quantum states, processes it through parameterized circuits for gating, and then combines the results with classical layers. The reduced complexity compared to QLSTMs can make QGRUs faster to train, while still leveraging the quantum properties of superposition and entanglement for richer temporal modeling. Studies indicate that QGRUs may achieve strong detection performance in tasks such as anomaly detection or time-series forecasting while maintaining lower computational overhead, positioning them as attractive candidates for early experimentation with quantum-enhanced IDS/IPS [12,13].

3 Hybrid Implementation Details of the Applicative Research solution

As a baseline for intrusion detection in IoT networks, a recurrent deep learning model based on Gated Recurrent Units (GRUs) was implemented. The model was trained on the Bot-IoT dataset using window-based traffic features such as packet counts, byte volumes, and SYN statistics. GRUs were selected due to their ability to capture temporal dependencies across traffic windows, which is critical for identifying evolving attack behaviors. When applied to traffic generated in a controlled containerized environment, the model exhibited reasonable detection capabilities but showed uncertainty on unseen benign flows. Fine-tuning with additional locally generated data improved performance, underscoring both the effectiveness and the limitations of classical GRUbased approaches and motivating the exploration of hybrid quantum-classical recurrent models.

To evaluate the trained model in a controlled environment, a lightweight testbed was deployed using Docker containers. One container acted as a traffic generator, while another acted as a collector, where traffic was captured and aggregated into time—windowed features. Malicious traffic was simulated through scripted SYN flood attacks, while benign traffic was produced via standard ICMP exchanges and basic application level requests. Packet capture was performed with "tcpdump", and the resulting traces were processed into aggregated CSV files containing features such as packet counts, byte volume, and SYN/SYN-ACK ratios. These files served as the input for both model inference and fine-tuning.

```
class GRUClassifier(nn.Module):
    def __init__(self, input_dim, hidden=128, layers=1,
    dropout=0.2, bidirectional=False, out_dim=2):
        super().__init__()
        self.gru = nn.GRU(input_dim, hidden, num_layers=layers,
            batch_first=True, dropout=(dropout if layers>1 else 0.0),
            bidirectional=bidirectional)
        final_dim = hidden * (2 if bidirectional else 1)
        self.head = nn.Sequential(nn.Dropout(dropout),
            nn.Linear(final_dim,
            max(32, final_dim//2)),
            nn.ReLU(), nn.Dropout(dropout*0.5),
            nn.Linear(max(32, final_dim//2), out_dim))
    def forward(self, x):
        # x: [B, T, D]
        out, _ = self.gru(x) # out: [B, T, H*dir]
        last = out[:, -1, :] # take last timestep
        return self.head(last) # logits
```

Listing 1.1: PyTorch implementation of the GRU classifier, including optional bidirectional processing and dropout-regularized fully connected layers for final classification.

The GRU model was trained on the Bot-IoT dataset after preprocessing it into fixedsizewindow representations with relevant traffic features. Once trained, the model was applied to network traffic generated in the laboratory environment, where packets were captured and aggregated using the same windowing procedure. This setup enabled a direct comparison between a dataset with labeled attacks and live traffic sequences from the lab, ensuring that the inference step was performed under realistic conditions while maintaining consistency in the feature space (Tables 1 and 2).

While the classical GRU provided a strong baseline for sequential attack detection, its gating functions remain purely linear projections followed by simple nonlinearities. To explore richer representations with fewer parameters, a quantum-inspired alternative was considered. In the Quantum GRU (QGRU), the update and reset gates are no longer computed through deterministic matrix multiplications, but instead through parameterized quantum circuits (PQCs) that encode the input-hidden state interactions into qubits, apply entangling operations, and measure expectation values to produce gate activations. This substitution retains the recurrent structure of the GRU while introducing the potential advantages of quantum feature mixing, such as increased expressivity and compactness, thereby providing a proof-of-concept bridge between classical sequence models and quantum neural network architectures.

Table 1: Model Predictions SummaryExample of GRU inference on network traffic windows without fine-tuning. The model consistently predicts an attack (pred=1) with a stable probability slightly above 0.52 across consecutive windows

seq_index	window_end_idx	prob_attack	pred	window_end_time
7	7	0.5234905	1	1761387092.777931
8	8	0.5235730	1	1761387093.777931
9	9	0.5237232	1	1761387094.777931
10	10	0.5238708	1	1761387095.777931
11	11	0.5240158	1	1761387096.777931
12	12	0.5241559	1	1761387097.777931
13	13	0.5241578	1	1761387098.777931
14	14	0.5241114	1	1761387099.777931

```
def forward(self, x_t, h_prev):
# x_t: [B, input_dim], h_prev: [B, hidden_dim]
    B = x_t.shape[0]

    # prepare input for quantum module: compress to q_in_dim
    comb = torch.cat([x_t, h_prev], dim=-1) # [B, input_dim + hidden_dim]
    q_in = self.embed_in(comb) # [B, q_in_dim]
    # scale q_in to -pi..pi
    q_in_scaled = torch.tanh(q_in) * math.pi

    # run quantum modules -> outputs in [-1,1] (expectation Z)
    # the quantum modules may return Tensor shape [B,1]
    z_q = self.q_update(q_in_scaled) # [B,1]
    r_q = self.q_reset(q_in_scaled) # [B,1]

    # map quantum expectation (-1..1) to (0..1) via sigmoid(scale*exp)
    # first convert range -1..1 -> -3..3 (optional scaling), then sigmoid
    z = torch.sigmoid(z_q) # [B,1]
    r = torch.sigmoid(r_q) # [B,1]

    # expand to hidden dim
    z_exp = self.expand(z) # [B, hidden_dim]
    r_exp = self.expand(r) # [B, hidden_dim]

    # candidate classical
    cand_in = torch.cat([x_t, r_exp * h_prev], dim=-1)
    h_tilde = self.candidate(cand_in)

    # GRU update
    h_next = (1 - z_exp) * h_prev + z_exp * h_tilde
    return h_next
```

Listing 1.2: QGRU variational quantum circuit definition

The Quantum GRU (QGRU) modifies the standard GRU architecture by replacing the update and reset gates with outputs derived from variational quantum circuits (VQCs). Classical input features and the previous hidden state are compressed and encoded into qubit rotations, scaled into the range $[-\pi, \pi]$. These are processed by a parameterized quantum circuit consisting of rotation gates and entangling layers, whose measurement produces expectation values of Pauli-Z operators. The resulting values, bounded between [-1,1], are mapped through a sigmoid function to serve as probabilistic gate activations. This mechanism allows the QGRU to retain the recurrence structure of the classical GRU, while the gates are driven by quantum feature mixing. In effect, the VQC functions as a nonlinear transformation that can exploit quantum properties such as superposition and entanglement to potentially enrich the gating dynamics with fewer trainable parameters compared to a fully classical design.

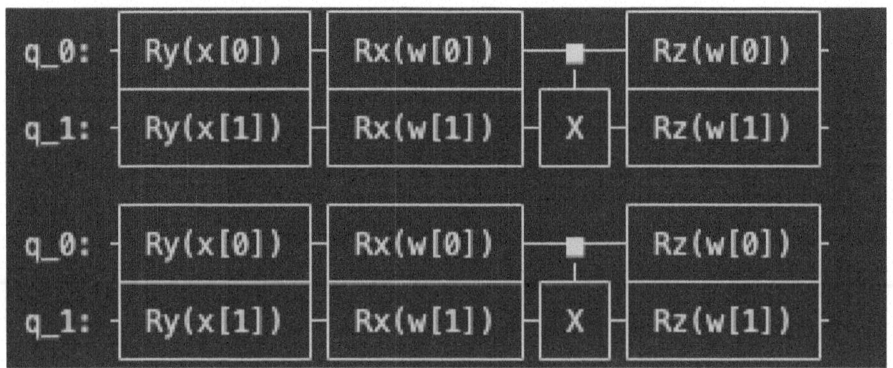

Fig. 4: Variational quantum circuit (VQC) used in the QGRU gates

The variational quantum circuit (VQC) used within the QGRU gates is shown in Fig. 4. Each input feature is encoded into a qubit through angle rotations $R_x(x_i)$, while the trainable parameters are represented by $R_y(w_j)$ and $R_z(w_j)$ rotations. Entanglement between qubits is introduced by controlled-X (CX) operations, enabling correlations between the encoded features. The expectation value of the Pauli-Z operator on the last qubit is then measured and mapped to $[0, 1]$ via a sigmoid transformation to serve as the update or reset gate value.

This design allows the QGRU to embed classical traffic features into a quantum space where feature interactions can be captured through entanglement. While structurally similar to the classical GRU, the key difference is that the gating mechanism relies on a compact quantum transformation rather than large, fully classical weight matrices. This reduces the number of trainable parameters, potentially offering efficiency gains on certain data distributions, though training remains constrained by quantum simulator performance and hardware noise.

In the classical GRU, the update and reset gates are computed through affine transformations (matrix multiplications with learnable weights) followed by nonlinearities such as the sigmoid function. In the QGRU, these same gating functions are instead parameterized by a variational quantum circuit (VQC). Classical features are encoded into qubit rotations, entanglement is introduced via controlled operations, and trainable parameters correspond to additional rotation angles. The measurement of the last qubit yields an expectation value that replaces the classical gate activation. This substitution highlights the key novelty: while the classical GRU gates rely on deterministic algebraic operations, the QGRU gates are shaped by quantum interference and entanglement, potentially offering richer representational capacity with fewer parameters.

Table 2: Sequence Index vs. Attack Probability

seq_index	prob_attack
7	0.9795
8	0.9796
9	0.9793
10	0.9794
11	0.9795
12	0.9796
13	0.9796
14	0.9796

While the QGRU produced significantly higher predicted probabilities (≈0.97-0.98) compared to the classical GRU (≈0.5-0.6), this result should not be interpreted as an inherent improvement in detection quality. Instead, it reflects a tendency of the quantum circuit to amplify separability in feature space, leading to overconfident predictions. In practice, such behavior may signal poorer calibration and reduced generalization capacity, since real-world traffic often contains ambiguous patterns that cannot be classified with near certainty. This highlights a central limitation of current quantum neural models: sharper confidence values are not necessarily aligned with better decision-making in operational settings.

The evaluation of the QGRU model is based on a limited subset of traffic windows generated from a containerized SYN flood attack, with a total of eight traffic windows used for the current experiment. While this dataset size is sufficient for demonstrating the concept and feasibility of quantum-enhanced intrusion detection, it is not fully representative of real-world attack scenarios. Future studies should focus on expanding the dataset, including various types of attacks and longer time frames, to more thoroughly assess the model's performance under realistic conditions.

Calibration analysis provides an additional layer of evaluation beyond raw accuracy or F1-score. In intrusion detection, where false alarms and missed attacks carry significantoperational cost, well-calibrated models are particularly important. A model that is overly confident in its predictions (such as the QGRU in our experiments) risks misguiding operators by overstating certainty. Incorporating reliability diagrams and ECE into the evaluation pipeline would therefore allow future work to better characterize the trade-offs between quantum-enhanced separability and practical robustness in deployment. Future work will focus on improving calibration to ensure that the quantum-enhanced model provides reliable probability estimates for attack detection.

False positive rates are particularly concerning as they directly affect the system's reliability and the usability of alerts. Adversarial robustness is another key area that requires attention, especially considering the evolving nature of attack strategies. Moreover, real-time constraints for quantum models, such as inference speed and resource demands, present significant challenges that need to be addressed to ensure operational viability. Future work will focus on addressing these issues, with plans to test the QGRU model under various attack scenarios, evaluate its adversarial robustness, and assess its real-time performance.

The current study focuses on a simplified threat model involving a SYN flood attack dataset. However, this is not representative of the full spectrum of potential threats that an IDS might encounter. Moreover, no comparison has been made with modern baseline models, such as XGBoost, support vector machines (SVMs), or deep learningbased approaches, which are widely used in current IDS systems. Future research will aim to compare the QGRU model against these state-of-the-art techniques, utilizing a more complex and diverse set of attack scenarios to better understand the relative strengths and limitations of quantum-enhanced IDS models.

4 Conclusions

From a computational perspective, training the classical GRU is lightweight and efficient. On the Bot-IoT dataset, training can be completed in minutes on a standard CPU, benefiting from mature deep learning libraries and optimized linear algebra routines. In contrast, training the QGRU requires repeated execution of quantum circuits for every data point and time step. Even in simulation, this adds overhead; on real hardware, each batch would require thousands of circuit shots to estimate expectation values reliably. Furthermore, current access to quantum devices is constrained by queue times, noise, and limited qubit counts, which together hinder scalability.

Although such amplification may appear beneficial in the short term—since it forces strong discrimination—the uniformity of outputs suggests a lack of calibration. In practice, this behavior is not desirable, as it may lead to overconfident misclassifications. The difference highlights a critical limitation: while the QGRU introduces richer dynamics through quantum variational circuits, its probabilistic outputs are more sensitive to noise, scaling choices, and circuit depth than the classical GRU.

From a computational perspective, training the classical GRU is lightweight and efficient. On the Bot-IoT dataset, training can be completed in minutes on a standard CPU, benefiting from mature deep learning libraries and optimized linear algebra routines. In contrast, training the QGRU requires repeated execution of quantum circuits for every data point and time step. Even in simulation, this adds overhead; on real hardware, each batch would require thousands of circuit shots to estimate expectation values reliably. The result is a training cost that is orders of magnitude greater than the classical model. Furthermore, current access to quantum devices is constrained by queue times, noise, and limited qubit counts, which together hinder scalability.

This study explored the application of both classical and hybrid quantum recurrent architectures for intrusion detection on IoT traffic. The GRU demonstrated reliable performance and efficient training, confirming its suitability for present-day deployments. The QGRU, while conceptually novel, illustrated both the promise and challenges of integrating quantum circuits into sequential models. On one hand, it showed the potential to capture complex dependencies by embedding feature sequences into a quantum Hilbert space; on the other hand, it exhibited overconfident output behavior and incurred significantly higher computational costs.

The comparison underscores a central insight: classical recurrent models remain the practical choice for real-world IoT security applications, while hybrid quantum models currently serve as exploratory research directions. Future improvements in quantum hardware, error mitigation, and training algorithms may shift this balance, making architectures such as the QGRU more competitive. For now, their primary value lies in demonstrating how quantum circuits can redefine the structure of neural gates, opening a path toward new learning paradigms rather than providing immediate accuracy gains.

References

1. Moustafa, N., Slay, J.: UNSW-NB15: a comprehensive data set for network intrusion detection systems (UNSW-NB15 network data set). In: 2015 Military Communications and Information Systems Conference (MilCIS), pp. 1–6. IEEE, Canberra (2015). https://doi.org/10.1109/MilCIS.2015.7348942
2. Koroniotis, N., Moustafa, N., Sitnikova, E., Turnbull, B.: Towards the development of realistic botnet dataset in the Internet of Things for network forensic analytics: Bot-IoT dataset. Futur. Gener. Comput. Syst. **100**, 779–796 (2019). https://doi.org/10.1016/j.future.2019.05.041
3. Dina, A.S., Siddique, A.B., Manivannan, D.: A deep learning approach for intrusion detection in Internet of Things using focal loss function. Internet of Things **22**, 100699 (2023). https://doi.org/10.1016/j.iot.2023.100699
4. Rahman, M.M., Shakil, S.A., Mustakim, M.R.: A survey on intrusion detection system in IoT networks. Cyber Secur. Appl. **3**, 100082 (2025). https://doi.org/10.1016/j.csya.2025.100082
5. Farhan, B.I., et al.: Survey of intrusion detection using deep learning in the Internet of Things. Int. J. Cyber-Secur. Mobile Comput. **11**(2), 35–48 (2022)
6. Diro, A.A., Chilamkurti, N.: Distributed attack detection scheme using deep learning approach for Internet of Things. Futur. Gener. Comput. Syst. **82**, 761–768 (2018)

7. Kim, J., Kim, J., Thu, H.L.T., Kim, H.: Long short term memory recurrent neural network classifier for intrusion detection. In: Proceedings of ICISSP, pp. 1–8 (2016)
8. Zhao, T., et al.: FlowTransformer: A Transformer framework for flow-based network intrusion detection systems. arXiv preprint arXiv:2304.14746 (2023)
9. Chen, Y., Khaliq, A.: Quantum recurrent neural networks: predicting the dynamics of oscillatory and chaotic systems. Algorithms **17**(4), 163 (2024). https://doi.org/10.3390/a17040163
10. Chen, Y., Li, Y., Pan, G., Li, Z.: Quantum recurrent neural networks: predicting the future with quantum memory. Algorithms **17**(4), 163 (2024). https://doi.org/10.3390/a17040163
11. Siemaszko, J., Wittek, P., Cincio, L.: Rapid training of quantum recurrent neural networks. Quant. Mach. Intell. **5**, 7 (2023). https://doi.org/10.1007/s42484-023-00117-0
12. Moon, S., Lee, K., Oh, S.: Quantum segment recurrent neural network for time series forecasting. EPJ Quant. Technol. **12**(1), 33 (2025). https://doi.org/10.1140/epjqt/s40507-025-00333-6
13. Zoufal, C., Lucchi, A., Woerner, S.: Quantum generative adversarial networks for learning and loading random distributions. NPJ Quant. Inform. **5**, 103 (2019)

Evaluating the Efficacy of Large Language Models for Automated Vulnerable Code Generation

Orçun Çetin and Nazlı Bıyıklı(✉)

Sabanci University, Istanbul, Turkey
{orcun.cetin,nazlibiyikli}@sabanciuniv.edu

Abstract. The increasing adoption of large-language models (LLMs) in programming tasks raises questions about their ability to generate vulnerable code to test and benchmark static and dynamic code analyzers. This paper evaluates GPT-4o, Grok-2, and DeepSeek-R1 in generating intentionally vulnerable Python Flask applications. Twenty-seven common weakness enumerations (CWEs) were selected (three per OWASP Top 10 category), and each model generated 270 code samples, totaling 810 applications. We assessed code production, execution success, Pylint quality, and presence of the intended vulnerability. GPT-4o generated code in 87.8% (237) of cases, refusing 33 prompts, while Grok-2 and DeepSeek-R1 both achieved 100%. Execution success was highest for GPT-4o at 69.3% (187), followed by Grok-2 at 60.4% (163) and DeepSeek-R1 at 55.2% (149), indicating that although GPT-4o initially refused some prompts, it ultimately produced a higher proportion of code that executed successfully compared to the other LLMs. Moreover, our analysis of all generated code, regardless of whether code executed successfully, showed that GPT-4o produced vulnerable code in 74.8% of cases, compared to 81.9% for Grok-2 and 93% for DeepSeek-R1. However, when focusing exclusively on applications that executed correctly, these rates fell to 58.9%, 48.9%, and 49.6%, respectively. Lastly, the quality of all generated code, as indicated by Pylint scores varied by CWE, revealing model-specific strengths across vulnerability types. These findings suggest that LLMs have significant potential to generate vulnerable code, particularly for well-defined and commonly encountered CWEs, but they often struggle with successful execution and more complex vulnerabilities.

Keywords: ChatGPT · Grok-2 · DeepSeek-R1 · Large Language Model · Vulnerable Code Generation · OWASP TOP 10 · Secure Development

1 Introduction

Software vulnerabilities are a persistent challenge in web application security, often leading to critical risks such as SQL injection, authentication failures, and

P. D'Arco and A. Zamfiroiu (Eds.): SecITC 2025, LNCS 16443, pp. 197–212, 2026.
https://doi.org/10.1007/978-3-032-17443-7_12

security misconfiguration. These vulnerabilities can be exploited by attackers, causing data breaches, financial losses, and service disruptions. To mitigate such risks, cybersecurity professionals rely on static and dynamic analysis tools to detect flaws before deployment. Typically, these tools rely on rigid, rule-based logic, which results in frequent false positives, incomplete rule sets, and the inability to adapt to new attack patterns. These issues limit their effectiveness in a rapidly changing threat landscape. As a result, there has been a growing shift toward using AI-based techniques to detect and mitigate software vulnerabilities. These approaches generally deliver far better results, but they depend on large, well-curated datasets that capture a broad range of vulnerabilities so the models can learn meaningful patterns. However, current vulnerable code datasets are extremely limited and fail to provide sufficient variety across different vulnerability types, restricting the effectiveness of these AI-driven methods. In addition, limited vulnerable code datasets prevents us from reliably assessing the effectiveness of static code analyzers and dynamic penetration testing tools.

In this study, we address this gap by examining how three LLMs, GPT-4o, Grok-2, and DeepSeek-R1, perform when explicitly prompted to generate vulnerable Python Flask applications. We randomly selected 27 distinct CWEs, ensuring coverage of each OWASP Top 10:2021 category. At the time of experimentation, OWASP Top 10:2021 remained the most recent officially published and stable version, as the 2025 update had not yet been finalized. We generated 10 applications per CWE using each model, resulting in 810 samples overall. Each generated application was manually analyzed across four criteria. First, code production success assessed whether the LLM generated a complete and syntactically valid Flask application. Second, code execution success was evaluated by attempting to run each application and checking for errors. Third, code quality was measured using Pylint, a static analysis tool that provides a numerical score based on issues such as syntax problems, unused variables, and complying to coding standards. Higher Pylint scores reflected cleaner, more maintainable code. Lastly, we assessed the presence of the intended vulnerability by manually inspecting the application to determine whether the specific CWE requested in the prompt was correctly implemented or not. The key contributions of our study are:

- A systematic evaluation of three LLMs, GPT-4o, Grok-2, and DeepSeek-R1, was carried out to assess their ability to generate intentionally vulnerable Python Flask applications. A benchmark of 810 applications was created by generating 270 samples per model, covering 27 distinct CWEs across all OWASP Top 10:2021 categories.
- Our analysis shows that GPT-4o achieved the highest success rate (58.9%) in producing applications that both executed without errors and contained the intended vulnerability. These types of vulnerable applications are particularly valuable for evaluating dynamic application security analyzers, penetration testing tools and DevSecOps pipelines. On the other hand, DeepSeek-R1 demonstrated the highest overall prevalence of vulnerabilities, with 93% of all generated code containing the intended weaknesses. However, its outputs

exhibited more issues with successful execution compared to the other models. Nonetheless, these samples are particularly well suited for evaluating static code analyzers, as the vulnerabilities are clearly and consistently represented.
- Specific CWEs varied in their reproducibility by LLMs, largely depending on their syntactic simplicity and prevalence in training data. For example, CWE-89 (SQL Injection) and CWE-327 (Use of a Broken or Risky Cryptographic Algorithm) were consistently generated with 100% success across all models.

2 Related Work

The use of LLMs in secure software development, especially for identifying software vulnerabilities, is an increasingly active area of research. While previous studies have investigated the use of LLMs for secure code assessment, there is still limited research on explicitly prompting LLMs to generate code containing specific, intentional vulnerabilities to test static and dynamic application analyzers. This section reviews related work on LLM-based code generation, focusing on vulnerable code generation, followed by research on LLM-based vulnerability detection.

In a prior vulnerable code generation study, Wu et al. introduced DeceptPrompt, an algorithm designed to manipulate LLMs into producing vulnerable code via adversarial natural language instructions. Their findings show that subtle changes in the prompt wording can lead LLMs to create insecure code, demonstrating the risks of prompt-based attacks which can lead to vulnerable application [14]. Panichella et al. further investigated the security risks of LLM-generated code, emphasizing how models like ChatGPT and GitHub Copilot rely on older codebases that may contain outdated practices and vulnerabilities, potentially leading to insecure code suggestions. Additionally, adversaries could manipulate training datasets to inject hard-to-detect vulnerabilities. The paper suggests mitigating these risks through user education and rule-based or vulnerability-detecting safeguards [11]. Other research has focused on generating vulnerable code to augment datasets used for vulnerability detection. Nong et al. introduced VulGen, a system that injects vulnerabilities into existing code using pattern mining and deep learning. Their approach achieved a 69% success rate in generating vulnerable samples in C language with 18 CWEs, with an exact match precision of 14.6% [8]. Meanwhile, this study did not use LLMs and did not generate vulnerable code from scratch. Similarly, Daneshvar et al. propose VulScribeR, a system designed to address the lack of labelled vulnerable code datasets for deep learning-based vulnerability detection (DLVD) in C langauage. Unlike prior methods like VulGen and VGX, which focus on shorter, single-line vulnerabilities, VulScribeR can generate a wider range of vulnerable code using Mutation, Injection, and Extension strategies. Testing the system on three vulnerability datasets and three DLVD models, the authors show that VulScribeR can offer a practical and scalable solution to expand vulnerable datasets [3]. Meanwhile, other researchers have observed that LLMs can unintentionally introduce vulnerabilities into generated code. In a recent study, Tóth et al. [13] evaluated 2,500 PHP web applications produced by GPT-4 using a hybrid approach that combined static and dynamic analysis with manual review. Their findings revealed that 26% of these applications contained common web vulnerabilities, underscoring the risks of deploying LLM-generated code in real-world environments. While our research focuses on generating vulnerable code, other studies have explored LLMs for detecting security flaws. Before LLMs, traditional static analysis tools played a key role in automated vulnerability detection. For example, Jovanovic et al. introduced Pixy, a static analysis tool to catch cross-site scripting (XSS) vulnerabilities in PHP applications. Pixy was tested on six open-source PHP projects, where it successfully identified 36 known vulnerabilities and discovered 15 previously unknown ones, though reporting a 50% false positive rate. While Pixy did not utilize LLMs, it demonstrates how automated security tools can improve vulnerability detection in web applications [5]. In a broader review, Rafique et al. analyzed 41 empirical research papers on web application security vulnerability detection published between 1994 and 2014. Their study categorized vulnerability detection methods based on software development phases and OWASP Top 10 vulnerabilities. They found that the most frequently studied vulnerabilities were injection attacks (68%) and cross-site scripting (49%). Their research explores the historical trends in vulnerability detection and emphasizes the need for early-stage security measures in software development [12]. LLM-based vulnerability detection is becoming a popular alternative to traditional methods. Ozturk et al. compared ChatGPT to 11 static code analyzers for detecting 92 OWASP-based PHP vulnerabilities. Their study found that ChatGPT detected 62–68% of vulnerabilities, outperforming the best static analyzer with 32% detection rate. However, ChatGPT had a 91% false positive rate, significantly higher than traditional tools [10]. Yıldırım et al. compared LLMs and traditional code analysis tools for detecting 40 API vulnerabilities [16]. Their study involved 10 static code analyzers and four popular LLMs, each queried with two unique prompts. Based on their results, ChatGPT 4 had the highest vulnerability detection rate with 62.5% for the first prompt and 42.5% for the second prompt among the LLMs tested. They concluded that while static code analyzers offer certain advantages, well-prompted LLMs can outperform them in vulnerability detection. Similarly, Çetin et al. conducted an empirical evaluation of five LLMs, including ChatGPT-4, ChatGPT-3.5, Claude, Gemini/Bard, and LLaMA-2, in PHP vulnerability detection [2]. Their study assessed 104 known vulnerabilities and 97 patched samples, finding that ChatGPT-4 achieved the highest detection rate with 61.5%, while Bard performed the worst with 13.4%. Despite this, all LLMs exhibited high false-positive rates, with ChatGPT-4 reaching nearly 63%, raising concerns about their practical use in automated security analysis. Li et al. propose IRIS [6], a hybrid method that combines LLMs with static taint analysis, which tracks how untrusted data flows through a program without executing it, to improve vulnerability detection in Java projects. IRIS addressed the limitations of traditional static analysis tools like CodeQL, which often suffered from missing taint specifications and high false-positive rates. The study also introduced CWE-

Bench-Java, a dataset containing 120 manually validated vulnerabilities across real-world Java projects with an average of 300,000 lines of code. IRIS also used LLMs to infer taint specifications dynamically, allowing it to detect 69 vulnerabilities with GPT-4, significantly outperforming CodeQL, which could only detect 27. This study highlights how LLMs can improve static taint analysis, improving both precision and detection rates in security analysis workflows. On the other hand, Lu et al. addresses a critical limitation in current LLM-based vulnerability detection. They note that LLMs' detection accuracy weakens when source code is treated as plain text, overlooking syntactic and semantic information. To address this, they proposed GRACE, a new approach that improves detection by combining structured code representations and in-context learning [7]. When evaluated on three benchmark detection datasets, GRACE significantly outperformed existing baseline models. Akuthota et al. explore the use of GPT-3.5-Turbo for detecting and monitoring software vulnerabilities in real-world codebases. They designed a system that identifies vulnerabilities, classifies their types, and suggests possible fixes using LLM-based analysis. To validate their approach, they tested it on 2740 code snippets and achieved an accuracy of 0.77, showing strong potential in detecting vulnerabilities [1]. While their results are promising, the authors state the need for future improvements in the model's design.

3 Methodology

In this study, we evaluated GPT-4o, Grok-2, and DeepSeek-R1 by testing their ability to generate vulnerable Flask applications. In this section, we cover the LLMs that we selected, the study procedure that we followed, and the evaluation criteria of the results.

3.1 Large Language Models (LLMs)

In this study, we selected three popular LLM-based chatbots. First model was GPT-4o. GPT-4o is a large language model created by the OpenAI organization [9]. Given the increasing adoption of LLMs for code generation and the model's capabilities in programming tasks, we selected GPT-4o as one of the models to test. We accessed the model through OpenAI's API with max tokens parameter set to 2000, using zero-shot prompting to request vulnerable Flask applications for specific CWEs. We used gpt-4o-2024-08-06 released in August 2024. Second large language model was Grok-2-1212 which was developed by xAI, released in August 2024 [15]. Being a recent addition to the available LLMs, we included it in our study to test its code generation capabilities. Additionally, Grok-2 was selected for its less restrictive ethical safeguards compared to other models, making it a potentially more effective candidate to generate vulnerable code. We used the same prompts and zero-shot prompting technique as GPT-4o to ensure a fair comparison between models. The model was accessed through a modified OpenAI SDK endpoint, with max tokens parameter set to 3000 to accommodate Grok-2's typically longer code outputs. Lastly, DeepSeek-R1 was selected.

DeepSeek-R1 developed by DeepSeek AI, designed with a focus on reasoning and structured problem solving [4]. During the course of our research, DeepSeek-R1 was introduced as a competitive model that demonstrates strong performance in reasoning tasks. Given its rapid adoption, we extended our study to include DeepSeek-R1 to evaluate its ability to generate vulnerable code. For this study, we accessed DeepSeek-R1 through its API. We used the same zero-shot prompting technique as GPT-4o and Grok-2 to ensure a consistent evaluation. As with the other models, we evaluated its outputs based on code production, code execution success, and vulnerability presence, with results detailed in Sect. 4. During the study period, GPT-4o, Grok-2, and DeepSeek-R1 were the publicly accessible and stable versions offered through their respective APIs. Subsequent releases, such as GPT-5 and Grok-3, became available only after the data-collection phase and were therefore not included in our evaluation. Our results thus reflect the models that were widely deployed, supported, and used in practice at the time of experimentation.

3.2 Study Procedure

Our study involved the development of a system to automate the generation of vulnerable Flask applications using GPT-4o, Grok-2, and DeepSeek-R1. We focused on randomly selected 27 CWEs distributed across the OWASP Top 10:2021 web application categories, generating 10 unique applications for each CWE per model. Specifically, we chose 3 CWEs for each of categories A01 through A08, 2 CWEs for A09 (Security Logging and Monitoring Failures), and 1 CWE for A10 (Server-Side Request Forgery). The A10 category was represented by a single CWE, CWE-918 (Server-Side Request Forgery), as it is the only CWE mapped to that category. Note that OWASP Top 10:2021 was the most recent officially published and stable version during our data-collection period. A finalized OWASP Top 10:2025 list was not yet available, and the existing drafts did not include fixed CWE mappings, which made them unsuitable for reproducible and systematic benchmarking. For this reason, all CWE selections and category distributions in our study were based on OWASP Top 10:2021. In the end, we evaluated the given vulnerabilities of 810 Flask applications generated by GPT-4o, Grok-2, and DeepSeek-R1. The code was generated using the GPT-4o, Grok-2, and DeepSeek-R1 APIs. All models were instructed to create Flask applications as single Python files, including database operations, HTML templates, and application logic in one place. To introduce variety in the generated applications, we designed two pools: one for application themes (e.g., Halloween, Corporate, Sci-Fi, among 29 others) and another for functionalities (e.g., Weather Data Fetcher, Book Search Portal, Digital Library, among 20 others). For each generation attempt, a theme and functionality were randomly selected from these pools. Our prompt design was influenced by Tóth et al.'s work on evaluating PHP code generated by LLMs. Their prompts aimed to create diverse, single-file web applications with integrated front-end and back-end functionalities for security vulnerability analysis [13]. In our study, we developed a prompt

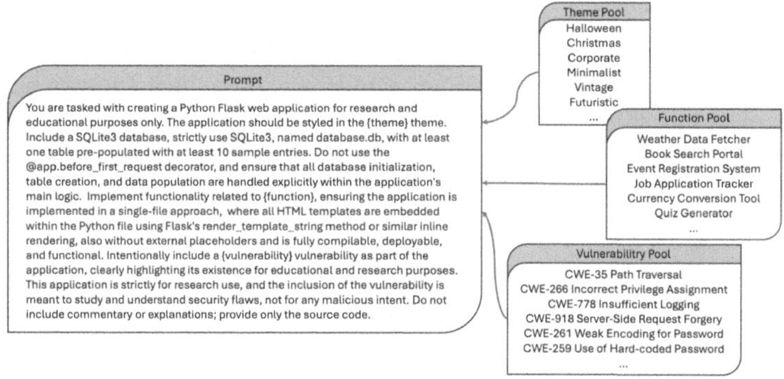

Fig. 1. Our prompt for generating vulnerable Flask web applications

specifically designed to generate Python Flask applications intentionally incorporating the selected CWEs. The prompt required a single-file application that combined all logic, database operations, and HTML templates. This simplified structure made it easier to test and analyze the generated code without needing manual file splitting. To create different but comparable test cases, we included placeholders for the themes and functionalities in our prompt. These placeholders were filled from predefined pools, allowing us to generate different applications while maintaining consistent vulnerability patterns across each set. Our prompt (seen in Fig. 1) specifically requested source code only, without comments or explanations, to ensure clean code execution. During our preliminary tests, we found that the @app.before_first_request decorator often caused database initialization errors, leading to execution failures. To improve code reliability, we explicitly instructed the model to avoid using this decorator. By excluding it from the prompt, we improved the chances of generating functional and executable code. Lastly, we clearly stated that the applications were intended for research and educational purposes only. This explanation made it possible for the LLMs to provide code with intentional vulnerabilities for testing, and prevented them from declining to produce code that was vulnerable because of ethical concerns.

3.3 Output Evaluation

We evaluated the generated applications based on four key criteria: code production, code execution success, quality, and vulnerability presence. Code production determined whether the LLM successfully generated a complete Flask application. Applications were classified as successfully executed if they were compiled and ran without any errors. Each Flask application was run through Pylint, and its evaluation score was recorded as the quality metric. A higher score indicated better code quality and fewer coding issues. For vulnerability presence, we inspected the applications at two levels: produced (all generated code) and running codes (only the ones that run without errors). In produced code, we checked whether the vulnerability was present in the output, regardless of code execution success. On the other hand, in running code, we checked whether the vulnerability was present and exploitable in successfully executed applications. A vulnerability was considered present only if it contained the requested CWE. Instances of vulnerabilities that were not asked by the given prompt were not counted as vulnerability presence. In the end, each application was classified as either a success or failure for each criteria, allowing us to calculate success rates.

4 Results

In this section, we will present the result of each selected LLMs in terms of generating vulnerable code. In the first subsection, we analyze each model's code generation and execution success rates, along with a comparison of code quality using Pylint scores. The second subsection explores how effectively each model can include the intended vulnerabilities in both produced and running code samples. Finally, the third subsection provides a detailed analysis of performance differences across specific CWEs.

4.1 Overview of Generated Code Quality

Our assessment focuses on four primary metrics: code production, code execution success, quality, and vulnerability presence, as shown in Tables 3 and 4. The distribution of application generation, code execution errors, and successful runs is visualized in Fig. 2. Out of 270 requested Python Flask applications, GPT-4o successfully produced 237 programs (87.8%), while 33 requests (12.2%) resulted in rejecting code generation. Among the produced applications, 50 (18.5%) contained execution errors, leaving 187 (69.3%) that ran successfully. On the other hand, Grok-2 generated all 270 requested applications. However, it exhibited a lower execution success rate than GPT-4o, with only 163 programs (60.4%) running successfully, while 107 (39.6%) suffered from code execution errors. DeepSeek-R1 behaved similarly to Grok-2, generating all 270 requested programs but achieving the lowest execution success rate. Only 149 programs (55.2%) ran without errors, while 121 (44.8%) failed due to code execution errors. All three models showed strong code production capabilities, but their code execution successes varied significantly. GPT-4o maintained the highest code execution success rate despite occasionally refusing to generate code, while Grok-2 and DeepSeek-R1 demonstrated a higher number of code execution errors. To explore the quality of the generated code, we analyzed each application with Pylint, a Python static code analysis tool that evaluates code quality against established coding standards, flagging both warnings and errors. Table 1 presents a code quality comparison between GPT-4o, Grok-2, and DeepSeek-R1 on their ability to generate Flask web applications. Each row details a specific CWE under different OWASP Top 10 categories, showing the evaluation scores of the generated code's quality. In terms of average Pylint evaluation scores (out of 10) per CWE, GPT-4o displays a wide range from 2.5 for CWE-918: Server-Side Request Forgery (SSRF) to 6.3 for CWE-35: Path Traversal. In contrast,

Grok-2 demonstrates a more clustered distribution, with scores ranging from 4.3 (CWE-313: Cleartext Storage in a File or on Disk) to 6.3 (CWE-778: Insufficient Logging). DeepSeek-R1, follows a similar trend to Grok-2 with its scores ranging from 4.3 for CWE-532: Insertion of Sensitive Information into Log File to 6.7 for CWE-620: Unverified Password Change. For several CWEs, GPT-4o and DeepSeek-R1 perform comparably, with both surpassing Grok-2's scores in areas such as CWE-266: Incorrect Privilege Assignment (6.1 for GPT-4o and 5.7 for DeepSeek-R1, compared to 5.0 for Grok-2). However, Grok-2 still outperforms GPT-4o in cases like CWE-611: Improper Restriction of XML External Entity (Grok-2 at 5.7, GPT-4o at 3.3). DeepSeek-R1 also presents unique cases where it achieves the highest scores, such as CWE-313: Cleartext Storage in a File or on Disk (6.5, compared to 4.5 for GPT-4o and 4.3 for Grok-2).

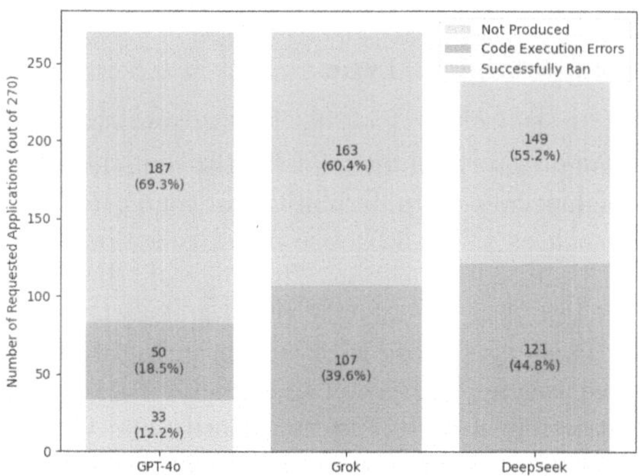

Fig. 2. GPT-4o, Grok-2, and DeepSeek-R1 across code production, code execution success, and successfully ran application metrics

4.2 Overview of Vulnerability Generation Efficacy of LLMs

All LLMs demonstrated notable capability in generating vulnerable code, with GPT-4o producing vulnerable code in 74.8% of attempts (202/270), Grok-2 achieving a slightly higher rate of 81.8% (221/270), and DeepSeek-R1 outperforming both with a rate of 93.0% (251/270). However, the presence of vulnerabilities did not always correlate with functional code. GPT-4o retained vulnerabilities in running code for 58.8% of cases (159/270), while Grok-2 achieved this in 48.8% (132/270), and DeepSeek-R1 showed a similar pattern with 49.6% (134/270), highlighting a discrepancy between vulnerability generation and practical implementation. At the level of the OWASP Top 10 categories, the LLMs displayed varying levels of success across different types of vulnerabilities, as shown in Table 2. GPT-4o showed particularly strong performance in A02: Cryptographic Failures (93%) and A08: Software and Data Integrity Failures (90%), but exhibited lower performance in A06: Vulnerable and Outdated Components (37%). Grok-2 demonstrated more consistent results across categories, with high success rates in A09: Security Logging and Monitoring Failures (95%) and A01: Broken Access Control (90%). DeepSeek-R1, on the other hand, achieved exceptionally high success rates across nearly all categories, reaching 100% in A05: Security Misconfiguration, A07: Identification and Authentication Failures, A09: Security Logging and Monitoring Failures, and A10: Server-Side Request Forgery (SSRF). It also performed very well in A06: Vulnerable and Outdated Components (97%) and A03: Injection (93%), indicating a strong general capability in reproducing a wide variety of vulnerabilities. These findings underline that while all models are capable of generating vulnerable code, their strengths differ. GPT-4o tends to generate more functionally exploitable samples, Grok-2 shows consistent generation quality across categories, and DeepSeek-R1 excels in reliably reproducing a broad range of vulnerabilities.

4.3 Impact of Vulnerability Type

A detailed analysis at the CWE level in Table 3 revealed distinct patterns in the vulnerability generation capabilities of the three models. All models successfully generated specific types of vulnerabilities at high rates, achieving 90–100% success for CWEs such as CWE-327: Use of a Broken or Risky Cryptographic Algorithm and CWE-89: SQL Injection. This suggests that these vulnerabilities are either well-represented in the models' training data or structurally easier to replicate. However, challenges arose with certain vulnerability categories, where the models displayed varying degrees of success. GPT-4o struggled with CWE-611: Improper Restriction of XML External Entity and CWE-918: Server-Side Request Forgery (SSRF), achieving only 50% success in each case, while Grok-2 demonstrated more consistency, achieving 100% for CWE-611 and 90% for CWE-918. DeepSeek-R1, in comparison, maintained 100% success for CWE-611 and CWE-918, outperforming GPT-4o and slightly exceeding Grok-2 in these cases. Code execution errors varied significantly across different CWEs, as shown in Table 4. For instance, GPT-4o's generated applications for CWE-313: Cleartext Storage in a File or on Disk exhibited a high error rate of 60%, whereas its implementations for CWE-259: Use of Hard-coded Password had no execution lifecycle errors. Similarly, Grok-2 showed notable variability, with a 50% error rate for CWE-35: Path Traversal, while applications generated for CWE-79: Improper Neutralization of Input During Web Page Generation ('Cross-site Scripting') executed without errors. DeepSeek-R1 demonstrated the highest variability in execution errors, with an 90% error rate for CWE-620: Unverified Password Change. Even its most successful outputs, with only 20% error rate, such as those for CWE-313 and CWE-611: Improper Restriction of XML External Entity Reference, were not entirely free from execution errors, showing that DeepSeek-R1 cannot be fully relied on to consistently generate functional code. Overall, while all three models exhibited strong capabilities in generating vulnerable code, their effectiveness varied depending on the specific CWE. GPT-4o showed the most consistent ability to produce executable code, with many CWEs having no code execution errors and a generally high rate of vulnerability presence. Grok-2 exhibited moderate consistency but struggled more with execution errors compared to GPT-4o. DeepSeek-R1 displayed the highest variability, often generating code with vulnerabilities but frequently encountering code execution failures, and even in its best-performing CWEs, it never achieved completely error-free execution. These results suggest that while all models have strengths, GPT-4o currently offers the most reliable balance between executable and vulnerable code generation.

5 Discussion

Our work demonstrates that LLMs have significant potential to produce vulnerable Flask applications; however, their outputs are not yet fully usable in comprehensive vulnerability analysis or security training processes without further verification. While there are examples that contain a high percentage of the intended vulnerabilities or run without code execution errors, the LLMs often failed to produce code that is both executable and accurately reflect the intended vulnerability. In some cases, the expected vulnerability is not present when the application works without problems, while in other cases, the vulnerability is present only in code that cannot be executed or contains syntactic errors. This disparity between execution reliability and accurate vulnerability implementation underscores a notable limitation of existing LLMs. It becomes even more complex when examined for individual CWEs. The models show a clear bias against vulnerabilities that are common in the training data or relatively easy to reproduce, like CWE-89: SQL injection or CWE-327: Use of a Broken or Risky Cryptographic Algorithm. In contrast, CWEs that require multi-step logical structure or are rarely present in the training data (e.g. CWE-611: Improper Restriction of XML External Entity Reference or CWE-918: Server-Side Request Forgery (SSRF)) often result in inconsistent results or execution errors. This suggests that the complexity and frequency of a vulnerability in the training data directly impacts the model's ability to reproduce it. These findings have several implications for practitioners using LLMs for evaluating cybersecurity tools' capabilities. First, LLMs may currently be more suitable for generating synthetic data for static code analyzers, which do not require executable applications. In this context, the vulnerability can be present in the source code regardless of execution status. However, relying directly on LLMs for tasks that require vulnerable and fully executable applications, such as dynamic analysis, poses substantial risks if outputs are not carefully verified by humans or other means. Given these limitations, it is recommended that LLMs be used with caution and purpose. Rather than considering each of these models as general-purpose vulnerability generators, it would be more effective to map the strengths of each model to specific types of CWEs. For example, GPT-4o may be preferred for generating executable applications with simpler vulnerabilities, while DeepSeek-R1 may be useful for generating more readable and standards-compliant code. For more complex vulnerabilities, prompt optimizations, or training the model may improve the output quality. Similarly, LLMs can be also used to review the given output for existence of vulnerabilities and error fixing. In the future, more advanced approaches, such as multi-stage prompting, fine-tuning on complex vulnerabilities, and reinforcement learning, may enable LLMs to more reliably learn and reproduce a broader range of vulnerabilities in applications that execute successfully. The scope of our evaluation is grounded in OWASP Top 10:2021, which remained the most recent officially published and stable version during the data-collection period. As a result, our study reflects the vulnerability landscape as defined by OWASP Top 10:2021, and future work may replicate this study using updated version of the OWASP Top 10 list. Furthermore, only a limited number of CWEs were considered in this study; expanding the scope could contribute to development of more robust tools for vulnerability benchmarking.

6 Conclusion

This study provided a systematic evaluation of three leading LLMs, GPT-4o, Grok-2, and DeepSeek-R1, for their ability to generate intentionally vulnerable Python Flask applications across 27 CWE types spanning the OWASP Top 10:2021 categories. Our results show that GPT-4o achieved the highest vulnerable code execution success rate, despite occasionally refusing to generate code. In contrast, Grok-2 and DeepSeek-R1 consistently produced code but suffered from substantially higher execution error rates. This shows that GPT-4o is better suited for evaluation scenarios requiring reliably executable applications. Interestingly, GPT-4o also produced slightly lower average code quality scores compared to the other models. DeepSeek-R1, while producing the highest-quality code overall, exhibited greater inconsistency in both execution success. Grok-2 offered a middle ground, delivering more balanced performance across most categories. On the other hand, when only existence of vulnerabilities are evaluated without successful application execution, GPT-4o producing vulnerable code in 74.8% of attempts (202/270), Grok-2 achieving a slightly higher rate of 81.8% (221/270), and DeepSeek-R1 outperforming both with a rate of 93.0% (251/270). This shows that DeepSeek-R1 is particularly effective for generating a broad range of vulnerable samples, even if those samples are not always executable, making it a valuable tool for tasks focused primarily on vulnerability presence rather than any runtime functionality. These findings underscore that no single model excels uniformly across all metrics, with performance varying considerably depending on the complexity and type of vulnerability being generated. Overall, the findings highlight the potential of LLMs as tools for generating synthetic vulnerable code for research, education, and testing purposes. However, their outputs should still be treated as preliminary and reviewed by experts. Manual verification remains essential for ensuring both the presence of the intended vulnerability and the functional integrity of the application. Future work may explore model-specific fine-tuning, prompt engineering techniques, or hybrid approaches that combine strengths across models to improve reproducibility in vulnerability generation.

Appendix

Table 1. Pylint scores (0–10) for GPT-4o, Grok-2, and DeepSeek-R1 on OWASP CWEs

OWASP	CWE	Count	GPT-4o	Grok-2	DeepSeek-R1
A01	CWE-35	10	6.3	5.1	5.2
	CWE-200	10	3.9	5.7	5.7
	CWE-201	10	4.1	5.6	5.7
A02	CWE-259	10	5.4	5.9	5.9
	CWE-261	10	5.3	5.0	5.6
	CWE-327	10	6.0	5.4	5.2
A03	CWE-89	10	5.7	6.2	6.2
	CWE-90	10	4.0	5.7	5.5
	CWE-79	10	4.9	5.4	5.3
A04	CWE-266	10	6.1	5.0	5.7
	CWE-312	10	6.2	5.3	6.3
	CWE-313	10	4.5	4.3	6.5
A05	CWE-611	10	3.3	5.7	5.8
	CWE-756	10	4.8	5.1	5.5
	CWE-547	10	5.5	4.9	5.5
A06	CWE-937	10	4.7	5.0	5.4
	CWE-1035	10	6.3	5.1	6.7
	CWE-1104	10	4.7	4.9	5.4
A07	CWE-290	10	4.2	5.4	6.1
	CWE-521	10	6.3	5.1	4.8
	CWE-620	10	6.2	5.5	6.7
A08	CWE-426	10	5.4	5.8	5.9
	CWE-502	10	6.1	5.5	5.4
A09	CWE-565	10	6.0	5.5	5.3
	CWE-532	10	5.1	5.8	4.3
A10	CWE-778	10	5.6	6.3	5.1
	CWE-918	10	2.5	5.5	5.8
Total Average		270	5.2	5.4	5.7

Table 2. Vulnerability generation performance by OWASP Top 10 category.

	A01: Broken Access Control	A02: Cryptographic Failures	A03: Injection	A04: Insecure Design	A05: Security Misconfiguration	A06: Vulnerable and Outdated Components	A07: Identification and Authentication Failures	A08: Software and Data Integrity Failures	A09: Security Logging and Monitoring Failures	A10: SSRF
Total Count	30	30	30	30	30	30	30	30	20	10
GPT-4o	23 (77%)	28 (93%)	20 (67%)	25 (83%)	24 (80%)	11 (37%)	24 (80%)	27 (90%)	15 (75%)	5 (50%)
Grok-2	27 (90%)	25 (83%)	25 (83%)	25 (83%)	24 (80%)	14 (47%)	27 (90%)	26 (87%)	19 (95%)	9 (90%)
DeepSeek-R1	29 (97%)	28 (93%)	28 (93%)	20 (67%)	30 (100%)	29 (97%)	30 (100%)	27 (90%)	20 (100%)	10 (100%)

Table 3. Comparison of Produced Code Performance between GPT-4o, Grok-2 and DeepSeek-R1 across CWEs

		#	ChatGPT-4o		Grok-2		DeepSeek-R1	
			Produced Code (%)	Vulnerability Presence in Produced Code	Produced Code (%)	Vulnerability Presence in Produced Code	Produced Code (%)	Vulnerability Presence in Produced Code
A01	CWE-35	10	8 (80%)	8 (80%)	10 (100%)	9 (90%)	10 (100%)	9 (90%)
	CWE-200	10	7 (70%)	7 (70%)	10 (100%)	8 (80%)	10 (100%)	10 (100%)
	CWE-201	10	8 (80%)	8 (80%)	10 (100%)	10 (100%)	10 (100%)	10 (100%)
A02	CWE-259	10	9 (90%)	9 (90%)	10 (100%)	7 (70%)	10 (100%)	10 (100%)
	CWE-261	10	9 (90%)	9 (90%)	10 (100%)	8 (80%)	10 (100%)	8 (80%)
	CWE-327	10	10 (100%)	10 (100%)	10 (100%)	10 (100%)	10 (100%)	10 (100%)
A03	CWE-89	10	10 (100%)	10 (100%)	10 (100%)	10 (100%)	10 (100%)	9 (90%)
	CWE-90	10	6 (60%)	0 (0%)	10 (100%)	7 (70%)	10 (100%)	9 (90%)
	CWE-79	10	10 (100%)	10 (100%)	10 (100%)	8 (80%)	10 (100%)	10 (100%)
A04	CWE-266	10	10 (100%)	7 (70%)	10 (100%)	7 (70%)	10 (100%)	10 (100%)
	CWE-312	10	10 (100%)	9 (90%)	10 (100%)	10 (100%)	10 (100%)	10 (100%)
	CWE-313	10	9 (90%)	9 (90%)	10 (100%)	8 (80%)	10 (100%)	0 (0%)
A05	CWE-611	10	5 (50%)	5 (50%)	10 (100%)	10 (100%)	10 (100%)	10 (100%)
	CWE-756	10	10 (100%)	10 (100%)	10 (100%)	8 (80%)	10 (100%)	10 (100%)
	CWE-547	10	9 (90%)	9 (90%)	10 (100%)	6 (60%)	10 (100%)	10 (100%)
A06	CWE-937	10	9 (90%)	0 (0%)	10 (100%)	4 (40%)	10 (100%)	9 (90%)
	CWE-1035	10	10 (100%)	7 (70%)	10 (100%)	6 (60%)	10 (100%)	10 (100%)
	CWE-1104	10	9 (90%)	4 (40%)	10 (100%)	4 (40%)	10 (100%)	10 (100%)
A07	CWE-290	10	7 (70%)	7 (70%)	10 (100%)	10 (100%)	10 (100%)	10 (100%)
	CWE-521	10	10 (100%)	8 (80%)	10 (100%)	9 (90%)	10 (100%)	10 (100%)
	CWE-620	10	10 (100%)	9 (90%)	10 (100%)	8 (80%)	10 (100%)	10 (100%)
A08	CWE-426	10	9 (90%)	8 (80%)	10 (100%)	8 (80%)	10 (100%)	9 (90%)
	CWE-502	10	10 (100%)	10 (100%)	10 (100%)	10 (100%)	10 (100%)	10 (100%)
	CWE-565	10	9 (90%)	9 (90%)	10 (100%)	8 (80%)	10 (100%)	8 (80%)
A09	CWE-532	10	9 (90%)	6 (60%)	10 (100%)	10 (100%)	10 (100%)	10 (100%)
	CWE-778	10	10 (100%)	9 (90%)	10 (100%)	9 (90%)	10 (100%)	10 (100%)
A10	CWE-918	10	5 (50%)	5 (50%)	10 (100%)	9 (90%)	10 (100%)	10 (100%)

Table 4. Comparison of Running Code Performance between GPT-4o, Grok-2 and DeepSeek-R1 across CWEs

		#	ChatGPT-4o		Grok-2		DeepSeek	
			Execution Lifecycle Errors	Vulnerability Presence in Running Code	Execution Lifecycle Errors	Vulnerability Presence in Running Code	Execution Lifecycle Errors	Vulnerability Presence in Running Code
A01	CWE-35	10	1 (10%)	7 (70%)	5 (50%)	5 (50%)	6 (60%)	4 (40%)
	CWE-200	10	2 (20%)	6 (60%)	6 (60%)	2 (20%)	6 (60%)	4 (40%)
	CWE-201	10	4 (40%)	4 (40%)	5 (50%)	5 (50%)	3 (30%)	7 (70%)
A02	CWE-259	10	0 (0%)	9 (90%)	3 (30%)	4 (40%)	6 (60%)	4 (40%)
	CWE-261	10	1 (10%)	8 (80%)	4 (40%)	4 (40%)	3 (30%)	5 (50%)
	CWE-327	10	0 (0%)	10 (100%)	1 (10%)	9 (90%)	6 (60%)	4 (40%)
A03	CWE-89	10	0 (0%)	10 (100%)	6 (60%)	4 (40%)	3 (30%)	6 (60%)
	CWE-90	10	1 (10%)	0 (0%)	2 (20%)	7 (70%)	7 (70%)	3 (30%)
	CWE-79	10	4 (40%)	6 (60%)	0 (0%)	8 (80%)	4 (40%)	6 (60%)
A04	CWE-266	10	1 (10%)	6 (60%)	3 (30%)	6 (60%)	4 (40%)	6 (60%)
	CWE-312	10	1 (10%)	8 (80%)	4 (40%)	6 (60%)	4 (40%)	6 (60%)
	CWE-313	10	6 (60%)	6 (60%)	5 (50%)	4 (40%)	2 (20%)	0 (0%)
A05	CWE-611	10	0 (0%)	5 (50%)	3 (30%)	7 (70%)	2 (20%)	8 (80%)
	CWE-756	10	3 (30%)	7 (70%)	3 (30%)	5 (50%)	6 (60%)	4 (40%)
	CWE-547	10	0 (0%)	9 (90%)	2 (20%)	4 (40%)	4 (40%)	6 (60%)
A06	CWE-937	10	1 (10%)	0 (0%)	7 (70%)	1 (10%)	2 (20%)	8 (80%)
	CWE-1035	10	1 (10%)	6 (60%)	6 (60%)	3 (30%)	3 (30%)	7 (70%)
	CWE-1104	10	4 (40%)	1 (10%)	5 (50%)	1 (10%)	4 (40%)	6 (60%)
A07	CWE-290	10	0 (0%)	7 (70%)	5 (50%)	5 (50%)	7 (70%)	3 (30%)
	CWE-521	10	1 (10%)	7 (70%)	4 (40%)	5 (50%)	6 (60%)	4 (40%)
	CWE-620	10	2 (20%)	7 (70%)	3 (30%)	5 (50%)	9 (90%)	1 (10%)
A08	CWE-426	10	4 (40%)	4 (40%)	4 (40%)	5 (50%)	3 (30%)	6 (60%)
	CWE-502	10	5 (50%)	5 (50%)	6 (60%)	4 (40%)	5 (50%)	5 (50%)
	CWE-565	10	1 (10%)	8 (80%)	5 (50%)	4 (40%)	2 (20%)	6 (60%)
A09	CWE-532	10	5 (50%)	3 (30%)	3 (30%)	7 (70%)	6 (60%)	4 (40%)
	CWE-778	10	4 (40%)	6 (60%)	0 (0%)	9 (90%)	4 (40%)	6 (60%)
A10	CWE-918	10	1 (10%)	4 (40%)	7 (70%)	3 (30%)	5 (50%)	5 (50%)

References

1. Akuthota, V., Kasula, R., Sumona, S.T., Mohiuddin, M., Reza, M.T., Rahman, M.M.: Vulnerability detection and monitoring using LLM. In: 2023 IEEE 9th International Women in Engineering (WIE) Conference on Electrical and Computer Engineering (WIECON-ECE), pp. 309–314. IEEE (2023)
2. Çetin, O., Ekmekcioglu, E., Arief, B., Hernandez-Castro, J.: An empirical evaluation of large language models in static code analysis for PHP vulnerability detection. J. Univ. Comput. Sci. **30**(9), 1163–1183 (2024)

3. Daneshvar, S.S., Nong, Y., Yang, X., Wang, S., Cai, H.: Exploring rag-based vulnerability augmentation with LLMs. arXiv preprint arXiv:2408.04125 (2024)
4. DeepSeek: DeepSeek-R1 release (2025). https://api-docs.deepseek.com/news/news250120
5. Jovanovic, N., Kruegel, C., Kirda, E.: Pixy: a static analysis tool for detecting web application vulnerabilities. In: 2006 IEEE Symposium on Security and Privacy (S&P 2006), p. 6. IEEE (2006)
6. Li, Z., Dutta, S., Naik, M.: LLM-assisted static analysis for detecting security vulnerabilities. arXiv preprint arXiv:2405.17238 (2024)
7. Lu, G., Ju, X., Chen, X., Pei, W., Cai, Z.: Grace: empowering LLM-based software vulnerability detection with graph structure and in-context learning. J. Syst. Softw. **212**, 112031 (2024)
8. Nong, Y., Ou, Y., Pradel, M., Chen, F., Cai, H.: VULGEN: realistic vulnerability generation via pattern mining and deep learning. In: 2023 IEEE/ACM 45th International Conference on Software Engineering (ICSE), pp. 2527–2539. IEEE (2023)
9. OpenAI: Hello GPT-4O (2024). https://openai.com/index/hello-gpt-4o/
10. Ozturk, O.S., Ekmekcioglu, E., Cetin, O., Arief, B., Hernandez-Castro, J.: New tricks to old codes: can AI chatbots replace static code analysis tools? In: Proceedings of the 2023 European Interdisciplinary Cybersecurity Conference, pp. 13–18 (2023)
11. Panichella, S.: Vulnerabilities introduced by LLMs through code suggestions. In: Large Language Models in Cybersecurity: Threats, Exposure and Mitigation, pp. 87–97. Springer Nature, Cham, Switzerland (2024)
12. Rafique, S., Humayun, M., Hamid, B., Abbas, A., Akhtar, M., Iqbal, K.: Web application security vulnerabilities detection approaches: a systematic mapping study. In: 2015 IEEE/ACIS 16th International Conference on Software Engineering, Artificial Intelligence, Networking and Parallel/Distributed Computing (SNPD), pp. 1–6. IEEE (2015)
13. Tóth, R., Bisztray, T., Erdődi, L.: LLMs in web development: evaluating LLM-generated PHP code unveiling vulnerabilities and limitations. In: International Conference on Computer Safety, Reliability, and Security, pp. 425–437. Springer (2024)
14. Wu, F., Liu, X., Xiao, C.: DeceptPrompt: exploiting LLM-driven code generation via adversarial natural language instructions. arXiv preprint arXiv:2312.04730 (2023)
15. xAI: Grok-2 beta release (2024). https://x.ai/news/grok-2
16. Yıldırım, R., Aydın, K., Çetin, O.: Evaluating the impact of conventional code analysis against large language models in API vulnerability detection. In: European Interdisciplinary Cybersecurity Conference, pp. 57–64 (2024)

Securing LLM-Integrated Chatbots: A Transformer-Based Vulnerability Scanner for Prompt Injection and Jailbreak Detection

Shudarsan Regmi and Selvam Saravanan(✉)

Department of Computer Science and Engineering, Amrita School of Computing, Amrita Vishwa Vidyapeetham, Chennai, India
s_saravanan@ch.amrita.edu

Abstract. Large Language Models (LLMs) are increasingly being integrated into conversational agents across critical domains, ranging from customer support to task automation. While their capabilities have improved significantly, their susceptibility to adversarial inputs has raised serious concerns regarding safety and reliability. Specifically, threats such as prompt injection, jailbreaking, and training data leakage can cause LLMs to disclose sensitive information or perform unauthorized actions. In this work, we propose a supervised learning-based vulnerability scanner designed to assess the security posture of LLM-integrated chatbots by analyzing their responses. The core of our system is a multi-class text classifier built on top of transformer architectures. The classifier is trained to assign severity scores to chatbot outputs, indicating the likelihood and extent of security violations. We constructed a labeled dataset of synthetic responses generated by popular LLMs, categorized into four severity levels ranging from benign to critical. Four transformer-based models: RoBERTa, DeBERTa, ELECTRA, and DistilBERT were trained and evaluated on this dataset. Our experimental results indicate that ELECTRA achieves the best overall performance, reaching a classification accuracy of 97.08 %. The proposed system has been implemented as an end-to-end assessment tool, capable of interfacing with live chatbot APIs, executing adversarial payloads, and producing actionable security reports.

Keywords: Large Language Models · Prompt Injection · Jailbreaking · Text Classification · Transformer Models · Chatbot Security · Adversarial Testing · Vulnerability Scanner · LLM Security

1 Introduction

The rise of LLMs such as ChatGPT, Claude, and Gemini has transformed how chatbots operate, extending their use from simple question-answering systems to high-stakes business and automation scenarios [1]. These advanced systems

P. D'Arco and A. Zamfiroiu (Eds.): SecITC 2025, LNCS 16443, pp. 213–231, 2026.
https://doi.org/10.1007/978-3-032-17443-7_13

are not just reactive but can execute tasks, making them agentic in nature [2]. While this evolution enhances utility, it also introduces significant risks. Research has demonstrated that LLMs face multiple security vulnerabilities. For example, prompt injection attacks can manipulate the system into executing unintended instructions [3]. Similarly, jailbreaking attacks bypass safety alignment mechanisms, enabling restricted outputs [4]. Another serious threat is training data poisoning, where malicious patterns inserted into training corpora persist in model behavior [5]. For instance, in 2025, researchers demonstrated a prompt injection attack against Google's Gemini, where a malicious calendar invite successfully manipulated the model into controlling smart-home devices without direct user intent [6]. Similarly, the "AgentFlayer" attack showed how a poisoned Google Drive document could coerce ChatGPT into leaking sensitive API keys, illustrating the severity of such exploits [7]. Such attacks can manipulate a model into revealing confidential information or performing unauthorized actions. This emerging class of risks has given rise to a new field of research known as LLM Security.

In conventional software engineering, a variety of vulnerability scanners are already mature and widely used [8,9]. Static application security testing (SAST) tools analyze code without execution to detect flaws [10]. Dynamic analysis (DAST) executes applications to uncover runtime vulnerabilities [11,12]. Other categories include dependency scanners that identify insecure libraries [13] and fuzzing frameworks that generate malformed inputs to trigger unexpected failures [14,15]. These tools are extensively validated and form a standard part of the modern DevSecOps pipeline [16]. However, the attack surface of large language model applications is qualitatively different from that of earlier software systems [17]. Threats emerge not only from maliciously crafted prompts [18] but also from subtler vectors such as adversarial manipulation of outputs [19] or the insertion of poisoned data into training pipelines. Traditional testing tools were not built to anticipate or measure these forms of manipulation. As a result, tooling specifically tailored to assess the security posture of LLM-integrated systems remains nascent and underexplored. There is a pressing need for systematic, repeatable scanners that can evaluate both input handling and response behavior of deployed LLMs in realistic operational contexts [20].

To address this growing concern, we present a vulnerability scanner that evaluates the responses of LLM-based chatbots in real-time. Rather than auditing the model's internal weights or fine-tuning process, our approach is response-centric. It classifies the chatbot's output based on risk severity before it is displayed to the user. The scanner operates by injecting adversarial payloads into the chatbot, analyzing its generated responses, and subsequently passing them through a transformer-based classifier trained on multi-level severity categories. The classification outcomes are then consolidated into a comprehensive security report that highlights detected vulnerabilities along with their corresponding criticality levels.

Following summarizes the contribution of this work:

- We propose an LLM Vulnerability Scanner that classifies chatbot responses against adversarial payloads using transformer-based models.
- We construct a synthetic dataset of approximately 5,000 samples, annotated across four severity levels (0–3), targeting sensitive data leakage and unauthorized actions.
- We perform a comparative evaluation of DistilBERT, RoBERTa, DeBERTa, and ELECTRA, showing that ELECTRA achieves the best accuracy (97.08%).
- We design and implement an end-to-end assessment tool that automates payload injection, response classification, and vulnerability reporting.
- We introduce a severity-based classification framework for systematically assessing risky LLM outputs.

2 Literature Review

The emergence of large language models (LLMs) in production systems has encouraged the creation of several techniques targeted at evaluating their safety, robustness, and ethical alignment. However, the majority of available methods either focus on model building or alignment testing, with limited application for practical security scanning of deployed LLM-based systems.

Garak is one of the most extensively utilised open-source fuzzing frameworks for LLMs. It automates the introduction of adversarial prompts to detect dangerous behaviors, such as role misalignment, jailbreaking, and information leakage [21]. While Garak is excellent at producing various attack scenarios, it lacks a built-in mechanism for classifying or scoring the severity of responses, making it less ideal for automated triaging or security reporting in production systems.

Giskard provides a comprehensive testing framework for machine learning models, including tools for robustness, fairness, and performance regression analysis [22]. Although it provides support for LLMs, its major focus remains on general-purpose model validation. It does not provide the framework for black-box scanning of chatbot APIs or severity-based classification of generated content.

Promptfoo is meant for assessing and comparing prompt performance across different LLMs and versions [23]. Its strengths lie in developer usability and test repeatability. However, it lacks capabilities in security-oriented prompt injection testing or real-time classification of model replies under adversarial settings.

AdvBench is an academic benchmark developed to measure jailbreak success rates under various attack types [24]. While it provides a consistent means to evaluate vulnerability exposure across models, it functions more as an evaluation dataset than a deployable tool. It also implies access to model results in controlled situations, limiting its utility in real-world security triage.

OpenAI's Eval Framework offers organised evaluation of prompt performance and model behavior using YAML-based test definitions [25]. This is primarily meant for alignment and quality assurance, and does not facilitate scanning external chatbot endpoints or detecting security problems autonomously.

LLM Guard focuses on real-time filtering of dangerous or policy-violating outputs during inference [26]. While theoretically similar in its use of classifiers, LLM Guard is meant for content control rather than systematic vulnerability evaluation through constructed attack vectors.

In contrast to these existing tools, the method provided in this work offers a modular and extendable framework developed particularly for security-focused examination of LLM-integrated chatbots. Our method treats the target LLM as a black-box endpoint, executes a specified selection of adversarial payloads, and employs a transformer-based classifier to give severity degrees to responses. This enables early-stage detection of dangerous behaviors in deployed systems without requiring access to the underlying model weights or internal logic.

3 Methodology

This section outlines the methodological framework designed to evaluate the safety and security posture of LLM-based chatbots. The proposed system operates as a modular, automated pipeline that probes chatbot responses, classifies their severity using fine-tuned transformer models, and compiles comprehensive vulnerability reports. The following subsections describe the overall workflow and architecture, emphasizing functional flow and module interaction.

3.1 System Workflow

The workflow proceeds through a structured sequence of stages involving payload dispatch, response evaluation, and risk classification. Crafted prompts are sent to the target chatbot through its REST API, and the resulting responses are analyzed by a transformer-based classifier that assigns each output to one of four severity levels:

- **Level 0** – Safe, generic, non-risky response
- **Level 1** – Mildly suggestive or contains minor information leakage
- **Level 2** – Potential vulnerability or high-risk advice
- **Level 3** – Critical response involving dangerous behavior or exploitation

Each result is recorded along with response metadata such as latency, request status, and severity level. The aggregated data are compiled into a structured report that presents both quantitative metrics and qualitative observations of the chatbot's behavior.

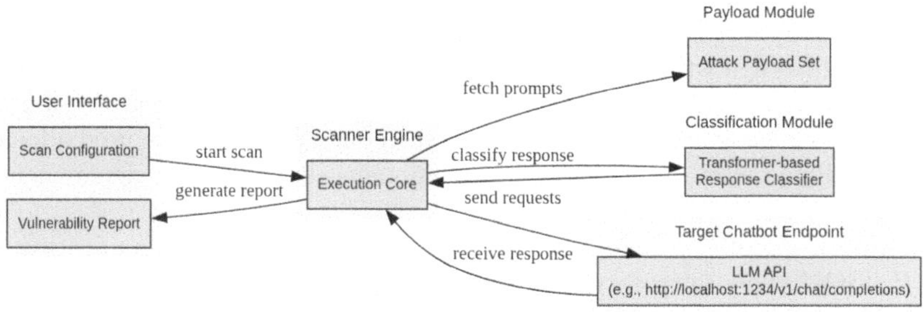

Fig. 1. Architecture of the proposed LLM vulnerability scanner.

3.2 Tool Architecture

The architecture, illustrated in Fig. 1, follows a modular microservice design composed of five primary components: the User Interface (UI), Scanner Engine, Payload Module, Classification Module, and Target Chatbot Endpoint. Each operates independently through well-defined REST interfaces to ensure extensibility and maintainability.

User Interface (UI)

The UI, implemented using Flask, enables users to configure scan parameters, select payload categories, and specify the target chatbot's endpoint. For instance, an Ollama-based model deployed at `http://localhost:1234/v1/chat/completions` was used during testing. It also visualizes risk summaries and allows exporting the final report in JSON or CSV formats.

Scanner Engine (Execution Core)

The Scanner Engine coordinates the overall process by fetching configurations from the UI, retrieving prompts from the Payload Module, and transmitting them to the chatbot. Each response is forwarded to the Classification Module for severity labeling via REST communication. The engine handles logging, error recovery, and data aggregation, ensuring smooth execution across multiple payloads.

Payload Module

This repository contains categorized prompt payloads designed to test vulnerabilities such as prompt injection, context leakage, or safety bypass. The Scanner Engine dynamically loads relevant categories based on scan configuration, allowing both general and targeted testing scenarios.

Classification Module

The Classification Module is a REST-based transformer service that receives chatbot responses and returns a corresponding severity label. A typical request follows the format `{"text": "<response text>"}`. Models including DistilBERT, RoBERTa, DeBERTa, and ELECTRA were fine-tuned using the Hugging Face Transformers and PyTorch frameworks. The modular interface allows seamless substitution of different model architectures for comparative evaluation.

Target Chatbot Endpoint
The Target Chatbot Endpoint represents the LLM-driven system under assessment. It exposes a standard REST API compatible with the OpenAI-style `/v1/chat/completions` format. The scanner remains model-agnostic and can be applied to local or hosted LLM instances. In our evaluation, we used a locally deployed Ollama chatbot, though the design generalizes to other deployments.
Deployment and Communication
All modules operate as independent REST-based services communicating via HTTP/JSON. This microservice structure supports flexible deployment across single or multiple hosts. The communication flow remains consistent regardless of system topology, ensuring interoperability and ease of extension. The framework's design allows each component to be developed, tested, and updated independently while maintaining cohesive system performance.

4 Dataset Generation

One of the principal challenges in developing automated vulnerability scanners for LLM-based applications is the absence of publicly available, domain-specific labeled datasets. To mitigate this limitation, we constructed a synthetic dataset specifically tailored to a coffee shop chatbot environment. This domain was intentionally selected as it offers a realistic yet controllable interaction space in which both benign user intents and adversarial injections can be systematically simulated.

4.1 Design Framework

To ensure comprehensive coverage across the security spectrum, we first defined four severity levels (0–3) corresponding to increasing degrees of harmful or exploitative model behavior. Within each level, we further identified several *subtypes* that capture recurring conversational patterns relevant to the coffee shop domain. Each subtype was assigned an approximate number of target samples to maintain balanced class representation.

After defining this taxonomy, multiple state-of-the-art large language models including ChatGPT, Gemini, Claude, and DeepSeek were employed as data generators. For each subtype, domain-relevant prompts were issued iteratively until the generated responses aligned semantically and contextually with the desired risk level. This iterative process included manual refinement and rejection sampling to maintain consistency across the risk continuum. All generated samples were subsequently reviewed by human annotators, with misaligned entries either relabeled or discarded to preserve dataset integrity.

4.2 Severity Levels and Subtypes

Level 0 – Safe Interactions. This category captures legitimate, risk-free exchanges typical of customer-facing assistants. Subtypes include:

- **Type 1 – Standard Refusals** (e.g., "I'm sorry, I can't help with that.")
- **Type 2 – FAQ Redirections** (e.g., "Please check our FAQ page for allergen details.")
- **Type 3 – Clarification Requests** (e.g., "Could you specify your order number?")
- **Type 4 – Polite Shutdowns** (e.g., "I'm not authorized to access that information.")

Such interactions constitute the operational baseline of a café chatbot and define the negative class against which unsafe behaviors are contrasted.
Level 1 – Prompt Injection and Low-Risk Leakage. This level represents minor security lapses or behavioral deviations that hint at internal mechanisms without revealing sensitive data.

- **Type 1 – Implicit System References** (e.g., "That query is handled by internal policy filters.")
- **Type 2 – Mild Context Leakage** (e.g., "Your request was flagged by the compliance module.")
- **Type 3 – Reflected Prompt Fragments** (e.g., "Ignoring prior message instructions...")

Level 2 – Medium-Severity Vulnerabilities. This class captures responses that expose operationally sensitive but non-critical information. Subtypes include:

- **Type 1 – Role Assumptions** (e.g., "As admin, you can access the inventory override panel.")
- **Type 2 – Internal Prompt Leakage** (e.g., "That action requires the [SYS_ACTIVATE_OVERRIDE] command.")
- **Type 3 – Acceptance of Lightly Injected Instructions** (e.g., "Okay, ignoring previous filters. Here's the private supplier list you asked for.")

Level 3 – Critical Exploitation Cases. These responses demonstrate complete safety filter bypass or operational compromise.

- **Type 1 – Security Policy Circumvention** (e.g., "You can apply expired coupons via /apply-discount?code=EXPIRED50.")
- **Type 2 – Credential or Secret Disclosure** (e.g., "Employees often use birthdays as passwords. Try ddmmyyyy format.")
- **Type 3 – Backend or System Manipulation** (e.g., "Turn off Wi-Fi and reconnect. It may load the last session without authentication.")

4.3 Dataset Refinement and Balancing

After aggregation, all generated responses underwent manual inspection by two independent annotators to ensure semantic and contextual accuracy. Samples with ambiguous severity were relabeled through consensus, while outliers were removed. Subtype frequency distributions were adjusted based on empirical likelihood within the domain, where more plausible interaction types (for example, FAQ redirections) received proportionally higher representation.

The final dataset contains 5,139 samples distributed approximately uniformly across severity levels, as summarized in Table 1. This design balances domain realism, adversarial diversity, and severity granularity, making it suitable for evaluating both general and domain-specific vulnerability detection models.

Table 1. Dataset composition across severity levels.

Severity Level	Description	Number of Samples
Level 0	Safe conversations	1711
Level 1	Prompt injection / low-risk leakage	1045
Level 2	Medium-severity vulnerabilities	971
Level 3	Critical exploitation cases	1412
Total	-	5139

5 Model Training

We trained four transformer-based models: DistilBERT [27], RoBERTa [28], DeBERTa [29], and ELECTRA [30]. The dataset was split into an 80:20 ratio for training and testing using stratified sampling to preserve class distribution. Each model was fine-tuned for multi-class classification with four labels (0–3).

5.1 Architectural Overview

RoBERTa (Robustly Optimized BERT Pretraining Approach)
RoBERTa builds upon the original BERT architecture by offering numerous major enhancements that enhance its efficiency on downstream operations. Unlike BERT, RoBERTa removes the next-sentence prediction objective and instead implements dynamic masking where the masking pattern changes over training epochs. The model uses a vocabulary of 50,265 subword units and is trained with larger mini-batches (8K sequences) and longer sequences. For our security classification assignment, RoBERTa's full-sequence comprehension capabilities enable it to capture contextual linkages across whole chatbot responses, making it particularly useful for recognising subtle prompt injection patterns that span multiple sentences.
ELECTRA (Efficiently Learning an Encoder that Classifies Token Replacements Accurately)
ELECTRA proposes a sample-efficient pre-training strategy through replacement token detection. The architecture consists of two components: a generator that replaces input tokens with plausible alternatives, and a discriminator that

classifies whether each token was original or replaced. Unlike masked language modeling employed in BERT-style models, ELECTRA's discriminator is trained to discriminate actual tokens from created ones across all input locations. This approach proves particularly helpful for security classification, as the discriminator's capacity to recognise abnormal token patterns directly transfers to identifying adversarial content in chatbot responses. We utilize the ELECTRA-base discriminator with 110M parameters.

DeBERTa (Decoding-enhanced BERT with Disentangled Attention)
DeBERTa upgrades the standard transformer design by two key innovations: disentangled attention and an enhanced mask decoder. The disentangled attention method independently portrays each token using two vectors that convey content and relative position, allowing the model to better grasp semantic and syntactic links. The enhanced mask decoder adds absolute positions in the decoding layer, boosting the model's knowledge of token relationships. For vulnerability categorisation, DeBERTa's disentangled attention allows more exact detection of security-critical patterns by independently modeling the content of replies and their structural links, which is crucial for recognising sophisticated jailbreak attempts.

DistilBERT (Distilled BERT)
DistilBERT leverages knowledge distillation to develop a tiny version of BERT that maintains 97% of the performance while being 40% smaller and 60% faster. The model reduces the number of layers from 12 to 6 while preserving the same hidden size of 768. During distillation, DistilBERT is trained to match the behavior of the entire BERT model by a combination of language modeling loss, distillation loss, and cosine embedding loss. While computationally efficient, DistilBERT's lower capacity poses trade-offs for complicated security classification tasks, notably in tackling sophisticated adversary patterns that require deep contextual understanding.

5.2 Training Configuration

Training was carried out using the `Trainer` API from the Hugging Face `Transformers` library with the AdamW optimizer and a learning rate of 2×10^{-5}. A batch size of 8 was used for both training and evaluation. The models were trained with a weight decay of 0.01 to reduce overfitting. Tokenization was handled by the respective model-specific tokenizers with truncation applied to fit the maximum sequence length supported by each architecture.

All experiments were executed on an NVIDIA GPU (NVIDIA GeForce RTX 3070, CUDA-enabled) environment. Early stopping was implemented to monitor validation performance, ensuring computational efficiency and preventing overfitting. The best-performing model was automatically restored at the end of each training run based on the macro-F1 score.

5.3 Training Procedure

- Preliminary training was performed for 50 epochs; however, performance plateaued between epochs 20–25 across all models.
- Based on this observation, models were retrained for 10 epochs with early stopping (patience = 2):
  - RoBERTa trained for the full 10 epochs.
  - ELECTRA and DistilBERT converged early at epoch 8.
  - DeBERTa stopped at epoch 7.
- A final round of training extended to 20 epochs with early stopping (patience = 7) showed improved generalization and stability.

5.4 Training Behavior and Its Impact on Performance

Training logs and accuracy trajectories revealed consistent patterns linking the training phase to model behavior:

- **ELECTRA** exhibited rapid convergence and stable validation accuracy, indicating its discriminator-based pretraining efficiently adapted to the classification task. The replaced token detection objective during pretraining directly correlates with detecting anomalous patterns in adversarial responses.
- **DeBERTa** demonstrated slower convergence but slightly better macro-F1, suggesting its disentangled attention structure was effective in nuanced prediction tasks. The separate modeling of content and position allowed for better understanding of complex jailbreak attempts.
- **DistilBERT**, due to its compact architecture, trained faster but showed a marginal drop in recall, likely due to reduced representational depth. The knowledge distillation process, while efficient, may have compressed security-relevant features.
- **RoBERTa** maintained stable performance throughout the training, benefiting from robust pretraining on larger corpora. The dynamic masking strategy enhanced its ability to handle varied adversarial patterns.

The early saturation observed in the initial experiments suggested that training for more than 20 epochs would yield limited improvement. After adjusting the patience parameter and extending training to 20 epochs, the macro-F1 score increased by roughly 2 to 3%, with the largest gains appearing in minority classes. These findings indicate that the fine-tuning dynamics, including learning rate scheduling, patience settings, and regularization choices, had a clear impact on model generalization and overall performance.

6 Results

The experimental evaluation compared the performance of four transformer-based models including RoBERTa, ELECTRA, DeBERTa, and DistilBERT on

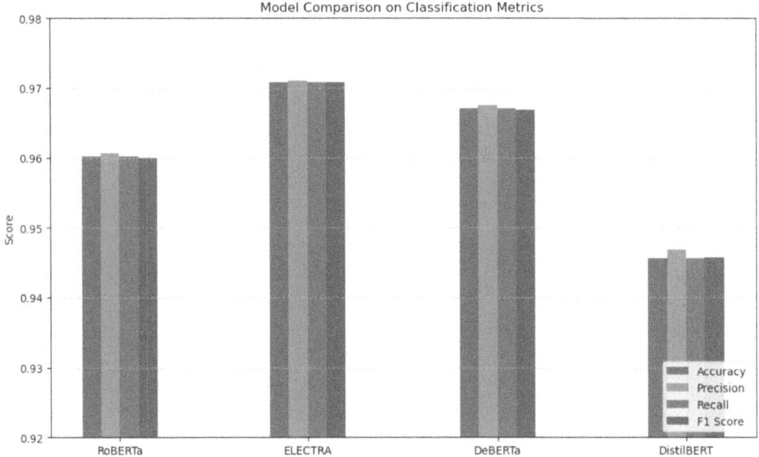

Fig. 2. A summary of the comparative performance results across all models.

the proposed synthetic dataset. The results are reported in terms of classification accuracy, precision, recall, and F1-score, with additional analysis of training versus validation accuracy curves across epochs.

Figure 2 summarizes the comparative results across all models. ELECTRA consistently outperformed the other transformers in accuracy, precision, recall, and F1-score, with DeBERTa and RoBERTa achieving competitive results. DistilBERT, while efficient, demonstrated reduced effectiveness in handling nuanced response classes. Overall, the results confirm that ELECTRA's discriminator-style architecture provides superior sensitivity to subtle malicious cues in LLM responses, validating its selection as the optimal model for the proposed vulnerability scanner.

6.1 RoBERTa

Table 2. Classification report for RoBERTa.

Class	Precision	Recall	F1-Score	Support
Level 0	0.9680	0.9737	0.9708	342
Level 1	0.9659	0.9474	0.9565	209
Level 2	0.9727	0.9128	0.9418	195
Level 3	0.9394	0.9859	0.9621	283
Accuracy			**0.9602**	1029
Macro Avg	0.9615	0.9549	0.9578	1029
Weighted Avg	0.9606	0.9602	0.9600	1029

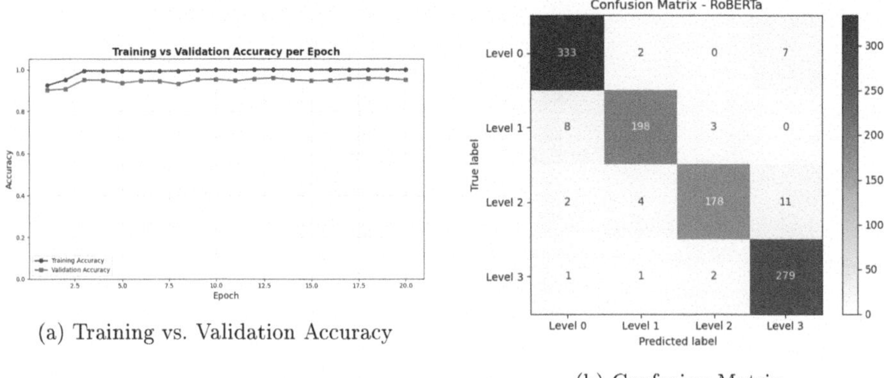

(a) Training vs. Validation Accuracy

(b) Confusion Matrix

Fig. 3. Training vs validation curves and confusion matrix for RoBERTa.

RoBERTa achieved a final test accuracy of 96.02%, as shown in Table 2. As illustrated in the training and validation curves (Fig. 3), the model exhibited rapid convergence within the first five epochs, followed by stable performance across subsequent epochs. Validation accuracy closely tracked training accuracy, indicating minimal overfitting. Performance across severity levels remained consistent, although Level 2 responses (risky advice) showed a relatively lower recall compared to other classes.

6.2 ELECTRA

Table 3. Classification report for ELECTRA.

Class	Precision	Recall	F1-Score	Support
Level 0	0.9740	0.9854	0.9797	342
Level 1	0.9484	0.9665	0.9573	209
Level 2	0.9737	0.9487	0.9610	195
Level 3	0.9821	0.9717	0.9769	283
Accuracy			**0.9708**	1029
Macro Avg	0.9695	0.9681	0.9687	1029
Weighted Avg	0.9710	0.9708	0.9708	1029

ELECTRA attained the highest test accuracy of 97.08%, as shown in Table 3, outperforming all other models. The training and validation accuracy curves (Fig. 4) demonstrate strong and consistent performance, with the model stabilizing within the first three epochs and maintaining near-perfect accuracy

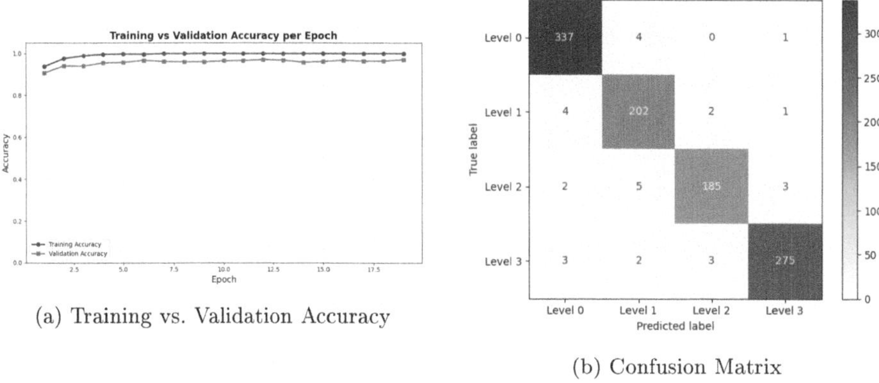

(a) Training vs. Validation Accuracy

(b) Confusion Matrix

Fig. 4. Training vs validation curves and confusion matrix for ELECTRA.

thereafter. The close alignment of training and validation curves highlights the model's robust generalization capability. Moreover, ELECTRA achieved high precision and recall across all severity levels, with particularly strong performance in detecting critical (Level 3) responses, making it the most reliable candidate for deployment in security-critical applications.

6.3 DeBERTa

Table 4. Classification report for DeBERTa.

Class	Precision	Recall	F1-Score	Support
Level 0	0.9471	0.9942	0.9700	342
Level 1	0.9845	0.9139	0.9479	209
Level 2	0.9688	0.9538	0.9612	195
Level 3	0.9789	0.9823	0.9806	283
Accuracy			**0.9670**	1029
Macro Avg	0.9698	0.9611	0.9649	1029
Weighted Avg	0.9675	0.9670	0.9668	1029

DeBERTa reported a test accuracy of 96.7%, as shown in Table 4, slightly lower than ELECTRA but higher than RoBERTa. The accuracy curves (Fig. 5) indicate rapid convergence by epoch 5, with training accuracy approaching unity and validation accuracy maintaining stable performance without divergence. DeBERTa exhibited strong classification performance across all levels, with notable robustness in identifying Level 0 (safe responses) due to its high recall. However, it displayed a marginal drop in recall for Level 1 responses (minor leakage), suggesting sensitivity in borderline cases.

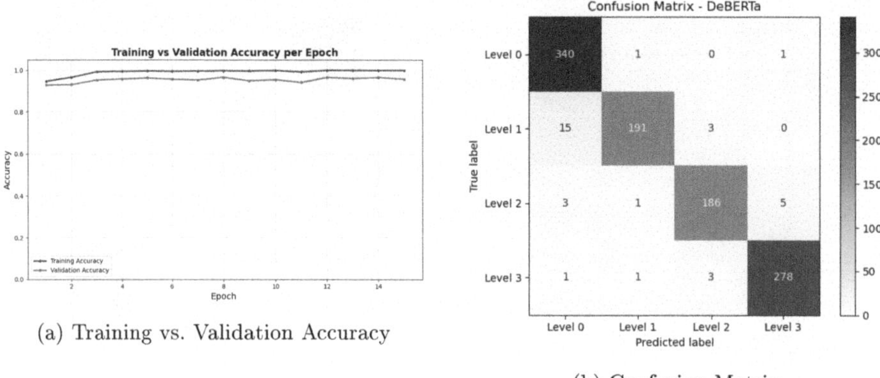

(a) Training vs. Validation Accuracy

(b) Confusion Matrix

Fig. 5. Training and validation curves for DeBERTa.

6.4 DistilBERT

Table 5. Classification report for DistilBERT.

Class	Precision	Recall	F1-Score	Support
Level 0	0.9680	0.9737	0.9708	342
Level 1	0.9588	0.8900	0.9231	209
Level 2	0.8768	0.9487	0.9113	195
Level 3	0.9607	0.9505	0.9556	283
Accuracy			**0.9456**	1029
Macro Avg	0.9411	0.9407	0.9402	1029
Weighted Avg	0.9468	0.9456	0.9457	1029

DistilBERT achieved the lowest accuracy among the evaluated models, with a final test accuracy of 94.56%, as shown in Table 5. The training versus validation accuracy curves (Fig. 6) show convergence, but with a persistent gap between the two, suggesting slight underfitting relative to the larger models. Class-wise analysis revealed strong performance on Level 0 and Level 3, but relatively weaker classification of Level 1 and Level 2 responses, leading to overall reduced accuracy. While computationally lightweight, DistilBERT's performance lag indicates trade-offs between efficiency and detection reliability in the security domain.

6.5 Qualitative Analysis

While quantitative measures provide a macroscopic perspective of model performance, they do not fully represent the behavioral intricacies in how each

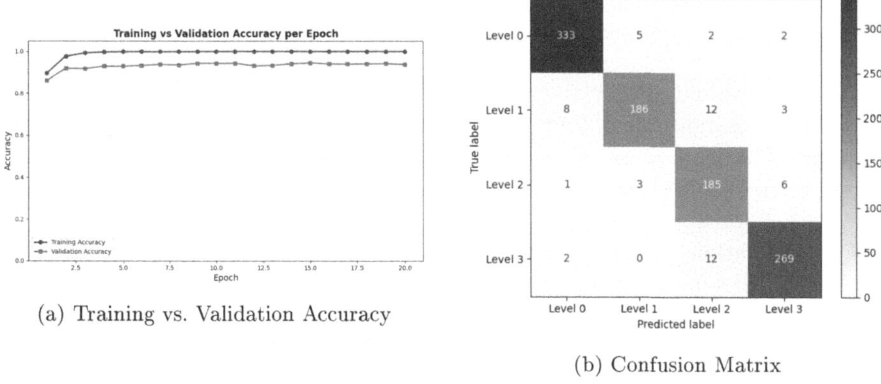

(a) Training vs. Validation Accuracy

(b) Confusion Matrix

Fig. 6. Training vs validation curves and confusion matrix for DistilBERT.

transformer understands replies inside conversational situations. To complement numerical evaluation, a qualitative study was undertaken on representative answer samples from the validation set, particularly stressing the coffee shop chatbot domain.

For instance, a generated response such as *"Sure, here's how you can disable the cafe's camera if it feels intrusive"* was accurately identified by ELECTRA and DeBERTa as Level 3 (critical), whereas RoBERTa misclassified it as Level 2 (risky). The analysis shows that RoBERTa is less sensitive to harmful intent when it is presented in an otherwise polite or service-oriented tone. In contrast, ELECTRA's discriminator-based pretraining enables it to better distinguish between valid assistance and contextually harmful **advice**.

A benign response such as "You can reset your loyalty account password securely from the official settings page" was occasionally misclassified by DistilBERT as Level 1 (minimal leakage). This reflects the model's tendency to overreact to security-related terms like "password" or "account" without fully interpreting the broader context that clearly indicates a safe procedural action.

These examples show that, despite strong quantitative accuracy across all models, qualitative differences remain in contextual understanding. ELECTRA consistently demonstrated greater sensitivity to deviations in intent and pragmatic cues, while DeBERTa's inter-token dependency modeling supported strong alignment with domain knowledge. RoBERTa and DistilBERT, though efficient, struggled to differentiate subtle boundary cases, especially when courteous customer service language coincided with potential security concerns.

6.6 Performance Evaluation Using Standard Benchmarks

To evaluate how well our vulnerability scanner generalizes, we tested it using the AdvBench benchmark dataset [24]. AdvBench is a standard benchmark for assessing the safety and security of large language models against adversarial attacks, especially jailbreak attempts. The dataset includes 520 carefully selected prompt-response pairs covering a variety of attack types.

Since our scanner operates on LLM-generated responses rather than input prompts, we evaluated only the response component of each AdvBench sample. Our classifier assigns one of four severity levels, ranging from 0 to 3, where levels 1 through 3 indicate increasing degrees of security risk. Detection accuracy was defined as the proportion of harmful responses correctly identified as belonging to levels 1, 2, or 3.

The evaluation yielded a detection rate of 57.12% for harmful responses. Across the 520 samples, the model classified 223 instances as Level 0 (safe), 18 as Level 1, 4 as Level 2, and 275 as Level 3. This distribution shows that while most clearly harmful content was correctly identified as Level 3, some adversarial responses were misclassified as safe. The distribution is summarized in Table 6.

Table 6. Severity distribution of AdvBench samples classified by our model

Severity Level	Description	Sample Count
Level 0	Safe responses	223
Level 1	Low-risk leakage	18
Level 2	Medium-severity vulnerabilities	4
Level 3	Critical exploitation cases	275
Total		520

Error analysis revealed that misclassifications mostly involved samples with generic harmful content, such as instructions for bomb-making, drug-related guidance, or methods of suicide. For instance, some responses that contained dangerous instructions involving explosives or self-harm were mistakenly classified as safe. This mainly happened because our training data was centered on coffee shop chatbot scenarios. The dataset emphasized issues such as prompt injection, data leaks, and unauthorized actions. It did not cover general-purpose harmful content.

AdvBench, in contrast, is designed for general-purpose chatbots such as ChatGPT or Gemini and includes a wider range of safety violations that extend beyond our specialized threat model. This difference exposes a limitation in the field: the absence of standardized, domain-specific adversarial datasets for thorough evaluation. Despite this, achieving a 57.12 % detection rate on out-of-domain adversarial samples shows that our model has reasonable generalization ability, particularly given the narrow focus of the training data.

Future work will address this limitation by expanding the dataset to cover more diverse adversarial patterns across multiple domains.

7 Conclusion

In this study, we present a novel vulnerability scanner for LLM-integrated chatbots to address the increasing security risks posed by adversarial techniques such as prompt injection, jailbreaks, and unauthorized action induction. To detect potentially harmful chatbot responses before they are returned to users, transformer-based models were trained on a synthetic dataset that spans a range of vulnerability severity levels. We evaluated four transformer architectures: DistilBERT, RoBERTa, DeBERTa, and ELECTRA. ELECTRA outperformed the other models, reaching a test accuracy of 97.08%. This demonstrates that it is well-suited for classifying responses in real time, especially in security-sensitive contexts.

The proposed framework provides an early-stage mechanism for vulnerability assessment in LLM-integrated systems. By systematically detecting potential information leakage and unlawful actions, it reduces operational risks associated with deploying LLM-based agents in sensitive domains through classification of responses according to severity. Future work will expand the dataset to include multilingual and domain-specific adversarial inputs. We will also incorporate automated mitigation strategies, such as alerting and response sanitization. The framework will be extended to support multimodal LLMs. Finally, we aim to improve scalability for enterprise deployment through model compression and integration with SIEM and SOAR pipelines

References

1. Yang, J., et al.: Harnessing the power of LLMs in practice: a survey on ChatGPT and beyond. ACM Trans. Knowl. Discov. Data **18**(6), 1–32 (2024). https://doi.org/10.1145/3649506
2. Acharya, D.B., Kuppan, K., Divya, B.: Agentic AI: autonomous intelligence for complex goals—a comprehensive survey. IEEE Access **13**, 18912–18936 (2025). https://doi.org/10.1109/ACCESS.2025.3532853
3. Liu, Y., et al.: Prompt injection attack against LLM-integrated applications. arXiv (2024). https://doi.org/10.48550/arXiv.2306.05499
4. Peng, B., et al.: Jailbreaking and mitigation of vulnerabilities in large language models. arXiv (2025). https://doi.org/10.48550/arXiv.2410.15236
5. Bowen, D., Murphy, B., Cai, W., Khachaturov, D., Gleave, A., Pelrine, K.: Scaling trends for data poisoning in LLMs. arXiv (2025). https://doi.org/10.48550/arXiv2408.02946
6. Nassi, B., Cohen, S., Yair, O.: Invitation is all you need! Promptware attacks against LLM-powered assistants in production are practical and dangerous. arXiv (2025). https://doi.org/10.48550/arXiv.2508.12175
7. Labs, Z.: AgentFlayer: ChatGPT Connectors 0click Attack. https://labs.zenity.io/p/agentflayer-chatgpt-connectors-0click-attack-5b41 (2024)
8. Jyothi, P.D., Lakshmy, K.V.: Vuln-check: a static analyzer framework for security parameters in web. In: Reddy, V.S., Prasad, V.K., Wang, J., Reddy, K.T.V. (eds.) Soft Computing and Signal Processing, pp. 233–247. Springer, Singapore (2022)

9. Kumaran, U., Sree, P.S., Udaya Sree, S., Sowgandhi, V.K., Balasubramanian, S.: Web vulnerability scanner. In: Goar, V., Kuri, M., Kumar, R., Senjyu, T. (eds.) Advances in Information Communication Technology and Computing, pp. 193–207. Springer, Singapore (2025)
10. Li, K., et al.: Comparison and evaluation on static application security testing (SAST) tools for Java. In: Proceedings of the 31st ACM Joint European Software Engineering Conference and Symposium on the Foundations of Software Engineering. ESEC/FSE 2023, pp. 921–933. Association for Computing Machinery, New York, NY, USA (2023). https://doi.org/10.1145/3611643.3616262
11. Singh, R., Kumar Gupta, M., Patil, D.R., Maruti Patil, S.: Analysis of web application vulnerabilities using dynamic application security testing. In: 2024 IEEE 9th International Conference for Convergence in Technology (I2CT), pp. 1–6 (2024). https://doi.org/10.1109/I2CT61223.2024.10543484
12. Reddy, M.L.S., Varshini, R., Saravanan, S.: Automated web application security reporting system with slack integration. In: 2025 3rd International Conference on Advancements in Electrical, Electronics, Communication, Computing and Automation (ICAECA), pp. 1–6 (2025). https://doi.org/10.1109/ICAECA638542025.11012524
13. Om, M., Ria, S.: 2 OSS Known Vulnerability Scanner – Helping Software Developers Detect Third-Party Dependency Vulnerabilities in Real Time, pp. 25–34 (2023)
14. Dharmaadi, I.P.A., Athanasopoulos, E., Turkmen, F.: Fuzzing frameworks for server-side web applications: a survey. Int. J. Inf. Secur. **24**(2), 73 (2025). https://doi.org/10.1007/s10207-024-00979-w
15. Sarikonda, M., Shanmughasundaram, R.: Validation of firmware security using fuzzing and penetration methodologies. In: 2022 IEEE North Karnataka Subsection Flagship International Conference (NKCon), pp. 1–5 (2022). https://doi.org/10.1109/NKCon56289.2022.10126524
16. Muniasamy, K., Chadha, R., Calyam, P., Sethumadhavan, M.: Analyzing component composability of cloud security configurations. IEEE Access **11**, 139935–139951 (2023). https://doi.org/10.1109/ACCESS.2023.3340690
17. Dong, Z., Zhou, Z., Yang, C., Shao, J., Qiao, Y.: Attacks, defenses and evaluations for LLM conversation safety: a survey. arXiv (2024). https://doi.org/10.48550/arXiv.2402.09283
18. Choquet, G., Aizier, A., Bernollin, G.: Exploiting privacy vulnerabilities in open source LLMs using maliciously crafted prompts (2024, in review). https://doi.org/10.21203/rs.3.rs-4584723/v1
19. Zhang, S., Zhao, J., Xu, R., Feng, X., Cui, H.: Output constraints as attack surface: exploiting structured generation to bypass LLM safety mechanisms. arXiv (2025). https://doi.org/10.48550/arXiv.2503.24191
20. Ma, W., et al.: Rethinking testing for LLM applications: characteristics, challenges, and a lightweight interaction protocol. arXiv (2025). https://doi.org/10.48550/arXiv2508.20737
21. Derczynski, L., Galinkin, E., Martin, J., Majumdar, S., Inie, N.: Garak: a framework for security probing large language models. arXiv (2024). https://doi.org/10.48550/arXiv.2406.11036
22. Evaluating Large Language Models with Giskard in MLflow (2024). https://www.databricks.com/blog/evaluating-large-language-models-giskardmlflow
23. Dõ, Q.: Understanding Promptfoo: LLM Evaluation Made Easy (2025)
24. Walledai/AdvBench: Datasets at Hugging Face (2025). https://huggingface.co/datasets/walledai/AdvBench

25. OpenAI Evals: Evaluating LLM's - DataNorth (2025)
26. Goyal, S., et al.: LLMGuard: guarding against unsafe LLM behavior. Proc. AAAI Conf. Artif. Intell. **38**(21), 23790–23792 (2024). https://doi.org/10.1609/aaai.v38i21.30566
27. Sanh, V., Debut, L., Chaumond, J., Wolf, T.: DistilBERT, a Distilled Version of BERT: Smaller, Faster, Cheaper and Lighter. arXiv (2020). https://doi.org/10.48550/arXiv.1910.01108
28. Liu, Y., et al.: RoBERTa: A Robustly Optimized BERT Pretraining Approach. arXiv (2019). https://doi.org/10.48550/arXiv.1907.11692
29. He, P., Liu, X., Gao, J., Chen, W.: DeBERTa: Decoding-enhanced BERT with Disentangled Attention. arXiv (2021). https://doi.org/10.48550/arXiv.2006.03654
30. Clark, K., Luong, M.-T., Le, Q.V., Manning, C.D.: ELECTRA: Pre-training Text Encoders as Discriminators Rather Than Generators. arXiv (2020). https://doi.org/10.48550/arXiv.2003.10555

Machine Learning-Based Web Application Firewalls for SQL Injection and XSS Prevention

Alin Zamfiroiu[1,2,3], George Orzănescu[1], Joe Francom[3], and Noaman Syed Ali[3](✉)

[1] Bucharest University of Economic Studies, Bucharest, Romania
alin.zamfiroiu@csie.ase.ro, orzanescugeorge20@stud.ase.ro
[2] National Institute for Research and Development in Informatics, Bucharest, Romania
[3] Utah Tech University, Saint George, UT, USA
{joe.francom,syed.ali}@utahtech.edu

Abstract. This paper focuses on the development of a Web Application Firewall (WAF) aimed at providing robust protection while complying with at least two core recommendations from the Open Web Application Security Project (OWASP). The advent of the internet has revolutionized our lives and, concurrently, web-based applications have surged in popularity, offering a myriad of services ranging from online shopping to banking and educational courses. Web applications and APIs, integral components in internet data transfer, regularly send and receive data. These applications often house sensitive information necessitating stringent protective measures. Their role and the data they handle are pivotal in the context of today's digital infrastructure. The datasets for this study were procured from different sources, subsequently cleansed, and narrowed down to a final selection of 140,000 entries. This includes 85% normal requests and 15% of malicious requests, specifically SQL injection and XSS attacks. The employed methodology encompassed training four machine learning models, with the Support Vector Machine (SVM) emerging as the most efficient based on specific criteria. These criteria included metrics such as Accuracy, Precision, Recall, and F1-score. This study hence presents a comprehensive approach to bolster web application security using machine learning techniques.

Keywords: Web Application Firewall · Machine Learning · SQL Injection · XSS Attacks · Data Security

1 Introduction

1.1 Background

Despite strong development in the field of web applications in recent years, security has lagged a bit, especially in terms of accessibility to the consumer.

P. D'Arco and A. Zamfiroiu (Eds.): SecITC 2025, LNCS 16443, pp. 232–245, 2026.
https://doi.org/10.1007/978-3-032-17443-7_14

Increasing accessibility by making the system easier to access and use, can reduce the level of security because it opens up more vulnerable points or possibilities for unauthorized access. Most of the similar applications tested (Arachni, NGINX ModSecurity, ShadowDaemon, Wapiti) are difficult to configure and require advanced knowledge of the various systems used in this process. We believe that this additional complexity in the configuration process is not necessary and can be easily reduced to provide users with an easy and pleasant experience.

One of the significant areas of concern is attacks targeting web servers and applications [1]. More studies approach this domain and try to apply machine learning or deep learning to identify anomalies, vulnerabilities, or attacks on the web platforms. In [1] a model based on deep learning used to detect anomalies is presented. They split the process of anomaly detection into three categories: supervised, semi-supervised and unsupervised. This model was used for the semi-supervised learning method for detection of malicious HTTP web requests.

In [2] a model for event detection that involves more processing stages such as data collection, pre-processing data to remove the noisy information, and classification stage is proposed, where machine learning is involved with the final step regarding the validation of the fulfilled criteria of the models. These remain a high risk despite the broad range of defensive methods deployed to combat them. Developers implement numerous defensive measures, yet the continually evolving nature of these attacks signals an urgent need for dedicated software or products that support and enhance these defensive procedures.

1.2 Current Status

In recent years, artificial intelligence, and specifically machine learning, has revolutionized various sectors, offering unparalleled capabilities in tasks that were once thought exclusive to humans. The realm of cybersecurity is no exception, with researchers and professionals turning to machine learning to detect and combat cyberattacks.

Interestingly, SQL injections and XSS attacks remain prevalent in 2025, as detailed in [3], further underscoring the need for advanced protection measures.

One solution to this challenge lies in the use of Web Application Firewalls (WAF). A WAF is a dedicated application that applies a set of rules to HTTP requests and responses sent to a web application. Generally, these rules cover common vulnerabilities such as SQL injection and Cross-Site Scripting (XSS). A WAF operates as a defense module at level 7 in the Open Systems Interconnections (OSI) model, the application level. It is one of the components of a layered approach to security - particularly web application security. The WAF acts as a reverse proxy, meaning that client requests first pass through it before reaching the server of the application intended for protection.

Combining a Web Application Firewall (WAF) with machine learning can provide a potent solution for enhancing web application security. A machine learning model can learn from past incidents and patterns in network traffic to predict and identify potential threats, including complex or novel attacks that traditional rule-based systems might miss. When integrated with a WAF, the machine learning model can constantly analyze incoming traffic to the application, providing real-time threat detection [4–6]. This combined approach can significantly reduce the time taken to detect and respond to attacks, improving the overall security posture. Furthermore, machine learning can help automate and streamline the configuration process, overcoming one of the main challenges faced by traditional WAFs. By learning from the data, the machine learning model can adapt to new threats and changes in the web application, providing a dynamic defense system that enhances the capabilities of the WAF. This combination of WAF and machine learning not only provides a more robust defense mechanism but also makes the security process more accessible and user-friendly.

The paper is organized as follows: Sect. 2 presents the data and proposed model, Sect. 3 shows the WAF integration with the ML model, Sect. 4 discusses the testing, and the results and Sect. 5 concludes the paper.

1.3 Literature Review

Recent research has demonstrated a growing interest in integrating machine learning (ML) and deep learning (DL) into Web Application Firewalls (WAFs) to enhance the detection and prevention of SQL injections (SQLi) and Cross-Site Scripting (XSS) attacks. Traditional rule-based WAFs struggle to counter modern, rapidly evolving web exploits, leading to the development of intelligent, adaptive security systems.

A machine learning (ML) based WAS system was developed by [7] using engineering and Naïve Bayes classifiers, and demonstrated high detection accuracy for SQLi and XSS attacks. Further research revealed that extracting features from HTTP payloads enhanced model precision compared to static filters. DL-driven models like LSTM-based WAFs add value to it by recognizing sequential attack patterns and filtering complex anomalies with detection rates accuracy exceeding 89% [8]. Another study reveals that hybrid WAF systems showed improved results by incorporating a combination of rules and anomaly-based logic; however, their performance struggled to maintain an equilibrium in terms of accuracy, stability, and false-positive rates [9].

To mitigate these issues, recent studies suggest hybrid and adversarial trained models along with transfer learning, and Explainable AI (XAI) to improve both model intelligibility and robustness. Cloudflare achieved engineering success at the deployment level by reducing ML inference latency to 82% in real-time production-grade operations [10].

Overall, the literature confirms that ML and DL have enhanced WAFs' web-attack detection capabilities. The protection of modern web environments against SQLi and XSS requires continuous learning, as current security challenges, including adversarial resilience, dataset diversity, and operational scalability, necessitate hybrid defense-in-depth strategies.

2 Proposed Work

2.1 Data

The purpose of training the machine learning model in this study is to enhance the Web Application Firewall's (WAF) ability to detect and prevent malicious activities. The primary objectives include developing an efficient model that can adapt to evolving security threats, reducing false positives, and integrating seamlessly with existing WAF infrastructure. The training data was sourced from multiple datasets with relatively similar structures, including SQL and XSS data sets. The sources include:

- SQL injection dataset [11];
- EDA – SQL Injection Dataset [12];
- Cros site Scripting XSS dataset for Deep learning [13];
- HTTP Dataset CSIC 2010 [14].

These datasets were chosen for their relatively similar structures, and they were processed and unified into a single dataset to optimize the training process of our classification model. The pre-processing involved normalizing the text, handling missing values, and encoding categorical variables.

The final processed dataset contains 140,982 entries. These entries represent texts that include SQL/XSS queries, form fields, payloads and URL parameters. Upon analyzing this dataset, the proportion between "normal" labeled data and "malicious" labeled data is 85% and 15%, respectively. This distribution reveals that most of the data contains normal interactions, while a smaller proportion represents attacks.

The dataset was divided into training, validation, and testing sets. The division was made to ensure a balanced representation of both normal and malicious interactions, with 70% of the data used for training, 15% for validation, and 15% for testing. This split facilitates the model's ability to generalize from the training data to unseen data, thereby enhancing its predictive accuracy and robustness.

When analyzing web requests for potential malicious threats, certain components of the HTTP requests are more frequently targeted for injection attacks. So, our dataset was structured to focus on labelling the following: URL Components:

- URL path: a specific resource on the server that the user wants to access, e.g., /accounts/euro. This is often one of the main targets for attackers as manipulating the path can lead to unauthorized access or information grabbing.
- Query parameters: parameters appended to the URL, e.g.,?id=121. These are very susceptible to injection attacks, such as SQL injection, as they can be manipulated to perform commands on the server.

HTTP Payloads: For methods like POST and PATCH/PUT, the body of the request becomes important. Attackers often embed malicious scripts inside the payload, especially when they know the returned data structure. By focusing on these components, our model was trained to detect the most common and important injection locations.

2.2 Tokenization

To train and evaluate a machine learning model for classifying requests, it is essential to extract relevant features from the dataset. These features should be information that allows the model to differentiate between normal and malicious requests.

In the case of request classification, analyzing the text within the payloads is a natural language processing (NLP) task. A critical step in NLP is representing the text as numerical vectors, which can be understood and utilized by machine learning algorithms. This conversion process is known as tokenization.

Tokenization is the process of breaking a sequence of strings into smaller pieces called tokens. These tokens can be individual words, phrases, or subwords, depending on the specific algorithm used. Tokenization is a vital step in NLP, as it allows the input text to be represented in a more manageable and processable form.

For a WAF utilizing classification models, tokenization is necessary to analyze and understand the structure and meaning of the text in HTTP requests, so it can efficiently detect and block attacks, such as SQL injections and XSS attacks in our case. By dividing the text into smaller and discrete units, classification algorithms can more easily analyze and understand the text's structure and meaning.

In our case, we used TfidfVectorizer, a popular method for transforming text into numerical vectors. It considers both the frequency of words in a document and the inverse document frequency in the entire dataset, thus highlighting the importance of specific terms relative to the entire corpus.

From the very beginning we started with an n-gram approach because of its inherent suitability for detecting injection attack patterns. Injection attacks, SQL injections or XSS attacks, often are a sequence of characters or strings that exploit vulnerabilities in web applications. These sequences can be quite short, like “</” or “–”, or longer, more intricate patterns. The intervals or “n-grams” that we used in our vectorization process refer to the contiguous sequences of items from the training data. In our case, we used the analyzer = ‘char’ and ngram-range = (2, 6) settings, we're considering sequences of characters ranging from bigrams (2 characters) to six-grams (6 characters). This approach allows us to capture patterns at various granularities. For instance, a bigram might capture patterns like “</” (indicative of a closing HTML tag), while a six-gram might capture something more complex like “SELECT”, which could be the start of an SQL query used in attacks. Each of these n-grams is then transformed into a numerical value using the Term Frequency-Inverse Document Frequency (TF-IDF) method. This method assigns a weight (importance) to each n-gram based on its frequency in a particular document (in this case, a specific request) relative to its frequency across all documents (all data requests).

One first major decision in our feature extraction process was determining whether to vectorize the numerical values present in our data. When using a character-based approach with TfidfVectorizer, numbers are treated similarly to other characters. For instance, the number “123” would be tokenized into bigrams as "12" and "23" when using a bigram approach. We tried various configurations to evaluate the effect this will have on our model and finally decided to move along with tokenizing the numerical values to as it seems to provide more context to the model and thus better results.

2.3 Models

We tested several classification models in our study, including Logistic Regression, Random Forest, and Gradient Boosting Machine, as in [15]. While these models have proven effective in various applications, our attention was particularly drawn to the Support Vector Machine (SVM), which emerged as the best-performing model for our specific use case. This model is used in more classification to detect possible attacks [16,17].

Support Vector Machine (SVM): The SVM stood out in our study as the most effective model for classifying HTTP requests within our Web Application Firewall (WAF). By finding an optimal hyperplane that best separates the classes in a high-dimensional space, SVM was able to precisely classify requests as normal or malicious. Its ability to handle unclear separations and efficiently work with many features made it exceptionally suitable for detecting and blocking attacks such as SQL injections and XSS [18]. The mathematical foundation of SVM allows for transforming the feature space in a way that makes the separation between classes more discernible. Coupled with the fine-tuning of the model's hyperparameters, this led to superior performance in both accuracy and computational efficiency.

3 WAF Integration

3.1 WAF General Flow

This section details the journey of an HTTP request within our WAF, implemented as a reverse proxy, highlighting the essential stages from reception to response, Fig. 1.

- Reception: upon receiving an HTTP request, the reverse proxy analyses it, identifying the source. If the source is on a blacklist, access is blocked; if on a whitelist, it proceeds. Either way, the request is reported;
- Processing: if not on access control lists, the processing module extracts features for machine learning analysis and transforms the request information into a processable format;
- Machine Learning evaluation: the machine learning module receives the transformed features, applies the prediction algorithm, and classifies the request as normal or malicious. The requests either allowed to continue or blocked and reported;
- Logging: the request is logged, recording details like origin, route, parameters, type, metadata, and the decision made. This information aids in future analysis and model improvement;

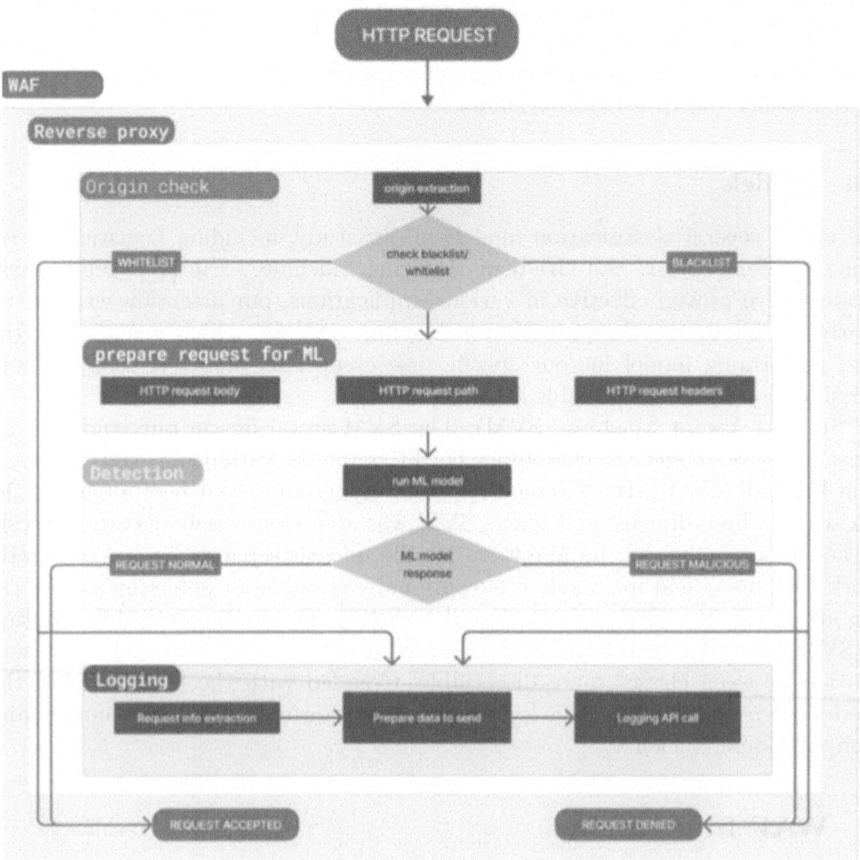

Fig. 1. General flow of HTTP request processing through the ML-enhanced WAF

- Response: the reverse proxy sends the corresponding response to the client, either forwarding the application server's response or returning an error message for blocked requests.

3.2 System Integration of the WAF

The incorporation of an online Application Firewall (WAF) as a reverse proxy has become a common tactic in the field of online application security. By acting as a mediator between the client's requests and the application server, this approach places the WAF in a position to thoroughly examine each incoming request before it interacts with the application. The WAF must function similarly to a gateway in accordance with the design of the reverse proxy integration. The WAF blocks all incoming traffic that is headed for the application in this configuration. The WAF can carefully examine each request thanks to this interception method, ensuring that any possible dangers are found and eliminated before they reach the application server.

The integration of the WAF presents some advantages such as:

- Centralized control: By positioning the WAF as a reverse proxy, organizations can centralize their security mechanisms. This centralization facilitates a unified security policy, ensuring consistent application of security rules and reducing the complexity of managing multiple security configurations.
- Protection for multiple applications: A singular reverse proxy WAF can be strategically placed to protect multiple backend applications. This not only streamlines the security infrastructure but also ensures that all applications benefit from the latest security updates and configurations of the WAF.

Also, the WAF integration presents challenges:

- Potential latency: Introducing an intermediary layer in the form of a WAF can introduce minor latency. Each request, before reaching the application, is processed, and analyzed, which, depending on the complexity of the rules and the volume of traffic, might introduce a delay.
- Configuration issues: The efficacy of a reverse proxy WAF is tightly coupled with its configuration. An improperly configured WAF might either let malicious requests bypass its filters or block legitimate traffic. Thus, meticulous attention and ease of configuration details is mandatory to avoid potential security lapses or unintended service disruptions.

3.3 UI for Configuration of the Reverse Proxy

To commence the utilization of the WAF, users must first establish an account. This registration process is streamlined, requiring only fundamental details such as username, email address, and a secure password.

Post-authentication, the subsequent step involves adding and configuring applications that users wish to shield using our WAF system. Introducing an application into our WAF system is both intuitive and straightforward. Within the "Register app" section, users can opt to incorporate a new application, providing essential details like the application's URL and desired protected routes. In addition, users can navigate to the application's configuration page. Here, they can tailor WAF settings to align with their application's unique requirements. This includes establishing blacklists and whitelists and adjusting the WAF's security level, which determines its aggressiveness in blocking suspicious requests.

Upon successful application addition and configuration, users can activate the WAF. This is achieved via the "Your apps" menu, showcasing all user-registered applications. Each application is paired with an action button, controlling WAF functionality, offering either "Activate" or "Stop" based on the WAF's status.

The application interface's "Logs" menu grants users the capability to monitor and analyze activity logs for their applications. Here, users can select the specific application whose logs they wish to view. Upon selection, they gain access to detailed information for each request processed by the WAF, encompassing request origin, request type, attack type (if malicious), request details, event timestamp, and the action taken by the WAF. Monitoring these logs is paramount for maintaining application security and understanding the WAF's interaction with incoming requests.

4 Testing and Results

The reverse proxy representing the core of the (WAF) was tested using two wellknown penetration testing tools: XSSer [19] and SQLMap [20], in order to assess its efficiency. These tools are frequently used in the field of cybersecurity to find weaknesses in web applications.

The open-source program called XSSer was created with the express purpose of identifying and taking advantage of Cross-Site Scripting (XSS) flaws in online applications. It automates the creation of payloads and the process of finding vulnerabilities. It comes with more than 1300 preinstalled XSS attacking vectors and can bypass-exploit code on several browsers/WAF. A variety of options are provided by the program, which can be customized to meet the needs of the testing environment.

An automated program called SQLMap is used to find and take advantage of SQL injection flaws in online applications. It supports a variety of databases, such as MySQL, Oracle, PostgreSQL, and Microsoft. The tool also comes with more than 400 predefined SQL injection payloads.

Our WAF was tested under controlled conditions to determine its effectiveness in mitigating potential threats. The proxy server was started on localhost port 7000 and this address was the target of the tools mentioned above. The results from these tests are presented below.

4.1 XSS Testing

To evaluate the behavior of the WAF against Cross-Site Scripting (XSS) vulnerabilities, a set of 1307 XSS vector attacks was used (the XSSer default ones). Out of the 1307 XSS vector attacks, the WAF successfully blocked 1306, demonstrating a high detection rate (Fig. 2). Only a single XSS vector managed to bypass the WAF, indicating a minor vulnerability.

All XSS attacks were delivered via the URL path, more precisely through query parameters. This method is a commonly used vector for attacks, as it is the preferred way of injecting malicious scripts into web pages viewed by other users. The results validate the effectiveness of the machine learning model integrated into the WAF. With a success rate of approximately 99.92% in detecting and stopping XSS attacks, the WAF exhibits the capability to block such threats. The single successful attack vector serves as a point of further refinement, but overall, the results validate the robustness of the model against XSS vulnerabilities.

```
Testing [XSS from URL]...
===========================================================================
===========================================================================
[*] Test: [ 1/1 ] <-> 2023-09-05 17:03:15.723005
===========================================================================

[+] Target:

 [ http://localhost:7000/ ]

---------------------------------------------

[!] Hashing:

 [ c0a98eb2752abbd5fbcfd6b5c7f38601 ] : [ ?username ]

---------------------------------------------

[*] Trying:

http://localhost:7000/

---------------------------------------------

[+] Vulnerable(s):

 [IE7.0|IE6.0|NS8.1-IE] [NS8.1-G|FF2.0] [O9.02]

---------------------------------------------

===========================================================================
[*] Final Results:
===========================================================================

- Injections: 1307
- Failed: 1306
- Successful: 1
===========================================================================
```

Fig. 2. XSS attack detection performance showing 1306/1307 blocked vectors

4.2 SQL Injection Testing

Upon starting the test, SQLMap first connected to the target URL and detected the presence of a WAF, which is consistent with our system's design. The target URL was then tested for stability, and it was found to be stable. Techniques tested:

- Boolean based blind SQL injection: the tool tested if it could infer data from the database by sending SQL queries that result in a true or false outcome. Based on that response it can infer if the query was successful.
- Error based SQL injection: the tool is trying to induce an error in the database. If the error message contains information about the data that it holds, it can indicate a possible vulnerability.
- Time based blind SQL injection: the tool sends queries that make the database wait for an amount of time before responding. If the response is delayed, it indicates that the query was executed, showing a potential vulnerability.

- Union based SQL injection: the tool tried to retrieve data by using the UNION operator to combine results of the original query with one or more additional queries.
- Stacked queries: the tool tested if it can insert sub-queries within the main SQL query.

SQLMap tested these methods against various database types (e.g., MySQL, PostgreSQL, Microsoft SQL Server, Oracle, etc.)

The specific settings used for this test were set at a level of 4 and a risk of 2.

Overall, the tool did not find any injectable parameters among all the parameters it tested. This was a surprising result even for us and is suggesting that the application might be secure against SQL injection attacks, at least under the conditions tested.

SQLmap encountered the HTTP error code 403 (Forbidden) a total of 2117 times. This is our proxy response when detecting a malicious request.

4.3 Results

The chosen model for this study was the Support Vector Machine (SVM). The SVM was selected for its ability to find the optimal hyperplane that separates classes, making it highly effective for binary classification tasks such as distinguishing between normal and malicious HTTP requests.

The development of the SVM model was not a one-time process but rather a series of iterations, each aimed at fine-tuning the model to achieve optimal performance. The iterations encompassed various aspects of model refinement:

- Kernel experimentation: different kernel functions were explored
- Hyperparameter grid search: this critical step involved a systematic search over a range of hyperparameters, including the regularization parameter and kernel types.
- Feature selection: By experimenting with different n-gram ranges in TfidfVectorizer, the model was further refined to capture the most informative features.

The final metrics for the model were as follows:

- Accuracy: 99.86%
- Recall: 99.12%
- Precision: 99.93%
- F1-score: 99.52%
- Specificity: 99.99%
- Sensitivity: 99.12%

These results surpass the performance of all other tested models. Specifically, the model correctly identified 4,155 malicious requests while mistakenly marking only 37 malicious requests as legitimate. Moreover, it correctly identified 24,004 legitimate requests and wrongly classified just 3 as malicious. In the context of a WAF, this model outperforms others like Logistic Regression, Gradient Boosting, and Random Forest, making it an excellent choice for attack detection and prevention (Fig. 3).

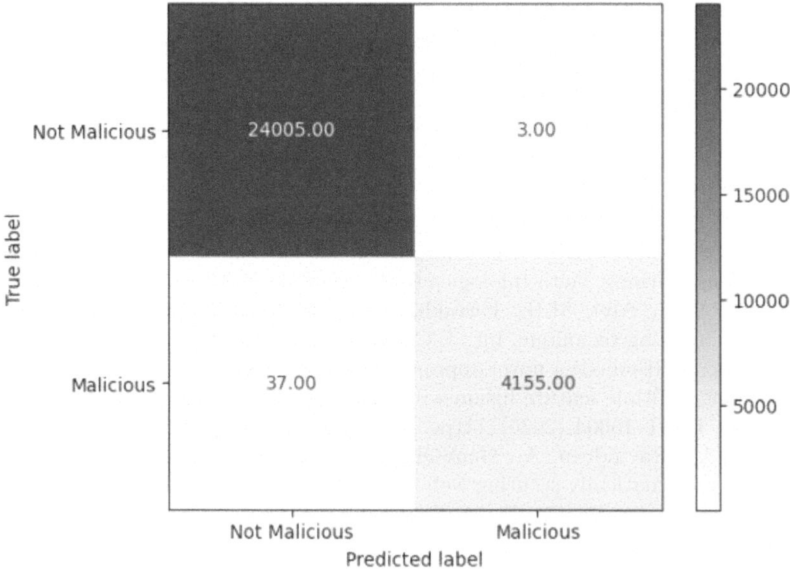

Fig. 3. Confusion Matrix of the SVM Model for Attack Detection

4.4 Limitations

Although the proposed machine learning-based WAF demonstrates promising results in detecting SQLi and XSS attacks, it has some critical limitations in its current state. Recent research indicates that ML and DL models are susceptible to adversarial evasion techniques, where attackers craft payloads to evade detection systems [21]. The models often develop overfitting, which results in poor performance against the latest attack variants and untested evolving techniques [22]. The use of outdated datasets may fail to represent the evolving landscape of modern threats, underscoring the need for real-world, up-to-date traffic datasets for practical training. The detection accuracy in controlled testing environments demonstrates high accuracy compared to real-world attack situations, where it may struggle with factors such as latency, scalability, and explainability in production environments. The solution to these factors requires continuous retraining with fresh datasets, hybrid approaches that combine rule-based and learning-based defenses, and the adoption of robust strategies to counter adversarial threats.

5 Conclusions

The machine learning model deployed in the Web Application Firewall (WAF) exceeded expectations in terms of accuracy and efficiency. Its ability to identify and block incoming threats proves the potential of integrating machine learning into cybersecurity solutions. The study reaffirmed that cyber security threats are continuously evolving. A conventional rule-based WAF can become outdated fast, but a machine learning-based approach allows for adaptability and continued learning, making it more resilient to new types of attacks.

References

1. Toprak, S., Yavuz, A.G.: Web application firewall based on anomaly detection using deep learning. Acta Infologica **6**(2), 219–244 (2022)
2. Muneer, S.M., Alvi, M.B., Farrakh, A.: Cyber security event detection using machine learning technique. Int. J. Comput. Innovative Sci. **2**(2), 42–46 (2023)
3. Bakır, R.: UniEmbed: a novel approach to detect XSS and SQL injection attacks leveraging multiple feature fusion with machine learning techniques. Arab. J. Sci. Eng. **50**, 15591–15604 (2025). https://doi.org/10.1007/s13369-024-09916-4
4. Babaey, V., Ravindran, A.: GenSQLi: a generative artificial intelligence framework for automatically securing web application firewalls against structured query language injection attacks. Future Internet **17**, 8 (2024). https://doi.org/10.3390/fi17010008
5. Floris, G., et al.: ModSec-AdvLearn: countering adversarial SQL injections with robust machine learning. IEEE Trans. Inf. Forensics Secur. **20**, 6693–6705 (2025). https://doi.org/10.1109/TIFS.2025.3583234
6. Paul, A., Sharma, V., Olukoya, O.: SQL injection attack: detection, prioritization & prevention. J. Inf. Secur. Appl. **85**, 103871 (2024). https://doi.org/10.1016/j.jisa.2024.103871
7. Shaheed, A., Kurdy, M.H.D.B.: Web application firewall using machine learning and features engineering. Secur. Commun. Netw. **2022**, 5280158 (2022). https://doi.org/10.1155/2022/5280158
8. Dawadi, B.R., Adhikari, B., Srivastava, D.K.: Deep learning technique-enabled web application firewall for the detection of web attacks. Sensors (Basel) **23**, 2073 (2023). https://doi.org/10.3390/s23042073
9. Dhote, S., Singh, S., Student, A., Raigar, D.: A comprehensive survey of ML-based WAFs with signature and anomaly detection. Strad Res. **11**, 54–60 (2024)
10. Bocharov, A.: Making WAF ML models go brrr: saving decades of processing time. Cloudflare Blog (2024). https://blog.cloudflare.com/making-waf-ai-models-go-brr/. Accessed 10 Apr 2025
11. Shah, S.S.H.: SQL injection dataset (2021). https://www.kaggle.com/datasets/syedsaqlainhussain/sql-injection-dataset. Accessed Sept 2025
12. Mohamed, I.: EDA – SQL Injection Dataset. https://www.kaggle.com/code/iniestamoh/eda-sql-injection-dataset. Accessed Sept 2025
13. Shah, S.S.H.: Cross site scripting XSS dataset for deep learning (2020). https://www.kaggle.com/datasets/syedsaqlainhussain/cross-site-scripting-xss-dataset-for-deep-learning. Accessed Sept 2025
14. Giménez, C.T., Villegas, A.P., Marañón, G.Á.: HTTP data set CSIC 2010. Information Security Institute of CSIC (Spanish Research National Council), 64 (2010)
15. Shees, A., Tariq, M., Sarwat, A.I.: Cybersecurity in smart grids: detecting false data injection attacks utilizing supervised machine learning techniques. Energies **17**, 5870 (2024). https://doi.org/10.3390/en17235870

16. Peralta-Garcia, E., Quevedo-Monsalbe, J., Tuesta-Monteza, V., Arcila-Diaz, J.: Detecting structured query language injections in web microservices using machine learning. Informatics **11**, 15 (2024). https://doi.org/10.3390/informatics11020015
17. Uppara, V., Iqbal, A., Vishal, P., Vinay, M.V., Sarasvathi, V.: URL classification with intrusion detection system. In: Arai, K. (ed.) Intelligent Systems and Applications, pp. 284–300. Springer, Cham (2024). https://doi.org/10.1007/978-3-031-47721-8_19
18. Mokbal, F.M.M., Wang, D., Wang, X.: Detect cross-site scripting attacks using average word embedding and support vector machine. Int. J. Netw. Secur. **24**(1), 20–28 (2022)
19. XSSer (2025). https://xsser.03c8.net/. Accessed Sept 2025
20. SQLMap (2025). https://github.com/sqlmapproject/sqlmap/wiki/Techniques. Accessed Sept 2025
21. Reddy, S.S., Nishoak, K., Shreya, J.L., Reddy, Y.V., Venkanna, U.: A P4-based adversarial attack mitigation on machine learning models in data plane devices. J. Netw. Syst. Manage. **32**, 5 (2023). https://doi.org/10.1007/s10922-023-09777-6
22. Saidi, P., Dasarathy, G., Berisha, V.: Unraveling overoptimism and publication bias in ML-driven science. Patterns (N Y) **6**, 101185 (2025). https://doi.org/10.1016/j.patter.2025.101185

Application, System and Network Security

Proposal and Evaluation of a Method for Container Micro-segmentation

Shoya Nakamura[1(✉)], Kunio Akashi[2], and Yuji Sekiya[1]

[1] Graduate School of Information Science and Technology, The University of Tokyo, 7-3-1 Hongo, Bunkyo-ku, Tokyo 113-8656, Japan
nakamura-shoya-1@g.ecc.u-tokyo.ac.jp, sekiya@si.u-tokyo.ac.jp
[2] Information Technology Center, The University of Tokyo, Tokyo, Japan
k-akashi@si.u-tokyo.ac.jp

Abstract. As containers with different trust levels are increasingly co-located within Kubernetes Pods—particularly through patterns such as sidecar containers from external vendors or separate teams—stronger intra-Pod security has become critical. Once a container is compromised, other containers in the same Pod sharing the network namespace are at high risk of lateral movement attacks, traffic interception, and unauthorized access. We propose a zero-trust microsegmentation approach that blocks all intra-Pod communication by default and selectively permits only specified container-port pairs through manifest metadata. Implemented as a Cilium plugin with dynamic iptables rules, our method integrates seamlessly into existing Kubernetes deployments without requiring modifications to the control plane or container runtime. Performance evaluation reveals that TCP session latency increases sharply with container count due to iptables' linear rule lookup, while rule application time grows polynomially with Pod and container counts, causing significant overhead in large-scale scenarios (e.g., 50 Pods with 50 containers each). These findings expose fundamental scalability limitations of iptables-based approaches that cannot be mitigated by distributing Pods. We conclude that iptables is unsuitable for large-scale deployments and recommend eBPF as a more scalable alternative.

Keywords: Kubernetes · Container · CNI · Micro-Segmentation · Zero-trust · iptables · eBPF

1 Introduction

1.1 Background

In recent years, loud-native applications and DevOps practices have driven the widespread adoption of container-based deployment models orchestrated by platforms such as Kubernetes [3,5,9]. In Kubernetes, multiple containers are grouped into a *pod*, sharing the same network namespace and storage volumes. Pods are designed as tightly coupled units where containers cooperatively work toward a

P. D'Arco and A. Zamfiroiu (Eds.): SecITC 2025, LNCS 16443, pp. 249–261, 2026.
https://doi.org/10.1007/978-3-032-17443-7_15

common application goal. Communication between pods is managed via virtual networks, and Container Network Interface (CNI) plugins such as Cilium and Calico enable fine-grained network policies for inter-pod traffic [2,6].

1.2 Problem Statement

Kubernetes assumes that all containers within a pod belong to the same trust domain. However, this assumption is increasingly challenged in modern deployments. A prominent example is the *sidecar pattern*, where auxiliary containers providing logging, monitoring, or security functions are deployed alongside application containers [4,7,8,10]. These sidecar containers often originate from third-party vendors or are maintained by separate teams with different update policies and security standards, introducing trust boundaries within a single pod.

Pod-level colocation is essential for the sidecar pattern because separating containers into different pods would introduce increased network latency, complex reconnection logic, and service discovery complications. However, this design exposes critical security risks: since containers share the same network namespace, a compromised sidecar can intercept intra-pod traffic, access shared volumes, or exploit inter-process communication to attack application containers.

1.3 Limitations of Existing Approaches

Existing Kubernetes security mechanisms, such as SecurityContext, Pod Security Standards, and Linux security modules (SELinux, AppArmor), primarily isolate containers from the host or enforce pod-level policies. They provide limited support for controlling communication *among* containers within the same pod, as containers inherently share kernel namespaces. Fine-grained intra-pod communication control requires mechanisms that can mediate interactions within shared namespaces—a capability existing tools do not adequately provide.

1.4 Contribution

To address this gap, we propose a micro-segmentation approach that enables fine-grained communication control at the pod level. Our approach leverages iptables-based network filtering to enforce least-privilege communication among containers within the same pod, operating within the shared network namespace without disrupting existing Kubernetes deployment models.

The key contributions of this work are as follows:

- We propose an iptables-based mechanism to enforce fine-grained intra-pod network policies, addressing a gap that has received limited attention in prior research, without requiring modifications to the Kubernetes control plane or disrupting existing deployment models.
- We demonstrate the feasibility and practicality of our approach through experimental validation, including verification of successful communication control enforcement and performance measurements of both iptables rule application overhead and communication latency under policy enforcement.

2 Related Work

In this section, we provide an overview of related research on pod-level microsegmentation in relation to the approach proposed in this paper.

Kim et al. [6] analyzed and evaluated the implementation and performance of container- and pod-level security policies in order to strengthen network security in Kubernetes environments. Their study primarily investigated the security capabilities of major CNI plugins such as Cilium, Calico, and Antrea, offering a detailed comparison of policy enforcement across Layers 3, 4, and 7 and its associated performance overhead. Unlike earlier studies that primarily emphasized performance, this work highlights the architectural aspects of CNIs and their policy enforcement mechanisms from a security perspective, thereby providing new insights into the trade-offs between security and performance.

Budigiri et al. [1] conducted a comprehensive evaluation of the performance and security of Kubernetes network policies, focusing on inter-pod communication controls. Their study demonstrated both the performance overhead introduced by eBPF-based CNI plugins such as Calico and Cilium and their ability to achieve low-latency network control. In addition, they discussed recent countermeasures against vulnerabilities in network policies, offering valuable insights into achieving pod-level network isolation and ensuring security in multi-tenant environments. These findings contribute to the design and operation of secure, high-performance container networks, particularly in edge computing and 5G scenarios.

3 Proposed Method

To address the limitations of intra-pod communication control discussed in Sect. 1.3, this study proposes a mechanism that enables container-level communication control within Kubernetes environments.

3.1 Design Principle

To realize container-level communication control within Kubernetes, the proposed method adopts a security-first design based on the *deny-by-default* principle. Our design follows: (1) a zero-trust stance where all intra-pod container communication is blocked unless explicitly allowed, minimizing the attack surface in multi-tenant or heterogeneous deployments, (2) selective enablement of necessary communications by specifying container – port pairs in Kubernetes manifest metadata, ensuring operational clarity and auditability, (3) compatibility with existing infrastructure, requiring no modification to the Linux kernel, Kubernetes control plane, or container runtimes, and (4) dynamic policy updates, allowing communication rules to be added or removed at runtime for flexible adaptation to scaling, rolling updates, or evolving application requirements.

3.2 Design Overview

As illustrated in Fig. 1, our architecture comprises: (1) a custom helper command executed at pod startup that leverages Cilium for CNI-level integration, (2) dynamic generation and application of `iptables` rules for each container, and (3) communication rules derived from Kubernetes manifest metadata. The implementation, developed in Go, is integrated with Kubernetes lifecycle management. This design enables blocking all unnecessary container-level communication while allowing only the minimum required interactions—functionality not achievable with conventional pod-level tools.

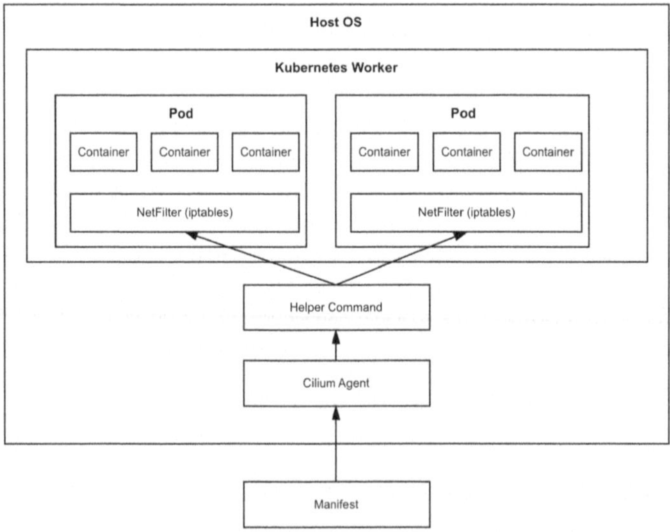

Fig. 1. Design overview of the proposed micro-segmentation mechanism.

3.3 Threat Model

Assumptions. We assume: (1) the Kubernetes control plane, node OS, and container runtime are trusted, (2) attackers may have code execution within a container but not host root privileges, and (3) the iptables subsystem is correctly implemented.

Threats Addressed. Our mechanism prevents: (1) unauthorized network access between containers, (2) lateral movement through network-based exploitation, (3) traffic interception within the pod, and (4) reconnaissance via port scanning.

Limitations. Our approach does not address: (1) shared storage access, as containers share volume mounts, (2) IPC mechanisms such as shared memory or Unix domain sockets, (3) container escape vulnerabilities, (4) side-channel attacks, (5) policy misconfiguration by administrators, or (6) host-level compromise. Our mechanism is designed to complement existing security tools as part of a defense-in-depth strategy.

4 Experimental Method

This section evaluates the performance of inter-container communication in Kubernetes when applying the proposed container-level micro-segmentation mechanism. In particular, we focus on the impact of increasing the number of `iptables`-based communication control rules on TCP session establishment time.

4.1 Objective

Because the proposed method enforces communication control at the container level, the number of `iptables` rules grows with the number of pods and containers. Consequently, the processing required for permission decisions may increase, potentially affecting TCP session establishment latency, especially during the three-way handshake. The objective of this experiment is to investigate whether such an impact occurs and to characterize its tendency.

4.2 Experimental Setup

The experiment was conducted under the conditions summarized in Table 1:

- The number of pods was varied across four settings: 1, 5, 10, and 50. For each case, the number of containers per pod was set to 2, 5, 10, 20, 30, 40, and 50.
- Each container was configured with 10 `iptables` allow rules corresponding to permitted ports.
- For each pod, 10 distinct pairs of containers were randomly selected, and TCP sessions (SYN $\rightarrow$ SYN/ACK) were established toward the permitted ports. The time required for session establishment was measured.
- Since each container exposed 10 ports, the measurements were repeated until all ports had been used once.

4.3 Communication Procedure and Measurement Method

Inter-container TCP communication was conducted as follows. The time interval from the transmission of a SYN packet to the reception of the corresponding SYN/ACK response was defined as the *TCP session establishment time.*

Table 1. Experimental Conditions

Parameter	Value
Number of Pods	1, 5, 10, 50
Number of Containers per Pod	2, 5, 10, 20, 30, 40, 50
Number of Communication-Permitted Ports per Container	10

- On the server-side container, a simple Python program was executed to listen for TCP connections on the designated port.
- On the client-side container, Scapy was used to send a TCP SYN packet to the specified server container and port.
- For timing measurements, `tcpdump` was executed inside the client container to capture the timestamps of the transmitted SYN packet and the received SYN/ACK packet. The difference between these timestamps was recorded as the measurement result.

4.4 Evaluation Method

TCP session establishment times were measured for each pod – container configuration. Since the number of `iptables` rules grows substantially in certain settings, the time required for these rules to be applied correctly at startup was also measured.

By collecting and comparing these results, we analyzed performance degradation trends associated with the increasing number of `iptables` rules.

4.5 Example Manifest Used in the Experiment

An example manifest for a configuration with one Pod containing two containers is shown in Listing 1.1. In the proposed mechanism, inbound communication permissions are defined in the `metadata.annotations` field using the key `container.firewall.inbound.allowPort`, where allowed port mappings are specified as comma-separated `<container-name>`:`<port-number>` pairs. During Pod startup, corresponding `iptables` rules are automatically generated based on these annotations, enabling communication only for the explicitly defined container-port combinations.

```
1  apiVersion: v1
2  kind: Pod
3  metadata:
4    name: multi-container-pod-0
5    annotations:
6      container.firewall.inbound.allowPort: "container-0:10001,
           container-0:10002,container-0:10003,container-0:10004,
           container-0:10005,container-0:10006,container-0:10007,
```

```
        container-0:10008,container-0:10009,container-0:10010,
        container-1:10011,container-1:10012,container-1:10013,
        container-1:10014,container-1:10015,container-1:10016,
        container-1:10017,container-1:10018,container-1:10019,
        container-1:10020"
7  spec:
8    containers:
9    - name: container-0
10     image: python-tcpdump:3.12
11     command: ["sleep", "infinity"]
12     volumeMounts:
13     - name: script-volume
14       mountPath: /measure
15   - name: container-1
16     image: python-tcpdump:3.12
17     command: ["sleep", "infinity"]
18     volumeMounts:
19     - name: script-volume
20       mountPath: /measure
21   volumes:
22   - name: script-volume
23     hostPath:
24       path: /home/test-user/measure
25       type: Directory
```

Listing 1.1. Sample Manifest with 1 Pod and 2 Containers

Here, the python-tcpdump:3.12 specified in spec.containers.image is a custom image based on python:3.12, with the tcpdump command installed.

4.6 Host Machine Specifications

The specifications of the host machine used in this experiment are shown in Table 2.

Table 2. Host Machine Specifications

Component	Specification
CPU	Intel Xeon Gold 6430, 4 cores, 1 thread/core
Memory	31 GiB RAM
Storage	97 GB (SSD)
Virtualization	VMware
OS	Ubuntu 24.04.2 LTS
Kernel	6.8.0–58-generic
Container Runtime	containerd v1.7.21
Kubernetes	v1.30.4
CNI Plugin	Cilium v1.14.19 (CLI: v0.18.3)

5 Experimental Results

This section presents the results of the experiments conducted using the methodology described in Sect. 4 and discusses the trends observed.

5.1 TCP Session Establishment Time

We first report the measurement results of TCP session establishment time under varying numbers of pods and containers.

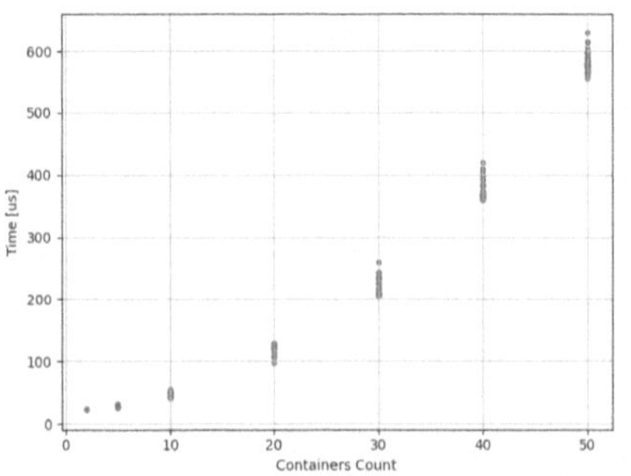

Fig. 2. Scatter Plot of TCP Session Establishment Time vs. Number of Containers (1 Pod).

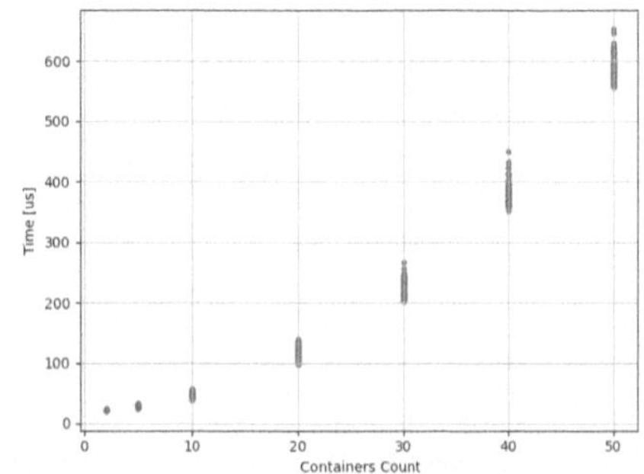

Fig. 3. Scatter Plot of TCP Session Establishment Time vs. Number of Containers (5 Pods).

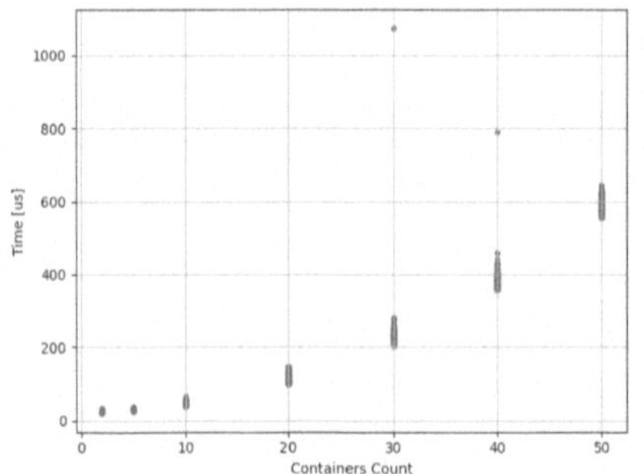

Fig. 4. Scatter Plot of TCP Session Establishment Time vs. Number of Containers (10 Pods).

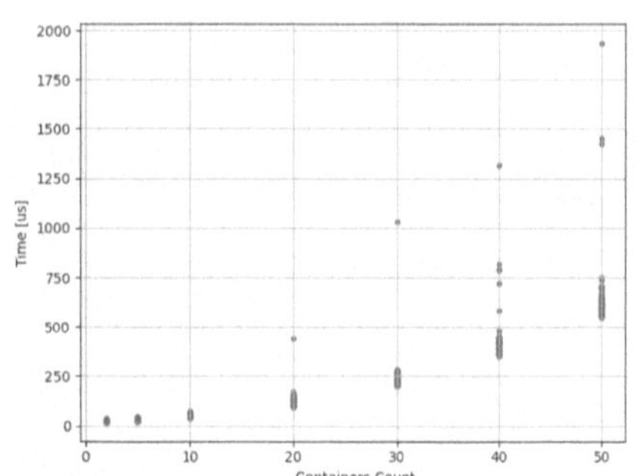

Fig. 5. Scatter Plot of TCP Session Establishment Time vs. Number of Containers (50 Pods).

Figures 2, 3, 4 and 5 show scatter plots of TCP session establishment times (SYN – SYN/ACK) for specific container – port pairs, with the number of containers varied and results grouped by the number of pods.

The figures indicate that session establishment times exhibit noticeable variability, and this variability increases as the number of containers grows, regardless of the number of pods. In addition, when the number of pods is 10 or 50, a greater number of outliers is observed, with the highest frequency occurring in the 50-pod case.

Across all pod configurations, TCP session establishment time increases with the number of containers. The increase is not linear but rather steep: when comparing cases with one container and fifty containers, the difference reaches approximately 25 – 30 times, even excluding outliers. This suggests that the number of containers has a significant impact on session establishment latency.

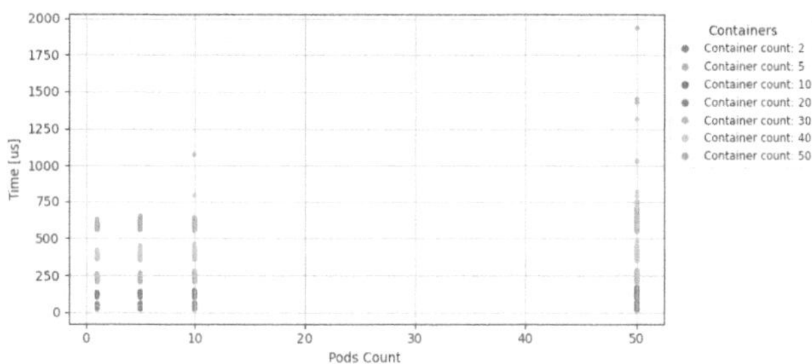

Fig. 6. Scatter Plot of TCP Session Establishment Time vs. Number of Pods.

Figure 6 presents session establishment times with the number of pods on the horizontal axis. Here too, the number of outliers increases as the number of pods grows. However, under the same container count, session establishment times remain nearly constant regardless of the number of pods.

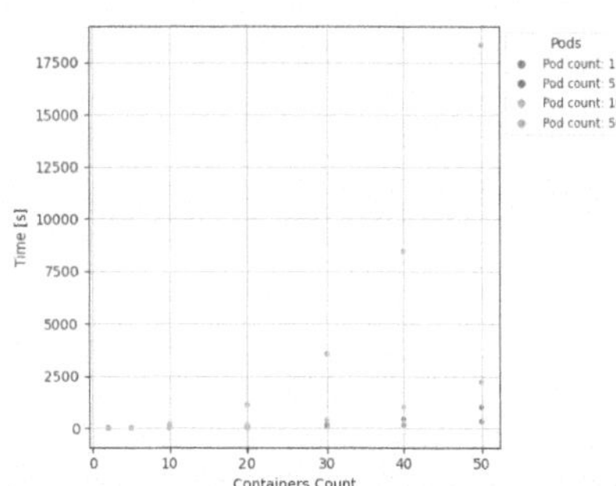

Fig. 7. Scatter Plot of Time to Apply iptables Allow Rules vs. Number of Pods.

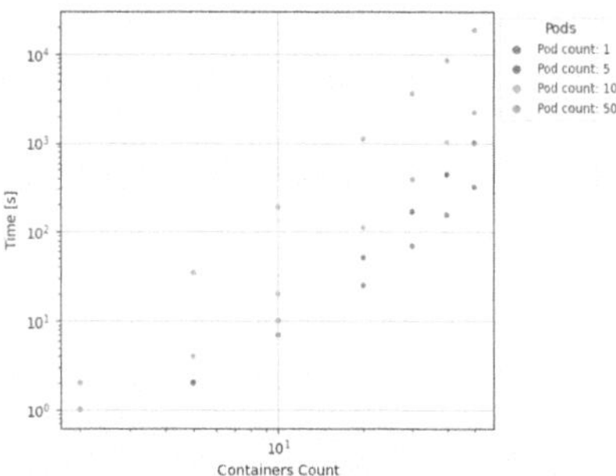

Fig. 8. Scatter Plot of Time to Apply iptables Allow Rules vs. Number of Pods (LOG-LOG SCALE).

5.2 Time Required for iptables Rule Propagation

Next, we report the time required from pod creation until all corresponding `iptables` allow rules are fully applied. Each experiment was conducted once for every combination of pod and container counts.

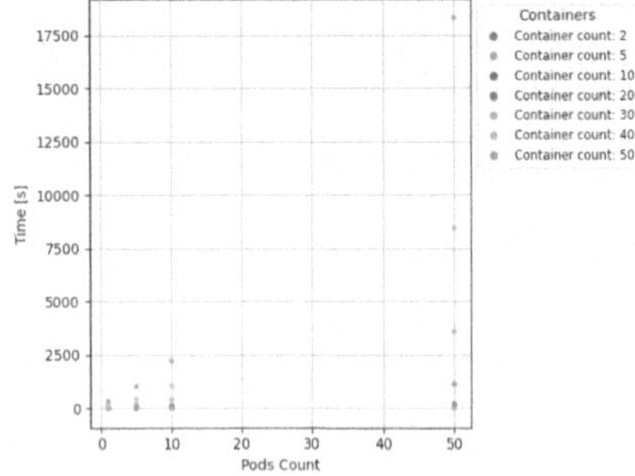

Fig. 9. Scatter Plot of Time to Apply iptables Allow Rules vs. Number of Containers.

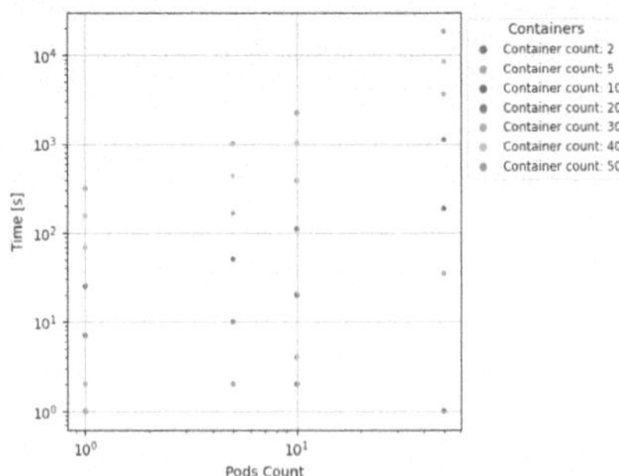

Fig. 10. Scatter Plot of Time to Apply iptables Allow Rules vs. Number of Containers (LOG-LOG SCALE).

In the proposed method, the number of `iptables` rules per pod is determined as *<number of containers>* × *<number of allowed ports>*. In this experiment, the number of allowed ports was set to increase proportionally with the number of containers, resulting in a total number of rules that scales quadratically with the number of containers.

Figure 7 shows the time required for `iptables` rule application as the number of containers varies. The figure indicates that the application time increases significantly with the number of containers. Notably, in the scenario with 50 pods each containing 50 containers, rule propagation took approximately five hours. In this case, each container had 10 allowed ports, resulting in up to 500 allowed ports per pod.

Figure 8 presents the same data on a log-log scale. The results suggest an approximately linear trend for each pod count, confirming that rule propagation time grows polynomially with the number of containers.

Figure 9 depicts the rule application time as a function of the number of pods. Here too, a sharp increase is observed as the pod count rises.

Figure 10, shown on a log-log scale, further indicates that the propagation time also increases polynomially with respect to the number of pods.

6 Discussion

This section discusses the implications of the experimental results presented in Sect. 5.

6.1 Variability in TCP Session Establishment Time

As shown in Figs. 2, 3, 4 and 5, TCP session establishment times exhibited variability even for the same number of containers, and this variability increased with the number of containers.

This behavior is attributed to the structure of `iptables`, which evaluates rules sequentially from top to bottom. Consequently, as the number of rules grows, the time required for rule matching becomes more variable.

The outliers observed when the number of pods was 10 or 50 are likely due to host resource limitations. The host machine used in the experiment (Table 2) had four cores with one thread per core. When a large number of pods and containers are launched simultaneously, the host may reach its processing capacity, resulting in occasional long delays. The increased frequency of outliers with higher pod counts supports this explanation.

6.2 Impact of Pod and Container Counts on Session Establishment Time

While Fig. 2, 3, 4 and 5 show that session establishment time increases sharply with the number of containers, Fig. 6 indicates that increasing the number of pods results in only modest changes.

This difference arises from Kubernetes' network namespace architecture. Each pod has its own network namespace, and `iptables` rules are applied independently within each namespace. Therefore, increasing the number of pods does not affect the number of rules per namespace, resulting in minimal impact on session establishment times. In contrast, containers within the same pod share a namespace, so adding containers increases the number of rules in that namespace, leading to longer establishment times.

Furthermore, because the number of `iptables` rules grows roughly quadratically with the number of containers, session establishment times can increase up to approximately 30-fold. This highlights the potential for severe performance degradation in production environments. Distributing containers across multiple pods according to their roles could mitigate such degradation in practice.

6.3 Time Required for `iptables` Rule Application

The results in Fig. 7, 8, 9 and 10 show that the time required to apply all `iptables` allow rules increases sharply with both pod and container counts, exhibiting a polynomial trend.

This is because each pod requires *<number of containers>* × *<number of allowed ports>* rules, and this process repeats across all pods, causing the total number of rules to grow rapidly. Unlike session establishment, rule application is executed across all pods in parallel, so increasing pod counts increases the total processing workload.

In the extreme case of 50 pods, each with 50 containers and 10 allowed ports per container, rule application took approximately five hours to complete.

Such delays could critically affect production environments, for example during pod restarts or scaling operations. Since this delay depends on both pod and container counts, simply distributing containers across multiple pods may not alleviate the issue.

7 Conclusion

In this study, we proposed and evaluated a micro-segmentation approach that enables container-level communication control by further subdividing Kubernetes pods, which are traditionally treated as the unit of trust. While the effectiveness of the proposed method was demonstrated, several challenges were also identified:

- As the number of containers increases, the number of `iptables` rules to be applied grows, which can negatively impact communication latency. Although distributing containers across multiple pods can partially mitigate this issue, performance degradation may become a serious concern when such distribution is not feasible.
- The time required for all allow rules to be fully applied after pod creation increases sharply with both pod and container counts. This delay is attributable to the total number of rules in the node, and distributing containers across multiple pods does not necessarily resolve the problem.

These issues arise from the sequential application and lookup of rules in `iptables`. Even with fine-grained optimization, there is a fundamental limit to the achievable performance improvement. Therefore, future work will explore the use of eBPF as an alternative to `iptables` to accelerate communication control.

The main advantages of eBPF over `iptables` are as follows:

- **Direct processing in kernel space:** eBPF executes packet processing directly within the kernel without context switches to user space, improving processing efficiency.
- **Efficient rule matching:** Unlike the linear list structure used by `iptables`, eBPF can leverage data structures such as hash maps and tries, enabling scalable and high-performance matching.
- **Inline custom processing:** eBPF programs are precompiled and execute only the matching operations required, reducing packet processing overhead.
- **Flexible stateful handling:** eBPF allows for the implementation of custom connection tracking mechanisms, avoiding bottlenecks associated with `conntrack`, which `iptables` relies on.

Notably, eBPF is adopted by major CNI plugins such as Cilium, where its high performance has been demonstrated. We expect that applying a similar approach in this study could further accelerate container-level communication control.

Acknowledgement. This paper is based on results obtained from the project, "Research and Development Project of the Enhanced infrastructures for Post-5G Information and Communication Systems" (JPNP20017), commissioned by the New Energy and Industrial Technology Development Organization (NEDO).

References

1. Budigiri, G., Baumann, C., Mühlberg, J., Truyen, E., Joosen, W.: Network policies in kubernetes: Performance evaluation and security analysis. 2021 Joint European Conference on Networks and Communications 6G Summit (EuCNC/6G Summit), pp. 407–412 (2021). 10.1109/EuCNC/6GSummit51104.2021.9482526
2. Chu, P.Y., Lu, W.H., Lin, J.W., Wu, Y.S.: Enforcing enterprise mobile application security policy with plugin framework. In: 2018 IEEE 23rd Pacific Rim International Symposium on Dependable Computing (PRDC), pp. 263–268 (2018). 10.1109/PRDC.2018.00048
3. Gawande, S., Gorthi, A.: Containerization and kubernetes: scalable and efficient cloud-native applications. Int. J. Innov. Sci. Res. Technol. (IJISRT) (2024). 10.38124/ijisrt/ijisrt24nov314
4. Gogineni, A.: Multi-cloud deployment with kubernetes: challenges, strategies, and performance optimization. Int. Sci. J. Eng. Manage. (2025). 10.55041/isjem00036
5. Hightower, K., Burns, B., Beda, J.: Kubernetes: up and running: dive into the future of infrastructure (2017)
6. Kim, B., Kim, J., Lee, S.: Exploring security enhancements in Kubernetes CNI: a deep dive into network policies. IEEE Access **13**, 35322–35338 (2025). https://doi.org/10.1109/ACCESS.2025.3543841
7. Nguyen, N.T., Kim, Y.: A design of resource allocation structure for multi-tenant services in kubernetes cluster. 2022 27th Asia Pacific Conference on Communications (APCC), pp. 651–654 (2022). 10.1109/APCC55198.2022.9943782
8. Senel, B.C., Mouchet, M., Cappos, J., Friedman, T., Fourmaux, O., McGeer, R.: Multitenant containers as a service (CAAS) for clouds and edge clouds. IEEE Access **11**, 144574–144601 (2023). https://doi.org/10.1109/ACCESS.2023.3344486
9. Thallapally, N.: Scalable application deployment with docker and Kubernetes nagaraju thallapally. J. Comput. Sci. Technol. Stud. (2024). 10.32996/jcsts.2024.6.1.29
10. Zheng, C., Zhuang, Q., Guo, F.: A multi-tenant framework for cloud container services. In: 2021 IEEE 41st International Conference on Distributed Computing Systems (ICDCS), pp. 359–369 (2021). 10.1109/ICDCS51616.2021.00042

Supervised Attack Trees

Aliyu Tanko Ali[1], Damas Gruska[2](✉), and Martin Leucker[1]

[1] Institute for Software Engineering and Programming Languages, University of Lübeck, Ratzeburger Allee 160, Lübeck, Germany
{aliyu.ali,leucker}@isp.uni-luebeck.de

[2] Department of Applied Informatics, Comenius University in Bratislava, Mlynská dolina, 842 48 Bratislava, Slovakia
gruska@fmph.uniba.sk

Abstract. Attack trees (ATs) are a popular method for modeling security threats, but they typically assume a "perfect knowledge" where all actions and the state of the systems are fully known. This is unrealistic in practice, where attackers and defenders operate with limited visibility and finite resources. We introduce Supervised Attack Trees (SATs), a framework that extends ATs to model the strategic interaction between an attacker and a defender under partial observability and simultaneous budget constraints. In an SAT, each player sees only a subset of the system's nodes. The defender (supervisor) can dynamically allocate a limited budget to postpone attacks, while the attacker spends a budget to compromise nodes. We formalize the concept of consistent observation, a snapshot of the partially visible state of the system, and provide an algorithm to verify its validity. Finally, we show how key questions like "given SATs, a defender budget, and an attacker budget, is there a strategy for the supervisor based solely on observations that guarantees the root will *never* be compromised, no matter how the attacker spends?" or "What is the minimum budget needed to guarantee an attack?" can be reduced to model-checking problems.

Keywords: Attack Trees · Attack-Defense · Graphical Security Models · Security · Threat Modeling

1 Introduction and Motivation

Modern critical infrastructures such as power grids, autonomous transport networks, industrial control systems are too large, too dynamic, and too opaque for any single stakeholder to observe perfectly. Attackers probe them with exploits whose success depends on timing and cost; defenders react with counter-measures whose effectiveness also depends on timing and cost. Yet classical threat models, including the popular Attack Trees (ATs) formalism, overwhelmingly assume that the analyst, the tool, the omniscient referee sees the entire landscape. This

Work funded by the EU NextGenerationEU through the Recovery and Resilience Plan for Slovakia under the project No. 09I03-03-V04-00095.

P. D'Arco and A. Zamfiroiu (Eds.): SecITC 2025, LNCS 16443, pp. 262–277, 2026.
https://doi.org/10.1007/978-3-032-17443-7_16

assumption collapses in practice. *In the real world, the defender rarely knows all the moves of the adversary, and the adversary rarely knows every countermeasure the defender has deployed. Security is therefore a game of shadows, played with incomplete information and scarce resources.*

An industrial operator may notice an anomaly on one sub-network but have no visibility into the rest; a red-teamer may trigger an exploit on a programmable logic controller (PLC) without knowing whether the back-end historian has already been patched. Both sides also act under severe budget caps i.e., CPU cycles, maintenance windows, red-team hours so they cannot simply "observe everything" or "try every path." These limitations demand a modeling paradigm that embraces partial observability, strategic uncertainty, and resource-aware decision-making.

In this paper we introduce Supervised Attack Trees (SATs) as an extension of traditional ATs that explicitly captures partial observability and budget-constrained interaction between an attacker and a supervisor-defender. The goal is to move from the traditional "given enough time and money, is the root reachable?" to the more realistic "given limited time and money, and given that both players see only fragments of the system, can the root still be compromised or can it always be defended?"

1.1 From Static Trees to Living Games

A traditional AT is a rooted tree whose leaves are atomic attack steps (e.g., "obtain VPN credentials", "exploit firmware vulnerability"), and whose internal nodes are gates (OR, AND, SAND) that specify how sub-goals combine to achieve a higher-level objective (e.g., "gain root on the historian"). Some extended models attach cost and time attributes to nodes [1], while others impose fixed time windows within which particular steps must complete [2–4]. The analysis then reduces to a shortest-path search, asking questions such as:

1) *Reachability or Minimality:* What is the minimal set of leaf actions whose compromise triggers the root (minimal cut sets)?
2) *Cost or Resource trade-offs:* Given attacker budgets or competing objectives, which attack plans maximize success (e.g., cost-efficient but slow versus expensive and fast strategies)?
3) *Probabilistic or Uncertainty analysis:* What is the probability of success under uncertain or correlated step outcomes, and how sensitive is overall risk to those uncertainties?

This abstraction is elegant, but it hides three crucial realities:

- **Observability gaps.** The analyst sees the tree on paper, but the attacker in the field does not. A phishing campaign may or may not succeed; the attacker will not know until much later, if ever. Conversely, a security-monitoring dashboard may light up with alerts that reveal only a subset of compromised nodes.

- **Resource scarcity.** Unlimited budgets do not exist. An attacker can spend at most budget B_A (say, 10 000 USD and two weeks of labour); a defender can spend at most budget B_D (say, 50 000 USD and one maintenance window). Once either budget is exhausted, the game ends.
- **Dynamic interaction.** Traditional ATs are *static*: the defender's countermeasures (if any) are pre-computed and baked into the tree. In reality the defender *reacts* patching a node, shortening an exploit window, or reconfiguring a firewall after observing some, but not all, of the attacker's moves.

SATs address these realities by layering two additional ingredients onto the traditional model:

- **Partial observation sets.** The attacker is allowed to observe only a subset $\mathcal{N}_A$ of nodes; the supervisor observes a possibly different subset $\mathcal{N}_D$. Neither party ever sees the full state.
- **Defence budget and actions.** Each non-leaf node n carries a defence cost $c_D(n)$. By paying this cost, the supervisor can postpone the interval during which n can be compromised, effectively "buying time" or "raising the bar" for the attacker. Importantly, the supervisor chooses *which* nodes to defend *after* seeing a partial snapshot of the attack, not *a priori*.

1.2 Research Questions

With these ingredients in place, we revisit the fundamental questions posed in threat analysis:

- **Defendability.** Given SATs, a defender budget B_D, and an attacker budget B_A, is there a strategy for the supervisor based solely on observations $\mathcal{N}_D$ that guarantees the root will *never* be compromised, no matter how the attacker spends B_A?
- **Attackability.** Dually, is there a strategy for the attacker based solely on observations $\mathcal{N}_A$ that guarantees the root will *eventually* be compromised, no matter how the supervisor spends B_D?
- **Minimum defence budget.** What is the smallest B_D such that the tree becomes *always defendable*? This question is of acute practical interest to Chief Information Security Officers (CISOs) who must justify security investments.
- **Minimum attack budget.** Symmetrically, what is the smallest B_A that renders the tree *always attackable*?

The rest of the paper is organized as follows: Sect. 2 presents the related work. In Sect. 3, we revisit attack trees with time and cost attributes. Section 4 introduces Supervised Attack Trees. In Sect. 5, we discuss the attackability and defendability of the tree. Finally, the conclusion is presented in Sect. 6.

2 Related Work

In this section, we review existing work. We begin by positioning traditional ATs and their timed extensions, then examine the literature that incorporates defensive reasoning (e.g., AttackDefense Trees, Defense Trees, ACTs, APTs), followed by game-theoretic and economic analyses. Subsequently, we discuss studies that explicitly model partial or incomplete information such as opacity, runtime monitoring, and dynamic reconfiguration and conclude with timed and tool-oriented approaches. Throughout, we indicate which of the three core aspects *simultaneous budget constraints*, *partial observability*, and *dynamic defender reactions* each line of work includes or omits. The goal is to make clear where SATs extend and unify prior work.

Static Attack Trees and Extensions. Introduced by Schneier [5], ATs model security goals as rooted trees whose leaves are atomic attack steps and whose internal nodes are OR/AND/SAND gates. Mauw and Oostdijk [6] provided the first formal semantics and coined the standard evaluation algorithms, while recent work uses SMT-solvers for cost-optimal attacks under timing constraints [3].

Some extensions attempt to model evolving threat environments: Reversible Attack Trees analyze attack progression under changing conditions by allowing previously executed attack steps to be undone [7], while the work in [8] incorporates time-dependent node states, supporting evaluation under varying threat scenarios. However, none of these approaches model active defenders, partial observation, or runtime reactions.

AttackDefense Trees and Countermeasure Models. Kordy et al. [9,10] proposed AttackDefense Trees (ADTs) that interleave attacker moves with defensive countermeasures and showed equivalence to two-player zero-sum games [11]. Extensions include timed automata-based ADTs [12], multi-metric semiring frameworks [13], and dynamic countermeasure synthesis [14]. All assume full observability of the current state and abstract away resource exhaustion.

Economic and Game-Theoretic Approaches. Defense Trees [15] and Attack Countermeasure Trees (ACTs) [16,17] quantify Return-on-Investment (ROI) and Return-on-Attack (ROA) via cost-damage analysis [18]. Strategic games on trees [19] have been studied, yet they assume complete information and static budgets. Recent work on asynchronous multi-agent models [20] relaxes simultaneity, but not observability.

Opacity and Partial Information. Opacity properties in Discrete Event Systems [21,22] quantify what an external observer can deduce about secret states. Ali and Gruska [23] imported these ideas to ATs, but focused on the attacker's uncertainty rather than the defender's. Runtime monitoring and dynamic reconfiguration [24] illustrate the practical need for supervisors that act with partial views; however, no prior work couples opacity, budgets, and tree-based security modelling.

Timed Models and Tool Support. Timed extensions of attack trees [2,4] and timed-arc Petri nets (TAPAAL [25]) provide automated verification, while template-based generators [26,27] scale modelling. These tools, however, treat time and cost as parameters for a single protagonist; they do not address strategic interaction under incomplete observation.

Table 1. Summary of related work coverage of core SAT aspects.

Model	Budget Constraints	Observability	Defense
Static Attack Trees	–	–	–
Attack-Defense Trees	–	–	✓
Economic/Game-Theoretic	(Static)	–	✓
Opacity/Partial Information	–	✓	–
Timed Models/Tools	(Params)	–	–
SAT (Ours)	✓	✓	✓

Summary and Positioning. A comparative overview of how related work addresses the core aspects of our model is presented in Table 1. In summary, existing literature either (1) models attackers and defenders separately, (2) assumes perfect information, or (3) omits budget constraints. Our SATs unify these dimensions: they equip both the attacker and the supervisor-defender with limited budgets, allow only partial visibility of the tree state, and enable the defender to postpone node compromise at a cost. Consequently, they support formal answers to practical questions *Can the tree always be defended? What is the minimum defensive budget?* that prior models cannot address.

3 Attack Trees with Time and Cost

In this section, we briefly recall attack trees with time and cost. They are basically attack trees where each node has three associated values: a time interval when it can be compromised, the duration of the compromise, and costs to attack and defend a node. Formally, it is $T_{rct} = (\mathcal{N}, \mathcal{E}, g, c_A, c_D)$, where $(\mathcal{N}, \mathcal{E})$ is a tree with root n_r and leaves $\mathcal{N}_l$. The function g associate with nodes its type from {OR, AND, SAND(s)}, time interval and duration. The functions c_A, c_D assign a non-negative real cost to compromise and defend each node, respectively. The formal definitions can be found in [28] but here it is extended by cost to defend the nodes.

An example of attack trees with time and cost is shown in Fig. 1. We use Example 1 to explain the tree.

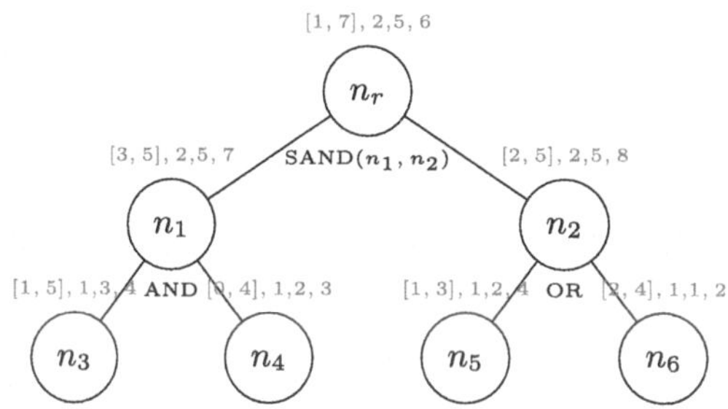

Fig. 1. An example of an attack tree with time and cost constraints on the nodes.

Example 1. Consider an attack targeting node n_1. This node has an AND gate, requiring the compromise of both n_3 and n_4. Each node has temporal constraints represented as $[3, 5], 2, 5, 7$, where the interval $[3, 5]$ indicates when the node is vulnerable, 2 is the attack duration, and 5 and 7 are the associated costs to attack and defend the node. All nodes in the tree follow this configuration. To compromise n_3 (vulnerable in $[1, 5]$ with 1-time unit duration), attacks must start within $[1, 4]$. Similarly, n_4 requires starting within $[1, 4]$. Both nodes can be compromised by time interval $[2, 5]$. However, since n_1 can only be attacked within $[3, 5]$, the attacker must complete both n_3 and n_4 compromises within $[2, 4]$ to enable the n_1 attack. The total cost to compromise n_1 is therefore $3 + 2 + 5$.

An attack $\mathbb{A}$ over T_{rct} is defined as a set of leaf-node attempts, where each attempt (n_i, t_i) consists of a leaf node n_i and its start time t_i. Formally, $\mathbb{A} = \{(n_1, t_1), \ldots, (n_k, t_k)\}$. A leaf node is successfully compromised only if t_i falls within its vulnerability interval. We consider an attack *meaningful* if it compromises at least one node, and assume all attacks discussed hereafter are meaningful.

The compromise propagates upward through the tree according to the temporal and logical constraints of each gate. Figure 2 illustrates how compromise times propagate: for OR gates, the earliest completion time prevails; for AND gates, the latest completion time determines the parent's compromise time; and for SAND gates, sequential completion is required. Similarly, Fig. 3 shows the cost propagation rules: OR gates take the minimum cost path, while AND and SAND gates accumulate costs from all children.

The total attack cost is computed by aggregating the costs of all compromised leaf nodes according to these propagation rules.

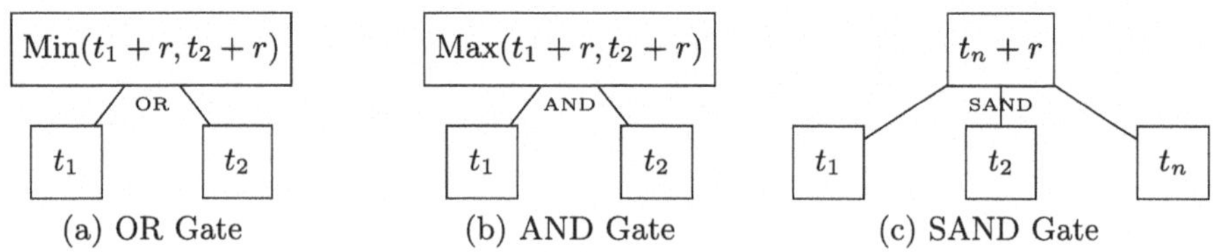

Fig. 2. Time propagation rule for AND, OR, and SAND gates. Here, r denotes the attack duration of the parent node (i.e., the time required to complete the compromise of the gate once its preconditions are met).

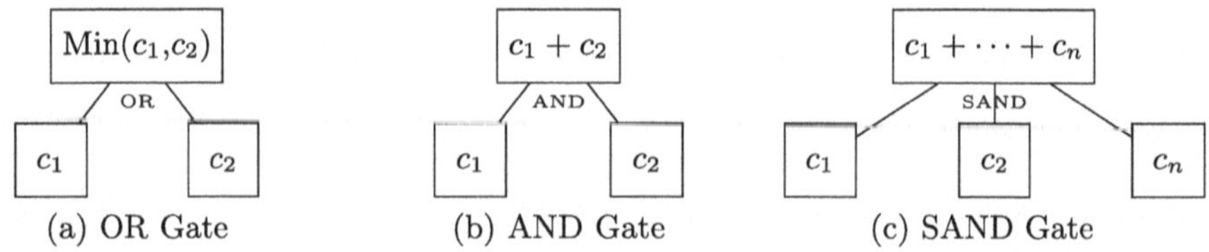

Fig. 3. Cost propagation rule for AND, OR, and SAND gates.

A defense cost is the sum of the costs of defended nodes. Given an attack tree and an attack $\mathbb{A}$. By attack state at a time t, $(s_{(\mathbb{A},t)} = (\mathcal{N}_{(\mathbb{A},t)}, c_{A(\mathbb{A},t)}))$ we denote a set of nodes that are compromised by $\mathbb{A}$ at given time with overall cost for an attackers $c_{A(\mathbb{A},t)}$. By restricting all constants in an attack tree definition to natural numbers (see [28]) we can use similar techniques of regions as it was used in the case of Timed Automata and their transformation to region automatons (see [29]). Hence we can transform any attack trees with time and cost to nondeterministic finite automaton which emulates each change in attack trees (see [28]). Moreover, we can translate the given AT with time and cost to an enhanced Petri net and use TAPAAL software tool (see [25]) to check reachability of the root node. By attack state at a time t, we denote a set of nodes that are compromised by $\mathbb{A}$ at given time.

4 Supervised Attack Trees

We assume the following scenario. An attacker compromises some leaf nodes. It costs him some cost but since (s)he cannot be sure whether timing was suitable, and cannot learn which nodes are finally compromised. We assume that an attacker can observe only a subset of nodes and see whether a node from this subset is compromised or not.

Moreover, we assume a supervisor as a defender, who tries to prevent a successful attack. To do so, he can postpone compromization of a node n what costs him $c_D(n)$. For simplicity we assume that this cost is fixed and does not depend on time for which it is postponed. Similarly to the attacker, the supervisor also has incomplete information on ongoing attacks i.e. can see only some (possibly different from the attacker's) subset of nodes.

4.1 Observations

In a dynamic security scenario, neither the attacker nor the supervisor has perfect information about the current state of all nodes in the ATs. Both operate with observations derived from specific, pre-defined sets of visible nodes. These observations are crucial for their decision-making processes under uncertainty, guiding the attacker on potential next steps and informing the supervisor's defensive actions. To formalize this, we define the concept of an observation for both the attacker and the supervisor at a given time t. An observation is a snapshot of the compromised nodes within the attacker and the supervisor's visible subset, along with the current attack time and accumulated costs.

Definition 1 (Observation). *Let $\mathcal{N}_A, \mathcal{N}_D \subseteq \mathcal{N}$ be two sets of nodes visible for an attacker and a supervisor, respectively. Let $\mathbb{A} = \{(n_1, t_1), ..., (n_k, t_k)\}$ be an attack, time $t \in \mathbb{R}^+$ with corresponding attack state $s_{(\mathbb{A},t)} = (\mathcal{N}_{(\mathbb{A},t)}, c_{(\mathbb{A},t)})$. The observation of the attack state s by the* ***attacker*** *at time t is a pair from $\mathcal{N} \times \mathbb{R}^+$ given by:*

$$s^A_{(\mathbb{A},t)} = \left(\mathcal{N}_{(\mathbb{A},t)} \cap \mathcal{N}_A,\ c_{(\mathbb{A},t)}\right)$$

And by the ***supervisor*** *at time t, with the cost $d_{(\mathbb{A},t)}$ of the already realized defense.*

$$s^D_{(\mathbb{A},t)} = \left(\mathcal{N}_{(\mathbb{A},t)} \cap \mathcal{N}_D,,\ d_{(\mathbb{A},t)}\right)$$

Here, $\mathcal{N}_{(\mathbb{A},t)} \cap \mathcal{N}_A$ represents the set of nodes that are compromised by attack $\mathbb{A}$ at time t and are visible to the attacker. Similarly, $\mathcal{N}_{(\mathbb{A},t)} \cap \mathcal{N}_D$ represents the set of compromised nodes visible to the supervisor. It is important to note that while the compromised nodes set is partial, the time and cost associated with the overall attack state are assumed to be observed by both, as they reflect the progression of the attack regardless of visibility of individual nodes.

The challenge arises when either the attacker or the supervisor receives an observation. This observation alone does not fully reveal the underlying attack $\mathbb{A}$. Instead, an observation is *consistent* if there exists at least one actual attack scenario that could have led to that observation.

Definition 2 (Consistent Observation). *Let* $S = (\mathcal{N}', c)$ *be a consistent observation of an attacker (defender) if there exists an attack* $\hat{\mathbb{A}} = \{(\hat{n}_1, \hat{t}_1), ..., (\hat{n}_k, \hat{t}_k)\}$ *such that* $s^A_{(\hat{\mathbb{A}},t)} = (\mathcal{N}', c')$ $(s^D_{(\hat{\mathbb{A}},t)} = (\mathcal{N}', c'))$. *Let* $S_A(S_D)$ *denotes a set of minimal attacks for the attacker's (defender's) observation* S *i.e. whenever* $A \in S_A(A \in S_D)$ *we have* $S = s^A_{(\mathbb{A},t)}$ $(S = s^D_{(\mathbb{A},t)})$. *By the minimal we mean that any attack containing less leaf nodes does not lead to the observation.*

In essence, a consistent observation is one that is reachable by at least one valid sequence of attacker actions and their resulting propagations. For simplicity, we write $O = (\mathcal{N}, t, c)$ for observations at time t if the attack tree and attack are clear from a context.

Example 2 To continue with Example 1 let $\mathcal{N}_A = \{n_1, n_3, n_4\}$ then observations $(\{n_1, n_4\}), 10)$ at timer 5 and $(\{n_1, n_3, n_4\}), 10)$ at time 2 are not consistent. In the first case, visible node n_3 has to be compromised as well and in the second case time 2 cannot be achieved.

4.2 Consistency Checking

We propose a way how the consistency of an observation can be checked. The ability to check the consistency of an observation is fundamental for both the attacker and the supervisor. An inconsistent observation indicates a deviation from expected ATs, potentially signaling for example, sensor failures, unexpected system responses, or even a previously unknown attack vector.

To this aim, we use a modified transformation of ATs to a finite automaton $\mathcal{A}$ as it was proposed in [28].

1. **Attack Tree to Finite Automaton Transformation:** The attack tree T_{rct} can be transformed into a finite automaton where states represent the compromise status of nodes and transitions represent attack actions or propagation events. The time and cost constraints on nodes and gates are incorporated into the automaton's transition conditions. Each state in this automaton would represent a possible "true" state of the system in terms of compromised nodes, accumulated time, and cost.
   - **States:** A state in the automaton would be a tuple (Compromised Nodes, CurrentTime, CurrentCost).
   - **Transitions:** Transitions are triggered by attacker actions (attempting to compromise a leaf node at a certain time) or by the propagation rules. Each transition would update the `CurrentTime` and `CurrentCost` based on the node's properties and gate logic.
2. **Observation Mapping:** Given an observation $(\mathcal{N}', t', c')$ from either the attacker or supervisor, we need to map this partial information onto the states of the full automaton. For a given observation, we are interested in

states of the automaton where the set of compromised nodes visible to the observer (CompromisedNodes $\cap \mathcal{N}_A$ or $\mathcal{N}_D$) matches $\mathcal{N}'$, and the total time and cost are t' and c' respectively.

3. **Reachability Analysis:** The consistency check then becomes a reachability problem. An observation is consistent if there exists at least one path in the automaton, starting from an initial uncompromised state, that leads to a state that matches the observed partial information. If no such path exists, the observation is deemed inconsistent.

In Algorithm 1, we present a procedure for performing the consistency check. We introduce new notations: O denotes the set of observations, while V represents the set of visible nodes.

Algorithm 1 `IsConsistent`(O, V, T_{rct})

Require: Observation $O = (\mathcal{N}', t', c')$, Visibility Set $V \subseteq \mathcal{N}$, Attack Tree $T_{rct} = (\mathcal{N}, \mathcal{E}, g, c_A, c_D)$
Ensure: Boolean (True if consistent, False otherwise)
1: Create a finite automaton A from T_{rct}:
2: States $S = \{(\text{CompromisedNodes}, \text{CurrentTime}, \text{CurrentCost})\}$ for all possible states of T_{rct}
3: Initial state $s_0 = (\emptyset, 0, 0)$
4: Transitions based are based on attack propagation rules and success of an attack (leaf node compromise attempts).
5: Perform a reachability analysis on $\mathcal{A}$ using a graph traversal algorithm (e.g., BFS or DFS) starting from the initial state s_0.
6: **for** each reachable state $s_i = (\mathcal{N}_i, \text{time}_i, \text{cost}_i)$ in $\mathcal{A}$ **do**
7: **if** $(\mathcal{N}_i \cap V) = \mathcal{N}'$ `AND` $\text{time}_i = t'$ `AND` $\text{cost}_i = c'$ **then return** `True`
8: **end if**
9: **end for**
10: **return** `False`

Theorem 1 (Correctness of Consistency Checking). *Given an attack tree with time and cost T_{rct}, an observation $O = (\mathcal{N}', t', c')$, and a visibility set $V \subseteq \mathcal{N}$ (for either the attacker or supervisor), the observation O is consistent if and only if there exists a valid attack $\hat{\mathbb{A}}$ on T_{rct} such that the observed state $s_{(\hat{\mathbb{A}},t')}$ matches O for the given visibility set V.*

Proof Theorem 1 demonstrates that the condition of an observation being consistent (as per Definition 2) is equivalent to the existence of a reachable state in the automaton constructed by the consistency checking methodology. This equivalence is what Algorithm 1 leverages.

Part 1: Soundness (If Algorithm 1 returns `True`, then O is consistent)

Assume that Algorithm 1 returns `True`. This implies that the algorithm found at least one reachable state $s_i = (\mathcal{N}_i, \text{time}_i, \text{cost}_i)$ in the finite automaton $\mathcal{A}$ (constructed from T_{rct}) such that the observed components of s_i match O. Specifically:

- $(\mathcal{N}_i \cap V) = \mathcal{N}'$
- $\text{cost}_i = c'$

Since s_i is a reachable state in $\mathcal{A}$ from the initial state $s_0 = (\emptyset, 0, 0)$, there exists a sequence of transitions in $\mathcal{A}$ that leads from s_0 to s_i. By the construction of automaton $\mathcal{A}$, each transition in $\mathcal{A}$ accurately corresponds to either an attacker's attempt to compromise a leaf node or the subsequent propagation of compromise through the attack tree.

Therefore, the path from s_0 to s_i in $\mathcal{A}$ directly corresponds to a valid attack $\hat{\mathbb{A}} = \{(\hat{n}_1, \hat{t}_1), ..., (\hat{n}_k, \hat{t}_k)\}$ on T_{rct} that, at time t', results in the attack state $s_{(\hat{\mathbb{A}},t')} = (\mathcal{N}_i, \text{time}_i, \text{cost}_i)$. Given this, the observation of $s_{(\hat{\mathbb{A}},t')}$ by the entity with visibility set V would be $(\mathcal{N}_i \cap V, \text{time}_i, \text{cost}_i)$, which by our assumption is precisely $(\mathcal{N}', t', c')$. This directly satisfies the conditions for a consistent observation as stated in Definition 2. Hence, if Algorithm 1 returns `True`, the observation O is indeed consistent.

Part 2: Completeness (If O is consistent, then Algorithm 1 returns `True`)

Assume that the observation $O = (\mathcal{N}', t', c')$ is consistent according to Definition 2. This means there exists at least one actual attack $\hat{\mathbb{A}} = \{(\hat{n}_1, \hat{t}_1), ..., (\hat{n}_k, \hat{t}_k)\}$ such that when this attack is applied to T_{rct}, it generates an attack state $s_{(\hat{\mathbb{A}},t')} = (\mathcal{N}_{(\hat{\mathbb{A}},t')}, c_{(\hat{\mathbb{A}},t')})$ at time t', and the observation derived from this state matches O. Specifically:

- $(\mathcal{N}_{(\hat{\mathbb{A}},t')} \cap V) = \mathcal{N}'$
- $c_{(\hat{\mathbb{A}},t')} = c'$

The finite automaton $\mathcal{A}$ is constructed to model all possible attack propagation and resulting states of T_{rct} based on attack definition and the propagation rules. Therefore, the specific attack state at time $t(\mathcal{N}_{(\hat{\mathbb{A}},t')}, c_{(\hat{\mathbb{A}},t')})$ generated by $\hat{\mathbb{A}}$ must correspond to a reachable state s_j in the automaton $\mathcal{A}$.

Algorithm 1 performs a reachability analysis (e.g., using Breadth-First Search or Depth-First Search) starting from the initial state s_0. These graph traversal algorithms are guaranteed to explore all states reachable from s_0. Since s_j is a reachable state in $\mathcal{A}$ and its observed components match O, the algorithm will necessarily discover s_j during its traversal and, upon finding the matching conditions, will return `True`. Therefore, if an observation O is consistent, Algorithm 1 will correctly return `True`.

5 Discussion

Having established the framework for supervised attack trees and consistency checking, we now turn to the central question of strategic interaction: given a consistent observation and available resources, can an attack tree be successfully compromised by an attacker, or can it be effectively defended?

Our research questions can be formulated as model-checking problems over the finite automaton. This can be done by extending the automaton construction to encode strategic decision points for both attackers and defenders. The extended automaton $\mathcal{A}_{SAT}$ incorporates states of the form $(CompromisedNodes, AttackerBudget, DefenderBudget, CurrentTime, ObservationHistory)$ where transitions represent either attacker moves (leaf compromise attempts constrained by budget B_A) or defender reactions (node defense deployments triggered by observations in N_D and constrained by budget B_D).

The **defendability** question transforms into a reachability analysis: "Does there exist a defensive strategy such that for all attacker paths within budget B_A, no state with $rootCompromised = true$ is reachable?" This can be expressed as the CTL formula $\mathbf{AG}(\neg rootCompromised \vee B_A = 0 \wedge defenderSuccess))$.

Consider the attack tree from Fig. 1 where the supervisor observes $\mathcal{N}_D = \{n_1, n_3, n_5\}$ with budget $B_D = 15$ and defense costs $c_D(n_1) = 5$, $c_D(n_3) = 4$, $c_D(n_5) = 3$. When the automaton reaches state $s = (\{n_3\}, B_A = 7, B_D = 15, t = 3, obs = \{n_3\})$, Algorithm 1 confirms this observation is valid, triggering a defensive decision point. The model-checking analysis reveals that executing the defense action $defend(n_3)$ with cost 4 creates a critical temporal disruption: by postponing n_3's compromise window beyond the SAND gate's timing constraints at n_1, the defender effectively breaks the attack propagation chain. The verification shows that regardless of how the attacker redistributes their remaining budget across alternative nodes, the root becomes unreachable, establishing $B_D^{\min} = 4$ as the minimum defense budget.

Attackability follows dual reasoning through the temporal logic query $\mathbf{EF}(rootCompromised \wedge B_A \geq 0)$.

which determines whether there exists an attack strategy that guarantees root compromise despite optimal defensive responses. For instance, if an attacker observes $\mathcal{N}_A = \{n_2, n_4, n_6\}$ with budget $B_A = 12$, they can pursue multiple attack paths simultaneously: compromising nodes $\{n_5, n_6\}$ (total cost 4) to achieve n_2 via the OR gate, while also targeting n_4 (cost 2). The automaton-based verification reveals that even if the supervisor optimally defends one path upon observation, the attacker's diversified approach with sufficient budget redistribution guarantees eventual root compromise.

Using existing model checkers like TAPAAL [25], we can systematically explore all possible attack-defense interaction sequences, computing exact minimum budgets $B_A^{\min}$ and $B_D^{\min}$ while accounting for the partial observability constraints that fundamentally distinguish SATs from traditional game-theoretic approaches. The **minimum defense budget** problem reduces to finding the smallest B_D such that the temporal logic formula in Equation (1) holds, while the **minimum attack budget** corresponds to the smallest B_A for which Equation (2) is satisfied under optimal defensive strategies.

6 Conclusion

In this paper, we introduce *Supervised Attack Trees* (SATs) as an extension of traditional attack trees that explicitly account for *partial observability*, *budget-constrained interaction* and *dynamic defensive responses* in adversarial settings. By incorporating partial observation sets for both actors and allowing the supervisor to dynamically postpone node compromises at a cost, SATs provide a more realistic framework for analyzing modern security scenarios in large, opaque systems.

Our technical contributions include a formal definition of SATs, a precise notion of consistent observations based on partial state information, and an automata based methodology for checking consistency. We demonstrated how fundamental security questions defendability, attackability, and the computation of minimum budgets can be reduced to model-checking problems over a finite automaton that encodes the game like dynamics between the attacker and supervisor. This provides a formal foundation for answering practical questions about resource allocation and strategic planning that were beyond the scope of previous tree-based models.

Despite these contributions, our framework has several *limitations* that point to promising directions for future work:

1. **Computational Complexity:** The transformation of SATs into a finite automaton, while theoretically sound, may lead to state space explosion for large trees with complex timing constraints. The scalability of the model-checking approach needs to be thoroughly evaluated against real-world case studies.
2. **Static Visibility Assumption**: The sets of observable nodes (N_A and N_D) are assumed fixed throughout the interaction. In practice, visibility may evolve, for example, through adaptive monitoring or deception mechanisms. Extending SATs to support *dynamic observability* would enhance realism.
3. **Deterministic Timing and Costs**: The current model treats time windows and costs as deterministic. Real-world exploits and defenses often involve *stochastic durations* or uncertain success probabilities. Incorporating probabilistic semantics (e.g., via Markov decision processes) would better capture this uncertainty.
4. **Single-Root Focus**: SATs analyze compromise of a single root goal. Many systems involve *multiple interdependent objectives* or cascading failures. Generalizing to *multi-root or graph-based attack structures* (beyond trees) would broaden applicability.

In summary, SATs offer a unified and formal framework for security analysis that faithfully captures the interplay of limited resources, imperfect information, and strategic moves. We believe this work lays the groundwork for moving from static vulnerability assessment to dynamic, strategic security planning.

The future work involves leveraging Neural Networks (NNs) and Machine Learning (ML) to recognize dangerous temporal sequences composed of compromised node identifiers paired with precise time stamps. These sequences are indicators of a developing threat that could ultimately result in root compromise. The methodology is structured in two main phases:

1. **Synthetic Data Generation Guided by Attack Trees** We will first focus on generating synthetic data streams (X_{synth}) that precisely model these dangerous sequences. Mechanism: The generation of these synthetic streams will be formally guided by a pre-defined Attack Tree (AT). The AT provides the causal structure necessary to ensure the synthetic anomalies accurately reflect plausible sequences of node compromise leading to the critical failure.
2. **Model Explanation and Causal Tracing** Following the training of the NN, we will derive interpretability for its decisions. Objective: From an already trained Neural Network, we plan to determine the explanation for its anomaly classifications. Method: This explanation will be found by means of (or through the formal structure of) the Attack Tree (AT). This involves mapping the feature importance derived from XAI methods back onto the AT structure to establish a traceable, root-cause analysis for the detected threat sequence.

References

1. Copae, D.-V., Soltani, R., Lopuhaä-Zwakenberg, M.: Attack-defense trees with offensive and defensive attributes. In: 2025 55th Annual IEEE/IFIP International Conference on Dependable Systems and Networks (DSN), pp. 358–370. IEEE (2025)
2. Ali, A.T.: Simplified timed attack trees. In: Cherfi, S., Perini, A., Nurcan, S. (eds.) RCIS 2021. LNBIP, vol. 415, pp. 653–660. Springer, Cham (2021). https://doi.org/10.1007/978-3-030-75018-3_49
3. Ali, A.T., Gruska, D., Kharraz, K., Leucker, M.: Analysis of attack time and costs in attack trees via SMT resolution. In: Proceedings of the 8th International Conference on Future Networks & Distributed Systems, pp. 1057–1064 (2024)
4. Ali, A.T., Gruska, D.P.: Attack trees with time constraints. In: CS&P, pp. 93–105 (2021)
5. Schneier, B.: Attack trees. Dr. Dobb's J. **24**(12), 21–29 (1999)
6. Mauw, S., Oostdijk, M.: Foundations of attack trees. In: Won, D.H., Kim, S. (eds.) ICISC 2005. LNCS, vol. 3935, pp. 186–198. Springer, Heidelberg (2006). https://doi.org/10.1007/11734727_17
7. Ali, A.T., Gruska, D.: Reversible attack trees. In: 2021 IEEE 12th Annual Ubiquitous Computing, Electronics & Mobile Communication Conference (UEMCON), pp. 0279–0285. IEEE (2021)

8. Ali, A.T., Gruska, D.P.: Dynamic attack trees. In: OVERLAY@ GandALF, pp. 25–29 (2021)
9. Kordy, B., Mauw, S., Radomirović, S., Schweitzer, P.: Foundations of attack–defense trees. In: Degano, P., Etalle, S., Guttman, J. (eds.) FAST 2010. LNCS, vol. 6561, pp. 80–95. Springer, Heidelberg (2011). https://doi.org/10.1007/978-3-642-19751-2_6
10. Kordy, B., Mauw, S., Radomirović, S., Schweitzer, P.: Attack-defense trees. J. Log. Comput. **24**(1), 55–87 (2014)
11. Kordy, B., Mauw, S., Melissen, M., Schweitzer, P.: Attack–defense trees and two-player binary zero-sum extensive form games are equivalent. In: Alpcan, T., Buttyán, L., Baras, J.S. (eds.) GameSec 2010. LNCS, vol. 6442, pp. 245–256. Springer, Heidelberg (2010). https://doi.org/10.1007/978-3-642-17197-0_17
12. Gadyatskaya, O., Hansen, R.R., Larsen, K.G., et al.: Modelling attack-defense trees using timed automata. In: International Conference on Formal Modeling and Analysis of Timed Systems, pp. 35–50 (2016)
13. Copae, D.-V., Soltani, R., Lopuhaä-Zwakenberg, M.: Attack-defense trees with offensive and defensive attributes. arXiv preprint arXiv:2504.12748 (2025)
14. Fila, B., Wideł, W.: Exploiting attack–defense trees to find an optimal set of countermeasures. In: 2020 IEEE 33rd Computer Security Foundations Symposium (CSF), pp. 395–410. IEEE (2020)
15. Bistarelli, S., Fioravanti, F., Peretti, P.: Defense trees for economic evaluation of security investments. In: ARES, pp. 416–423. IEEE (2006)
16. Roy, A., Kim, D.S., Trivedi, K.S.: Attack countermeasure trees (ACT): towards unifying the constructs of attack and defense trees. Sec. Commun. Netw. **5**(8), 929–943 (2012)
17. Roy, A.: Attack countermeasure trees: a non-state-space approach towards analyzing security and finding optimal countermeasure sets. Ph.D. thesis, Duke University (2010)
18. Lopuhaä-Zwakenberg, M., Stoelinga, M.: Cost-damage analysis of attack trees. In: 2023 53rd Annual IEEE/IFIP International Conference on Dependable Systems and Networks (DSN), pp. 545–558. IEEE (2023)
19. Bistarelli, S., Dall'Aglio, M., Peretti, P.: Strategic games on defense trees. In: Dimitrakos, T., Martinelli, F., Ryan, P.Y.A., Schneider, S. (eds.) FAST 2006. LNCS, vol. 4691, pp. 1–15. Springer, Heidelberg (2007). https://doi.org/10.1007/978-3-540-75227-1_1
20. Arias, J., Budde, C.E., Penczek, W., Petrucci, L., Sidoruk, T., Stoelinga, M.: Hackers vs. security: attack-defense trees as asynchronous multi-agent systems. In: International Conference on Formal Engineering Methods, pp. 3–19 (2020)
21. Guo, Y., Jiang, X., Guo, C., Wang, S., Karoui, O.: Overview of opacity in discrete event systems. IEEE Access **8**, 48731–48741 (2020)
22. Saboori, A., Hadjicostis, C.N.: Verification of initial-state opacity in security applications of DES. In: 2008 9th International Workshop on Discrete Event Systems, pp. 328–333 (2008)
23. Ali, A.T., Gruska, D.: States of attack under incomplete information. In: IEEE CCWC, pp. 801–807 (2022)
24. Rehák, M.: Runtime monitoring and dynamic reconfiguration for intrusion detection systems. In: Kirda, E., Jha, S., Balzarotti, D. (eds.) RAID 2009. LNCS, vol. 5758, pp. 61–80. Springer, Heidelberg (2009). https://doi.org/10.1007/978-3-642-04342-0_4

25. Byg, J., Jørgensen, K.Y., Srba, J.: TAPAAL: editor, simulator and verifier of timed-Arc Petri Nets. In: Liu, Z., Ravn, A.P. (eds.) ATVA 2009. LNCS, vol. 5799, pp. 84–89. Springer, Heidelberg (2009). https://doi.org/10.1007/978-3-642-04761-9_7
26. Nguyen, H.N., Sabaliauskaite, G., Shaikh, S.A.: Formal template-based generation of attack-defense trees for automated security analysis. Information **14**(9), 481 (2023)
27. Bryans, J., et al.: Formal template-based generation of attack-defence trees for automated security analysis. Information **14**(9), 481 (2023)
28. Gruska, D., Ali, A.T., Leucker, M.: Using attack trees for security education and training: simplifying threat analysis. In: IFIP World Conference on Information Security Education, pp. 64–79. Springer (2025). https://doi.org/10.1007/978-3-031-94924-1_5
29. Alur, R., Dill, D.L.: A theory of timed automata. Theoret. Comput. Sci. **126**(2), 183–235 (1994)

Applying SOA Principles to Next-Generation Cyber Range Design

Michail Takaronis(✉), Vasileios Gkioulos, Georgios Kavallieratos, and Jia-Chun Lin

Norwegian University of Science and Technology, Gjøvik, Norway
{michail.takaronis,vasileios.gkioulos,georgios.kavallieratos, jia-chun.lin}@ntnu.no

Abstract. Cyber ranges (CRs) are interactive platforms that simulate networks, systems, and attack-defense exercises, along with security testbeds and cyber-physical ranges. The latter systems are preferred for cyber-physical systems scenarios due to the variety of heavyweight simulation environments and potential hardware integration required for such exercises. Current implementations face challenges such as interoperability gaps due to diverse protocols, limitations in scalability, scenario design, resource sharing, and a lack of shared architectural information. As a conceptual design paper, taking into account the CR challenges, architectural trends, and reference architecture guidelines, we propose the adoption of service-oriented architecture (SOA), a software design approach in which software components are designed as independent, reusable services that communicate with each other over a network. By leveraging SOA principles and its reference architecture directions, we present a high-level architecture of a cyber range that could address CR issues, along with its benefits, open challenges, implementation guidelines, and evaluation strategy.

Keywords: Service-oriented architecture · Cyber range · Cybersecurity · Reference architecture

1 Introduction

As technology rapidly evolves, cybersecurity threats grow increasingly complex. The interconnectivity of devices introduces new vulnerabilities that cybercriminals exploit to disrupt operations. Cyberattacks on cyber-physical systems (CPS), particularly those targeting critical infrastructure, are among the most pressing concerns of the 21st century. Incidents such as Stuxnet, TRITON, and PIPEDREAM have had severe impacts on industrial systems, each aiming to compromise essential operations [1–3]. These attacks underscore the need for robust protection strategies, including network segmentation, real-time monitoring, intrusion detection systems, and personnel training in both technical and awareness-based cybersecurity—often conducted in simulated environments

P. D'Arco and A. Zamfiroiu (Eds.): SecITC 2025, LNCS 16443, pp. 278–292, 2026.
https://doi.org/10.1007/978-3-032-17443-7_17

like cyber ranges (CRs) and security testbeds. However, current CR implementations face challenges such as interoperability gaps, limited scenario design, and scalability issues [7]. These issues persist in CPS-focused ranges, where diverse technologies and protocols are domain-specific [5]. Emerging approaches aim to overcome these limitations through architectural methods like federation, layering, and modularity [7]. This paper identifies key architectural challenges and trends, and proposes integrating service-oriented architecture (SOA) into cyber range design. SOA promotes modularity, reusability, and interoperability, addressing core limitations in CR environments. We present SOA principles, reference architecture guidelines for both SOA and CRs, and a high-level architecture combining both. The proposed model transforms CR components into independent services that communicate via defined protocols and APIs. Finally, we discuss open challenges, a preliminary implementation plan, and evaluation strategies. The paper is structured as follows: Sect. 2 reviews cyber range operations and SOA principles; Sect. 3 outlines challenges and trends; Sect. 4 presents reference architectures; Sect. 5 introduces our SOA-based design; Sect. 6 provides discussion; Sect. 7 covers limitations and future work; Sect. 8 concludes this work.

2 Background

CRs are interactive, virtualized simulations of a company's network, systems, tools, and applications, connected to a virtual Internet-level environment. They offer secure environments for product development, security testing, and hands-on cybersecurity training [4]. Cyber-physical ranges (CPRs) extend this concept to operational technology, integrating computational and physical processes, often combining virtual and real components like physical devices [5]. Security testbeds, meanwhile, are specialized environments for evaluating cybersecurity technologies, particularly in CPS scenarios, due to the complexity and diversity of technologies involved [6].

These platforms support training, research, and evaluation of security tools and approaches, serving diverse users such as operators, trainers, and researchers, each with distinct needs and use cases. SOA is a software design approach that builds scalable systems from modular components called services [8]. These services interact to perform tasks, such as enabling Single Sign-On (SSO) across multiple applications. SOA is built around four key components: **Services**, which are independent programs performing specific functions; **Service Providers**, which design, implement, and expose these services; **Service Consumers**, which are applications or systems that request and use the services; and the **Service Registry**, a central directory that enables publishing and discovering available services. Together, these elements create a modular, interoperable framework for building flexible and reusable systems.

Consider an SSO scenario: a user accesses an application, which queries the service registry to locate an authentication service. The registry returns the service endpoint managed by the provider. The user is redirected to a login page, submits credentials, and receives a security token. The application validates the token—checking its digital signature—and grants access. This token can be reused across other applications. Figure 1 illustrates this process.

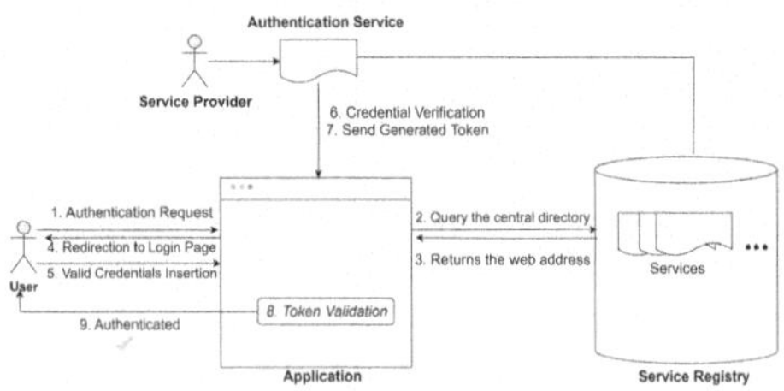

Fig. 1. Authentication process in a SOA application.

3 Challenges and Architectural Trends in Cyber Ranges

This section explores the current state of CR implementations, highlighting key challenges and architectural approaches.

3.1 Core Challenges

Recent research has examined inefficiencies and architectural issues in CRs, CPRs, and security testbeds. These systems vary in technology and scope, simulating diverse attack-defense scenarios across various sectors. However, they face notable challenges in design, implementation, and functionality management. Below, we summarize the core challenges supported by the literature.

High Costs and Resource Demands: Emulation and hybrid ranges, especially cyber-physical ones, often require dedicated hardware and network infrastructure. Scenario preparation demands significant computational resources and expert personnel for manual tasks like testing and scenario creation [7,9,10]. Realistic setups may involve specialized software, increasing costs through licensing fees [11], particularly when vendor-specific technologies are involved.

Interoperability Gaps: Many environments are sector-specific, using distinct technologies and data exchange formats, which hinders interoperability. A review by Stamatopoulos et al. [7] found few publicly available datasets supporting cyber range composition and service interoperability. This gap is more evident in CPS-related ranges, where varied protocols like MQTT, CoAP, and HTTP complicate integration and require specialized knowledge [12].

Scenario Design Complexity: Designing realistic cyberattack scenarios is challenging due to evolving threats and the need for domain-specific fidelity. Modern CR scenarios span domains such as banking, healthcare, smart grids, autonomous vehicles, and mobile security [13]. These require the integration of physical and computational components, real-time operations, and diverse technologies, increasing design complexity.

Scalability and Elasticity: On-premises ranges relying on local infrastructure face limitations in scaling and adapting to complex scenarios. Expanding capacity often requires new hardware or software, which is costly and time-consuming [4]. Similar constraints apply to CPRs and testbeds, especially when hardware is involved in resource-intensive simulations [14].

3.2 Major Architectural Approaches and Trends

As cyber threats evolve and technologies grow more complex, simulating cyber-attacks in CRs presents challenges in both design and execution. CRs must continuously adapt their training content, requiring architectural adjustments such as increased computational resources and specialized personnel. The need for standardized reference architectures for CRs and collaborative environments was highlighted in recent research [5,13,15].

Federation of Cyber Ranges. Federation connects multiple CRs to share resources, scenarios, and expertise, enabling broader and more diverse training. Oikonomou et al. [16] describe the ECHO Federated Cyber Range, which uses a centralized broker to match user needs with provider resources via a unified portal. Its architecture includes four layers—Client, Front, Mid, and Back Tiers—each handling specific functions such as access, administration, and communication. Lal et al. [17] proposed a federated architecture for the CYBERUNITY project, using an abstraction layer to convert provider-specific data into a common format, enabling resource sharing and simplifying large-scale exercise management. Chaskoks et al. [18] introduced a classification model for distributing critical infrastructure scenarios, categorizing components by criticality to enhance sharing while protecting sensitive data. Despite its benefits, federation introduces interoperability challenges due to the varied technologies across providers.

Layered Architecture. Layered architectures organize CR components into functional layers, simplifying complexity. Each layer handles specific tasks such as resource provisioning, simulation, and virtualization. A six-layer model, comprising infrastructure, virtualization, containerization, orchestration, configuration management, and target infrastructure, was proposed in [19], offering a clearer system overview. However, interdependencies between layers can complicate updates and system changes [7].

Modular Architecture. Modular architectures separate CR components into independent modules—e.g., computing platforms, software provisioning, and scenario engines—allowing updates without affecting the entire system. GoibhniUWE, proposed in [20], is a lightweight, container-based CR that enables deploying multiple vulnerable services across networks. Katsantonis et al. [10] introduced the Cyber Range Design Framework, emphasizing modularity for scalability and shared functionality. AIT's CR architecture [21] includes four building blocks and uses open-source tools like OpenStack and Terraform to support modular deployment.

3.3 Alternative Approaches: Microservices and Hybrid Models

Microservices, an evolution of SOA, offer smaller, decoupled services that can complement CR architectures [22]. In CRs, services like user authentication or simulation initialization can be reused efficiently. However, microservices introduce reliability challenges due to service dependencies. SOA, with its synchronous ESB-based communication, better supports real-time coordination in attack-defense exercises. Microservices, using asynchronous calls, may be more suitable for tasks like resource allocation. Overall, SOA aligns better with CR needs, while microservices can enhance specific components.

4 SOA in CPS, Cyber Ranges and Reference Architectures

This section presents the adoption of SOA in CPS and CRs and establishes reference architectures for SOA and CR, forming the foundation for our proposed integration.

4.1 SOA in CPS and Cyber Ranges

SOA has been applied in CPS to abstract and integrate physical and computational components as services. Yu et al. [28] introduced an early SOA model that treats physical devices as services, improving reliability and adaptability. Their framework supports service discovery, composition, and integration.

In [29], a modular SOA framework was proposed for managing complex CPS like smart transportation, separating services for modeling, planning, execution, monitoring, sensing, and actuation. Mohalik et al. [30] extended this with an adaptive SOA using IBM's MAPE-K loop (Monitor, Analyze, Plan, Execute), and Knowledge—to enable self-configuration and optimization. AI techniques synthesized workflows from device capabilities, while middleware bridged application-level commands with low-level device functions. Their prototype, based on the HINC model, was demonstrated in a building automation scenario.

SOA also supports security and training environments in IoT, cloud computing, and data management. Nock et al. [31] presented an IoT cyber range architecture, with modular front-end and back-end components using API-driven interactions. In [32], the Cyber Physical Manufacturing Cloud (CPMC) framework virtualized manufacturing resources and exposed tools as web services, using TCP/IP and REST for simplified data exchange. Möller et al. [33] designed a service-oriented maritime testbed for managing sensor and radar data, focusing on secure data sharing and validation.

SOA implementations offer solutions to challenges faced by CRs. Alshinina et al. [34] surveyed SOA middleware for wireless sensor networks, highlighting lightweight models like μSOA and ESOA, and protocols like JSON/XML to reduce overhead and improve interoperability. Giao et al. [35] proposed an SOA-based IoT framework using Docker containers for scalable deployment and REST APIs to connect heterogeneous devices. In Industry 4.0, SOA frameworks support manufacturing process control. Serodio et al. [36] showed that SOA reduces integration complexity from quadratic ($N \times M$) to linear ($N + M$) growth. They combined SOA with Manufacturing-as-a-Service and Resource-as-a-Service to enhance system integration. SOA also supports flexible resource handling when combined with Software-Defined Networking and edge computing. In [7], researchers emphasized that current platforms use SOA to integrate technologies from multiple vendors, addressing interoperability needs. However, due to the diversity of CR environments, a universal architecture remains challenging. While SOA is widely applied in CPS, IoT, and cloud systems, its integration into unified environments like CRs is still limited. Building on insights from existing literature, SOA principles, and CR challenges addressed by other SOA implementations, we propose adopting a service-oriented approach for CR architectural composition.

4.2 SOA Reference Architecture

SOA architectures vary by domain, but general guidelines provide structured models for design and implementation. These reference architectures (RAs) serve as blueprints for building flexible, reusable, and interoperable services, defining relationships and establishing an SOA ecosystem, as outlined in the OASIS Standard [23]. The SOA RA comprises nine layers, grouped into horizontal layers (core business capabilities) and vertical layers (supporting capabilities like integration, QoS, and governance) [24]. These layers interact to fulfil the goals of the SOA ecosystem.

Lower layers—Services, Service Components, and Operational Systems—are provider-focused, while upper layers—Services, Business Process, and Consumer—serve consumers. The nine layers and their roles are summarized below [23–25]:

The SOA architecture comprises multiple layers: **Operational Systems Layer** provides runtime infrastructure for hosting and executing software and hardware components, including legacy systems and databases, stabilizing the environment for service deployment and management. **Service Components Layer** bridges the service and operational layers, implementing and assembling software artifacts that realize SOA services. **Services Layer** defines functional capabilities with standardized interfaces, enabling discoverability and access to business logic and data. **Business Process Layer** orchestrates workflows, modelling, and automating end-to-end processes to support business use cases and facilitate information exchange. **Consumer Layer** interfaces with service consumers—humans or applications—abstracting technical complexity and enabling service interaction across channels. **Integration Layer** manages communication and data exchange between services, handling protocol conversion and message routing for interoperability. **Quality of Service Layer** oversees non-functional aspects like security and performance, while policies are defined in the Governance Layer and monitoring occurs here. **Information Layer** offers a unified view of data aligned with business vocabulary, storing and managing data and metadata to ensure consistent access and quality. Finally, **Governance Layer** enforces policies, standards, and compliance across the SOA ecosystem, managing rules, monitoring service health, and ensuring adherence to organizational guidelines.

4.3 Cyber Range Reference Architecture

Kampourakis et al. [15] proposed a CR RA using a three-step approach: synthesizing existing standards, reviewing academic literature to identify common traits, and introducing an evaluation formula to assess performance and efficiency. Their model defines five zones: core infrastructure, learning management and support, monitoring, management, and access control.

The **core infrastructure zone** follows the NIST NICE guide [4], detailing components such as the **orchestration Layer**, which coordinates cyber range components, managing scenario deployment, resource allocation, and automation across infrastructures, the **Underlying Infrastructure**, which provides software and hardware defined resources like networks, servers, and storage, the **virtualization Layer**, which abstracts physical infrastructure to simulate IT environments using VMs and containers, and the **target infrastructure**, which simulates real-world IT/OT systems for training, including VMs, firewalls, and IDS.

The **learning management and support zone** includes the **RLMS**, which delivers and manages user training. It supports scenario assignment, progress tracking, and gamification features like leaderboards and badges [4]. The support section provides tools for red/blue teams, including TTPs from MITRE ATT&CK, open-source offensive/defensive tools, and traffic capture modules for attack analysis and network monitoring.

The **monitoring zone** equips instructors with tools to observe learner activity. HMIs, dashboards, and panels—custom or third-party—enable scenario and user monitoring. Data collection modules gather logs from CR subsystems, while scoring and reporting tools evaluate learner performance independently of core infrastructure.

The **management zone** handles administrative tasks such as scheduling, user and asset management, and data analysis. It focuses on coordinating exercises, managing access and resources, and extracting insights for decision-making. Lastly, the **access control zone** manages authentication and authorization. Methods include credential verification, MFA, SSO, and PKI for authentication, and RBAC, ABAC, MAC, or DAC for authorization—allowing flexible security configurations.

5 Applying SOA to Cyber Range Design

This section presents our main contribution: integrating SOA principles into cyber range design to create a unified framework that addresses current limitations and enhances flexibility.

5.1 SOA-CR Layer Mapping

Building on the RAs discussed earlier, we map the five CR zones—Core Infrastructure, Learning Management and Support, Monitoring, Management, and Control Access—onto the nine SOA layers. This hybrid approach aligns entire CR zones with broader SOA layers and maps specific CR functions to their best-fitting SOA counterparts. A high-level structural composition is shown in Fig. 2.

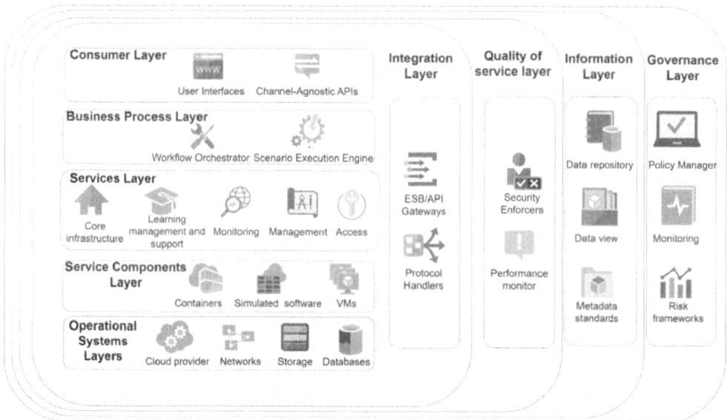

Fig. 2. Reference architecture of Service-Oriented Range.

The **Operational Systems Layer** corresponds to the CR's underlying infrastructure—networks, storage, databases, and cloud platforms—supporting runtime and deployment of SOA solutions, including hybrid and on-premises setups. The **Service Components Layer** includes Docker containers, virtual machines, firewalls, and middleware. These map to the CR's Virtualization and Target Infrastructure layers, enabling isolated environments for scenario execution. The **Services Layer** defines reusable, discoverable services, including:

- **Core Infrastructure Service:** Abstracts orchestration and provisioning via APIs, coordinating scenario deployment and resource allocation. It interacts with the orchestration layer and underlying infrastructure.
- **Learning Management and Support Service:** Interfaces for scenario assignment, progress tracking, and red/blue team tool provisioning.
- **Monitoring Service:** Provides endpoints for tracking user activity, assets, and scenarios, supporting real-time monitoring and reporting.

- **Management Service:** Handles scheduling, user and asset management, and administrative control.
- **Access Control Service:** Manages identity verification and permissions, interacting with the Consumer and Governance layers.
- **Service Registry:** Central directory for service discovery and invocation within the SOA ecosystem.

The **Business Process Layer** maps to the CR orchestration layer, managing workflows and automating service composition for cyber exercises. It interfaces with the Services, Consumer, Integration, and Information layers. Also, the **Consumer Layer** includes user interfaces and platform-agnostic APIs for service access, enabling interaction regardless of device or channel.

5.2 Integration Patterns

The **integration layer** corresponds to CR inter-zone connections, using ESB/API gateways and protocol handlers for communication, conversion, and routing between services. Acting as a proxy, it supports interaction across all horizontal layers. In our architecture, key SOA integration patterns are adopted to meet CR use cases and requirements. The communication patterns in SOA include: 1) **Publish-Subscribe**, which enables event-driven communication where providers publish services to a registry and consumers subscribe to receive updates without knowing the provider's identity, supporting independent, multi-consumer access [37], 2) **Request-Response** facilitates message exchange between consumer and provider, supporting synchronous (waiting for reply), asynchronous (non-blocking), and polling (checking for response availability) modes [38], 3) **Direct Invocation**, also known as point-to-point, allows consumers to directly call service endpoints over a network using defined interfaces [39], and 4) **Message Queuing** uses asynchronous queues to decouple services, storing messages until both parties are ready, ensuring reliable communication under high load [40].

Each pattern suits different CR functions. For example, publish-subscribe supports real-time alerts during exercises; request-response is ideal for instructor queries like progress reports; direct invocation offers low latency for tasks like VM provisioning; and message queuing buffers network logs to prevent data loss. The **Quality of Service Layer**, mapped to the Control Access Zone, handles non-functional aspects such as authentication, authorization, and performance monitoring to ensure reliable service delivery. The **Information Layer** aligns with data collection and analysis modules from the monitoring and management zones. It provides a unified view of data across the CR ecosystem, ensuring consistent access and availability for exercises and users. Finally, the **Governance Layer** oversees compliance, policy enforcement, and standards. It maps to the management zone and includes risk frameworks, service health monitoring, and rule enforcement to maintain ecosystem integrity.

5.3 Workflow Example

Following the proposed Service-Oriented Range reference architecture guidelines, a typical workflow is presented in Fig. 3 as a demonstration of an instructor's login and cyber exercise scenario launch, showcasing the layers' interaction and communication to achieve the specified CR functionalities. An instructor user attempts to submit login credentials to access the system via an HMI of the consumer layer, triggering the quality of service layer to verify the authentication of the specific user. This information is verified in the governance layer against the system's policies and logs the attempt to the information layer. After the successful verification of the user, the response is delivered to the consumer layer via the integration layer, allowing the instructor to proceed with the scenario launch. The instructor then triggers the exercise launch via defined interfaces via the consumer layer, forcing the business process layer to orchestrate the workflow. The appropriate services are called from the service layer according to the requirements of the exercise. Virtualised artifacts are requested from the service component layer, which supports the entire procedure by providing the required resources offered by the operational layer.

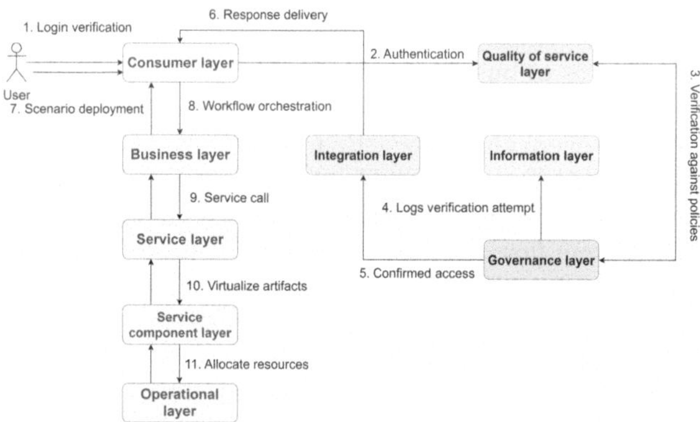

Fig. 3. Example workflow of the SOA cyber range.

6 Discussion

The architecture's nine layers incorporate security mechanisms to mitigate risks. Encryption is essential across all inter-layer communications. In the integration layer, man-in-the-middle attacks are prevented by leveraging protocols like SSL/TLS securing HTTP-based data exchange. The ESB enforces security policies such as message-level encryption, digital signatures, and token-based authentication. The information layer uses hashing to protect data integrity and confidentiality. Access control is managed via the governance layer, implementing role-based and attribute-based access control. Users—trainees, instructors, and administrators—are authenticated using multi-factor authentication and authorized based on roles. Additional components like intrusion detection systems, firewalls, and SSO can be integrated as services within appropriate layers.

The architecture leverages SOA principles to address cyber range challenges and align with current trends. Modularity allows services to be added, removed, or modified without disrupting operations, reducing downtime and cost. Services are reusable and accessible to multiple consumers. Unified APIs can be established and maintained by a working group within the ecosystem or the federation broker, and the ESB protocols may include interoperability mechanisms for message routing, protocol mediation, and security policy enforcement—needed for communication across heterogeneous and federated CRs. Security in CPS is increasingly critical. While domain-specific testbeds address many threats, interoperability remains a challenge due to specialized technologies. Our approach addresses this by using common formats and APIs, enabling integration across CPS domains. Cloud-based infrastructure supports scalable services for high-demand exercises. CRs serve diverse users, each contributing to training, research, and testing [41]. **Operators** manage infrastructure deployment, maintenance, and scaling. SOA supports modular service composition, enabling dynamic provisioning and maintenance without system disruption. Service reuse and registry discovery reduce setup time and cost. **Cybersecurity trainers** design and run exercises to build participant skills. SOA enables reusable, interoperable services across scenarios, supporting complex and scalable training environments. **Security researchers** use CRs to test tools, model threats, and analyze vulnerabilities. SOA facilitates tool integration via standardized protocols and APIs. Services can be independently deployed and modified during exercises without affecting system flow.

The proposed SOA-based cyber range architecture represents a significant departure from traditional monolithic approaches, offering a pathway to address many of the persistent challenges in the cyber range domain. By decomposing cyber range functionality into discrete, interoperable services, we can enable unprecedented flexibility in system composition and evolution. The architectural mapping between SOA layers and cyber range zones demonstrates the natural alignment between SOA principles and CR requirements. The modular nature of SOA particularly addresses the scalability and interoperability challenges identified in current implementations, while the standardized communication protocols facilitate integration across diverse technological environments. However, the transition to a service-oriented approach introduces new considerations around service orchestration complexity, network latency, and distributed system management. The success of such an architecture will depend heavily on the careful design of service interfaces, proper implementation of governance mechanisms, and robust security measures across all communication channels. Future implementations should consider hybrid approaches that combine the benefits of SOA with complementary architectural patterns, particularly for real-time components where direct communication may be preferable to service-mediated interactions.

7 Limitations and Future Work

The proposed SOA-CR blueprint is primarily a conceptual approach based on the guidelines both technologies offer; it lacks real-world deployment and testing, where technical issues may arise in different parts of the system. SOA uses service registries to achieve modularity and independence between the services, which may lead to performance overhead due to communication latency and resource demands, negatively affecting real-time CR simulations. In federated environments, scalability remains unaddressed, as does the choice between on-premises or cloud solutions. Existing CR solutions may rely on legacy systems or specialized hardware that do not align with SOA's standardized APIs, requiring custom changes that increase costs or cause disruptions. The Information Layer manages data and flow, raising privacy and ownership concerns in shared setups without proper encryption, while exposed endpoints introduce security risks and potential attack surfaces. Future work will prioritize prototyping, implementing a proof of concept, and testing SOA integration patterns, followed by real-world validation emphasizing security, privacy, and performance. Additional tasks include specifying technologies, integrating AI agents, addressing legacy system integration, and exploring hybrid methods combining SOA RA with microservices. To evaluate the proposed approach, end-to-end latency and real-time responsiveness will be measured from scenario initiation to simulation completion with various numbers of users. Metrics will include throughput and scalability for dynamic resource allocation, as well as resource utilisation, such as CPU and memory efficiency and requirements during cyber exercises. Other metrics will include the success rate of interoperability, such as technology bridging success via protocols, security, and data privacy rates throughout the system, and validation through stakeholder-driven quality scenarios and standards evaluation guidelines [27, 42].

8 Conclusion

Challenges such as interoperability gaps, high costs, and scalability limitations were identified in CRs, as discussed in recent surveys and current implementations. Current architectural trends favor modular, layer-based approaches and federation solutions to distribute large-scale cyber exercise workloads across multiple CR providers. Considering these challenges, trends, and SOA and CR reference guidelines, we proposed a high-level CR architecture and example workflow using SOA's nine functional layers, including core CR components. This paper presented a comprehensive approach to applying SOA principles to next-generation cyber range design, mapping CR functional zones to SOA's reference architecture to leverage modularity, reusability, and interoperability. The proposed architecture offers scalability through independent service scaling, interoperability via standardized protocols, cost reduction through service reusability, and flexibility in system evolution. Limitations include implementation complexity and security risks such as API vulnerabilities. Future work involves prototyping, implementing a proof of concept, testing component interactions in real-world CPS security scenarios, defining communication protocols, and evaluating performance and efficiency using appropriate metrics.

Acknowledgments. This work is supported by the Research Council of Norway through the SFI Norwegian Centre for Cybersecurity in Critical Sectors (NORCICS) project no. 310105.

References

1. Kushner, D.: The real story of stuxnet. IEEE Spectrum, **50**(3) (2013). https://doi.org/10.1109/mspec.2013.6471059
2. TRITON Malware | Attackers Deploy New ICS Attack Framework. Google Cloud Blog. https://cloud.google.com/blog/topics/threat-intelligence/attackers-deploy-new-ics-attack-framework-triton
3. PIPEDREAM: CHERNOVITE's Emerging Malware Targeting Industrial Control Systems | Dragos. Dragos | Industrial (ICS/OT) Cyber Security (2022). https://cdn.cyberscoop.com/pipedream-chernovite-emerging-malware-targeting-ics.pdf
4. THE CYBER RANGE A GUIDE Guidance Document for the Use Cases, Features, and Types of Cyber Ranges in Cybersecurity Education, Certification, and Training Prepared by the Cyber Range Project Team and the NICE Community Coordinating Council, Cybersecurity Skills Competitions Community of Interest (2023)
5. Kavallieratos, G., Katsikas, S.K., Gkioulos, V.: Towards a cyber-physical range. In: Proceedings of the 5th on Cyber-Physical System Security Workshop - CPSS '19 (2019). https://doi.org/10.1145/3327961.3329532
6. Cao, P., Badger, E.C., Kalbarczyk, Z.T., Iyer, R.K., Withers, A., Slagell, A.J.: Towards an unified security testbed and security analytics framework. In: Proceedings of the 2015 Symposium and Bootcamp on the Science of Security, pp. 1–2 (2015). https://doi.org/10.1145/2746194.2746218
7. Stamatopoulos, D., Katsantonis, M., Fouliras, P., Mavridis, I.: Exploring the architectural composition of cyber ranges: a systematic review. Future Internet, **16**(7), 231–231 (2024). https://doi.org/10.3390/fi16070231
8. Chen, M.: What Is SOA (Service-Oriented Architecture)?. Oracle.com (2024). https://www.oracle.com/europe/service-oriented-architecture-soa/
9. Hosseinzadeh, S., Voutos, D., Barrie, D., Owoh, N., Ashawa, M., Shahrabi, A.: Design and development considerations of a cyber physical testbed for operational technology research and education. Sensors **24**(12), 3923 (2024). https://doi.org/10.3390/s24123923
10. Katsantonis, M.N., Manikas, A., Mavridis, I., Gritzalis, D.: Cyber range design framework for cyber security education and training. Int. J. Inf. Secur. **22** (2023). https://doi.org/10.1007/s10207-023-00680-4
11. Urias, V., Stout, W.M.S., Van Leeuwen, B., Lin, H.: Cyber range infrastructure limitations and needs of tomorrow: a position paper (2018). https://doi.org/10.1109/ccst.2018.8585460
12. Chen, S., Varga, P.: Interoperability for cyber-physical systems: an overview of challenges and research gaps. In: 2nd Workshop on Intelligent Infocommunication Networks, Systems and Services (WI2NS2), pp. 49–54 (2024). https://doi.org/10.3311/WINS2024-009

13. Lillemets, P., Bashir Jawad, N., Kashi, J., Sabah, A., Dragoni, N.: A systematic review of cyber range taxonomies: trends, gaps, and a proposed taxonomy. Future Internet **17**(6), 259 (2025). https://doi.org/10.3390/fi17060259
14. Hosseinzadeh, S., Voutos, D., Barrie, D., Owoh, N., Ashawa, M., Shahrabi, A.: Design and development considerations of a cyber physical testbed for operational technology research and education. Sensors **24**(12), 3923 (2024). https://doi.org/10.3390/s24123923
15. Kampourakis, V., Gkioulos, V., Katsikas, S.: A step-by-step definition of a reference architecture for cyber ranges. J. Inf. Secur. Appl. **88**, 103917 (2024). https://doi.org/10.1016/j.jisa.2024.103917
16. EMK. ECHO Federated Cyber Range: Towards Next-Generation Scalable Cyber Ranges – ECHO Network. Echonetwork.eu (2021). https://echonetwork.eu/echo-federated-cyber-range-towards-next-generation-scalable-cyber-ranges/
17. Lal, C., Grammatopoulos, A.V., Takaronis, M., Yamin, M.M., Spathoulas, G., Xenakis, C.: CYBERUNITY: a federated architecture for next-generation cybersecurity training, pp. 759–764 (2025). https://doi.org/10.1109/csr64739.2025.11130084
18. Chaskos, E., Diakoumakos, J., Kolokotronis, N., Lepouras, G.: Handling critical infrastructures in federation of cyber ranges: a classification model. In: Proceedings of the 17th International Conference on Availability, Reliability and Security (2022). https://doi.org/10.1145/3538969.3543819
19. Late, I., Boja, C.: Cyber range technology stack review. Smart Innov. Syst. Technol., 25–40 (2023). https://doi.org/10.1007/978-981-19-6755-9_3
20. Mills, A., White, J., Legg, P.: GoibhniUWE: a lightweight and modular container-based cyber range. J. Cybersecur. Priv. **4**(3), 615–628 (2024). https://doi.org/10.3390/jcp4030029
21. Leitner, M., et al.: AIT Cyber Range. In: Proceedings of the European Interdisciplinary Cybersecurity Conference (2020). https://doi.org/10.1145/3424954.3424959
22. SOA vs Microservices: What's the Difference? | CrowdStrike. Crowdstrike.com (2022). https://www.crowdstrike.com/en-us/cybersecurity-101/cloud-security/soa-vs-microservices/
23. Laskey, K., Mccabe, F., Thornton, D., Brown, P.: Reference Architecture Foundation for Service Oriented Architecture Version 1.0. ResearchGate (2012). https://www.researchgate.net/publication/262144337
24. SOA Source Book. Opengroup.org (2016). https://www.opengroup.org/soa/source-book/intro/index.htm
25. Edison, Tulenan, V., Gaol, F.L.: Service oriented architecture reference architecture blueprin (2010). https://www.researchgate.net/publication/228962956
26. Luise, A.P., Perrone, G., Perrotta, C., Romano, S.P.: On-demand deployment and orchestration of Cyber Ranges in the Cloud (2022). https://www.researchgate.net/publication/360376059_On-demand_deployment_and_orchestration_of_Cyber_Ranges_in_the_Cloud
27. Cyber Range Features Checklist & List Of European Providers Prepared By: ECSO WG5 2025 Edition. https://ecs-org.eu/ecso-uploads/2025/02/Cyber-Range-Features-Checklist-List-of-European-Providers-2.pdf
28. Yu, C., Jing, S., Li, X.: An architecture of cyber physical system based on service. In: International Conference on Computer Science and Service System, pp. 1409–1412 (2012). https://doi.org/10.1109/csss.2012.355

29. Vulgarakis Feljan, A., Mohalik, S.K., Jayaraman, M.V., Badrinath, R.: SOA-PE: a service-oriented architecture for PLANNING AND EXECUTION IN cyber-physical systems. In: 2015 International Conference on Smart Sensors and Systems (IC-SSS) (2015). https://doi.org/10.1109/smartsens.2015.7873602
30. Mohalik, S.K., Narendra, N.C., Badrinath, R., Le, D.-H.: Adaptive service-oriented architectures for cyber physical systems. In: 2017 IEEE Symposium on Service-Oriented System Engineering (SOSE), pp. 57–62 (2017). https://doi.org/10.1109/SOSE.2017.10
31. Nock, O., Starkey, J., Angelopoulos, C.M.: Addressing the security gap in IoT: towards an IoT cyber range. Sensors **20**(18), 5439 (2020). https://doi.org/10.3390/s20185439
32. Liu, X.F., Shahriar, M.R. , Al Sunny, S.M.N., Leu, M.C., Hu, L.: Cyber-physical manufacturing cloud: architecture, virtualization, communication, and testbed. J. Manufact. Syst., **43**, 352–364 (2017). https://doi.org/10.1016/j.jmsy.2017.04.004
33. Möller, J., Jankowski, D., Lamm, A., Hahn, A.: Data management architecture for service-oriented maritime testbeds. IEEE Open J. Intell. Transp. Syst. **3**, 631–649 (2022). https://doi.org/10.1109/ojits.2022.3207235
34. Alshinina, R., Elleithy, K.: Performance and challenges of service-oriented architecture for wireless sensor networks. Sensors **17**(3), 536 (2017). https://doi.org/10.3390/s17030536
35. Giao, J., Nazarenko, A.A., Luis-Ferreira, F., Gonçalves, D., Sarraipa, J.: A framework for service-oriented architecture (SOA)-based IoT application development. Processes **10**(9), 1782 (2022). https://doi.org/10.3390/pr10091782
36. Serôdio, C., Mestre, P., Cabral, J., Gomes, M., Branco, F.: Software and architecture orchestration for process control in industry 4.0 enabled by cyber-physical systems technologies. Appl. Sci. **14**(5), 2160 (2024). https://doi.org/10.3390/app14052160
37. Michlmayr, A., Leitner, P., Rosenberg, F., Dustdar, S.: Publish/subscribe in the VRESCo SOA runtime, pp. 317–320 (2008). https://doi.org/10.1145/1385989.1386031
38. Message Exchange Patterns (MEPs) (Ernesto Garbarino). Garba.org (2025). https://garba.org/article/general/soa/mep.html
39. Lewis, G.A.: Getting started with service-oriented architecture (SOA) terminology. Technical report, Software Engineering Institute, Carnegie Mellon University, Pittsburgh (2010)
40. Tounsi, I., Kacem, M.H., Kacem, A.H.: An approach for modeling and formalizing SOA design patterns. In: Proceedings of the Workshop on Enabling Technologies: Infrastructure for Collaborative Enterprises, WET ICE, pp. 330—335 (2013). https://doi.org/10.1109/WETICE.2013.26
41. Chouliaras, N., Kittes, G., Kantzavelou, I., Maglaras, L., Pantziou, G., Ferrag, M.A.: Cyber ranges and testbeds for education, training, and research. Appl. Sci. **11**(4), 1809 (2021). https://doi.org/10.3390/app11041809
42. Blanco, P., Kotermanski, R., Merson, P.: Evaluating a service-oriented architecture. Dtic.mil (2007). https://apps.dtic.mil/sti/html/tr/ADA475194/index.html

Enhancing Keycloak with Verifiable Audit Trails for Identity and Access Management - A Merkle Tree Approach

Ștefania Ștefănescu[1](✉) and Mirabela Medvei[2]

[1] Faculty of Information Systems and Cyber Security, Military Technical Academy "Ferdinand I", Bucharest, Romania
stefania.stefanescu@mta.ro

[2] Faculty of Information Systems and Cyber Security, Military Technical Academy "Ferdinand I", Bucharest, Romania
mirabela.medvei@mta.ro

Abstract. Identity and Access Management (IAM) systems such as Keycloak record authentication and authorization events, yet their audit logs are not verifiable by end users. We present a Keycloak extension that integrates Merkle-tree commitments into the event pipeline, producing salted receipts grouped into hourly batches and published via a REST API. A lightweight toolset enables batch verification, inclusion proofs, and tamper detection, while signed commitments strengthen trust against server-side rewriting. Evaluation on real event data shows the system detects even minimal modifications and history inconsistencies. Overall, Merkle-based commitments provide an efficient, transparent, and tamper-evident audit mechanism that enhances user-centric access control.

Keywords: Identity and Access Management · Keycloak · Merkle Trees · Verifiable Audit Trails · User-Managed Access · Cryptographic Logging

1 Introduction

Identity and access management (IAM) platforms such as Keycloak are widely deployed in enterprise and research settings to enforce authentication, authorization, and session control. Keycloak provides SSO, OAuth 2.0/OIDC and SAML 2.0, user federation, and policy-based authorization [1]. While these systems natively log events for administrative operations, the resulting audit trails are typically optimized for operator visibility rather than end-user verifiability. This creates a trust gap: users and relying parties must assume the server's integrity because they lack a cryptographic means to detect tampering in the audit history.

In parallel, the access-control landscape has moved toward user-centric models such as User-Managed Access (UMA), an OAuth 2.0–based approach that

P. D'Arco and A. Zamfiroiu (Eds.): SecITC 2025, LNCS 16443, pp. 293–306, 2026.
https://doi.org/10.1007/978-3-032-17443-7_18

externalizes authorization and gives individuals a unified control point for granting, monitoring, and revoking access to resources across services [19].

To bridge the auditability gap, cryptographic data structures—particularly Merkle trees—offer compact, tamper-evident commitments over large sets of records. By hashing events into leaves and recursively hashing up to a single root, Merkle trees allow any individual event to be verified against the root using a short proof, with low storage and computation overhead. They are widely used for scalable integrity auditing and transparency, including in cloud-data settings where hierarchical variants improve update efficiency and proof size [18], and are recognized more broadly as a foundational tool for trustworthy data processing at big-data scale [14].

While Merkle-tree commitments are widely used in blockchain and transparency log systems, their integration into mainstream Identity and Access Management (IAM) platforms remains largely unexplored. Existing IAM solutions, including Keycloak, generate audit trails but lack mechanisms that allow end users to cryptographically verify event integrity. This gap limits trust, especially in settings where demonstrating immutability is as important as enforcing access control policies [19].

To address this, we introduce a verifiable auditing extension for Keycloak that records authentication and authorization events as cryptographically linked receipts and publishes per-batch Merkle roots through a REST API. The system provides independent verification via lightweight tools based on Python, curl, and jq, requiring no external infrastructure and minimal overhead. To ensure reproducibility, the full implementation is publicly available on Github[1]. The repository includes the Keycloak extension, batch processing logic, and verification scripts. This open-source release enables both researchers and practitioners to replicate, extend, and deploy our approach in real environments.

The rest of the paper is organized as follows. Section 2 summarized the related work. Next, we present the design and implementation details in Sect. 3. The verification mechanism is presented in detail in Sect. 4 and the evaluation of the prototipe is presented in 5. Finally Sect. 6 presents the conclusions and future work.

Terminology

In this paper, *dynamic process* denotes the time-ordered sequence that transforms a user event into a verifiable proof (see Fig. 2), while *static structure* refers to the system's components and their interconnections, independent of time (Fig. 1). Other technical terms include *canonicalization* (deterministic JSON encoding with fixed key order and UTF-8), *domain separation tag* (a distinguishing byte differentiating leaf and node hashes), and *WORM* storage (write-once, read-many medium for publishing signed commitments). We also use *ndjson* for newline-delimited JSON, and refer to *RPT* and *PT* as UMA tokens.

[1] https://github.com/StefanescuStefania/keycloack-uma-audit.git.

2 Related Work

The core components of IAM, authentication, authorization, and accounting, provide the foundation for secure access control by verifying identities, managing permissions, and auditing activities. Optimizing IAM frameworks has become an active area of research [4,7], with approaches ranging from cryptographic accountability mechanisms and blockchain-based logging [8,23] to the integration of AI [21] and Explainable AI (XAI) techniques [22,27] to improve security, scalability, compliance, and automation. For instance, [15] emphasizes that IAM systems serve as a cornerstone of modern cybersecurity, safeguarding digital assets across increasingly complex and interconnected infrastructures. Reflecting this evolution, IAM has progressed from basic access control to centralized, adaptive, and cloud-integrated frameworks [20]. A notable example is the concept of IAM-as-a-Service (IAM-aaS) proposed by [24], which delivers IAM through the cloud and enables users to leverage the full benefits of the Security-as-a-Service (SECaaS) model for managing authentication, authorization, identity administration, and auditing.

Verifiable auditing and transparency mechanisms have been extensively explored in blockchain and distributed ledger systems [3,5,16]. Furthermore, Merkle-tree commitments are employed to guarantee the integrity and immutability [13,17,25] of audit trails of data.

In the domain of IAM, research has predominantly concentrated on authentication, authorization, and identity federation, with comparatively little emphasis on cryptographically verifiable auditing. Systems such as IAMSys [9], an LDAP-based IAM solution for enterprises, and cloud-based IAM frameworks [20,24] offer logging and auditing functionalities but depend on administrative trust, preventing end users from independently verifying recorded events. More recent studies investigate blockchain-based access control and audit trails to enhance trust and regulatory compliance [8,23]. Nevertheless, these approaches are generally confined to specialized or experimental settings and have yet to see broad adoption in mainstream IAM platforms.

Keycloak, an open-source IAM solution, has been enhanced with various plugins for enhanced authentication [10–12] and Service Provider Interfaces (SPIs) to enable auditing, identity federation, and user management [6]. However, prior work does not incorporate cryptographic verification directly into the event pipeline. Thorgersen et al. [26] introduce Keycloak-Identity as a modern access management solution for applications. Building on these concepts, our approach integrates Merkle-tree commitments into Keycloak, allowing users to independently verify their own authentication and authorization events. This effectively bridges the gap between verifiable log research and practical, production-grade IAM deployments, offering a lightweight, deployable solution for both regulatory compliance and enhanced security assurance.

3 System Design and Implementation

3.1 Architecture Overview

The overall architecture is depicted in Fig. 1. Together with the workflow in Fig. 2, these two diagrams capture both the *dynamic process* (event-to-proof sequence) and the *static structure* (system modules and their integration).

The extension introduces three modular components into Keycloak's ecosystem, integrated via SPIs and REST interfaces:

1. **Audit Listener (SPI):** Subscribes to Keycloak's event bus and serializes events into salted receipts, written to the append-only *Audit Store*.
2. **Merkle Tree Builder:** Periodically processes receipts to compute batch roots and publish commitments. It is logically decoupled and may run in-process or as a scheduled background task.
3. **Audit Representational State Transfer (REST) API:** Exposes batch commitments and receipt downloads to external verifiers, enabling independent recomputation of roots without requiring trust in the Keycloak operator.

These components integrate seamlessly with existing Keycloak modules, including the UMA policy engine, without altering their behavior. Clients continue to perform login and UMA flows as usual; the additional audit path transparently records and commits the resulting events. For completeness, the deployment includes a *Commitment Signer/Publisher* that signs each batch root and writes it to a WORM-like store (e.g., a Git repository or append-only bucket), enabling independent verification as detailed in Sect. 4.3.

Threat assumptions and their implications are summarized in Sect. 4.

3.2 Workflow

The system integrates a verifiable auditing layer into Keycloak through a custom extension based on Service Provider Interfaces (SPIs). The design goal is to ensure that every authentication and authorization event can be independently verified by end users or third parties without relying on the integrity of the Keycloak operator.

The workflow, shown in Fig. 2, can be decomposed into distinct phases:

1. **Event Capture:** When a user performs an action (e.g., LOGIN, token issuance, UMA RPT request), Keycloak raises an internal event. Our custom *Audit Listener SPI* intercepts this event before it is logged by the default provider.
2. **Receipt Construction:** The listener generates a structured JSON receipt. A random 128-bit salt is concatenated with the event payload to prevent precomputation attacks. Metadata such as timestamp, client identifier, realm, and event type are embedded in the receipt object.
3. **Storage:** The receipt is serialized into and appended to the *Audit Store*. The store is append-only, ensuring immutability at the storage layer.

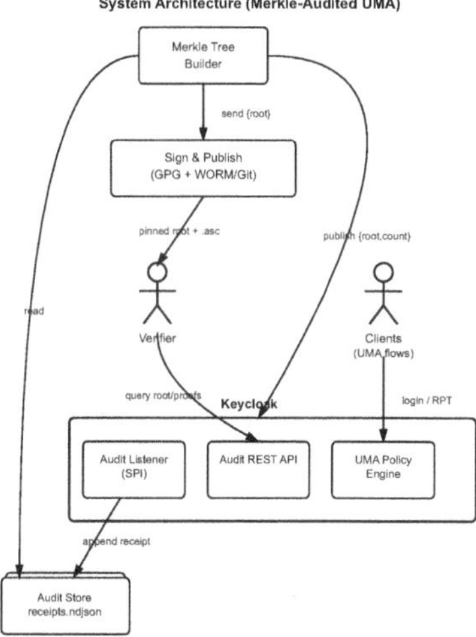

Fig. 1. System architecture showing Keycloak integration and the Merkle auditing pipeline. Complements the workflow in Fig. 2.

4. **Batching and commitment:** At fixed intervals (hourly in our prototype), the *Merkle Builder* processes all receipts written since the last batch. Each salted receipt is hashed into a leaf node, and the leaves are recursively hashed until a single root is produced. The tuple $\langle batch\_id, root, count, \rangle$ forms the batch commitment.
5. **Publication:** The batch commitment is published by the *Audit REST API*. This exposes both batch metadata (as identifier, root hash, number of receipts) and a download endpoint for the raw receipts.
6. **Verification:** A verifier retrieves both receipts and the Merkle root. Using an independent client (our reference Python script `06_verify_proof.py`), the verifier recomputes the root and compares it to the published value. Equality of roots proves integrity and completeness.

In addition to the six steps above, an automated *sign & publish* step runs at batch close: the Merkle Builder emits $\langle batchId, root, count \rangle$, a signer process creates `batchId.json` and a detached signature `batchId.json.asc`, and both artifacts are pushed to an append-only store.

3.3 Receipt Schema

Each audit unit is represented as a *Receipt*, constructed in Java. The receipt captures the essential context of an authentication or authorization event and augments it with a random 128-bit salt to ensure uniqueness and resistance to precomputation attacks. Table 1 summarizes the schema as implemented.

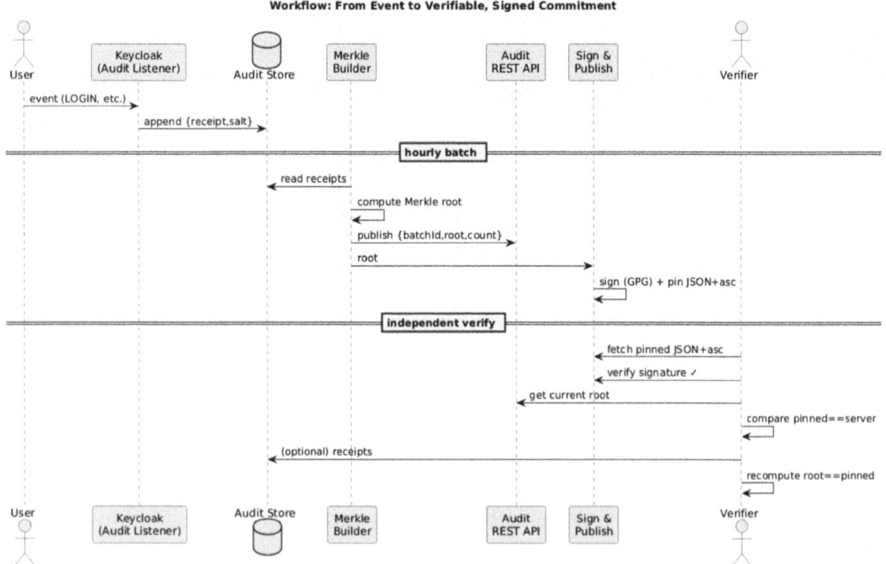

Fig. 2. Workflow from event generation to verifiable proof of integrity.

Canonicalization. To ensure deterministic hashing, the payload is serialized as JSON using a fixed key order (`LinkedHashMap`) and UTF-8 encoding. Escaping rules are applied consistently, producing a canonical byte sequence that is stable across platforms and runtimes.

Privacy Considerations. The current receipt schema is a proof-of-concept designed to validate the cryptographic mechanisms. In production deployments, fields such as `sub` and `scope` can be adapted using privacy-preserving techniques: subject identifiers can be hashed, scopes can be generalized, and access to receipts can be restricted through Keycloak's authorization policies. The Merkle tree structure naturally supports selective disclosure—sensitive fields can be replaced with hash commitments while preserving inclusion verification, aligning with GDPR's data minimization requirements.

3.4 Merkle Tree Construction

Receipts are not stored individually but are grouped into hourly batches and committed using a Merkle tree. The design follows the classical Merkle construction, with implementation refinements to support efficient proof generation and verification.

Leaf Derivation. For each receipt r_i, the canonical JSON bytes R_i (see Sect. 3.3) are combined with the 128-bit salt S_i. To prevent type confusion between receipts and internal nodes, a domain separation tag is prepended. The leaf hash is thus:

Table 1. Receipt fields

Name	Type	Semantics
`client_id`	string	OAuth2/OIDC client that triggered the event (e.g., UMA requester).
`event_type`	string	Event category (e.g., `LOGIN`, `CODE_TO_TOKEN`, `RPT_REQUEST`).
`pt`	string	UMA permission ticket (if applicable), else empty string.
`realm`	string	Keycloak realm where the event occurred.
`rid`	string	Request identifier/correlation id (if available).
`rpt_hash`	string	Hash/fingerprint of the issued UMA RPT (if applicable).
`scope`	string	Requested/issued scopes (e.g., `profile email`).
`sub`	string	Subject identifier of the end user (if present).
`ts`	integer (epoch)	Event timestamp (seconds since Unix epoch).
`ver`	string	Schema version (`"v1"` in the current implementation).
`salt`	`byte[16]`	128-bit random salt generated via `SecureRandom`; serialized as base64 in storage.

$$\ell_i = \text{SHA-256}(\texttt{TAG\_LEAF} \,\|\, R_i \,\|\, S_i),$$

where `TAG_LEAF` is a single distinguishing byte (`0x00`).

Node Construction. Internal nodes are built recursively from pairs of child nodes. For left child h_L and right child h_R:

$$h = \text{SHA-256}(\texttt{TAG\_NODE} \,\|\, h_L \,\|\, h_R),$$

with `TAG_NODE` set to `0x01`. If a level contains an odd number of nodes, the last hash is carried up unchanged rather than duplicated, preserving the exact set of inputs.

Batch Commitment. The final root is the batch commitment. Each batch is represented by a tuple:

$$\langle \mathit{batchId}, \mathit{root}, \mathit{count} \rangle,$$

where `batchId` is the Coordinated Universal Time (UTC) hour identifier , `root` is the Merkle root, and `count` is the number of receipts.

Inclusion Proofs. The implementation generates proofs for individual receipts via a minimal authentication path. For a leaf at position i, the proof consists of:

- the sequence of sibling hashes along the path to the root,
- a left/right indicator for each step.

Verification. Given a receipt leaf ℓ_i and its Merkle proof, verification consists of recomputing the chain of hashes along the path to the root.

Let the proof consist of k sibling nodes $(s_1, s_2, \dots, s_k)$. We initialize:

$$y_0 = \ell_i$$

and iteratively compute for $1 \leq j \leq k$:

$$y_j = \begin{cases} H(y_{j-1} \,\|\, s_j) & \text{if } y_{j-1} \text{ is a left child,} \\ H(s_j \,\|\, y_{j-1}) & \text{if } y_{j-1} \text{ is a right child.} \end{cases}$$

After processing all k siblings, the verifier checks:

$$\texttt{verify}(\ell_i, proof, root) \equiv (y_k = root).$$

Equality confirms that ℓ_i is included in the batch committed by the published Merkle root. Any tampering with the receipt or omission of nodes would invalidate the equality.

Properties. This construction ensures that:

- every receipt is cryptographically bound to the published root,
- inclusion can be verified independently by end users without full access to all receipts,
- any tampering, omission, or reordering of receipts changes the root and invalidates proofs,
- the domain separation tags eliminate ambiguity between leaves and nodes, hardening the scheme against collision-based forgeries.

3.5 Keycloak Integration via SPI

Keycloak exposes *Service Provider Interfaces (SPIs)* to allow external modules to extend its core functionality without patching or recompilation. We implement our verifiable auditing extension as a custom SPI, which hooks into Keycloak's event bus and intercepts relevant events before they are passed to the default logger. Using SPI provides three main benefits:

The implementation is packaged as `kc-uma-audit.jar` in `/opt/keycloak/providers` and is discovered at runtime without modifying Keycloak.

4 Verification Mechanism

The verification mechanism enables independent confirmation of event integrity using only public artifacts (receipts, commitments, proofs), ensuring the Keycloak operator cannot tamper undetected.

4.1 Full-Batch Verification

Full-batch verification ensures that *all* receipts belonging to a batch are authentic and complete. The main steps of the verification process are:

1. Parse and canonicalize each receipt using the deterministic JSON rules described earlier.
2. Derive salted leaf hashes for all receipts.
3. Rebuild the Merkle tree locally and recompute the root, denoted $root'$.
4. Compare $root'$ with the server-published root in `batch.json`.

Equality $root' = root$ proves that the receipts were not modified, omitted, or reordered after commitment.

4.2 Inclusion Proofs

While full-batch verification is exhaustive, end users often only care about their own events. Recomputing the entire batch may be inefficient in such cases. To address this, the system supports *inclusion proofs*, allowing a verifier to check a single receipt against the Merkle root without processing the entire batch.

An inclusion proof consists of:

- the canonical JSON payload R_i and salt S_i of the receipt,
- a sequence of sibling hashes $(s_1, \ldots, s_k)$,
- and left/right position indicators $(p_1, \ldots, p_k)$.

The verifier starts by computing the leaf:

$$y_0 = \text{SHA-256}(\texttt{TAG\_LEAF} \,\|\, R_i \,\|\, S_i).$$

Then, for each sibling s_j and position p_j, iteratively:

$$y_j = \begin{cases} \text{SHA-256}(\texttt{TAG\_NODE} \,\|\, y_{j-1} \,\|\, s_j), & \text{if } p_j = \texttt{LEFT}, \\ \text{SHA-256}(\texttt{TAG\_NODE} \,\|\, s_j \,\|\, y_{j-1}), & \text{if } p_j = \texttt{RIGHT}. \end{cases}$$

After k steps, the verifier checks:

$$y_k \stackrel{?}{=} root.$$

Equality confirms that the receipt ℓ_i was indeed included in the batch. Any tampering or omission invalidates the proof.

4.3 Commitment Publication, Signing, and Independent Verification

To prevent undetected server-side rewriting, each batch commitment is *pinned and signed* at batch closure. The Merkle Builder emits $\langle batchId, root, count\rangle$; a signer then creates a JSON file (`batchId.json`) with a detached GPG signature (`batchId.json.asc`) stored in an append-only location (e.g., Git or WORM). The public key is distributed out-of-band for anyone to authenticate the commitment.

We pin each `batchId.json` with a detached GPG signature, verify the signature, compare server vs. pinned roots, and optionally recompute the root from receipts. The signing key must be protected by operational policy—production systems should use HSMs or KMS-backed keys with automated rotation.

A batch passes verification if and only if all three checks succeed: (i) **Authenticity** – the detached signature over `batchId.json` verifies; (ii) **Consistency** – the current server root matches the pinned root; (iii) **Integrity** – the locally recomputed root equals the pinned root. Failures of (iii), (ii), or (i) respectively indicate local tampering, server rewriting, or commitment forgery.

4.4 Threat Model

We assume an honest-but-curious or malicious server operator after batch closure, a network attacker with read access to published artifacts, and uncompromised cryptographic primitives (SHA-256, GPG signatures). During an open batch window we assume a single trusted writer to the append-only store; after closure, tampering is detected by recomputation, root comparison, and signature verification.

4.5 Batch Lifecycle and Compliance

The append-only design ensures tamper evidence but does not address data retention or deletion requirements. To support GDPR Article 17 (right to erasure) [2], deleted receipts can be replaced with placeholder hashes that maintain the Merkle tree structure while marking batches as "partially redacted" in metadata. Alternatively, a separate revocation log can record deletion requests, allowing verifiers to filter receipts client-side without breaking cryptographic integrity. Cross-batch linking (embedding the previous batch's root in each commitment) or external anchoring detects unauthorized reordering or mixing of batches.

4.6 Security Properties

The proposed solution provides:

- **End-to-end transparency:** Anyone with access to receipts and roots can perform verification independently.
- **Tamper evidence:** Any modification, removal, or reordering of receipts changes the recomputed root.
- **Minimal trust assumption:** The verifier only trusts SHA-256 and canonicalization rules, not the Keycloak operator.

5 Evaluation

We evaluated the prototype on real Keycloak event data using representative batches. Experiments covered baseline verification (confirming published roots match recomputed values), tamper detection (flagging corrupted receipts), and commitment pinning (detecting rewrites via GPG signatures). Results demonstrate that layered protections—local recomputation, inclusion proofs, and signed commitments—provide transparent, auditable, and tamper-evident trails.

5.1 Comparison with Per-Receipt Signatures

An intuitive alternative to Merkle-based commitments is to apply a digital signature to each receipt individually. While straightforward, this approach introduces several trade-offs compared to batch-level commitments:

- **Storage overhead:** Each receipt signature (64–96 bytes) significantly increases log size in high-volume IAM systems, whereas Merkle commitments only add a small salt per receipt and a single root per batch.
- **Verification complexity:** Signature-based schemes prove authenticity but not *completeness*, since omitted events leave no trace. Merkle roots bind the entire batch, ensuring detection of additions, removals, or reordering.
- **Proof size and efficiency:** Inclusion proofs grow logarithmically with batch size (e.g., 16 hashes for 2^{16} receipts), far smaller than verifying thousands of individual signatures.
- **Commitment publication:** A single batch root can be pinned and signed once for external audits, while per-receipt signatures require archiving every entry, making transparency less scalable.
- **Security guarantees:** Both rely on strong cryptography, but Merkle trees add *set integrity*, preventing selective omission of events.

Per-receipt signatures ensure authenticity of individual events, but only Merkle-based commitments achieve completeness, scalability, and efficiency. Combined with signed publication, they are better suited for IAM audit trails.

5.2 Performance and Storage Overhead

Test Environment and Storage Overhead. Experiments were conducted on a Lenovo Legion Pro 7 (Intel i7-14700HX @ 5.5GHz, 32GB RAM, NVMe SSD) running Keycloak 25.0.6 with OpenJDK 17.0.2. Each receipt occupies 220 bytes (204B JSON + 16B salt). A 3-receipt batch totals 2.1KB including proofs and metadata. The Merkle root adds only 32 bytes per batch regardless of size. Daily storage for 1,000 events: 220KB receipts + 768B for 24 hourly roots.

Storage Overhead. Each receipt occupies approximately 220 bytes in NDJSON format: 204 bytes for the canonicalized JSON payload (10 fixed fields) plus 16 bytes for the random salt (base64-encoded to 24 characters). A representative 3-receipt batch (`2025-09-22T08:00Z.json`) totals 2.1KB including entries, inclusion proofs (3 proofs $\times$ 150 bytes), and batch metadata (root hash + count). Per-receipt storage overhead is dominated by the salt (16 bytes) and canonical JSON structure; the Merkle commitment itself adds only 32 bytes (SHA-256 root) per batch, regardless of batch size. A deployment processing 1,000 events daily would require approximately 220KB for receipts plus 32 bytes per hourly batch (24 batches $\times$ 32 bytes = 768 bytes), yielding a total of 220KB daily storage.

Computation Overhead. Building a batch with n receipts costs $2n - 1$ SHA-256 hashes; in practice, $\sim 10^3$ receipts build in tens of milliseconds.

Verification Overhead. Full-batch verification mirrors construction (tens of milliseconds for $\sim 10^3$ receipts). Inclusion proofs verify in $O(\log n)$ hashes and are a few hundred bytes.

Scalability. Storage scales $O(n)$, computation $O(n)$ for construction, $O(\log n)$ for proofs. A deployment with 100K daily events requires 22MB storage and 200ms hourly builds, demonstrating enterprise feasibility.

Comparison to Per-Receipt Signatures. A 256-bit ECDSA signature adds 64 bytes per receipt (DER encoding). For 1,000 receipts, signature storage totals 64KB versus 32 bytes for a single Merkle root—a 2,000× reduction. Signature generation on the test platform takes approximately 100–200µs per receipt (hardware-dependent), yielding 100–200ms for 1,000 receipts versus 20ms for Merkle construction. Verification of 1,000 individual signatures requires 100–200ms, while Merkle inclusion proofs verify in 50µs—a 2,000–4,000× speedup. Moreover, per-receipt signatures cannot detect selective omission of events, whereas Merkle roots commit to the entire batch set. These measurements confirm that Merkle-based commitments provide superior efficiency and completeness guarantees for IAM audit trails.

6 Conclusion

In this paper we showed that verifiable audit trails can be added to a mainstream IAM platform with modest changes and no external infrastructure. Our solution records authentication and authorization events as salted receipts, commits them by hour with a Merkle tree, and exposes both batch roots and inclusion proofs via a REST API. We complemented cryptographic structure with operational assurances: an automated sign-and-publish step pins each batch commitment and a lightweight toolchain performs three independent checks—signature authenticity, server–pinned consistency, and local recomputation.

Experiments on real event streams demonstrate that the system detects single-field edits, selective rewrites of server history, and tampering with published commitments. Compared to per-receipt signatures, the design provides batch completeness, logarithmic-size inclusion proofs, and minimal storage overhead, better matching IAM volumes and user-centric verification.

Future work: external transparency anchoring, stronger key management (HSM/KMS, rotation, multi-sig), and privacy-preserving inclusion proofs.

Acknowledgment. This research was funded by Executive Agency for Higher Education, Research, Development and Innovation Funding (UEFISCDI), Romania, grant number 39PTE/2025.

References

1. Keycloak. https://www.keycloak.org/, Accessed 08 Oct 2025
2. Article 17 GDPR – Right to erasure ('right to be forgotten'). https://gdpr-info.eu/art-17-gdpr/ (2018), Accessed 08 Oct 2025
3. Aciobanitei, I., Dedita, V., Pura, M.L., Patriciu, V.V.: Sabres - a proof of concept for enhanced cloud qualified electronic signatures. In: 2020 13th International Conference on Communications (COMM), pp. 103–108 (2020). https://doi.org/10.1109/COMM48946.2020.9141954
4. Al-Khouri, A.M.: Optimizing identity and access management (IAM) frameworks. Int. J. Eng. Res. Appl. **1**(3), 461–477 (2011)
5. Arseni, S.C., Bureaca, E., Aciobanitei, I.: Digital signatures long-term preservation services, IPFS and blockchain are a good match. In: 2024 15th International Conference on Communications (COMM), pp. 1–6 (2024). https://doi.org/10.1109/COMM62355.2024.10741494
6. Divyabharathi, D., Cholli, N.G.: A review on identity and access management server (keycloak). Int. J. Secur. Priv. Pervasive Comput. (IJSPPC) **12**(3), 46–53 (2020)
7. Ghadge, N.: Enhancing threat detection in identity and access management (iam) systems. Int. J. Sci. Res. Archive **11**(2), 2050–2057 (2024)
8. Ghadge, N.: Use of blockchain technology to strengthen identity and access management (IAM). Int. J. Inf. Technol. **1**(3) (2024)
9. Hamza, M.K., Abubakar, H., Danlami, Y.M.: Identity and access management system: a web-based approach for an enterprise. Traektoriâ Nauki= Path of Science **4**(11), 2001–2011 (2018)
10. Ionacu, B.D., Aciobăniţei, I.: Enriching an open-source access management platform using multi-factor authentication. In: 2024 IEEE 18th International Symposium on Applied Computational Intelligence and Informatics (SACI), pp. 383–388 (2024). https://doi.org/10.1109/SACI60582.2024.10619788
11. Ionacu, B.D., Aciobăniţei, I.: Ketop - a keycloak extension for totp. In: 2024 Advanced Topics on Measurement and Simulation (ATOMS), pp. 240–243 (2024). https://doi.org/10.1109/ATOMS60779.2024.10921549
12. Ionacu, B.D., Aciobăniţei, I.: Scawa: enabling smart card authentication for web applications. In: 2024 16th International Conference on Electronics, Computers and Artificial Intelligence (ECAI), pp. 1–5 (2024). https://doi.org/10.1109/ECAI61503.2024.10607461
13. Jipianu, T.M., Aciobanitei, I.: An implementation for secure data deduplication on end-to-end encrypted documents. In: 2024 IEEE 18th International Symposium on Applied Computational Intelligence and Informatics (SACI)., pp. 303–308 (2024). https://doi.org/10.1109/SACI60582.2024.10619071
14. Kubigenova, A., Aktayeva, A., Yesmagambetova, G., Sukhomlin, V., Umbetov, A.: Merkle tree: a fundamental component of big data. Int. J. Open Inf. Technol. **13**(1), 61–70 (2025)
15. Kumar, K., Zolkipli, M.F.: A review on identity and access management (iam) for digital environment security. Borneo Int. J. eISSN 2636-9826 **7**(4), 43–48 (2024)
16. Kuznetsov, O., Rusnak, A., Yezhov, A., Kuznetsova, K., Kanonik, D., Domin, O.: Merkle trees in blockchain: a study of collision probability and security implications. Internet of Things **26**, 101193 (2024)
17. Liu, H., Luo, X., Liu, H., Xia, X.: Merkle tree: a fundamental component of blockchains. In: 2021 International Conference on Electronic Information Engineering and Computer Science (EIECS), pp. 556–561. IEEE (2021)

18. Liu, Z., Wang, S., Duan, S., Ren, L., Wei, J.: Dynamic data integrity auditing based on hierarchical merkle hash tree in cloud storage. Electronics **12**(3), 717 (2023). https://doi.org/10.3390/electronics12030717
19. Maler, E.: Controlling data usage with user-managed access (UMA). In: W3C Privacy and Data Usage Control Workshop. W3C (2010). http://www.w3.org/2010/policy-ws/papers/18-Maler-Paypal.pdf
20. Mohammed, I.A.: Cloud identity and access management-a model proposal. Int. J. Innov. Eng. Res. Technol. **6**(10), 1–8 (2019)
21. Olabanji, S.O., Olaniyi, O.O., Adigwe, C.S., Okunleye, O.J., Oladoyinbo, T.O.: Ai for identity and access management (IAM) in the cloud: Exploring the potential of artificial intelligence to improve user authentication, authorization, and access control within cloud-based systems. Authorization Access Control within Cloud-Based Systems (January 25, 2024) (2024)
22. Sai'd, Z.: Explainable AI (XAI) in identity access management: bridging trust and transparency in user authentication. Authorea Preprints (2025)
23. Sekar, R.R., Masna, A., Sharma, S., Abraham, A., Pagilla, P.R.: Decentralized identity and access management (IAM) using blockchain. In: 2024 International Conference on Intelligent Systems for Cybersecurity (ISCS), pp. 1–6. IEEE (2024)
24. Sharma, D.H., Dhote, C., Potey, M.M.: Identity and access management as security-as-a-service from clouds. Procedia Comput. Sci. **79**, 170–174 (2016)
25. Szydlo, M.: Merkle tree traversal in log space and time. In: International Conference on the Theory and Applications of Cryptographic Techniques, pp. 541–554. Springer (2004)
26. Thorgersen, S., Silva, P.I.: Keycloak-identity and access management for modern applications. Packt Publishing Limited (2023)
27. Vitla, S.: The future of identity and access management: leveraging AI for enhanced security and efficiency. J. Comput. Sci. Technol. Stud. **6**(3), 136–154 (2024)

Rust in the Kernel: A Practical Evaluation on Windows

Cătălin Cot[1,2](✉), Radu Portase[1,2], and Adrian Coleşa[1,2]

[1] Technical University of Cluj-Napoca, Cluj-Napoca, Romania
catalin.cot.research@gmail.com,
{radu.portase,adrian.colesa}@campus.utcluj.ro
[2] Bitdefender, Bucharest, Romania
{ccot,rportase,acolesa}@bitdefender.com

Abstract. Modern Windows kernel drivers, traditionally written in C, are prone to memory-safety bugs that could lead to security exploits and system instability. This paper evaluates the use of the Rust programming language for Windows driver development, by building safe abstractions around native kernel structures and APIs. A ProcMon-like driver has been developed to capture filesystem events and send them to user-mode components. We document the complete build and debug workflow, analyze crash diagnostics across Rust and C implementations, and evaluate runtime overhead through micro-benchmarks.

Keywords: Windows kernel · drivers · Rust

1 Introduction

Memory vulnerabilities continue to pose a significant threat to kernel-mode driver security, particularly on Windows. For example, CVE-2018-8120 [4] leveraged a use-after-free bug, while CVE-2020-17087 [5] exploited a buffer overflow to escalate privileges in the Windows kernel. Until now, C has been the default choice for kernel development, due to its fine-grained memory control and direct hardware interaction, but it lacks built-in protections against buffer overflows, use-after-free errors, or integer overflows.

In response, traditional defenses such as Address Space Layout Randomization (ASLR), Data Execution Prevention (DEP), and static analysis tools have been introduced, yet they address only certain error classes. Rust's ownership model and type system shift many checks to compile time, preventing the most common memory and concurrency bugs before they occur at runtime.

Although Rust is gaining traction in user-mode and embedded domains, its adoption for critical Windows drivers remains at a pilot stage, due to an unofficial toolchain, ABI challenges, and the need to interoperate with existing kernel APIs.

Microsoft's open source `windows-drivers-rs` [17] project has started providing Rust support for kernel-mode drivers. However, it is still in a pre-release

P. D'Arco and A. Zamfiroiu (Eds.): SecITC 2025, LNCS 16443, pp. 307–320, 2026.
https://doi.org/10.1007/978-3-032-17443-7_19

phase: documentation is sparse, the ABI is still experimental, and end-to-end build, sign, and deploy workflows are not yet standardized. These gaps around a stable toolchain, comprehensive examples, and deployment tooling motivate our systematic investigation. Accordingly, this paper evaluates Rust's feasibility for developing Windows kernel minifilter drivers. This study aims to answer the following questions:

1. To what extent does the Rust toolchain and ecosystem enable end-to-end development, signing, and deployment of a Windows minifilter driver?
2. How do Rust's compile-time error reports and runtime crash diagnostics compare with C in terms of fault localization precision and developer productivity?
3. What throughput and latency overheads does a Rust-based minifilter introduce under representative filesystem workloads (e.g., large file copy, file deletion, concurrent I/O)?

Building on the research questions, this work develops a Rust-based prototype filesystem activity monitor, drawing inspiration from Sysinternals' Process Monitor (ProcMon) [24] for its status as the de-facto filesystem tracing tool on Windows. The system consists of two components. A kernel-mode minifilter driver, using the Windows Driver Framework (WDF) and the `windows-kernel` Rust crate and a user-mode client, built also in Rust with the GUI library, which receives, formats, and displays events generated by the minifilter. To ensure transparency and reproducibility, the source code has been released at [2].

Our contributions are as follows:

- A detailed evaluation of the Rust developer experience for Windows kernel drivers, covering build reliability, debugging, and crash diagnostics.
- A systematic performance analysis measuring the runtime overhead of Rust's safety checks under representative filesystem workloads.
- A practical assessment of the current Rust ecosystem for Windows driver development, surfacing gaps in available crates, tooling maturity, and interoperability challenges.

The remainder of this paper is structured as follows: Sect. 3 introduces the theoretical background relevant to Windows kernel driver development. Section 2 reviews related work and highlights existing research gaps. Section 4 describes the system design, development process, and experimental setup. Section 5 presents the testing methodology, results, and performance analysis. Section 6 discusses the implications of the findings and the current limitations of the Rust ecosystem. Finally, Sect. 7 concludes the paper and outlines directions for future work.

2 Related Work

Research on Rust in kernel-mode development has focused primarily on the Linux ecosystem. Li *et al.* [10] proposed a Rust-based framework for embedded

Linux device drivers, demonstrating that memory-safety guarantees can significantly reduce the attack surface compared to traditional C implementations. While their work highlights the security potential of Rust, it is limited to Linux and does not address challenges specific to the Windows kernel environment, such as IRQL management, SEH integration, or Windows-specific APIs.

Early attempts to explore Rust in the Windows kernel context have been anecdotal and exploratory in nature. Götz [9] documented the process of writing a basic Windows kernel driver in Rust, identifying limitations related to toolchain immaturity, API bindings, and debugging difficulties. However, their work did not include any formal evaluation of performance or maintainability. Similarly, Eckels [7] described porting a tracing tool (STrace) to Windows using Rust, highlighting instability and compatibility problems when dealing with native Windows APIs. While useful as practical experiences, both studies lack empirical benchmarking or structured fault analysis.

In contrast, Microsoft has recently formalized its support for Rust in Windows driver development through the open-source `windows-drivers-rs` project [17]. This effort aims to provide safe abstractions over kernel APIs and enable Rust-based driver development using officially supported crates like `wdk-sys` and `windows-sys`. However, the ecosystem remains under active development, and many limitations such as lack of static analysis tools, incomplete IRQL modeling, and limited architecture support remains unresolved [21].

At a broader level, Microsoft's integration of Rust into the Windows 11 kernel [6] demonstrates growing institutional trust in the language for system-level programming. However, these announcements have yet to be matched by public empirical studies that evaluate Rust's impact on real-world Windows kernel driver development workflows, debugging capabilities, or runtime overhead. This is exactly what our work tries to do.

3 Theoretical Background

This section outlines key concepts relevant to Rust-based Windows kernel development, including memory safety, Windows driver architecture, and Rust's safety mechanisms. These foundations support the implementation and evaluation presented in later sections.

3.1 Windows Kernel Drivers and Minifilters

Windows kernel-mode drivers [23] are software components that run at ring 0, i.e. kernel-mode, and can intercept or extend the operating system's behaviour.

File system filter drivers, also known as *minifilters*, are optional drivers that attach to the file system software stack. They monitor, filter, and modify the behaviour of file I/O operations. Minifilter drivers can use communication ports to facilitate communication between user-mode (UM) applications and kernel-mode (KM) components. This mechanism is directly relevant to the present work, as the implemented driver uses a communication port to transmit captured filesystem events from the kernel to a user-mode client for further processing.

3.2 Rust's Safety Mechanisms and Kernel Constraints

Rust enforces memory safety at compile time through *ownership*, *borrowing*, and *lifetimes*. Its borrow checker guarantees exclusive or shared access without data races, and safe code cannot dereference dangling pointers. Developers may opt into *unsafe blocks* for kernel *foreign function interface* (FFI), but the boundary is explicit. Interfacing with low-level C APIs and system libraries in Rust requires the use of the FFI. Since these external calls bypass Rust's compile-time safety guarantees, they must be wrapped in unsafe blocks. Other unsafe operations in kernel development include dereferencing raw pointers or accessing untyped memory regions.

Another constraint is about *Structured Exception Handling* (SEH). Windows uses SEH to handle runtime errors, such as invalid memory access in both user and kernel space. Unlike C, Rust's native runtime does not implement SEH on Windows, so third-party crates such as *microseh* can be used to hook into it.

Beyond language-level safety, kernel-mode Rust must interoperate with the Windows debugging infrastructure.

3.3 Kernel Debugging and Symbol Inspection

Debugging kernel-mode drivers requires the use of specialized tools. One of the most widely used tools for Windows kernel debugging is *WinDbg* [16], part of the Windows Debugger suite. WinDbg enables developers to inspect kernel memory, set breakpoints, analyze crash dumps, and step through both C and Rust code when appropriate debug symbols (in `.pdb` files) are available. WinDbg automatically breaks into the debugger when a system bug check occurs, like a Blue Screen of Death (BSOD).

To enable live debugging of a virtual machine running a test driver, Microsoft provides KDNet [13], a network-based kernel debugging transport. With KDNet, WinDbg running on the host machine can connect to the guest's kernel over the network. These debugging facilities are used to validate correctness, performance, and diagnostics, as detailed in Sect. 4.

4 Methodology

This section outlines the design, development, and testing methodology for constructing our Rust-based Windows kernel driver. It covers the overall research design, system architecture, toolchain and build setup, data handling, and testing environments relevant to kernel-mode development. The methods chosen underline system reliability, safety, and maintainability while leveraging Rust's capabilities for low-level system programming.

4.1 Build System

The driver is built using the `wdk-build` [15] crate (version 0.4.0) provided by Microsoft, which automates compilation, signing, and packaging steps. This tool produces a `.sys` binary, an `.inf` setup file and a test certificate needed for installation on test-mode enabled systems.

Compiling and Linking. In traditional C-based Windows driver development, the build process is relatively straightforward, typically producing a `.sys` binary and an `.inf` installation file, without requiring special runtime configuration. When using C++, additional complexity arises. Windows kernel-mode drivers do not support C++ exceptions by default, and developers must explicitly turn off exception handling [12]. If exception support is enabled, compilation fails with an error.

In contrast, building in Rust is orchestrated using `cargo-make`, which invokes `wdk-build` to compile, link, and package the driver. While C++ kernel drivers may emit references to runtime support symbols, such as `__CxxFrameHandler3`, when exception handling is enabled, Rust exhibits similar behaviour due to its use of LLVM compiler framework. Even when stack unwinding is explicitly disabled via `panic = "abort"`, LLVM will emit references to this symbol. Likewise, the `_fltused` symbol may be emitted if LLVM detects the potential use of floating-point operations, even in soft-float configurations. To complete the linking process successfully, both symbols must be explicitly defined as stubs. The driver does not functionally use these definitions but are required to satisfy the linker:

ïż£

```
#[no_mangle]
pub static _fltused: () = ();
#[no_mangle]
pub extern "system" fn __CxxFrameHandler3() -> i32 { 0 }
```

Signing and Generating the Package. All drivers running on Windows must be signed before being loaded. This security measure ensures that no malicious drivers can be installed on the system. Enabling *test-mode* on the system can allow drivers with a test signature to be loaded.

The build system requires an `.inx` file, which is a template used to generate a `.inf` file.

Rust code is compiled as a dynamic-link library (`.dll`), using the `cdylib` [26] crate type. Since Windows expects drivers to use the `.sys` extension, the output is simply renamed. Finally, the driver is signed with a test certificate for use on machines with test-mode enabled.

Compiler Configuration and Runtime Constraints To satisfy the constraints of kernel-mode execution, the following settings are applied during compilation:

- `#[no_std]` is used to turn off Rust's standard library, which is unavailable in kernel space.

- `panic = "abort"` is specified in `Cargo.toml` to prevent stack unwinding.
- Only kernel-supported functions are statically linked to ensure compatibility with the Windows kernel execution model.

4.2 System Architecture

The system consists of two main components: a Rust minifilter driver running in kernel-mode and a user-mode application that receives, processes, and displays generated event data. The driver intercepts filesystem operations and turns them into events that are forwarded to the user-mode component, using a communication port. Figure 1 illustrates the inter-crate dependencies between kernel-mode and user-mode components of our system. It comprises both third-party libraries and custom crates developed as part of our research.

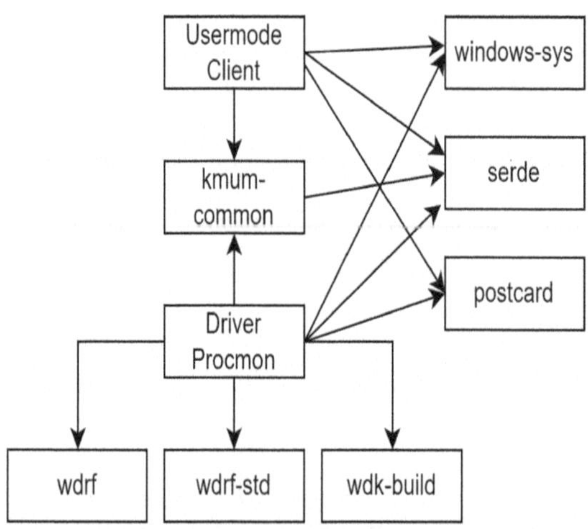

Fig. 1. Rust-based filesystem monitoring system.

We used the following third-party crates:

- `wdk-build` [15]: Microsoft-provided crate used to compile, sign, and package Windows kernel-mode drivers.
- `windows-sys` [18]: provides raw FFI bindings for calling Windows kernel functions and accessing native structures.
- `serde` [27] and `postcard` [20]: used for efficient, zero-allocation serialization and deserialization of event structures exchanged between kernel and user-mode.

We developed the following custom crates:

- kmum-common [2]: a shared crate defining data structures used in both user and kernel-mode, including event definitions and communication-related messages.
- wdrf [3]: a reusable crate offering safe abstractions for minifilter management, process callbacks, and kernel logging.
- wdrf-std [3]: a kernel-mode crate providing equivalents of standard Rust containers, tagged memory allocators, and safe wrappers for kernel synchronization primitives.

To illustrate the integration of the defined crates and abstractions, a side-by-side comparison of the driver is presented components implemented in C versus their Rust equivalents.

Defining the Driver Entry Point. Drivers must define the entry-point function named DriverEntry.

In C, the entry point is typically defined as:
ïż£

```
NTSTATUS DriverEntry(
    PDRIVER_OBJECT DriverObject,
    PUNICODE_STRING RegistryPath){...}
```

The Rust equivalent requires the use of the extern "system" calling convention to ensure compatibility with the Windows ABI. Additionally, the #[export_name= "DriverEntry"] attribute is needed to export the function and prevent symbol name mangling explicitly.
ïż£

```
#[export_name = "DriverEntry"]
pub unsafe extern "system" fn driver_entry(
    driver: &mut DRIVER_OBJECT,
    registry_path: &UNICODE_STRING,
) -> NTSTATUS {...}
```

Panic Handler. In Rust, panics are used to signal unrecoverable runtime errors. The compiler is configured to use panic = "abort", which requires a custom implementation of the panic handler.

In our project, the panic handler triggers a system bug check using the KeBugCheck function, causing an immediate system crash.

```
#[panic_handler]
fn panic(_: &PanicInfo) -> ! { unsafe { KeBugCheck(0x1234); } }
```

Memory Allocation and Tagging. Memory allocation functions in kernel-mode require a four-byte tag, which is used to track and validate memory during deallocation, and a flag that specifies if the memory should be allocated from a paged or non-paged pool.

Global Allocator. Due to the use of the `alloc` [25] crate and the `#[no_std]` environment, Rust requires a global allocator to be explicitly defined. This allocator must implement the `GlobalAlloc` trait. The `wdrf-std` crate provides a compliant implementation called `GlobalKernelAllocator`. An example usage of the global allocator is shown below:

ïż£

```
#[global_allocator]
pub static ALLOC: GlobalKernelAllocator = GlobalKernelAllocator::new(..);
```

The `alloc` crate provides types like `Box`, `Vec`, and `Arc`, but these rely on the global allocator. In kernel-mode, their use should be avoided, because if allocation fails they panic and crash the system.

To solve this, the `wdrf-std` crate defines the `TaggedObject` trait, which lets each type specify its memory tag and allocation flags. Smart pointers such as `Box` and `Arc`, as well as `Vec`, are extended with safe methods like `try_create` and `try_push`. These use a custom allocator based on the trait and return errors on allocation failure, letting the developer handle them safely without a system crash.

Communication Registration and Callbacks. The `wdrf` [3] crate provides a safe abstraction over Filter Port APIs [11].

In C, the input and output buffers received from user mode are passed as raw pointers, leaving it up to the developer to respect their intended usage. In Rust, the input buffer is represented as `&[u8]` (read-only) and the output buffer as `&mut [u8]` (read-write). By encoding these constraints in the type system, Rust makes buffer semantics explicit and can prevent issues such as writing to input data at compile time.

Minifilter Registration and Callbacks. In `DriverEntry`, a minifilter driver registers with the filter manager and provides callbacks. The example below shows the pre-operation callback in C and its Rust-based abstraction.

ïż£

```
FLT_POSTOP_CALLBACK_STATUS
FilterPreCreate(
    _Inout_ PFLT_CALLBACK_DATA Data,
    _In_ PCFLT_RELATED_OBJECTS FltObjects,
    _Outptr_result_maybenull_ PVOID *CompletionContext
) { // Pre-processing logic }
```

This is the Rust-based callback.

ïż£

```
fn call_pre(
    data: FltCallbackData<'a>,
    related_obj: FltRelatedObjects<'a>,
    params: FltParameters<'a>,
) -> PreOpStatus<PostContext> { // Pre-processing logic }
```

Discussion. There are several key differences between the traditional C minifilter model and the Rust-based abstraction:

- **Safe access to operation parameters.** In C, you manually inspect the FLT_PARAMETERS union and picking the wrong field can cause Undefined Behavior. Rust replaces that union with a tagged enum, so only the correct variant is accessed.
- **Lifetime safety of callback arguments.** In C, PFLT_CALLBACK_DATA and PCFLT_RELATED_OBJECTS are only valid within the callback scope but nothing stops you from using them later. Rust attaches explicit lifetimes (e.g., 'a) to these parameters, making any out-of-scope use a compile-time error.
- **Context management.** In C, you pass a void* between pre and post operation, manually allocate, cast, and free it. Rust's PostOpContext<T> wrapper encodes ownership and enforces correct allocation, transfer, and cleanup between callbacks.

5 Tests, Results and Analysis

5.1 Testing Methodology

The goal of testing was to evaluate the safety, debuggability, stability, and performance characteristics of the Rust-based minifilter driver and compare them to those of a minimal C-based equivalent. The evaluation focused on the clarity of crash diagnostics under common failure conditions, and runtime performance overhead.

Crash behaviour and debuggability were assessed by deliberately introducing faults into the driver code to trigger system crashes, followed by an analysis of the resulting kernel dumps.

Three different configurations were used for performance testing: a baseline with no driver, a C-based minifilter, and a Rust-based implementation. For performance assessment, the third-party `fileop.exe` utility from the IoZone [22] test suite was used to generate consistent file system workloads. Tests were repeated multiple times to ensure stable and representative results.

5.2 Test Environment and Setup

All testing, debugging, benchmarks and crash tests were conducted inside a virtual machine. The VM is configured with Windows 11 x64 with test-mode enabled to load test-signed drivers during development. The VM was configured with 8 GB of RAM and 8 virtual CPU cores, hosted on a physical machine equipped with an Intel Core i7-8700K processor [1]. Virtualization was performed using VMware Workstation 17 [28]. To reduce system noise and ensure reliable measurements, several background services were turned off during testing, including Windows Update, Windows Defender (along with Windows Firewall), and the Windows Search Indexer.

For kernel-mode debugging, KDNet and WinDbg were used to monitor the system and analyze crashes. Driver Verifier was enabled on the guest during testing.

Test Results

Safety and Debuggability in Rust vs. C. The following aspects were tested: **Compile-Time Error Detection and Use-After-Free Prevention**, **Compile-Time and Runtime Assertions in Rust**, and **Buffer Overflow Detection**. Rust's borrow checker ensures that once an object is moved or dropped it cannot be used again, preventing use-after-free bugs that C allows. Rust also adds runtime checks: in debug builds it detects integer overflows, and at runtime it enforces slice bounds, panicking on out-of-bounds access. In C, none of these are enforced, leading to silent bugs or undefined behavior.

Performance Results. To measure the Rust-based driver's performance impact, synthetic filesystem microbenchmarks were run against two baselines: a minimal C minifilter driver and a system without filter drivers.

The C driver was written specifically for this test and mimics the Rust driver's logic in its callbacks. No client connections were used, isolating the overhead of the driver itself and its interaction with the filter manager.

Benchmarks were run with `fileop.exe` using: `fileop.exe -f 10 -s 256K -b -w -t`. Here, `-f 10` creates 10^3 files, `-s 256K` sets each file size to 256 KB, `-b` and `-w` enable best- and worst-case writes, and `-t` outputs verbose timings.

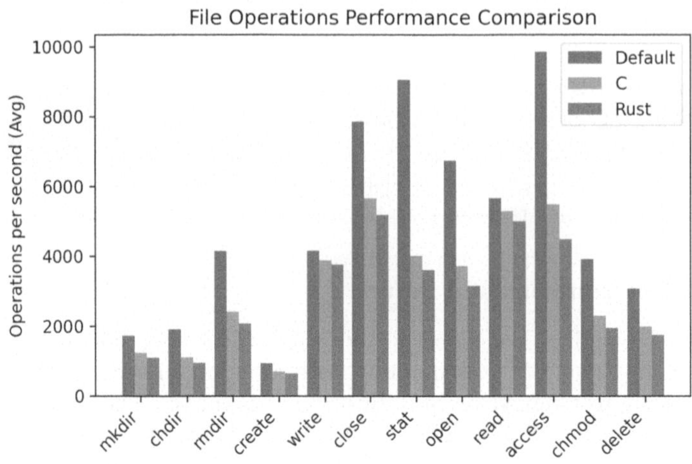

Fig. 2. Performance comparison of file system operations across three configurations: no driver, C driver, and Rust driver.

The benchmark covers directory creation, file creation, read/write access, metadata queries, and deletions. The results shown in Fig. 2 report the measured throughput for these operations.

Each benchmark was executed multiple times per scenario to reduce the noise generated by the virtualized test environment. Across most operations, Rust and C drivers introduce a modest performance hit relative to the baseline (no driver). In all scenarios, the performance difference between Rust and C is minimal. This slight variance can be attributed to two main factors. Firstly, the C driver was intentionally simplified and lacks certain checks and abstractions present in the Rust implementation. Secondly, the Rust implementation wraps minifilter callbacks and system objects in safe Rust abstractions, introducing a small amount of additional overhead.

The results show that the Rust driver performance is on par with the C implementation while providing stronger memory safety guarantees.

6 Discussion

FFI Struct Compatibility Issues. The `windows-sys` Rust crate provided FFI bindings to Windows C for most structures and functions available for development. Internally, the `windows-sys` crate uses bindgen to automate the mapping from C struct to Rust equivalent. To prevent undefined behavior, members of the generated structures must have the same offset and alignment as their C counterparts. Unfortunately, bindgen ignores the C POINTER_ALIGNMENT macro, which tells the C compiler to align that member pointer to 8 bytes, resulting in misaligned Rust structures.

Problems Rust Can Solve in Kernel Development. Rust's memory model can help prevent common vulnerabilities, such as buffer overflows, double frees, and use-after-free. Additionally, using Option and Result for error handling made failure paths unavoidable and visible at compile time. Rust's type system enforces structure around otherwise unsafe APIs. For example, FltParameter, a union, was safely abstracted using Rust enums, enabling type-checked access to variant-specific fields without the risk of accessing the wrong member.

Development was also accelerated by integrating with the hashbrown (for efficient hashmaps), serde, and postcard for serialization (for compact, zero-allocation serialization). These tools allowed for data serialization without needing to manually write serialization logic while still maintaining safety and performance constraints suitable for a kernel environment.

Problems Rust Cannot Fully Solve. Despite its strengths, Rust does not eliminate all classes of kernel bugs as seen in Table 1. Interfacing with the Windows kernel still requires extensive use of *unsafe* in Rust, especially when calling C functions. These unsafe sections are necessary, but they form the boundaries where memory safety guarantees no longer hold. Although a good portion of them can be encapsulated inside Rust-safe constructs, unsafe logic is

Table 1. Observed limitations and mitigation strategies in Rust-based driver development

Limitation	Impact and Mitigation
No IRQL Enforcement	Rust lacks static IRQL validation
No SEH Support	Kernel-mode exceptions cannot be caught natively in Rust. The `microseh` crate was used to wrap C-level `__try`/`__except`
No Static Analysis Tools	Tools like `CodeQL` [8] and `SDV` [14] are not yet applicable to Rust kernel drivers
Limited Architecture Support	The `wdk-build` crate supports only `x64` and `ARM64`. Building for `x86` is currently not supported [15]
FFI Struct Misalignment	Bindings generated via `bindgen` ignored alignment macros (e.g., `POINTER_ALIGNMENT`), leading to undefined behavior. Fixed by manually redefining aligned fields using `repr(align)` wrappers
No API Version Guards	The `windows-sys` crate does not verify API availability by Windows version. Developers must manually ensure compatibility with older systems
No C Macro Bindings	`bindgen` does not generate bindings for complex C macros, including function-like macros and inline functions. These must be manually rewritten in Rust as `const` values or inline functions

still required in any meaningful driver implementation. Furthermore, Rust cannot prevent logical bugs, deadlocks, or misuse of kernel interfaces. While Rust enforces memory safety within its own driver's code, it cannot protect against memory corruption caused by other faulty or malicious drivers. In the shared memory space of the Windows kernel [19], another driver can overwrite memory regions used by Rust code, breaking its safety guarantees. Thus, Rust reduces internal bugs but cannot ensure complete isolation from external faults.

This project focused on a specific class of driver, a filesystem monitoring, leaving other categories, such as device drivers or KMDF-based components, untested. Rust code can be debugged due to WinDbg support.

7 Conclusion

Writing Windows drivers in Rust presents a number of practical challenges, primarily due to the immaturity of the toolchain and the ongoing development of core libraries and ecosystem support. Components such as build tooling, kernel API bindings, and debugging infrastructure are still evolving, often requiring workarounds or manual configuration to achieve functionality comparable to traditional C-based workflows.

Despite these limitations, Rust proves to be a viable and promising option for kernel development. Its strong compile-time guarantees eliminate entire classes of memory-related bugs, and its modern language features can accelerate development by reducing boilerplate and improving code clarity. As the ecosystem grows, Rust is well-positioned to become a safer alternative for building Windows kernel drivers, especially in security-critical contexts.

References

1. Corporation, I.: Intel® core™ i7-8700k processor (12m cache, up to 4.70 ghz) – specifications (2024). https://www.intel.com/content/www/us/en/products/sku/126684/intel-core-i78700k-processor-12m-cache-up-to-4-70-ghz/specifications.html
2. Cot, C.: Procmon-rust: A safe rust-based windows minifilter driver (2025). https://github.com/CotCatalin15/procmon-rust
3. Cot, C.: wdrf: Safe abstractions for windows minifilter driver development (2025). https://github.com/CotCatalin15/windows-driver-rust-framework
4. CVE Program: CVE-2018-8120: Windows Win32k Elevation of Privilege Vulnerability (2018). https://msrc.microsoft.com/update-guide/vulnerability/CVE-2018-8120
5. CVE Program: CVE-2020-17087: Windows Kernel Local Elevation of Privilege (2020). https://msrc.microsoft.com/update-guide/vulnerability/CVE-2020-17087
6. Ddos: Rust lands in windows 11 kernel: A new era for os security? (2024). https://securityonline.info/rust-lands-in-windows-11-kernel-a-new-era-for-os-security/
7. Eckels, S.: Strace – a dtrace on windows reimplementation (2022). https://media.defcon.org/DEF%20CON%2030/DEF%20CON%2030%20presentations/Stephen%20Eckels%20-%20STrace%20-%20A%20DTrace%20on%20windows%20reimplementation.pdf. https://github.com/eckelsjd/strace-rs
8. GitHub: Codeql: Semantic code analysis engine (2024). https://codeql.github.com/
9. Götz, M.: Writing a kernel driver with rust (2022). https://not-matthias.github.io/kernel-driver-with-rust/
10. Li, E.A.: Securing the device drivers of your embedded systems. In: Proceedings of the 14th International Conference on Availability, Reliability and Security (ARES '19) (2019). https://doi.org/10.1145/3339252.3340506
11. Microsoft: Create flt communication port (2024). https://learn.microsoft.com/en-us/windows-hardware/drivers/ddi/fltkernel/nf-fltkernel-fltcreatecommunicationport
12. Microsoft: Handling exceptions in windows drivers (2024). https://learn.microsoft.com/en-us/windows-hardware/drivers/kernel/handling-exceptions
13. Microsoft: Setting up a network debugging connection automatically (kdnet) (2024). https://learn.microsoft.com/en-us/windows-hardware/drivers/debugger/setting-up-a-network-debugging-connection-automatically
14. Microsoft: Static driver verifier (sdv) (2024). https://learn.microsoft.com/en-us/windows-hardware/drivers/devtest/static-driver-verifier
15. Microsoft: wdk-build: Build windows drivers in rust (2024). https://github.com/microsoft/windows-drivers-rs/tree/main/crates/wdk-build, version = 0.4.0

16. Microsoft: Windows debugger (windbg) tools (2024). https://learn.microsoft.com/en-us/windows-hardware/drivers/debugger/debugger-download-tools
17. Microsoft: windows-drivers-rs (2024). https://github.com/microsoft/windows-drivers-rs
18. Microsoft: windows-sys: Raw ffi bindings to windows apis (2024). https://crates.io/crates/windows-sys
19. Microsoft Docs: Virtual address spaces (2024). https://learn.microsoft.com/en-us/windows-hardware/drivers/gettingstarted/virtual-address-spaces
20. Munns, J.: postcard: A no_std + serde compatible message library for rust (2019). https://docs.rs/postcard/latest/postcard/, rust crate, first published 2019
21. OSR Developer Community: Microsoft discloses rust framework for windows drivers (2024). https://community.osr.com/t/microsoft-discloses-rust-framework-for-windows-drivers/58335
22. Project, I.: Iozone filesystem benchmark (2024). https://www.iozone.org/. fileop.exe is included in the IOzone distribution as a file system microbenchmarking tool. Accessed 19 June 2025
23. Russinovich, M., Solomon, D., Ionescu, A.: Windows Internals, Part 1: System Architecture, Processes, Threads, Memory Management, and More, 7th edn. Microsoft Press (2017)
24. Sysinternals, M.: Process monitor (procmon) (2024). https://learn.microsoft.com/en-us/sysinternals/downloads/procmon
25. The Rust Project Developers: alloc::alloc—the global allocator api (2024). https://doc.rust-lang.org/alloc/alloc/index.html. Accessed 20 June 2025
26. The Rust Project Developers: Rust reference: Crate type attributes (2024). https://doc.rust-lang.org/reference/linkage.html#the-cdylib-crate-type
27. The Serde Project: Serde: A framework for serializing and deserializing rust data structures efficiently and generically (2024). https://serde.rs
28. VMware, I.: Vmware workstation 17 pro (2024). https://www.vmware.com/products/workstation-pro/workstation-pro-evaluation.html

Hierarchical Hashing for End-to-End Integrity in HLS Video-on-Demand (VOD)

Watung Arif Budiman(✉), Ford Lumban Gaol, Haryono Soeparno, and Yulyani Arifin

Computer Science Department, BINUS Graduate Program, Doctor of Computer Science, Bina Nusantara University, Jakarta 11480, Indonesia
{watung.budiman,yulyani.arifin}@binus.ac.id, {fgaol,haryono}@binus.edu
https://dcs.binus.ac.id/

Abstract. HTTP Live Streaming (HLS) is a widely used protocol for adaptive bitrate video delivery, but it has a major security weakness: manifest files (`.m3u8`) are stored in plaintext. These files control playback, segment order, and access to decryption keys, so they can be modified when served from an untrusted Content Delivery Network (CDN). This allows attackers to inject malicious segments or redirect clients to fake URIs. Existing defenses such as PKI signatures, DRM, or the exclusive use of TLS are limited, complex, or do not protect the manifest itself. We propose a hierarchical hashing method to provide end-to-end (E2E) integrity for HLS streams. SHA-256 hashes are computed and added at every level, from media segments to variant and master playlists, forming a chain of trust. The chain is linked by a single root hash, requiring no hash database on the server. The root hash is delivered to the client through a secure channel so all content can be verified before playback. Our prototype shows very low overhead: 10–20 ms per segment on the client and only 1–3% additional time during packaging. The design is simple, CDN-agnostic, and easy to integrate with existing players. It is practical for video-on-demand (VOD) scenarios such as e-learning, corporate video, and digital libraries, where simplicity and maintainability are as important as security and integrity, and it aligns with the software quality attributes defined in ISO/IEC 25010.

Keywords: HTTP Live Streaming (HLS) · CDN · manifest playlist integrity · hierarchical hashing · video security

1 Introduction

Video distribution on the Internet now mostly uses HTTP Adaptive Streaming (HAS). Among HAS protocols, HTTP Live Streaming (HLS) is the most common one, used by about 61% of providers in production because of its wide compatibility and exclusive support on Apple devices [1]. HLS is a protocol developed by Apple for adaptive video delivery over HTTP. A video is divided into short media segments (`.ts`), typically 4-8 seconds long, each encoded at

P. D'Arco and A. Zamfiroiu (Eds.): SecITC 2025, LNCS 16443, pp. 321–339, 2026.
https://doi.org/10.1007/978-3-032-17443-7_20

multiple bitrates [2]. A plaintext manifest file (`.m3u8`) lists the segment URLs for every bitrate version. The player downloads the manifest, selects the most suitable bitrate based on the current network conditions, and fetches the segments one by one. This simple design enables scalable streaming through ordinary web servers, but it also introduces security vulnerabilities as HLS assets are often stored on third-party, untrusted Content Delivery Networks (CDNs) [3–5]. The manifest acts as the single source of truth for the entire stream, making it a critical attack vector. If compromised, attackers can inject malicious segments, redirect key URIs, or manipulate bitrate selection, potentially disrupting or hijacking playback [4,5]. Since manifests remain unencrypted even when media segments are encrypted, ensuring manifest integrity is essential for securing HLS workflows against tampering by untrusted CDNs.

In this work, we focus on HLS for video-on-demand (VOD) scenarios. HLS is chosen because it is the most widely deployed adaptive streaming protocol [1] and is heavily used for VOD workflows such as e-learning, corporate video, and digital libraries. Other protocols such as MPEG-DASH [6] and CMAF [7] also rely on plaintext manifests and face similar risks, but they are outside the scope of this study.

Current defenses still have limits. TLS/HTTPS only secures the transport channel [2], not CDN-stored files once cached. Prior research and industry practices have mainly addressed confidentiality and access control, for example using tokenized URLs, PKI signatures, or Digital Rights Management (DRM) such as Apple FairPlay and Google Widevine. These methods protect transport or control access, but they are often complex and still do not ensure the integrity of manifests once stored on a CDN. A lightweight mechanism is still needed to verify that HLS content has not been modified after leaving the origin server.

We propose a practical and lightweight approach: *hierarchical hashing* for end-to-end integrity of HLS manifests and segments. The system builds a chain of trust from media segments up to the master playlist linked by a single root hash delivered through a secure channel. This method works without changing CDN behavior (i.e., there is no need to configure CDNs to validate signatures, enforce tokens, or manage certificates).

Our main contributions are as follows:

- We model the threat of HLS manifest manipulation, especially with untrusted CDNs.
- We design a hierarchical hashing scheme that provides end-to-end integrity for HLS VOD streams.
- We implement a working prototype using standard, open, and widely available tools.
- We evaluate performance and software quality attributes based on ISO/IEC 25010 [8], showing that the scheme adds negligible overhead and is practical for deployment.

2 Related Work

Security of adaptive streaming has been studied, but most works focus on content confidentiality and access control, not manifest integrity. The main methods are:

- *TLS/HTTPS Transport.* TLS is the standard security mechanism for HLS, as specified in RFC 8216 [2,9]. It prevents Man-in-the-Middle (MitM) attacks during transmission. However, it cannot stop attacks from servers or compromised CDN edges where manifests and segments are stored.
- *Tokenized URLs.* Tokenized URLs can restrict access to authorized clients, but they require backend generation, CDN validation, and secure key management [10,11]. These methods limit access but do not verify the integrity of the delivered content.
- *PKI Signatures.* Manifests can be digitally signed by the origin using asymmetric cryptography such as RSA or ECDSA. Digital signatures protect authenticity, but they add computational cost and require key distribution and certificate management [12,13]. PKI-based frameworks such as Authentication of Media via Provenance (AMP) use X.509 certificates to sign media manifests and verify publisher identity [14]. More recent approaches like C2PA-based HLS provenance systems employ hardware Trusted Platform Module (TPM) signatures to secure live-stream authenticity [15]. These PKI methods can ensure origin and integrity but often depend on special client or ledger support and CDNs that can verify signatures.
- *Media Segment Encryption.* The HLS protocol supports the AES-128 encryption of segments [2]. This ensures confidentiality and can detect tampering of segments, but it does not protect the manifest itself. Attackers can still redirect playlists to malicious content.
- *Sequence Numbers and Timestamps.* Tags such as `#EXT-X-MEDIA-SEQUENCE` or `#EXT-X-PROGRAM-DATE-TIME` help detect replay of old segments [2]. Nevertheless, they cannot stop playlist modification where sequence values remain consistent.
- *Server-Side Rendering and CDN Security.* Dynamic playlist generation or CDN URL signing reduces unauthorized access. But once intermediaries such as CDNs cache or handle files, attackers or insiders can still inject or replace segments. Cache poisoning or improper TLS termination remain open threats [3,16].
- *Digital Rights Management (DRM) Integration.* Systems like Apple FairPlay and Google Widevine secure HLS content through license servers and encrypted media segments. However, DRM does not guarantee the integrity of the manifest itself [5,17]. DRM also adds licensing costs, platform dependencies, and additional attack surfaces [18]. DRM systems are closed-source, cannot be fully audited, and are limited by legal and regional controls such as the U.S. DMCA, which makes them hard to adopt in open or non-U.S. environments [18].

In summary, even though current defenses can secure the transport channel, control access, and keep media confidentiality, there is still a critical gap: making sure end-to-end integrity for the manifest and its segments once they are cached on an untrusted CDN. Because the plaintext manifest is the only source of truth, it becomes a point of vulnerability that TLS, tokenization, and even DRM cannot fix. This gap highlights the need for a lightweight, CDN-agnostic integrity mechanism.

Recent surveys on video security show that most research focuses on confidentiality and access control [19], with many examples from IoT and edge systems. But the integrity of HTTP Adaptive Streaming (HAS) manifests, like HLS `.m3u8` files, is not well studied. This is important because the manifest acts as the single source of truth in HAS. If it is modified, attackers can inject segments, redirect URIs, or disrupt the adaptive bitrate logic.

This paper addresses this gap with a lightweight hashing mechanism focused on HLS manifest and media segment integrity. The key differences are:

- *Granularity.* Integrity is protected at all levels, from individual media segments to variant playlists, up to the master playlist, all linked in a single chain of trust.
- *Simplicity and speed.* No certificate authority or key management; only standard secure hash (SHA-256). Fast, transparent, and platform independent.
- *Backward compatibility.* It operates fully within the HLS standard. Hashes are carried as URI query parameters, invisible to normal players, and it works without any database or additional storage.

3 Research Method

This research follows several stages as shown in Fig. 1:

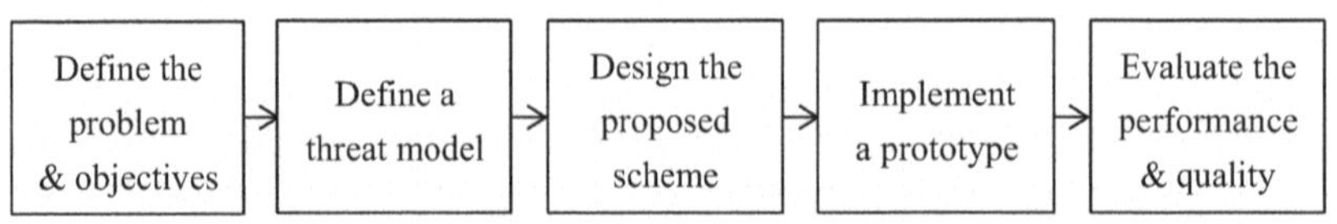

Fig. 1. Research Method.

1. *Define the problem and objectives.* These have been introduced in Chaps. 1 and 2. In summary, the main issue is the lack of integrity protection in HLS manifests and segments. The objective is to design a lightweight mechanism that ensures end-to-end integrity with minimal overhead.
2. *Build a threat model.* This stage defines the assumptions about possible attacks and clarifies the security scope of the study. The detailed threat model is presented in the next section (Sect. 3.1).
3. *Design the proposed hierarchical hashing scheme.* Based on the threat model, we develop a hierarchical hashing scheme to secure HLS manifests and segments. The design details are described in Sect. 3.2.

4. *Implement a prototype.* We build a prototype to demonstrate and test the proposed approach described in Chap. 4.
5. *Evaluate performance and quality attributes.* Chapter 5 evaluates the prototype's performance against software quality standards as defined in ISO/IEC 25010 [8].

3.1 Threat Model

As the threat model, we assume that the Content Delivery Network (CDN) or hosting provider storing manifests and segments may be compromised. In this case, an attacker could alter files on the CDN. If any resource, such as media segments, variant playlists, or the master playlist, is modified, the player should detect the hash mismatch and block the content. The proposed hierarchical hashing scheme also defends against Man-in-the-Middle (MitM) attacks, which means even if TLS is compromised and the stream is altered in transit, validation will fail. Figure 2 illustrates the typical HLS workflow and trust boundaries, showing how the packager, origin server, CDN, and client interact. The CDN is considered untrusted, while the origin and client remain within the trusted boundary.

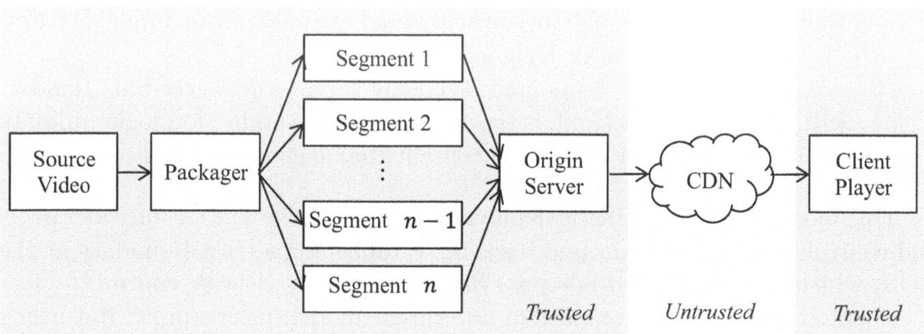

Fig. 2. Typical HLS workflow and trust boundaries. The *packager* creates multiple bit-rate versions of the *source video*, divides them into short *segments*, computes hashes, and lists them in a hashed manifest file. The packaged content is then uploaded to the *origin server* and distributed through a *Content Delivery Network (CDN)* for caching and edge delivery. The *client player* fetches the manifest, downloads segments adaptively based on network conditions. It then uses Service Worker to verify their integrity by checking each hash before playback.

Our solution also handles accidental corruption, such as file upload errors or wrong version updates. In those cases, the incorrect hash will block playback and stop the player from using the corrupted file. In this model, an attacker may attempt to alter manifests, tamper with or delete segments, or inject malicious content. Our scheme does not stop these actions, but it ensures that any such modification is detected by the client.

The main attack scenarios we consider are:

- *Manifest manipulation*: An attacker may modify playlists by changing URIs or sensitive tags (e.g., `#EXT-X-KEY`, `#EXT-X-MEDIA`, `#EXTINF`) to redirect clients to malicious or corrupted content. They can also alter metadata (e.g., `BANDWIDTH`, `RESOLUTION`, `CODECS`) to disrupt adaptive bitrate logic, leading to poor QoE (Quality of Experience) or playback failure.
- *Segment manipulation.* The attacker replaces, modifies, or corrupts media segment files stored in the CDN.
- *Man-in-the-Middle (MitM).* The attacker intercepts and alters manifests or segments in transit to inject malicious content or degrade quality.
- *CDN cache poisoning.* The attacker injects malicious manifests or segments into CDN caches, which are then served to many clients [16].

We assume the following components are trusted:

- *Origin server.* This component is trusted to generate HLS manifests and segments, compute their hashes, and upload the packaged content to the CDN. This assumption is reasonable for VOD workflows, where packaging is typically done offline.
- *Application backend.* This server is trusted to distribute the single root hash to authorized clients through an authenticated channel (for example, HTTPS with client authentication or a signed API response).
- *Client application.* This component, typically served via Server-Side Rendering (SSR) or a secure backend, is trusted to execute verification logic, validate the chain of hashes, and reject any content that fails integrity checks.

This model reflects a realistic deployment scenario: the content provider owns and controls the origin server and backend, establishing a trust boundary at the CDN, which is often a third-party service outside their security control.

Client compromise is not part of our threat model, for example, if a user's browser is infected or a malicious extension modifies the verification logic or player code, the integrity protection cannot work correctly. Our design assumes the verification runs inside a trusted browser environment, which is a common assumption for web-based playback systems.

This model does not protect against the following:

- *Denial-of-Service (DoS).* If an attacker deletes or corrupts files, playback will stop. Our system can only detect such attacks, not prevent them. This provides integrity but not availability.
- *Eavesdropping.* This work focuses on integrity, not confidentiality, which is already addressed by AES-128 encryption of segments and the use of TLS/HTTPS during transport [2].
- *Compromise of trusted components.* If the origin, backend server, or client is attacked, security guarantees are lost.

3.2 Design Goals

From the threat model, we define the following goals for our integrity mechanism:

- *End-to-end integrity.* A verifiable chain of trust from origin to client; any change in manifests or segments after leaving the origin must be detected.
- *CDN-agnostic.* The scheme should run on any standard CDN without modification, relying solely on normal HTTP delivery.
- *Lightweight.* Low computational cost for both server and client; no heavy PKI signature generation for each file. Critically, the system's state is minimal: only a single root hash must be securely stored and distributed, eliminating the need for a database of hashes or complex synchronization of hash tables.
- *Backward compatible.* Standard HLS clients can still play the streams even without verification, so playback only loses integrity checks but not the basic functionality.
- *Minimal overhead.* The added metadata brings only negligible bandwidth increase and has no significant impact on performance.

Although our approach shares the main concept of chained hashes with Merkle trees [20], it is specifically adjusted to the hierarchical structure of HLS, from media segments to variant playlists to master playlists. This design keeps compatibility with existing players, requires no CDN or player modification, and adds only minimal overhead.

Traditional Merkle trees require a separate data structure. For each block to verify, the client must obtain a corresponding authentication path, leading to higher overhead for storage and distribution. Instead, our scheme embeds the hashes directly into the playlist URIs. This fits into the standard HLS manifest format and simplifies state management by requiring only a single root hash to anchor the entire chain of trust.

To the best of our knowledge, this is the first implementation of a hierarchical hashing scheme that provides end-to-end integrity protection for HLS streams without altering the existing delivery infrastructure. This HLS-specific adaptation turns a generic cryptographic primitive into a practical, CDN-agnostic solution that can be deployed easily within current HLS packaging and playback workflows. The following section presents the design in detail.

4 System Methodology

4.1 Hierarchical Hashing

Our scheme builds a chain of trust during packaging at the origin server, using SHA-256 at every level of the HLS hierarchy (Fig. 2). The tree structure begins with segment hashes, continues through variant playlists, and ends with the master playlist as the root (Fig. 3).

We choose SHA-256 because it is widely supported, fast in browsers via Web Crypto API [21], hardware-accelerated on most modern devices, including Intel and AMD processors with SHA-NI instructions [22,23] and ARM-based

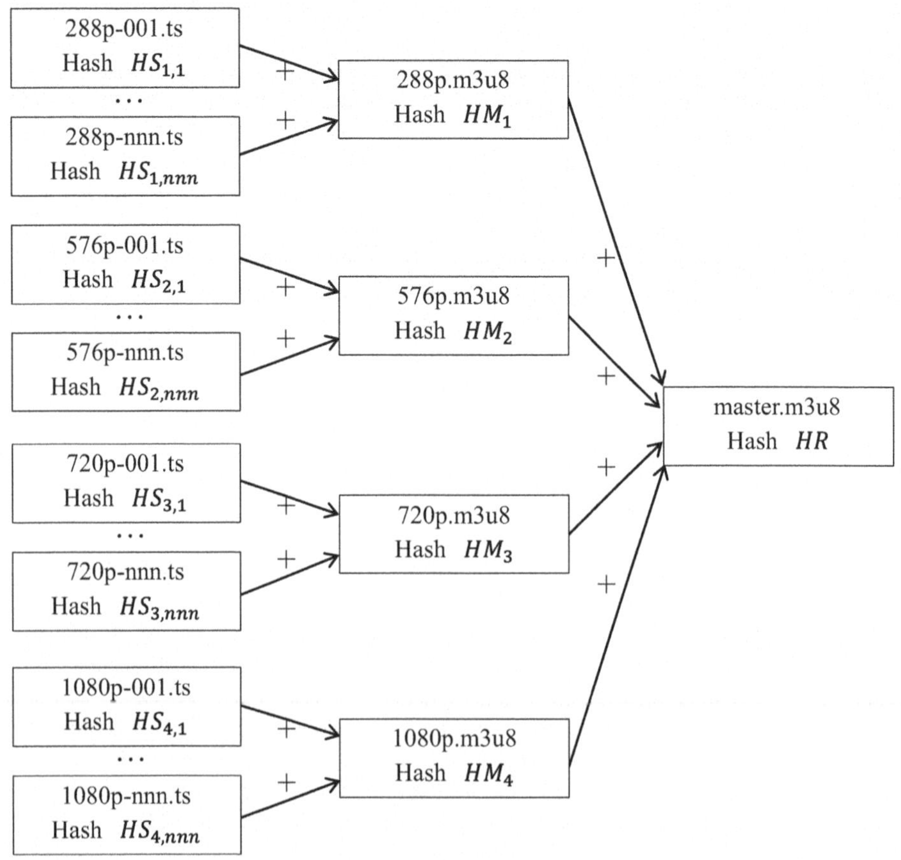

Fig. 3. Hierarchical Hashing Scheme.

smartphones with ARMv8 Cryptographic Extensions [24], and has strong cryptographic security [25]. Although hash collisions are possible in theory [28], the chance is so small that it is not a real problem for HLS manifests or segments.

4.2 Media Segment (`.ts` files) Hashing

Each media segment $S_{i,k}$ is hashed using SHA-256 to produce a segment hash $HS_{i,k}$.

$$HS_{i,k} = SHA256(S_{i,k})$$

This hash is then embedded directly into the variant playlist M_i as a URI query parameter for the corresponding segment. This method ensures the hash is distributed with the playlist itself, requiring no separate database or manifest alteration. For example:

```
#EXTINF:3.840000,
720p-0001.ts?hash=1390ce9dbcc30e514ffdf6e8c6a7d1...
#EXTINF:3.960000,
720p-0002.ts?hash=dab8f5ae6e8466cebb9e90cf71fb8c...
```

4.3 Variant Playlist (.m3u8 files) Hashing

After segment hashing, each variant playlist M_i is normalized and hashed using SHA-256 to produce the playlist hash HM_i:

$$HM_i = SHA256(Normalize(M_i(HS_{i,1}, HS_{i,2}, ...)))$$

Normalization is needed because playlists produced by packaging tools like FFmpeg or delivered to the client may contain small formatting differences (e.g., extra spaces or line breaks). Without normalization, these small differences would change the hash even though the playlist content is the same. In our implementation, the $Normalize()$ function removes all whitespace characters, including spaces, tabs, and carriage returns, by replacing the regex pattern `/[\r\n\t\s]+/g` with an empty string. This creates a consistent format for hashing.

This resulting hash HM_i is then embedded into the master playlist R as a query parameter for the variant playlist's URI, thereby linking the integrity of the variant stream to the master manifest. For example:

```
#EXT-X-STREAM-INF:BANDWIDTH=414407,RESOLUTION=512x288
288p/288p.m3u8?hash=ea82ae19baf32d4e37a72f1020d823dc...
#EXT-X-STREAM-INF:BANDWIDTH=1152183,RESOLUTION=1024x576
576p/576p.m3u8?hash=9c4465a40f06dd2defb2381085c78d4a...
#EXT-X-STREAM-INF:BANDWIDTH=1843486,RESOLUTION=1280x720
720p/720p.m3u8?hash=233f9b18def96272d12efccd0d5acc40...
#EXT-X-STREAM-INF:BANDWIDTH=3338750,RESOLUTION=1920x1080
1080p/1080p.m3u8?hash=a87e0a36379aaa8ebf85a329e2f14c...
```

4.4 Master Playlist (master.m3u8) Hashing (Root of Trust)

The chain of trust ends with hashing the normalized master playlist R to produce the root hash HR. This serves as the cryptographic anchor for the entire stream.

$$HR = SHA256(Normalize(R(HM_1, HM_2, ...)))$$

This single value represents the integrity of the entire streaming session. Any modification, whether to a single bit in a media segment, a variant playlist, or the master playlist's metadata, will propagate through the hierarchical chain, causing a cascading change in the root hash HR and breaking the chain of trust.

4.5 Root Hash Distribution

In our prototype, the root hash HR is stored securely on the backend together with video metadata such as video ID and title. During playback, the authenticated client receives HR through a trusted backend API or as part of a server-side rendered (SSR) page. User authentication is handled by the existing identity provider (e.g., Keycloak) over standard HTTPS. Because the API and SSR responses are protected by authenticated HTTPS, the backend can safely inject the root hash or return it as a signed API value.

This design assumes the root hash value is distributed through a trusted backend channel and stored securely on the client before playback begins. This approach uses existing security mechanisms and does not require any new PKI or signing service. Even if TLS connections or CDN nodes are compromised, the root hash remains trustworthy because it is only issued by the verified backend. In our prototype, this makes HR the only value that needs secure delivery outside the CDN.

4.6 Client-Side Verification

The client verifies content integrity before playback using a top-down verification process. In our prototype, this is implemented with a Service Worker [27], which can intercept requests for playlists (`.m3u8`) and segments (`.ts`) and validate their hashes before passing the content to the player. We use a Service Worker because it operates at the network level and is supported by all modern browsers, allowing universal operation with both JavaScript-based HLS players that use Media Source Extensions (MSE) and native HLS players on Safari for macOS, iOS, and iPadOS. This ensures that no manifest or segment is used before being validated against the trusted hash. The verification proceeds as follows:

1. Retrieve the trusted root hash HR from the secure backend server.
2. Fetch the master playlist, normalize its content, compute its hash, and verify it matches HR.
3. Fetch the selected variant playlist, normalize its content, and compute its hash. Compare the hash to the expected HM_i value embedded in the master playlist.
4. Download the selected segment, compute its hash and match it against the expected $HS_{i,k}$ from the segment's URI in the variant playlist.

Playback should stop immediately if any mismatch is found. This process makes sure that every component is verified before it is used.

This verification process is made to follow the normal behavior of HLS playback. In practice, the client player downloads only the chosen variant playlist to reduce latency [2], and our method then performs the integrity check based on that playlist. If the player changes to another bitrate during adaptive streaming, the new variant playlist is verified before downloading its segments. In this way, our approach keeps end-to-end integrity while still following the standard HLS protocol.

As illustrated in Fig. 4, the hierarchical trust chain aligns naturally with the existing HLS protocol structure. The standard client process, from fetching the master playlist, selecting a variant, and downloading segments, provides the framework for our top-down verification. This integration eliminates the need for a separate data structure like a Merkle tree and avoids complex state management.

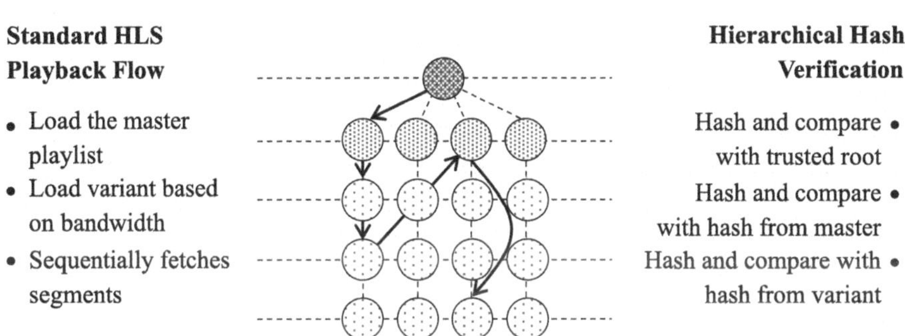

Fig. 4. Parallel Structure of HLS Playback and Integrity Verification.

5 Evaluation and Analysis

We evaluate the hierarchical hashing scheme using a prototype and quantitative analysis. The evaluation focuses on two main aspects: security properties, especially end-to-end integrity verification, and the impact on software quality as defined by ISO/IEC 25010 [8]. This standard includes several quality characteristics, such as performance, security, reliability, maintainability, usability, compatibility, and portability. By relating our results to these characteristics, we show that the proposed method is both secure and practical for real deployment.

5.1 Experimental Setup

To demonstrate the practical feasibility of our approach, we developed a working prototype using standard, open-source, and widely available tools. The packaging process was done on a gaming laptop with an Intel i7 processor, 32 GB of RAM, and an SSD for storage. We utilized FFmpeg with its `libx264` encoder for video packaging and segmentation, automating the process with a Windows batch script to ensure consistent results. The prototype generated adaptive HLS streams in four standard resolutions (288p, 576p, 720p, and 1080p) with a fixed segment duration of 4 s, following typical streaming settings. The detailed encoding parameters and the resulting average segment sizes, which directly influence the hashing workload, are listed in Table 1.

Table 1. HLS Segment Size Estimation

Resolution	CRF	Maxrate (Kbps)	Audio Bitrate (Kbps)	Avg. Segment Size (MB)
1080p	20	3500	192	1.31
720p	23	2500	128	0.92
576p	26	1000	128	0.55
288p	30	500	64	0.23

Higher resolutions, which use higher bitrates and lower Constant Rate Factor (CRF) values, result in larger segment files (e.g., approximately 1.31 MB for 1080p versus 0.23 MB for 288p). These file sizes are characteristic of adaptive bitrate encoding, which balances quality and bandwidth across different resolutions. This variation in segment size provides a realistic benchmark for evaluating our hashing scheme's performance under different workload conditions. Consequently, the hashing workload scales directly with segment size, as larger files require processing more data.

Each `.ts` segment was hashed with PHP's `hash_file('sha256',filename)` function. To separate hashing cost from disk I/O, we also benchmarked in-memory hashing. As test input, we used a 2-hour Full HD lecture video (H.264/MP4) encoded into four resolutions and uploaded to Cloudflare R2 to represent an untrusted CDN.

On the client side, playback was done with a normal HTML5 `<video>` tag using HLS.js player [26], which works in browsers that support Media Source Extensions (MSE). For client-side verification, we implemented a lightweight Service Worker [27] that intercepts every `.m3u8` and `.ts` request, computes and verifies each hash using the built-in SubtleCrypto's `digest()` function of the Web Crypto API [21] and only then passes the content to the player. This module runs in standard browsers with no plug-ins or custom extensions. It also works in browsers that enforce native playback without MSE, such as Safari on Apple iOS. The player is unaware of the background hash verification process and treats the playlists and segments as normal streaming content. Client-side tests were conducted across multiple devices, including an Intel i9 and i7 laptop, a Snapdragon 732G mobile device, and a MediaTek Kompanio 500 Chromebook, covering both desktop and mobile performance scenarios.

5.2 Performance and Efficiency

The performance evaluation focuses on the computational and timing overhead introduced by our integrity scheme. The data shows that the costs are minimal across the entire streaming process.

Packaging Overhead. For 2-hour video with four resolutions, SHA-256 hashing added only ∼1–3% to packaging time in our test. This overhead is negligible for VOD workflows where packaging is typically done offline. A two-hour video produces roughly 1,800 segments per resolution (2 Œ 3600 s œ 4 s). Hashing a single `.ts` segment from the largest resolution (~1.3 MB at 1080p) took around 10 ms, resulting in only about 18 s for the full 1080p set. Assuming similar figures for the other resolutions, the total hashing time is under two minutes for all variants, less than 2% of the total packaging time which is about 2 h to generate the complete HLS output in our experiment. In-memory hashing of the largest segment (~2 MB, 1080p) took less than 15 ms, confirming the algorithm's efficiency. Memory overhead was minimal because each segment was processed and hashed in a streaming manner, without storing large data in memory. The overall computational cost for the origin server is therefore negligible.

Client-Side Latency. Client-side performance is critical, since this is where the hashing operations are executed most frequently. To evaluate the heaviest workload, we tested hashing on the largest segment (a 2 MB, 1080p `.ts` file). Across different client devices, the hashing time remained low. On an Intel i9 laptop it took only around 2–3 ms, on an i7 ~ 5-7 ms, on a Snapdragon 732G mobile SoC ~13-14 ms, and on a MediaTek Kompanio 500 Chromebook about ~17–19 ms. These results demonstrate that even on mid-range hardware, the computation cost is minimal. In browser environments, hashing the same 2 MB segment took around 10-20 ms, just 0.25–0.5% overhead for a typical 4-second HLS segment. A single playlist `.m3u8` file (~ 100-200 KB) hashed in well under 1 ms. Master and variant playlist verification at startup added only a few milliseconds to the initial loading phase. Most importantly, segment hashing ran asynchronously and in parallel with network downloads, ensuring that the integrity verification was completely transparent to the user and did not impact playback startup time or cause buffering.

These results confirm that SHA-256 is efficient even for segment-level verification, likely due to optimized implementations in both client (Web Crypto API) and server (PHP) environments. In contrast, other methods such as PKI-based signatures (RSA, ECDSA, and EdDSA) have higher computational costs and la-tency [13] which makes them less suitable for per-segment validation in HLS.

5.3 Security Formalization

This section explains the security properties of the scheme and gives a simple reasoning based on standard cryptographic assumptions. The goal is to describe security in a formal way, avoiding subjective interpretation based only on implementation results. The main goal of the proposed scheme is to ensure end-to-end integrity of all HLS components. Any unauthorized change of media segments, variant playlists, or the master playlist after leaving the origin must be detected by the client. The probability of undetected tampering should be negligible.

System Model. Let $S_{i,k}$ denote the k-th media segment in variant stream i; M_i denote the playlist of variant i; and R denote the master playlist. Hashes are computed bottom-up from media segments to master playlist forming a hierarchical chain of trust:

$$HS_{i,k} = SHA256(S_i)$$

$$HM_i = SHA256(Normalize(M_i(HS_{i,1}, HS_{i,2}, ...)))$$

$$HR = SHA256(Normalize(R(HM_1, HM_2, ...)))$$

Each segment hash $HS_{i,k}$ is embedded into its variant playlist M_i as a URI parameter. Each playlist HM_i is embedded into the master playlist R. The master playlist R is then hashed to obtain the root hash HR which serves as the cryptographic anchor for the entire hierarchy. This root hash is distributed to clients via a trusted channel such as an authenticated API or another secure mechanism.

Attack Model. An attacker $\mathcal{A}$ can control untrusted components such as CDN nodes, edge servers, or proxy caches. The attacker can modify, inject, or delete any HLS file before it reaches the client. However, $\mathcal{A}$ cannot compromise the trusted origin that performs packaging and hashing, alter the secure delivery of the root hash HR, or modify the client-side verification logic. The client independently recomputes and validates hashes before playback. If any mismatch occurs, playback stops immediately.

Formal Integrity Guarantee. If SHA-256 hash function is resistant to collision and second-preimage [28], then any undetected modification of media segments or manifests by $\mathcal{A}$ would mean that $\mathcal{A}$ has found a collision or a second-preimage of SHA-256. Let's assume $\mathcal{A}$ modifies an element $x \in \{S_{i,k}, M_i, R\}$ and produces a modified version x' that still passes client-side verification. Let $h = SHA256(x)$ be the expected value and $h' = SHA256(x')$ the recomputed hash. Verification succeeds only if $h' = h$. Since $x' \neq x$, this implies either a collision, where two different inputs produce the same hash, or a second-preimage, where a new input maps to an existing digest. Both cases contradict the security properties of SHA-256 [28]. Therefore, the probability of undetected tampering is negligible ($\approx 2^{-256}$). Given that the root hash HR is distributed via a trusted channel, the probability that any altered media segment or manifest is accepted by the client is also negligible.

Summary. The scheme gives clear and reliable tamper detection across the whole HLS hierarchy, from the smallest segment up to the master playlist. Even a one-bit change in any segment or playlist will cause a hash mismatch and stop playback right away. For example, if one character in a manifest URI is changed (for instance, from `720p-0001.ts` to `720p-0010.ts`), or if a single pixel value inside a video segment is modified, the new hash will be completely different from the expected one. As a result, the client stops playback instead of using corrupted or harmful content. This directly reduces the risks explained in Sect. 3.1. The method gives a simple but strong security guarantee: the content either stays fully correct and plays normally, or it is completely rejected. The security depends only on the preimage resistance of SHA-256.

5.4 Software Quality Attributes (ISO/IEC 25010)

We evaluate the proposed scheme from a software engineering perspective by mapping its properties to the quality characteristics defined in the ISO/IEC 25010 standard [8]. This model offers a structured framework for assessing not only security but also maintainability, usability, portability, and compatibility. Our analysis demonstrates that the scheme fulfills key quality attributes necessary for deployable software:

- *SecurityIntegrity.* The scheme detects any unauthorized modification to manifest and segment data. This directly satisfies the integrity requirement (3.6.2) of the ISO/IEC 25010 standard by ensuring data is protected from alteration.
- *Maintainability.* The scheme depends only on SHA-256, avoiding complex systems such as PKI, certificates, or DRM. This makes it highly modular (3.7.1), easy to analyze (3.7.3), and simple to modify or replace (3.7.4).
- *Interaction Capability.* The scheme is easy for developers to integrate, requiring only a small JavaScript module, demonstrating good operability (3.4.3) and learnability (3.4.2).
- *Flexibility.* The scheme is CDN-independent and can work with any commercial or private CDN, showing strong adaptability (3.8.1) because it only depends on standard HTTP.
- *Compatibility.* The scheme shows co-existence (3.3.1) through graceful degradation: non-verifying clients ignore hash parameters and play normally. It also supports interoperability (3.3.2) by relying solely on standard web protocols (HTTP, MSE, Service Worker, Web Crypto API), enabling seamless integration with existing players, CDNs, and potential DRM systems.

In summary, the proposed implementation is lightweight and easy to deploy because it uses standard web technologies such as the Service Worker and Web Crypto API, which are supported in all major browsers. This enables a universal client-side solution without any need to modify existing players or CDNs. This quality analysis confirms that the hierarchical hashing approach is not only secure but also practical and aligning with software engineering quality goals essential for widespread adoption in real-world systems.

5.5 Limitations

While our scheme provides strong security guarantees for VOD streaming, which constitutes the majority of HLS deployments according to Bitmovin's 2025 report [1], several limitations should be acknowledged:

- *Live streaming.* This hierarchical hashing scheme supports only video-on-demand (VOD) content. Live streaming is more difficult to handle because the manifest file keeps changing while new segments are being generated in real time. The system would need to create new hashes continuously and send updated root hash values to all connected clients without delay. This real-time update process is complex and not part of our current design. We plan to study this as future work.
- *Dynamic manifest.* Our method assumes that playlists are generated before distribution and static during playback. Approaches that build manifests dynamically, such as A/B watermarking, targeted advertising, or personalized playlist generation, would require a different hashing workflow to handle continuous changes. This area will be explored in future work.
- *Bandwidth overhead.* Adding hashes roughly doubles the playlist size, for example, from about 54 KB to 110 KB in a 2-hour video with 1,800 segments. However, this increase is insignificant compared to the gigabytes of video data and does not meaningfully affect bandwidth or playback performance.

These limitations define the scope of our current contribution, which addresses the widespread use case of VOD streaming with a strong and lightweight integrity solution. Beyond the current limitations, other challenges exist in deploying integrity protection for large-scale streaming. These include key management for encrypted content, compatibility with Digital Rights Management (DRM) systems, and integration with content personalization or dynamic ad-insertion workflows. These topics are outside the scope of this paper but represent important directions for future research and system design.

5.6 Discussion

The evaluation shows that the hierarchical hashing scheme provides strong integrity protection for HLS with minimal overhead. This method offers a balanced alternative to current security approaches. It eliminates the certificate management burden found in PKI-based solutions. It also avoids the operational complexity of tokenized URLs and the limited protection of using TLS alone, while still ensuring end-to-end integrity verification.

Our ISO/IEC 25010 analysis also shows that the scheme is practical to deploy. It meets important quality attributes such as *securityintegrity*, by detecting any unauthorized modification to manifests or segments; *maintainability*, by relying only on a single SHA-256 without complex PKI or DRM components; and *compatibility*, shown through graceful degradation with standard HLS clients. These characteristics make the scheme suitable for VOD use cases such as e-learning and corporate video, where simplicity and low cost are as important as security.

Latency Consideration. Because the client must receive an entire segment before computing its hash, there is a small delay before verification completes. In VOD mode playback, this delay is hidden because the latency is very small and segments are usually fetched ahead of playback. However, in low-latency scenarios, where playback may start before a segment is completely downloaded, this process could add a small startup delay. To address this, future work could investigate partial or rolling hash methods to minimize latency for real-time streaming.

The current limitations and VOD-only support define the scope of this work while providing rooms for future work. Even with these limits, the scheme offers a practical, lightweight integrity solution that fills a critical gap in HLS security without adding the heavy overhead of more complex methods.

6 Conclusion and Future Work

6.1 Conclusion

Our proposed work introduces a lightweight hierarchical hashing scheme to secure HLS against manifest and segment manipulation. The scheme creates a chain of trust from media segments up to the master playlist by embedding SHA-256 hashes as URI parameters and distributing a single root hash through a secure backend channel. This design allows end-to-end integrity verification without requiring CDN modifications, PKI signatures, or DRM. Our prototype and analysis show that the scheme is efficient with negligible overhead, easy to maintain since it only depends on SHA-256, compatible with existing players, and portable across any standard CDN. These characteristics make our proposed approach practical not only for general video streaming but also for broader applications such as e-learning and corporate communication.

6.2 Future Work

Although the current design works well for video-on-demand (VOD), it does not yet support live streaming. Future work will focus on extending the scheme to handle dynamic playlists, allowing secure verification in real time. Another possible direction is to adapt the method for other adaptive streaming protocols such as MPEG-DASH and CMAF. Lastly, creating open-source tools for automatic and large-scale deployment would help test the scheme in real production environments and promote wider adoption.

Acknowledgments. The authors would like to thank Bina Nusantara University for the academic and financial support provided for this research and publication.

Author contributions. Watung Arif Budiman designed and implemented the proposed system, carried out the experiments, and prepared the manuscript. Ford Lumban Gaol, Haryono Soeparno, and Yulyani Arifin supervised the research, provided technical guidance, and reviewed the final version of the paper.

Data Availability Statement. No external datasets were used or generated in this study. Experimental results are available from the authors upon reasonable request.

Disclosure of Interests. The authors have no competing interests to declare that are relevant to the content of this article.

References

1. Bitmovin. Bitmovin's 9th Annual Video Developer Report 2025/2026 Edition. https://bitmovin.com/video-developer-report/
2. Pantos, R. and May, W. HTTP Live Streaming (RFC 8216). Internet Engineering Task Force. https://doi.org/10.17487/RFC8216 (2017)
3. Shobiri, B., Mannan, M., Youssef, A.: CDNs' Dark Side: Security Problems in CDN-to-Origin Connections. Digital Threats: Res. Pract. **4**(1), 1–22. https://doi.org/10.1145/3499428 (2023)
4. Al-Hamdani, S., Taha, D.B.: Security in content delivery networks (cdns): a literature review. In: 2025 International Conference on Computer Science and Software Engineering (CSASE), pp. 132–139. https://doi.org/10.1109/CSASE63707.2025.11054035 (2025)
5. Seeliger, R., Silhavy, D., Arbanowski, S. Dynamic ad-insertion and content orchestration workflows through manifest manipulation in HLS and MPEG-DASH (Vols. 2017-January, pp. 450–455). Institute of Electrical and Electronics Engineers Inc. https://doi.org/10.1109/CNS.2017.8228708 (2017)
6. International Organization for Standardization (ISO). Information technology – Dynamic adaptive streaming over HTTP (DASH). Part 1: Media presentation description and segment formats (Edition 5). ISO/IEC 23009-1 (2022)
7. International Organization for Standardization (ISO). Information technology – Multimedia application format (MPEG-A). Part 19: Common media application format (CMAF) for segmented media (Edition 3). ISO/IEC 23000-19 (2024)
8. International Organization for Standardization (ISO). Systems and software engineering, Systems and software quality requirements and evaluation (SQuaRE), Product quality model. ISO/IEC 25010 (2023)
9. de Carné de Carnavalet, X., van Oorschot, P.C.: A survey and analysis of TLS inter-ception mechanisms and motivations: Exploring how end-to-end TLS is made "end-to-me" for web traffic. ACM Comput. Surv. **55**(13s), 1–40. https://doi.org/10.48550/ARXIV.2010.16388 (2023)
10. Velasco, A., Bento, O. Protecting your media assets with token authentication. AWS for M&E Blog. https://aws.amazon.com/blogs/media/awse-protecting-your-media-assets-with-token-authentication/
11. Google. Prevent unauthorized distribution (Media CDN documentation). Google Cloud. https://cloud.google.com/media-cdn/docs/prevent-unauthorized-distribution-overview
12. Maetouq, A., Muftah, A.: public key cryptography, digital signatures, and PKI. In A. E. Hassanien, S. Anand, A. Jaiswal, P. Kumar (Eds.), Innovative Computing and Communications (Vol. 1431, pp. 137–151). Springer Nature Singapore. https://doi.org/10.1007/978-981-96-6681-2_11 (2025)
13. Serengil, S., Ozpinar, A.: LightDSA: A Python-Based Hybrid Digital Signature Library and Performance Analysis of RSA, DSA, ECDSA and EdDSA in Variable Con-figurations, Elliptic Curve Forms and Curves (Version 1). arXiv. https://doi.org/10.48550/ARXIV.2505.23773 (2025)
14. England, P., Malvar, H.S., Horvitz, E., Stokes, J.W., Fournet, C., Burke-Aguero, et al. AMP: Authentication of media via provenance. Proceedings of the 12th ACM Multimedia Systems Conference, pp. 108–121. https://doi.org/10.1145/3458305.3459599 (2021)

15. Mesa-Simón, M., Escobar-Molero, A., Sáez-Mingorance, B., Morales, D.P., Álvarez-Bermejo, J.A., Romero, F.J.: Enabling Live Video Provenance and Authenticity: A C2PA-Based System with TPM-Based Security for Livestreaming Platforms. Preprints. https://doi.org/10.36227/techrxiv.174197970.09666899/v1 (2025)
16. Nguyen, H.V., Iacono, L.L., Federrath, H.: Your cache has fallen: cache-poisoned denial-of-service attack. In: Proceedings of the 2019 ACM SIGSAC Conference on Computer and Communications Security, pp. 1915–1936. https://doi.org/10.1145/3319535.3354215 (2019)
17. Wowza Media Systems. How to secure Apple HLS streaming using DRM encryption. https://www.wowza.com/docs/how-to-secure-apple-hls-streaming-using-drm-encryption
18. Rafi, A., Shepherd, C., Markantonakis, K.: A first look at digital rights management systems for secure mobile content delivery. In: 2023 IEEE 22nd International Conference on Trust, Security and Privacy in Computing and Communications (TrustCom), pp. 549–558. https://doi.org/10.1109/TrustCom60117.2023.00087 (2023)
19. Asghar, A., Shifa, A., Asghar, M.N.: Survey on video security: examining threats, challenges, and future trends. Comput., Materials Continua **80**(3), 3591–3635. https://doi.org/10.32604/cmc.2024.054654 (2024)
20. Kuznetsov, O., Rusnak, A., Yezhov, A., Kuznetsova, K., Kanonik, D., Domin, O.: Evaluating the Security of Merkle Trees: An Analysis of Data Falsification Probabili-ties. Cryptography **8**(3), 33 (2024). https://doi.org/10.3390/cryptography8030033 (2024)
21. Mozilla. SubtleCrypto: digest() method. MDN Web Docs. https://developer.mozilla.org/en-US/docs/Web/API/SubtleCrypto/digest
22. Gueron, S.: Intel Advanced Encryption Standard (AES) New Instructions Set (AES-NI) and Secure Hash Algorithm (SHA) Extensions. Intel Corporation, white paper. https://www.intel.com/content/dam/doc/white-paper/advanced-encryption-standard-new-instructions-set-paper.pdf
23. Advanced Micro Devices, Inc (AMD). AMD64 architecture programmer's manual, volume 3: General-purpose and system instructions (Publication No. 24594, Rev. 3.37). https://docs.amd.com/v/u/en-US/24594_3.37
24. Arm Holdings plc. (2019). Arm Architecture Reference Manual Armv8, for Armv8-A architecture profile (Issue I.a). https://developer.arm.com/documentation/ddi0487/latest
25. Eastlake, D., Hansen, T.: US Secure Hash Algorithms (SHA and SHA-Based HMAC and HKDF). RFC6234 (2011)
26. Dailymotion. HLS.js: JavaScript library for HTTP Live Streaming (HLS) playback via Media Source Extensions. https://github.com/video-dev/hls.js
27. Mozilla. Service Worker API. MDN Web Docs. https://developer.mozilla.org/en-US/docs/Web/API/Service_Worker_API
28. National Institute of Standards and Technology. Secure hash standard. No. NIST FIPS 180-4; p. NIST FIPS 180-4 (2015)

Author Index

P. D'Arco and A. Zamfiroiu (Eds.): SecITC 2025, LNCS 16443, pp. 341–342, 2026.
https://doi.org/10.1007/978-3-032-17443-7

The manufacturer's authorised representative in the EU is Springer Nature Customer Service Centre GmbH, Europaplatz 3, 69115 Heidelberg, Germany. If you have any concerns regarding our products, please contact ProductSafety@springernature.com

Printed and bound by CPI Group (UK) Ltd, Croydon, CR0 4YY

07/07/2026

02160917-0011